PEOPLE'S COMPANION

to the

BREVIARY

VOLUME I

Revised and Expanded Edition
of the
New Companion to the Breviary with
Seasonal Supplement

The Liturgy of the Hours with Inclusive Language

CONTENTS

Volume I

HOW TO USE THIS BOOK

This *People's Companion to the Breviary* contains the four-week psalter and seasonal prayers for Advent, Christmas, Epiphany, Lent, Easter, Sundays of the Year, and Special Feasts and Commemorations. A calendar indicates the proper week of the psalter to use for the years from 1997–2020.

Each **Psalm** follows a given antiphon. The **Antiphon** from the four-week Psalter or from the Season is generally prayed before and after the psalm. Three Psalms are used for each office. If two or more people are praying together, the verses of the psalms are alternated, i.e., one person or a group of persons prays a verse, then another person or group prays the following verse.

After the psalms, a suggested **Reading** is given for silent meditation or faith sharing among those praying together. Other readings may be substituted. The **Responsory** is begun by the leader and the group repeats the prayer as indicated by the parts printed in bold print.

After the antiphon for the **Canticle** is prayed, one may use the Canticle of Zechariah (on the last page) or the Canticle of Mary (on the inside back cover). Traditionally the Canticle of Zechariah is prayed in the morning and the Canticle of Mary is prayed in the evening, but the office chosen may dictate the preference of the group.

The **Intercessions** are begun by the leader and the group prays the response together. It is suggested that those praying add their own petitions after reading the intercessions given.

The **Prayer** can be prayed by the leader or in unison.

ACKNOWLEDGMENTS

We thank Don Brophy of Paulist Press, and Patricia Kline of Harper, San Francisco, for their encouragement and advice, and a special debt of gratitude to Pete Piazza and Steve Cole for their generosity.

Grateful acknowledgment is also made to the following publishers/copyright holders for permission to reprint material copyrighted or controlled by them. All rights are reserved.

(1) Paulist Press · 997 Macarthur Blvd. · Mahwah, NJ 07430.

Abraham Isaac Kook: The Lights of Penitence, The Moral Principles, Lights of Holiness, Essays, Letters, and Poems. © 1978 by Ben Zion Bokser. Translation and Introduction by Ben Zion Bokser and Preface by Jacob Agus and Rivka Schatz.

Augustine of Hippo: Selected Writings. © 1984 by Mary T. Clark. Translation and Introduction by Mary T. Clark and Preface by Goulven Madec.

Barry, William A., SJ. © 1990 by The New England Province of the Society of Jesus. 'Now Choose Life:" Conversion as the Way to Life.

Bastin, Marcel, Ghislain Pinckers and Michel Teheux. English translation © 1985 by the Missionary Society of St. Paul the Apostle in the State of New York. God Day by Day. Vol 4. Translated by David Smith.

Bernard of Clairvaux: Selected Works. © 1987 by Gillian R. Evans. Translation and Forward by G.R. Evans. Introduction by Jean Leclercq, OSB and Preface by Ewert H. Cousins.

Bonaventure: The Soul's Journey into God, The Tree of Life, The Life of St. Francis. © 1978 by the Missionary Society of St. Paul the Apostle in the State of New York. Translation and Introduction by Ewert Cousins and Preface by Ignatius Brady, OFM.

Brennan, Walter T., OSM. © 1988 by Walter Brennan. The Sacred Memory of Mary.

Brueggemann, Walter, Sharon Parks, and Thomas H. Groome. © 1986 by Walter Brennan, Sharon Parks, and Thomas H. Groome. To Act Justly, Love Tenderly, Walk Humbly: An Agenda for Ministers.

Burghardt, Walter J., SJ.© 1984 by Walter J. Burghardt, SJ. Still Proclaiming Your Wonders: Homilies for the Eighties.

Burghardt, Walter J., SJ. © 1988 by the New York Province of the Society of Jesus. Lovely in Eyes Not His: Homilies for an Imaging of Christ.

Carr, Anne. © 1989 by Saint Mary's College, Notre Dame, IN. Mary: Model of Faith. In Mary of Nazareth: Biblical and Theological Perspectives. Edited by Doris Donnelly.

Catherine of Siena: The Dialogue. © 1980 by the Missionary Society of St. Paul the Apostle in the State of New York. Translation and Introduction by Suzanne Noffke, OP and Preface by Giuliana Cavallini.

Day, Dorothy. © 1970 by the Missionary Society of St. Paul the Apostle in the State of New York. Meditations. Selected and arranged by Stanley Vishnewski.

Dumm, Demetrius, OSB. © 1987 by Demetrius Dumm. Flowers in the Desert: A Spirituality of the Bible.

Early Anabaptist Spirituality: Selected Writings. © 1994 by Daniel Liechty. Translated, Edited, and with an Introduction by Daniel Liechty and Preface by Hans J. Hillerbrand.

English, John, SJ. © 1978 by the Missionary Society of St. Paul the Apostle in the State of New York. Choosing Life.

Evdokimov, Paul. © 1966 by the Missionary Society of St. Paul the Apostle in the State of New York. The Struggle with God. Translated by Sister Gertrude, SP.

Faricy, Robert, SJ. © 1990 by the Society of the Sacred Heart, US Province. The Heart of Christ in the Writings of Teilhard de Chardin. In Spiritualities of the Heart. Edited by Annice Callahan, RSCJ.

Fischer, Kathleen. © 1988 by Kathleen Fischer. Women at the Well: Feminist Perspectives on Spiritual Direction.

Francis and Clare: The Complete Works. © 1982 by the Missionary Society of St. Paul the Apostle in the State of New York. Translation and Introduction by Regis J. Armstrong, OFM.CAP and Ignatius C. Brady, OFM and Preface by John Vaughn, OFM.

Francisco de Osuna: The Third Spiritual Alphabet. © 1981 by the Missionary Society of St. Paul the Apostle in the State of New York. Translation and Introduction by Mary E. Giles and Preface by Kieran Kavanaugh, OCD.

George Herbert: The Country Parson, The Temple. © 1981 by the Missionary Society of St. Paul the Apostle in the State of New York. Edited, with an Introduction by John N. Wall, Jr. and Preface by A.M. Allchin.

Gertrude of Helfta: The Herald of Divine Love. © 1993 by Margaret Winkworth. Translated and Edited by Margaret Winkworth. Introduced by Sister Maximilian Marnau and Preface by Louis Bouyer.

Gorsuch, John P. © 1990 by John P. Gorsuch. An Invitation to the Spiritual Journey.

Grant, W. Harold, Magdala Thompson and Thomas E. Clarke. © 1983 by Thomas E. Clarke, Magdala Thompson and W. Harold Grant. From Image to Likeness: A Jungian Path in the Gospel Journey.

Håring, Bernard, C.SS.R. © 1986 by Bernard Håring. The Healing Power of Peace and Nonviolence.

Haughton, Rosemary. © 1981 by Rosemary Haughton. The Passionate God.

Hildegard of Bingen: Scivias. © 1990 by the Abbey of Regina Laudis: Benedictine Congregation Regina Laudis of the Strict Observance, Inc. Translated by Mother Columba Hart and Jane Bishop, Introduced by Barbara J. Newman and Preface by Caroline Walker Bynum.

Ibn 'Ata' Illah: The Book of Wisdom and Kwaja Abdullah Ansari: Intimate Conversations. © 1978 by the Missionary Society of St. Paul the Apostle in the State of New York. Introduction, Translation and Notes of The Book of Wisdom by Victor Danner and of Intimate Conversations by Wheeler M. Thackston. Preface by Annemarie Schimmel.

Jacob Boehme: The Way to Christ. © 1978 by the Missionary Society of St. Paul the Apostle in the State of New York. Translation and Introduction by Peter Erb and Preface by Winfried Zeller.

John and Charles Wesley: Selected Prayers, Hymns, Journal Notes, Sermons, Letters and Treatises. © 1981 by the Missionary Society of St. Paul the Apostle in the State of New York. Edited, with an Introduction by Frank Whaling and Preface by Albert C. Outler.

Johnson, Elizabeth. © 1989 by Saint Mary's College, Notre Dame, IN. Reconstructing a Theology of Mary. In Mary of Nazareth: Biblical and Theological Perspectives. Edited by Doris Donnelly.

Julian of Norwich: Showings. © 1978 by the Missionary Society of St. Paul the Apostle in the State of New York. Translated, with an Introduction by Edmund Colledge, OSA and James Walsh, SJ and Preface by Jean Leclercq, OSB.

v

Acknowledgments

Kasper, Walter. © 1976 by Search Press Limited. *Jesus the Christ*. Translated by V. Green.

Kelsey, Morton. T. © 1976 by the Missionary Society of St. Paul the Apostle in the State of New York. *The Other Side of Silence: A Guide to Christian Meditation.*

Lee, Bernard. © 1976 by the Missionary Society of St. Paul the Apostle in the State of New York. The Lord's Supper. In *Religious Experience and Process Theology: The Pastoral Implications of a Major Modern Movement.* Edited by Harry James Cargas and Bernard Lee.

Lozano, John M. © 1991 by John M. Lozano. *Grace and Brokenness in God's Country: An Exploration of American Catholic Spirituality.*

Madeleva, Sister M., CSC. Candlemas Day. © 1987 by Paul Ramsey. In *Contemporary Religious Poetry*. Edited, with Introduction by Paul Ramsey.

Marie of the Incarnation: Selected Writings. © 1989 by the Ursuline Community of St. Teresa. Translated and Edited by Irene Mahoney, OSU.

McNamara, William, OCD. © 1977 by the Missionary Society of St. Paul the Apostle in the State of New York. *Mystical Passion: Spirituality for a Bored Society.*

Meister Eckhart: The Essential Sermons, Commentaries, Treatises, and Defense. © 1981 by the Missionary Society of St. Paul the Apostle in the State of New York. Translation and Introduction by Edmund Colledge, OSA and Bernard McGinn and Preface by Huston Smith.

Mische, Gerald and Patricia. © 1977 by Gerald Mische and Patricia Mische. *Toward a Human World Order: Beyond the National Security Straitjacket.*

Moore, Sebastian. © 1977 by Sebastian Moore. *The Crucified Jesus is No Stranger.*

Native North American Spirituality of the Eastern Woodlands: Sacred Myths, Dreams, Visions, Speeches, Healing Formulas, Rituals and Ceremonials. © 1979 by the Missionary Society of St. Paul the Apostle in the State of New York. Edited by Elisabeth Tooker and Preface by William C. Sturtevant.

Padovano, Anthony T. © 1987 by Anthony T. Padovano. *Christmas to Calvary: Life and Memories of Jesus.*

Penrose, Mary E. © 1995 by the Benedictine Sisters Benevolent Association. *Roots, Deep and Strong: Great Men and Women of the Church.*

Principe, Walter, CSB. © 1990 by the Society of the Sacred Heart, US Province. Affectivity and the Heart in Thomas Aquinas' Spirituality. In *Spiritualities of the Heart.* Edited by Annice Callahan, RSCJ.

Pseudo-Dionysius: The Complete Works. © 1987 by Colm Luibheid. Translation by Colm Luibheid. Foreword, Notes, and Translation Collaboration by Paul Rorem. Preface by Rene Roques. Introductions by Jaroslav Pelikan, Jean Leclercq, and Karlfried Froehlich.

Quaker Spirituality: Selected Writings. © 1984 by Douglas V. Steere. Edited and Introduced by Douglas V. Steere and Preface by Elizabeth Gray Vining.

Raguin, Yves, SJ. © 1982 by the Missionary Society of St. Paul the Apostle in the State of New York. *Attention to the Mystery: Entry into the Spiritual Life.* Translation by Kathleen England, OSU.

Richard Rolle: The English Writings. © 1988 by Rosamund S. Allen. Translated, Edited, and Introduced by Rosamund S. Allen. Preface by Valerie M. Lagorio.

Schneiders, Sandra M., IHM. © 1986 by Sandra M. Schneiders, IHM. *New Wineskins: Re-Imaging Religious Life Today.*

Stuhlmueller, Carroll, CP. © 1978 by the Missionary Society of St. Paul the Apostle in the State of New York. *Biblical Meditations for Lent.* Introduction by Roger Mercurio, CP.

Stuhlmueller, Carroll, CP. © 1980 by the Missionary Society of St. Paul the Apostle in the State of New York. *Biblical Meditations for Advent and the Christmas Season.* Introduction by Most Rev. Thomas J. Gumbleton.

Sullivan, Paula Farrell. © 1991 by Paula Farrell Sullivan. *The Mystery of My Story: Autobiographical Writing for Personal and Spiritual Development.*

The Cloud of Unknowing. © 1981 by the Missionary Society of St. Paul the Apostle in the State of New York. Edited, with an Introduction by James Walsh, SJ and Preface by Simon Tuwell, OP.

The Shakers: Two Centuries of Spiritual Reflection. © 1983 by Robley Edward Whitson. Edited, with an Introduction by Robley Edward Whitson and Preface by Gertrude M. Soule.

Wright, Wendy M. © 1985 by Wendy M. Wright. *Bond of Perfection: Jeanne de Chantal & Francis de Sales.*

(2) The Crossroad Publishing Company · 370 Lexington Avenue · New York, NY 10017.

Fiorenza, Elisabeth Schüssler. © 1983 by Elisabeth Schüssler Fiorenza. *In Memory of Her: A Feminist Theological Reconstruction of Christian Origins.* Used by permission of The Crossroad Publishing Company and SCM Press Ltd.

Johnson, Elizabeth A. © 1990 by Elizabeth A. Johnson. *Consider Jesus: Waves of Renewal in Christology.* Used by permission of The Crossroad Publishing Company and Cassell PLC.

Johnson, Elizabeth A. © 1992 by Elizabeth A. Johnson. *She Who Is: The Mystery of God in Feminist Theological Discourse.*

Morneau, Robert F. © 1996 by Robert F. Morneau. *Ashes to Easter: Lenten Meditations.*

Rahner, Karl. © 1985. *I Remember: An Autobiographical Interview with Meinold Krauss.* Translated by Harvey D. Egan, SJ. Used by permission of The Crossroad Publishing Company and SCM.Press Ltd.

Rahner, Karl. © 1993. *The Great Church Year: The Best of Karl Rahner's Homilies, Sermons, and Meditations.* Edited by Alber Raffelt. Translation edited by Harvey D. Egan, SJ.

Rahner, Karl. © 1983. *The Love of Jesus and the Love of Neighbor.* Translated by Robert Barr. Used by permission of The Crossroad Publishing Company and St. Pauls, Slough, UK.

Rahner, Karl. © 1983. *The Practice of Faith: A Handbook of Contemporary Spirituality.* Used by permission of The Crossroad Publishing Company and SCM.Press Ltd.

Rahner, Karl. © 1983 by The Crossroad Publishing Company, © 1978 by Benziger Verlag, © 1983 by Darton, Longman & Todd Ltd. *Theological Investigations.* Vol. XVIII: *God and Revelation.* Translated by Edward Quinn. Used by permission of The Crossroad Publishing Company.

Hewitt Suchocki. Revised Edition © 1989 by Marjorie Hewitt Suchocki: *God Christ Church: A Practical Guide to Process Theology,* New Revised Edition.

(3) ICS Publications · 2131 Lincoln Road, NE · Washington, DC 20002.

Edith Stein: Self-Portrait in Letters, 1916-1942. © 1993 by the Washington Province of Discalced Carmelites, Inc. Translated by Josephine Koeppel, OCD.

Acknowledgments

Edith Stein: The Hidden Life: Hagiographic Essays, Meditations, Spiritual Texts. © 1992 by the Washington Province of Discalced Carmelites, Inc. Translated by Waltraut Stein, PhD.

Saint Thérèse of Lisieux: General Correspondence. Vol. II: 1890-1897. © 1988 by the Washington Province of Discalced Carmelites, Inc. Translated by John Clarke, OCD.

The Collected Works of Saint John of the Cross. Revised Edition. © 1991 by the Washington Province of Discalced Carmelites Friars, Inc. Translated by Kieran Kavanaugh, OCD and Otilio Rodriquez, OCD. Revisions and Introductions by Kieran Kavanaugh, OCD.

The Collected Works of St. Teresa of Avila. Vol. 1: The Book of Her Life, Spiritual Testimonies, Soliloquies. © 1976 by the Washington Province of Discalced Carmelites, Inc. Translated by Kieran Kavanaugh, OCD and Otilio Rodriguez, OCD.

The Collected Works of St. Teresa of Avila. Vol. 2: The Way of Perfection, Meditations on the Song of Songs, The Interior Castle. © 1980 by the Washington Province of Discalced Carmelites, Inc. Translated by Kieran Kavanaugh, OCD and Otilio Rodriguez, OCD.

The Story of a Soul: The Autobiography of St. Thérèse of Lisieux. Translation © 1976 by the Washington Province of Discalced Carmelites, Inc. Translated by John Clarke, OCD.

(4) Living Prayer · Contemplative Review Inc. · RR 2 Box 4784 · Barre, VT 05641.

Boersig, Teresa M., OCD. 1986. Christmas reverie. November-December. 21-22. Reprinted by permission of the author.

Coff, Pascaline, OSB. 1986. Many mansions. November-December: 34-35. Reprinted by permission of the author.

Finley, Mitch and Kathy. 1989. The home front. March-April. 30-31. Reprinted by permission of the authors.

Giallanza, Joel, CSC. 1988. Loving attention to the Lord. May-June. 15-17. Reprinted by permission of the author.

Gumbleton, Bishop Thomas J. 1988. Worth pondering.... January-February: 14-15.Reprinted by permission of the author.

Harkness, Paul H. 1986. Our journey to the cradle. November-December: 29-30. Reprinted by permission of the author.

Maish, Alma L. 1995. Master and servant. March-April. 23-24. Reprinted by permission of the author.

Martos, Joseph and Richard Rohr, 1991. Mary in Luke's gospel. November-December. 3-7. Reprinted by permission of the authors.

Rochelle, Jay C. 1989. The environment of prayer. May-June. 19-23. Reprinted by permission of the author.

Roman, Mary, OCD. 1995. Christian: wimp or saint? March-April. 37. Reprinted by permission of the author.

Ruffing, Janet, RSM. 1995. As refined by fire. March-April. 3-7. Reprinted by permission of the author.

Seelaus, Vilma, OCD. 1995. Kenosis in the Carmelite tradition. September-October. 15-18. Reprinted by permission of the author.

Teasdale, Wayne. 1991. The mystery of forgiveness. November-December. 22-26. Reprinted by permission of the author.

Thurston, Bonnie Bowman, PhD. 1986. Paul's fundamentals of faith: Philippians 4: 4-7. November-December: 18-20. Reprinted by permission of the author.

Winchester, Kay. 1995. The home front. March-April. 30-31. Reprinted by permission of the author.

(5) Sheed and Ward · 115 E. Armour Blvd. · PO Box 419492 · Kansas City, MO 64141 · (800) 333-7373.

Carmelites of Indianapolis. © 1995 by the Carmelites of Indianapolis. *Hidden Friends: Growing in Prayer.*

Houselander, Caryll. © 1944. *The Reed of God.*

Morneau, Robert F. © 1991 by Robert F. Morneau. *Mantras from a Poet: Jessica Powers.*

Oliver, Mary, IBVM. © 1959. *Mary Ward: 1585-1645.* Introduction and Epilogue by Maisie Ward.

Siegfried, Regina, ASC. and Robert F. Morneau. © 1989. *Selected Poetry of Jessica Powers.*

The Complete Works of Saint Teresa of Jesus. Vol. I. © 1957. Translated and edited by E. Allison Peers.

The Letters of Caryll Houselander: Her Spiritual Legacy. © 1965. Edited by Maisie Ward.

Theologians Today: Hans Urs Von Balthasar. © 1972. Selected and Edited by Martin Redfern.

von Le Fort, Gertrude. © 1953. *Hymns to the Church.* Translated by Margaret Chanler.

(6) Carmelite Monastery · 275 Pleasant Street · Concord, NH 03301-2590.

Frangrance from Alabaster: Thoughts of Reverend Mother Aloysius of the Blessed Sacrament. 1961.

(7) Cistercian Publications · WMU Station · Kalamazoo, MI 49008.

Cummings, Charles. © 1987. The Motherhood of God According to Julian of Norwich. In *Medieval Religious Women. Vol. 2: Peaceweavers.* Edited by Lillian Thomas Shank and John A Nichols.

Dorgan, Margaret. © 1987. St. Teresa of Avila: A Guide for Travel Inward. In *Medieval Religious Women. Vol. 2: Peaceweavers.* Edited by Lillian Thomas Shank and John A. Nichols.

Gertrud the Great of Helfta: Spiritual Exercises. Translation © 1989. Translation, Introduction, Notes and Indexes by Gertrud Jaron Lewis and Jack Lewis.

Howe, Jean Marie. © 1987. Epilogue: Cistercian Monastic Life/Vows: A Vision. In *Medieval Religious Women. Vol. 2: Peaceweavers.* Edited by Lillian Thomas Shank and John A. Nichols.

Leclerq, Jean. © 1987. Solitude and Solidarity: Medieval Women Recluses. In *Medieval Religious Women. Vol. 2: Peaceweavers.* Edited by Lillian Thomas Shank and John A. Nichols.

Muto, Susan. © 1987. Foundations of Christian Formation in the Dialogue of St. Catherine of Siena. In *Medieval Religious Women. Vol. 2: Peaceweavers.* Edited by Lillian Thomas Shank and John A. Nichols.

Wright, Wendy M. © 1987. Two Faces of Christ: Jeanne de Chantal. In *Medieval Religious Women. Vol. 2: Peaceweavers.* Edited by Lillian Thomas Shank and John A. Nichols.

(8) Fides Publishers, Inc. · Notre Dame, IN 46556 (Reprinted by permission of **Claretian Publications · 205 W. Monroe Street · Chicago, IL 60606**).

Häring, Bernard. © 1975. *Prayer: The Integration of Faith and Life.*

(9) Liturgical Press · St. John's Abbey · PO Box 7500 · Collegeville, MN 56321-7500.

Days of the Lord: The Liturgical Year. Vol. 1. © 1991 by the Order of St. Benedict, Collegeville, MN. Translation by Gregory LaNave and Donald Molloy and Preface by Godfried Cardinal Danneels.

Days of the Lord: The Liturgical Year. Vol. 3. © 1993 by the Order of St. Benedict, Collegeville, MN. Translation by Gregory LaNave and Donald Molloy.

viii   Acknowledgments

(10) Religious Sisters of St. Joseph, · **9 Mount Street, North Sydney, NSW 2059, Australia.**
All quotations of Bl. Mary MacKillop are from unpublished manuscripts. Reprinted by permission.

(11) Carmelites of Indianapolis · **2500 Cold Spring Road, Indianapolis, IN 46222.**

(12) Edizioni Carmelitane · **Via Sforza Pallavicini, 10·00193** · **Roma, Italia.**
Essays on Titus Brandsma: Carmelite, Educator, Journalist, Martyr. © 1985 by Institutum Carmelitanum. Edited by Redemptus Maria Valabek, O.Carm.

(13) The Newman Press · **Westminster, MD** (Reprinted by permission of **Paulist Press**).
Callan, Louise, RSCJ. © 1957. *Philippine Duchesne: Frontier Missionary of the Sacred Heart, 1769-1852.* Introduction by The Most Reverend Joseph E. Ritter, STD.
Löhr, Aemiliana. © 1958 by Longmans, Green & Co Ltd. *The Mass Through the Year. Vol. 1.* Translated by I. T. Hale and Forward by Damasus Winzen, OSB.
Smulders, Piet, SJ. © 1967. *The Design of Teilhard de Chardin: An Essay in Theological Reflection.* Introduction by Christian d'Armagnac, SJ and Translated by Arthur Gibson.
The Conferences of St. Vincent de Paul to the Sisters of Charity. Vol. 1. © 1952. Translated by Joseph Leonard, CM.
The Exercises of Saint Gertrude. © 1956. Introduction, Commentary and Translation by A Benedictine Nun of Regina Laudis.

(14) HarperCollins Publishers · **10 E. 53rd Street** · **New York, NY 10022-5299).**
McBrien, Richard, P. *Catholicism: Study Edition.* © 1981 by Richard P. McBrien. Reprinted by permission of HarperCollins Publishers.
Teilhard de Chardin, Pierre. © 1957 by Éditions du Seuil, Paris. English translation © 1960 by Wm. Collins Sons & Co., London, and Harper & Row Publishers, Inc., New York. Renewed © 1988 by Harper & Row Publishers, Inc. *The Divine Milieu.* Reprinted by permission of HarperCollins Publishers, Inc. and Éditions du Seuil.
Teilhard de Chardin, Pierre. © 1961 by Éditions du Seuil, Paris. English translation © 1965 by Wm. Collins Sons & Co, Ltd., London and Harper & Row Publishers, Inc., New York. © Renewed. *Hymn of the Universe.* Reprinted by permission of HarperCollins Publishers, Inc. and Éditions du Seuil.

(15) Addison Wesley Longman Group Ltd. · **Edinburgh Gate** · **Harlow, Essex CM20 2JE** · **UK.**
The Spirit of Saint Jane Frances de Chantal as Shown by Her Letters. © 1922. Translated by The Sisters of the Visitation, Harrow-on-the-Hill.
Monahan, Maud. © 1946. *Life and Letters of Janet Erskine Stuart: Superior General of the Society of the Sacred Heart, 1857 to 1914.* Introduction by Cardinal Bourne.

(16) New Directions Publishing Corp. · **80 Eighth Avenue** · **New York, NY 10011.**
Merton, Thomas. © 1961 by The Abbey of Gethsemani, Inc. . *New Seeds of Contemplation.* Reprinted by permission of New Directions Publishing Corp. and Laurence Pollinger, Ltd.
The Asian Journal of Thomas Merton. © 1975 by The Trustees of the Merton Legacy Trust. Edited by Naomi Burton, Brother Patrick Hart and James Laughlin. Amiya Chakravarty, Consulting Editor. Reprinted by permission of New Directions Publishing Corp. and Laurence Pollinger, Ltd.
The Collected Poems of Thomas Merton. © 1948 by New Directions Publishing Corporation, © 1977 by The Trustees of the Merton Legacy Trust. Reprinted by permission of New Directions Publishing Corp. and Laurence Pollinger, Ltd.
The Wisdom of the Desert: Sayings from the Desert Fathers of the Fourth Century. © 1960 by The Abbey of Gethsemani, Inc. Translated by Thomas Merton. Reprinted by permission of New Directions Publishing Corp. and Laurence Pollinger, Ltd.

(17) Alba House · **2187 Victory Boulevard** · **Staten Island, NY 10314-6603.**
Miller, Charles E., C.M. and Grindel, John A., C.M. © 1972 by the Society of St. Paul. *Until He Comes: Reflections and commentaries on the New Liturgical Readings for the Weekdays of Advent.*

(18) Bishop Neumann Center · **Philadelphia, PA.** (Reprinted by permission of the **Redemptorist Fathers of the Baltimore Province** · **Brooklyn, NY 11209.**)
Curley, Rev. Michael J., C.SS.R. © 1952 by the Redemptorist Fathers of the Baltimore Province. *Bishop John Neumann, C.SS.R.: Fourth Bishop of Philadelphia.*

(19) Loyola University Press · **3441 N. Ashland Avenue** · **Chicago, IL 60657.**
Letters of St. Ignatius of Loyola. © 1959. Selected and Translated by William J. Young, SJ.
The Autobiography of Venerable Marie of the Incarnation, OSU: Mystic and Missionary. © 1964. Translated by John J. Sullivan, SJ and Preface by James Brodrick, SJ.

(20) Mary Brian Durkin, OP · **Rosary College** · **River Forest, IL 60305.**
Durkin, Mary Brian, OP. © 1995. Teresian wisdom in selected writings of Evelyn Underhill. *Spiritual Life,* Spring. 20-31. Reprinted by permission of the author.

(21) Templegate Publishers · **302 East Adams** · **PO Box 5152** · **Springfield, IL 62705.**
The Dorothy Day Book. © 1982. Edited by Margaret Quigley and Michael Garvey.

(22) Orbis Books · **PO Box 308** · **Maryknoll, NY 10545-0308**
Boff, Leonardo. © 1987. *Passion of Christ, Passion of the World: The Facts, Their Interpretation, and Their Meaning Yesterday and Today.* Translated by Robert R. Barr.
Donders, Joseph G. © 1990 by Joseph G. Donders. *Risen Life: Healing a Broken World.*
Galilea, Segundo. English translation © 1981. *Following Jesus.* Translated by Sister Helen Phillips, MM.
Sobrino, Jon, Ignacio Elacuria, and Others. © 1990. *Companions of Jesus: The Jesuit Martyrs of El Salvador.*
Williams, Delores S. © 1993 by Delores S. Williams. *Sisters in the Wilderness: The Challenge of Womanist God-Talk.*

Acknowledgments

(23) America Press Inc. · 106 West 56th Street · New York, NY 10019.
Feeney, Leonard, S.J. © 1927. *In Towns and Little Towns: A Book of Poems.*

(24) Fortress Press · (Augsburg Fortress Publishers) · 426 S. Fifth Street · Box 1209 · Minneapolis, MN 55440-1209.
Proclamation 4: Aids for Interpreting the Lessons of the Church Year: Epiphany, Series C. © 1988 by Fortress Press. Edited by Walter E. Rast. Used by permission of Augsburg Fortress.

(25) Sheed and Ward · Kansas City, MO. (Reprinted by permission of **Mrs. John Farrow · c/o Carl L. Zanger, P.C. · 152 W. 57th Street · New York, NY 10019.**)
Farrow, John. © 1937. Copyright renewed © 1964 by Mrs. John Farrow. *Damian the Leper.*

(26) Editions Fleurus · 11, rue Duguay-Trouin · 75006 Paris · France.
Richomme, Agnes. *The Wonderful Story of a Great Missionary: Anne-Marie Javouhey.*
Sigaut, Marie-Hélène. *At the Service of the Elderly: Jeanne Jugan and the Little Sisters of the Poor.* Texts by René Berthier in collaboration with the Little Sisters of the Poor.

(27) Benziger Brothers (The following books are no longer under copyright protection).
A Member of the Congregation. 1904. *Life and Life-Work of Mother Theodore Guérin, Foundress of the Sisters of Providence at St.-Mary-of-the-Woods, Vigo County, Indiana.*
Rivaux, The Abbé. 1897. *Life of Rev. Mother St. John Fontbonne, Foundress and First Superior-General of the Congregation of the Sisters of St. Joseph in Lyons.*

(28) The Criterion · Archdiocese of Indianapolis · 1400 North Meridian · Indianapolis, IN 46202.
Bosler, Raymond T. 1992. *New Wine Bursting Old Skins: Memories of an Old Priest Longing for a New Church.*

(29) NAL Penguin Inc. · 375 Hudson Street · New York, NY 10014-3657.
Underhill, Evelyn. © 1961 by E.P. Dutton. *Mysticism: A Study in the Nature and Development of Man's Spiritual Consciousness.* Used by permission of Dutton Signet, a division of Penguin Books USA, Inc. and Tessa Sayle Agency, London.

(30) Farrar, Straus and Giroux, Inc. · 19 Union Square West · New York, NY 10003.
Dirvin, Jospeh, I. CM. © 1962, 1975 by Farrar, Straus and Giroux, Inc. *Mrs. Seton: Foundress of the American Sisters of Charity.*

(31) Fidelity Publishing Company · St. Clair, MI (Used by permission of **Alt Publishing Company · PO Box 400 · Green Bay, WI 54305**).
Derum, James Patrick. © 1960 by James Patrick Derum. *Apostle in a Top Hat: The Story of Frederic Ozanam: Founder of the Society of St. Vincent de Paul.*

(32) The Way · Heythrop College · Kensington Square · London W8 5HQ · UK.
Callahan, Annice, RSCJ. © 1989 by Editors of The Way. Traditions of spiritual guidance: Karl Rahner's insights for spiritual direction. October. 341-47.

(33) Grail Publication · St. Meinrad, IN (Used by permission of **Abbey Press · Hill Drive · St. Meinrad, IN 47577**).
Benedictine Monks of St. Meinrad's Abbey. © 1950. *The Holy Rule of Our Most Holy Father Saint Benedict.*

(34) The Oratory · 3800 Queen Mary · Montreal H3V 1H6.

(35) Herder and Herder · New York, NY (Used by permission of **The Society of the Sacred Heart · United States Province · 4389 West Pine Blvd. · St. Louis, MO 63108**).
Williams, Margaret, RSCJ. © 1965. *St. Madeleine Sophie: Her Life and Letters.*

(36) The Jesus Journal · PO Box 15304· Tallahassee, FL 32317-5304.
McCarthy, Emmanuel Charles. 1993. The man who chose to see. Winter, No. 69. 2-8.
McCarthy, Emmanuel Charles. 1995. Stations of the cross of non-violent love. No. 79. 9-23.

(37) Little, Brown and Company
R.V.C. Bodley. © 1953. *The Warrior Saint.*

(38) McGraw-Hill Companies, Inc. · 1221 Avenue of the Americas · New York, NY 10020.
Pope John XXIII: The Journal of a Soul. English translation © 1965 by Geoffrey Chapman Ltd. Translated by Dorothy White.

(39) Mother Katharine Drexel Guild · Bensalem, PA 19020.
Duffy, Sister Consuela Marie, SBS. © 1987. *Katharine Drexel: A Biography.*

(40) Mary Gleason, SP · 622 S.W. 129 · Seattle, WA 98146.

(41) Vincentian Studies Institute · 2233 N. Kenmore Avenue · Chicago, IL 60614.
Papers from the Symposium Louise de Marillac: A Legacy of Charity, 1591-1991, Saint Louis, Missouri 21-25 June 1991.

(42) St. Mary's Press · 702 Terrace Heights · Winona, MN 55987-1320
Durka, Gloria. © 1991. *Companions for the Journey: Praying with Hildegard of Bingen.*
Gibson, Audrey and Kieran Kneaves. © 1995. *Companions for the Journey: Praying with Louise de Marillac.*

(43) Thames and Hudson Ltd. · 30, Bloomsbury Street · London WC1B 3QP · UK.
De Breffny, Brian. © 1982. *In the Steps of St. Patrick.* Photographs by George Mott.

Acknowledgments

(44) Archives of the Sisters of Notre Dame de Namur · Boston Province · 36 Newcastle Road · Brighton, MA 02135.
Themes of Julie Billiart, Record Group 12. Unpublished manuscript. Reprinted by permission.

(45) Longmans, Green and Co. · New York. (Reprinted by permission of **Sheed and Ward, Ltd. · 14 Coopers Row · London EC3N 2BH · UK.**)
Ghéon, Henri. © 1929. *The Secret of the Curé D'Ars. Translated by F.J. Sheed.*

(46) The Wicklow Press · New York, NY (Used by permission of **The Society of Jesus · 114 Mount Street · London W1Y 6AH · UK**).
Brodrick, James, SJ. © 1952. *St. Francis Xavier (1506 - 1552).*

(47) Bruce Publishing Company · Milwaukee, WI. (Reprinted by permission of the **Missionary Sisters of the Sacred Heart of Jesus · 701 Ft. Washington Avenue · New York, NY 10040.**)
Maynard, Theodore. © 1945. *Too Small a World: The Life of Francesca Cabrini.*

(48) Doubleday and Co. Inc. · 1540 Broadway · New York, NY 10036-4094.
The Confessions of St. Augustine. © 1960. Translation, Introduction and Notes by John K. Ryan.

(49) The Westminster/John Knox Press · 100 Witherspoon Street · Louisville, KY 40202-1396.
Cobb, John B.,Jr. © 1976. *God and the World.*

(50) St. Anthony Messenger Press · Cincinnati, OH 45210
Turpin, Joanne. © 1990 by Joanne Turpin. *Women in Church History: 20 Stories for 20 Centuries.*

(51) Source Books · Trabuco Canyon, CA 92678-0794
Gateley, Edwina. © 1981 by Edwina Gateley. *Psalms of a Laywoman.*

(52) Southern Illinois University Press · PO Box 3697 · Carbondale, IL 62902.
Wieman, Henry N. © 1946. *The Source of Human Good.*

(53) TAN Books and Publishers, Inc · PO Box 424 · Rockford, IL 61105
Cruz, Joan Carroll. © 1993. *Miraculous Images of Our Lady: 100 Famous Catholic Statues and Portraits.*

(54) Mary Jo Weaver · 1030 South Mitchell Road · Bloomington, IN 47401.

(55) Liguori Publications · 1 Liguori Drive · Liguori, MO 63057-9999.
Hâring, Bernard, C.SS.R. © 1983. *Heart of Jesus: Symbol of Redeeming Love.*

(56) Maryknoll Sisters · Maryknoll, NY 10545.
Kennedy, Camilla, MM. © 1987. *To the Uttermost Parts of the Earth: The Spirit and Charism of Mary Josephine Rogers.*

(57) Liguorian Magazine · 1 Liguori Drive · Liguori, MO 63057-9999.
DeCelles, Charles, PhD.© 1968. A tribute to a pioneer educator. February. 34-38.

(58) Sisters of St. Joseph of Peace · 1225 Newton Street, NE · Washington, DC 20017.
Vidulich, Dorothy A., CSJP. © 1990 by Dorothy A. Vidulich. *Peace Pays a Price: A Study of Margaret Anna Cusack, The Nun of Kenmare.*

(59) The Merton Legacy Trust · New York, NY 10025.
Merton, Thomas. © 1971. *Contemplation in a World of Action.* Introduction by Jean Leclercq, OSB.
Merton, Thomas. *Nonviolent Alternative.* Reprinted by permission.

(60) Georges Borchardt, Inc., · 136 E. 57 Street · New York, NY 10022.
Teilhard de Chardin, Pierre. © 1968 by Éditions Bernard Grasset. English translation © 1968 by William Collins Sons & Co. Ltd., London, and Harper & Row, Publishers, Inc., New York. *The Prayer of the Universe. (Écrits du Temps de la Guerre).* Translation by René Hague and Introduction by Robert Speaight. Reprinted by permission of Georges Borchardt, Inc. and Éditions Bernard Grasset.

(61) Pope Paul VI. February 2, 1974. Apostolic Exhortation *Marialis Cultus,* On Rightly Grounding and Increasing Marian Devotion, DOL 467.

(62) Morehouse Publishing Company · 871 Ethan Allen Highway · Ridgefield, CT 06877-2801.
Underhill, Evelyn. © 1984 by the estate of Evelyn Underhill, Harrisburg, PA. *The Spiritual Life.* Reprinted by permission of Morehouse Publishing Co. and Cassell PLC.

(63) The Sisters of Mercy Diocese of Cork and Ross · Ireland.
The Correspondence of Catherine McAuley: 1827-1841. © 1989. Edited by Sister M. Angela Bolster, RSM.

An exhaustive effort has been made to locate all copyright holders and to clear reprint permissions. This process has been complicated, and if any required acknowledgments have been omitted, or any rights overlooked, it is unintentional and forgiveness is requested. If notified we will be pleased to rectify any omission in future editions.

The Carmelites of Indianapolis.

WEEK I

SUNDAY, EVENING PRAYER I

Ant 1 Let my prayer rise as incense before you.

Psalm 141:1-9

I call upon you, O God; make
haste to help me;
give ear to my voice, when I call
to you.
Let my prayer rise as incense
before you,
and the lifting up of my hands as
an evening sacrifice!

Set a guard over my mouth, O
God,
keep watch over the door of my
lips!
Do not incline my heart to evil,
that I not busy myself with
wicked deeds
in company with those who work
iniquity;
let me not partake of their
dainties!

Let a good person strike or
rebuke me in kindness,
but let the oil of wickedness
never anoint my head;
for my prayer is constantly
against wicked deeds.

When those who do evil are given
over to those who condemn
them,
then they shall learn that your
word is true.—

***Glory to you, Source of all
Being, Eternal Word and Holy
Spirit,**

**As it was in the beginning is
now and will be forever. Amen.**

As a rock which one holds and
shatters on the ground,
so shall their bones be strewn at
the mouth of the grave.

But my eyes are turned toward
you, O God;
in you I seek refuge; leave me not
defenseless!
Keep me from the trap which evil
lays before me,
and from the snares of my own
wickedness. **Glory*...**

**Ant 2 You are my refuge, O
God; my portion in the land of
the living.**

Psalm 142

I cry out with my voice to you, O
God,
with my voice I make supplication
to you.
I pour out my complaints before
you,
before you I place all my troubles.
When my spirit is faint, you, O
God, know my way!

In the path where I walk
hidden traps surround me.
I look to the right and watch,
but no one takes notice of me;
no human refuge remains for me,
no one cares for my soul.

I cry out to you, O God;
I say, you are my refuge,
my portion in the land of the
living.
Give heed to my cry;
for I am brought low, indeed!

Deliver me from those who would
  hurt me;
for they are too strong for me!
Bring me out of my distress,
that I may give thanks to your
  name!
Let your holy ones surround me;
for you will deal graciously with
  me. **Glory*...**

**Ant 3 Every tongue will
  proclaim the glory of God.**

Cant: Phil 2:6–11

Though he was in the form of
  God,
Jesus did not count equality with
  God
something to be grasped at.

But emptied himself—

taking the form of a slave,
being born in human likeness.

Being found in human estate,
he humbled himself and became
  obedient,
obediently accepting death,
even death on a cross!

Therefore God has highly exalted
  him
and bestowed on him the name
above every other name.

So that at the name of Jesus
every knee should bow,
in heaven, on the earth,
and under the earth,
and every tongue proclaim
to the glory of God:
Jesus Christ is Lord! **Glory*...**

READING

We can apply...what Christ says about the narrow gate to the sensitive
part of the human person, and what he says about the constricting way
to the spiritual or rational part. Since he proclaims that few find it, we
ought to note the cause: Few there are with the knowledge and desire to
enter into this supreme nakedness and emptiness of spirit. As this path
on the high mount of perfection is narrow and steep, it demands
travelers who are neither weighed down by the lower part of their nature
nor burdened in the higher part. This is a venture in which God alone is
sought and gained; thus only God ought to be sought and gained.

John of the Cross, *The Ascent of Mount Carmel*, II.7:3, (3)

RESPONSORY

In love and thanksgiving, we praise you, Holy God. **—In love...**
Your name is written in our hearts; **—we praise...**
Glory to you, Source of all Being, Eternal Word and Holy Spirit.
    —In love...

CANTICLE OF MARY

Ant. Forever I will sing your praise.

INTERCESSIONS

Heaven and earth will pass away, but your word will remain, O God;
  —let this promise of eternal life in you give meaning to our lives and energize us in your service.
You bless your people with a variety of talents, O God;
  —give us the courage to develop our gifts for your glory and the good of all.
Jesus, you foresaw the stark reality of the future, and you encouraged your followers to have patience;
  —help us to live the gospel so faithfully that our lives will be a beacon of hope to others.
We are your children and you look upon us with love.
  —help us to refrain from judging others negatively and to temper justice with mercy.
Prayer is your invitation to realize our union with you;
  —awaken us to your presence in us; teach us what it means to pray always.

PRAYER: Most loving God, you pursue creation with your love and rescue us with your mercy. Look upon us, your people, this evening with tenderness and compassion. Especially do we pray for all world leaders. May they all find strength in your love and courage in your wisdom. We ask this through the holy name of Jesus. Amen.

MORNING PRAYER

Ant. 1 As morning breaks I call upon your name, O God.

Psalm 63:1–9

O God, you are my God, I long for you;
my soul thirsts for you;
My body seeks for you
as in a dry and weary land without water.
So I have looked upon you in the sanctuary,—

beholding your power and your glory.

For your constant love is better than life.
My lips will sing your praises.
So I will bless you as long as I live;
I will lift up my hands and call on your name.

My soul feasts on you and my mouth praises you,
as I think of you upon my bed,
and meditate on you in the watches of the night;—

for you have been my help,
In the shadow of your wings I sing
for joy.
My soul clings to you; your hand
upholds me. **Glory*...**

**Ant. 2 Not fearing the flames the
three young men cried out with
one voice: Blessed be God,
(alleluia).**

Cant: Daniel 3:57–88, 56

All you works of God, praise our
God.
Praise and exalt God above all
forever.
All you angels, sing God's praise,
you heavens and waters above.
Sun and moon, and stars of
heaven,
sing praise with the heavenly
hosts.

Every shower and dew, praise our
God.
Give praise all you winds.
Praise our God, you fire and heat,
cold and chill—dew and rain.
Frost and chill, praise our God.
Praise God, ice and snow.
Nights and days, sing hymns of
praise,
light and darkness,
lightnings and clouds.

Let all the earth bless our God.
Praise and exalt God above all
forever.
Let all that grows from the earth
give praise
together with mountains and hills.
Give praise you springs,
you seas and rivers,
dolphins and all water creatures.
Let birds of the air,—

beasts wild and tame,
together with all living peoples,
praise and exalt God above all
forever.

O Israel praise our God.
Praise and exalt God above all
forever.
Give praise, you priests,
servants of the Most High,
spirits and souls of the just.
Holy ones of humble heart,
sing your hymns of praise.
Hananiah, Azariah, Mishael,
praise our God.
Praise and exalt God above all
forever.

Let us bless our God, Holy
Mystery,
Source of All Being, Word, and
Spirit.
Let us praise and exalt God above
all forever.
Blessed are you, O God, in the
firmament of heaven.
Praiseworthy and glorious and
exalted above all forever.

**Ant. 3 Let the people of Zion
rejoice, (alleluia).**

Psalm 149

Sing a new song to our God.
Give praise in the assembly of the
faithful.
Let Israel be glad in its maker;
let Zion's heirs exult in the Most
High.
Let them praise God's name with
dancing,
and make music with timbrel and
harp.

For you take delight in your
people, O God.—

You adorn the humble with victory.
Let the faithful exult in their glory, in their rest, let them sing for joy.
Let the praises of God be on their lips
and two-edged swords in their hands,
to wreak vengeance on all that is wicked,
and chastisement on all injustice;
to bind what is evil in chains
and oppression in fetters of iron;
to carry out the sentence pre-ordained;
this is glory for all God's faithful ones. **Glory*...**

READING

[I], John looked, and there was a great multitude that no one could count, from every nation, from all tribes and peoples and languages, standing before the throne and before the Lamb, robed in white, with palm branches in their hands. They cried out in a loud voice, saying, "Salvation belongs to our God who is seated on the throne, and to the Lamb!" And all the angels stood around the throne and around the elders and the four living creatures, and they fell on their faces before the throne and worshipped God, singing, "Amen! Blessing and glory and wisdom and thanksgiving and honor and power and might be to our God forever and ever! Amen."

Rev 7:9–12

RESPONSORY

Christ, living word in our midst, hear our morning prayer.
    —**Christ...**
You are the light of the world; —**hear our...**
Glory to you, Source of all Being, Eternal Word and Holy Spirit.
    —**Christ...**

CANTICLE OF ZECHARIAH

Ant. Most gracious God, may you bless us all our days.

INTERCESSIONS

The earth is your masterpiece, O God, and you have made us its stewards;
    —give us eyes to see your handiwork in every creature.
Creator is your name, and all that comes from your hand is good;
    —cleanse our hearts and enlighten our minds that our
        choices may enhance and magnify your work in our world.
Your measuring rod is love;
    —give us a love that takes us out of and beyond ourselves.

Jesus, you know the strengths and weaknesses of the human heart;
  —share with us your patience and compassion; remind us
    that another may carry a cross beyond our imagining.
Death is our last chance on earth to say yes to you, O God;
  —make us one with your will day by day.

PRAYER: O loving God we take delight in your people and all of creation. Together we unite our hearts and voices to sing your praise. Be with us this day and help us to treat each other and all living creatures with respect and appreciation. Grant this in the name of Jesus who is our way, our truth, and our life. Amen.

DAYTIME PRAYER

Ant. 1 O God, to whom shall we go? You alone are our refuge.
Psalm 118
I

We give thanks to you, for you are good,
and your steadfast love endures forever.
Let the descendants of Israel say:
"Your steadfast love endures forever."
Let the descendants of Aaron say:
"Your steadfast love endures forever."
Let those who fear you say:
"Your steadfast love endures forever."

In my distress, I called to you;
you answered me and set me free.
With you at my side I do not fear.
What can anyone do against me?
You are at my side to help me:
I shall withstand all evildoers.

It is better to take refuge in you,
than to trust in people:—

it is better to take refuge in you
than to trust in our leaders.
    Glory*...

Ant. 2 God's holy hand has raised me up, (alleluia).
II

All wickedness surrounded me;
in your name I crushed it.
It surrounded me, surrounded me
  on every side;
in your name I cut it off.
It surrounded me like bees;
it blazed like a fire among thorns.
In your name I crushed it.

I was pushed hard, and was falling
but you came to help me.
You are my strength and my song;
you are my salvation.

O God, you have triumphed;
your reign is exalted.
You have triumphed over all;
I shall not die, I shall live
and recount your wondrous deeds.
You have chastened me sorely,—

but have not given me over to death. **Glory*...**

Ant. 3 Our God has let the light of the Most High to shine upon us, (alleluia).

III

Open to me the gates of justice,
that I may enter and give thanks.
This is your gate, O God;
the just shall enter through it.
I thank you for you have answered me
you alone are my salvation.

The stone which the builders rejected
has become the cornerstone.
This is your doing, O God,
it is marvelous in our eyes.—

This is the day which you have made;
let us rejoice and be glad in it.

Save us, we beseech you, O God!
O God, grant us success.
Blessed are those who enter
in your holy name.
For you O God, are our God,
and you have given us light.

Let us go forward in procession with branches,
up to your holy altar.
You are my God, I thank you.
You are my God, I praise you.
We give thanks to you for you are good;
and your steadfast love endures forever. **Glory*...**

PRAYER: Most holy God, we rejoice in your gift of life as shared with us in the paschal mystery. On this day of remembrance, help us to enter more deeply into the mystery of your life lived among us, your people. We ask this in the name of Jesus who lived as one of us and through your Spirit who enlivens us. Amen.

EVENING PRAYER II

Ant. 1 God's reign will last forever.

Psalm 110:1-5, 7

God's revelation to the Anointed One:
"Sit at my side:
till I put injustice beneath your feet."

God will send forth from Zion
your scepter of power:
rule in the midst of your foes.

Your people will give themselves freely
on the day you lead your host
upon the holy mountains.
From the womb of the morning
your youth will come like dew.

God has sworn an oath that will not be changed.
"You are a priest forever,
after the order of Melchizedek."

The Anointed standing at your side,—

will shatter rulers on the day of
wrath.

Drinking from your streams by the
wayside
shall the Chosen One be
refreshed. **Glory*...**

**Ant. 2 Tremble, O earth, at the
presence of your God.**

Psalm 114

When Israel went forth from Egypt,
Jacob's heirs from an alien people,
Judah became God's sanctuary,
Israel, the dominion of the Most
High.

The sea looked and fled,
Jordan turned back on its course.
The mountains skipped like rams,
the hills like yearling lambs.

What ails you, O sea, that you
flee?
O Jordan, that you turn back?
Mountains, that you skip like
rams,
hills, like yearling lambs?

Tremble, O earth, at the presence
of God,
at the presence of the God of your
ancestors,
who turns the rock into a pool,
the flint into a spring of water.
Glory*...

**Ant. 3 All power is yours, O God,
creator of all.**

Cant: Rev 19:1, 5-7

Salvation, glory, and power belong
to you,
your judgments are honest and
true.

All of us, your servants, sing
praise to you,
we worship you reverently, both
great and small.

You, our almighty God, are Creator
of heaven and earth.
Let us rejoice and exult, and give
you glory.

The wedding feast of the Lamb has
begun,
And the bride has made herself
ready. **Glory*...**

READING

Blessed be the God...of our Lord Jesus Christ, the [God] of mercies and
the God of all consolation, who consoles us in all our affliction, so that
we may be able to console those who are in any affliction with the
consolation with which we ourselves are consoled by God. For just as
the sufferings of Christ are abundant for us, so also our consolation is
abundant through Christ. If we are being afflicted, it is for your
consolation and salvation; if we are being consoled, it is for your
consolation, which you experience when you patiently endure the same
sufferings that we are also suffering. Our hope for you is unshaken; for
we know that as you share in our sufferings, so also you share in our
consolation.

2 Cor 1:3–7

RESPONSORY

Incline my heart to praise your goodness all the days of my life.
     —Incline...
For my prayer is always before you; **—all the...**
Glory to you, Source of all Being, Eternal Word and Holy Spirit.
     —Incline...

CANTICLE OF MARY

Ant. You fill us with goodness and mercy.

INTERCESSIONS

Spirit of God, you lead each of us in a direction that is life-giving
and fruitful;
     —help us to silence all that would deafen us to your call.
As the possibilities of science continue to expand;
     —remind us of our creaturehood and give us humble hearts.
Life is your gift to us, O God, and your love for us gives meaning
to your gift;
     —show yourself to those who are tempted to despair.
Jesus, you knew the cares of family life;
     —encourage and strengthen heads of families who face the
       special challenges of our culture.
Jesus you healed on the Sabbath and were persecuted for it;
     —be with our present day prophets who make unpopular
       decisions for the cause of justice and truth.

PRAYER: You, O God, are our place of refuge; you continue to
          call us forth to be your people in a world of division
          and distress. Help us to be people of faith, joy, and love
          in the midst of chaos. This we ask through the
          intercession of Jesus, Mary, and Joseph, who imaged
          community in a captive and oppressed land. Amen.

MONDAY

MORNING PRAYER

Ant 1 Give heed to my words, O God, and listen to my morning prayer.

Psalm 5:1–9, 11–12

Give ear to my words, O God,
give heed to my groaning.
Attend to the sound of my cry,
O God, Most High.

For it is you to whom I pray.
In the morning you hear my
　voice;
I prepare a sacrifice for you,
watching and waiting.

You are not a God delighting in
　evil;
no sinner is your companion.
The boastful may not stand before
　you,
before your holy face.

You hate all that is evil;
you destroy all that is false.
The deceitful and the bloodthirsty
you chastise, O God.

But I through the abundance of
　your love
will enter your holy house.
I will worship at your holy temple,
filled with awe.

Lead me, O God, in your justice;
there are those who seek to
　seduce me,
make clear your way before me.

For there is no truth in their
　mouth,
their heart is destruction,
their throat is a wide-open grave,
all flattery their speech.

Let all be glad who take refuge in
　you,
forever, sing out their joy.
Shelter those who love your
　name;
May they ever exult in you.

For you it is, who bless the just;
you cover them with favor,
　as with a shield. **Glory*...**

Ant. 2 We sing your praises from generation to generation.

Cant: 1 Chron 9:10b–13

Blessed may you be,
O God of Israel,
from eternity to eternity.

Yours, O God, are grandeur and
　power,
majesty, splendor, and glory.

For all in heaven and on earth is
　yours;
yours, O God, is the sovereignty;
you are exalted as head over all.

Riches and honor are from you;
you have dominion over all.
In your hands are power and
　might;
it is yours to give grandeur and
　strength to all.

Therefore, our God, we give you
　thanks
and we praise the majesty of
　your name. **Glory*...**

Ant. 3 You are the Alpha and the Omega, the first and the last, the beginning and the end.

Psalm 29

O give to God, you heavenly
  beings,
give to God glory and power;
give glory to God's holy name.
Worship your God in holy array.

For God's voice is heard on the
  waters,
thundering on many waters;
the voice of God is powerful,
God's voice, full of splendor.

Your voice shatters the cedars,—

it shatters the cedars of Lebanon;
you make Lebanon skip like a calf
and Sirion like a young wild ox.

Your voice, O God flashes flames
  of fire.
Your voice shakes the wilderness
  of Kadesh;
it makes the oak trees whirl,
and strips the forests bare.

The God of glory thunders!
In your temple all cry: "Glory!"
You sit enthroned over the flood;
you sit, our sovereign forever.

May you give strength to your
  people,
and bless your people with peace.
  Glory*...

READING

Do as perfectly as you can the tasks of your every day life, even the most trivial. It is quite simple. Follow our Lord [Jesus] like a little child. I skip after him as best I can. I put my trust in him and abandon all care.

The Beatification of Father Titus Brandsma, Carmelite, p. 46, (12)

RESPONSORY

Shelter us, O God, in the safety of your dwelling place. **—Shelter...**
Your name is forever blessed; **—in the...**
Glory to you, Source of all Being, Eternal Word and Holy Spirit.
  —Shelter...

CANTICLE OF ZECHARIAH

Ant. You are faithful to your word, forever.

INTERCESSIONS

O God, you bow to our weakness and need;
  —deliver us from temptation and guide us in the way of truth.
Your Spirit prays in us for what we know not how to ask;
  —let that same Spirit draw us to a maturity worthy of you.
Jesus, you drew your disciples to yourself and taught them eternal truths;

—bless the young people who must live in our streets,
    jobless and tempted to crime and despair.
Our minds and hearts are pulled in many directions;
    —let the words of your gospel unify and direct our lives.
The sick and the poor were drawn to you;
    —help us to find ways to care for all who are terminally ill.

PRAYER: O Holy God, you continue to bless us with your gifts of creation. We give thanks to you for your kindness to your people and take delight in the gifts we share to bring about the fullness of your life in our world. All praise to you, Most Blessed Trinity, living in us and among us through all generations. Amen.

DAYTIME PRAYER

Ant. 1 Teach us to love you and our neighbor, so as to fulfill your law.
Psalm 19:7-14

Your law, O God, is perfect,
reviving the soul.
Your testimony is to be trusted,
making the simple wise.

Your precepts are right,
rejoicing the heart.
Your command is pure,
giving light to the eyes.

The fear of God is holy,
enduring forever.
God's ordinances are true,
and all of them just.

More to be desired are they than
  gold,
more than the purest gold,
and sweeter are they than honey,
than drippings from the comb.

By them your servant finds
  instruction;
great reward is in their keeping.
But who can detect all one's
  errors?—

From hidden faults acquit me.

Restrain me from presumptuous
  sins,
let them not have rule over me!
Then shall I be blameless,
and clean from serious sin.

Let the words of my mouth,
the thoughts of my heart,
be acceptable in your sight,
O God, my rock and my
  redeemer. **Glory*...**

Ant. 2 Judge me, O God, according to your law.

Psalm 7
I

O God, in you I take refuge;
Save me from my pursuers and
  rescue me,
lest they tear me to pieces like a
  lion,
dragging me off with none to
  rescue me.

O God, if I have done this,
if my hands have done wrong,
if I have paid my friend with evil
or plundered without cause,—

then let my foes pursue me and
  seize me,
let them trample my life to the
  ground
and lay my soul in the dust.

Let the assembly of nations
  gather round you,
taking your seat above them on
  high.
For you, O God, are judge of the
  peoples.

Judge me, O God, according to
  my justice,
and according to the integrity
  that is mine.
Put an end to the evil of the
  wicked;
and make the just stand firm,
you who test the mind and heart,
you, our most just God!
  Glory*...

**Ant. 3 Search me, O God, and
know my heart; cleanse me
from all sin.**

II

God is the shield that protects
  me,
who saves the upright of heart.—

God is a just judge
slow to anger;
challenging the wicked every day,
those who are slow to repent.

God sharpens the sword,
bends the bow that is strung,
prepares deadly weapons for
  wickedness,
and barbs the arrows with fire.
Behold those who are pregnant
  with malice,
who conceive evil and bring forth
  lies.

They dig a pitfall, dig it deep;
and fall into the trap they have
  made.
Their malice will recoil on
  themselves;
on their own heads their violence
  will fall.

I will give thanks to you, God,
for your justice;
and will sing to your name,
  O Most High. **Glory*...**

PRAYER: As we pause to remember your fidelity to us, O Source
of Life, continue to abide with us this day. We give
thanks for all people working for justice and peace, and
we ask you, O God, to come in power to give your
people courage and strength. We ask this through the
intercession of Jesus and all who have given their lives
in the cause of justice. Amen.

EVENING PRAYER

Ant. 1 Teach us how to act justly, and to walk humbly with one another.

Psalm 11

In God I have taken my refuge.
How can you say to my soul:
"Fly like a bird to the mountains.

See the wicked bending the bow;
they have fitted their arrows on
the string
to shoot the upright in the dark.
If the foundations are destroyed,
what can the righteous do?"

But you are in your holy temple,
you, whose throne is in heaven.
Your eyes look down on the
world;
your gaze tests mortal flesh.

God tests the just and the
wicked,
scorned by the lovers of violence.
God will chastise those who do
evil;
a scorching wind shall be their
lot.

You are just and love justice;
the upright shall behold your
face. **Glory*...**

Ant. 2 Create in me an upright spirit that I may serve you in others.

Psalm 15

Who shall visit in your tent,
and dwell on your holy
mountain?

They who walk blamelessly,
and do what is right,
who speak the truth from their
hearts;—

and do not slander with their
tongues;

they who do no wrong to each
other,
nor cast reproaches on their
neighbors,
who pray the godless to repent,
and honor those who fear the
Most High;

they who keep their pledge, come
what may;
who take no profit from injustice,
nor accept bribes against the
innocent.
Such as these will stand firm
forever. **Glory*...**

Ant. 3 We are your people, chosen before the foundation of the world.

Cant: Ephesians 1:3–10

Praised be the God
of our Lord Jesus Christ,
who has blessed us in Christ
with every spiritual blessing in
the heavens.

God chose us in him
before the foundation of the
world,
that we should be holy
and blameless in God's sight.

We have been predestined
to be God's children through
Jesus Christ,
such was the purpose of God's
will,
that all might praise the glorious
favor
bestowed on us in Christ.

In Christ and through his blood,
we have redemption,—

the forgiveness of our sins,
according to the riches of God's
  grace lavished upon us.

For God has made known to us
in all wisdom and insight,
the mystery of the plan set forth
  in Christ.

A plan to be carried out in Christ,
in the fullness of time,
to unite all things in Christ,
things in heaven and things on
  earth. **Glory*...**

READING

If love is the soul of Christian existence, it must be at the heart of
every other Christian virtue. Thus, for example, *justice* without love is
legalism; *faith* without love is ideology; *hope* without love is self-
centeredness; *forgiveness* without love is self-abasement; *fortitude*
without love is recklessness; *generosity* without love is extravagance;
care without love is mere duty; *fidelity* without love is servitude. Every
virtue is an expression of love. No virtue is really a virtue unless it is
permeated, or informed, by love (1 Cor 13).

Richard P. McBrien, *Catholicism: Study Edition*, p. 977, (14)

RESPONSORY

Look upon us graciously, O God, and have mercy on us. **—Look...**
For you are our source of love; **—have**...
Glory to you, Source of all Being, Eternal Word and Holy Spirit.
   —Look...

CANTICLE OF MARY

Ant. I long for you, God of my life.

INTERCESSIONS

Jesus, you loved the land of your birth;
   —bless all nations torn by war and division.
You were filled with the Holy Spirit, the very Wisdom of God;
   —enlighten and guide all who labor to discover insights
      toward our spiritual and physical healing and growth.
Many believed in you because of your miracles;
   —let our love for you and for one another be the sign that
      draws others to you.
You welcomed outcasts and dined with them;
   —teach us how to reverently minister to those who are
      rejected today.
Your gospel is a call to life;
   —bring its message of peace to those who are dying.

PRAYER: Most loving God, you love justice. Help us to be open to your ways of mercy, compassion, and truth that we may call forth in ourselves and in one another your ways of wisdom and truth. We ask this through the Holy Spirit of Wisdom living in you through all eternity. Amen.

TUESDAY
MORNING PRAYER

Ant. 1 Blessed are the pure of heart, for they shall see God.

Psalm 24

Yours is the earth and its fullness,
the world and all who dwell there;
for you have founded it upon the
  seas,
and established it upon the rivers.

Who shall climb your mountain, O
  God?
Who shall stand in your holy
  place?
Those with clean hands and pure
  hearts,
who do not desire what is vain,
who have not sworn so as to
  deceive their neighbors.

They shall receive blessings from
  the Most High,
and reward from the God who
  saves them.
Such are those who seek after the
  Holy One;
who seek the face of the God of
  their ancestors.

O gates, lift up your heads;
grow higher, ancient doors.
Let enter the God of glory!

Who is this God of glory?
The One who is mighty and
  valiant,
valiant against all injustice.

O gates, lift up your heads;
grow higher, ancient doors.
Let enter the God of glory!

Who is this God of glory?
You, the God of hosts,
You, O God, are the God of glory.
  Glory*...

Ant. 2 Turn to me, O God, and show me your face.

Cant: Tobit 13:1b–8

Blessed be God who lives forever,
whose realm lasts for all ages.

For you scourge, O God, and then
  have mercy;
you cast down to the depths of the
  nether world,
and bring up from the great abyss.
No one can escape your hand.

Praise God, you Israelites, before
  the Gentiles,
for though you are scattered
  among them,
you have seen God's greatness
  even there.

Exalt God before every living
  being,
because you, O God, are the Most
  High,
our God forever and ever.

God has scourged you for your
  iniquities,—

but will again have mercy on you
all.
Gathering you from all the
Gentiles
among whom you have been
scattered.

When you turn back to God with
all your heart,
to do only what is right,
then God will turn back to you,
God's face will no longer be
hidden.

So now consider what has been
done for you,
and give praise with full voice.
Bless the God of righteousness,
and exalt the Ruler of the ages.

In the land of my exile I praise
you, O God,
and show your power and majesty
to a sinful nation.
"Turn back, you sinners! Do what
is right:
perhaps God may look with favor
upon you
and show you mercy.

As for me, I exult in my God,
and my spirit rejoices.
Let all speak of God's majesty,
and sing God's praises in
Jerusalem." **Glory*...**

**Ant. 3 Blessed are those who
hear your word and keep it.**

Psalm 33

Rejoice in God, O you just;
praise is fitting for loyal hearts.
We give thanks to you with the
lyre,
make melody with ten-stringed
harps.
Let us sing a song that is new,
and play skillfully, full of gladness.

For your words, O God are faithful
and all your works to be trusted.
You love justice and
righteousness,
and fill the earth with your
steadfast love.

By your word the heavens were
made,
by the breath of your mouth all
the stars.
You gather the waters of the
oceans;
you store up the depths of the
seas.

Let all the earth fear you, O God,
all who live in the world, stand in
wonder.
For you spoke; and it came to be.
You commanded; it sprang into
being.

You frustrate the designs of the
nations,
you upset the plans of the peoples.
Your own designs stand forever,
the plans of your heart to all
generations.

Happy are they whose God you
are,
the peoples you have chosen for
your heritage.
From the heavens you look forth,
and see all the peoples of the
earth.

From the place where you dwell
you gaze
on all the dwellers of this earth,
you who fashion the hearts of
them all
and observe all their deeds.

Rulers are not saved by their
armies,
nor leaders preserved by their
strength.—

A vain hope for safety are our
  weapons;
despite their power they cannot
  save.

Look on those who reverence you,
on those who hope in your love,
to deliver their souls from death,
and keep them alive in famine.

Our souls are waiting for you;
you are our help and our
  shield.
In you do our hearts find joy;
we trust in your holy name.

Let your love be upon us, O God,
as we place all our hope in you.
Glory*...

READING

Humanly speaking a genuine gift is given freely, out of love and not
out of necessity; its reception is occasion for gratitude and joy. In the
divine freedom to be present to all creatures, empowering them to
birth and rebirth in the midst of the antagonistic structures of reality,
the Spirit is intelligible as the first gift, freely given and giving. Her
loving in the world is gracious and inviting, never forcing or using
violence but respectfully calling to human freedom, as is befitting a
gift.

Elizabeth Johnson, *She Who Is*, p. 143, (2)

RESPONSORY

You call us each by name, for we are blessed in you. **—You call...**
Faithful to your promise; **—for we are...**
Glory to you, Source of all Being, Eternal Word and Holy Spirit.
   —You call...

CANTICLE OF ZECHARIAH

Ant. You are our God and holy is your name.

INTERCESSIONS

Jesus, you enabled your disciples to hear your call and to follow
you;
   —enable all Christians to discern the promptings of your
     Spirit and to respond wholeheartedly.
Through your death and rising, we have become your body; your
Spirit lives on in us;
   —awaken us to our responsibility as your people; let us meet
     each other with openness and good will.
Your apostle Paul prayed for an end to division within his
community;

—teach us positive ways to heal our differences and to
cultivate peace of mind for ourselves and our children.
Jesus, our Savior, you were taught and nourished by the words
of Scripture;
—may our hearing of the word of God today help us to bring
quality of life to those who are imprisoned, the oppressed,
and the disabled.
O God, time after time you spoke to your people and drew them
to conversion of heart;
—grant us the ability to read the signs of the times, that we
may hear your call to a change of heart as individuals and
as a people.

PRAYER: Most compassionate God, touch our hearts this
morning with your mercy and love. Help us to be a
source of love and light to those who are suffering this
day. May all who die today experience the joy of being
in your presence. Grant this through the intercession
of all who suffered persecution for the sake of justice.
Amen.

DAYTIME PRAYER

Ant. 1 The just shall praise you with upright hearts.

Psalm 119:1-8

Blessed are they whose way is
blameless,
who follow your law, O God!
Blessed are they who do your will,
who seek you with all their hearts,
who never do anything wrong,
but walk in your ways.

You have laid down your precepts
to be diligently kept.
O that my ways may be firm
in obeying your statutes.
Then I shall not be put to shame
as I heed your commands.

I will praise you with an upright
heart
as I learn your decrees.—

I will obey your statutes;
do not forsake me. **Glory*...**

Ant. 2 My heart rejoices in your saving grace, O God.

Psalm 13

How long, O God? Will you forget
me forever?
How long will you hide your face?
How long must I bear pain in my
soul,
and sorrow in my heart day and
night?
How long shall my oppressors
prevail?

Look at me, answer me, my God!
Lighten my eyes lest I sleep the
sleep of death,—

lest my oppressors say: "I have
  overcome you";
lest they rejoice to see me shaken.

As for me, I trust in your merciful
  love.
My heart rejoices in your
  salvation;
I will sing to you for your
  goodness,
because you are gracious to me.
  Glory*...

**Ant. 3 Give us your wisdom that
we may follow your way.**

Psalm 14

Fools say in their hearts:
"There is no God!"
They are corrupt, their deeds,
  depraved;
there are none that do good.

But you look down from heaven,
upon the peoples of the earth,—

to see if any are wise,
if any seek God.

All seem to have gone astray,
depraved, every one;
there are none that do good,
no, not even one.

Do evildoers have no knowledge?
They eat up God's people
as though they were eating bread;
do they never call upon the Most
  High God?

There they shall be in great terror,
for God is with the just.
You may mock the hope of the
  poor,
but their refuge is the Most High
  God.

O that Israel's salvation might
  come from Zion!
When God delivers the people from
  bondage,
then Jacob shall rejoice and Israel
  be glad. **Glory*...**

PRAYER: Gentle God, you remind us that you are our faithful
friend, and that you will deliver us from bondage.
Look upon us, your people, and deliver us from the
chains that keep us from the fullness of life. We pray
this in love and confidence in Jesus' name. Amen.

EVENING PRAYER

**Ant. 1 Only in you, O God, will
my soul be at rest.**

Psalm 20

May God answer in time of
  trouble!
May the name of our God protect
us.

Send your help, O God, from your
  sanctuary,
and give your support from Zion.
May you remember all our
  offerings
and receive our sacrifice with
  favor.

May you give us our heart's desire
and fulfill every one of our plans.-

May we ring out our joy at your
victory
and rejoice in your name, O God.
May you grant all our prayers.

Now I know that you, O God,
will give victory to your anointed;
you will reply from your holy
heaven
with the help of your hand.

Some trust in chariots or horses,
but we trust in your holy name.
They will collapse and fall,
but we shall rise and stand firm.

Give victory to your Anointed,
give answer on the day we call.
Glory*...

**Ant. 2 To know you, O God, is
to possess eternal life.**

Psalm 21:2-8, 14

O God, your strength gives joy to
your people;
how your saving help makes them
glad!
You have granted them the desire
of their hearts;
you have not refused the prayer of
their lips.

You came to meet them with
goodly blessings,
you have set blessings on their
heads.
They asked you for life and this
you have given,
length of days forever and ever.

Your saving help has given them
glory.—

Splendor you bestow upon them.
You grant your blessings to them
forever.
You gladden them with the joy of
your presence.

They put their trust in you:
through your steadfast love, they
shall stand firm.
O God, we exult in your strength;
we shall sing and praise your
goodness. **Glory*...**

**Ant. 3 O God, you have made us
in your own image.**

Cant: Rev 4:11, 5:9, 10, 12

Worthy are you, O God, our God,
to receive glory and honor and
power.

For you have created all things;
by your will they came to be and
were made.

Worthy are you to take the scroll
and to open its seals,

For you were slain, and by your
blood,
you purchased for God
saints of every race and tongue,
of every people and nation.

You have made of them a kindom,
and priests to serve our God,
and they shall reign on the earth.

Worthy is the Lamb who was slain
to receive power and riches,
wisdom and strength,
honor and glory and praise.
Glory*...

READING

As happiness lies in the ultimate perfection we all hope for, so there is
virtuous, contented rest in having accomplished the purpose for which

we begin a good work, and we should not linger in the task but take
heart in the promise of satisfaction and joy in the happy conclusion that
we trust our [God] will give to the good work begun.

Francisco de Osuna, The Third Spiritual Alphabet, p. 35, (1)

RESPONSORY

In you, Word of God, I place my trust and love.**—In you...**
For you are our redeemer; **—I place...**
Glory to you, Source of all Being, Eternal Word and Holy Spirit.
    —In you...

CANTICLE OF MARY

Ant. My soul will sing your praises.

INTERCESSIONS

O God, you are ever calling us to greater freedom, to walk in the
light, to grow and to deepen our lives;
    —give us the desire and the courage to respond fully to your
        goodness; make our lives pleasing to you.
Your compassion is boundless; you uphold your gift of freedom to
us;
    —deliver us from timidity and all that would keep us from
        turning to you.
Jesus, you respected those who worked with their hands; some
became your disciples;
    —preserve the dignity of those who work for others; deliver
        them from harassment of any kind.
You prayed with your people and read to them from the
Scriptures;
    —may all who lend their gifts to liturgical service enrich
        our lives and be blessed in their sharing.
You promised to be with us till the end of time;
    —may the words of your gospel keep hope alive in our hearts.

PRAYER: At the close of our day, we turn to you, our God, and
        with hearts of gratitude, we ask you to remember our
        deeds of goodness and to have mercy upon our
        shortcomings. May all who have died this day find
        peace in you and may all the sorrowing find comfort in
        those around them and in your compassionate heart.
        We ask this mindful of your mercy and forgiveness.
        Amen.

WEDNESDAY

MORNING PRAYER

Ant 1 You are the light of the world.

Psalm 36

Sin speaks to the wicked
in the depths of their hearts.
There is no fear of God
before their eyes.

They so flatter themselves in their
own eyes
that they know not their own
guilt.
In their mouths are mischief and
deceit.
They no longer act wisely or good.

They plot the defeat of goodness
as they lie on their beds.
They set their feet on evil ways,
and do not spurn what is evil.

But your steadfast love extends to
the heavens,
your faithfulness to the skies.
Your justice is like the mountain,
your judgments like the great
deep.

To both human and beast you give
salvation.
How precious is your love.
The children of this earth
take refuge in the shadow of your
wings.

They feast on the riches of your
house;
and drink from the stream of your
delight.
In you is the fountain of life
and in your light we see light.

Keep on loving those who know
you,
giving salvation to upright hearts.
Let the foot of the proud not crush
me
nor the hand of the wicked drive
me away.

There the evildoers lie prostrate!
Thrust down, they are unable to
rise. **Glory*...**

**Ant. 2 Let all creation bow down
before you.**

Cant: Judith 16:1, 13–15

Strike up the instruments,
a song to my God with timbrels,
chant to the Most High with
cymbals.
Sing a new song,
exalt and acclaim God's name.

A new hymn I will sing to you.
O God, great are you and glorious,
wonderful in power and
unsurpassable.

Let your every creature serve you;
for you spoke, and they were
made,
you sent forth your spirit, and
they were created;
no one can resist your word.

The mountains to their bases, and
the seas, are shaken;
the rocks, like wax, melt before
your glance.
But to those who fear you,
you are very merciful. **Glory*...**

Ant. 3 We sing praise to you, Most High.

Psalm 47

Clap your hands, all you peoples,
shout to God with songs of joy!
For the Most High we must fear,
great ruler over all the earth!

O God, you subdue evil
  oppression,
and challenge unjust nations.
You chose our heritage for us,
gave it to us out of love.

You go up with shouts of joy;
O God, with trumpet blast.—

We sing praise to you, sing
  praise,
sing praise to you, Most High.

For your realm is all the earth.
We sing to you our hymns of
  praise!
Your reign is over all the nations;
Over all the peoples of this earth.

The leaders of the peoples gather
with the people of Abraham's
  God.
May all leaders of the earth pay
  heed,
to God who reigns over all.
   Glory*...

READING

My [God], you are my hope; you the glory; you the joy; you my
blessedness. You are the thirst of my spirit; you the life of my soul, you
the jubilation of my heart. Where above you could my wonder lead me,
my God? You are the beginning and the consummation of all the good,
and in you all those who are glad have, as it were, a dwelling-place
together. You are the praise in my heart and mouth. You glow altogether
red in the spring-like loveliness of the festival of your love. May your
most outstanding divinity magnify and glorify you because you are the
source of light and the fountain of life forever.
                      Gertrud the Great of Helfta, *Spiritual Exercises*, p. 101, (7)

RESPONSORY

Living source of light and wisdom, be with us always. —**Living...**
In you we find new life; —**be with...**
Glory to you, Source of all Being, Eternal Word and Holy Spirit.
   —**Living...**

CANTICLE OF ZECHARIAH

Ant. You are faithful to your promise, God of all the ages.

INTERCESSIONS

O God, you know our coming and our going, and you bless our
every effort to live justly;
   —help us to remember your faithfulness and that our
     inspiration and strength is your gift.

You have power over all that you have created;
—enable warring nations to redeem the wounds of the past
and to discover creative ways to peace.
Jesus, you were rejected by your own people;
—direct each of us to a milieu that is receptive of our gifts.
Love is patient and kind, but a stressful world can thin our
resources;
—have mercy on parents who are overworked and fearful;
guide and protect teen-agers who run away from home.
Mindful that you call us to be a light in darkness, we pray;
—be with us in our poverty and need.

PRAYER: O God, source of our light, you are ever with us to
reveal the way of truth and justice. Be with us this day
as we struggle to ease the burdens of our sisters and
brothers. We ask this in Jesus who is our way, our
truth, and our life. Amen.

DAYTIME PRAYER

Ant. 1 Your law is written on my heart.
Psalm 119:9–16

How shall the young remain
sinless?
By living according to your word.
I have sought you with all my
heart;
let me not stray from your
commands.

I carry your word in my heart
lest I sin against you.
Blessed are you, O God;
teach me your statutes.

With my lips I have recounted
all the decrees of your mouth.
I delight to do your will
as though all riches were mine.

I will meditate on your precepts
and fix my eyes on your ways.
I will delight in your statutes;—

I will not forget your word.
Glory*...

Ant. 2 You are a light to my eyes, a lamp for my feet.

Psalm 17

O God, hear a cause that is just,
attend to my cry.
Give ear to my prayer
from lips free of deceit.

If you should try my heart
or visit me by night;
if you should test me,
you will find no deceit in me;
my tongue has not deceived.

Because of the word of your
mouth
I have avoided the ways of the
violent.
My steps have held fast to your
paths,
my feet have not slipped.

I call upon you, for you will hear
me.
Turn your ear to me; hear my
words.
Show your steadfast love,
to all who seek refuge
in the shelter of your hand.

Keep me as the apple of your eye.
Hide me in the shadow of your
wings
from the wicked who seek to
destroy. **Glory*...**

**Ant. 3 You are my portion, the
God of my life.**

II

They close their hearts to pity;
with their mouths they speak
arrogantly.
They track me down, surrounding
me;
setting their eyes to cast me to
the ground—

as though they were a lion eager
to tear,
as a young lion lurking in
ambush.

Arise, O God, confront them,
strike them down!
Deliver my life from the wicked;
by your hand, O God, rescue me
from evildoers,
from those whose portion is of
this world.

May they be filled from the
abundance of your storehouse;
may their children have more
than enough;
may their wealth extend to their
offspring.

As for me, in my justice I shall
see your face;
when I awake, I shall be filled
with the sight of your glory.
Glory*...

PRAYER: God of wisdom, enlighten us with your spirit that we
may work to bring about your love and justice within
our hearts and in the hearts of all your people.
Strengthen us with insight to be faithful to your word
revealed among us. Grant this through the
intercessions of all those who faithfully heard your
word and kept it. Amen.

EVENING PRAYER

**Ant. 1 You are my dwelling
place, in you I take my rest.**

Psalm 27

O God, you are my light and my
help;
whom shall I fear?
You are the stronghold of my life;
before whom shall I be afraid?

When evildoers assail me
uttering slanders against me,
it is they, my enemies and foes,
who shall stumble and fall.

Though an army encamp against
me
my heart shall not fear.
Though war break out against me
yet will I trust.

One thing I have asked of you,
for this will I seek,
that I may dwell in your holy
  house
all the days of my life,
to behold the beauty of your
  countenance
and the holiness of your temple.

In your shelter you will hide me
in the day of trouble;
you will conceal me under the
  cover of your tent,
you will set me high upon a rock.

And now my head shall be raised
above my foes who surround me;
and I will offer in your tent
sacrifices with songs of joy.
I will sing and make music to my
God. **Glory*...**

**Ant. 2 It is you, O God that I
seek.**

II

Hear my voice when I cry aloud,
be gracious to me and give
  answer!
You say to me: "Seek my face,
Seek the face of your God."

"Your face, O God, I do seek."
Hide not your face from me.
Do not dismiss me in anger;
you have been my help.

Do not cast me off or forsake me,
O God, my help!
Though father and mother
  forsake me,
You, O God, will receive me.

Teach me your way, O God;
lead me on a level path.
Give me not up to the will of
  evildoers;
who bear false witness and
  breathe out violence.

I believe I shall see your goodness
in the land of the living.
Hope in God, be strong and take
  heart.
Hope in God, the Most High!
    Glory*...

**Ant. 3 Jesus is the image of the
invisible God.**

Cant: Colossians 1:12-20

Let us give thanks to God
for having made us worthy
to share the inheritance of the
  saints in light.

God has delivered us
from the power of darkness
and transferred us
into the kindom of God's beloved
  Son, Jesus,
in whom we have redemption,
the forgiveness of our sins.

Jesus is the image of the invisible
  God,
the first-born of all creation;
in him all things were created,
in heaven and on earth,
things visible and invisible.

All things were created through
  him;
all were created for him.
He is before all else that is.
In him all things hold together.

He is the head of the body, the
  church!
He is the beginning,
the firstborn from the dead,
that in everything, he might be
  above all others.

In him all the fullness of God was
  pleased to dwell,
and through him, to reconcile all
  things to himself,—

whether on earth or in heaven,
making peace by the blood of his
   cross. **Glory*...**

READING

Certainly when [I] lie in jail thinking of these things, thinking of war and
peace, and the problems of human freedom...and the apathy of great
masses of people who believe that nothing can be done, I am all the
more confirmed in my faith in the little way of St. Thérèse. We do the
minute things that come to hand, we pray our prayers, and beg also for
an increase of faith—and God will do the rest.

The Dorothy Day Book, p. 59, (21)

RESPONSORY

Hold me gently, O God, in the palm of your hand. **—Hold...**
In you I find my rest; **—in the...**
Glory to you, Source of all Being, Eternal Word and Holy Spirit.
   —Hold...

CANTICLE OF MARY

**Ant. You have done great things for us and holy is your
    name.**

INTERCESSIONS

Faith, hope, and love are the things that last;
   —O God, make us good stewards of what we have, and grant
    us the help we need to be a sign of your kindom.
You created our bodies as temples of the Holy Spirit;
   —send your healing to victims of rape, incest, and every
    form of violence that destroys and deforms.
You call each one of us to be holy;
   —help us to reflect the divine imprint of your creativity in our
    lives.
You bless those who bear insult and persecution;
   —give wise advocates to those who are falsely accused; make
    us humble and just in our speech.
In the many voices that cry out for attention, help us to recognize
you and to pray;
   —"Speak, O God, for your servant is listening."

PRAYER: In the evening we come to you, O God, to thank you for
          the blessings of this day. May we be ever mindful of
          your love in the midst of life's joys and burdens, and

may all your people experience your peace this night. This we ask placing ourselves in your care, Most Blessed Trinity. Amen.

THURSDAY

MORNING PRAYER

Ant. 1 In the early hours of the morning, my heart will sing your praise.

Psalm 57

Have mercy on me, have mercy,
for in you my soul takes refuge.
In the shadow of your wings I take refuge
till the storms of destruction pass by.

I cry to God the Most High,
to God who has always been my help.
May you send from heaven and save me
and shame those who trample upon me.
O God, send your truth and your love.

My soul lies down among lions,
who greedily devour the peoples of the earth.
Their teeth are spears and arrows,
their tongues a sharpened sword.

Be exalted, O God, above the heavens;
let your glory be over all the earth!

They laid a snare for my steps,
my soul was bowed down.
They dug a pit in my path
but they fell in it themselves.

My heart is steadfast, O God,
my heart is steadfast.
I will sing and make melody!—

Awake, my soul,
awake, lyre and harp!
I will awake the dawn!

I will give thanks to you among the peoples,
I will praise you among the nations
for your love reaches to the heavens
your faithfulness to the skies.

Be exalted, O God, above the heavens!
let your glory be over all the earth!
Glory*...

Ant. 2 You are the bread of life; you are the cup of salvation.

Cant: Jeremiah 31:10–14

Hear the word of God, O nations,
proclaim it on distant coasts and say:
God who scattered Israel, now gathers them together,
and guards them as shepherds guard their flocks.

God will ransom the chosen people
and redeem them from the hands of their conquerors.

Shouting, they shall mount the heights of Zion,
they shall come streaming to God's blessings:
the grain, the wine, and the oil,—

the sheep and the oxen;
they themselves shall be like
  watered gardens,
never again shall they languish.

Then the young shall make merry
  and dance,
old men and women as well.
I will turn their mourning into joy,
I will console and gladden them
  after their sorrows.
I will lavish choice portions upon
  them,
and my people shall be filled with
  my blessings,
says our God. **Glory*....**

**Ant. 3 Let us build the city of
God!**

Psalm 48

O God, you are great and worthy
  to be praised
in your holy city.
Your holy mountain rising in
  beauty,
is the joy of all the earth.

Mount Zion, in the far north,
your holy city!
Within its citadels,
you show yourself its stronghold.

For invaders assembled together,
together they advanced.—

As soon as they saw it, they were
  astounded;
in panic they took to flight.

Trembling took hold of them there,
like the anguish of a woman giving
  birth;
By the east wind you have
  shattered the ships of Tarshish.

As we have heard, so we have seen
in the city of our God,
in the city of the Most High
which God establishes forever.

O God, we ponder your love
in the midst of your temple.
Your praise, like your name
reaches to the ends of the earth.

With justice your hands are filled.
Let Mount Zion be glad!
The people of Judah rejoice
because of your judgments.

Walk through Zion, walk all round
  it;
number its towers.
Review its ramparts,
examine its citadels;

that you may tell the next
  generation
that this is our God,
our God forever and ever.
You will always be our guide.
    Glory*...

READING

It is with the moral infirmities we may see in one another—our defects
of character or temperament, our faults, our failings—that I think we
should try to be watchful to exercise charity in thought, word, and
deed. It is so easy and so natural to criticize; yet we cannot do so even
interiorly without detriment to our soul. Such thoughts consented to,
certainly retard our progress in the perfection of charity, if they do not
offend God.

Mother Aloysius Rogers, OCD, Fragrance from Alabaster, p. 18, (6)

RESPONSORY

I have seen the glory of God, in the land of the living. **—I have...**
You are with us always; **—in the...**
Glory to you, Source of all Being, Eternal Word and Holy Spirit.
   —I have...

CANTICLE OF ZECHARIAH

Ant. In love let us ponder your word forever.

INTERCESSIONS

O God, the path to holiness includes times of emptiness and
darkness;
   —let us realize that you are with us as you walked with
      Jesus on his journey toward the cross.
Holy, holy, holy are you, O God; the whole earth is full of your
glory;
   —help us to live compatibly with our environment.
The voice of God said, "Whom shall I send, and who will go for
us";
   —with your help, may I answer: "Here I am! Send me."
Jesus, you healed many who were sick with various diseases;
   —be with all healers and health care personnel as they give
      of themselves to care for us.
Jesus, you have called us to preach the good news by the
statement of our lives;
   —help us to live the truth with compassion.

PRAYER: Most gracious God and Father, you are with us as we
   make our journey throughout this day. Help us to
   look lovingly upon all people and events that come
   into our lives today and to walk gently upon our land.
   Grant this through Jesus who lives and walks among
   us ever present at each moment. Amen.

DAYTIME PRAYER

Ant. 1 I am a sojourner on earth; Open my eyes that I may behold
   teach me your ways. the wonders of your law.

Psalm 119:17–24 I am a sojourner on earth;
hide not your commands from
Bless your servant that I may live me!—
and obey your word.—

My soul is consumed with longing
forever, for your decrees.

You rebuke the insolent,
who turn from your commands.
Relieve me of their scorn and
  contempt
for I have kept your word.

Though others sit plotting against
  me
I ponder on your statutes.
Your will is my delight;
your decrees are my counselors.
  Glory*...

**Ant. 2 Lead me in your truth,
  and guide me in the path of
  salvation.**
Psalm 25

To you, O God, I lift up my soul.
In you, I trust, let me not be put to
  shame;
let not the wicked exult over me.
Those who wait on you shall not be
  put to shame;
but only those who wantonly break
  faith.

Make me know your ways, O God;
Teach me your paths.
Lead me in your truth, and teach
  me,
for you are God, my savior.
For you I wait all the day long.

Remember your mercy, O God,
and your steadfast love,
which you have given from of old.
Remember not the sins of my
  youth, or my transgressions;
But in your goodness, remember
  me
according to your steadfast love!

You, O God, are good and upright.
You instruct sinners in your way.
You lead the humble in the right
  path;
you teach your way to the poor.

All your ways are loving and
  constant
for those who keep your covenant
  and your decrees.
For your name's sake, O God,
pardon my guilt, for it is great.
  Glory*...

**Ant. 3 Say but the word, and I
  shall be healed.**
II

Those who fear you, O God,
you will instruct in the way they
  should choose.
They shall abide in prosperity,
and their children shall possess
  the land.
Your friendship is for those who
  revere you;
make known to them your
  covenant.

My eyes are ever turned toward
  you,
for you rescue my feet from the
  snare.
Turn to me and be gracious to me;
for I am lonely and afflicted.

Relieve the troubles of my heart
and bring me out of my distress.
See my affliction and my troubles,
and forgive all my sins.

See how many are my faults,
with what violence they pursue me.
Preserve my life and deliver me;
let me not be put to shame,—

for I take refuge in you.
May integrity and uprightness
  preserve me:
for my hope is in you.

Redeem Israel, O God, from all its
  troubles. **Glory*...**

PRAYER: To you, O God, we lift up our hearts at this midday
prayer. We ask you to remember us and all those who
are troubled at this time. Help us to reach out in
justice and charity to those in need among us. Grant
this through the intercessions of all who served you in
serving your poor. Amen.

EVENING PRAYER

**Ant. 1 You heal my affliction;
you restore my soul to life!**
Psalm 30

I will praise you, O God, you have
  rescued me
and have not let evil triumph over
  me.

O God, I cried to you for help
and you have healed me.
You have raised my soul from the
  dead,
restored me to life from among
  those gone down to the grave.

We sing praises to you, we your
  people,
and give thanks to your holy
  name.
For your anger lasts but a
  moment,
your favors for a lifetime.
At night there may be weeping,
but joy comes with the morning.

I said to myself in my prosperity,
"Nothing will ever disturb me."
By your favor, O God,
you have made me strong as a
  mountain;
when you hide your face, I am
  dismayed.

O God, to you I cried,
to you I make supplication:
"What profit is there in my death,
if I go down to the grave?
Can dust praise you, or tell of your
  faithfulness?"

Hear, O God, and be gracious to
  me!
O God be my help!
You have turned my mourning
  into dancing;
you have removed my sackcloth
  and clothed me with gladness,
that I may praise you with full
  voice,
and give thanks to you forever.
    Glory*...

**Ant. 2 In the integrity of my
heart, I lay my guilt before you.**

Psalm 32

Happy are they whose faults are
  forgiven,
whose sins are covered.
Happy are they to whom our God
  imputes no guilt,
in whose spirits there is no deceit.

When I declared not my sin,
my body wasted away—

with groanings all the day long.
For day and night your hand was
heavy upon me;
my strength was dried up as by
the heat of summer.

When I acknowledged my sin to
you,
and did not hide my guilt;
I said: "I will confess my sins to
you, O God."
Then you did forgive me the guilt
of my sin.

So let all who acclaim you offer
prayers;
in times of distress, the rush of
the flood waters will not reach
them.
For you are a hiding place for me,
you preserve me from trouble;
you surround me with deliverance.

I will instruct you and teach you
the way you should go;
I will counsel you with my eye
upon you.
Be not like a horse or a mule,
without understanding,
which must be curbed with bit and
bridle else it will not keep you.

Many are the sorrows of the
wicked;
but faithful love surrounds those
who trust in you.
We rejoice in you and are glad.
Let all the upright in heart rejoice
and shout for joy.
   Glory*...

**Ant. 3 Behold the Lamb of God,
   who takes away the sins of the
   world.**
   **Cant: Rev 11: 17–18;
      12:10b–12a**

We praise you, God Almighty,
who is and who was.
You have assumed your great
power,
you have begun your reign.

The nations have raged in anger,
but then came your day of wrath
and the moment to judge the
dead;
the time to reward your servants
the prophets
and the holy ones who revere you,
the great and the small alike.

Now have salvation and power
come,
your reign, O God, and the
authority of your Anointed One.
For the accusers of our loved ones
have been cast out,
who night and day accused them.

By the blood of the Lamb have
they been defeated,
and by the testimony of your
servants;
love for life did not deter them
from death.
So rejoice, you heavens,
and you that dwell therein!
   Glory*...

READING

Jesus gives [his disciples] a simple, clear example of what discipleship
is all about: service. Washing one another's feet, feeding the hungry,
clothing the naked—here is the core of the Eucharist, our great miracle
of love.... God's table is large, as large as creation. All are invited, all are

to have access to the necessity of food and the miracle of love. Both are essential to the fullness of life. Without food, the body languishes and dies; without love, our souls wither and are filled with despair. The leftovers in our lives? What are they and who will get them? So many people can live off our leavings if we would only share. This is hardly sufficient. Disciples of Christ give abundantly in imitation of the Master who gave his very self.

Robert F. Morneau, Ashes to Easter, p. 107, p. 108, (2)

RESPONSORY

You gather us together in the bosom of your love. **—You...**
As a mother hen, **—in the...**
Glory to you, Source of all Being, Eternal Word and Holy Spirit. **—You...**

CANTICLE OF MARY

Ant. In you I rejoice all the days of my life.

INTERCESSIONS

Jesus, in the days of your ministry, many traveled far to listen to you;
   —keep alive our search for truth and our efforts to live by it.
You tell us not to be afraid;
   —let your Spirit guide the oppressed as they seek ways to freedom.
You call us "salt of the earth";
   —make us your true followers, one with the suffering of the world, and calling down God's blessing on your people.
You withdrew to lonely places, praying in the night;
   —remind us that you are with us in light or darkness, joy or sorrow—the abiding guest of our hearts.
Spirit of God, source of our deepest desires for good;
   —show us ways to be light for the world.

PRAYER: You, Mother and God, are our safety in times of distress. Show us your ways of peace that we may gather one another into your loving embrace, into your dwelling place. May you be with us this night and may all those in darkness walk in your light. Grant this, Spirit of Comfort, through Jesus, our brother. Amen.

FRIDAY

MORNING PRAYER

Ant 1 Create in me a clean heart, O God.
Psalm 51

Have mercy on me, O God,
according to your steadfast love;
in your abundant mercy blot out
my sins.
Wash me thoroughly from my
offenses,
and cleanse me from my sin!

For I know my offenses,
and my sin is ever before me.
Against you, you alone, have I
sinned,
and done what is evil in your
sight,
so you are justified in your
sentence
and blameless in your judgment.
Behold, I was brought forth in a
sinful world.

For you desire truth in my
innermost being;
teach me wisdom in the depths of
my heart.
O purify me, and I shall be clean;
O wash me, I shall be whiter than
snow.
Fill me with joy and gladness;
let the bones you have broken
rejoice.
Hide your face from my guilt,
and blot out all my offenses.

Create in me a clean heart,
put a steadfast spirit within me.
Cast me not from your presence,
take not your spirit from me.
Give me again the joy of your
salvation,
with a willing spirit uphold me.

Then I will teach transgressors
your ways
and sinners will return to you.
Deliver me from death,
O God of my salvation,
and my tongue will sing out your
saving help.

Open my lips and my mouth will
sing your praises.
For you take no delight in
sacrifice;
were I to give a burnt offering,
you would not be pleased.
A broken spirit you accept;
a contrite heart, you will not
despise.

In your goodness, show favor to
Zion;
rebuild the walls of Jerusalem.
Then you will delight in just
sacrifices,
in gifts offered on your altar.
   Glory*...

Ant. 2 You are our God, there is no other besides you.

Cant: Isaiah 45:15-25

Truly you are a God who is
hidden,
the God of Israel, the savior!
They are put to shame and
disgraced,
the makers of idols are put to
confusion.

Israel, you are saved by the Most
High,
with everlasting salvation!
You shall never be put to shame
or disgraced for all eternity.

For thus says the Most High,
the creator of the heavens,
who is God,
the designer and maker of the
  earth,
who established it,
not creating it as chaos,
but designing it to be lived in.

I am God, and there is no other.
I have not spoken in secret,
in a land of darkness;
I have not said to the
  descendants of my people,
"Look for me in chaos."
I, your God, speak the truth,
I declare what is right.

Come and assemble, gather
  together,
you survivors of the nations!
They are without knowledge who
  bear wooden idols
and pray to gods that cannot
  save.

Come here and declare in counsel
  together!
Who declared this from the
  beginning
and foretold it from of old?
Was it not I, your God?
There is no other besides me,
a just and saving God!

Turn to me and be saved,
all you ends of the earth,
for I am God; there is no other!
By myself I have sworn,
uttering my just decree—

and my word which cannot be
  changed.

To me every knee shall bend;
by me every tongue shall swear,
saying, "Only in you, our God, are
  justice and righteousness.

You, O God, shall be the
  vindication and the glory
of all the descendants of Israel."
  Glory*...

**Ant. 3 We are your people, the
sheep of your pasture.**

Psalm 100

All the earth cries out to you with
  shouts of joy, O God,
Serving you with gladness;
coming before you, singing for
  joy.

You, Creator of all, are God.
You made us, we belong to you,
we are your people, the sheep of
  your pasture.

We enter your gates with
  thanksgiving,
and your courts with songs of
  praise!
We give you thanks and bless
  your name.

Indeed, how good you are,
enduring, your steadfast love.
You are faithful to all generations.
  Glory*...

READING

...Ask grace not instruction, desire not understanding, the groaning of
prayer not diligent reading, the Spouse not the teacher, God not
[people], darkness not clarity, not light but the fire that totally inflames
and carries us into God by ecstatic unctions and burning affections.

This fire is God, and [God's] furnace is in Jerusalem; and Christ enkindles it in the heat of his burning passion...

Bonaventure, *The Soul's Journey into God*, p. 115, (1)

RESPONSORY

You are the Good Shepherd, have compassion on us. —**You are...**
In you we find mercy; —**have...**
Glory to you, Source of all Being, Eternal Word and Holy Spirit.
   —**You are...**

CANTICLE OF ZECHARIAH

Ant. You teach us the way of peace.

INTERCESSIONS

O God, you are Truth itself;
   —give us discerning hearts that we may live full and creative
      lives.
Jesus, you walked among the outcasts of your day, healing them
and drawing them to yourself;
   —help us to walk in your ways that those who are shunned
      by society may know your love and healing through us.
Jesus, you bless with a hundredfold our endeavors to serve you;
   —give us the generosity to enable and support one another.
Spirit of God, you pray within us for needs we hardly know;
   —make our prayer one with yours that we may be one with
      you.
Eternal Shepherd, every person and the future of us all is
precious to you;
   —bless those who are tempted to take negative or destructive
      paths this day.

PRAYER: Forgiving God, look not upon our sins but upon our
desire to serve you and one another. Dispel our
darkness, and help us to embrace our failings in
loving union with your goodness. Heal us this day,
and may we be a source of strength and courage for
others. Grant this through the intercession of all
those who fill up what is wanting in the sufferings of
Christ. Amen.

DAYTIME PRAYER

Ant. 1 I cling to your will, O God.

Psalm 119:25-32

My soul cleaves to the dust;
revive me according to your word!
I told of my ways and you
  answered me;
teach me your statutes.

Make me understand the way of
  your precepts
and I will ponder on your wonders.
My soul pines with sorrow;
strengthen me by your word.

Keep me from the way of
  falsehood;
and teach me your law!
I have chosen the way of
  faithfulness,
I set your decrees before me.

I cling to your will, O God;
let me not be put to shame!
I will run in the way of your
  commands;
when you enlighten my
  understanding. **Glory*...**

**Ant. 2 I trust in God without
  wavering.**

Psalm 26

Judge me, O God, for I walk in the
  way of integrity,
I trust in you without wavering.

Examine me, O God, and try me;
test my heart and my mind,
for your steadfast love is before
  me,
and I walk to you in faithfulness.

I do not sit with the wicked,
nor conspire with those who cause
  trouble;—

I avoid the company of evildoers;
and those who speak falsehood.

I wash my hands in innocence,
and gather around your altar,
singing a song of thanksgiving,
and telling of all your wonders.

I love the house where you live,
the place where your glory dwells.
Do not sweep me away with
  sinners,
nor my life with those who
  oppress,
who plot evil deeds,
whose hands are full of bribes.

As for me, I walk the path of
  integrity.
Redeem me, and be gracious to
  me.
My foot stands on level ground;
I will bless you in the assembly.
    Glory*...

**Ant. 3 I call to you, O God, hear
  the sound of my voice.**

Psalm 28:1-3, 6-9

To you, O God, I call,
my rock, be not deaf to me.
If you turn your ear away from me,
I become like those in the grave.

Hear the voice of my pleading
as I cry to you for help,
as I lift up my hands in prayer
to your holy sanctuary.

Do not take me away with the
  wicked,
with those who are workers of evil,
who speak peace with their
  neighbors,
while evil is in their hearts.

I bless you, for you have heard
the voice of my supplication.
You are my strength and my
  shield;
in you my heart trusts.
I am helped, and my heart exults,
with my song I give you thanks.

You are the strength of your
  people,
you are the refuge of your
  anointed.
Save your people; and bless your
  heritage;
be their shepherd and carry them
  forever. **Glory*...**

PRAYER: Jesus, our Redeemer, you brought us into life by dying
upon the cross. May we search for new ways to
alleviate suffering among all creatures that your name
be glorified and that peace may find a home in us. We
ask this in the name of all creation that groans for your
salvation to be realized within its being. Amen.

EVENING PRAYER

**Ant. 1 Be gracious to me, O
God, for I have sinned.**

Psalm 41

Blessed are they who consider
  the poor!
O God, you deliver them in the
  day of trouble;
you guard them and give them
  life;
they are called blessed in the
  land;
you do not give them up to
  temptation.
You sustain them on their
  sickbeds;
you heal them of all their
  infirmities.

As for me, I said: "O God, be
  gracious to me,
heal me, for I have sinned against
  you."
Some could say of me in malice:
"When will you die and your
  name perish?"—

They come to see me, uttering
  empty words,
while their hearts gather
  mischief;
and spread it abroad.
They whisper about me,
  imagining the worst of me.

They say, "A deadly thing has
  come upon you;
you will not rise from where you
  lie."
Even my friend in whom I
  trusted,
who ate of my bread, has turned
  against me.

But you, O God, be gracious to
  me.
Raise me up in your great mercy.
By this I shall know that you are
  pleased with me,
that evildoers have not
  triumphed.
You have upheld me in my
  integrity,—

and set me in your presence
forever.

Blessed are you, God of Israel,
from everlasting to everlasting.
Amen. Amen. **Glory*...**

**Ant. 2 In the stillness we will
hear your voice.**

Psalm 46

God is our refuge and strength,
a helper in time of trouble.
We shall not fear though the
earth should rock,
though the mountains fall into
the depths of the sea,
though its waters rage and foam,
though the mountains tremble
with its tumult.

There is a river whose streams
gladden the city of God,
the holy place of the Most High.
God is within, it shall not be
moved;
God will help it at the dawning of
the day.
Nations rage, sovereignties are
shaken;
at the sound of God's voice, the
earth melts away.

The God of hosts is with us;
the God of our ancestors is our
refuge.

Come, behold the works of our
God,
who has wrought wonders on the
earth.
Making wars cease to the ends of
the earth;
breaking the bow, snapping the
spear,
burning the chariots with fire.
"Be still, and know that I am God,
I am exalted among the nations,
I am exalted on the earth!"

The God of hosts is with us;
the God of our ancestors is our
refuge. **Glory*....**

**Ant. 3 You are the ruler of all
the ages, O God.**

Cant: Rev 15:3-4

Great and wonderful are your
works,
God the Almighty One!
Just and true are your ways,
Ruler of all the ages!

Who shall refuse you honor,
or the glory due your name?

For you alone are holy,
all nations shall come and
worship in your presence.
Your judgments are clearly seen.
Glory*...

READING

I asked the earth, the sea and the deeps, heaven, the sun, the moon
and the stars.... My questioning of them was my contemplation, and
their answer was their beauty.... They do not change their voice, that is
their beauty, if one person is there to see and another to see and to
question.... Beauty appears to all in the same way, but is silent to one
and speaks to the other.... They understand it who compare the voice
received on the outside with the truth that lies within.

The Confessions of St. Augustine (adapted), pp. 234-35, (48)

RESPONSORY

In the spirit of Jesus, we give praise to our God. **—In the...**
For our sins are forgiven; **—we give...**
Glory to you, Source of all Being, Eternal Word and Holy Spirit.
   —In the...

CANTICLE OF MARY

Ant. Your covenant is one of mercy and forgiveness.

INTERCESSIONS

The law of God is perfect, refreshing the soul;
   —let your love, O God, be our law of life and perfect guide.
Your forgiveness of humankind flows from generation to
generation;
   —heal the nations that continue to seek vengeance; teach us
      all how to forgive in the name of Jesus.
Jesus, you stayed in desert places, strengthened there by God.
   —In time of pain or trouble, help us to find God in the solitude
      of our hearts.
You are our hope in life and in death;
   —help us to live our belief in you for the strength and courage
      of all in need of your truth.
Spirit of God, your gifts abound in humankind;
   —bless the poor whose creativity is buried by a raw search
      for survival.

PRAYER: Jesus, you heal the sick and brokenhearted. Let your
            mercy be upon us so that we may be a sign of your
            mercy in our world. We thank you for your forgiveness
            and for bringing us to this time of our lives. May all
            those who died find rest in you. Grant this through the
            intercession of all who died forgiving those who
            oppressed them. Amen.

SATURDAY

MORNING PRAYER

Ant. 1 Before the dawn, O God, hear my call for help.

Psalm 119: 145–152

With all my heart, I cry to you;
answer me, O God.
I cry to you; save me,
that I may observe your will.

I rise before dawn and cry for help;
I hope in your words.
My eyes watch throughout the
night
meditating on your promises.

Hear my voice in your steadfast
love;
in your justice preserve my life.
Those who persecute me draw
near;
they are far from your law.

But you, O God, are near at hand,
all your commands are true.
Long have I known that your will
endures forever. **Glory*...**

Ant. 2 Bring me to your holy mountain, the place of your dwelling.

Cant: Exodus 15:1–4a, 8–13, 17–18

I will sing to you, O God, for you
are gloriously triumphant;
horse and rider you have cast into
the sea.

You are my strength and my
courage,
you are my salvation.
You are my God, I praise you;
God of my ancestors, I extol you.

Pharaoh's chariots and army you
cast into the sea.
At a breath of your anger the
waters piled up,
the floods stood up in a heap;
the floods congealed in the midst
of the sea.

The enemy boasted, "I will pursue
and overtake them;
I will divide the spoils and have
my fill of them;
I will draw my sword; my hand
shall destroy them!"
When your wind blew, the sea
covered them;
they sank as lead in the mighty
waters.

Who is like you, among the gods?
Who is like you, majestic in
holiness,
terrible in glorious deeds, worker
of wonders?
You stretched out your hand, the
earth swallowed them!

In your love you led the people
you redeemed;
you guided them to your holy
dwelling.

You bring them in and plant them
on your mountain,
the place you have made for your
abode,
the sanctuary which your hands
have established.
You, O God, will reign forever and
ever. **Glory*...**

Ant. 3 O praise God all you nations.

Psalm 117

Praise our God, all you nations!
Acclaim the Most High, all you
    peoples!

For great is your love for us;
and your faithfulness endures
    forever. **Glory*...**

READING

Mindful now of our own rich tradition of meditation and contemplative
prayer and eager to learn what is "true and holy" in other religions, the
time is right for us to learn from one another, from whatever culture
and religion, all that is helpful in moving toward a simpler life, a
deeper life, and a more authentic life in which the inner experience of
God is primary and energizing and centering!

Pascaline Coff, osb, "Many Mansions," (4)

RESPONSORY

Your love is round about me; in you I find my life. **—Your love...**
Forever I will sing your praise; **—in you...**
Glory to you, Source of all Being, Eternal Word and Holy Spirit.
    —Your love...

CANTICLE OF ZECHARIAH

Ant. You are the light of my salvation.

INTERCESSIONS

O God, your son Jesus prayed that we all may be one;
    —help us to love one another as you love us.
All of creation cries out for healing;
    —make us instruments of your peace.
You are the Center of all that is;
    —teach us to listen to your life within us.
Many do not know your love and care for us;
    —let our lives bear witness to your unending mercy.
You call us to live in freedom and happiness;
    —give hope and peace of heart to all in prison or bondage
    of any kind.

PRAYER: You give and sustain our lives, O God, and in you we
    find our sanctuary. May all displaced people find a
    place of sanctuary and safety in our hearts and

homes this day, and may all those who seek you find
you in the living word among us. Grant this through
Jesus who lives and reigns among us. Amen.

DAYTIME PRAYER

Ant. 1 Incline my heart to your decrees.

Psalm 119:33–40

Teach me the way of your
　precepts
and I will keep them to the end.
Give me understanding,
that I may keep your law
and observe it with all my heart.

Guide me in the path of your
　commandments,
for there is my delight.
Incline my heart to your will
and not to love of profit.

Turn my eyes from what is vain;
by your ways, give me life.
Keep the promise you have made
to those who reverence you.

Turn away the reproach which I
　dread;
for your decrees are good.
Behold, I long for your precepts;
in your justice, give me life!
　Glory*...

Ant. 2 O taste and see the goodness of our God!

Psalm 34

I will bless you, O God, at all
　times,
your praise always on my lips.
My soul makes its boast in you;
the afflicted shall hear and be
　glad.
Glorify our God with me.—

Together let us praise God's
　name.

I sought you, and you answered
　me;
and delivered me from all my
　fears.
Look towards the Most High, and
　be radiant;
let your faces not be ashamed.
These poor ones cried; you heard
　them,
and saved them from all their
　troubles.

Your angel, O God, is encamped
around those who revere you, to
　deliver them.
Taste and see that God is good!
Happy are they who take refuge
　in you.

May all the saints revere you, O
　God.
Those who revere you, have no
　want!
Young lions suffer want and
　hunger;
but those who seek you lack no
　blessing. **Glory*...**

Ant. 3 Blessed are those who seek after peace.

II

Come, children, listen to me,
I will teach you to reverence the
　Most High.
Who among you longs for life
and many days to enjoy
　prosperity?

Keep your tongue from evil,
your lips from speaking deceit.
Turn aside from evil and do good;
seek peace and pursue it.

God's eyes are turned to the
  righteous,
God's ears toward their cry.
God's face turns away from evil,
that it not be remembered on
  earth.

When the just cry, the Most High
  hears,
and delivers them from their
  troubles.
God is close to the
  brokenhearted;—

saving those whose spirits are
  crushed.

Many are the afflictions of the
  just;
they will be delivered from them
  all.
God will keep guard over all their
  bones,
not one of them shall be broken.

Evil shall be its own destruction;
oppression shall be condemned.
You redeem the lives of your
  servants;
those who take refuge in you
  shall not be condemned.
  Glory*...

PRAYER: Most provident God, you graciously give us all good
gifts. Teach us to care for our earth: to till our soil
responsibly, to keep our air pure, to free our waters
from pollution, to harvest the warmth of our sun, and
to respect the rights of all species. May we willingly
share the gifts of your goodness with one another. We
ask this of you, God of our universe. Amen.

WEEK II

SUNDAY, EVENING PRAYER I

Ant. 1 Your word, O God, is a light for my path.

Psalm 119:105-112

O God, your word is a lamp to my feet
and a light for my path.
I have sworn an oath and confirmed it
to observe your commandments.

I am sorely afflicted:
give me life according to your word!
Accept my offerings of praise,
and teach me your decrees.

Though I hold my life in my hands,
I do not forget your law.
Though the wicked try to ensnare me,
I do not stray from your precepts.

Your will is my heritage forever,
the joy of my heart.
I incline my heart to carry out your will forever, to endless ages. **Glory*...**

Ant. 2 I have given you as a covenant to the people.

Psalm 16

Preserve me, O God, for in you I take refuge.—

*Glory to you, Source of all Being, Eternal Word, and Holy Spirit.

As it was in the beginning is now and will be forever. Amen.

I say to you: "You are my God;
I have no good apart from you."
All my delight is in your saints;
the faithful who dwell in your land.

Those who choose other gods increase their sorrows;
their offerings of blood I will not pour out
or take their names upon my lips.

You are my portion and my cup;
you are my fortune, my prize.
The lines have fallen for me in pleasant places;
I have been given a welcome heritage.

I will bless you who give me counsel;
in the night my heart instructs me.
I keep you always before me;
because you are near, I shall stand firm.

Therefore my heart is glad, and my soul rejoices;
even my body rests securely.
For you do not give me up to death,
or let your faithful see the grave.

You will show me the path of life;
in your presence there is fullness of joy,
in your hands, happiness forever.
Glory*...

Ant. 3 For me to live is Christ and to die is gain.

Cant: Phil 2:6–11

Though he was in the form of God,
Jesus did not count equality with God
something to be grasped at.

But emptied himself
taking the form of a slave,
being born in human likeness.

Being found in human estate,
he humbled himself and became obedient,—

obediently accepting death, even death on a cross!

Therefore God has highly exalted him
and bestowed on him the name above every other name.

So that at the name of Jesus
every knee should bow,
in heaven, on the earth,
and under the earth,
and every tongue proclaim
to the glory of God:
Jesus Christ is Lord! **Glory*...**

READING

[O loving God], help us to be masters of the weapons that threaten to master us. Help us to use science for peace and plenty, not for war and destruction. Show us how to use atomic power to bless our children's children, not to blight them. Save us from the compulsion to follow our adversaries in all that we most hate, confirming them in their hatred and suspicion of us. Resolve our inner contradictions, which now grow beyond belief and beyond bearing. They are at once a torment and a blessing; for if you had not left us the light of conscience, we would not have to endure them. Teach us to be long-suffering in anguish and insecurity, teach us to wait and trust. Grant light, grant strength and patience to all who work for peace...grant us prudence in proportion to our power, wisdom in proportion to our science, humaneness in proportion to our wealth and might. And bless our earnest will to help all races and peoples to travel, in friendship with us, along the road to justice, liberty and lasting peace.... (Merton's Prayer for Peace)

Thomas Merton, *Nonviolent Alternative*, (59)

RESPONSORY

We call to you in our need, O God, for you hear the cry of the poor.
  —**We call...**
You will not leave us orphans; —**for you...**
Glory to you, Source of all Being, Eternal Word and Holy Spirit.
  —**We call...**

CANTICLE OF MARY

Ant. Be mindful of your mercy to us, O loving God.

INTERCESSIONS

O God, you grieve for all that afflicts us;
  —give those who struggle with addictions the courage and
   perseverance they need.
You are father and mother to us, and we bask in your love;
  —inspire persons of integrity and compassion to care for
   children who are separated from their parents.
You bless those who employ the talents you have given them;
  —give all in research the insight they need to develop the good
   you desire for us.
Jesus, you loved the land and fields of flowers;
  —bless farmers and all who are stewards of the soil.
You taught your followers to travel lightly through life;
  —call our consumer culture to a change of heart—to values
   that lead to life.

PRAYER: O God, we long to love you with all our heart and mind
and soul, but we know we are divided. Give us a single
heart. Make us one as you are one with Jesus and your
Holy Spirit. Amen.

MORNING PRAYER

**Ant. 1 You are members of the
household of God.**

Psalm 118

We give thanks to you, for you are
good,
and your steadfast love endures
forever.

Let the descendants of Israel say:
"Your steadfast love endures
forever."
Let the descendants of Aaron say:
"Your steadfast love endures
forever."
Let those who fear you say:
"Your steadfast love endures
forever."

In my distress, I called to you;
you answered me and set me free.
With you at my side, I do not fear.
What can anyone do against me?
You are at my side to help me:
I shall withstand all evildoers.

It is better to take refuge in you,
than to trust in people:
it is better to take refuge in you
  than to trust in our leaders.

All wickedness surrounded me;
in your name I crushed it.
It surrounded me like bees;
it blazed like a fire among thorns.
In your name I crushed it.

I was pushed hard, and was falling
but you came to help me.
You are my strength and my song;
you are my salvation.

O God, you have triumphed;
your reign is exalted.
You have triumphed over all;
I shall not die, I shall live
and recount your wondrous deeds.
You have chastened me sorely,
but have not given me over to
  death.

Open to me the gates of justice,
that I may enter and give thanks.
This is your gate, O God;
the just shall enter through it.
I thank you for you have answered
  me
you alone are my salvation.

The stone which the builders
  rejected
has become the cornerstone.
This is your doing, O God;
it is marvelous in our eyes.
This is the day which you have
  made;
let us rejoice and be glad in it.

Save us, we beseech you, O God!
O God, grant us success.
Blessed are those who enter in
  your holy name.
For you O God, are our God,
and you have given us light.

Let us go forward in procession
  with branches,
up to your holy altar.
You are my God, I thank you.
You are my God, I praise you.
We give thanks to you for you are
  good;
and your steadfast love endures
  forever. **Glory*...**

**Ant. 2 How glorious is your name
over all the earth.**

Cant: Daniel 3:52–57

Blessed are you, God of our
  ancestors,
praiseworthy and exalted above all
  forever.

Blessed be your holy and glorious
  name,
praiseworthy and exalted above all
  for all ages.

Blessed are you in the temple of
  your glory,
praiseworthy and exalted above all
  forever.

Blessed are you on the throne of
  your kindom,
praiseworthy and exalted above all
  forever.

Blessed are you who look into the
  depths
from your throne upon the
  cherubim,
praiseworthy and exalted above all
  forever.

Blessed are you in the firmament of
  heaven,
praiseworthy and glorious forever.

Blessed are you by all your works.
We praise and exalt you above all
  forever. **Glory*...**

**Ant. 3 Let us praise God's infinite
greatness.**

Psalm 150

We praise you, O God, in your holy
  sanctuary;
we praise you in your mighty
  heavens.—

We praise you for your powerful
deeds;
we praise you according to your
greatness.

We praise you with trumpet sound;
We praise you with lute and harp!
We praise you with strings and
pipe!

We praise you with sounding
cymbals,
We praise you with clashing
cymbals!
Let everything that breathes,
give praise to you, O God.
Glory*...

READING

I will sprinkle clean water upon you, and you shall be clean from all
your uncleanness, and from all your idols I will cleanse you. A new
heart I will give you, and a new spirit I will put within you; and I will
remove from your body the heart of stone and give you a heart of flesh. I
will put my spirit within you, and make you follow my statutes and be
careful to observe my ordinances. Then you shall live in the land that I
gave to your ancestors; and you shall be my people and I will be your
God.

Ezek 36:25–28

RESPONSORY

Our hearts are restless, O God, till they rest in you. —**Our...**
Searching and waiting; —**till they...**
Glory to you, Source of all Being, Eternal Word and Holy Spirit.
—**Our...**

CANTICLE OF ZECHARIAH

Ant. May you give light to those who sit in darkness.

INTERCESSIONS

God revealing, forgiving, ever recreating us;
  —we thank you for your abiding care, and we pray for those who
  do not know your love.
You are a God of the living, and your Spirit brings us joy;
  —let our lives bear witness to the resurrection of Jesus.
Minorities, countries, the earth itself—all cry out for liberation as
never before;
  —Spirit of God, flood our lives with the wisdom to make all
  things new.
You raise up prophets today;
  —open our hearts, our church, and our world to their message.

Jesus, your message calls for the new wineskins of openness to your word;
   —help us to free ourselves from what is merely familiar and comfortable.

PRAYER: O God, on this first day of the week, we join all creation and people of all ages in praising you. Your kindness and forgiveness flow like a river through the centuries refreshing our faith, our hope and our love. May you be forever praised throughout all the ages. Amen.

DAYTIME PRAYER

Ant. 1 You restore my soul in your living waters.

Psalm 23

O God, you are my shepherd;
I shall not want.
You make me to lie in green
   pastures.
You lead me to restful waters,
to restore my soul.

You guide me in paths of
   righteousness
for the sake of your name.
Even though I walk through the
   valley of the shadow of death,
I fear no evil;
for you are with me;
your crook and your staff
give me comfort.

You prepare a table before me
in the presence of my foes;
you anoint my head with oil,
my cup overflows.

Surely goodness and mercy shall
   follow me
all the days of my life;
and I shall dwell in your holy
   house forever and ever. **Glory*...**

Ant. 2 Lead a life worthy of God, who calls you to glory.

Psalm 76

In Judah you are made known, O
   God,
your name is great in Israel.
Your abode is established in
   Jerusalem,
your dwelling place in Zion.
There you broke the flashing
   arrows,
the shield, the sword, the weapons
   of war.

You, O God, are glorious,
more majestic than the mountains.
The stouthearted were stripped of
   their spoil;
they sank into sleep;
all the provokers of war
were unable to use their hands.
At your rebuke, O God, our God,
both rider and horse lay stunned.
   Glory*...

Ant. 3 Do not let the sun go down on your anger, for God is a forgiving God.

II

You, you alone, strike terror.
When your anger is aroused,
who can stand before you?
From heaven you utter judgment;
the earth feared and stood still,—

when you arose to give judgment
to save the oppressed of the earth.

Our anger will serve to praise you;
its residue gird you round.
We fulfill the vows made before
  you;
you whom we revere,
who cut short the lives of leaders,
who strike terror in unjust rulers.
    Glory*...

PRAYER: O God, you have created us to be free. Only through the power of your love do you reign over us. Help us to be worthy of the gift of freedom, and teach us to respect all creation as the work of your hands. We ask this, Creator God, giver of all good gifts, through Jesus who taught us the way. Amen.

EVENING PRAYER II

Ant. 1 You are a priestly people according to the order of Melchizedeck.

Psalm 110:1-5, 7

God's revelation to the Anointed
  One:
"Sit at my side:
till I put injustice beneath your
  feet."

God will send forth from Zion
your scepter of power:
rule in the midst of your foes.

Your people will give themselves
  freely
on the day you lead your host
upon the holy mountains.
From the womb of the morning
your youth will come like dew.

God has sworn an oath that will
  not be changed.—

"You are a priest forever,
after the order of Melchizedek."

The Anointed standing by your
  side,
will shatter rulers on the day of
  wrath.

Drinking from your streams by
  the wayside
shall the Chosen One be
  refreshed. **Glory*...**

Ant. 2 The heavens belong to you, but the earth has been given to us.

Psalm 115

Not to us, O God, not to us,
but to your name give glory
for the sake of your love and your
  truth!
Why should the nations say,
"Where is their God?"

But you are in the heavens;
you do whatever you please.
Their idols are silver and gold,
the work of human hands.

They have mouths, but cannot
  speak;
eyes, but cannot see;
they have ears, but cannot hear;
noses, but cannot smell.

They have hands, but cannot feel;
feet, but cannot walk.
No sound comes from their
  throats.
Those who make them are like
  them;
so are all who trust in them.

Descendants of Abraham, trust in
  God,
who is your help and your shield.
Descendants of Sarah, trust in
  God,
who is your help and your shield.
You who fear, trust in God,
who is your help and your shield.

You remember us and will bless
  us,
blessing the descendants of
  Abraham,
blessing the descendants of
  Sarah.
God will bless those who fear,
the little no less than the great.

May God give you increase,—

you and all your children.
May you be blessed by the Most
  High,
who made heaven and earth!

The heavens belong to God,
but the earth has been given to
  us.
The dead do not praise you,
nor those who go down into
  silence.
But we who live, bless you,
both now and forever. Amen.
  Glory*...

**Ant. 3 We come to join in your
  holy banquet, O God.**

Cant: Rev 19:1, 5–7

Salvation, glory, and power
  belong to you,
your judgments are honest and
  true.

All of us, your servants, sing
  praise to you,
we worship you reverently, both
  great and small.

You, our almighty God, are
  Creator of heaven and earth.
Let us rejoice and exult, and give
  you glory.

The wedding feast of the Lamb
  has begun,
And the bride has made herself
  ready. **Glory*...**

READING

But we must always give thanks to God for you, brothers and sisters
beloved by the [Lord Jesus], because God chose you as the first fruits
for salvation through sanctification by the Spirit and through belief in
the truth. For this purpose [God] called you through our proclamation of
the good news, so that you may obtain the glory of our Lord Jesus
Christ.

                                                        2 Thess 2:13–14

RESPONSORY

How can we repay you, O God, for your goodness to us?
  —How can...
We will sing your praise; **—for your...**
Glory to you, Source of all Being, Eternal Word and Holy Spirit.
  —How can...

CANTICLE OF MARY

Ant. My spirit rejoices in God, my Savior.

INTERCESSIONS

Rain and clouds are your gifts of life and beauty to us, O God;
  —teach us how to use and preserve the waters of the earth.
You surround us with beauty on earth and in the sky;
  —bless those who have lost the gift of sight.
You are always with us, silently guiding and encouraging us;
  —help us to quiet our lives with moments for listening to your
    voice in our hearts.
You love justice, and all your ways are true;
  —give us the insight and courage to face our prejudices and
    blind spots.
Jesus is your supreme gift to us;
  —let the words of his gospel be woven into our daily lives,
    coming easily to mind for our inspiration and your glory.

PRAYER: God of mystery, God of love, send your Spirit into our
hearts with gifts of wisdom and peace, fortitude and
charity. We long to love and serve you. Faithful God,
make us faithful. This we ask through the intercession
of all your saints. Amen.

MONDAY

MORNING PRAYER

**Ant 1 When from this exile
shall we behold you face to
face?**

Psalm 42

Like the deer that yearns
for flowing streams,—

so my soul is longing
for you, my God.

My soul is thirsting for God,
the living God.
When shall I come and see,
the face of God?

My tears have become my food,
by night and day,
while I hear it said all day,
"Where is your God?"

These things will I remember
as I pour out my soul:
how I led the throng,
to the house of God,
with shouts of gladness and
 songs of thanksgiving,
the multitude keeping festival.

Why are you cast down my soul,
why disquieted within me?
Hope in God; I will again praise
 you,
my help and my God.

My soul is cast down within me,
therefore I think of you
from the land of Jordan and of
 Hermon,
from Mount Mizar.

Deep calls to deep,
in the thunder of your waters;
all your waves and your billows
have swept over me.

By day you will send me
your steadfast love;
and at night your song is with
 me,
a prayer to the God of my life.

I will say to you my rock:
"Why have you forgotten me?
Why do I go mourning
because of oppression?"

As with a deadly wound,
my adversaries taunt me,
saying to me all the day long:
"Where is your God?"

Why are you cast down, my soul,
why disquieted within me?
Hope in God; for I shall praise
 again,
my savior and my God.
    Glory*...

**Ant. 2 Worker of wonders,
 show forth your splendor!**

Cant: Sirach 36:1–5, 10–13

Come to our aid, O God of the
 universe,
and put all the nations in dread
 of you!
Raise your hand toward the
 heathen,
that they may realize your power.

As you have used us to show
 them your holiness,
so now use them to show us your
 glory.
Thus they will know, as we know,
that there is no God but you.

Give new signs and work new
 wonders;
show forth the splendor of the
 works of your hands.

Gather all the tribes of Jacob,
that they may inherit the land as
 of old.
Show mercy to the people called
 by your name;
Israel, whom you named your
 first-born.

Take pity on your holy city,
Jerusalem, your dwelling place.
Fill Zion with your majesty,
your temple with your glory.
    Glory*...

Ant. 3 The courts of heaven ring with the praise of our God.

Psalm 19a

The heavens tell of your glory, O God,
and the firmament proclaims your handiwork.
Day unto day pours forth the story
and night unto night reveals its knowledge.

No speech, no word, no voice is heard;—

yet their voice goes out to all the earth,
their words to the end of the world.

In them you set a tent for the sun;
it comes forth like a bridegroom leaving his chamber,
rejoices like a champion running its course.

Its rising is from the end of the heavens,
and its course to the end of them;
there is nothing concealed from its heat. **Glory*...**

READING

I saw that [God] is everything which is good, as I understand. And in this [God] showed me something small, no bigger than a hazelnut, lying in the palm of my hand, as it seemed to me, and it was as round as a ball. I looked at it with the eye of my understanding and thought: What can this be? I was amazed that it could last, for I thought that because of its littleness it would suddenly have fallen into nothing. And I was answered in my understanding: It lasts and always will, because God loves it; and thus everything has being through the love of God.

Julian of Norwich, *Showings*, p. 183, (1)

RESPONSORY

You are present to us, O God, in all creation. **—You are...**
Enriching our lives; **—in all...**
Glory to you, Source of all Being, Eternal Word and Holy Spirit.
    —You are...

CANTICLE OF ZECHARIAH

Ant. Blessed be God who has visited us and saved us.

INTERCESSIONS

O God, you ask us to keep your words in our minds and hearts and so we pray:
    —give us the grace to hear you in turmoil and in silence.
Help us to recognize our sinfulness and to be grateful for your gifts of grace;
    —give us the strength and courage to act in humility and truth.

God of wisdom and source of all that is sacred;
—help teachers to value and nourish the wisdom and goodness
of children.
Jesus, you came to serve and not to be served;
—bless all who serve us daily, in inclement weather, in
dangerous jobs, and at work that is tedious or monotonous.
We are blessed by the words of your gospel;
—make us aware of the ways we shield ourselves from its
challenge to us.

PRAYER: O God, you have made us in your image and we long to
see your face. Quiet our minds and enkindle our hearts
that walking the way of your truth we may leave the
imprint of your goodness throughout the world. Grant
this in the name of Jesus. Amen.

DAYTIME PRAYER

Ant. 1 Make love your aim, and desire every spiritual gift.

Psalm 119:41–48

O God, let your love come upon me,
your salvation according to your promise;
Then I have answer for those who taunt me
for I trust in your word.

Take not truth from my mouth,
for my hope is in your decrees.
I shall always keep your law
forever and ever.

I shall walk in the path of freedom
for I have sought your precepts.
I will speak of your will before rulers
and shall not be put to shame;

for my delight is in your commandments;
these I have loved.—

I revere your precepts,
and will ponder on your statutes.
Glory*...

Ant. 2 My delight is to do your will, O God.

Psalm 40:2–14, 17–18

I waited patiently for you, O God
and you stooped down to me;
and heard my cry.

You drew me from the desolate pit,
out of the miry clay,
and set my feet upon a rock,
making my steps secure.

You put a new song in my mouth,
a song of praise to you.
Many shall see and fear
and place their trust in you.

Happy are we who have placed our trust in you, O God,
who do not turn to the proud,
to those who follow false gods!

For us you have multiplied, O
God, my Creator,
your wondrous deeds and plans;
none can compare with you!
Were I to proclaim and tell of
them,
they are more than can be
numbered.

Sacrifice and offering you do not
desire;
but you have given me an open
ear.
Burnt offering and sin offering
you have not required.

Therefore, I said, "Here I am;
In the scroll of the book it is
written of me:
my delight is to do your will;
your law is within my heart."
    Glory*...

**Ant. 3 Your mercy is from age
to age toward those who
revere you.**
              II

Your deliverance I have
proclaimed
in the great assembly.
I have not restrained my lips,
as you well know, O God.

I have not concealed your saving
help within my heart;
but have spoken of your
faithfulness, and your salvation;
I have not hidden your steadfast
love nor your faithfulness
from the great assembly.

O God, you will not withhold
your mercy from me.
Your steadfast love and
faithfulness always surround
me.

For evils without number have
encompassed me;
My sins have overtaken me,
till I cannot see.
They are more than the hairs of
my head;
my heart fails me.

Be pleased, O God, to deliver me!
O God, make haste to help me!

May all who seek you rejoice and
be glad;
May all who love your salvation
say evermore: "Great is our God!"

As for me, I am poor and needy;
but you take thought of me.
You are my help, my deliverer;
O God, do not delay.
    Glory*...

PRAYER: God of justice, God of mercy, bless all those who are
surprised with pain this day from suffering caused by
their own weakness or that of others. Let what we
suffer teach us to be merciful; let our sins teach us to
forgive. This we ask through the intercession of Jesus
and all who died forgiving those who oppressed them.
Amen.

EVENING PRAYER

Ant. 1 O God, how great is your wisdom, so far beyond my understanding.

Psalm 139:1-18, 23-24

O God, you have searched me
and you know me,
you know when I sit and when I
stand;
you discern my thoughts from
afar.
You mark when I walk or lie
down,
with all my ways you are
acquainted.

Before a word is on my tongue,
behold, O God, you know the
whole of it.
Behind and before you besiege
me,
You lay your hand upon me.
Such knowledge is too wonderful
for me:
too high, beyond my reach.

O where can I go from your spirit,
or where can I flee from your
presence?
If I climb to heaven, you are
there!
If I lie in the grave, you are there!

If I take the wings of the morning
and dwell in the depths of the
sea,
even there your hand shall lead
me,
your hand shall hold me fast.

If I say: "Let darkness cover me,
and the light around me be
night,"
even darkness is not dark to
you,—

and the night is as bright as the
day;
for darkness is as light to you.
Glory*...

Ant. 2 You search the mind and probe the heart, giving to each as we deserve.

II

For it was you who formed my
inmost parts,
knit me together in my mother's
womb.
I praise you for the wonder of my
being,
for the wonder of all your works.

Already you knew me well;
my body was not hidden from
you,
when I was being made in secret
and molded in the depths of the
earth.

Your eyes beheld my unformed
substance;
in your book they all were
written,
the days that you had formed for
me
when none of them yet were.

How precious to me are your
thoughts!
How vast the sum of them!
If I count them, they are more
than the sand.
When I awake, I am still with you.

Search me, O God, and know my
heart!
O test me and know my thoughts!
See that I follow not the wrong
way,—

and lead me in the way of life
eternal. **Glory*...**

**Ant. 3 May Christ dwell in our
hearts through faith that we
may be rooted in love.**

Cant: Ephesians 1:3–10

Praised be the God
of our Lord Jesus Christ,
who has blessed us in Christ
with every spiritual blessing in
the heavens.

God chose us in him
before the foundation of the
world,
that we should be holy
and blameless in God's sight.

We have been predestined
to be God's children through
Jesus Christ,—

such was the purpose of God's
will,
that all might praise the glorious
favor
bestowed on us in Christ.

In Christ and through his blood,
we have redemption,
the forgiveness of our sins,
according to the riches of God's
grace lavished upon us.

For God has made known to us
in all wisdom and insight,
the mystery of the plan set forth
in Christ.

A plan to be carried out in Christ,
in the fullness of time,
to unite all things in Christ,
things in heaven and things on
earth. **Glory*...**

READING

God knows the best human instruments to use in the work of making
us saints, which is the work of making us God-like; and they must
necessarily be those who will cause us to put aside our own ways and
desires and views to take on [God's own]. It is a matter of...following the
Holy Spirit instead of our own spirit, of letting that mind be in us that
was in Christ Jesus.

Mother Aloysius Rogers, OCD, *Fragrance from Alabaster*, p. 3, (6)

RESPONSORY

You create us in your image, O God, we are co-creators with you.
—**You create...**
We are nothing without you; —**we are...**
Glory to you, Source of all Being, Eternal Word and Holy Spirit.
—**You create...**

CANTICLE OF MARY

Ant. I rejoice in your greatness, O God.

INTERCESSIONS

O God, you invite us to: "Let light shine out of darkness";
  —give us the courage to embrace the darkness and walk with
  you toward the light.
You hear the prayers of those in need;
  —give us the grace to open our hearts, our homes, and our
  spaces of worship to those who are in distress.
You marveled at the faith of the Centurion;
  —help us to recognize that truth and wisdom are often found
  where we least expect it.
Spirit of God, guide us in our use of power;
  —let our methods be constructive and sensitive to the needs
  of all.
May we realize that life itself is a blessing;
  —comfort those who are preparing for the blessings of
  eternal life.

PRAYER: God of wisdom, God of our way, we have walked with
you from early morning. Renew our strength this night
that we may rise to serve you and one another with
clear vision and strong hope. We pray especially for all
who will awake this night to the vision of your glory.
This we ask through Jesus who is the light of the
world. Amen.

TUESDAY

MORNING PRAYER

Ant. 1 O God, let us walk as people of light, that we may know what is pleasing to you.

Psalm 43

Defend me, O God, and plead my
  cause against a godless nation.
From the deceitful and the unjust
rescue me, O God.

For in you I take refuge;
why have you cast me off?
Why do I go mourning
because of oppression?

O send out your light and your
  truth;
let these be my guide.
Let them bring me to your holy hill
and to your dwelling place.

Then I will go to the altar of God,
to God, my exceeding joy;
and I will praise you with the lyre,
O God, my God.

Why are you cast down, my soul,
why groan within me?
Hope in God;—

I shall again praise, my savior and my God. **Glory*...**

Ant. 2 Seek first the reign of God, and all things shall be yours as well.

Cant: Isaiah 38:10–14, 17b–20

Once I said,
"In the noontime of life, I must depart!
I am consigned to the gates of death for the rest of my years."

I said, "I shall not see God
in the land of the living.
No longer shall I see my companions
among the dwellers of this world."

My dwelling is plucked up and removed from me
like a shepherd's tent;
like a weaver I have rolled up my life;
being cut off from the loom.

Day and night you give me over to torment;
I cry for help until daybreak;
like a lion you break all my bones;
day and night you give me over to torment.

Like a swallow or crane, I clamor,
I moan like a dove.
My eyes grow weary gazing upward.
I am oppressed; be my security!

Restore me to health, make me live!
It was for my welfare that I had great bitterness;
you have held back my life from the pit of destruction,
you have cast all my sins behind your back.

For the nether world cannot thank you,
death cannot praise you;
those who go down to the pit cannot hope for your faithfulness.

The living, the living give you thanks, as I do this day;
Parents make known to their children,
O God, your faithfulness.

You, O God, will save us;
we will sing to stringed instruments
all the days of our lives,
in your holy dwelling.
Glory*...

Ant. 3 Consider the lilies of the field; they neither toil nor spin.

Psalm 65

Praise is due to you,
O God in Zion;
and to you shall vows be made,
to you who hear our prayer.

To you shall all flesh come because of its sins.
When our offenses bear us down,
you forgive them all.

Blessed are we whom you choose and draw near,
to dwell in your courts!
We are filled with the goodness of your house,
your holy temple!

With wonders you deliver us,
O God of our salvation.
You are the hope of all the earth
and of far distant seas.

By your strength, you established the mountains,
girded with might;—

you still the roaring of the seas,
the roaring of their waves,
and the tumult of the peoples.

Those who dwell at earth's farthest
  bounds
stand in awe at your wonders;
you make the sunrise and sunset
  shout for joy.

You care for the earth, give it water,
you fill it with riches.
Your river in heaven brims over
to provide its grain.

You visit the earth and water it,
greatly enriching it;—

you level it, soften it with showers,
blessing its growth.

You crown the year with your
  bounty;
Abundance flows in your path.
The pastures of the wilderness
  flow,
the hills gird themselves with joy,
the meadows clothe themselves
  with flocks,
the valleys deck themselves with
  grain,
they shout and sing together for
  joy. **Glory*...**

READING

It is so thoughtful and commendable to thank those who do us favors
that if we glance around, we will find this truth naturally inheres in all
creatures who, even though unable to speak, offer better thanks to their
benefactors through action than we humans do in word. We see that
when earth is regaled by heaven's waters and sunlight, it sends forth
grass and flowers in grateful payment for the gift. Very tenderly the
gardener cares for [the] trees so that, having grown quite tall, they bend
down their fruit...to pick, almost as if to say: "Take this fruit in return
for your kind care."

Francisco de Osuna, *The Third Spiritual Alphabet*, p. 68, (1)

RESPONSORY

You know our frailty, O God; give us strength. **—You know...**
You fill us with hope; **—give...**
Glory to you, Source of all Being, Eternal Word and Holy Spirit.
   —You know...

CANTICLE OF ZECHARIAH

Ant. You, O God, have raised up a horn of salvation for us.

INTERCESSIONS

Jesus, tax collectors and public sinners experienced your
goodness and changed their lives;
   —help us to enable others to grow and realize their worth.

You had compassion on the weak and sorrowful;
—open our eyes and hearts to the ways we can comfort others.
You were a gift to all who came to you in faith;
—fill us with love that is creative and fruitful for your people
and the world.
No one is beyond the reach of your care;
—bless those in refugee camps and all who are uprooted from
their homes and land.
Make us wise as serpents and simple as doves;
—make us a people after your own heart.

PRAYER: All loving God, let us know your presence as we begin
this day. Guide us as we strive to choose what is good
and just. Lift up our hearts to you when the demands
of the day threaten to lead us astray. This we ask
through Jesus who is our way, our truth and our life.
Amen.

DAYTIME PRAYER

Ant. 1 Blessed are they who hear your word and keep it.

Psalm 119:49–56

Remember your word to your
servant
by which you gave me hope.
This is my comfort in my affliction
that your promise gives me life.

Though the proud utterly deride
me,
I do not turn from your law.
When I think of your precepts of
old,
I take comfort, O God.

I am seized with indignation
because of the wicked
who forsake your law.
Your statutes have been my songs
in the house of my pilgrimage.

I remember your name in the night,
and keep your law.—

This blessing has been given to me,
the keeping of your precepts.
Glory*...

Ant. 2 You free us from the bondage of sin and restore us to life.

Psalm 53

Fools say in their hearts:
"There is no God."
They are corrupt, doing wicked
things;
there are none that do good.

God looks down from heaven
on the peoples of the earth,
to see if any are wise,
if any seek God.

They have all fallen away;
they are all alike depraved;
there are none that do good,
no, not even one.

Have the evildoers no
understanding,
who eat up my people just as they
eat bread,
and do not call upon God?

There they are, in great terror,
such terror as has not been!
For God will chastise the
oppressors;
they will be put to shame.

O that salvation might come from
Zion!
When you restore the fortunes of
your people,
Jacob will rejoice and Israel be
glad. **Glory*...**

**Ant. 3 O God, my eyes rejoice in
your salvation.**

Psalm 54:1-6, 8-9

Save me, O God, by your name;
deliver me by your might.
O God, hear my prayer;
give ear to the words of my mouth.

For the insolent have risen against
me,
the ruthless seek my life;
they set themselves before you.
But I have you for my helper;
You uphold my life.

With a willing heart I make
sacrifice;
and give thanks to your name.
You deliver me from all trouble,
my eyes rejoice in your salvation.
Glory*...

PRAYER: O God, you sent your son, Jesus, to call us to your
realm of mercy and love. Let our memories of his words
and deeds overflow into our lives, that following him,
we may lead others to salvation. We ask this through
the intercession of all those who lived as true disciples
and now live eternally with you. Amen.

EVENING PRAYER

**Ant. 1 Our riches lie in the glory
of God.**

Psalm 49

Hear this, all you peoples!
Give heed, all dwellers of the world,
you, both low and high,
rich and poor together!

My lips will speak words of wisdom;
my heart will ponder your ways.
I will incline my ear to a proverb;
I will solve my riddle on the lyre.

Why should I fear in times of
trouble,
when the malice of my foes
surrounds me,
those who trust in their wealth,
and boast of the vastness of their
riches?

For we cannot buy our own
ransom,
or give to God the price for our
lives.
The ransom of our lives is beyond
us.—

It can never be enough,
to avoid going to the grave.

Both the wise and the foolish must
perish
and leave their wealth to others.
Their graves are their homes
forever,
their dwelling places to all
generations,
though their names spread wide
through the land.
They are like the beasts that
perish. **Glory*...**

**Ant. 2 Be not afraid, I go before
you.**

II

This is the fate of those with foolish
confidence,
the end of those who are pleased
with their portion.
Like sheep they are driven to the
grave;
death shall be their shepherd;
straight to the grave they descend,
and their form shall waste away;
the grave shall be their home.

But you will ransom my soul from
the power of the grave,
for you will receive me.

Be not afraid when people grow
rich,
when the glory of their houses
increases.
They carry nothing with them when
they die,
their glory will not go down with
them.

Though while they lived, they
thought themselves happy,
and thought themselves praised for
their success,
they will go to join their ancestors,
who will never more see the light.

People cannot abide in insolence;
they are like the beasts that perish.
Glory*...

**Ant. 3 Worthy is the Lamb who
was slain.**

Cant: Rev 4:11, 5:9, 10, 12

Worthy are you, O God, our God,
to receive glory and honor and
power.

For you have created all things;
by your will they came to be and
were made.

Worthy are you to take the scroll
and to open its seals,
For you were slain, and by your
blood,
you purchased for God
saints of every race and tongue,
of every people and nation.

You have made of them a kindom,
and priests to serve our God,
and they shall reign on the earth.

Worthy is the Lamb who was slain
to receive power and riches,
wisdom and strength,
honor and glory and praise.
Glory*...

READING

We are truly on the way with Christ, our Hope and our Promise, if we
live a life of thanksgiving for all that God has already revealed and done,

and of vigilance for what [God] wants us to do in the present moment, even if [God] wants to surprise us and lead us where we did not want to go. For those who put their trust in Christ, everything, even the most insignificant or the most unpleasant event, becomes a sign of grace and hope, a school of vigilance for the coming of our Lord.

Bernard Häring, Prayer: The Integration of Faith and Life, p. 29, (8)

RESPONSORY

Your compassion, O God, calls us to repentance.—**Your...**
Your love heals us, and —**calls us...**
Glory to you, Source of all Being, Eternal Word and Holy Spirit.
—**Your...**

CANTICLE OF MARY

Ant. My spirit rejoices in God, my Savior.

INTERCESSIONS

Eternal God, you create us and call us to realize our union with you;
—help us to rise above all that undermines our calling.
Jesus, you were called a fool for our sake;
—let us bear the inevitable humiliations of life with equanimity.
You brought joy and a new beginning to those who received you;
—give us a hunger for your presence and your truth.
Spirit of God, your realm of love encompasses all of creation;
—in times of temptation and doubt, draw us ever closer to you.
Your love is eternal;
—bless and heal those who are burdened with hatred or unforgiveness.

PRAYER: Spirit of God, promise of Jesus, come to our help at the close of this day. Come with forgiveness and healing love. Come with light and hope. Come with all that we need to continue in the way of your truth. So may we praise you in the Trinity forever. Amen.

WEDNESDAY

MORNING PRAYER

Ant 1 You, O God, are faithful; all your ways are holy.

Psalm 77

I cry aloud to you, my God,
cry aloud that you may hear me.

In the day of my trouble I seek
you,
in the night I stretch out my hand
without tiring;
my soul refuses to be consoled.

I remember you and I moan;
I ponder, and my spirit faints.
You hold my eyelids from closing;
I am so troubled, I cannot speak.

I consider the days of old,
I remember the years long past.
I converse with my heart in the
night;
I ponder and search my spirit:

"God, will you spurn us forever,
and never again show us favor?
Has your love vanished forever?
Are your promises at an end for
all time?
Have you forgotten to be
gracious?
Has your anger withheld your
compassion?"

I say: "This is the cause of my
grief;
that the way of the Most High has
changed."
I will call to mind your deeds;
I will remember your wonders of
old,
I will meditate on all your works,
and ponder your mighty deeds.

Your ways, O God, are holy.
What god is great as our God?
You are the God who works
wonders,
who shows your power among the
peoples.
Your strong arm redeemed your
people,
the descendants of Jacob and
Rachel.

When the waters saw you, O God,
when the waters saw you, they
were afraid,
the depths were moved with
terror.
The clouds poured out water;
the skies gave forth thunder;
your arrows flashed to and fro.

Your thunder crashed in the
whirlwind;
your flashes lighted up the world;
the earth trembled and shook.
Your way was through the sea,
your path through the great
waters;
yet your footprints were not seen.

You led your people like a flock
by the hands of Moses and
Miriam. **Glory*...**

Ant. 2 My heart exults in God, the joy of my salvation.

Cant: 1 Samuel 2:1–10

My heart exults in the Most High,
my strength is exalted in my God.
My lips renounce all that is evil,
because I rejoice in your
salvation.

There is no Holy One like You;
there is no Rock like our God.
Speak no longer so boastfully,
nor let arrogance come from your
   mouth.
For God is a God of knowledge,
a God who weighs our deeds.

The bows of the mighty are
   broken,
but the feeble are circled with
   strength.
The full hire themselves out for
   bread,
while the hungry cease to
   hunger.
The barren have borne seven
   children,
but those who have many are
   forlorn.

O God, you put to death and give
   life;
you cast down to the grave and
   raise up.
You make poor and make rich;
you bring low, you also exalt.

You raise up the poor from the
   dust;
you lift the needy from the ash
   heap,
to seat them with those of renown
and inherit a seat of honor.

For the pillars of the earth are
   yours,
on them you set the world.
You will guard the steps of your
   faithful ones,
but wickedness shall perish in
   darkness.
For not by strength shall we
   prevail.

Against evil you will thunder on
   high.
You will judge the ends of the
   earth;
you will give strength to just
   leaders
and exalt the power of your
   anointed ones! **Glory*...**

**Ant. 3 Rejoice, our God comes
to save us.**

Psalm 97

You reign over all; let the earth
   rejoice;
let the many coastlands be glad!
Clouds and thick darkness are
   round about you;
righteousness and justice the
   foundation of your throne.

Fire goes before you,
burning up all that is evil.
Your lightnings lighten the world,
the earth sees and trembles.

Mountains melt like wax before
   you,
before you, Creator of all the
   earth.
The heavens proclaim your
   justice;
all peoples behold your glory.

All who pay homage to idols,
who boast in worthless gods,
are put to shame.
All gods bow down before you.

Zion hears and is glad;
the people of Judah rejoice,
because of your judgments, O
   God.
For you are most high over all the
   earth;
exalted far above all gods.

You love those who hate evil;
you preserve the lives of your
saints;
you deliver them from
wickedness.

Light dawns for the just
and joy for the upright of heart.
Rejoice in God, you that are just,
and give thanks to God's holy
name. **Glory*...**

READING

This path of self-knowledge must never be abandoned, nor is there on this journey a soul so much a giant that it has no need to return often to the stage of an infant and a suckling.... There is no stage of prayer so sublime that it isn't necessary to return often to the beginning. Along this path of prayer, self-knowledge and the thought of one's sins is the bread with which all palates must be fed no matter how delicate they may be; they cannot be sustained without this bread. It must be eaten within bounds, nonetheless.

Teresa of Avila, *Life*, 13.15, (3)

RESPONSORY

O God, you are One, you love the singlehearted. **—O God,...**
The pure of heart shall see you; **—you love...**
Glory to you, Source of all Being, Eternal Word and Holy Spirit.
—O God,...

CANTICLE OF ZECHARIAH

Ant. Deliver us, O God, from all that is evil.

INTERCESSIONS

O God, you have made a covenant of love with us;
   —dispel from our minds and hearts the fear that belies your
    care for us.
You have hidden yourself in every blade of grass and every
towering mountain;
   —give us eyes to see your creative love at work in our world.
Jesus, you responded to women with affirmation and love;
   —show us how to encourage and support women when
    others would prevent them from serving you.
You allowed the words of Scripture to form you and to guide your
life;
   —let the word of your life be the foundation of all we do and the
    guide for our lives.

Spirit of God, you are the very life of the church;
 —invade us all with the wisdom, fortitude, and generosity to be
  the people of God in deed and truth.

PRAYER: O God, our Creator, each morning we praise the
  wonder of your love. Your tender care measures our
  strength and calls us to grow. You give us courage
  before the challenge of the day. O Eternal God, make
  us worthy of the time you have given us. This we ask
  for ourselves and for all of creation through Jesus, our
  brother and friend. Amen.

DAYTIME PRAYER

Ant. 1 Be gracious to me according to your promise.

Psalm 119:57–64

You, O God, are my portion;
I promise to obey your words.
I entreat your favor with all my
 heart;
be gracious to me according to
 your promise.

When I think of your ways,
I turn my feet to your will;
I hasten and do not delay
to keep your commandments.

Though the cords of the wicked
 ensnare me
I do not forget your law.
At midnight I rise to praise you,
because of your just decrees.

I am a friend of all who revere
 you,
of those who obey your precepts.
The earth is full of your steadfast
 love;
teach me your statutes.
  Glory*...

Ant. 2 Shelter me in the shadow of your wings.

Psalm 55:1–19, 22–24

O God, give ear to my prayer;
hide not from my supplication!
attend to me and answer me;
I am overcome by my troubles.

I am distraught by the lure of
 corruption,
at oppression caused by
 wickedness.
The evil that brings trouble upon
 me,
and whose anger weighs on my
 soul.

My heart is in anguish within me,
the terrors of death fall upon me.
Fear and trembling come upon
 me,
and horror overwhelms me.

O that I had wings like a dove!
I would fly away and be at rest;
indeed, I would wander afar,
I would take refuge in the
 wilderness,
I would haste to find me a shelter
from the raging wind and
 tempest.

Overthrow this oppression, O
  God,
confuse all who seek to destroy.
For I see violence and strife all
  around me.
Day and night it patrols our
  cities;
They are full of wickedness and
  evil,
ruin is in their midst;
oppression and fraud do not
  depart
from their market places.
  Glory*...

**Ant. 3 Let us walk together in
the ways of our God.**
  II

It is not our enemies who cause
  this;
then I might bear it;
it is not our foes who oppress,
I might hide from them.

But it is ourselves, our
  companions,
our familiar and intimate friends.
We used to speak together of
  justice;
We walked together in
  companionship in the ways of
  our God.

I will call out to you, O God,
and you will save me.
Evening, morning and at noon
I utter complaint and lament;
you will hear my voice.

You will deliver my soul in safety
in the attack waged all around;
for many things can bring me
  down,
but you will hear my cry.

You will give ear, and chastise us,
you, who reign from of old;
because we have not kept your
  law,
and have not revered you.

Cast your burdens on our God,
and you will be supported.
Never will God permit
the just ones to falter.

But you, O God, will bring down
to the pit of the grave,
all that is wicked and evil;
that oppresses the poor and the
  needy.

O God, we will trust in you.
  Glory*...

PRAYER: O God, our daily burdens weigh us down and fear for
our future is no stranger to us. Help us to remember
the life and death of Jesus, that strengthened by his
hope, we too may become totally open to your will.
Grant this in Jesus' name. Amen.

EVENING PRAYER

Ant. 1 In silence and stillness, my heart waits for you.

Psalm 62

For God alone my soul waits in
 silence;
From God comes my salvation.
God alone is my rock and my
 stronghold,
my fortress; I shall not be moved.

How long will you set upon me
to break me down,
as though I were a leaning wall,
or a tottering fence?

They only plan to destroy.
They take pleasure in falsehood.
They bless with their mouths,
but inwardly they curse.

For God alone my soul waits in
 silence,
for my hope comes from the Most
 High.
God alone is my rock and my
 stronghold,
my fortress; I shall not be moved.

In you alone is my deliverance,
my mighty rock, my refuge.
We trust in you at all times
and pour out our hearts before
 you;
for you are our refuge.

Common folk are but a breath,
great persons are a delusion.
Placed on the scales, they go up;
together they are lighter than a
 breath.

Put no confidence in extortion,
set no vain hopes on robbery;—

do not set your heart on riches,
even if they should increase.

Once God has spoken; twice have
 I heard this:
that power belongs to God;
and to you, O God, steadfast love.
For you repay us according to our
 deeds. **Glory*...**

Ant. 2 Your spirit, O God, moves upon the face of the earth.

Psalm 67

O God, be gracious to us and
 bless us
and make your face shine upon
 us.
That your ways be known upon
 earth,
your saving power among all
 nations.
Let the peoples praise you, O
 God;
let all the peoples praise you.

Let the nations be glad and sing
 for joy,
for you judge the peoples with
 equity
and guide the nations on earth.
Let the peoples praise you, O
 God;
let all the peoples praise you.

The earth has yielded its
 increase;
God, our God, has blessed us.
You, indeed, have blessed us;
let all the earth revere you!
 Glory*...

**Ant. 3 You are God's temple;
God's spirit dwells in you.**

Cant: Colossians 1:12–20

Let us give thanks to God
for having made us worthy
to share the inheritance of the
  saints in light.

God has delivered us
from the power of darkness
and transferred us
into the kindom of God's beloved
  Son, Jesus,
in whom we have redemption,
the forgiveness of our sins.

Jesus is the image of the invisible
  God,
the first-born of all creation;
in him all things were created,
in heaven and on earth,
things visible and invisible.

All things were created through
  him;
all were created for him.
He is before all else that is.
In him all things hold together.

He is the head of the body, the
  church!
He is the beginning,
the firstborn from the dead,
that in everything, he might be
  above all others.

In him all the fullness of God was
  pleased to dwell,
and through him, to reconcile all
  things to himself,
whether on earth or in heaven,
making peace by the blood of his
  cross. **Glory*...**

READING

My God, how can You leave me to myself, for You are responsible for me?
And how could I be harmed while You are my Ally? Or how could I be
disappointed in You, my Welcomer? Here I am seeking to gain access to
You by means of my need of You. How could I seek to gain access to You
by means of what cannot possibly reach You? Or how can I complain to
You of my state, for it is not hidden from You? Or how can I express
myself to You in *my* speech, since it comes from You and goes forth to
You? Or how can my hopes be dashed, for they have already reached
You? Or how can my states not be good, for they are based on You and
go to You? My God how gentle You are with me in spite of my great
ignorance, and how merciful You are with me in spite of my ugly deeds!

Ibn 'Ata' Illah, The Book of Wisdom, p.120, (1)

RESPONSORY

You love the poor, O God; you feed them with your word.
  —You love...
They call to you for life; **—you feed...**
Glory to you, Source of all Being, Eternal Word and Holy Spirit.
  —You love...

CANTICLE OF MARY

Ant. Most holy be your name.

INTERCESSIONS

O God, you long to draw us to yourself in a realm of peace;
  —bless all who struggle with relationships in the home and in
  the workplace.
Your gift of faith to us grows by use and for the asking;
  —make us aware of this treasure; let us taste and share its
  fruits.
Jesus, you knew the sins of your followers, but you forgave and
encouraged them in the way of love;
  —let our awareness of our faults lead us to encourage one
  another to turn to you.
You eased the burdens of so many by healing their sickness and
wounds;
  —give nurses and doctors the skill and compassion they need to
  do the same.
The alien and stranger are dear to your heart;
  —give us the humility and generosity to welcome those who are
  different from us.

PRAYER: O God, we live in constant need. To whom shall we go
but to you? You are both father and mother to us,
tending our days with delicate care. We thank you for
your love and mercy this day, and we ask you to help
us to forgive as we have been forgiven; to give as we
have received. This we, your children, ask of you in
your tender mercy. Amen.

THURSDAY

MORNING PRAYER

Ant. 1 I am the vine, you are the branches. The one who abides in me will bear much fruit.

Psalm 80

Give ear, O Shepherd of Israel,
you who lead Joseph like a flock!—

You who are enthroned upon the
  cherubim,
shine before Ephraim, Benjamin
  and Manasseh!
Stir up your might and come to
  save us!

Restore us, God of hosts;
let your face shine, that we may be
saved.
God of hosts, how long will you be
angry
with your people's prayers?
You fed them with the bread of
tears,
and gave them tears to drink in full
measure.
You made us the scorn of our
neighbors,
our enemies laugh among
themselves.

Restore us, God of hosts;
let your face shine, that we may be
saved.

You brought a vine out of Egypt;
you drove out the nations to plant
it.
You cleared the ground before it;
it took root and filled the land.

The mountains were covered with
its shade,
the mighty cedars with its
branches;
it sent out its branches to the sea,
and its roots to the Great River.

Then why have you broken down
its walls?
so that all who pass by pluck its
fruit?
It is ravaged by the boar of the
forest,
devoured by the beasts of the field.

Turn again, O God of hosts!
Look down from heaven, and see;
have regard for this vine,
the vine you have planted.
It has been burnt with fire and cut
down.

Let your hand be on those you
have chosen,
those you make strong for yourself!
Then we will never forsake you;
give us life, and we will call on your
name.

Restore us, God of hosts!
let your face shine, that we may be
saved. **Glory*...**

**Ant. 2 God is the joy of my
salvation.**

Cant: Isaiah 12:1-6

I will give thanks to you, O God;
for though you were angry with me,
your anger turned away,
and you did comfort me.

Behold, you are my savior;
I will trust, and will not be afraid;
you are my strength and my song,
you have become my salvation.

With joy we will draw water from
the wells of salvation.
We will say on that day:
"We give you thanks and call upon
your name;
make known your deeds among the
nations,
proclaim how exalted is your name.

"We sing our praise to you,
for all your glorious deeds;
let this be known in all the earth."
Shout, and sing for joy, O people of
Zion,
for great in your midst
is the Holy One of Israel!
  Glory*...

Ant. 3 Today if you should hear God's voice, harden not your heart.

Psalm 81

Sing aloud to God our strength;
shout for joy to the God of our
  people.

Raise a song and sound the
  timbrel,
the sweet-sounding harp and the
  lyre.
Blow the trumpet at the new moon,
when the moon is full on our feast.

For this is a statute for Israel,
a command of our God.
Who made it a decree with Joseph,
when he went against the land of
  Egypt.

A voice I had not known said to me:
"I relieved your shoulder of the
  burden;
your hands were freed from the
  basket.
In distress you called, and I
  delivered you;
I answered you, concealed in the
  storm cloud,
I tested you at the waters of
  Meribah.

Hear, O my people, while I
  admonish you!
O Israel, if only you would listen to
  me!
There shall be no strange god
  among you;

You shall not worship an alien god.
I am the Most High, your God,
who brought you up out of the land
  of Egypt.
Open wide your mouth, and I will
  fill it.

But my people did not listen to my
  voice;
Israel would have none of me.
So I gave them over to their
  stubborn hearts,
to follow their own counsels.

O that my people would listen to
  me,
that Israel would walk in my ways!
I would soon subdue their
  enemies,
and turn my hand against their
  foes.

I would feed you with the finest
  wheat,
and with honey from the rock I
  would fill you." **Glory*...**

READING

Within the Christian story it is possible to see that divine self-emptying
in the incarnation and passion of Christ is not an uncharacteristic
divine action. Rather, this historical moment discloses the pattern of
Sophia-God's love always and everywhere operative. Divine freely self-
giving love did not begin with God's personal entering into human
history but is so typical that it plays out at the dawn of creation itself.

Elizabeth Johnson, She Who Is, p. 234, (2)

RESPONSORY

O God, you promise life eternal, asking only that we love.—**O God...**

You are kind to the brokenhearted; —**asking...**
Glory to you, Source of all Being, Eternal Word and Holy Spirit.
—**O God...**

CANTICLE OF ZECHARIAH

Ant. Let us serve our God in holiness.

INTERCESSIONS

O God, only you know the whole truth about us and our deeds;
  —guide us with your wisdom and compassion in our
  relationships with one another.
Every person and thing that you have created is precious to you;
  —bless those who are handicapped and all who assist them.
Jesus, you crossed the sea and encountered its dangers;
  —bless sailors and all who travel the waters of our world.
We know the story of your life, O Christ, yet mystery abounds;
  —let our search for truth keep us open to the inspiration of the
  Holy Spirit.
Spirit of God, joy is among your many gifts to us;
  —bless artists of every kind—all who lift up our hearts and fill
  the world with beauty and light.

PRAYER: God of the universe, you speak to us in all of creation,
but you call to us most surely in the depths of our
hearts. Help us to listen for your voice today, gentling
our work, our recreation, and our relationships with
others in ways that let us hear you. Deepen in us our
faith in your presence to us. Grant this through the
intercession of all your prophets who listened in
sincerity and truth. Amen.

DAYTIME PRAYER

**Ant. 1 Teach me discernment
that I may know your ways.**

Psalm 119:65–72

You have been good to your servant,
according to your word, O God.—

Teach me discernment and
  knowledge,
for I trust in your commands.

Before I was afflicted I went astray;
but now I keep your word.
You are good and your deeds are
  good;
teach me your commandments.

The proud smear me with lies,
yet I keep your precepts.
Their hearts are closed to good
but I delight in your law.

It was good for me to be afflicted,
that I might learn your statutes.
The law of your mouth is better to
  me
than silver and gold.   **Glory*...**

**Ant. 2 Take heart, it is I; have no
  fear.**
          Psalm 56:1–7b, 9–14

Be gracious to me, O God,
some there are who crush me;
they trample upon me all day long,
for many fight proudly against me.

When I am afraid,
I put my trust in you.
In you, whose word I praise,
In you I trust without fear.
What can mortal flesh do to me?

All day long they injure my cause,
all their thoughts are for evil.
They band together, they lurk,
they watch my steps.

You have kept count of my
  wanderings;
you have kept a record of my tears!
Are they not written in your book?
Then my foes will be turned back
in the day when I call to you.

This I know, that God is with me.
In God, whose word I praise,
in the Holy One, whose word I
  praise,
in God I trust without a fear.
What can mortal flesh do to me?

My vows to you I will make, O God.
I will render you thanks.—

For you delivered my soul from
  death,
my feet from falling,
that I may walk before you
in the light of life.   **Glory*...**

**Ant. 3 My heart is steadfast; I
  will praise you all my days.**
          Psalm 57

Have mercy on me, have mercy,
for in you my soul takes refuge.
In the shadow of your wings I take
  refuge
till the storms of destruction pass
  by.

I cry to God the Most High,
to God who has always been my
  help.
May you send from heaven and
  save me
and shame those who trample
  upon me.
O God, send your truth and your
  love.

My soul lies down among lions,
who greedily devour the peoples of
  the earth.
Their teeth are spears and arrows,
their tongues sharpened swords.

Be exalted, O God, above the
  heavens;
let your glory be over all the earth!

They laid a snare for my steps,
my soul was bowed down.
They dug a pit in my path
but they fell in it themselves.

My heart is steadfast, O God,
my heart is steadfast.
I will sing and make melody!
Awake, my soul,
awake, lyre and harp!
I will awake the dawn!

I will give thanks to you among the peoples,
I will praise you among the nations
for your love reaches to the heavens
your faithfulness to the skies.

Be exalted, O God, above the heavens!
let your glory be over all the earth!
Glory*...

PRAYER: O God, you bless those who hunger and thirst for justice. We ask for the gift of this desire. Imprint on our minds and in our hearts the longings of your son, Jesus, that our labor this day may be done justly and that we too may bless those who labor for the sake of justice. This we ask in Jesus who is our Way, our Truth, and our Life. Amen.

EVENING PRAYER

Ant. 1 You are the salt of the earth; you are the light of the world.

Psalm 72

Give justice to your Anointed, O God,
and righteousness to those Chosen!
That your people may be judged in righteousness,
and your poor with justice.

Let the mountains bring forth peace for the people,
and the hills, justice!
May your Anointed
defend the cause of the poor,
give deliverance to the needy,
and punish the oppressor!

May your Anointed endure like the sun,
and as long as the moon, through all ages,
like rain that falls on the mown grass,
like showers that water the earth.

In that day justice shall flourish
and peace till the moon be no more!
Your Anointed shall rule from sea to sea,
from the River to the ends of the earth!

May evil bow down before the Holy One,
and wickedness lick the dust!
The kings of Tarshish and of the isles shall render tribute.

May rulers of Sheba and Seba bring gifts.
All will fall down before the Anointed,
all nations serve and pay homage.
Glory*...

Ant. 2 God will save the poor from oppression and violence.

II

The Anointed delivers the needy when they call,
the poor and those who are helpless.—

Having pity on the weak and the
　needy,
saving the lives of the poor.

From oppression and violence they
　are redeemed;
and precious is their blood.
Long may your Chosen One live,
may gold of Sheba be given
to the one you have anointed,
and prayers be made without
　ceasing,
and blessings all the day!

May there be abundance of grain in
　the land,
waving on the tops of the
　mountains;
may its fruit be like Lebanon;
may people flourish in the cities
like the grass in the field!

May the name of your Anointed
　endure forever,
and continue as long as the sun!
Every tribe shall be blessed in the
　one you have chosen,
all nations bless your name.

Blessed be the God of Israel,
who alone does wondrous things.
Blessed be your name forever;
may your glory fill the earth.
Amen! Amen!　**Glory*...**

**Ant. 3 Lamb of God, you take
away the sin of the world.
Cant: Rev 11:17–18;
12:10b–12a**

We praise you, God Almighty,
who is and who was.
You have assumed your great
　power,
you have begun your reign.

The nations have raged in anger,
but then came your day of wrath
and the moment to judge the dead;
the time to reward your servants
　the prophets
and the holy ones who revere you,
the great and the small alike.

Now have salvation and power
　come,
your reign, O God, and the
　authority of your Anointed One.
For the accusers of our loved ones
　have been cast out,
who night and day accused them.

By the blood of the Lamb have they
　been defeated,
and by the testimony of your
　servants;
love for life did not deter them from
　death.
So rejoice, you heavens,
and you that dwell therein!
　　Glory*...

READING

In order to practice the virtues it is not necessary to be attentive to all of
them all of the time. In fact, this tends to turn one's thoughts and
affections back on oneself so that they become entangled. Humility and
charity are the dominant chords; all the other virtues are overtones of
these. It's only necessary that these two be carefully observed: one very
lowly, the other very lofty. The preservation of an entire structure
depends upon the foundation and the roof. If you continue the exercise
of these two with conviction, when you come up against the others, they

won't give you any difficulty. These are the mothers of the virtues; the others follow them as little chicks follow mother hens. (François de Sales)

Wendy Wright, *Bond of Perfection*, p. 81, (1)

RESPONSORY

You are bountiful, O God; all of your desires for us are good.
  —You...
Everything is a grace; **—all of...**
Glory to you, Source of all Being, Eternal Word and Holy Spirit.
  —You...

CANTICLE OF MARY

Ant. You have shown your power, O God; you have scattered the proud in their hearts' fantasy.

INTERCESSIONS

You hear our prayers and guide and protect us, O God;
  —be praised and thanked for all that we take for granted and for hidden gifts.
You offer us the grace to become a new person in Christ;
  —in times of boredom, awaken us to the world of the Spirit we so often ignore.
Jesus, you were content to hide your glory and to give in secret;
  —strengthen our inward self that we may find our true peace beyond the measure of others.
You challenged the status quo; you died for being different;
  —give courage and peace to all who live on the fringes of society.
You promised a peace that the world cannot give;
  —banish war from our world.

PRAYER: Jesus, our Savior and Guide, you gave yourself to us through a meal at the end of a day, at the end of your life. Be with us at the end of this day as we dedicate ourselves to all that you call us to be. Help us to say to God with you, "Thy will be done." Let us conclude this day strengthened by the remembrance of your total gift of self. We ask this through the power of your name. Amen.

FRIDAY

MORNING PRAYER

Ant 1 A contrite heart, O God, is pleasing in your sight.
Psalm 51

Have mercy on me, O God,
according to your steadfast love;
in your abundant mercy blot out my sins.
Wash me thoroughly from my offenses,
and cleanse me from my sin!

For I know my offenses,
and my sin is ever before me.
Against you, you alone, have I sinned,
and done what is evil in your sight,
so you are justified in your sentence
and blameless in your judgment.
Behold, I was brought forth in a sinful world.

For you desire truth in my innermost being;
teach me wisdom in the depths of my heart.
O purify me, and I shall be clean;
O wash me, I shall be whiter than snow.
Fill me with joy and gladness;
let the bones you have broken rejoice.
Hide your face from my guilt,
and blot out all my offenses.

Create in me a clean heart,
put a steadfast spirit within me.
Cast me not from your presence,
take not your spirit from me.
Give me again the joy of your salvation,
with a willing spirit uphold me.

Then I will teach transgressors your ways
and sinners will return to you.
Deliver me from death,
O God of my salvation,
and my tongue will sing out your saving help.

Open my lips and my mouth will sing your praises.
For you take no delight in sacrifice;
were I to give a burnt offering,
you would not be pleased.
A broken spirit you accept;
a contrite heart, you will not despise.

In your goodness, show favor to Zion;
rebuild the walls of Jerusalem.
Then you will delight in just sacrifices,
in gifts offered on your altar.
  Glory*...

Ant. 2 Your mercy reaches to the heavens; your mercy covers the earth.
Cant: Habakkuk 3:2-4, 13a, 15-19

O God, I have heard your renown,
and your work, O God, do I revere.
In the course of the years renew it;
in the course of the years make it known;
in your wrath remember mercy!

God came from Teman,
and the Holy One from Mount Paran.—

Your glory covered the heavens,
O God,
and the earth was full of your
praise.

Your brightness was like the
light,
rays flashed forth from your
hand;
there you veiled your power.
You went forth to save your
people,
for the salvation of your anointed.

You trampled the sea with your
horses,
the surging of mighty waters.
I hear, and my body trembles,
my lips quiver at the sound.

Decay enters my bones,
my legs totter beneath me.
I wait for the day of trouble
to come on those who oppress us.
    Glory*...

**Ant. 3 Hear the word of God, O
people.**
        Psalm 147:12–20

O praise the Most High,
Jerusalem!
Praise your God, O Zion!

For God strengthens the bars of
your gates,
blessing your children within
you,
establishing peace in your
borders,
feeding you with the finest of
wheat.

You send out your word to the
earth;
your command runs swiftly,
giving snow like wool,
scattering hoarfrost like ashes.

You cast forth your ice like
crumbs;
who can stand before your cold?
You send forth your word, and
melt them;
you make the wind blow, and the
waters flow.

You make your word known to
your people,
your statutes and decrees to
Israel.
You have not dealt thus with any
other nation;
you have not taught them your
decrees. **Glory*...**

READING

Sometimes, as we look at the night sky, a single bright star will appear.
In its brightness it transforms the night; every star in the sky is changed
in relation to this new appearance. It is as if this one star, in
unparalleled beauty, crowns the entire beauty of the night. Christ in
God is like that bright star, illumining the actuality of the primordial
nature through the beauty of his manifestation of that nature in our
history. Through Christ the depths of God are touched for the world;
new possibilities for reflecting divine harmony in human history shine
out for us. The church is born.

Marjorie Hewitt Suchocki, *God, Christ, Church*, p. 132, (2)

RESPONSORY

Who will deliver us, O God, from our weakness and sin?
  —**Who will...**
Jesus Christ has saved us —**from our...**
Glory to you, Source of all Being, Eternal Word and Holy Spirit.
  —**Who will...**

CANTICLE OF ZECHARIAH

**Ant. You are compassionate, O God, and forever faithful to
    your promise.**

INTERCESSIONS

O God, you have created us for what eye has not seen and ear has
not heard;
  —give us open minds and largeness of heart that we may see
  and serve beyond ourselves.
Jesus, you served and saved others—ridicule did not shrink your
compassion;
  —make us singlehearted in our care for others.
With religious authority against you and disciples slow to
understand, you stayed your course to the end;
  —give perseverance to the new and creative in our culture,
  that your message may live on in us.
Jesus, you knew the innocence and vulnerability of childhood;
  —guide and protect the children of our disturbed and violent
  world.
Spirit of God, you promote progress—you make all things new;
  —give us the vision we need to develop for the better without
  destroying our vital heritage.

PRAYER: O God, your son, Jesus, died giving the message of
      your love to us. Have mercy on us. Give us the courage
      to die rather than cause the death of another. Help us
      to allow his death to mean new life for us. Never let us
      stand in the way of your saving grace. Grant this
      through the intercession of Jesus and all who have
      given their lives for others. Amen.

DAYTIME PRAYER

Ant. 1 Blessed be God who comforts us in all our affliction.

Psalm 119:73-80

Your hands have made me and
have fashioned me;
give me understanding that I may
learn your commandments.
Those who revere you will see me
and rejoice,
because I have hoped in your
word.

I know that your judgments are
right,
that in faithfulness you afflicted
me.
Let your love be ready to comfort
me
according to your promise.

Let your mercy come to me, that I
may live;
for your law is my delight.
Let the godless be put to shame,
who have corrupted me with
guile,
while I will ponder on your
precepts.

Let those who revere you turn to
me,
that they may know your will.
May my heart be blameless in
your commandments,
that I may not be put to shame!
Glory*...

Ant. 2 We have a treasure in earthen vessels, to show the power of God.

Psalm 59:1-5, 10-11, 17-18

Deliver me from evil, O my God,—

protect me from those who
oppress me,
deliver me from all that is wicked,
and save me from all cruelty.

Calamity lies in wait for my life;
misfortune bands together
against me.
For no offense or sin of mine,
for no fault, they run and make
ready.
Rouse yourself, come to my aid
and see!

O my Strength, I will sing praises
to you;
for you, O God, are my
stronghold.
In your steadfast love you will
meet me;
O God, come to my aid,
let me triumph over oppression.

As for me, I will sing of your
might;
each morning sing of your love.
For you have been to me a
stronghold
and a refuge in the day of
distress.

O my Strength, I will sing praises
to you,
for you, O God, are my
stronghold,
the God who shows me love
without end. **Glory*...**

Ant. 3 Blessed are you, O God; you heal us while wounding us.

Psalm 60

O God, you have rejected us and
broken our defenses;—

You have turned your face;
   restore us.
You have made the land to quake,
   torn it open;
Repair its breaches for it totters.
You have made your people suffer
   hard things,
and have given us wine that
   made us reel.

You have set up a signal for those
   who fear you,
to rally to it from the bow.
That your faithful ones may be
   delivered,
help us by your hand and give
   answer!

You have spoken from your
   sanctuary:
"With exultation I will divide
   Shechem—

and portion out the Vale of
   Succoth.

Gilead is mine and Manasseh;
Ephraim is my helmet,
Judah is my scepter.

Moab is my washbasin;
upon Edom I cast my shoe.
Over Philistia I will shout in
   triumph."

Who will bring me to the fortified
   city?
Who will lead me to Edom?
Have you not rejected us, O God?
You did not go forth with our
   armies.

Give us help against the foe,
for human help is vain.
With you we shall do valiantly;
it is you who will tread down
   oppression. **Glory*...**

PRAYER: Lord Jesus Christ, the marvel of your love lives on and
challenges everyone who comes to know you. In you we
know the love of God; through you we know the will
and ways of God. Be with us now that we may live for
one another as you have lived and died for us. Grant
this through your Spirit of Love. Amen.

EVENING PRAYER

**Ant. 1 You are gracious, O God,
and full of compassion.**

Psalm 116:1–9

I love you, O God, for you have
   heard
my voice and my supplications.
You have inclined your ear to me,
I will call on you as long as I live.

The snares of death encompassed
   me;—

the pangs of the grave laid hold
   on me;
I suffered distress and anguish.
Then I called on your name, O
   God:
"O God, I pray you, save my life!"

Gracious are you and just;
merciful and full of compassion.
You preserve those with simple
   hearts;
when I was brought low, you
   saved me.

Return my soul, to your rest;
for God has dealt kindly with you,
delivering my soul from death,
my eyes from tears,
my feet from stumbling.

I will walk before you, O God,
in the land of the living.
Glory*...

**Ant. 2 God is my comforter and
help in time of need.**

Psalm 121

I lift up my eyes to the hills.
From whence comes my help?
My help comes from you, O God,
who made heaven and earth.

You will not let my foot stumble,
you, who preserve me, will not
sleep.
Behold, you who keep Israel
will neither slumber nor sleep.

You, O God, are our keeper;
you are our shade.—

The sun shall not smite us by
day,
nor the moon by night.

You will guard us from all evil;
you will preserve our lives.
You will protect our goings and
comings
both now and forever.
Glory*...

**Ant. 3 Ruler of all the ages, just
and true are your ways.**

Cant: Rev 15:3–4

Great and wonderful are your
works,
God the Almighty One!
Just and true are your ways,
Ruler of all the ages!

Who shall refuse you honor,
or the glory due your name?

For you alone are holy,
all nations shall come and
worship in your presence.
Your judgments are clearly seen.
Glory*...

READING

I would have you know that every virtue of yours and every vice is put
into action by means of your neighbors. If you hate me, you harm your
neighbors and yourself as well (for you are your chief neighbor), and the
harm is both general and in particular. I say general because it is your
duty to love your neighbors as your own self. In love you ought to help
them spiritually with prayer and counsel, and assist them spiritually
and materially in their need—at least with your good will if you have
nothing else. If you do not love me you do not love your neighbors...but
it is yourself you harm most, because you deprive yourself of grace.

Catherine of Siena, *The Dialogue*, p. 33, (1)

RESPONSORY

Lord Jesus Christ, your yoke is easy and your burden is light.
—Lord Jesus...
In you we will find rest; **—for your yoke...**

Glory to you, Source of all Being, Eternal Word and Holy Spirit.
—Lord Jesus...

CANTICLE OF MARY

**Ant. You put down the mighty from their throne and lift up
the lowly.**

INTERCESSIONS

Jesus, you washed the feet of your followers;
   —teach all civic and religious leaders how to govern with
   humility and reverence.
You did not call your disciples servants but friends;
   —help us to establish your kindom by mutual collaboration and
   loving respect.
You shared a meal with one who had betrayed you;
   —give us the desire to set aside our mistrust of one another.
Jesus, you came into the world to testify to the truth;
   —make us credible witnesses to the truth of your gospel.
You suffered at the hands of those you served;
   —enable us to serve one another selflessly without regard for
   human success.

PRAYER: Holy Spirit, Living Love of God, you are in the world
healing the wounds of sin and death. Warm the hearts
of those embittered by sorrow and pain, encourage
those crushed by failure, enlighten the minds of those
dulled by pleasure or fatigue. Awaken in us all the
remembrance of the overwhelming love of God made
known to us in the life and death of Jesus. Help us to
continue with renewed trust. This we ask of you, Life-
giving Spirit, in the name of your Christ, God among
us. Amen.

SATURDAY

MORNING PRAYER

Ant. 1 We acclaim your love in the morning and your faithfulness at night.

Psalm 92

It is good to give thanks to you,
to sing praises to your name, Most High,
to declare your love in the morning,
and your faithfulness by night,
to the music of the lute and the harp,
to the melody of the lyre.

For you make me glad by your deeds;
at the work of your hands I sing for joy.
How great are your works, O God!
Your thoughts are very deep!

The foolish ones cannot know;
the stupid cannot understand this:
though the wicked spring up like grass
and all evildoers flourish,
they are doomed to their own devices.
But you, O God, are on high forever.
All wickedness shall perish;
all oppression be wiped out.

You give me the strength of the wild ox;
you pour oil over my head.
My eyes have seen the downfall of evil,
my ears have heard the doom of corruption.
The just shall flourish like the palm tree
and grow like a cedar in Lebanon.

They are planted in your holy house,
they flourish in your courts.
They still bring forth fruit in old age,
they are ever full of sap and green,
to show that you, O God, are just;
you are my rock; in you there is no injustice. **Glory*...**

Ant. 2 We declare your greatness, O God.

Cant: Deut 32:1-12

Give ear, O heavens, while I speak;
let the earth hear the words of my mouth.
May my teaching soak in like the rain,
and my speech permeate like the dew,
like a gentle rain upon the tender grass,
like a shower upon the herbs.

For I will proclaim your name, O God.
Declare your holy greatness!
"My Rock, your work is faultless;
all your ways are justice.
A faithful God, without deceit,
how just and right you are!

Yet basely have you been dealt with by your sinful children,
a perverse and crooked generation.
Is God to be thus requited,
you foolish and senseless people?
Is God not your source, who created you,
who made you and established you?

Remember the days of old,
Consider the years of many
  generations;
Ask your parents and they will
  inform you,
ask your elders and they will tell
  you.

When the Most High gave the
  nations their inheritance,
separating the children of the
  earth,
the Most High fixed the boundaries
  of the peoples
according to the number of those in
  your court.
But your portion, O God, is your
  people,
Jacob, your allotted heritage.

You found them in a desert land,
in the howling waste of the
  wilderness;
encircling them and caring for
  them,
guarding them as the apple of your
  eye.

Like an eagle that stirs up its nest,
that flutters over its young,
so you spread your wings to catch
  them,
and bear them on your pinions.
You alone were their leader,
no strange god was with our God."
    Glory*...

**Ant. 3 How great is your name in
  all the earth.**

Psalm 8

How great is your name, O God,
in all the earth!

You whose glory above the heavens
is chanted on the lips of babes,
have founded a defense against
  your foes,
to silence the cries of the rebels.

When I look at the heavens,
the work of your hands,
the moon and the stars which you
  established;
who are we that you should keep
  us in mind,
mortal flesh that you care for us?

Yet you have made us little less
  than God,
and crowned us with glory and
  honor.
You entrust us with the works of
  your hands,
to care for all your creation.

All sheep and oxen,
and even the beasts of the field,
the birds of the air, and the fish of
  the sea,
whatever passes along the paths of
  the sea.

How great is your name, Creator
God,
in all the earth!   **Glory*...**

READING

I feel the *vocation* of the WARRIOR, THE PRIEST, THE APOSTLE, THE
DOCTOR, THE MARTYR. Finally, I feel the need and the desire of
carrying out the most heroic deeds for *You, O Jesus....* I feel in me the
vocation of the PRIEST. With what love, O Jesus, I would carry You in
my hands when, at my voice, You would come down from heaven. And
with what love would I give you to souls!... I would like to travel over the

whole earth to preach your Name...one mission alone would not be enough for me. I would want to preach the Gospel on all the five continents simultaneously and even to the most remote isles. I would be a missionary, not for a few years only but from the beginning of creation until the consummation of the ages. But above all, O my Beloved Savior, I would shed my blood for You even to the last drop.

Thérèse of Lisieux, *Story of a Soul*, p. 192, (3)

RESPONSORY

Those who wait for you, O God, shall never be disappointed.
—Those who...
They shall see you face to face; **—and shall...**
Glory to you, Source of all Being, Eternal Word and Holy Spirit.
—Those who...

CANTICLE OF ZECHARIAH

Ant. Guide our feet into the way of peace.

INTERCESSIONS

O God, you know of what we are made, and you give us all that we need;
—let us mirror your compassion to one another.
Jesus, many dismissed your teaching because of your common origin;
—help us to look beyond surface impressions to the true value of each person.
Our attachments and addictions lay heavy burdens upon us;
—teach us how to listen to your freeing word written in our hearts.
You knew rejection and derision;
—give us the desire to serve all and the grace to be at peace when we cannot please everyone.
Our culture tends to reward the strong and powerful and to dismiss the weak;
—make all that we do reflect your gospel—your good news to the poor.

PRAYER: Merciful God, we often stray from your call and our own good intentions, but you meet us with forgiveness and creative love. Give us the gift of patience and understanding that we too may lure others to new life.

May all who die this day enjoy life with you as they see you face to face. Grant this through Mary, who brought new life to us in Jesus. Amen.

DAYTIME PRAYER

Ant. 1 In your love spare my life, that I may keep your decrees.

Psalm 119:81–88

My soul pines for your salvation;
I hope in your word.
My eyes fail with watching for
  your promise;
"When will you comfort me?"

Though parched and exhausted
  with waiting
I have not forgotten your
  commands.
How long must your servant
  endure?
When will you requite me?

Evil waits to entrap me
to sin against your law.
All your commandments are sure;
then help me when oppressed by
  falsehood!

Death lurks to make an end of
  me;
but I forsake not your precepts.
In your steadfast love spare my
  life,
that I may do your will. **Glory*...**

Ant. 2 O God, you are my refuge, my stronghold against evil.

Psalm 61

Hear my cry, O God,
listen to my prayer;
from the end of the earth I call,
when my heart is faint.

Set me on the rock that is higher
  than I;
for you are my refuge,
my stronghold against evil.

Let me dwell in your tent forever!
Hide me in the shelter of your
  wings!
For you, O God, have heard my
  vows,
you have given me the heritage
of those who love your name.

May you lengthen the lives of just
  rulers:
may their years cover many
  generations!
May they ever be enthroned
  before you;
bid love and truth watch over
  them.

So will I ever sing your praises,
as I pay my vows day after day.
  Glory*...

Ant. 3 O God, preserve my life from corruption.

Psalm 64

Hear my voice, O God, in my
  complaint;
preserve my life from all that is
  evil,
hide me from the tempter's snare,
from the scheming wiles of my
  heart.

Evil sharpens its tongue like a
  sword;—

aiming bitter words like arrows
shooting from ambush at the
  innocent,
shooting suddenly and without
  fear.

Holding fast to its evil purpose;
conspiring to lay secret snares
thinking: "Who can see us?
Who can search out our crimes?"

But you know well our inmost
  thoughts,
the depth of the heart and
  mind!—

You will shoot your arrow at
  them;
they will be wounded suddenly.
Our own tongues bring us to ruin.

Then let all people fear;
they will tell what you have
  wrought,
and ponder what you have done.
The just will rejoice in you, O God,
and fly to you for refuge.
Let the upright in heart exult.
  Glory*...

PRAYER: Another week has passed, O God, and we see all that
we have done and what we might have done differently.
We give all of our endeavors to you. Bless the good and
heal the faulty. Inspire us to do your will more
creatively and generously in the week to come. We ask
this through Jesus who shows us the way. Amen.

WEEK III

SUNDAY, EVENING PRAYER I

Ant 1 Your glory is above the heavens; we praise your name.

Psalm 113

We your servants, praise you!
Praise your holy name!
Blessed be your name, O God,
from now and forevermore!
From the rising of the sun to its
    setting
your name is to be praised!

You are high above all nations,
and your glory above the
    heavens!
Who is like unto you, O God,
who is seated upon the heights,
who looks far down upon us,
upon the heavens and the earth?

You raise the poor from the dust,
lift the needy from the ash heap,
to set them in the company of
    rulers,
with the rulers of your people.
To the barren you give a home,
and gladden their hearts with
    children. **Glory*...**

Ant 2 I will lift up the cup of salvation and call on your holy name.

Psalm 116:10–19

I kept faith, even when I said:
"I am greatly afflicted;"—

*Glory to you, Source of all Being, Eternal Word and Holy Spirit,

As it was in the beginning is now and will be forever. Amen.

I said in my dismay,
"No one can be trusted."

What shall I render to you,
for all your goodness to me?
I will lift up the cup of salvation
and call on your holy name.

I will make my vows to you
in the presence of all your people.
Precious in your sight
is the death of your faithful ones.

Indeed, I am your servant;
you have loosened my bonds.
I will offer sacrifice of
    thanksgiving
and call on your holy name.

I will make my vows to you
in the presence of all your people,
in the courts of your holy house,
in the midst of all your saints.
    Glory*...

Ant 3 Every tongue will proclaim: Jesus Christ is Lord!

Cant: Phil 2:6–11

Though he was in the form of
    God,
Jesus did not count equality with
    God
something to be grasped at.

But emptied himself
taking the form of a slave,
being born in human likeness.

Being found in human estate,
he humbled himself and became
    obedient,
obediently accepting death,
even death on a cross!

Therefore God has highly exalted him
and bestowed on him the name above every other name.

So that at the name of Jesus every knee should bow,—

in heaven, on the earth,
and under the earth,
and every tongue proclaim
to the glory of God:
Jesus Christ is Lord! **Glory***...

READING

...What we believe we understand about our own soul is, after all, only a fleeting reflection of what will remain God's secret until the day all will be made manifest. My great joy consists in the hope of that future clarity. Faith in the secret history must always strengthen us when what we actually perceive (about ourselves or about others) might discourage us.

Edith Stein: Self-Portrait in Letters, p. 331, (3)

RESPONSORY

We sing to you, O God, and bless your name. **—We sing...**
Tell of your salvation day after day; **—and bless...**
Glory to you, Source of all Being, Eternal Word and Holy Spirit.
   —We sing...

CANTICLE OF MARY

Ant. You have helped your servant, Israel, remembering your mercy.

INTERCESSIONS

O God, you speak to us in many ways;
   —keep us open to your guidance from sources however
   great or humble.
We cherish our call to serve you, and we endeavor to be faithful;
   —deliver us from the plethora of idols that beckon to us
   daily.
Bless all who are united in marriage;
   —let the grace of the sacrament enable them to love and
   support one another.
Jesus, you knew the challenge of choosing your direction in life;
   —send your Spirit to guide those who struggle with
   vocational choices.
Spirit of God, grant wisdom, understanding, and fortitude to all
involved in the media;

—let the highest values and principles govern their decisions and programs.

PRAYER: All holy, ever present God, at the close of this day we offer to you the world's struggle toward wholeness. We are confident that our darkness and sin have been redeemed through the life and death of Jesus and that your mercy has no limit. Give us the gift of mercy for ourselves and for others. We ask this in Jesus' name. Amen.

MORNING PRAYER

Ant 1 Glory to God in the highest.

Psalm 93

O God, you are our Sovereign,
you are robed in majesty;
you are girded with strength.
The world is made firm;
it shall never be moved;
your throne is established from of
    old;
from all eternity, you are.

The waters have lifted up, O God,
the waters have lifted up their
    voice,
the waters have lifted up their
    thunder.
Mightier than the roaring of the
    waters,
mightier than the surgings of the
    sea,
You, O God, are glorious on high!

Your decrees are to be trusted.
Holiness befits your house,
O God, for evermore.
    Glory*...

Ant 2 Praise and exalt God above all, forever.

Cant: Daniel 3:57–88, 56

All you works of God, praise our
    God.
Praise and exalt God above all
    forever.
All you angels, sing God's praise,
you heavens and waters above.
Sun and moon, and stars of
    heaven,
sing praise with the heavenly
    hosts.

Every shower and dew, praise our
    God.
Give praise all you winds.
Praise our God, you fire and heat,
cold and chill–dew and rain.
Frost and chill, praise our God.
Praise God, ice and snow.
Nights and days, sing hymns of
    praise,
light and darkness,
lightnings and clouds.

Let all the earth bless our God.
Praise and exalt God above all
    forever.
Let all that grows from the earth
    give praise—

together with mountains and hills.
Give praise, you springs,
you seas and rivers,
dolphins and all water creatures.
Let birds of the air,
beasts, wild and tame,
together with all living peoples,
praise and exalt God above all
  forever.

O Israel, praise our God.
Praise and exalt God above all
  forever.
Give praise, you priests,
servants of the Most High,
spirits and souls of the just.
Holy ones of humble heart,
sing your hymns of praise.
Hannaniah, Azariah, Mishael,
  praise our God.
Praise and exalt God above all
  forever.

Let us bless our God, Holy
  Mystery,
Source of All Being, Word and
  Spirit.
Let us praise and exalt God above
  all forever.
Blessed are you, O God, in the
  firmament of heaven.
Praiseworthy and glorious and
  exalted above all forever.

**Ant 3 Praise God from the
  heavens.**

Psalm 148

Praise God from the heavens,
Praise God in the heights!—

Praise God, all you angels,
Praise God, you heavenly hosts!

Praise God, sun and moon,
Praise God, shining stars.
Praise God, highest heavens,
and the waters above the heavens!

Let them praise the name of God,
who commanded and they were
  created.
God established them forever;
fixed their bounds which will not
  pass away.

Praise God, all you on earth,
sea monsters and all deeps,
fire and hail, snow and frost,
stormy winds that obey God's
  word!

Mountains and all hills,
fruit trees and all cedars!
Beasts, wild and tame,
reptiles and birds on the wing!

All earth's rulers and peoples,
leaders and those of renown!
Young men and women,
the old together with children!

Let us praise your name, O God,
for your name alone is exalted;
your glory above heaven and
  earth.

You exalt the strength of your
  people,
you are praise for all your saints,
for all the faithful near to you.
Glory*...

READING

Thus says the [Most High God]: I am going to open your graves, and
bring you up from your graves, O my people; and I will bring you back
to the land of Israel. And you shall know that I am [your God], when I
open your graves, and bring you up from your graves, O my people. I

will put my spirit within you, and you shall live, and I will place you on your own soil; then you shall know that I, [your God], have spoken and will act," says the [Most High].

Ezek 37:12–14

RESPONSORY

Our hearts rejoice, O God, in your tender care. **—Our hearts...**
We live in peace; **—in your...**
Glory to you, Source of all Being, Eternal Word and Holy Spirit.
    —Our hearts...

CANTICLE OF ZECHARIAH

Ant. You have visited and redeemed your people, O God.

INTERCESSIONS

O God, we are one in you, and all that we do affects the whole;
    —make us aware of our power to seed the world with
        good or ill by every thought, word, and deed.
Our hearts are torn by the realization of the sufferings of others;
    —grant that we may never be a stumbling block to others
        or a culpable cause of their pain.
Jesus, you chose laborers, and tax collectors, to be your
companions;
    —preserve us from deciding what people are by what they
        do, and let us see the worth of every person and the
        value in every kind of work.
Bless those who have lost their life companion through death or
divorce;
    —let the people of God be a saving support and comfort to
        them.
Spirit of God, enlighten the minds and renew the hearts of the
hierarchy of the churches;
    —let their ministry be a healing service for all of your people.

PRAYER: God of the universe, you create the night as well as
        the day. You are with us in good fortune and bad
        times. You order all things for our well being and you
        lure us to truth and holiness. For these and all your
        gifts to us we sing your praise through Jesus Christ
        who is our way, our truth and our life. Amen.

DAYTIME PRAYER

Ant. 1 You are my companion, my helper on the way.

Psalm 118

I

We give thanks to you, for you are good,
and your steadfast love endures forever.
Let the descendants of Israel say:
"Your steadfast love endures forever."
Let the descendants of Aaron say:
"Your steadfast love endures forever."
Let those who fear you say:
"Your steadfast love endures forever."

In my distress, I called to you;
you answered me and set me free.
With you at my side I do not fear.
What can anyone do against me?
You are at my side to help me:
I shall withstand all evildoers.

It is better to take refuge in you,
than to trust in people:
it is better to take refuge in you
than to trust in our leaders.
    Glory*...

Ant. 2 You are my saving God; you chastise and you bless.

II

All wickedness surrounded me;
in your name I crushed it.
It surrounded me, surrounded me
on every side;
in your name I cut it off.
It surrounded me like bees;
it blazed like a fire among thorns.
In your name I crushed it.

I was pushed hard, and was falling
but you came to help me.—

You are my strength and my song;
you are my salvation.

O God, you have triumphed;
your reign is exalted.
You have triumphed over all;
I shall not die, I shall live
and recount your wondrous deeds.
You have chastened me sorely,
but have not given me over to
death. **Glory*...**

Ant. 3 Blessed is the one who comes in the name of our God.

III

Open to me the gates of justice,
that I may enter and give thanks.
This is your gate, O God;
the just shall enter through it.
I thank you for you have answered
me
you alone are my salvation.

The stone which the builders rejected
has become the cornerstone.
This is your doing, O God,
it is marvelous in our eyes.
This is the day which you have
made;
let us rejoice and be glad in it.

Save us, we beseech you, O God!
O God, grant us success.
Blessed are those who enter
in your holy name.
For you O God, are our God,
and you have given us light.

Let us go forward in procession
with branches,
up to your holy altar.
You are my God, I thank you.
You are my God, I praise you.

We give thanks to you for you are good;— and your steadfast love endures forever. **Glory*...**

PRAYER: God of mercy, your goodness encompasses the great and the small. Help us to know your presence in the most hidden suffering, the most secret pain. Remind us again of your unfailing love and give us new hope. This we ask through the intercession of all who suffered in hope and now live with you. Amen.

EVENING PRAYER II

Ant. 1 God revealed to the Anointed One, "Sit at my side."

Psalm 110:1-5, 7

God's revelation to the Anointed One:
"Sit at my side:
till I put injustice beneath your feet."

God will send forth from Zion your scepter of power:
rule in the midst of your foes.

Your people will give themselves freely
on the day you lead your host upon the holy mountains.
From the womb of the morning your youth will come like dew.

God has sworn an oath that will not be changed.
"You are a priest forever,
after the order of Melchizedek."

The Anointed standing by your side,
will shatter rulers on the day of wrath.

Drinking from your streams by the wayside
shall the Chosen One be refreshed. **Glory*...**

Ant. 2 In your gracious mercy, you cause us to remember your wonderful works.

Psalm 111

I will give thanks to you with all my heart,
in the company of the great assembly.
Great are the works of the Most High;
pondered by all who delight in them.

Full of honor and majesty is your work,
your justice endures for ever.
You enable us to remember your wonders;
you are gracious and merciful.

You give food to those who fear you;
you are mindful of your covenant.
You have shown your people the power of your works,
by giving them the heritage of the nations.

Your works are faithful and just;
your precepts are all trustworthy,
they are established forever and ever,—

to be done in uprightness and truth.

You sent redemption to your people,
and commanded your covenant forever.
Holy and awesome is your name!

To fear you is the beginning of wisdom;
all who do so prove themselves wise.
Your praise endures forever!
Glory*...

Ant. 3 We rejoice and exult in you.

Cant: Rev 19:1, 5–7

Salvation, glory, and power belong to you,—

your judgments are honest and true.

All of us, your servants, sing praise to you,
we worship you reverently, both great and small.

You, our almighty God, are Creator of heaven and earth.
Let us rejoice and exult, and give you glory.

The wedding feast of the Lamb has begun,
And the bride has made herself ready. **Glory*...**

READING

Blessed be the God...of our Lord Jesus Christ! By [God's] great mercy God has given us a new birth into a living hope through the resurrection of Jesus Christ from the dead, and into an inheritance that is imperishable, undefiled, and unfading, kept in heaven for you, who are being protected by the power of God through faith for a salvation ready to be revealed in the last time. In this you rejoice, even if now for a little while you have had to suffer various trials, so that the genuineness of your faith—being more precious than gold that, though perishable, is tested by fire—may be found to result in praise and glory and honor when Jesus Christ is revealed.

1 Pet 1:3–7

RESPONSORY

You create and sustain us, O God, with your love. —**You...**
From generation to generation —**with your...**
Glory to you, Source of all Being, Eternal Word and Holy Spirit.
—**You...**

CANTICLE OF MARY

Ant. Blessed are you among women and blessed is the fruit of your womb.

INTERCESSIONS

Life after death is a mystery to us, O God;
—let the resurrection of Jesus and his Spirit among us
witness to your eternal love and care for us.
You ask us to give, to empty ourselves, and to follow you in faith;
—only to fill us with solid nourishment that enables us to
live the journey of the gospel.
We know well your law of love; your Spirit lives within us;
—let no other rule take precedence in our lives.
You came to us bringing peace and reconciliation;
—may your gospel be the bridge that reconciles us—families,
communities, and nations.
Bless all who have a great fear of death;
—grant them peace of heart and friends to support them.

PRAYER: God of wisdom, your steadfast love gives meaning to
our lives. Remembering your goodness from ages past,
we have hope. Our very desire for you is a gift of your
love. Holy Mystery, we do believe; help our unbelief.
This we ask for ourselves, but especially for those
without hope and those who know no love. Hear our
prayer in Jesus' name. Amen.

MONDAY

MORNING PRAYER

Ant 1 My soul is longing for the living God.

Psalm 84

How lovely is your dwelling place,
O God of hosts!

My soul longs and yearns
for the courts of the Most High;
my heart and lips sing for joy
to you, the living God.

Even the sparrow finds a home,
and the swallow a nest for its
brood,
where it may lay its young,
at your altars, O God of hosts!

Blessed are those who dwell in
your house,
forever singing your praise!
Blessed are those whose strength
you are,
in whose hearts are the roads to
Zion.

As they go through the Bitter
Valley,
they make it a place of springs;
the early rain covers it with pools.
They go from strength to
strength;
the God of gods will be seen in
Zion.

O God of hosts, hear my prayer;
give ear, O God of Jacob!
Look upon our shield, O God;
look on the face of your Anointed!

For one day in your courts is
  better,
than a thousand anywhere else.
I would rather stand at your
  threshold,
than dwell in the tents of
  wickedness.

For you are a sun and a shield;
you bestow favor and honor.
No good do you withhold
from those who walk uprightly.

O God! God of hosts!
Blessed are those who trust in
  you! **Glory*...**

**Ant. 2 Let us walk in your light,
  O God.**

Cant: Isaiah 2:2-5

It shall come to pass in days to
  come,
that the mountain of the house of
  God
shall be established as the
  highest mountain,
and be raised above the hills.

All nations shall flow to it;
many peoples shall come and say:
"Come, let us go up to the
  mountain of God,
to the house of the God of Jacob;
that we may be taught in God's
  ways,
and walk in God's paths."

For from Zion shall go forth the
  law,
and the word of the Most High
  from Jerusalem.—

God shall judge between the
  nations,
and shall decide for many
  peoples;
they shall beat their swords into
  plowshares,
and their spears into pruning
  hooks;
nation shall not lift up sword
  against nation,
nor shall they teach war any
  more.

O house of Jacob, come,
let us walk in the light of our
  God! **Glory*...**

**Ant. 3 Let all things exult in
  your presence for you come to
  judge the earth.**

Psalm 96

O sing to God a new song;
sing to God, all the earth!
Sing and bless God's name.

We proclaim your salvation day
  by day,
declare your glory among the
  nations,
your wonders among all the
  peoples.

You are great and worthy to be
  praised;
to be feared above all gods.
The gods of the nations are idols;
but you made the heavens.
Honor and majesty are before
  you;
strength and beauty, in your
  sanctuary.

Give to God, you families of
  peoples,
give to God glory and power!
Give glory to God's holy name;—

bring an offering, and enter God's
courts!
Worship in the temple of the Most
High.
O earth, tremble before the
Almighty.

We proclaim to all nations:
"You, O God, are sovereign.
The world you established:
it shall never be moved;
you will judge the peoples with
equity."

Let the heavens be glad and the
earth rejoice;—

let the sea thunder, and all that
fills it;
let the field exult, and everything
in it!
Then shall all the trees of the
wood sing for joy
at your presence, O God, for you
come,
you come to judge the earth.

You will judge the world with
justice,
and the peoples with your truth.
Glory*...

READING

The advice [of François de Sales] was simple—she [Jeanne de Chantal]
was to learn to love beyond her present capacity. She was eventually to
learn to love all that life presented to her. By doing this she would open
herself radically to the presence of God in all events. She, like the Savior
she adored, would stretch out her arms to embrace all her "crosses,"
knowing that in the act of authentic loving, resignation in its most
profound sense, she was being fashioned in the image she loved and
bringing that image into the world.

Wendy Wright, *The Bond of Perfection*, p. 70, (1)

RESPONSORY

There is no limit, O God, to your love for us. **—There is...**
All that you do attests **—to your...**
Glory to you, Source of all Being, Eternal Word and Holy Spirit.
    —There is...

CANTICLE OF ZECHARIAH

Ant. Blessed be the great God of Israel.

INTERCESSIONS

You are our Creator, O God, our lives are in your hands;
    —make us humble and reverent of heart as we unravel
        some small part of the mystery of creation.
Jesus, people were drawn to you for you spoke with authority.
    —bless our public officials with insight for our good, and
        protect them from all that is not just in your sight.

You often spoke to those who were closed to your teaching;
—give us a contemplative attitude and the grace to
hear and live your message.
Spirit of God, you hovered over chaos and called forth a world of
life;
—calm us in times of anxiety; teach us how to live one
moment at a time in your loving presence.
Our hearts are drawn to glorify you, O God, and you receive our
humble praise;
—bless composers, singers and all musicians who enable
us to express our love and gratitude to you.

PRAYER: O God, we long to follow in the footsteps of Jesus,
bringing about your reign of love. Our weakness and
sinfulness stop us over and over again. Help us to
cooperate with your personal design for each of us and
by your strength to embrace your will and to grow in
love. Grant this through the intercession of all your
saints who inspire, challenge, and call us to the praise
of your glory now and forever. Amen.

DAYTIME PRAYER

Ant. 1 I will not forget your precepts; by them you give me life.
Psalm 119:89–96

Forever, O God, your word
is firmly fixed in the heavens.
Your faithfulness endures to all
generations;
you established the earth,
it will not be moved.

By your decree it stands to this
day;
for all things are your servants.
If your law had not been my
delight,
I would have died in my affliction.

I will never forget your precepts;
by them you have given me life.
Save me, for I am yours;—

I have sought your precepts.

Wickedness waits to destroy me;
but I ponder your will.
I have seen a limit to all
perfection,
but your commandment is
exceedingly broad.
Glory*...

Ant. 2 You are my hope; my trust from the days of my youth.
Psalm 71

In you, O God, I take refuge;
let me never be put to shame!
In your justice deliver and rescue
me;
incline your ear to me and save
me.

Be to me a rock of refuge,
a stronghold to save me,
for you are my rock and my
stronghold.
Rescue me from the throes of
oppression,
from the grip of injustice and
greed.

For you, O God, are my hope,
my trust, O God, from my youth.
Upon you I have leaned from my
birth;
from my mother's womb you
claimed me.
I praise you forever and ever.

I have been a portent to many;
but you are my strong refuge.
My lips are filled with your praise,
with your glory all the day.
Do not cast me off in old age;
forsake me not when my strength
is spent.

O God, be not far from me;
O God, make haste to help me!
Let evil see its own destruction,
and injustice turn on itself.
    Glory*...

**Ant. 3 Even in old age, O God,
    do not forsake your servant.**
                II

But as for me, I will always hope
and praise you more and more.
My lips will tell of your justice,
of your salvation all the day,
for your goodness cannot be
numbered.

I will declare your mighty deeds,
I will proclaim your justice.
You have taught me from my
youth,
and I proclaim your wonders still.

Now that I am old and gray-
headed,
O God, do not forsake me,
till I proclaim your power
to generations to come.
Your power and your justice, O
God,
reach to the highest heavens.

You have done marvelous things,
O God, who is like you?
You who have made me see many
sore troubles
will revive me once again;
from the depths of the earth you
will raise me.
You will exalt and comfort me
again.

So I will praise you with the harp
for your faithfulness, O God;
I will sing praises to you with the
lyre,
O Holy One of Israel.

My lips will shout for joy,
when I sing praises to you;
my soul also, which you have
redeemed.
My tongue will tell of your justice
all the day long,
for evil is put to rout, and all that
sought to harm me.
    Glory*...

PRAYER: Help us, O God, to reach out to those in need. The poor,
the elderly, the imprisoned, those who are ill call out to
us as they fill out what is wanting in the suffering of
Jesus. Give us the wisdom and generosity to minister

to them and to manifest your love. Grant this for Jesus' sake who came to set us free. Amen.

EVENING PRAYER

Ant. 1 Our eyes look to you till you have mercy upon us.

Psalm 123

To you I lift up my eyes,
you who are enthroned in the
heavens!
Behold like the eyes of servants
look to the hand of their master,

Like the eyes of a maid
look to the hand of her mistress,
so our eyes look to you, O God,
till you have mercy upon us.

Have mercy on us, O God, have
mercy,
for we are filled with contempt.
Too long has our soul been sated
with the scorn of the arrogant,
the contempt of the proud.
Glory*...

Ant. 2 You will wipe away every tear from our eyes and death shall be no more.

Psalm 124

If you had not been on our side,
let Israel now say:
if you had not been on our side,
when oppression overwhelmed
us,
then would we be swallowed
alive,
when injustice raged against us.

Then the flood would have swept
us away,
the torrent would have gone over
us;—

over us would have gone the
raging waters.

Blessed be God who did not give
us
a prey to its teeth!
We have escaped like a bird
from the snare of the fowler;
indeed the snare is broken,
and we have escaped.

Our help is in the name of the
Most High,
who made heaven and earth.
Glory*...

Ant. 3 O God, you chose us in Jesus to be your children.

Cant: Ephesians 1:3–10

Praised be the God
of our Lord Jesus Christ,
who has blessed us in Christ
with every spiritual blessing in
the heavens.

God chose us in him
before the foundation of the
world,
that we should be holy
and blameless in God's sight.

We have been predestined
to be God's children through
Jesus Christ,
such was the purpose of God's
will,
that all might praise the glorious
favor
bestowed on us in Christ.

In Christ and through his blood,
we have redemption,—

the forgiveness of our sins,
according to the riches of God's
  grace lavished upon us.

For God has made known to us
in all wisdom and insight,—

the mystery of the plan set forth
  in Christ.

A plan to be carried out in Christ,
in the fullness of time,
to unite all things in Christ,
things in heaven and things on
  earth. **Glory*...**

READING

What is that sweetness that is accustomed to touch me from time to
time and affects me so strongly and deliciously that I begin in a way to
be completely taken out of myself, and to be carried away I know not
where? All at once I am renewed and entirely changed; I begin to feel
well in a way that lies beyond description. Consciousness is lifted on
high, and all the misery of past misfortunes is forgotten. The intellectual
soul rejoices; the understanding is strengthened, the heart is
enlightened, the desires satisfied. I already see myself in a different
place that I do not know. I hold something within love's embrace, but I
do not know what it is. (Hugh of St. Victor)

Meister Eckhart, p. 139, (1)

RESPONSORY

Your mercy, O God, calls us to mercy. **—Your mercy...**
It manifests your greatness; **—and calls...**
Glory to you, Source of all Being, Eternal Word and Holy Spirit.
    —Your mercy...

CANTICLE OF MARY

Ant. Your regard has blessed me, O God.

INTERCESSIONS

In you, O God, resides all creative energy, and we receive our lives
from you;
    —inspire us with great desires, and let our hope be larger
      than our doubt.
We are a wounded people, afflicted by sin and ignorance;
    —guide and protect our police and all who are missioned
      to protect us; arm them with wisdom and compassion.
Jesus, for you and your people, hospitality was a sacred duty;
    —help us to transform our world into a place that is safe
      for mutual aid and neighborliness.

You were content to let weeds grow among wheat until harvest
time;
　　—give us the patience to live with our own shortcomings
　　　　and those of others.
Our days are often filled with interruptions;
　　—teach us how to reap the good fruit of patience from
　　　　these times.

PRAYER: God our Creator, you have called us by name; we
　　　　　belong to you. Help us to believe in your truth, hope in
　　　　　your mercy, and love all people as you call us to love.
　　　　　Let our lives give joy to you and encouragement to one
　　　　　another. May our efforts to live in love give you praise
　　　　　this night and every day of our lives through all
　　　　　eternity. Amen.

TUESDAY
MORNING PRAYER

**Ant. 1 O God, forgive the sins of
your people.**
Psalm 85

O God, once you favored your
　land,
restoring the fortunes of Rachel
　and Jacob.
You forgave the guilt of your
　people;
you pardoned all their sins.
You withdrew your wrath;
you calmed the heat of your anger.

Restore us again,
O God our salvation,
put away your grievance against
　us!
Will you be angry with us forever,
Will you prolong it to all
　generations?

Will you not restore us again,
that your people may rejoice in
　you?—

Show us your steadfast love,
and grant us your salvation.

Let me hear what you have to say,
for you will speak peace to your
　people,
to those who are near you,
and who turn to you in their
　hearts.
Your salvation is near for those
　who fear you,
that glory may dwell in our land.

Mercy and truth have embraced;
justice and peace will kiss.
Truth shall spring out of the earth,
and justice will look down from
　heaven.

You will give what is good,
our land will yield its increase.
Justice shall go before you
and make a path for your steps.
　　Glory*...

Ant. 2 O God, grant peace to all peoples.

Cant: Isaiah 26:1b–4, 7–9, 12

A strong city have we, O God;
you set up salvation
like walls and ramparts.
Open the gates
that the nation which keeps faith
may enter in.

You keep those in perfect peace,
whose minds are fixed on you,
because they trust in you,
trust in you forever.
For you are our God,
an everlasting Rock.

The way of the just is level;
you make smooth the path of the
   just.
In the path of your judgments,
we wait for you;
your name remembered from of
   old,
is the desire of our souls.

My soul yearns for you in the
   night,
my spirit within me keeps vigil;
when your judgments abide in the
   earth,
the inhabitants of the world learn
   justice.

O God, you ordain peace for all
   people,
you accomplish all our works.
   Glory*...

**Ant. 3 In the light of your face
there is life, O God.**

Psalm 67

O God, be gracious to us and bless
   us
and make your face shine upon
   us.
That your ways be known upon
   earth,
your saving power among all
   nations.
Let the peoples praise you, O God;
let all the peoples praise you.

Let the nations be glad and sing
   for joy,
for you judge the peoples with
   equity
and guide the nations on earth.
Let the peoples praise you, O God;
let all the peoples praise you.

The earth has yielded its increase;
God, our God, has blessed us.
You, indeed, have blessed us;
let all the earth revere you!
   Glory*...

READING

Considering the mystical body of the Church, I had not recognized
myself in any of the members...or rather I desired to see myself in
them *all. Charity* gave me the key to my *vocation.* I understood that if
the Church had a body composed of different members, the most
necessary and most noble of all could not be lacking to it, and so I
understood that the Church *had a Heart and that this Heart was
BURNING WITH LOVE. I understood it was Love alone* that made the
Church's members act, that if *Love* ever became extinct, apostles
would not preach the Gospel and martyrs would not shed their blood. I

understood that LOVE COMPRISED ALL VOCATIONS, THAT LOVE
WAS EVERYTHING, THAT IT EMBRACED ALL TIMES AND
PLACES....IN A WORD, THAT IT WAS ETERNAL! Then, in the excess of
my delirious joy, I cried out: O Jesus, my Love...my *vocation*, at last I
have found it...MY VOCATION IS LOVE!

Thérèse of Lisieux, *Story of a Soul*, p. 194, (3)

RESPONSORY

It is good to give thanks to you and sing praise to your name.
  —**It is good...**
At the works of your hands I shout for joy, —**and sing...**
Glory to you, Source of all Being, Eternal Word and Holy Spirit.
  —**It is good...**

CANTICLE OF ZECHARIAH

**Ant. I will praise you from the rising of the sun to its going
    down.**

INTERCESSIONS

O God, you have blessed humankind with understanding,
imagination and memory;
  —show us how to learn from the past and to plan for the
    future.
The gifts of the earth are distributed unevenly, and we long to lift
up those in need;
  —soften the hearts of those who place personal or national
    gain above the good of the whole.
Jesus, you have gifted us with the revelation of God's love;
  —let your love bear abundant fruit in our lives.
You preached to the crowds, inviting them to sit on grassy
hillsides;
  —open our eyes to the beauty of our world, and make us
    understand the need to protect our environment.
Spirit of God, life-giving presence to every person;
  —make your compassion and love known to those who
    suffer abuse, torture, and sub-human conditions.

PRAYER: Giver of hope, we begin a new day confident that you
        come to us in all circumstances and make all things
        work for the fulfillment of your purposes. We praise

you for your wonderful works through Christ who has
shown us the way. Amen.

DAYTIME PRAYER

**Ant. 1 I will ponder your law
within my heart.**

Psalm 119:97–104

How I love your law, O God!
It is my meditation all the day.
Your commandment makes me
    wiser than the learned,
for it is ever with me.

I have more understanding than
    all my teachers,
for your will is my meditation.
I have more understanding than
    the aged,
for I keep your precepts.

I turn my feet from evil ways,
to obey your word.
I turn not aside from your decrees,
for you, yourself, have taught me.

How sweet are your words to my
    taste,
sweeter than honey to my mouth!
Through your precepts I gain
    understanding;
therefore I hate every false way.
    Glory*...

**Ant. 2 Restore your dwelling
place within us.**

Psalm 74

Why have you cast us off forever?
Why blaze with anger against the
    sheep of your pasture?
Remember your people whom you
    chose from of old,—

which you redeemed as your
    heritage!
Remember Mount Zion where you
    made your dwelling.

Direct your steps to the eternal
    ruins,
everything destroyed in your
    sanctuary!
Evil has roared in your house of
    prayer,
setting up its signs for symbols.

At the upper entrance they hacked
the wooden trellis with axes.
With hatchets and hammers,
broke down its carved wood.
The sanctuary they set on fire,
desecrating the place where you
    dwell.

They said to themselves, "We will
    utterly crush them;"
and burned all the shrines in the
    land.
We do not see our signs any more;
there is no longer a prophet,
no one knows how long it will last.

How long, O God, is evil to
    conquer?
Is your name to be scoffed forever?
Why do you hold back your hand,
Why do you keep your hand
    concealed?

Yet you are our ruler from of old,
working salvation in the midst of
    the earth.   **Glory*...**

Ant. 3 Yours is the day, yours is the night; all things are in your hands.

II

It was you who divided the sea by
your might,
who shattered the heads of the
monsters in the sea.

You crushed the heads of
Leviathan,
and gave them as food to the
creatures of the wilderness.
You split open springs and brooks;
dried up the ever-flowing streams.

Yours is the day and yours is the
night;
you fixed the stars and the sun.
You established all the bounds of
earth;
you made both summer and
winter.

Remember then, how evil scoffs,
and how your name is reviled.
Do not deliver your dove to the
hawk:
do not forget the lives of your poor.

Remember your covenant of old;
for violence dwells in every corner
of the land.
Let not the downtrodden be put to
shame;
let the poor and the needy bless
your name.

Arise, O God, defend your cause!
Remember how you are reviled all
the day.
Quiet those who clamor against
you,
who clamor against you day after
day. **Glory*...**

PRAYER: God of love, you gave us this universe filled with your
gifts. Help us to reverence all of your creation,
respecting the rights of all species, and the integrity of
the elements. Teach us to realize in our hearts as well
as in our minds that we praise you when we use your
gifts as you meant them to be used. May we unite with
all suffering creation in the struggle for liberation from
all that seeks to destroy. Grant this that all creation
may live with you for all eternity. Amen.

EVENING PRAYER

**Ant. 1 You are round about your
people, both now and forever.**

Psalm 125

Those who put their trust in you
are like Mount Zion;
it cannot be moved, but stands
forever.

As the mountains are round about
Jerusalem,
so are you round about your
people,
both now and forever.

For the scepter of wickedness
shall not rest
over the land of the just,—

lest the just put forth their hands
to turn to evil ways.

Do good, O God, to those who are
   good,
to those who are upright of heart!
But those who turn to evil ways,
will be chastised and punished!

On Israel, peace! **Glory*...**

**Ant. 2 Blessed are those who are
   pure of heart.**

Psalm 131

O God, my heart is not lifted up,
my eyes are not raised too high;
I have not occupied myself
with marvels beyond me.

I have calmed and quieted my
   soul,
like a child at its mother's breast;
like a child in its father's arms,
even so my soul.

O Israel, hope in your God
both now and forever.
   Glory*....

**Ant. 3 Let all creation serve you,
   for you created all things.**

Cant: Rev 4:11, 5:9, 10, 12

Worthy are you, O God, our God,
to receive glory and honor and
   power.

For you have created all things;
by your will they came to be and
   were made.

Worthy are you to take the scroll
   and to open its seals,

For you were slain, and by your
   blood,
you purchased for God
saints of every race and tongue,
of every people and nation.

You have made of them a kindom,
and priests to serve our God,
and they shall reign on the earth.

Worthy is the Lamb who was slain
to receive power and riches,
wisdom and strength,
honor and glory and praise.
   Glory*...

READING

Happy, indeed, is [the one] to whom it is given to share this sacred
banquet, to cling with all her heart to [God] whose beauty all the
heavenly hosts admire unceasingly, whose love inflames our love, whose
contemplation is our refreshment, whose graciousness is our joy, whose
gentleness fills us to overflowing, whose remembrance brings a gentle
light, whose fragrance will revive the dead, whose glorious vision will be
the happiness of all the citizens of the heavenly Jerusalem.

Clare of Assisi, *Francis and Clare*, p. 204, (1)

RESPONSORY

Teach us to number our days that we may gain wisdom
   of heart.—**Teach us...**
Let your works be manifest to your servants; —**that we...**

Glory to you, Source of all Being, Eternal Word and Holy Spirit.
   —Teach us...

CANTICLE OF MARY

Ant. You who are mighty have done great things for me.

INTERCESSIONS

O God, the wonders of communication have made our world
smaller but more complex;
   —bless the United Nations with wise and magnanimous
      leaders.
Jesus, you teach us of the realm of God with wonderful and
effective images;
   —inspire teachers and writers with the creativity they need
      to expand our minds and hearts.
Ask, knock, seek is your invitation to us to take our needs to God;
   —make us quick to respond to the needs of those who ask;
      make us aware of those so needy they cannot ask.
Spirit of God, you take flesh in us and for us;
   —keep us open to all who inspire us to grow; prophets,
      athletes, philosophers, artists, and all who serve us in
      your name.
Time is your gift to us, O God; let us not take it for granted;
   —show us efficient ways to use and share it.

PRAYER: O God, you are both mother and father to us. Help us
            to reverence all people with whom we share such great
            love, and show us the way to peace in our world. We
            ask this as your children through Jesus, our brother.
            Amen.

WEDNESDAY

MORNING PRAYER

**Ant 1 Gladden my soul, O God;
for to you I lift up my heart.**

Psalm 86

Incline your ear and give answer,
for I am poor and needy.
Preserve my life, for I am
   faithful:—

save the servant who trusts in
   you.

You are my God, have mercy on
   me,
for to you I cry all the day.
Gladden the soul of your servant,
for to you I lift up my soul.

O God, you are good and
forgiving,
abounding in love to all who call.
Give ear to my prayer;
hearken to my supplication.
In the day of my trouble I call on
you,
for you will answer me.

There is none like you among the
gods,
nor works to compare with yours.
All the nations you made
shall come and bow down,
shall glorify your name.
For you are great and do
wondrous things,
you alone are God.

Teach me your way, O God,
that I may walk in your truth;
cause my heart to fear your
name.
I give thanks to you with all my
heart,
and glorify your name forever.
For great toward me is your love;
you deliver my soul from the
grave.

Pride has risen against me;
corruption pursues my life,
evil pays you no heed.
But you are merciful and
gracious,
slow to anger, abounding in love.

Turn to me and take pity;
give strength to your servant,
and save your handmaid's child.
Show me a sign of your favor;
let injustice be put to shame,
help me and give me your
comfort. **Glory*...**

**Ant. 2 Blessed are the just, who
speak the truth.**

Cant: Isaiah 33:13–16

Hear, you who are far off,
what I have done;
you who are near,
acknowledge my might.

The sinners in Zion are afraid;
trembling grips the impious;
"Who of us can live with the
devouring fire?
Who of us can live with the
everlasting flames?"

Those who walk justly and speak
honestly,
who spurn what is gained by
oppression,
who shake their hands,
free of contact with a bribe;
who stop their ears,
lest they hear of bloodshed,
who close their eyes,
lest they look on evil.

They shall dwell on the heights;
their place of refuge
shall be the rocky fortress;
their food will be given,
their water will be sure.
Glory*...

**Ant. 3 Let us sing a joyful song
in the presence of our God.**

Psalm 98

We sing to you a new song,
for you have done wonderful
things!
Your saving hand and your holy
arm
have given the victory.

You have made known your
salvation;
have revealed your justice to the
nations.
You have remembered your love
and your faithfulness
for the house of Israel.
All the ends of the earth have
seen
the salvation of our God.

Make a joyful noise, all the earth;
break forth into joyous song!
Sing praise to God with the harp,
with the lyre and the sound of
music!—

With trumpets and the sound of
the horn
make a joyful noise to our God.

Let the sea roar and all that fills
it;
the world and those who dwell in
it!
Let the rivers clap their hands;
and the hills ring out their joy.

All creation sings before God
who comes to judge the earth.
God will judge the world with
justice
and the peoples with equity.
Glory.

READING

Rahner asserts that to speak of the human is to speak of the divine
and vice versa. He describes God as the mystery in human experience.
For him, then, God is the depth dimension in experiences such as
solitude, friendship, community, death, hope and, as such, is the
orientation toward the future. Rahner goes so far as to say that
loneliness, disappointments and the ingratitude of others can be graced
moments because they open us to the transcendent. The silence of God,
the toughness of life and the darkness of death can be graced events.
This mystery of grace discloses itself as a forgiving nearness, a hidden
closeness, our real home, a love which shares itself, something familiar
which we can turn to from the alienation of our own empty and perilous
lives. When we are in touch with ourselves authentically, we experience
God.

Annice Callahan, RSCJ, *Traditions of Spiritual Guidance*, p. 341, (32)

RESPONSORY

Satisfy us in the morning with your steadfast love, that we may
rejoice and be glad all our days. **—Satisfy us...**
Let the favor of God be upon us; **—that we...**
Glory to you, Source of all Being, Eternal Word and Holy Spirit.
—Satisfy us...

CANTICLE OF ZECHARIAH

Ant. Remember the mercy you promised long ago.

INTERCESSIONS

Jesus, you preached a kindom not of this world, but you were
ever mindful to provide food for your followers;
>—grant success to those who draw food from our waters and
>fields; keep them safe and their methods environmentally
>sound.

You blessed little children and warned us against misleading
them;
>—give wisdom to those who become parents while they are
>still children themselves.

O God, you call us all to unity through Jesus;
>—show yourself to those who are estranged from one
>another, and bridge their differences with the fire of your
>love.

Jesus, you frowned upon the ambitions of your apostles;
>—let our ambition and goal be to offer you a life of love and
>dedicated service as we care for one another.

Bless the ministers of your church;
>—guide them to serve as you have served.

PRAYER: God of unity and peace, may the gift of your life within
us show itself in concrete ways so that we may make
clear with our lives the good news of Jesus Christ.
Especially today we pray for all the children of this
world, that they may know your love and the hope of
peace on earth. Grant this prayer that all may know
the gift you gave in Jesus. Amen.

DAYTIME PRAYER

**Ant. 1 Your Word is the true
light that enlightens all who
come into the world.**

Psalm 119:105–112

O God, your word is a lamp to my
feet
and a light for my path.
I have sworn an oath and
confirmed it
to observe your commandments.

I am sorely afflicted:
give me life according to your
word!
Accept my offerings of praise,
and teach me your decrees.

Though I hold my life in my
hands,
I do not forget your law.
Though the wicked try to ensnare
me,
I do not stray from your precepts.

Your will is my heritage forever,
the joy of my heart.
I incline my heart to carry out
your will forever, to endless
ages. **Glory***...

**Ant. 2 Hear my prayer and
hasten to help me.**
Psalm 70

Be pleased, O God, to save me!
O God, make haste to help me!
Fill me with shame and confusion
if I turn away from life!

O let me turn back in confusion,
when I delight in wrongdoing!
Let me retreat in my shame,
when I trifle with evil.

May all who seek you
rejoice and be glad!
May those who love your
salvation
proclaim, "Our God is great!"

But I am poor and needy;
hasten to me, O God!
You are my help, my deliverer;
O God, do not delay. **Glory***...

**Ant. 3 You know the hearts of
all; your judgment is right and
true.**
Psalm 75

We give thanks to you, O God;—

we give you thanks;
we call on your name
and recount your wondrous
deeds.

"At the time which I appoint
I will judge with equity.
When the earth totters,
and all its inhabitants,
it is I who steady its pillars.

To the boastful I say: 'Do not
boast,'
to the wicked, 'Do not flaunt your
strength,
do not flaunt your strength on
high,
or speak with insolent pride.'"

For not from the east or from the
west,
or from the wilderness comes
judgment,
but you, O God, are the judge,
putting down one, lifting up
another.

But I will rejoice forever,
I will sing praises to you on high.
You shall break the power of
wickedness,
while the strength of the just
shall be exalted. **Glory***...

PRAYER: O God, you both comfort us and disturb our
complacency through your Spirit. May we recognize
the blind, the lame and the prisoner in the
circumstances of our lives, and understand our
call to proclaim the good news to the poor. We
ask this through Jesus who is our way, our truth,
and our life. Amen.

EVENING PRAYER

Ant. 1 You will not reject me; you will fill my mouth with laughter.

Psalm 126

When God restored the fortunes of Zion,
it seemed like a dream.
Then our mouth was filled with laughter,
and our tongue with shouts of joy;

Then they said among the nations,
"God has done great things for them."
You have done great things for us!
Indeed we are glad.

Restore our fortunes, O God,
like the streams in the desert!
May those who sow in tears
reap with shouts of joy!

They that go forth weeping,
bearing seed for the sowing,
shall come home with shouts of joy,
bringing their sheaves with them.
     Glory*...

Ant. 2 Wisdom has built herself a house!

Psalm 127

If God does not build the house,
its builders labor in vain.
If God does not watch over the city,
in vain is the vigil kept.

It is vain to rise up early
and go late to rest,
eating the bread of anxious toil:—

for you, O God, give sleep to your beloved.

Truly children are a gift from the Most High,
the fruit of the womb, a blessing.
Like arrows in the hand of a warrior
are the children of one's youth.

Happy the couple who have their quiver full of them!
They shall not be put to shame
when they encounter distress.
     Glory*...

Ant. 3 Jesus is the image of the invisible God.

Cant: Colossians 1:12–20

Let us give thanks to God
for having made us worthy
to share the inheritance of the saints in light.

God has delivered us
from the power of darkness
and transferred us
into the kindom of God's beloved Son, Jesus,
in whom we have redemption,
the forgiveness of our sins.

Jesus is the image of the invisible God,
the first-born of all creation;
in him all things were created,
in heaven and on earth,
things visible and invisible.

All things were created through him;
all were created for him.
He is before all else that is.
In him all things hold together.

He is the head of the body, the church!
He is the beginning,
the firstborn from the dead,
that in everything, he might be above all others.

In him all the fullness of God was pleased to dwell,
and, through him, to reconcile all things to himself,
whether on earth or in heaven,
making peace by the blood of his cross. **Glory*...**

READING

...These things that come home to us and hurt our self-love and humble us in the dust, these are some of God's best graces, full of promise, and never think that you are at the end of them. There will come more revelations ever more humbling, ever more intimate and ever more true. But never let them cast you down. Remember that they are birthdays, the putting away of the things of a child. And your vocation beaten by storms, will come out all the truer. (Janet Erskine Stuart, RSCJ)

Maud Monahan, *Life and Letters of Janet Erskine Stuart*, p. 499, (15)

RESPONSORY

You will cover us with your pinions, and under your wings we will find refuge. —**You will...**
We will not fear the terror of the night; —**and under...**
Glory to you, Source of all Being, Eternal Word and Holy Spirit.
—**You will...**

CANTICLE OF MARY

Ant. Holy is the name of our God.

INTERCESSIONS

Jesus, you knew a laborer's day;
  —bless those who live by the work of their hands; help all to find the employment they need.
The world still longs for the peace that only you can give;
  —guard and protect those whose work is to keep the peace in lands torn by war and revolution.
In your kindom the last shall be first and the first last;
  —encourage and liberate minorities, those whose lot is mostly last.
Enlighten and encourage those committed to you in religious vocations;
  —let their lives reflect their calling.

Have mercy on all who are touched by the drug epidemic in our world;
—lead them to freedom through the good news enfleshed in those who reach out to them.

PRAYER: Jesus, light of the world, for the many who have followed you today through the darkness of temptation, doubt, or pain, you are the promise of an eternal dawn. We give thanks for all that has been given to us through you, and we ask for the grace to be your faithful disciples. May we praise you all the days of our lives. Amen.

THURSDAY

MORNING PRAYER

Ant. 1 Blessed are those who delight in your law, O God.

Psalm 1

Blessed are those who walk not in
  the counsel of the wicked,
nor stand in the way of sinners,
nor sit with those who scoff;
but delight in your law, O God,
pondering it day and night.

They are like a tree
planted by streams of water,
that yields its fruit in due season,
and whose leaves never fade.
May they prosper in all they do.

It is not so with wickedness.
Like chaff the wind drives it away.
Evil cannot stand before you,
nor injustice before your face.

For you guide the path of the
  faithful,
but renounce the way of
  oppression. **Glory*...**

Ant. 2 God will come with justice for all the people.

Cant: Isaiah 40:10–17

Behold, you come with power,
O God, the Almighty,
ruling with your strong arm;
behold, your reward is with you,
and your recompense before you.

You will feed your flock like a
  shepherd,
you will gather the lambs in your
  arms,
carrying them in your bosom,
gently leading the ewes with
  young.

Who else had measured the waters
in the hollows of their hands,
and marked off the heavens with a
  span,
enclosed the dust of the earth in a
  measure
weighed the mountains in scales
and the hills in a balance?

Who has directed your spirit,
or who has been your
  counselor?—

Whom did you consult for
  enlightenment,
who taught you the path of justice,
or showed you the way of
  understanding?

Behold, the nations are like a drop
  from a bucket,
accounted as dust on the scales;
you take up the isles like powder.

Lebanon would not suffice for fuel,
nor its beasts be enough for burnt
  offering.
All the nations are as nothing
  before you,
as nothing and void are they
  accounted. **Glory*...**

**Ant. 3 We worship and give
praise to you, Most High.**

Psalm 99

O God, you reign on high;
let all the peoples tremble!
You are throned on the cherubim;
let the earth quake!
You are great in Zion.

You are exalted over all peoples.
Let them praise your name,—

awesome and great!
Holy are you over all!

Mighty Sovereign, lover of justice,
you have established equity;
you have ruled with justice.
We extol you, Most High God;
worshipping at your footstool!
You alone are holy.

Moses and Aaron were among
  your priests,
among your petitioners, Judith
  and Esther.
They invoked you, and you
  answered.
You spoke to them in the pillar of
  cloud;
they kept your will,
and the precepts that you gave
  them.

O God, our God, you answered
  them;
you were a forgiving God to them,
yet you punished their offenses.

We extol you, Most High God,
and worship on your holy
  mountain;
for you alone are holy.
    Glory*...

READING

Let us look at our own shortcomings and leave other people's alone;
for those who live carefully ordered lives are apt to be shocked at
everything and we might well learn very important lessons from the
persons who shock us. Our outward comportment and behavior may
be better than theirs, but this, though good, is not the most important
thing; there is no reason why we should expect everyone else to travel
by our own road, and we should not attempt to point them to the
spiritual path when perhaps we do not know what it is.... It is better to
attempt to...live in silence and in hope, and [God] will take care of
[God's] own.

Teresa of Avila, *Interior Castle*, p. 229, (5)

RESPONSORY

No one who practices deceit shall dwell in your house.
    —No one...
They who walk in the way that is blameless **—shall dwell...**
Glory to you, Source of all Being, Eternal Word and Holy Spirit.
    —No one...

CANTICLE OF ZECHARIAH

Ant. Guide our feet, O God, into the way of peace.

INTERCESSIONS

O God, we praise you for the gift of faith and for all that our
baptism means to us;
    —help us to keep our commitment to you alive and active
        and to cherish and remember special moments of insight.
You answer our prayers and fulfill our needs;
    —make us aware of the needs of others and generous in
        ministering to them.
Jesus, you were called the carpenter's son, an attempt to
discredit you;
    —give us the grace we need to see one another in truth, to
        hold each other's heritage with reverence, and to realize
        that we are one in you.
Your disciples left all to follow you;
    —be praised in the missionaries who leave all that is
        familiar to them to give your message to the world.
You are resurrection and life to all who hope in you;
    —give courage and peace to those who await your coming.

PRAYER: O God, we are the work of your hands, and you have
made us for communion with you and one another. As
we begin the business of this day, we recall that you
alone can fill our hearts. We ask to remain by love in
your holy presence with Jesus who incarnated your
presence among us. Amen.

DAYTIME PRAYER

Ant. 1 Sustain me, O God, according to your promise.

Psalm 119:113-120

I have no love for the half-hearted,
but I love your law.
You are my shelter, my shield;
I hope in your word.

Rid me of all that is evil,
that I may keep your
    commandments.
Uphold me according to your
    promise,
that I may live in your way,
let my hopes not be in vain!

Sustain me and I shall be safe
and ever observe your statutes.
Help me spurn all that is evil;
let its cunning be in vain!

You overthrow all that is wicked;
therefore I love your will.
I tremble before you in awe,
I am afraid of your judgments.
    Glory*...

Ant. 2 Rescue us, O God, for the sake of your name.

Psalm 79:1-5, 8-11, 13

O God, the nations have invaded
    our land,
they have defiled your holy temple;
Jerusalem is in ruins.
They have given the bodies of your
    servants
as food to the birds of the air,
and the flesh of your faithful
    to the beasts of the earth.

They have poured out blood like
    water round about Jerusalem,
no one is left to bury the dead.—

We have become the taunt of our
    neighbors,
mocked and derided by those
    round about us.

How long, O God? Will you be
    angry forever,
how long will your anger burn like
    fire?
Do not hold against us the guilt of
    our ancestors;
Let your compassion hasten to
    meet us;
for we are brought very low.

Help us, O God, our savior,
for the glory of your name;
deliver us, and forgive us our sins,
rescue us for the sake of your
    name.

Why should the nations say,
"Where is their God?"
Let us see oppression overthrown,
may justice come to Jerusalem!
Let the groans of the prisoners
    come before you;
let your strong arm preserve those
    condemned to die!

Then we your people, the flock of
    your pasture,
will give you thanks for ever;
from generation to generation
we will recount your praise.
    Glory*...

Ant. 3 O God, you are the vinedresser; prune the vine that it may bear fruit.

Psalm 80

Give ear, O Shepherd of Israel,
you who lead Joseph like a flock!
You who are enthroned upon the
    cherubim,—

shine forth before Ephraim,
Benjamin and Manasseh!
Stir up your might and come to
save us!

Restore us, God of hosts;
let your face shine, that we may be
saved.
God of hosts, how long will you be
angry
with your people's prayers?
You fed them with the bread of
tears,
and gave them tears to drink in
full measure.
You made us the scorn of our
neighbors,
our enemies laugh among
themselves.

Restore us, God of hosts;
let your face shine, that we may be
saved.

You brought a vine out of Egypt;
you drove out the nations to plant
it.
You cleared the ground before it;
it took root and filled the land.

The mountains were covered with
its shade,—

the mighty cedars with its
branches;
it sent out its branches to the sea,
and its roots to the Great River.

Then why have you broken down
its walls?
so that all who pass by pluck its
fruit?
It is ravaged by the boar of the
forest,
devoured by the beasts of the field.

Turn again, O God of hosts!
Look down from heaven, and see;
have regard for this vine,
the vine your own hand has
planted.
It has been burnt with fire and cut
down.

Let your hand be on those you
have chosen,
those you make strong for
yourself!
Then we will never forsake you;
give us life, and we will call on
your name.

Restore us, God of hosts!
let your face shine, that we may be
saved. **Glory*...**

PRAYER: Renew in our hearts, O God, the gift of your Holy
Spirit, so that we may love you fully in all that we do
and love one another as Christ loves us. May all that
we do proclaim the good news that you are God with
us. Amen.

EVENING PRAYER

**Ant. 1 Let us enter your courts
with shouts of praise.**

Psalm 132

O God, remember David,—

all the many hardships he
endured;
the oath he swore to you,
his vow to the Strong One of
Jacob.

"I will not enter my house or get
  into my bed;
I will give no sleep to my eyes,
or slumber to my eyelids,
till I find a place for my God,
a dwelling for the Strong One of
  Jacob."

We heard of it in Ephrathah,
we found the ark in the fields of
  Jaar.
"Let us go to the place of God's
  dwelling;
let us worship at God's footstool."

Go up, O God, to the place of your
  rest,
you and the ark of your might.
Let your priests be clothed with
  justice,
and your faithful shout for joy.
For the sake of David your servant
do not reject your anointed.
    Glory*...

**Ant. 2 You, O God, have chosen
  Zion as your dwelling place.**
    II

You swore an oath to David;
from which you will not turn back:
"A son, the fruit of your body,
I will set upon your throne.

If your offspring keep my covenant
  in truth,
and my laws which I shall teach
  them,
their descendants also forever
shall sit upon your throne."

For you have chosen Zion;
you desired it for your dwelling:
"This is my resting place forever;
here I have desired to dwell.

I will abundantly bless its
  provisions;—

I will satisfy its poor with bread.
I will clothe its priests with
  salvation
and its faithful will shout for joy.

There David's stock will flower:
I will prepare a lamp for my
  anointed.
Treacherous plots will be put to
  shame,
but on him my crown shall shine."
    Glory*...

**Ant. 3 The glory of God is the
  light of the city and its lamp is
  the Lamb.**
    **Cant: Rev 11:17–18;
        12:10b–12a**

We praise you, God Almighty,
who is and who was.
You have assumed your great
  power,
you have begun your reign.

The nations have raged in anger,
but then came your day of wrath
and the moment to judge the
  dead;
the time to reward your servants
  the prophets
and the holy ones who revere you,
the great and the small alike.

Now have salvation and power
  come,
your reign, O God, and the
  authority of your Anointed One.
For the accusers of our loved ones
  have been cast out,
who night and day accused them.

By the blood of the Lamb have
  they been defeated,
and by the testimony of your
  servants;
love for life did not deter them
  from death.—

So rejoice, you heavens,
and you that dwell therein!
Glory*...

READING

As long as persons are constrained to wait for a time when the creative
spirit will inspire them, and then they will create, meditate, sing—this is
an indication that their souls have not yet been illuminated. Surely the
soul sings always. It is robed in might and joy, it is surrounded by a
noble delight, and persons must raise themselves to the height of
confronting the soul, of recognizing its spiritual imprints, the rushing of
its wings that abound in the majesty of the holy of holies, and...always
be ready to listen to the secret of its holy discourse. Then they will know
that it is not at one time rather than another, on one occasion rather
than another, that the soul engenders in us new thrusts of wisdom and
thought, song and holy meditation. At all times, in every hour, it
releases streams of precious gifts. And the streams that flow from it are
holy treasures, fountains of understanding, stored with good sense.
God's compassions are new each morning, great is God's faithfulness.

Abraham Isaac Kook, *Lights of Holiness*, p. 214, (1)

RESPONSORY

How great are your works, O God. Your thoughts are very deep.
    —How great...
The dull of heart will never know. **—Your thoughts**
Glory to you, Source of all Being, Eternal Word and Holy Spirit.
    —How great...

CANTICLE OF MARY

Ant. Your mercy endures through all generations.

INTERCESSIONS

Jesus, you invited Peter to follow you in ways beyond his courage;
    —increase our faith, that we may be ready and willing
        instruments of your love.
You caution us over and over again to stay awake, to be on guard;
    —give us the gift of discernment; help us to live consciously,
        learning from the past as we plan for the future.
O God, bless those whom you call to the single life;
    —let their commitment to the gospel be a joy to you,
        enrichment for them, and a service to others that mirrors
        your Christ.

O God, give us a desire for true and lasting values;
—let our faith in you inform all that we are and do.
Spirit of God, you bring both peace and fire to our hearts;
—teach us how to challenge and affirm one another in a
spirit of harmony.

PRAYER: Most gentle God, you have fed us this day with your
holy Word and life-giving Bread. May we continue to
discern your calls in life, family, community and in the
movements of our hearts. May we always be among
those who worship you in spirit and in truth. We ask
this through the intercession of all those who gave their
lives that others may have bread and a better quality of
life. Amen.

FRIDAY

MORNING PRAYER

**Ant 1 A humble, contrite heart,
O God, you will not despise.**

Psalm 51

Have mercy on me, O God,
according to your steadfast love;
in your abundant mercy blot out
my sins.
Wash me thoroughly from my
offenses,
and cleanse me from my sin!

For I know my offenses,
and my sin is ever before me.
Against you, you alone, have I
sinned,
and done what is evil in your
sight,
so you are justified in your
sentence
and blameless in your judgment.
Behold, I was brought forth in a
sinful world.

For you desire truth in my
innermost being;—

teach me wisdom in the depths of
my heart.
O purify me, and I shall be clean;
O wash me, I shall be whiter than
snow.
Fill me with joy and gladness;
let the bones you have broken
rejoice.
Hide your face from my guilt,
and blot out all my offenses.

Create in me a clean heart,
put a steadfast spirit within me.
Cast me not from your presence,
take not your spirit from me.
Give me again the joy of your
salvation,
with a willing spirit uphold me.

Then I will teach transgressors
your ways
and sinners will return to you.
Deliver me from death,
O God of my salvation,
and my tongue will sing out your
saving help.

Open my lips and my mouth will
sing your praises.
For you take no delight in
sacrifice;
were I to give a burnt offering,
you would not be pleased.
A broken spirit you accept;
a contrite heart, you will not
despise.

In your goodness, show favor to
Zion;
rebuild the walls of Jerusalem.
Then you will delight in just
sacrifices,
in gifts offered on your altar.
   Glory*...

**Ant. 2 You bring us to springs of
water; you will wipe away
every tear from our eyes.**

Cant: Jeremiah 14:17-21

Let my eyes stream with tears
night and day, without rest,
for the virgin daughter of my
people
is smitten with a great wound,
with a very grievous blow.

If I walk out into the field,
behold those slain by the sword!
If I enter the city,
behold the diseases of famine!
Both the prophet and the priest
ply their trade throughout the
land,
ignorant of their doings.

Have you utterly rejected Judah?
Is Zion loathsome to you?
Why have you smitten us—

so that there is no healing?
We looked for peace to no avail;
for a time of healing,
but terror comes instead.
We acknowledge our wickedness,
and the guilt of our ancestors,
for we have sinned against you.

Spurn us not for your name's
sake;
do not dishonor your glorious
throne;
remember your covenant with us,
and break it not. **Glory*...**

**Ant. 3 We are your people, the
sheep of your pasture.**

Psalm 100

All the earth cries out to you with
shouts of joy, O God,
Serving you with gladness;
coming before you, singing for joy.

You, Creator of all, are God.
You made us, we belong to you,
we are your people, the sheep of
your pasture.

We enter your gates with
thanksgiving,
and your courts with songs of
praise!
We give you thanks and bless
your name.

Indeed, how good you are,
enduring, your steadfast love.
You are faithful to all generations.
   Glory*...

READING

I went into the garden before Prime, and, sitting down beside the pool, I
began to consider what a pleasant place it was. I was charmed by the
clear water and flowing streams, the fresh green of the surrounding

trees, the birds flying about, especially the doves. But most of all, I loved the quiet, hidden peace of this secluded retreat. I asked myself what more was needed to complete my happiness in a place that seemed to me so perfect, and I reflected that it was the presence of a friend, intimate, affectionate, wise, and companionable to share my solitude. And then you, my God, source of ineffable delights, who, as I believe, did but inspire the beginning of this meditation to lead it back to yourself, made me understand that, if I were to pour back like water the stream of graces received from you in that continual gratitude I owe you; if, like a tree, growing in the exercise of virtue, I were to cover myself with the leaves and blossoms of good works; if, like the doves I were to spurn earth and soar heavenward; and if, with my senses set free from passions and worldly distractions, I were to occupy myself with you alone; then my heart would afford you a dwelling most suitably appointed from which no joy would be lacking.

Gertrude of Helfta, The Herald of Divine Love, p. 97, (1)

RESPONSORY

Return, O God! How long? Have pity on your servants. —**Return...**
Satisfy us in the morning with your steadfast love. —**Have...**
Glory to you, Source of all Being, Eternal Word and Holy Spirit.
   —**Return...**

CANTICLE OF ZECHARIAH

Ant. Give light to those in darkness and the shadow of death.

INTERCESSIONS

O God, a humble heart is more pleasing to you than sacrifice;
   —lift up all who are humiliated and despised because of
      their own faults or those of others.
Faith is your free gift to us, O God;
   —enlighten us with ways of sharing it with others.
O God, your love is eternal, and we fail you "seven times a day";
   —preserve us from measuring you by our own pettiness;
      never let fear keep us from turning to you.
Jesus, you have made yourself as available to us as bread;
   —help us to realize our need to live in your presence and to
      listen to the voice of your spirit in our hearts.
Spirit of God, love is your gift to us and the gift you desire from us;
   —receive our desire and poor efforts to offer you our lives
      this day.

PRAYER: Direct our activity this day, O merciful God, that we may reflect your goodness and love to our companions. Help us to be mindful of the many people who are oppressed, and may we be aware of the ways that we oppress others. We ask this in the name of Jesus who died to set us free. Amen.

DAYTIME PRAYER

Ant. 1 The servant of God was stricken; smitten by God, and afflicted.

Psalm 22

O God, my God, why have you forsaken me?
Why are you so far from helping me,
from the sound of my groaning?
I cry out by day, but you do not answer;
by night, but find no rest.

Yet you alone are holy,
enthroned on the praises of Israel.
In you our ancestors trusted;
they trusted and you delivered them.
To you they cried, and were saved;
In you they trusted,
and were not disappointed.

But I am a worm and not human,
scorned and despised by the people.
All who see me mock at me,
they curl their lips, they wag their heads;
"You trusted in God, let God save you;
let God rescue you
for God delights in you!"

Yet it was you who took me from the womb;
you kept me safe upon my mother's breasts.
Upon you was I cast from my birth,
since my mother's womb you have been my God.
Be not far from me in my distress;
there is no one else to help.
      Glory*...

Ant. 2 By oppression and judgment, the just one was cut off from the land of the living.

II

Many bulls encompass me,
strong bulls of Bashan surround me;
they open wide their mouths,
like a ravening and roaring lion.

I am poured out like water,
disjointed are all my bones;
my heart has become like wax,
melted within my breast;
my strength is dried up like burnt clay,
my tongue cleaves to my jaws;
you lay me in the dust of death.

Many dogs are round about me;
a band of evildoers encircles me;
they pierce my hands and my feet;—

I can count every one of my
bones.
They stare and gloat over me;
they divide my garments among
them,
for my raiment they cast lots.

But you, O God, be not far off!
O my help, hasten to my aid!
Deliver my soul from the sword,
my life from the grip of the dog!
Save me from the jaws of the lion,
my poor soul from the horns of
the wild ox!

I will tell of your name to my
kinsfolk
and praise you in the assembly.
Glory*...

**Ant. 3 For a moment I hid my
face, but I will have
compassion on you.**
III

You who fear God, give praise!
You descendants of Jacob, give
glory!
Stand in awe, children of Israel!

For you, O God, have not
despised
nor scorned the affliction of the
poor;—

you have not hid your face from
them,
but heard them when they cried
to you.

To you comes praise from the
great assembly;
my vows I will pay before those
who fear you.
The poor shall eat and be
satisfied;
those who seek you shall sing
your praise!
May their hearts live forever and
ever!

All the earth shall remember
and turn to you, O God;
all families of the nations
shall worship before you.
For sovereignty belongs to you;
you rule over the nations.

All the mighty of the earth
bow down before you;
before you shall bow
all who go down to the dust.

Posterity shall serve you;
They shall tell of you
to generations yet to come,
and proclaim your deliverance
to a people yet unborn:
"These things our God has done."
Glory*...

PRAYER: Look upon us, most gracious God, as we gather at
midday. Bless the work of our hands and hearts. May
all peoples be blessed with the dignity of work, with an
understanding of their gifts, and with generous spirits
so that together we may further your reign among us.
Help all who are unemployed and those who are
disabled. May all know their worth and dignity. Grant
this is Jesus' name. Amen.

EVENING PRAYER

Ant. 1 Our God is high above all other gods.

Psalm 135

We praise your name, O God,
all your servants give praise,
those who stand in your holy
house,
in the courts of your house, O
God!

We praise you, for you are good.
Sing to your name for you are
gracious!
For you have chosen Jacob for
yourself,
Israel as your own possession.

For I know that you are great,
that you are high above all gods.
You do whatever you please,
in heaven and on earth,
in the seas and all the deeps.

You summon clouds from the end
of the earth,
make lightning for the rain,
and bring forth wind from your
storehouse.

You smote the firstborn of Egypt,
both of human and beast alike.
Signs and wonders you worked
in the midst of the land of Egypt,
against Pharaoh and all his
servants.

You smote many nations
and slew mighty rulers,
Sihon, king of the Amorites,
Og, the king of Bashan,
and all the kingdoms of Canaan.
You gave their land as a heritage,
a heritage to your people.
     Glory*...

Ant. 2 You are the living God come down from heaven.

II

O God, your name endures
forever,
your renown throughout all ages.
You will work justice for your
people,
and have compassion on your
servants.

The idols of the nations are silver
and gold,
the work of human hands.
They have eyes, but they cannot
see;
they have ears, but they cannot
hear;
nor is there any breath on their
lips.
Like them be those who make
them!
And everyone who trusts in them!

Descendants of Israel, bless our
God!
Descendants of Aaron, bless our
God!
Descendants of Levi, bless our
God!
You who fear, bless the Most
High!

Blessed are you from Zion, O
God,
you who dwell in Jerusalem!
     Glory*...

Ant. 3 Behold I make all things new!
     Cant: Rev 15:3-4

Great and wonderful are your
works,
God the Almighty One!—

Just and true are your ways,
Ruler of all the ages!

Who shall refuse you honor,
or the glory due your name?

For you alone are holy,
all nations shall come and
worship in your presence.
Your judgments are clearly seen.
Glory*...

READING

On the one hand, Jeanne de Chantal's life appears as one of unfolding
potential, a life of a woman whose circumstance allowed her to gain the
fullness of her personal vision. While this is true, it is also true that the
backdrop behind this vocational scenario was the experience of great
personal loss. It should be remembered that this was a woman with
deep affection for those closest to her. Life did not spare her grief on
that account. The death of her adored husband was only one in a long
series of losses that were to cut cruelly through the fabric of her life....
To this sad history of loss must be added the experience of loss in the
interior life.... For most of her adult life she suffered from what she
called 'temptations', doubts of faith that merged into an intense
experience of inner pain and turbulence. But this constant interior
suffering was not reflected in her daily life. Her letters, the advice she
gave others, the reports of those nearest her suggest that this was a
hidden experience.

Wendy Wright, "Two Faces of Christ: Jeanne de Chantal," pp. 355–56, (7)

RESPONSORY

When the cares of my heart are many, your consolations cheer
   my soul. —**When the...**
You have become my stronghold; —**your...**
Glory to you, Source of all Being, Eternal Word and Holy Spirit.
   —**When the...**

CANTICLE OF MARY

Ant. Fill the hungry with bread of earth and bread of heaven.

INTERCESSIONS

You are our Creator, O God, and you know of what we are made;
   —have mercy on those who are forced to work beyond their
      strength or to bear their limit of suffering.
We thank and praise you for the talents you have given to those
who make our lives less burdensome by invention and more
delightful through art;
   —give them the grace to live balanced and holy lives.

The future is always a mystery to us; our lives are in your hands;
—grant us a childlike peace as we place our trust in you
and do our best to serve you.
Jesus, you prayed for unity on the night before you died for us;
—heal us of our prejudices, and grant success to our efforts
toward ecumenism.
You radiated the joy that is the sign of the Spirit;
—let our joy and good humor reveal your presence in our
lives.

PRAYER: Most loving God, at evening's end we pray for all who
near the evening of their lives. Grant them your peace
and reconciliation with all who love them. May they
know the hope and joy that awaits them when they see
you face to face. This we ask through the intercession
of Joseph and of all who died in your embrace. Amen.

SATURDAY

MORNING PRAYER

**Ant. 1 You are near at hand, O
God, and all your ways are true.**

Psalm 119: 145–152

With all my heart, I cry to you;
answer me, O God.
I cry to you; save me,
that I may observe your will.

I rise before dawn and cry for help;
I hope in your words.
My eyes watch throughout the
night
meditating on your promises.

Hear my voice in your steadfast
love;
in your justice preserve my life.
Those who persecute me draw
near;
they are far from your law.

But you, O God, are near at hand,
all your commands are true.—

Long have I known that your will
endures forever.
Glory*...

**Ant. 2 Give us your Spirit of
Wisdom in all our affairs.**

Cant: Wisdom 9:1–6, 9–11

God of our ancestors, God of
mercy,
you who have made all things by
your word
and in your wisdom have
established us
to care for the creatures produced
by you,
to govern the world in holiness
and justice,
and to render judgment in
integrity of heart.

Give us Wisdom, the attendant at
your throne,—

and reject us not from among your children;

for we are your servants; weak and short-lived

and lacking in comprehension of judgment and of laws.

Indeed, though some be perfect among all the peoples of this earth,

if Wisdom, who comes from you, be not with them,

they shall be held in no esteem.

Now with you is Wisdom, who knows your works

and was present when you made the world;

who understands what is pleasing in your eyes

and what is conformable with your commands.

Send her forth from your holy heavens—

and from your glorious throne dispatch her

that she may be with us and work with us,

that we may know what is your pleasure.

For she knows and understands all things,

and will guide us discreetly in our affairs

and safeguard us by her glory. **Glory*....**

Ant. 3 O God, your faithfulness endures forever.

Psalm 117

Praise our God, all you nations! Acclaim the Most High, all you peoples!

For great is your love for us; and your faithfulness endures forever. **Glory*...**

READING

Simplicity means that we live close enough to the limits of our resources so that we can rely on God's providence and appreciate the beauty of life. Simplicity fosters spontaneity, truthfulness, and clear speech. Simplicity also is required of anyone who seeks justice, peace, and equitable stewardship of resources. Simplicity is not a simple way to live. It requires serious reflection to sort out what is necessary and what is luxury. With all the pressures to buy this and have that, it is difficult to be satisfied with having just enough to be generous and caring. It is not simple to speak plainly and truthfully. We are tempted to equivocate, massage the truth, and manipulate our speech. Only conscious and consistent meditation, prayer, and examination can help us live the simplicity of Jesus.

Audrey Gibson and Kieran Kneaves, *Praying with Louise de Marillac*, p. 84, (42)

RESPONSORY

I will give heed to the way that is blameless. When will you come to me? —**I will...**

I will walk with integrity of heart within my house. —**When...**

Glory to you, Source of all Being, Eternal Word and Holy Spirit.
—I will...

CANTICLE OF ZECHARIAH

Ant. May we serve you in holiness all the days of our lives.

INTERCESSIONS

Jesus, you taught your followers the deepest lessons of life;
  —show us how to teach our children your ways of forgiveness,
    reverence for one another, and mutual support.
To all who would listen, you revealed God as a tender mother
and an understanding father;
  —teach us how to develop and balance the feminine and
    masculine aspects of our lives.
O God, our desires are boundless, but we are limited on every
side;
  —let the discipline of reality be a spur to our creativity.
Bless all children; let their school years be maturing and fruitful
ones for them;
  —inspire our teachers with ways to draw out the best in all.
You left your mother to follow the call of the Spirit;
  —be with those who must leave their families to find work
    in other countries.

PRAYER: You are a God of Wonder, Most Holy One, as you call
us into being and set us free in your loving plan. Help
us to grow in understanding the meaning of our
freedom, so that we may discern wisely and respect
the gift of freedom in all our sisters and brothers.
Grant this through the intercession of all who have
died that others may be free. Amen.

DAYTIME PRAYER

**Ant. 1 Deal with us according to
the greatness of your love.**

Psalm 119:121–128

I have done what is right and
just:
let me not be oppressed.—

Guarantee the goodness of your
servant
let not the proud oppress me.

My eyes grow weak watching for
salvation,
and the fulfillment of your
promise.—

Treat your servant according to
the greatness of your love,
and teach me your statutes.

I am your servant; give me
knowledge,
that I may know your will!
It is time for you to act, O God,
for your law has been broken.

Therefore I love your
commandments
more than finest gold.
I guide my steps by your
precepts:
I hate the ways of falsehood.
Glory*...

**Ant. 2 Happy are those who
take refuge in you.**

Psalm 34

I will bless you, O God, at all
times,
your praise always on my lips.
My soul makes its boast in you;
the afflicted shall hear and be
glad.
Glorify our God with me.
Together let us praise God's
name.

I sought you, and you answered
me;
and delivered me from all my
fears.
Look towards the Most High, and
be radiant;
let your faces not be ashamed.
These poor ones cried; you heard
them,
and saved them from all their
troubles.

Your angel, O God, is encamped
around those who revere you, to
deliver them.—

Taste and see that God is good!
Happy are they who take refuge
in you.

Revere the Most High, all you
saints.
Those who revere you, have no
want!
Young lions suffer want and
hunger;
but those who seek you lack no
blessing. **Glory*...**

**Ant. 3 Deliver the
brokenhearted from all their
troubles.**

II

Come children, listen to me,
I will teach you to reverence the
Most High.
Who among you longs for life
and many days to enjoy
prosperity?

Keep your tongue from evil,
your lips from speaking deceit.
Turn aside from evil and do good;
seek peace and pursue it.

God's eyes are turned to the
righteous,
God's ears toward their cry.
God's face turns away from evil,
that it not be remembered on
earth.

When the just cry, the Most High
hears,
and delivers them from their
troubles.
God is close to the
brokenhearted;
saving those whose spirits are
crushed.

Many are the afflictions of the
just;—

they will be delivered from them all.
God will keep guard over all their bones,
not one of them shall be broken.

Evil shall be its own destruction; oppression shall be condemned.
You redeem the lives of your servants;
those who take refuge in you shall not be condemned.
Glory*...

PRAYER: You gather us together in faith, O God, as a loving mother and a gentle father. Help us to remember that your dwelling place is built upon love and peace, and that to bring about your reign on earth we must follow your way of peace. We pray for all governments and legislatures that they may be mindful of the rights of all peoples of this world to live in peace and dignity. Grant this is the name of Jesus. Amen.

WEEK IV

SUNDAY, EVENING PRAYER I

Ant 1 Peace be within you!

Psalm 122

I was glad when they said to me:
"let us go to the house of God!"
And now our feet are standing
within your gates, O Jerusalem!

Jerusalem, built as a city
bound firmly together,
to which the tribes go up,
the tribes of our God,
as was decreed for Israel,
to give thanks to your holy name.
There thrones for judgment were
  set,
the thrones of the house of David.

Pray for the peace of Jerusalem!
"Peace be to your homes!
Peace be within your walls,
and security within your borders!

For love of my family and friends
I will say: "Peace be within you!"
For the sake of the house of our
  God,
I seek your good. **Glory*...**

**Ant 2 From sunrise to sunset,
my soul waits for you.**

Psalm 130

Out of the depths I cry to you,
O God, hear my voice!
Let your ears be attentive
to the voice of my supplication.

***Glory to you, Source of all
Being, Eternal Word and Holy
Spirit,**

**As it was in the beginning is
now and will be forever. Amen.**

If you should mark our iniquities,
O God, who could stand?
But with you is found
  forgiveness:
for this we revere you.

My soul waits for you,
in your word I hope;
my soul waits for you
more than those who watch for
  daybreak.

Let Israel hope in you!
For with you there is love,
and fullness of redemption.
And you will redeem Israel
from all its iniquities.
    Glory*...

**Ant 3 Let every knee bow at
the name of Jesus.**

Cant: Phil 2:6–11

Though he was in the form of
  God,
Jesus did not count equality with
  God
something to be grasped at.

But emptied himself
taking the form of a slave,
being born in human likeness.

Being found in human estate,
he humbled himself and became
  obedient,
obediently accepting death,
even death on a cross!

Therefore God has highly exalted
  him
and bestowed on him the name
above every other name.

So that at the name of Jesus
every knee should bow,
in heaven, on the earth,
and under the earth,—

and every tongue proclaim
to the glory of God:
Jesus Christ is Lord! **Glory*...**

READING

"Christ is risen!" does not mean that Jesus lives on in history as Lenin
lives on in his revolution.... Jesus does not live on because people
have faith in him and proclaim his teaching. The reverse is true.
People have faith in him and proclaim his teaching because he lives....
When the ointment bearing women went to the tomb on that first
Easter morning they only expected to see the dead body of Jesus.
When they heard the words, "...He is not here, He is risen!", all life
radically changed for them forever—and so it must be for us.
Everything in our lives that is not based on a Resurrection faith in
Jesus and his message must be rejected. Once one has found the
"pearl of great price" he or she automatically sells everything of lesser
value to procure it.

Emmanuel Charles McCarthy, "Stations of the Cross of Non-Violent Love," p. 22, (36)

RESPONSORY

From daybreak to sunset, we praise your name, O God.
—From daybreak...
Your glory fills the heavens; **—we praise...**
Glory to you, Source of all Being, Eternal Word and Holy Spirit.
—From daybreak...

CANTICLE OF MARY

Ant. Blessed are the pure of heart, for they shall see God.

INTERCESSIONS

O God, your invitation to grow is ever before us;
—free us from the need to control; deepen our trust in your
desire for our good.
Nothing is impossible for you;
—let our desires be your own, then grant our requests.
Jesus, you promise to raise up those who have died with you;
—help us to remember that the suffering of life is not
meaningless.
Bless those who break under the stress of life;
—give them understanding and compassionate mentors.
Help the agencies of the world that help others;
—enable them to find homes and sustenance for all refugees.

PRAYER: All-loving God, you restored your people to eternal life by raising Jesus from the dead. Make our faith strong and our hope sure. May we never doubt that you will fulfill the promises you have made to us and to all the peoples of this world. Grant this through the prayers of all who without seeing have believed and now enjoy the gift of eternal life. Amen.

MORNING PRAYER

Ant. 1 We praise you for your steadfast love.

Psalm 118

I

We give thanks to you, for you are good,
and your steadfast love endures forever.

Let the descendants of Israel say:
"Your steadfast love endures forever."
Let the descendants of Aaron say:
"Your steadfast love endures forever."
Let those who fear you say:
"Your steadfast love endures forever."

In my distress, I called to you;
you answered me and set me free.
With you at my side I do not fear.
What can anyone do against me?
You are at my side to help me:
I shall withstand all evildoers.

It is better to take refuge in you,
than to trust in people:
it is better to take refuge in you
than to trust in our leaders.

All wickedness surrounded me;
in your name I crushed it.
It surrounded me, surrounded me
on every side;
in your name I cut it off.—

It surrounded me like bees;
it blazed like a fire among thorns.
In your name I crushed it.

I was pushed hard, and was falling
but you came to help me.
You are my strength and my song;
you are my salvation.

O God, you have triumphed;
your reign is exalted.
You have triumphed over all;
I shall not die, I shall live
and recount your wondrous deeds.
You have chastened me sorely,
but have not given me over to
death.

Open to me the gates of justice,
that I may enter and give thanks.
This is your gate, O God;
the just shall enter through it.
I thank you for you have answered
me
you alone are my salvation.

The stone which the builders
rejected
has become the cornerstone.
This is your doing, O God,
it is marvelous in our eyes.
This is the day which you have
made;
let us rejoice and be glad in it.

Save us, we beseech you, O God!
O God, grant us success.—

Blessed are those who enter
in your holy name.
For you O God, are our God,
and you have given us light.

Let us go forward in procession
with branches,
up to your holy altar.
You are my God, I thank you.
You are my God, I praise you.
We give thanks to you for you are
good;
and your steadfast love endures
forever. **Glory*...**

**Ant. 2 May all your works bless
you, (alleluia).**
Cant: Daniel 3:52-57

Blessed are you, God of our
ancestors,
praiseworthy and exalted above all
forever.

Blessed be your holy and glorious
name,
praiseworthy and exalted above all
for all ages.

Blessed are you in the temple of
your glory,
praiseworthy and exalted above all
forever.

Blessed are you on the throne of
your kindom,
praiseworthy and exalted above all
forever.

Blessed are you who look into the
depths
from your throne upon the
cherubim,
praiseworthy and exalted above all
forever.

Blessed are you in the firmament
of heaven,
praiseworthy and glorious forever.

Blessed are you by all your works.
We praise and exalt you above all
forever. **Glory*...**

**Ant. 3 You are wonderful in all
your works, O God.**
Psalm 150

We praise you, O God, in your holy
sanctuary;
we praise you in your mighty
heavens.
We praise you for your powerful
deeds;
we praise you according to your
greatness.

We praise you with trumpet
sound;
We praise you with lute and harp!
We praise you with strings and
pipe!

We praise you with sounding
cymbals,
We praise you with clashing
cymbals!
Let everything that breathes,
give praise to you, O God.
Glory*...

READING

Remember Jesus Christ, raised from the dead, a descendant of David.
The saying is sure: If we have died with him, we will also live with him; if
we endure, we will also reign with him; if we deny him, he will also deny
us; if we are faithless, he remains faithful—for he cannot deny himself.

2 Tim 2:8a, 11-13

RESPONSORY

We praise your goodness, O God, with songs of thanksgiving.
   —We praise...
We rejoice in your presence; **—with songs...**
Glory to you, Source of all Being, Eternal Word and Holy Spirit.
   —We praise...

CANTICLE OF ZECHARIAH

Ant. Give us this day our daily bread.

INTERCESSIONS

O God, the whole world was changed and raised up by the coming
of your son;
   —let us never take his life or gospel for granted.
You give us the power to be light or darkness for one another on
the way to salvation;
   —show us how to transform the stumbling blocks in our lives
     to ladders of grace for ourselves and for others.
There are many who do not know you or your Christ;
   —send laborers into your harvest.
Jesus, you ate with sinners and stayed with them;
   —let the Eucharist that we share remind us of your forgiveness
     and constant presence in our lives.
Spirit of God, lead us to wholesome recreations that delight and
nourish us;
   —keep us safe as we play, and let us do so with moderation
     and gratitude.

PRAYER: O God of the morning, you call us to a new day and to a
life of resurrection and union with you. Help us to live
this day as a people of hope in a world of chaos. May
all who face oppression, terror, abuse, or suffering in
any way know that you call us to life and happiness in
this world as well as the world to come. We ask this
through the intercession of all who lived as people of
hope in the midst of despair and now live with you in
everlasting peace. Amen.

DAYTIME PRAYER

Ant. 1 You are the bread of life, (alleluia).

Psalm 23

O God, you are my shepherd;
I shall not want.
You make me to lie in green
  pastures.
You lead me to restful waters,
to restore my soul.

You guide me in paths of
  righteousness
for the sake of your name.
Even though I walk through the
  valley of the shadow of death,
I fear no evil;
for you are with me;
your crook and your staff
give me comfort.

You prepare a table before me
in the presence of my foes;
you anoint my head with oil,
my cup overflows.

Surely goodness and mercy shall
  follow me
all the days of my life;
and I shall dwell in your holy
  house forever and ever.
  Glory*...

Ant. 2 More glorious are you than the everlasting mountains, (alleluia).

Psalm 76

O God, you are known in Judah;
Your abode you established in
  Jerusalem,
your dwelling place in Zion.—

There you broke the flashing
  arrows,
the sword, and the weapons of
  war.

Glorious are you, more majestic
than the everlasting mountains.
Warriors were stripped of their
  spoil,
sinking into death;
those engaged in war, made
  powerless at your word.
At your rebuke, O God,
the makers of war lay stunned.
  Glory*...

Ant. 3 God arose in judgment to save the oppressed on earth, (alleluia).

II

You, alone, O God, strike terror!
Who can stand before you
when your anger is aroused?
From the heavens you utter
  judgment;
the earth feared and was still,
when you rose to establish
  judgment
to save the oppressed of the
  earth.

Human anger will serve to praise
  you;
its residue gird you round.
We make vows to you, and fulfill
  them.
Let your faithful bring you gifts;
you, who are worthy of awe,
who cut short the lives of leaders
who strike terror in the rulers of
  the earth. **Glory*...**

PRAYER: Creator of all, by the paschal mystery you touch our
  lives with the healing power of your love. You have

given us the freedom of the children of God. May all people know this freedom in their hearts and in their lives, so that they may celebrate your gift and find joy in it now and forever. Amen.

EVENING PRAYER II

Ant. 1 We are a priestly people; let us give thanks, (alleluia).

Psalm 110:1–5, 7

God's revelation to the Anointed
   One:
"Sit at my side:
till I put injustice beneath your
   feet."

God will send forth from Zion
your scepter of power:
rule in the midst of your foes.

Your people will give themselves
   freely
on the day you lead your host
upon the holy mountains.
From the womb of the morning
your youth will come like dew.

God has sworn an oath that will
   not be changed.
"You are a priest forever,
after the order of Melchizedek."

The Anointed standing by your
   side,
will shatter rulers on the day of
   wrath.

Drinking from your streams by
   the wayside
shall the Chosen One be
   refreshed. **Glory*...**

Ant. 2 Those who give to the poor will have treasure in heaven.

Psalm 112

Happy are they who fear the Most
   High,
who greatly delight in God's
   commands.
Their children will be mighty in
   the land;
the offspring of the upright will be
   blessed.

Wealth and riches are in their
   homes;
their justice endures forever.
Light rises in the darkness for the
   upright:
God is gracious, merciful and
   just.

It is well for those who are
   generous and lend,
who conduct their affairs with
   justice.
The upright will never be moved;
they will be remembered forever.

They have no fear of evil tidings;
their hearts are firm, trusting in
   God.
With steadfast hearts, they will
   not fear;
they will withstand all deception.

Open-handed, they give to the
   poor;
their justice endures forever.
Their power is exalted in glory.

The wicked see and are angry,
gnash their teeth and melt away;
the desire of the wicked comes to
nought. **Glory*...**

**Ant. 3 May all who serve you,
give you praise, (alleluia).**

Cant: Rev 19:1, 5–7

Salvation, glory, and power
belong to you,
your judgments are honest and
true.

All of us, your servants, sing
praise to you,
we worship you reverently, both
great and small.

You, our almighty God, are
Creator of heaven and earth.
Let us rejoice and exult, and give
you glory.

The wedding feast of the Lamb
has begun,
And the bride has made herself
ready. **Glory*...**

READING

Those who are seized by the peace of Christ and who preserve peace in
their hearts, radiate peace, give witness to peace and cooperate as much
as possible in making peace attainable, are assured of great beatitude.
"They shall be called sons and daughters of God" (Mt 59). They reveal
themselves as genuine brothers and sisters of Jesus Christ, Prince of
Peace. They find security and joy in God. For them it is happiness to
lead people to God's peace, and to peace among themselves. "The
[kindom] of heaven is theirs", for the [kindom] of God is justice, peace,
and joy, inspired by the Holy Spirit" (Rom 14:17).

Bernard Häring, *The Healing Power of Peace and Nonviolence*, p. 23, (1)

RESPONSORY

Glorious are your works, God of the universe. **—Glorious...**
Nothing can surpass your greatness; **—God...**
Glory to you, Source of all Being, Eternal Word and Holy Spirit.
—Glorious...

CANTICLE OF MARY

Ant. Blessed are the meek, for they shall inherit the earth.

INTERCESSIONS

O God, you are present to us, yet our minds cannot contain the
mystery of your being;
—let what we know of you in the life and love of Jesus draw
us to you in ever deepening faith.
It is difficult to wait with hope for what we think is good and just;

—increase our faith, and help us to hold fast to our
    dedication to you.
Let the harvest of our land yield enough for all;
    —banish famine from our world; teach us to share.
Eye has not seen, nor ear heard, what you have prepared for
those who love you;
    —let the hundredfold that we seek be only to love you totally
    with grateful hearts.
Jesus, you prayed that we all might be one;
    —help us to recognize those who differ from us as our sisters
    and brothers sharing this one earth that you came to save.

PRAYER: O holy God, as evening falls remain with us. Remember
our good deeds and forgive our failings. Help us to
reflect upon and live according to your covenant of
love. Be with our lonely and elderly sisters and
brothers in the evening of their lives. May all who long
to see you face to face know the comfort of your
presence. This we ask in union with Simeon and Anna
and all who have gone before us blessing and
proclaiming you by the fidelity of their lives. Amen.

MONDAY

MORNING PRAYER

**Ant 1 Give success to the work
of our hands, O God.**

Psalm 90

O God, you have been our shelter
from one generation to the next.
Before the mountains were
    formed,
or the earth or the world brought
    forth,
from everlasting to everlasting
you are God.

You turn us back to dust, and
    say:
"Go back, peoples of the earth!"
For a thousand years in your
    sight—

are like yesterday, when it is
    past,
no more than a watch in the
    night.

You sweep us away like a dream,
like grass which is renewed in the
    morning:
in the morning it flowers and is
    renewed;
in the evening it fades and
    withers.

So we are consumed by your
    anger;
by your wrath we are
    overwhelmed.—

You set our iniquities before you,
our secret sins in the light of your
   face.
All our days pass away in your
   anger.
Our years are over like a sigh.
The years of our life are seventy,
or eighty for those who are
   strong;
yet their span is but toil and
   trouble;
they pass swiftly and we are gone.

Who understands the power of
   your anger
and fears the strength of your
   wrath?
Teach us to number our days
that we may gain wisdom of
   heart.

Relent, O God! How long?
Have pity on your servants!
In the morning, fill us with your
   love,
that we may rejoice and be glad
   all our days.
Balance with joy our days of
   affliction,
and the years when we knew
   misfortune.

Let your word be manifest to your
   servants,
your glorious power to their
   children.
Let your favor, O God, be upon
   us:
give success to the work of our
   hands,
give success to the work of our
   hands. **Glory*...**

Ant. 2 **You turn darkness into
light and make the rough ways
smooth!**

Cant: Isaiah 42:10–16

Sing to our God a new song,
Sing praise from the ends of the
   earth!

Let the sea and what fills it
   resound,
the coastlands and their
   inhabitants.
Let the desert and its cities cry
   out,
the villages where Kedar dwells.

Let the inhabitants of Sela exult,
let them shout from the top of the
   mountains.
Let them give glory to the Most
   High,
and declare God's praise in the
   coastlands.

You go forth, O God, like a hero,
like a warrior you stir up your
   fury;
crying out and shouting aloud,
against the oppression of your
   poor.

For a long time I held my peace,
I kept still and restrained myself;
now, I will cry like a woman in
   labor, gasping and panting.

I will lay waste mountains and
   hills,
and dry up all their herbage;
I will turn the rivers into islands,
and dry up all the streams.

I will lead the blind on their
   journey,
in a way that they know not,
in unknown paths I will guide
   them.—

I will turn darkness before them
  into light,
and rough places into level
  ground. **Glory*...**

**Ant. 3 You are gracious, O God;
you call us to be your people.**

Psalm 135

We praise your name, O God,
all your servants give praise,
those who stand in your holy
  house,
in the courts of your house, O
  God!

We praise you, for you are good.
Sing to your name for you are
  gracious!
For you have chosen Jacob for
  yourself,
Israel as your own possession.

For I know that you are great,
that you are high above all gods.–

You do whatever you please,
in heaven and on earth,
in the seas and all the deeps.

You summon clouds from the
  ends of the earth,
make lightning for the rain,
and bring forth wind from your
  storehouse.

You smote the firstborn of Egypt,
both of human and beast alike.
Signs and wonders you worked
in the midst of the land of Egypt,
against Pharaoh and all his
  servants.

You smote many nations
and slew mighty rulers,
Sihon, king of the Amorites,
Og, the king of Bashan,
and all the kingdoms of Canaan.
You gave their land as a heritage,
a heritage to your people.
  Glory*...

READING

We live in a culture of achievement and production which believes that people should and do get what they deserve. As Christians we know that this is not so. The infinite bounty of God begins with the gift of life itself and continues with everything that sustains it. Our activity is not so much an earning our way as a cooperating with the Creator God in transforming history into God's reign of justice and love. Building this attitude of grateful response into our lives requires a constant cultivation of faith against the seeming self-evident "way things are" around us.

Sandra M. Schneiders, IHM, *New Wineskins*, p. 186, (1)

RESPONSORY

All nations rejoice and praise God our creator. —**All...**
Sing with joy to the Most High; —**and praise...**
Glory to you, Source of all Being, Eternal Word and Holy Spirit.
  —**All...**

CANTICLE OF ZECHARIAH

Ant. Come to us this day and set your people free.

INTERCESSIONS

Jesus, you preached a gospel of love and forgiveness;
   —may those who hear your word be freed from unfounded
     guilt and a misguided conscience.

You healed those who could not hear or speak;
   —may we close our ears to falsehood and endeavor to speak
     the truth in love.

We know well how to plan for the things we want;
   —help us to plan as surely for ways to open ourselves to
     your Spirit within us.

O God, mobility is a sign of our times; the whole world is within
our reach;
   —protect us all, and guide those who are responsible for our
     trips on land, sea, and in the air.

You desire our good, and you have compassion on all who suffer;
   —be merciful to those who are in constant pain; comfort and
     sustain them.

PRAYER: O God of life, you bring us to this day and we are
grateful for your gift. Enable us to be and to work for
one another in order that justice may reign, that the
needs of the poor be met, and that the oppressed may
be liberated. We pray this in the name of Jesus who
came that we may be free. Amen.

DAYTIME PRAYER

**Ant. 1 Teach me to follow in
your steps, that I may be your
disciple.**

Psalm 119:129–136

Your will is wonderful indeed;
therefore will I obey it.
The unfolding of your words gives
  light;
it imparts wisdom to the simple.

I open my mouth and I sigh
as I yearn for your
    commandments.
Turn to me and be gracious,
treat me as one who loves your
  name.

Keep my steps steady in your
  way,
according to your promise;
let no iniquity rule over me.—

Redeem me from human
oppression,
that I may keep your precepts.

Let your face shine on your
servant
and teach me your statutes.
My eyes shed streams of tears,
because your law is disobeyed.
Glory*...

**Ant. 2 Blessed are the merciful,
mercy shall be theirs.**

Psalm 82

God stands in the divine
assembly;
holding judgment in the midst of
the gods:

"How long will you judge unjustly
and favor the cause of the
wicked?
Give justice to the weak and the
orphan;
defend the afflicted and the
needy.
Rescue the weak and the
destitute;
deliver them from the hand of the
wicked."

They have neither knowledge nor
understanding,
they walk about in darkness;—

the foundations of the world are
shaken.

God says, "You are gods,
children of the Most High, all of
you;
yet, you shall die like human
beings,
and fall like any of their leaders."

Arise, O God, judge the earth;
for to you belong all the nations.
Glory*...

**Ant. 3 Guide us in your way of
peace.**

Psalm 120

In my distress, I cry to you,
that you may answer me:
"Deliver my soul from lying lips,
and from a deceitful tongue."
What shall be given you in
return,
you deceitful tongue?
The warrior's arrows sharpened
and coals, red-hot blazing.

Alas, that I sojourn in Meshech,
dwell among the tents of Kedar!
Too long have I had my dwelling
among those who hate peace.
I am for peace; but when I speak,
they are for war! **Glory*...**

PRAYER: O God, in your love you have given each of us gifts and
talents to serve the common good. Help us to use them
generously and lovingly, for we are your children. Free
us from the desire to serve only our own interests, and
help us to grow in the spirit of love that makes us
sisters and brothers. This we ask for the sake of all
who are in bondage through our selfishness and that of
our governments. Grant us our prayer that your love
and peace may reign now and forever. Amen.

EVENING PRAYER

Ant. 1 Your love, O God, endures forever.

Psalm 136

We give thanks to you, for you are
good,
for your love endures forever.
We thank you, O God of gods,
for your love endures forever.
We thank you, Creator of the
universe,
for your love endures forever.

You alone have done great
wonders,
for your love endures forever.
Your wisdom made the heavens,
for your love endures forever.
You spread out the earth upon
the waters,
for your love endures forever.

It was you who made the great
lights,
for your love endures forever.
the sun to rule over the day,
for your love endures forever.
the moon and the stars to rule
over the night,
for your love endures forever.
Glory*...

**Ant. 2 With outstretched arm
you lead us out of darkness.**
II

The first born of the Egyptians
you smote,
for your love endures forever;
and brought Israel out from their
midst,
for your love endures forever;—

with arm outstretched and power
in your hand,
for your love endures forever.

You divided the Red Sea in two,
for your love endures forever;
you made Israel pass through the
midst,
for your love endures forever;
you flung Pharaoh and his host in
the sea,
for your love endures forever.

You led your people through the
desert,
for your love endures forever.
Nations in their greatness you
struck,
for your love endures forever.
Rulers in their splendor you slew,
for your love endures forever.

Sihon, king of the Amorites,
for your love endures forever;
and Og, the king of Bashan,
for your love endures forever.

Their land you gave as a heritage,
for your love endures forever;
a heritage to your faithful people,
for your love endures forever.

You remembered us in our
distress,
for your love endures forever;
and you rescued us from
oppression,
for your love endures forever.
You give food to all living things,
for your love endures forever.

We give thanks to you, God of
heaven,
for your love endures forever.
Glory*...

Ant. 3 In Christ, God's grace is revealed.

Cant: Ephesians 1:3-10

Praised be the God
of our Lord Jesus Christ,
who has blessed us in Christ
with every spiritual blessing in
the heavens.

God chose us in him
before the foundation of the
world,
that we should be holy
and blameless in God's sight.

We have been predestined
to be God's children through
Jesus Christ,
such was the purpose of God's
will,—

that all might praise the glorious
favor
bestowed on us in Christ.

In Christ and through his blood,
we have redemption,
the forgiveness of our sins,
according to the riches of God's
grace lavished upon us.

For God has made known to us
in all wisdom and insight,
the mystery of the plan set forth
in Christ.

A plan to be carried out in Christ,
in the fullness of time,
to unite all things in Christ,
things in heaven and things on
earth. **Glory*...**

READING

Meister Eckhart wrote, "As thou art in church or cell, that same frame of mind carry out into the world, into its turmoil and its fitfulness." Deep within us all there is an amazing inner sanctuary of the soul, a holy place, a Divine Center, a speaking Voice, to which we may continuously return. Eternity is at our hearts, pressing upon our time-torn lives, warming us with intimations of an astounding destiny, calling us home unto Itself.

Thomas R. Kelly, *Quaker Spirituality*, p. 290, (1)

RESPONSORY

O God, receive our prayer which is lifted up to you. **—O God,...**
Like the fragrance of incense, **—which is...**
Glory to you, Source of all Being, Eternal Word and Holy Spirit.
—O God,...

CANTICLE OF MARY

Ant. Blessed are the merciful, for they shall obtain mercy.

INTERCESSIONS

O God, slavery is a reality in our world in many forms;
—grant us a new consciousness of the equality of all people.

You created a new covenant of peace through your Son, Jesus, yet
we live in fear of one another;
>   —show us how to re-seed the world with trust; help us to
>   put love where there is no love.

You delight in those who receive your gifts with gratitude;
>   —bless all who endeavor to develop their talents; encourage
>   and enlighten all students, and keep them in your care.

Jesus, you revealed yourself to a woman of Samaria, an
unwelcoming land;
>   —enable world leaders to overcome national rivalries and
>   centuries of mutual retaliation.

You gave us the power to bind and to loose;
>   —free us from our need to control, and give us the grace to
>   free others from our expectations.

PRAYER: O God, as darkness falls, remain with us as our light.
Help us to meet you in the scriptures that we read, in
the bread that we break, and in the neighbor that we
welcome into our hearts. Grant this prayer that your
reign will come, that your will be done in us as it was
in Jesus, now and forever. Amen.

TUESDAY

MORNING PRAYER

**Ant. 1 Look with favor upon us
that we may dwell with you
forever.**

Psalm 101

I sing of fidelity and justice;
to you, O God, I will sing.
I will pay heed to the way that is
blameless.
Oh when will you come to me?

I will walk with integrity of heart
within my house;
I will not set before my eyes
anything that is base.

I renounce the ways of
wrongdoers;—

they shall not adhere to me.
Perverseness of heart shall be far
from me;
I will know nothing of evil.

Those who slander their neighbor
secretly
I will ignore.
Those of haughty looks and proud
hearts
I will not endure.

I will look with favor on all who
are faithful,
that they may dwell with me;
they who walk in the way that is
blameless
shall minister to me.

No one who practices deceit shall
dwell in my house;
no one who utters lies shall
remain in my presence.

Morning by morning I will
renounce
all the oppression in the land,
uprooting from the city of God all
that is evil. **Glory*...**

**Ant. 2 Look upon us with
compassion, O God, and heal
us.**
Cant: Daniel 3:26, 27, 29, 34–41

Blessed are you, and
praiseworthy,
O God of our ancestors,
and glorious forever is your
name.

For you are just in all you have
done;
all your deeds are faultless, all
your ways right,
and all your judgments proper.

For we have sinned and
transgressed
by departing from you,
and we have done every kind of
evil.

For your name's sake, do not
deliver us up forever,
or make void your covenant.

Do not take away your mercy
from us,
for the sake of those beloved by
you:
Sara and Abraham, Rebecca and
Isaac, Rachel and Jacob, your
holy ones,

To whom you promised to
multiply their offspring
like the stars of heaven,
or the sands on the shore of the
sea.

For we are reduced beyond any
other nation,
brought low everywhere in the
world this day because of our
sins.

We have in our day no ruler,
prophet, or leader,
no holocaust, sacrifice, oblation,
or incense,
no place to offer first fruits, to
find favor with you.

But with contrite heart and
humble spirit let us be received;
as though it were holocausts of
rams and bullocks, or
thousands of fat lambs,
so let our sacrifice be in your
presence today as we follow you
unreservedly;
for those who trust in you cannot
be put to shame.

And now we follow you with our
whole heart,
we fear you and we pray to you.
Glory*...

**Ant. 3 O God, you are my
shield. In you I take refuge.**
Psalm 144:1–10

Blessed are you, O God, my rock,
who trains my hands for war,
and my fingers for battle.

You are my rock and my fortress,
my stronghold and my deliverer,
my shield in whom I take refuge,
You bring peoples under your
rule.

Who are we that you care for us,
mortal flesh, that you keep us in
mind?
We, who are merely a breath,
whose days are like a passing
shadow.

Lower your heavens and come
down!
Touch the mountains that they
smoke!
Flash your lightnings and scatter
them,
shoot your arrows and put them
to flight.

Stretch forth your hand from on
high,
rescue me from the mighty
waters,
from the hands of alien foes,
whose mouths are filled with lies,
and whose hands are raised in
perjury.

To you will I sing a new song.
On a ten-stringed harp I will play
to you, who give rulers their
victory,
who rescue David, your servant.
Glory*...

READING

For Mary MacKillop God's will was her guiding principle.... "To me the
Will of God is a dear book which I am never tired of reading, which has
always some new charm for me.... I cannot tell you what a beautiful
thing the Will of God seems to me."

When overcome by sadness she clung to the Will of God as her only
support: "...[I] was so weary of the struggle, and felt so utterly alone,
could not pray or say my ordinary Rosaries, only offered my weary
heart's trials to my God...."

Bl. Mary MacKillop, RSJ, (10)

RESPONSORY

Answer my plea, O God; I trust in your word. **—Answer...**
Before the first rays of dawn, I come to you. **—I trust...**
Glory to you, Source of all Being, Eternal Word and Holy Spirit.
    —Answer...

CANTICLE OF ZECHARIAH

**Ant. Protect us from the grasp of evil, and lead us not into
    temptation.**

INTERCESSIONS

O God, your love is greater than our guilt;
    —have mercy on those who are sentenced to death.
Too often our faith exists only in our minds and words;
    —awaken us to new and practical ways to enflesh our
        commitment to your will.

Our lives are fragile, and you surround us with men and women
in life-preserving professions;
—guard and guide our police, fire fighters, rescue workers,
and all who labor and risk their lives for our safety.
Open our minds to the ways that we are destroying the gifts of the
earth;
—bless again the land and water and all of the life that
sustains us.
Jesus, you knew the sweetness of friendship, and you gave new
life to those who received you;
—keep us faithful to you and to one another.

PRAYER: O God, you call us to begin this day in dedication to
you. May all who need your help today experience your
love and compassion through us and through all who
have come to know you. Bless all the children of this
world; protect them from abuse. May they come to
know their worth and dignity as your children, rightful
citizens of this earth. This we ask in union with all the
innocent and pure of heart who stand in your presence
now and forever. Amen.

DAYTIME PRAYER

**Ant. 1 You are true to your
promise in which I delight.**

Psalm 119:137–144

Just are you, O God,
and right are your judgments.
You have decreed your will in
justice
and in all faithfulness.

I am consumed with zeal
because your words are forgotten.
Your promise is tried in the fire,
the delight of your servant.

Though I am weak and despised
I do not forget your precepts.
Your justice is righteous forever,
and your law is true.

Trouble and anguish come upon
me,
but your commands are my
delight.
The justice of your will is eternal;
give me understanding that I may
live. **Glory*...**

**Ant. 2 Listen to the sound of
my call, O God, I cry for your
help.**

Psalm 88

My God, I call for help by day;
I cry out in the night before you.
Let my prayer come into your
presence,
incline your ear to my cry!
For my soul is full of troubles,—

and my life draws near to the
  grave.

I am reckoned as one in the
  tomb;
I have reached the end of my
  strength,
like one forsaken among the
  dead,
like the slain that lie in the grave,
like those you no longer
  remember,
for they are cut off from your
  hand.

You have laid me in the depths of
  the tomb,
in the regions dark and deep.
Your anger lies heavy upon me,
you overwhelm me with all your
  waves. **Glory*...**

**Ant. 3 Hide not your face from
  me, O God, in time of distress.**
                    II

All my companions now shun me;
to them I am a thing of horror.
I am shut in so that I cannot
  escape;
my eye grows dim through
  sorrow.

Every day I call upon you;
to you I stretch out my hands.
Do you work wonders for the
  dead?
Do phantoms rise up to praise
  you?

Is your love declared in the grave,
or your faithfulness in the
  bottomless pit?
Are your wonders known in the
  darkness,
or your salvation in the land of
  forgetfulness?

But I, O God, cry out to you:
in the morning my prayer comes
  before you.
Why do you cast me off, O God?
Why hide your face from me?

Afflicted and close to death from
  the days of my youth,
I suffer your trials; I am helpless.
Your chastisements swept over
  me;
your dread assaults destroy me.

They surround me like a flood all
  day long;
they close in upon me together.
Friend and neighbor shun me;
my companions are in darkness.
  Glory*...

PRAYER: Loving God, you sent the Holy Spirit to the early
Christians as their source of courage and fidelity. Send
your Spirit to us that we, too, may be witnesses of your
love to all peoples on this earth. We pray especially for
the homeless, the displaced, the nameless, the ignored.
May all come to know your love and care, for you are
both mother and father to us all. Help us to recognize
all as our sisters and brothers. We ask this in union
with Jesus, our friend and brother. Amen.

EVENING PRAYER

Ant. 1 May we remember your covenant in this land of exile.

Psalm 137:1–6

By the waters of Babylon,
we sat down and wept,
when we remembered Zion.
On the willows there we hung up
our harps.

For there our captors required of
us songs,
and our tormentors, mirth,
saying,
"Sing us one of the songs of
Zion!"

How shall we sing God's song in a
foreign land?
If I forget you, Jerusalem,
let my hand wither!

Let my tongue cleave to the roof
of my mouth,
if I do not remember you,
if I do not set Jerusalem above all
my joys! **Glory*...**

Ant. 2 Your name and your word are above all forever.

Psalm 138

I give you thanks with all my
heart;
before the gods I sing your praise;
I bow down before your holy
temple
and give thanks to your name
for your steadfast love and your
faithfulness;
for exalted above all are your
name and your word.

On the day I called, you answered
me;
you increased the strength of my
soul.

All of earth's rulers shall praise
you
for they have heard the words of
your mouth;
they shall sing of your ways for
great is your glory, O God.
Though you are high, you look on
the lowly
and the haughty you know from
afar.

Though I walk in the midst of
trouble,
you preserve my life;
you stretch out your hand and
save me.
You will fulfill your purpose for
me;
your steadfast love endures
forever.
Do not forsake the work of your
hands. **Glory*...**

Ant. 3 Salvation and glory belong to our God, (alleluia)!

Cant: Rev 4:11, 5:9, 10, 12

Worthy are you, O God, our God,
to receive glory and honor and
power.

For you have created all things;
by your will they came to be and
were made.

Worthy are you to take the scroll
and to open its seals,—

For you were slain, and by your
  blood,
you purchased for God
saints of every race and tongue,
of every people and nation.

You have made of them a kindom,
and priests to serve our God,—

and they shall reign on the earth.

Worthy is the Lamb who was
  slain
to receive power and riches,
wisdom and strength,
honor and glory and praise.
Glory*...

READING

Saint Teresa says prayer is not thinking much but loving much.
Everything becomes simple when we realize that here we are dealing
with what is, first of all, a matter of the heart. It is not then a case of
straining the mind, but simply of uniting our hearts to God.... It seems
to be often [God's] way, however, not to let us see results, and even to
let us be aware of our lack of success; but this can keep us humble. All
the while [God] continues to work within our souls, though in darkness
and in silence.

Mother Aloysius Rogers, OCD, Fragrance from Alabaster, p. 7, (6)

RESPONSORY

In your presence, O God, I will find all my joy.—**In your...**
When I see you face to face; —**I will...**
Glory to you, Source of all Being, Eternal Word and Holy Spirit.
  —**In your...**

CANTICLE OF MARY

Ant. Blessed are the poor in spirit, the reign of God is theirs.

INTERCESSIONS

O God, you have created us free, but our prisons are full;
    —help us to cultivate an environment that inspires life-
      giving choices.
You have created us to choose the good;
    —bless our children that they may know the good and
      pursue it.
You have created us in your image;
    —give us the joy of radiating your goodness, truth, and
      beauty.
Jesus, you experienced the worst of human weakness;
    —grant heroic courage and strength to those who are
      tortured; erase this horror from our world.

You promised to be with us to the end of the world;
—let us never lose hope in you, and help us to trust one
another.

PRAYER: O gracious God, open our hearts and our eyes to the
wonders of your presence among us. May we see the
signs of your beauty within and about us and ever be
in awe of the simple gifts of life. Help us to reach
beyond ourselves and to give thanks for all of your
creation that shares this universe with us: peoples of
every nation, animals of every species, all forms of
vegetation, the planets, stars, and all the elements. We
pray this in union with the incarnate Word of God in
whose image all was created. May you be blessed
throughout the ages and for all eternity. Amen.

WEDNESDAY

MORNING PRAYER

**Ant 1 I will give thanks to you
among the peoples.**

Psalm 108

My heart is steadfast, O God, my
heart is steadfast!
I will sing and make melody!
Awake, my soul!
Awake, lyre and harp!
I will awake the dawn!

I will give thanks to you among
the peoples,
I will sing praises to you among
the nations.
For your steadfast love is great
above the heavens,
your faithfulness reaches to the
clouds.

Be exalted, O God, above the
heavens!
Let your glory be over all the
earth!—

That your beloved may be
delivered,
give help with your hand, and
answer me!

You have promised in your
sanctuary:
"With exultation I will divide up
Shechem,
and portion out the Vale of
Succoth.
Gilead is mine, and Manasseh;
Ephraim is my helmet;
Judah my scepter.
Moab is my washbasin;
upon Edom I cast my shoe;
over Philistia I shout in triumph."

Who will bring me to the fortified
city?
Who will lead me to Edom?
Have you not rejected us, O God?
You no longer go forth with our
armies.—

Give us help against this
oppression,
for human help is vain!
With you, we shall do valiantly;
it is you who will conquer
injustice. **Glory*...**

**Ant. 2 Justice and peace will
spring forth before all nations.**

Cant: Isaiah 61:10–62:5

I will greatly rejoice in you, O
God,
in you my soul shall exult;
for you clothe me with garments
of salvation,
you cover me with the robe of
justice,
like a bridegroom bedecked with
a garland,
like a bride adorned with her
jewels.

As the earth brings forth its
shoots,
and a garden makes its seeds
spring up,
so will you make justice and
praise
to spring forth before all the
nations.

For Zion's sake I will not be
silent,
for Jerusalem's sake I will not
rest,
until its vindication shines forth
like the dawn
and its salvation like a burning
torch.

Nations shall behold its
vindication,
and all rulers see its glory;
it shall be called by a new name—

which your own mouth will give.
It shall be a crown of beauty,
a royal diadem held in your hand,
O God.

No more shall they call it
"Forsaken,"
or its land be termed "Desolate;"
but it shall be called "My delight,"
and its land "Espoused;"
for you, O God, delight in it,
and take it as a spouse.

For as young lovers are espoused,
so shall its children espouse
Zion,
and as newlyweds rejoice in each
other,
so shall you rejoice over Zion.
Glory*...

**Ant. 3 You set us free, O God,
from the chains that bind us.**

Psalm 146

My soul, give praise to my God!
I will praise the Most High as long
as I live;
I will sing praises to my God
while I have being.

Put no trust in sovereigns,
in mortal flesh in whom there is
no help.
When their breath departs they
return to the earth;
on that day their plans perish.

Happy are they whose help is the
Most High,
whose hope is in the Creator of
all,
who alone made heaven and
earth,
the seas, and all that is in them;
who keeps faith forever;—

who executes justice for the
oppressed;
who gives food to the hungry.

For you, O God, set prisoners
free;
you open the eyes of the blind.
You lift up those who are bowed
down;—

you love the upright of heart.
You watch over the sojourners;
uphold the bereaved and the
orphaned.

O God, you will reign forever and
ever,
through all generations.
Glory*...

READING

This prayer is called "recollection," because the soul collects its faculties
together and enters within itself to be with its God.... Those who by
such a method can enclose themselves within this little heaven of our
soul, where the Maker of heaven and earth is present, and grow
accustomed to refusing to be where the exterior senses in their
distraction have gone or look in that direction should believe they are
following an excellent path and that they will not fail to drink water from
the fount; for they will journey far in a short time.

Teresa of Avila, *Way of Perfection*, 28, 4–5, (3)

RESPONSORY

I will sing your praise, O God, every day of my life. **—I will...**
From sunrise to sunset, **—every day...**
Glory to you, Source of all Being, Eternal Word and Holy Spirit.
—I will...

CANTICLE OF ZECHARIAH

Ant. In joy and holiness let us serve God our Savior.

INTERCESSIONS

You invite us to be co-creators with you, O God; work is our
privilege;
 —bless employers with all they need to provide safe and
 satisfying work for people in their service.
You have given us stewardship over the earth;
 —make us all responsible workers in time's "vineyard."
Jesus, you teach us to serve one another and to shun ambitious
pride;
 —help us to realize that our nobility lies in our relationship
 to God, whom you have revealed to us.
You knew loneliness and misunderstanding;

•

—comfort and sustain those who have been betrayed or abandoned.

You came to serve and not to be served;

—let all who are elected to leadership rise to the responsibility of their office and serve with justice and integrity.

PRAYER: See in us, O God, the face of your Christ, and forgive us our sins. Help all who must live with the strain of broken and tense relationships. Give us the courage to love in spite of loss and the mercy to forgive all who have injured us in any way. May our work this day bring us and all the world nearer to the quality of life to which you call us. Grant this through the intercession of the Holy Family and of all the families like them that image your life in the trinity of love. Amen.

DAYTIME PRAYER

Ant. 1 Day and night I hope in your words.

Psalm 119:145-152

With all my heart, I cry to you;
answer me, O God.
I cry to you; save me,
that I may observe your will.

I rise before dawn and cry for
  help;
I hope in your words.
My eyes watch throughout the
  night
meditating on your promises.

Hear my voice in your steadfast
  love;
in your justice preserve my life.
Those who persecute me draw
  near;
they are far from your law.

But you, O God, are near at hand,
all your commands are true.—

Long have I known that your will
endures forever.
  Glory*...

Ant. 2 Do good to those who hate you, bless those who curse you, pray for those who abuse you.

Psalm 94

O God, avenging God,
avenging God, appear!
Judge of the earth, arise,
render injustice its deserts!
How long, O God, shall
  oppression,
how long shall oppression exult?

They bluster with arrogant
  speech,
they boast, all the evildoers.
They crush your people, O God,
they afflict the ones you have
  chosen.—

They kill the helpless and the poor,
and murder the parentless child.
They say: "God does not see;
their God pays no heed!"

Understand, O dullest of people!
Fools, when will you be wise?
Can God who made the ear, not hear?
The one who formed the eye, not see?
Will God who chastens nations, not punish?
God who imparts knowledge knows our thoughts,
knows they are no more than a breath. **Glory*...**

Ant. 3 Judge not, and you will not be judged; condemn not and you will not be condemned.

II

Happy are those whom you chasten,
whom you teach by means of your law
to give them respite from days of trouble,
until oppression is no more.
You will not abandon your people;—

you will not forsake your heritage;
for justice will return to the righteous,
and the upright in heart will follow it.

Who will rise against oppression?
Who will stand against injustice?
If you had not been my help,
I would soon dwell in the land of silence.

When I think: "My foot is slipping,"
your steadfast love upholds me.
When the cares of my heart are many,
your consolations cheer my soul.

Can unjust rulers be your friends,
who do injustice under cover of law?
They attack the life of the helpless,
and condemn the innocent to death.

But you have become my stronghold,
my God, the rock of my refuge.
Injustice will turn on itself,
and evil will destroy evil.
Glory*...

PRAYER: Compassionate God, we pause to rest in your presence. May the work we have begun this day find fulfillment in you for our good and the good of all people on this earth. We ask this is in the name of Jesus who is our way, our truth, and our life. Amen.

EVENING PRAYER

Ant. 1 Behold, I am with you always.

Psalm 139:1-18, 23-24

O God, you have searched me
  and you know me,
you know when I sit and when I
  stand;
you discern my thoughts from
  afar.
You mark when I walk or lie
  down,
with all my ways you are
  acquainted.

Before a word is on my tongue,
behold, O God, you know the
  whole of it.
Behind and before you besiege
  me,
You lay your hand upon me.
Such knowledge is too wonderful
  for me:
too high, beyond my reach.

O where can I go from your spirit,
or where can I flee from your
  presence?
If I climb to heaven, you are
  there!
If I lie in the grave, you are there!

If I take the wings of the morning
and dwell in the depths of the
  sea,
even there your hand shall lead
  me,
your hand shall hold me fast.

If I say: "Let darkness cover me,
and the light around me be
  night,"
even darkness is not dark to
  you—

and the night is as bright as the
  day;
for darkness is as light to you.
  Glory*...

Ant. 2 O God, I praise you for the wonder of my being.

II

For it was you who formed my
  inmost parts,
knit me together in my mother's
  womb.
I praise you for the wonder of my
  being,
for the wonder of all your works.

Already you knew me well;
my body was not hidden from
  you,
when I was being made in secret
and molded in the depths of the
  earth.

Your eyes beheld my unformed
  substance;
in your book they all were
  written,
the days that you had formed for
  me
when none of them yet were.

How precious to me are your
  thoughts!
How vast the sum of them!
If I count them, they are more
  than the sand.
When I awake, I am still with you.

Search me, O God, and know my
  heart!
O test me and know my thoughts!
See that I follow not the wrong
  way
and lead me in the way of life
  eternal. **Glory*...**

Ant. 3 Christ is the firstborn of all creation.

Cant: Colossians 1:12–20

Let us give thanks to God
for having made us worthy
to share the inheritance of the
saints in light.

God has delivered us
from the power of darkness
and transferred us
into the kindom of God's beloved
Son, Jesus,
in whom we have redemption,
the forgiveness of our sins.

Jesus is the image of the invisible
God,
the first-born of all creation;
in him all things were created,—

in heaven and on earth,
things visible and invisible.

All things were created through
him;
all were created for him.
He is before all else that is.
In him all things hold together.

He is the head of the body, the
church!
He is the beginning,
the firstborn from the dead,
that in everything, he might be
above all others.

In him all the fullness of God was
pleased to dwell,
and, through him, to reconcile all
things to himself,
whether on earth or in heaven,
making peace by the blood of his
cross. **Glory*...**

READING

Over and over again, [Rahner] urges simple fidelity to duty and daily
humdrum love.... [His] contemplative approach to the mystery of God in
human experiences can enable us who are convinced that we live in a
world of grace to speak of God in secular terms. His understanding of
the Christian life as a mysticism of everyday faith can free us to seek
and find God not only in times of formal prayer, but also in times of
suffering, celebrations, service, and self-emptying, which we can view as
opportunities for faith. His experience of prayer as surrender of the
heart can help us to concentrate on its fruits, the ways we let go of all
that can keep us from being open to the mystery of God in our lives....

Annice Callahan, RSCJ, *Traditions of Spiritual Guidance*, p. 347 (32)

RESPONSORY

Keep us, O God, on the path to life. **—Keep us...**
May your hand ever guide us **—on the path...**
Glory to you, Source of all Being, Eternal Word and Holy Spirit.
    —Keep us...

CANTICLE OF MARY

Ant. Blessed are they who mourn for they shall be comforted.

INTERCESSIONS

Your justice is governed by mercy, O God;
  —strengthen those whose work exposes them to temptations
    of greed or unjust dealings.
Inspire those who can to give aid to worthy endeavors;
  —let their hundredfold be a deepened awareness of your
    presence in their lives.
Have mercy on abused spouses and children and on those who
abuse them;
  —help us to enable them to begin life anew.
Spirit of God, joy and peace are your gifts to us;
  —bless all who lighten our burden by their thoughtfulness,
    humor, and creativity.
Jesus, you remind us that we cannot serve two masters;
  —give us a single heart that seeks what is good, receiving all
    from God with trust.

PRAYER: O God, look upon the poverty of our hearts with
compassion and love. Enable us to give lovingly and
freely of our possessions and gifts. May those who work
with the poor and needy receive joy in this life and
fullness of life forever. This we ask through the
intercession of all the saints, especially of those whose
legacy of service we carry on today. Grant that we may
be faithful as they were faithful so that we too may live
with you forever. Amen.

THURSDAY

MORNING PRAYER

Ant. 1 In the early morning, O God, I remember your steadfast love.

Psalm 143:1–11

Hear my prayer, O God;
give ear to my supplication!
In your justice and faithfulness
  answer me!—

Do not call your servant to
  judgment
for no one is righteous before
  you.

For evil pursues my soul,
crushing my life to the ground,
making me dwell in darkness
like the dead, long forgotten.—

Therefore my spirit faints within
  me;
my heart within me is appalled.

I remember the days gone before,
I ponder on all you have done;
I muse on what you have
  wrought.
To you I stretch out my hands;
my soul thirsts for you like
  parched land.

O God, make haste to answer me!
My spirit fails within me!
Hide not your face from me,
lest I be like those who go down
  to the grave.

Let me hear in the morning of
  your steadfast love,
for in you I put my trust.
Teach me the way I should go,
for to you I lift up my soul.

Deliver me, O God, from all evil!
I have fled to you for refuge!
Teach me to do your will,
for you are my God!
Let your good spirit lead me
in ways that are level and
  smooth!

For your name's sake, save my
  life!
In your justice bring me out of
  trouble. **Glory*...**

**Ant. 2 I have sheltered you as a
hen shelters her brood!**

Cant.: Isaiah 66:10–14a

"Rejoice with Jerusalem, and be
  glad for her, all you who love
  her;
rejoice with her in joy,
all you who mourn over her;—

that you may suck and be
  satisfied with her consoling
  breasts;
that you may drink deeply with
  delight from the abundance of
  her glory."

For thus says God Most High:
"Behold, I will extend prosperity
  to her like a river,
and the wealth of the nations like
  an overflowing stream.

As nurslings, you shall be carried
  upon her hip,
and fondled on her lap.

As a parent comforts a child,
  so will I comfort you;
you shall be comforted in
  Jerusalem.

You shall see, and your hearts
  shall rejoice;
your beings flourish like the
  grass. **Glory*...**

**Ant. 3 Through you, the blind
  see, the lame walk, and the
  poor hear your good news.**

Psalm 147:1–11

It is good to sing praise to you;
for you are gracious and merciful;
to you our praise is due.

You, O God, build up Jerusalem;
you gather the outcasts of Israel.
You heal the broken-hearted,
and bind up their wounds.
You fix the number of the stars,
and give to each its name.

You are great and almighty,
your wisdom beyond all measure.
For you lift up the poor and
  downtrodden,
you put oppression to rout.

We sing to you with thanksgiving;
make melody upon the lyre!

You cover the heavens with clouds,
you prepare rain for the earth,
make mountains sprout with grass.
You provide beasts with their food,—

and the young ravens that cry.
You delight not in the strength of the horse,
nor take pleasure in human indulgence;
but you delight in those who revere you,
in those who hope in your love.
    Glory*...

READING

Transformation through immersion and consciousness depends on our capacity to be penetrated by the Mystery of Christ. Our being, our substance, must be porous in order for the Mystery to enter, to penetrate. That is the crux of the matter. It is not enough simply to be immersed in...life. We must let ourselves be plowed so that the furrows of our person become deeper and deeper, so that our earth becomes softer and softer. This is something our being craves, but this plowing is *kenosis* [emptying, the death which must precede new life, rebirth] and *kenosis* is not easy. In the measure that our being becomes porous, open, grace can penetrate us. Depth is possible. Transformation is possible. Thus an ever deepening penetration by the Mystery can fill us with spiritual being.

Jean-Marie Howe, "Cistercian Monastic Life/Vows: A Vision," p. 367, (7)

RESPONSORY

O God, you have made of us a priesthood, baptized in the blood of
    Christ. **—O God...**
You send us to all nations; **—baptized...**
Glory to you, Source of all Being, Eternal Word and Holy Spirit.
    —O God...

CANTICLE OF ZECHARIAH

Ant. Send your light and your truth to those who dwell in darkness.

INTERCESSIONS

O God, no one is beyond the reach of your love;
    —help us to appreciate one another as we are, not expecting
        more than we can do or give.

Our culture is heavy with the lure of material gain;
—deliver us from the temptation to use others for our own
profit.
Jesus, your Spirit dwells in our hearts;
—keep us open to the wisdom and gifts of everyone.
Wealthy men and women were among your followers, and they
supported your mission;
—show us how to use whatever we have in keeping with your
gospel.
We have walked on the moon, and technology reaches deeper and
deeper into the galaxies;
—may scientific research deepen our thirst for the wisdom and
knowledge of God.

PRAYER: O God, you call us to be your people and to minister to
one another. Look with pity on all who are held captive
by the bonds of addiction. Free us from our own
destructive impulses that we may choose life and
enable others to find what is life-giving for them. Give
discernment and wisdom to all who minister to those
seeking liberation from any forms of addiction, that we
may all know the joy of the freedom that is ours as
your children. This we ask of you, who are our Mother,
our Father, our Guardian, our God, Creator and
Preserver of us all, both now and in eternity. Amen.

DAYTIME PRAYER

Ant. 1 Give me life according to your justice.

Psalm 119:153-160

Look on my affliction and deliver
me,
for I remember your law.
Plead my cause and redeem me;
give me life according to your
promise!

Salvation is far from the wicked,
for they do not seek your
statutes.—

Great is your mercy, O God;
give me life according to your
justice.

Though my foes and oppressors
are many,
I have not swerved from your will.
I look at evil with disgust,
because it seeks to snare me.

See how I love your precepts!
Preserve my life in your love.
The whole of your word is truth;
your decrees are eternal.
Glory*...

**Ant. 2 Bless the work of our
hands, O God.**

Psalm 128

Blessed are they who fear you, O
  God,
and walk in your ways!

By the labor of their hands they
  shall eat.
A husband will be happy and
  prosper;
a wife like a fruitful vine
  in the heart of her house;
their children like olive shoots
  around their table.

Indeed thus shall be blessed
those who fear you, O God.

May you bless them from Zion
all the days of their lives!
May they see their children's
  children in a happy Jerusalem!
    Glory*...

**Ant. 3 Deliver me for the sake
of your love.**
Psalm 6

O God, rebuke me not for my
  frailties,—

nor chastise me in my weakness.
Be gracious to me for I am
  languishing;
heal me, for my bones are
  troubled.
My soul is sorely troubled.
But you, O God—how long?

Turn, O God, save my life;
deliver me for the sake of your
  love.
For in death there is no
  remembrance of you;
in the grave who can give you
  praise?

I am weary with my moaning;
every night I flood my bed with
  tears;
I drench my couch with my
  weeping.
My eyes waste away because of
  my grief,
they grow weak because of my
  misfortune.

Let this darkness depart from me;
hear the sound of my weeping.
You will hear my supplication;
you will accept my prayer.
    Glory*...

PRAYER: Bountiful God, you nourish us daily with the bread of
life and the bread that is the work of our hands. May
all the peoples and creatures of this earth have the
nourishment they need to live their lives fully. Help us
to solve the problems of food distribution, drought,
expanding deserts, malnutrition, famine, and disease,
that all may share in the banquet and none will be in
want. We ask this through Jesus, our Bread of Life.
Amen.

EVENING PRAYER

Ant. 1 I will sing a new song to you, for you are my refuge.

Psalm 144:1-10

Blessed are you, O God, my rock,
who train my hands for war,
and my fingers for battle.

You are my rock and my fortress,
my stronghold and my deliverer,
my shield in whom I take refuge,
You bring peoples under your
rule.

Who are we that you care for us,
mortal flesh, that you keep us in
mind?
We, who are merely a breath,
whose days are like a passing
shadow.

Lower your heavens and come
down!
Touch the mountains that they
smoke!
Flash your lightnings and scatter
them,
shoot your arrows and put them
to flight.

Stretch forth your hand from on
high,
rescue me from the mighty
waters,
from the hands of alien foes,
whose mouths are filled with lies,
and whose hands are raised in
perjury.

To you will I sing a new song.
On a ten-stringed harp I will play
to you, who give rulers their
victory,
who rescue David, your servant.
Glory*...

Ant. 2 Happy are the people whose God is our God.

II

To you I will sing a new song;
I will play on the ten-stringed
harp,
to you who give rulers their
victory,
who set David your servant free.

You set him free from the evil
sword,
and delivered him from alien foes,
whose mouths were filled with
lies,
whose hands were raised in
perjury.

Let our sons in their youth be like
plants full grown,
our daughters like graceful
columns
adorned as though for a palace.

Let our granaries be full, with
crops of every kind;
may our sheep bring forth
thousands
and ten thousands in our fields;
may our cattle be heavy with
young,
suffering no mischance in
bearing.

May there be no ruined wall, no
exile,
no cry of distress in our streets.
Happy the people with such
blessings!
Happy the people whose God is
our God. **Glory*...**

Ant. 3 Now is the time of salvation for those who revere your name.

Cant: Rev 11: 17–18; 12:10b–12a

We give thanks to you, God
  Almighty,
who is and who was.
You have assumed your great
  power,
you have begun your reign.

The nations raged, but your
  wrath came,
and the time for the dead to be
  judged,
for rewarding your servants, the
  prophets and saints,—

and those who revere your name,
the great and small alike.

Now the salvation, the power and
  the reign have come,
of God and of the Christ,
for the accusers of our loved ones
  have been thrown down,
who accuse them day and night.

They have been conquered by the
  blood of the Lamb,
and by the word of their
  testimony,
for love of life did not deter them
  from death.
Rejoice then, O heavens,
and you that dwell therein!
  Glory*...

READING

If you will it,...observe the light of the divine presence that pervades all existence. Observe the harmony of the heavenly realm, how it pervades every aspect of life, the spiritual and the material, which are before your eyes of flesh and your eyes of the spirit. Contemplate the wonders of creation, the divine dimension of their being, not as a dim configuration that is presented to you from the distance but as the reality in which you live. Know yourself, and your world; know the meditations of your heart, and of every thinker; find the source of your own life, and of the life beyond you, around you, the glorious splendor of the life in which you have your being.

Abraham Isaac Kook, Lights of Holiness, p. 207, (1)

RESPONSORY

You bless the peacemakers, and call them your children.
    —You bless...
You give them your spirit, **—and call...**
Glory to you, Source of all Being, Eternal Word and Holy Spirit.
    —You bless...

CANTICLE OF MARY

Ant. Blessed are the peacemakers, for they shall be called children of God.

INTERCESSIONS

O God, creator of all that is;
  —bless the work of our hands.
Jesus, revelation of God to us;
  —teach us to speak and live the truth.
Holy Spirit, dwelling in our hearts;
  —deepen our love for God and for one another.
Triune God, Eternal Love;
  —bless our families, communities, and the nations of the
    world.
Holy God, Holy Available One;
  —never let us be separated from you.

PRAYER: God of the nations, look upon the lands devastated by war and show us the way to peace. Turn our guns into plows and our bombs into bread. Remove hatred from our hearts and vengeance from our memories. Give us the wisdom and the will to end terrorism and war whether in lands far or near, or in the confines of our families and communities. Help us to remember that we are one world and one family. Grant this through the intercession of all the peacemakers of all times and all places, especially those who suffered persecution and death for the sake of justice and peace. Amen.

FRIDAY

MORNING PRAYER

Ant 1 Remember me, O God, make yourself known in time of affliction.

Psalm 51

Have mercy on me, O God,
according to your steadfast love;
in your abundant mercy blot out
  my sins.
Wash me thoroughly from my
  offenses,
and cleanse me from my sin!

For I know my offenses,
and my sin is ever before me.
Against you, you alone, have I
  sinned,
and done what is evil in your
  sight,
so you are justified in your
  sentence
and blameless in your judgment.
Behold, I was brought forth in a
  sinful world.

For you desire truth in my
innermost being;
teach me wisdom in the depths of
my heart.
O purify me, and I shall be clean;
O wash me, I shall be whiter than
snow.
Fill me with joy and gladness;
let the bones you have broken
rejoice.
Hide your face from my guilt,
and blot out all my offenses.

Create in me a clean heart,
put a steadfast spirit within me.
Cast me not from your presence,
take not your spirit from me.
Give me again the joy of your
salvation,
with a willing spirit uphold me.

Then I will teach transgressors
your ways
and sinners will return to you.
Deliver me from death,
O God of my salvation,
and my tongue will sing out your
saving help.

Open my lips and my mouth will
sing your praises.
For you take no delight in
sacrifice;
were I to give a burnt offering,
you would not be pleased.
A broken spirit you accept;
a contrite heart, you will not
despise.

In your goodness, show favor to
Zion;
rebuild the walls of Jerusalem.
Then you will delight in just
sacrifices,
in gifts offered on your altar.
    Glory*...

**Ant. 2 Your love and your
kindness extend to all the
nations of the earth.**

Cant: Tobit 13:8–11, 13–15

Let all speak of your majesty, O
God,
and sing your praises in
Jerusalem.

O Jerusalem, holy city,
God scourged you for the works
of your hands,
but will again pity the children of
the righteous.

Praise the goodness of God,
and bless the Sovereign of the
ages,
so that the holy tent may be
rebuilt in you with joy.

May God gladden within you all
who were captives;
cherishing within you all who
were ravaged
for all generations to come.

A bright light will shine to all
parts of the earth;
many nations shall come to you
from afar,
and the inhabitants of all the
limits of the earth,
drawn to you by the name of the
Most High God,
bearing in their hands their gifts
for the Almighty.

Every generation shall give joyful
praise to you,
and shall call you the chosen
one,
through all ages forever.

Go, then, rejoice over the children
of the righteous,—

who shall all be gathered together
and shall bless the God of the
ages.

Happy are those who love you,
and happy those who rejoice in
your prosperity.
Happy are they who shall grieve
over you,
over all your chastisements,
for they shall rejoice in you
as they behold your joy forever.

My spirit blesses you, my God.
Glory*...

**Ant. 3 You feed us with the
finest wheat.**

Psalm 147:12-20

O praise the Most High,
Jerusalem!
Praise your God, O Zion!

For God strengthens the bars of
your gates,
blessing your children within
you,—

establishing peace in your
borders,
feeding you with the finest of
wheat.

You send out your word to the
earth;
your command runs swiftly,
giving snow like wool,
scattering hoarfrost like ashes.

You cast forth your ice like
crumbs;
who can stand before your cold?
You send forth your words, and
melt them;
you make the wind blow, and the
waters flow.

You make your word known to
your people,
your statutes and decrees to
Israel.
You have not dealt thus with any
other nation;
you have not taught them your
decrees. **Glory*...**

READING

She [Teresa of Avila] is a guide for the heights, those moments on the
mount of unitive embrace; for the lowlands, when we wonder if we can
ever climb up again; for the plateaus, when we would just as soon set
up a tent and stop moving. In every situation, positive or negative,
Teresa is with us, urging us to see where we are as simply another
starting point for further journeying inward to God. "And if [a] person
should do no more than take one step, the step will contain in itself so
much power that [they] will not have to fear losing it, nor will [they] fail
to be very well paid." (Teresa of Avila, *Way of Perfection*)

Margaret Dorgan, "St. Teresa of Avila: A Guide for Travel Inward," pp. 351-52, (7)

RESPONSORY

O God, freedom is your gift to all, whether rich or poor.
   —O God...
You care for all peoples of the earth, **—whether...**

Glory to you, Source of all Being, Eternal Word and Holy Spirit.
—**O God...**

CANTICLE OF ZECHARIAH

Ant. Heal the wounds of our sins and grant us new life.

INTERCESSIONS

O God, you have planted the seed of your word in our lives;
—let its nourishment be the deciding factor in what we choose
to see and hear.
Faith as small as a mustard seed is enough for us;
—give us an appreciation of what we have, living in your
presence day by day.
We long to be instruments of unity and peace in the world;
—teach us how to support husbands and wives in their efforts
to be faithful; show us ways to make our culture supportive.
Jesus, again and again you assured your followers with a
calming, "Fear not!"
—Grant your peace to those who live in fear for their lives or
dignity, those for whom fear is an abiding reality.
Bless the aging who live alone, with family, or in nursing homes;
—reveal your love for them through those who care for them.

PRAYER: O God, look with mercy on those who are in prison.
Fill their hearts with courage and peace, and let those
who minister to them do so with justice built on
compassion. Free political prisoners, prisoners of
conscience, and all those who are imprisoned unjustly.
Grant this through Jesus who was unjustly condemned
but now lives and reigns with you forever and ever.
Amen.

DAYTIME PRAYER

**Ant. 1 Your word is my
treasure, O God.**

Psalm 119:161–168

Rulers oppress me without cause
but my heart stands in awe of
your words.—

I rejoice in your word
like one who finds great treasure.

I hate and abhor falsehood, but I
love your law.
Seven times a day I praise you for
your just decrees.

Great peace have those who love
your law;
nothing can make them stumble.
I hope for your salvation, O God,
I fulfill your commandments.

My soul obeys your will and loves
it exceedingly.
I obey your precepts and your
will,
for all my ways are before you.
Glory*...

Ant. 2 Let us love one another for love is of God.

Psalm 133

How good and how pleasant it is,
when we live together in unity!

It is like precious oil upon the
head,
running down upon the beard of
Aaron,
running down the collar of his
robes!

It is like the dew of Hermon
which falls on the mountains of
Zion!
For there God gives us the
blessing,
life for evermore. **Glory*...**

Ant. 3 Guard me, O God, from the snares of darkness.

Psalm 140:1–9, 13–14

Rescue me from evil;
preserve me from violence.
Deliver me from an unclean
heart,
from the chaos of a troubled
mind.
Preserve me from a malicious
tongue,
from sharp and poisonous words.

Guard me, O God, from my
darkness,
and from those who lure me to
evil,
who darken my light with gloom.
Pride and arrogance lay a snare;
greed and covetousness spread a
net;
by my pathway they lie in wait.

I say to you: "You are my God."
Give ear to my supplication!
O God, my strong deliverer,
you shield my head in battle.
Grant not the desires of
darkness;
protect me against its snares.

I know you uphold the afflicted,
you effect justice for the needy.
Surely the just shall give thanks
to your name;
the upright shall dwell in your
presence. **Glory*...**

PRAYER: O God, we remember the agonizing death of Jesus. In your compassion deliver those who suffer from the cruelty of others, and heal the minds and hearts of those who inflict pain. Give us a sensitivity to others that is worthy of your children. This we ask through the intercession of all who suffered persecution and death for the sake of others. Amen.

EVENING PRAYER

Ant. 1 Every day I will bless you and praise your name forever.

Psalm 145

I will extol you, O God my God,
and bless your name forever and
  ever.

Every day I will bless you,
and praise your name forever.
For you are great and highly to be
  praised,
your greatness is unsearchable.

Age to age shall proclaim your
  works,
and declare your mighty deeds.
I will ponder your glorious
  splendor,
and the wonder of all your works.

Your people will proclaim the
  might of your deeds,
and I will declare your greatness.
They will pour forth the fame of
  your goodness,
and sing with joy of your justice.

You are gracious and merciful,
slow to anger, abounding in love.
Your compassion extends to all
  you have made;
how good you are to all!

All your works shall give you
  thanks;
all your friends shall bless you!
They shall speak of the glory of
  your creation,
and declare your marvelous
  might,
to make known to the children of
  earth the glory of your deeds,
and the glorious splendor of all
  you have made.

Yours is an everlasting realm,
and your dominion endures
  through all generations.
  Glory*...

Ant. 2 You are near to all who call to you with sincere and upright hearts.

II

O God, you are faithful in all your
  words,
and gracious in all your deeds.
You uphold all who are falling,
and raise up all who are bowed
  down.

The eyes of all creatures look to
  you,
to give them their food in due
  season.
You open wide your hand,
and satisfy the desires of every
  living thing.

You are just in all your ways,
and loving in all your deeds.
You are near to all who call on
  you,
who call on you from their hearts.

You fulfill the desires of those
  who revere you,
you hear their cries and save
  them.
You protect all who love you, O
  God;
but evil you will utterly destroy.

Let me speak your praises, O
  God,
let all humankind bless your
  name forever,
for ages unending.   **Glory*...**

Ant. 3 **Your works, O God, are great and wonderful.**

Cant: Rev 15:3–4

Great and wonderful are your
  works,
God the Almighty One!
Just and true are your ways,
Ruler of all the ages!

Who shall refuse you honor,
or the glory due your name?

For you alone are holy,
  all nations shall come and
    worship in your presence.
Your judgments are clearly seen.
Glory*...

READING

Nowadays I always feel transported into Napoleonic times, and I can
imagine in what tension people lived then everywhere in Europe. I
wonder: will we live to see the events of our days become "history"? I
have a great desire to see all this sometime in the light of eternity. For
one realizes ever more clearly how blind we are toward everything. One
marvels at how mistakenly one viewed a lot of things before, and yet the
very next moment one commits the blunder again of forming an opinion
without having the necessary basis for it.

Edith Stein: Self-Portrait in Letters, p. 315, (3)

RESPONSORY

Your ways are mysterious, O God, but your love is our light.
  —Your ways...
Your Word became flesh; **—your love...**
Glory to you, Source of all Being, Eternal Word and Holy Spirit.
  —Your ways...

CANTICLE OF MARY

Ant. **Guide us in your truth lest we go astray.**

INTERCESSIONS

O God, you adorn the earth with the beauty of each season;
  —awaken us to your loving care as you lift up our hearts
    with color and surprise.
You share your life with us through the talents you give us;
  —make us worthy stewards, eager to grow, mindful of our
    use of time.
Your Spirit dwells in our hearts, the very power of your love;
  —let us remember that you are at work in us, never asking
    what is beyond our power.

Lord Jesus, teach us to pray as you taught your apostles;
—show us how to live quietly and to know how to
distinguish want from need.
Heart of Jesus, once in agony,
—have pity on the dying.

PRAYER: God, source of all life, have pity on the dying and on
those who mourn. Help them to experience this
transition as a birth to new life; this loss in time as a
realization of eternity. Ease their pain and grant them
your peace which Jesus proclaimed after that first
Good Friday. We ask this in his name. Amen.

SATURDAY

MORNING PRAYER

Ant. 1 We proclaim your love in the morning and your faithfulness at night.

Psalm 92

It is good to give thanks to you, O God,
to sing praise to your name, O Most High,
to proclaim your love in the morning,
and your faithfulness by night,
to the music of the lute and the harp,
to the melody of the lyre.

For you make me glad by your deeds;
at the work of your hands I sing for joy.
O God, how great are your works!
Your thoughts are very deep!

The foolish ones cannot know this,
and the dull cannot understand:
though wickedness sprouts like grass—

and evil seems to flourish,
they are doomed to destruction forever.
But you are forever on high.

You exalt my strength like that of the ox;
you pour over me fresh oil.
My eyes looked in triumph over evil,
my ears heard the doom of oppression.

The just will flourish like the palm tree
and grow like a cedar of Lebanon.
They are planted in your holy house,
they flourish in your courts, O God.
They still bring forth fruit in old age,
they are ever full of sap and green,
to show that you are just;
you are my rock, in you is no injustice. **Glory*...**

Ant. 2 Give us hearts of flesh, O God, that we may serve you.

Cant: Ezekiel 36:24–28

I will take you from the nations,
and gather you from foreign
   countries,
and bring you back to your own
   land.

I will sprinkle clean water upon
   you
to cleanse you from all your
   impurities,
and from all your idols I will
   cleanse you.

A new heart I will give you,
and a new spirit I will put within
   you;
and I will take out of your body
   the heart of stone
and give you a heart of flesh.

I will put my spirit within you,
and make you live by my
   statutes,
careful to observe my decrees.

You shall dwell in the land which
   I gave to your ancestors;
you shall be my people,
and I will be your God.

   Glory*...

Ant. 3 Your name is great in all the earth.

Psalm 8

How great is your name, O God,
   in all the earth!

You, whose glory above the
   heavens
is chanted on the lips of babes,
have found a defense against
   your foes,
to silence the cries of the rebels.

When I look at the heavens,
the work of your hands,
the moon and the stars which
   you established;
who are we that you should keep
   us in mind,
mortal flesh that you care for us?

Yet you have made us little less
   than God,
and crowned us with glory and
   honor.
You entrust us with the works of
   your hands;
to care for all your creation.

All sheep and oxen,
and even the beasts of the field,
the birds of the air, and the fish
   of the sea,
whatever passes along the paths
   of the sea.

How great is your name, Creator
   God, in all the earth!   **Glory*...**

READING

In order for thanksgiving and the voice of praise, which are one and the same, to be found in your soul, you must rejoice and be glad in the [One] who created it, and then from joy and gladness proceed to the thanksgiving of which we speak and which is so perfect that for good reason Our Lady is said to have invented the manner of speech used by all religious when they say *Deo gratias,* which means "let us give thanks to God."

Francisco de Osuna, *The Third Spiritual Alphabet,* p. 72, (1)

RESPONSORY

O God, you are father and mother to us; your love never ceases.
   —O God,...
We have sinned against you; **—your love...**
Glory to you, Source of all Being, Eternal Word and Holy Spirit.
   —O God,...

CANTICLE OF ZECHARIAH

Ant. Fill our days with peace that we may sing your praise.

INTERCESSIONS

O God, time often leaves us longing for more, for we are created
for eternity;
   —help us to find you within, where time and eternity are more
      clearly one.
Your commandments are guides for our way to fullness of life;
   —remind us that law follows life.
Our short lives are a history of your gifts to us;
   —may all that we do give you thanks and praise.
You are ever present to us in our need;
   —let us never be indifferent to the suffering of others.
Spirit of God, our advocate and guide;
   —teach us how to be an effective voice for the powerless.

PRAYER: O God, your love is truth, yet we so often fear you.
         You regard us with mercy, yet we see you as judge.
         Open our eyes to your goodness and let us realize the
         life to which we are called. We ask this through the
         intercession of Mary, mother of Jesus, who knew and
         proclaimed your goodness to all generations. Amen.

DAYTIME PRAYER

Ant. 1 I delight in your law; teach me discernment according to your will.

Psalm 119:169–176

Let my cry come before you, O God;—

give me discernment according to your word.
Let my supplication come before you;
deliver me as you have promised.

My lips will pour forth praise because you teach me your commands.—

My tongue will sing of your
promise,
for all your commands are just.

Let your hand be ready to help
me,
for I have chosen your precepts.
I long for your saving help
and your law is my delight.

Let me live, that I may praise you,
and let your precepts help me.
I have gone astray like a lost
sheep;
seek your servant, for I do not
forget your commands.
Glory*...

**Ant. 2 Listen to my prayer, O
God.**

Psalm 61

Hear my cry, O God,
listen to my prayer;
from the end of the earth I call,
when my heart is faint.

Set me on the rock that is higher
than I;
for you are my refuge,
my stronghold against evil.

Let me dwell in your tent forever!
Hide me in the shelter of your
wings!
For you, O God, have heard my
vows,
you have given me the heritage
of those who love your name.

May you lengthen the lives of just
rulers:
may their years cover many
generations!
May they ever be enthroned
before you;
bid love and truth watch over
them.

So will I ever sing your praises,
as I pay my vows day after day.
Glory*...

**Ant. 3 The needy fly to you for
refuge.**

Psalm 64

Hear my voice, O God, in my
complaint;
preserve my life from all that is
evil,
hide me from the tempter's snare,
from the scheming wiles of my
heart.

Evil sharpens its tongue like a
sword;
aiming bitter words like arrows
shooting from ambush at the
innocent,
shooting suddenly and without
fear.

Holding fast to its evil purpose;
conspiring to lay secret snares
thinking: "Who can see us?
Who can search out our crimes?"

But you know well our inmost
thoughts,
the depth of the heart and mind!
You will shoot your arrow at
them;
they will be wounded suddenly.
Our own tongues bring us to
ruin.

Then let all people fear;
they will tell what you have
wrought,
and ponder what you have done.
The just will rejoice in you, O
God,
and fly to you for refuge.
Let the upright in heart exult.
Glory*...

PRAYER: Deliver us, O God, from those who would hurt us and from our own selfishness. Guard us from all that would prevent our growth, and let us not be stumbling blocks to others. We ask this in the name of Jesus who is our way, our truth and our life. Amen.

INVITATORY

Psalm 95

O come, let us sing to our God;
let us make a joyful noise to the rock
   of our salvation!

We come into your presence with thanksgiving,
rejoicing with songs of praise!
For you, O God, are our God,
a great Ruler over all other gods.
In your hands are the depths of the earth;
the heights of the mountains as well.
The sea is yours, for you made it;
and your hands formed the dry land.

We bow down before you and worship,
kneeling before you, our Maker!
For you are our God, and we are your people,
the flock that you shepherd.

Today let us hearken to your voice:
"Harden not your hearts, as at Meribah,
as on the day at Massah in the desert,
when your ancestors tested me,
and put me to the test,
though they had seen my works."
  Glory...

FIRST SUNDAY OF ADVENT
(Psalms from Sunday, Week I, p. 1)

EVENING PRAYER I

Ant 1 Behold I bring you glad tidings; our God and Savior is coming.

Ant 2 Our God is coming, bringing salvation to all. Let us rejoice! Alleluia.

Ant 3 God will come, the Holy One of Israel.

READING

"Are you he who is to come [the Messiah], or shall we look for another?" (Mt. 11:3). Are you the one I am supposed to proclaim, the long-awaited of the ages? John's puzzlement is a rough lesson for our Advent waiting. It is not always easy to recognize Christ. He comes in unexpected ways, ways you and I are not prepared for. If you were living in Palestine at Christ's first coming, and some prophet told you the Messiah would be coming soon, would you have looked for a baby wrapped in straw? Would you have looked for him on a cross? Would you have expected him to come to you looking like bread, tasting like bread?

Walter J. Burghardt, SJ, *Still Proclaiming Your Wonders*, pp. 21–22, (1)

RESPONSORY

O God, guide us into the way of peace and love. **—O God...**
And give light to our darkness; **—into...**
Glory to you, Source of all Being, Eternal Word and Holy Spirit.
    —O God...

CANTICLE OF MARY

Ant The favors of God I will sing forever; through all generations my mouth shall proclaim your faithfulness.

INTERCESSIONS

In anticipation of your promise, O God, we pray:
    Drop down dew, you heavens from above;
    let the clouds rain down the Just One.

Gentle God, you satisfy our thirsty hearts;
    —may we respond to the needs of those thirsting for justice.
Loving God, you give us bread for our table and bread for our spirit;

—may we share our bread generously; may it never be used as
a weapon in the hands of the powerful.
Peaceful God, you desire harmony for us;
—may we be free from our selfish and defensive ways.
Comforting God, you give sight to the blind;
—may we see with new eyes your life in our midst.
Liberating God, you set the captives free;
—may we support those people who are imprisoned for the sake
of justice.

PRAYER: We wait for you, most gracious God, for eye has not
seen and ear has not heard the wonders of your deeds.
In gratitude we thank you for the gift of Jesus to our
world. Grant us the eyes to see beyond our limited
vision and the ears to hear the joy of your message. We
thank you for being one with us in your covenant of
love. Amen.

MORNING PRAYER

Ant 1 On that day, the Most High will bring forth power and
glory and the fruit of the earth will be the splendor of
Israel.

Ant 2 God will show mercy to a nation endangered by war and
division.

Ant 3 There shall be everlasting joy for those who keep faith.

READING

You know what time it is, how it is now the moment for you to wake
from sleep. For salvation is nearer to us now than when we became
believers; the night is far gone, the day is near. Let us then lay aside the
works of darkness and put on the armor of light....

Rom 13:11–12

RESPONSORY

Behold the Lamb of God, who comes to bring us salvation. **—Behold**...
Clothed in a mantle of justice; **—who**...
Glory to you, Source of all Being, Eternal Word and Holy Spirit.
—Behold...

CANTICLE OF ZECHARIAH

Ant You will have joy and gladness, and many will rejoice at the savior's birth.

INTERCESSIONS

In hope we have waited for your coming, O Jesus; in confidence we pray:

Most Holy One, bring us your salvation!

Strengthen our hearts and hands;
—help us to appreciate the wonder of birth and bless the wombs of all expectant mothers.
Open our eyes to your ways;
—assist us to see beyond the borders of our vision and to cut through the prejudices that keep us in isolation.
Release us from bondage;
—may we be ready to free ourselves and others from the oppression that keeps us in slavery.
Loosen our tongues to sing your praise;
—may we proclaim your message in the way we speak to and treat one another.
Free our ears to hear your word;
—grant us a readiness to listen attentively to your voice, and assist all pastoral ministers to bear witness to your word among the poor.

PRAYER: We wait for you, most gracious God, for eye has not seen and ear has not heard the wonders of your deeds. In gratitude we thank you for the gift of Jesus to our world. Grant us the eyes to see beyond our limited vision and the ears to hear the joy of your message. We thank you for being one with us in your covenant of love. Amen.

DAYTIME PRAYER

Ant 1 Comfort, comfort my people, says our God.

Ant 2 Every valley shall be lifted up, and every mountain shall be made low, and the glory of God shall be revealed.

Ant 3 The grass withers, the flower fades; but the word of our God will live forever.

(Prayer as in Morning Prayer)

EVENING PRAYER II

Ant 1 Rejoice, nations of the earth; our God comes, alleluia.

Ant 2 Jesus Christ will come to us, taking away our sins.

Ant 3 Do not lose heart, says our God; soon you will walk in my light, alleluia.

READING

The days are surely coming, says [our God], when I will fulfill the promise I made to the house of Israel and the house of Judah. In those days and at that time I will cause a righteous Branch to spring up for David; and he shall execute justice and righteousness in the land. In those days Judah will be saved and Jerusalem will live in safety. And this is the name by which it will be called: "The [Most High God] is our righteousness."

Jer 33:14–16

RESPONSORY

Show us, O God, your steadfast love, and grant us your salvation.
    —Show us...
Restore us again that we may rejoice, **—and grant...**
Glory to you, Source of all Being, Eternal Word and Holy Spirit.
    —Show us...

CANTICLE OF MARY

Ant Hail Mary full of grace, our God is with you, alleluia.

INTERCESSIONS

Jesus, you are the one born of Mary, and in joy we pray with eager hearts:
    Maranatha! Come, Lord Jesus!

You, Jesus, are our savior;
    —may we proclaim your message willingly and participate in bringing about your reign in our world.
You are the fountain of living water;
    —be with all peoples who are preparing to receive baptism.

You are the Holy One of Israel;
  —grant shelter to the homeless, especially children, who need
  food, care, and companionship.
You are hope in our weariness;
  —free us from our selfishness and give courage to all children
  and adults who are handicapped.

PRAYER: We wait for you, most gracious God, for eye has not
seen and ear has not heard the wonders of your deeds.
In gratitude we thank you for the gift of Jesus to our
world. Grant us the eyes to see beyond our limited
vision and the ears to hear the joy of your message. We
thank you for being one with us in your covenant of
love. Amen.

FIRST MONDAY OF ADVENT
(Psalms and antiphons from Week I, p. 10)
MORNING PRAYER
READING

Think often of our Lady of the Incarnation and of the reverent, silent
love with which she listened to the Divine Word as she awaited the
moment when He would reveal Himself to her human gaze. This same
Divine Word dwells within our soul, and with Him the overshadowing
Spirit that formed His Sacred Humanity within our Lady.

Mother Aloysius Rogers, OCD, *Fragrance from Alabaster*, p. 1, (6)

RESPONSORY

Sing to God a new song, give praise from the ends of the earth.
  —Sing to...
Mountains and deserts rejoice; **—give**...
Glory to you, Source of all Being, Eternal Word and Holy Spirit.
  —Sing to...

CANTICLE OF ZECHARIAH

Ant Look up, Jerusalem, and see the power of your God; your
savior comes to free you.

INTERCESSIONS

O God, you share your life with us in the mystery of the Word
Incarnate. In joy, let us pray:
Come, hope of all peoples!

In your light, Christ Jesus, we can walk in freedom;
  —may we follow your way of truth without counting the cost.
Our hearts are open to receive you;
  —enable us to be compassionate in working with one another.
You come as a fragile child;
  —empower religious leaders to respond effectively from the
    experience of their personal vulnerability.
Teach us your law of love and mercy;
  —assist all missionaries in their efforts to give birth to your
    love.

PRAYER: O Giver of Peace, you invite us to beat our swords into
plowshares and our spears into pruning hooks. Enable
us to translate your message into our daily living and
to be people of peace and nonviolence. Grant this
request in the name of Jesus who comes to be peace
with us. Amen.

DAYTIME PRAYER

Ant 1 Comfort, comfort my people, says our God.

Ant 2 Every valley shall be lifted up, and every mountain shall be
made low, and the glory of God shall be revealed.

Ant 3 The grass withers, the flower fades; but the word of our
God will live forever.

(Prayer as in Morning Prayer)

EVENING PRAYER

READING

Advent is always a new beginning. It is actually a beginning and an
ending. We are beginning a new life with Christ at the center, a life that
is full with Christ. We are leading and ending an old life. This must be
so. There must be this movement.... We need to relinquish and empty
ourselves, so that the newness Christ brings can enter and have a place
to stay. We as Advent pilgrims on the way to the manger—to the great
newness that the child brings—must allow ourselves to pass through
the desert where John is preaching.

                              Paul H. Harkness, "Our Journey to the Cradle," (4)

RESPONSORY

Come to deliver us, gentle and loving God; — **Come...**
Turn your face to us and save us; —**gentle**...
Glory to you, Source of all Being, Eternal Word and Holy Spirit.
   — **Come**...

CANTICLE OF MARY

Ant Gabriel announced God's favor to Mary, and she conceived
   by the power of the Spirit of God.

INTERCESSIONS

In you, O God, we rejoice, for you invite us to new heights and to
climb your holy mountain. In joy we proclaim:
   Let us walk in your light, O God!

You are our refuge in time of need;
   —protect the homeless and give refuge to those who leave their
   homelands to find peace.
You are our shade in the heat of the day;
   —give hope to the elderly so that they may experience fullness
   in their years of apparent diminishment.
You are a light to guide us on our journey;
   —may your people find meaning in their youthful years, and a
   desire to create a peaceful future.
You are our shelter from storm and rain;
   —grant us the insight to see your provident care in all our
   struggles.
You are the source of our peace;
   —may all who die today experience peace in your light.

PRAYER: O Giver of Peace, you invite us to beat our swords into
            plowshares and our spears into pruning hooks. Enable
            us to translate your message into our daily living and
            to be people of peace and nonviolence. Grant this
            request in the name of Jesus who comes to be peace
            with us. Amen.

FIRST TUESDAY OF ADVENT
(Psalms and antiphons from Week I, p. 16)

MORNING PRAYER

READING

[Faith] brings us to believe divinely revealed truths that transcend every
natural light and infinitely exceed all human understanding. As a result
the excessive light of faith bestowed on [one] is darkness...; a brighter
light will eclipse and suppress a dimmer one. The sun so obscures all
other lights that they do not seem to be lights at all when it is shining,
and instead of affording vision to the eyes it overwhelms, blinds, and
deprives them of vision. ...Similarly, the light of faith in its abundance
suppresses and overwhelms that of the intellect. For the intellect, by its
own power, extends only to natural knowledge....

John of the Cross, *The Ascent of Mt. Carmel*, II. 3, 1, (3)

RESPONSORY

Sing to God a new song, give praise from the ends of the earth.
  —Sing to...
Mountains and deserts rejoice; **—give**...
Glory to you, Source of all Being, Eternal Word and Holy Spirit.
  —Sing to...

CANTICLE OF ZECHARIAH

Ant There shall come forth a shoot from the stump of Jesse, and
    God's delight will fill the earth.

INTERCESSIONS

O Giver of all gifts, you continue to reveal your goodness to us
and in faith we pray:
         May your spirit rest gently upon us!

O Spirit of Wisdom, you give us insight;
  —grant all people the wisdom to choose effective ways to
    develop their human potential through their respective
    governments.
O Spirit of Understanding, you show us mercy;
  —help us to reach out in compassion to one another.
O Spirit of Counsel and of Strength, you give us courage;
  —may we be open to your loving challenges and strengthened in
    our desire to be of service.

O Spirit of Knowledge, you instruct us in your ways;
—assist us to know ourselves and to be open to your
continuous revelation in our midst.

PRAYER: O God of Compassion, you come to be with us in our
humanity. Enable us to move beyond our stagnant
places to embrace your life giving waters of new birth.
We ask you to bless us in the name of the Eternal
Word, who was, who is, and who will always be. Amen.

DAYTIME PRAYER

Ant 1 Comfort, comfort my people, says our God.

Ant 2 Every valley shall be lifted up, and every mountain shall be
made low, and the glory of God shall be revealed.

Ant 3 The grass withers, the flower fades; but the word of our
God will live forever.

(Prayer as in Morning Prayer)

EVENING PRAYER

READING

Our Lord shows us both the difficulty of the way and the reward of the
labor. "I am the way, the truth and the life" (Jn 14:6). The way, he says,
is humility, which leads to truth. The first is labor; the second is the
reward for the labor (1 Cor 3:8). But, you ask, how do I know that he is
speaking of humility when he says only, "I am the way"? Listen to this
clearer statement, "Learn from me, for I am meek and humble of heart"
(Mt 11:29). He offers himself as an example of humility, a model of
gentleness. If you imitate him you will not walk in darkness; you will
have the light of life (Jn 8:12).

Bernard of Clairvaux, *On Humility and Pride*, p. 102, (1)

RESPONSORY

Come to deliver us, gentle and loving God; — **Come...**
Turn your face to us and save us; —**gentle**...
Glory to you, Source of all Being, Eternal Word and Holy Spirit.
— **Come...**

CANTICLE OF MARY

Ant Jesus said to his disciples: Blessed are the eyes that see what you see!

INTERCESSIONS

O God of Love, hear the cry of the poor; listen to us as we pray:
Come and save your people!

O God, you invite us to work in the vineyard;
  —may all peoples know the true dignity of work.
You call us to serve one another in love;
  —may we be open to hear the needs of those around us.
You give us the image of peace, the wolf as a guest of the lamb;
  —grant us the courage to work for peace and to support all
    peacemakers.
You love justice and are close to the afflicted;
  —assist all women and men in their search for just institutional
    structures.

PRAYER: O God of Compassion, you come to be with us in our humanity. Enable us to move beyond our stagnant places to embrace your life giving waters of new birth. We ask you to bless us in the name of the Eternal Word, who was, who is, and who will always be. Amen.

FIRST WEDNESDAY OF ADVENT
(Psalms and antiphons from Week I, p. 23)
MORNING PRAYER

READING

Since serving the child Jesus did not hinder the Virgin Our Lady, nor did his presence so distract her that her memory was scattered or she was pulled out of recollection in God, which state was more perfect in her than in any holy person, it follows that the most blessed Humanity of Our Lord does not obstruct the soul's lofty recollection in God.

Francisco de Osuna, *The Third Spiritual Alphabet*, p. 39, (1)

RESPONSORY

Sing to God a new song, give praise from the ends of the earth.
  —Sing to...

Mountains and deserts rejoice; —**give**...
Glory to you, Source of all Being, Eternal Word and Holy Spirit.
   —**Sing to**...

CANTICLE OF ZECHARIAH

Ant This is our God, for whom we have waited; let us rejoice in
   our salvation.

INTERCESSIONS

God of our salvation, you come bringing us nourishment and joy
and we exclaim:
   Jesus, you are the joy of our salvation!

Jesus, you are the light in our darkness;
   —may we see meaning in our struggles.
You bring bread to feed us;
   —assist us to move beyond our selfish desires and to be a
   leaven for others.
In healing and forgiveness you wipe away our tears;
   —help us to be a sign of healing within the brokenness around
   us.
You made this earth your home;
   —enlighten us to discover creative ways for preserving and
   renewing our environment.
You taught us to have a deep respect for life;
   —be with all expectant parents and enable them to bring forth
   life.

PRAYER: Most compassionate God, you share your life with us
   in Jesus, who brings us light, healing and salvation.
   We are grateful for being invited to the eternal banquet.
   May we share generously the life we have received in
   your holy name. Amen.

DAYTIME PRAYER

Ant 1 Comfort, comfort my people, says our God.

Ant 2 Every valley shall be lifted up, and every mountain shall be
   made low, and the glory of God shall be revealed.

Ant 3 The grass withers, the flower fades; but the word of our
God will live forever.

(Prayer as in Morning Prayer)

EVENING PRAYER

READING

...if we say that we are believers in the One Sent, professing that Jesus
comes to liberate us from the worst of our human condition, then our
search for meaning and fulfillment is over. To paraphrase a popular
song, "The search is over. You were with us all the while." The Good
News is that God's seal has been set upon Jesus Christ. We must fasten
our eyes on him alone, for in him God has spoken and revealed all, and
in him we will discover even more than we ask for or desire.

Carmelites of Indianapolis, Hidden Friends, p. 71, (5)

RESPONSORY

Come to deliver us, gentle and loving God; — **Come...**
Turn your face to us and save us; —**gentle**...
Glory to you, Source of all Being, Eternal Word and Holy Spirit.
  — **Come...**

CANTICLE OF MARY

Ant Great crowds came to Jesus and he healed them; all were
filled with awe and glorified God.

INTERCESSIONS

You, O God, are a loving father and mother as you share your life,
your table, and your inheritance with us. In gratitude we pray:
Show us the way, O God!

You promise us a banquet of choice food;
  —may all people find the food they need this day.
You give us guidance in your compassionate understanding;
  —assist us to discern faithfully your word for us.
You invite us to choose freely the way we use our gifts and the
fruits of the earth;
    —help us to allow our sisters and brothers the opportunity to
    live in your freedom and love.
You are a God of hospitality and you welcome us to share in your
inheritance;

—enable us to be faithful to your invitation to growth, freedom, and love.

PRAYER: Most compassionate God, you share your life with us in Jesus, who brings us light, healing and salvation. We are grateful for being invited to the eternal banquet. May we share generously the life we have received in your holy name. Amen.

FIRST THURSDAY OF ADVENT
(Psalms and antiphons from Week I, p. 29)
MORNING PRAYER

READING

The celebration of the Word made flesh, is also the celebration of all women and men who have incarnated the message of Jesus in their lives. We tell the stories of prophets, liberators, and martyrs of not so long ago whose lives challenge us to hold to our commitment to God and to be open to the Spirit who frees us from the bondage of our addictions and fears. Remembering Jesus, we make him a part of our lives. Remembering those who have followed him unites us with them.

Elizabeth Meluch, OCD, (11)

RESPONSORY

Sing to God a new song, give praise from the ends of the earth.
   —Sing to...
Mountains and deserts rejoice; **—give**...
Glory to you, Source of all Being, Eternal Word and Holy Spirit.
   —Sing to...

CANTICLE OF ZECHARIAH

Ant Trust in God forever, for God is an everlasting rock.

INTERCESSIONS

O God of Goodness, you invite us to a covenant of peace and love. In faith we pray:
Show us your kindness forever!

O God, you call us to be one in you;
   —give us the grace to live in your love.
You walk among us in the poor and lonely;
   —help us to serve you in our sisters and brothers.

You bless the Church with the gift of your Spirit;
  —may we place our gifts at the service of all.
You are our messenger of light;
  —assist us with the courage to share our faith life with one
    another.

PRAYER: O God of peace, you weave your way through our
            hearts to share with us your covenantal love. May we
            broaden our understanding of being peacemakers in
            our world today. Grant this in the name of Jesus whose
            birth heralded peace on earth. Amen.

DAYTIME PRAYER

Ant 1 Comfort, comfort my people, says our God.

Ant 2 Every valley shall be lifted up, and every mountain shall be
           made low, and the glory of God shall be revealed.

Ant 3 The grass withers, the flower fades; but the word of our
           God will live forever.

(Prayer as in Morning Prayer)

EVENING PRAYER

READING

Capacity for love is perhaps the only indispensable natural foundation
for holiness. I must possess the power and impetus, the wings of the
soul, to forget myself for another's sake, to prize another more than
myself, to face fear and pain for another, and to risk my life. Friendship
with God depends on this.

William McNamara, OCD, *Mystical Passion*, p. 44, (1)

RESPONSORY

Come to deliver us, gentle and loving God; — **Come...**
Turn your face to us and save us; —**gentle**...
Glory to you, Source of all Being, Eternal Word and Holy Spirit.
  — **Come**...

CANTICLE OF MARY

Ant Those who hear my words are like one whose house is built
         on rock.

INTERCESSIONS

Christ, you are the Light that the darkness cannot overcome; in confidence we pray:

Come, Light of Life!

You were present at the creation of the world;
—by your coming as one of us renew the earth.
You who dwell in the heart of God;
—come and teach us the love of God.
John the Baptist was imprisoned for the cause of truth;
—free those imprisoned for the sake of your name.
You are always attentive to us in our every need;
—help us to comfort the poor by our loving efforts.

PRAYER: O God of peace, you weave your way through our hearts to share with us your covenantal love. May we broaden our understanding of being peacemakers in our world today. Grant this in the name of Jesus whose birth heralded peace on earth. Amen.

FIRST FRIDAY OF ADVENT
(Psalms and antiphons from Week I, p. 36)
MORNING PRAYER

READING

The scriptures frequently present sinfulness in terms of blindness, and redemption in terms of seeing. In this context Isaiah wrote, "Out of gloom and darkness the eyes of the blind will see." Because of the coming of Jesus Christ we live in the age of redemption. In baptism our eyes were opened to see the Lord in faith. But do we keep our eyes open? God is present for us to see everywhere, especially in people.... Every human person has something of the goodness of God within.... What a shame it is to close our eyes to God's presence, to live in darkness and gloom, when all we have to do is open our eyes in faith to see....

Charles E. Miller, CM and John A. Grindel, CM, *Until He Comes*, p. 18, (17)

RESPONSORY

Sing to God a new song, give praise from the ends of the earth.
—**Sing to**...

Mountains and deserts rejoice; —**give**...
Glory to you, Source of all Being, Eternal Word and Holy Spirit.
   —**Sing to**...

CANTICLE OF ZECHARIAH

Ant When the reign of God appears, the deaf shall hear, the blind
   shall see, and the poor shall rejoice.

INTERCESSIONS

Gracious Spirit, you share with us your life and light; in trust we
say:
                    Have mercy on us!

Christ, you gave us the commandment to love one another;
   —help us to live in this covenant of love.
You send your Spirit of hope into our hearts;
   —may our lives be signs of hope for others.
Give world leaders the wisdom to work for justice;
   —that peace may become a reality for all people.
We await the celebration of Christ's birth;
   —may every family experience joy and harmony.

PRAYER: O loving God, you remind us that living in faith is a
         special gift. Increase our faith in you so that we may
         open ourselves to the mystery of your love in our lives.
         We ask this in the name of Jesus, who lives and reigns
         with you and with the Holy Spirit forever. Amen.

DAYTIME PRAYER

Ant 1 Comfort, comfort my people, says our God.

Ant 2 Every valley shall be lifted up, and every mountain shall be
   made low, and the glory of God shall be revealed.

Ant 3 The grass withers, the flower fades; but the word of our
   God will live forever.

(Prayer as in Morning Prayer)

EVENING PRAYER

READING

God has favored us by giving us faith in Jesus. This gift, however, is not to be hoarded as if it were too precious to be shared with others. Faith is different from material things. If you give someone money, you necessarily have less yourself. If you give someone your faith, you not only do not have less, you actually have more. In fact, to grow in our Christian life we must share with others this most precious gift from God. We associate with people every day who do not enjoy our gift of faith. While we must respect their own personal convictions, we should never be reluctant to try to draw them to full faith in Jesus Christ by our words, our good example, our interest, our own obvious sense of conviction and dedication.

Charles E. Miller, CM and John A. Grindel, CM, *Until He Comes*, p. 22, (17)

RESPONSORY

Come to deliver us, gentle and loving God; — **Come...**
Turn your face to us and save us; —**gentle**...
Glory to you, Source of all Being, Eternal Word and Holy Spirit.
　— **Come**...

CANTICLE OF MARY

Ant　Jesus cured the blind, saying: According to your faith, be
　　healed.

INTERCESSIONS

We rejoice in you, the God of our salvation; you call our blindness to sight and our deafness to hearing. In joy we proclaim:
Hear our prayer, O God!

God of Love, you invite us to trust in your saving mercy;
　—help us to be confident of your continuous love for us,
　　especially in times of doubt and distress.
God of Light, increase our vision;
　—help us to see the beauty around us and to celebrate it each
　　day.
God of Wonders, you come to us in simplicity;
　—enable us to be content with our basic needs.
God of Joy, increase our openness to celebrating life;
　—may all children experience acceptance, love, and care.

PRAYER: O loving God, you remind us that living in faith is a special gift. Increase our faith in you so that we may open ourselves to the mystery of your love in our lives. We ask this in the name of Jesus, who lives and reigns with you and with the Holy Spirit forever. Amen.

FIRST SATURDAY OF ADVENT
(Psalms and antiphons from Week I, p. 43)
MORNING PRAYER
READING

Be generous in cooperating with God, whatever the moments hold of things pleasant or painful. It can be an unlooked for service asked when your day is already planned, an experience when all seems to go wrong. Look upon such an occasion not as a trial, but as an opportunity, and embrace it with all the ardor of a lover who sees at hand a gift for the Beloved. I ask this grace for you from our Lady. It will be to share in the grace of her spirit of "handmaid of the Lord," ready for whatever [God] wants and whenever [God] wants it.

Mother Aloysius Rogers, OCD, Fragrance from Alabaster, p. 35, (6)

RESPONSORY

Sing to God a new song, give praise from the ends of the earth.
   —Sing to...
Mountains and deserts rejoice; **—give**...
Glory to you, Source of all Being, Eternal Word and Holy Spirit.
   —Sing to...

CANTICLE OF ZECHARIAH

Ant   God will be gracious to you at the sound of your cry and will answer you.

INTERCESSIONS

God of our Delight, invite us to walk in your way. In faith we pray:
                    Heal us, O God!

You are the voice that sounds in our ears;
   —help us to hear the prophetic people around us.
You are the gentle rain that brings forth the seed of life;
   —enable us to be fruitful bearers of your word.

You are the bread that nourishes our being;
  —may we share our wheat, and respect the rights of
  agricultural workers.
You are the ointment that heals our wounds;
  —assist us to be compassionate with our sick, elderly and
  handicapped sisters and brothers.
You are the gift given to us for our liberation;
  —strengthen us to embrace your gift of life lovingly.

PRAYER: You came among us, Jesus, to heal the broken-hearted
and to show us the way to God, our Mother and Father.
Help us to extend your compassion to our world. May
you bless us with your generative love, for you are God-
with-us, now and forever. Amen.

DAYTIME PRAYER

Ant 1 Comfort, comfort my people, says our God.

Ant 2 Every valley shall be lifted up, and every mountain shall be
made low, and the glory of God shall be revealed.

Ant 3 The grass withers, the flower fades; but the word of our
God will live forever.

(Prayer as in Morning Prayer)

SECOND SUNDAY OF ADVENT
(Psalms from Sunday, Week II, p. 47)
EVENING PRAYER I

Ant 1 Bring comfort to my people, says our God.

Ant 2 Have courage, do not fear; our God is coming; the glory of
God shall be revealed.

Ant 3 A savior will come to you, O Zion; the time for laughter and
rejoicing is near, alleluia.

READING

This waiting for the Promised One we recapture in Advent, we relive it,
we re-present it. But as Christians, we know that this aspect of the
liturgy, Christ's first coming, is a fact of history; he has already come.

He came on a midnight clear, in infant powerlessness. What we actually await now is his second coming, "with great power and glory" (Mk 13: 26). That is why St. Paul's [message] is so appropriate: "I am sure that he who began a good work in you will bring it to completion at the day of Jesus Christ" (Phil 1:6), the day when Christ will return and the present age will end.

Walter J. Burghardt, sj, *Still Proclaiming Your Wonders*, p. 26, (1)

RESPONSORY

O God, guide us into the way of peace and love. **—O God**...
And give light to our darkness; **—into**...
Glory to you, Source of all Being, Eternal Word and Holy Spirit.
  —O God...

CANTICLE OF MARY

Ant   On that day it shall be said: your God is in your midst.
    Rejoice, O Jerusalem!

INTERCESSIONS

God of a New Dawn, you are born of Mary. In confidence let us pray:
    Come, Lord Jesus, and be one with us.

You became human and were born in a troubled land;
  —come and liberate all peoples suffering oppression.
Like us, you faced the reality of death;
  —be our comfort at the hour of death, and give courage to the
    terminally ill.
You came to judge the poor with justice;
  —save us from our blindness and place a new spirit within us.
You came as a child to call us to gentleness and simplicity;
  —free us from false pretenses and from the burden of self-
    aggrandizement.
Your death brought us the hope of resurrection; grant new life
  —to all who have died this day.

PRAYER: O loving God, within and about us a voice cries out to
      prepare a way in the wilderness. You come to restore
      us to new life with you and with one another. Help us
      to be open to every opportunity to prepare a way for
      you. We ask this in the name of Jesus. Amen.

MORNING PRAYER

Ant 1 I will rejoice and go up to the house of my God.

Ant 2 Open wide your gates, O Jerusalem, and receive your savior.

Ant 3 In Zion I will make my salvation known, alleluia.

READING

A shoot shall come out from the stump of Jesse, and a branch shall grow out of his roots. The spirit of the [Most High] shall rest on [the Anointed One], the spirit of wisdom and understanding, the spirit of counsel and might, the spirit of knowledge and the fear of the [Most High]. The wolf shall live with the lamb, the leopard shall lie down with the kid, the calf and the lion and the fatling together, and a little child shall lead them. The cow and the bear shall graze, their young shall lie down together; and the lion shall eat straw like the ox. The nursling child shall play over the hole of the asp, and the weaned child shall put its hand on the adder's den. They will not hurt or destroy on all my holy mountain; for the earth will be full of the knowledge of the [Most High God] as the waters cover the sea.

Is 11:1-2, 6-9

RESPONSORY

Behold the Lamb of God, who comes to bring us salvation. —**Behold**...
Clothed in a mantle of justice, —**who**...
Glory to you, Source of all Being, Eternal Word and Holy Spirit.
   —**Behold**...

CANTICLE OF ZECHARIAH

Ant Do not be afraid, Mary; you will conceive and bear a child.

INTERCESSIONS

We await your coming and with joyful hearts we pray:
        Come, Lord Jesus!

You come to bring us hope and courage;
   —may we support people who feel rejected and hopeless in their present struggles.
You come as a radiant reflection of God's love;
   —assist us to be prayerful and reflective women and men before we take steps of action for the sake of justice.

You come to speak the human word of God's care and tenderness;
—help us to show our care for one another, our environment
and all our endangered species.

You come to show us how to be more fully human in our giving to
a needy world;
—may we share our gifts freely and willingly in a manner that
gives dignity to the poor among us.

PRAYER: O loving God, within and about us a voice cries out to
prepare a way in the wilderness. You come to restore
us to new life with you and with one another. Help us
to be open to every opportunity to prepare a way for
you. We ask this in the name of Jesus. Amen.

DAYTIME PRAYER

Ant 1 Comfort, comfort my people, says our God.

Ant 2 Every valley shall be lifted up, and every mountain shall be
made low, and the glory of God shall be revealed.

Ant 3 The grass withers, the flower fades; but the word of our
God will live forever.

(Prayer as in Morning Prayer)

EVENING PRAYER

Ant 1 Look up to the heavens to see the power of God, alleluia.

Ant 2 O God, you will come and your word is true, alleluia.

Ant 3 Jesus Christ will come to heal us, alleluia.

READING

A voice cries out: "In the wilderness prepare the way of the [Most High],
make straight in the desert a highway for our God. Every valley shall be
lifted up, and every mountain and hill be made low; the uneven ground
shall become level, and the rough places a plain. Then the glory of [God]
shall be revealed, and all people shall see it together, for the mouth of
[the Most High] has spoken."

Is 40:3–5

RESPONSORY

Lift up your eyes, Jerusalem; the glory of God is dawning on you.
  —**Lift up**...
Darkness has covered the earth and thick clouds the people;
  —**the glory of**...
Glory to you, Source of all Being, Eternal Word and Holy Spirit.
  —**Lift up**...

CANTICLE OF MARY

Ant Blessed indeed is Mary who trusted that God's words to her
  would be fulfilled, alleluia.

INTERCESSIONS

O God of Wisdom, you come to walk with us and give us the
opportunity to choose the good and the holy each day, and so we
pray:
We rejoice in your coming, Jesus!

O Jesus, our brother, grant us the gift of understanding;
  —may we welcome the stranger in our midst.
O Word of God, you have come to be one with us in our humanity;
  —assist us to be open to our individual and communal
    differences.
O Light of God's radiance, you come to enlighten our darkness;
  —enable us to hear the prophets of our time and to discern
    their message.
Proclaimer of God's love, you come to invite us to share your
covenantal love;
  —grant us the grace to be faithful in our commitments and
    covenants with one another.

PRAYER: O loving God, within and about us a voice cries out to
prepare a way in the wilderness. You come to restore
us to new life with you and with one another. Help us
to be open to every opportunity to prepare a way for
you. We ask this in the name of Jesus. Amen.

SECOND MONDAY OF ADVENT

(Psalms and antiphons from Week II, p. 55)

MORNING PRAYER

READING

Be aware all the time that above all else God desires the love of one's heart, and therefore try harder to love [God] than to perform any act of self-denial, because unreasonable self-denial is not worth very much, and even nothing at all, yet love is always best, whether the acts of self-sacrifice you are performing are great or small. Be striving with all your strength to make sure of being so disposed within you to the love of Jesus Christ that nothing anyone can do or say can make you unhappy because of the spiritual joy in your soul, and that your mind is inwardly fed only by the sweetness of Christ's love and not by the delightfulness of earthly recreations, nor by the admiration of people should they begin to speak well of you, [nor] by frivolous merriment. Trust in God and [God] will give you what you are [praying]...for in a responsible way.

Richard Rolle, *The English Writings*, p. 146, (1)

RESPONSORY

Sing to God a new song, give praise from the ends of the earth.
 —Sing to...
Mountains and deserts rejoice; **—give**...
Glory to you, Source of all Being, Eternal Word and Holy Spirit.
 —Sing to...

CANTICLE OF ZECHARIAH

Ant Our God proclaims: Repent, the reign of God is upon you, alleluia!

INTERCESSIONS

In joyful song we prepare for your coming as we say:
 Come and abide with us.

As we prepare for your coming among us;
 —free our hearts from selfish desires.
Your prophets announced the joy of your coming;
 —may our lives give witness to your presence among us.
You come to us as a sign of reconciliation;
 —help all who are living in division and dissension to experience your forgiveness.

You bring a promise of abundance of life in our deserts;
—give hope to prisoners and to those who are imprisoned by
their fears.
You turn our sorrow into gladness;
—may all who die this day experience the fullness of your joy.

PRAYER: O God, open our hearts to prepare the way for the
coming of Christ. Instruct us in your ways of
compassion so that we may extend your love and mercy
to all people. We ask this in the name of Jesus, the
Eternal Word, who lives with you and the Holy Spirit
forever. Amen.

DAYTIME PRAYER

Ant 1 Comfort, comfort my people, says our God.

Ant 2 Every valley shall be lifted up, and every mountain shall be
made low, and the glory of God shall be revealed.

Ant 3 The grass withers, the flower fades; but the word of our
God will live forever.

(Prayer as in Morning Prayer)

EVENING PRAYER

READING

No matter which gospel text we take to consider the life of Jesus, we are
confronted with one who consistently manifests the love to which he
calls others. He breaks down all partitions that divide humans from
each other; he embodies a love that is just, and a love that therefore
variously exhibits judgment, affirmation, service, or sharing, depending
upon the context of love. But this is the life that reveals the nature of
God for us; this is the life that offers a concrete vision of the reality to
which God calls us. This is the revelation of God to us for the sake of
conforming us to that divine image. If we see in Jesus a revelation of
God for us, then the way Jesus loves us is the way God loves.

Marjorie Hewitt Suchocki, *God, Christ, Church,* pp. 97–98, (2)

RESPONSORY

Come to deliver us, gentle and loving God; — **Come**...
Turn your face to us and save us; —**gentle**...
Glory to you, Source of all Being, Eternal Word and Holy Spirit.
   — **Come**...

CANTICLE OF MARY

Ant Look to see the Messiah's coming, breaking the bonds of our
   sinfulness.

INTERCESSIONS

Most provident God, you call us to be strong and not to fear for
you are with us always. In trust we say:
                     Our God is here.

That the desert shall rejoice and bloom is the promise you give to
us;
   —may all people find sufficient water of truth and spirit to
   satisfy their thirsty hearts.
The eyes of the blind shall be opened;
   —may you, O God of Wonders, grant us the gift to recognize our
   own blindness.
Your highway shall be called the holy way;
   —grant us, O holy God, the understanding and courage to
   share in the burden of our companions on the journey.
The grass shall become reeds and rushes;
   —may you, O caring Provider, continue to give us the fruits of
   this earth and may we use them wisely.
Everlasting joy shall be upon their heads;
   —may you be a source of comfort to all who mourn.

PRAYER: O God, open our hearts to prepare the way for the
   coming of Christ. Instruct us in your ways of
   compassion so that we may extend your love and mercy
   to all people. We ask this in the name of Jesus, the
   Eternal Word, who lives with you and the Holy Spirit
   forever. Amen.

SECOND TUESDAY OF ADVENT
(Psalms and antiphons from Week II, p. 62)

MORNING PRAYER

READING

Because hidden souls do not live in isolation...their impact and affinity
can remain hidden from themselves and others for their entire earthly
lives. But it is also possible for some of this to become visible in the
external world. This is how it was with the persons and events
intertwined in the mystery of the Incarnation. Mary and Joseph,
Zechariah and Elizabeth, the shepherds and the kings, Simeon and
Anna—all of these had behind them a solitary life with God and were
prepared for their special tasks before they found themselves together in
those awesome encounters and events, and in retrospect, could
understand how the paths left behind led to this climax. Their
astounded adoration in the presence of these great deeds of God is
expressed in the songs of praise that have come down to us.

Edith Stein: The Hidden Life, p. 110, (3)

RESPONSORY

Sing to God a new song, give praise from the ends of the earth.
   —Sing to...
Mountains and deserts rejoice; **—give...**
Glory to you, Source of all Being, Eternal Word and Holy Spirit.
   —Sing to...

CANTICLE OF ZECHARIAH

Ant A voice cries in the wilderness to make straight a highway for
   our God.

INTERCESSIONS

You gather us together carefully, as a mother hen gathers her
chicks. In confidence, we pray:
   Be merciful to us, O God!

You show us your love for all creation;
   —may we be sensitive to all living creatures.
You search after the one who wanders away;
   —help us to confront the manner in which we wander from your
   way.
You call us to praise and glorify you, Creator God;
   —enable us to show our gratitude in songs of thanksgiving.

You comfort the sorrowing and give strength to the weary;
  —grant all in health service professions the gift of compassion.
You come to bring life to the lonely;
  —be with them and touch them with transforming joy and hope.

PRAYER: O God of Tenderness, you gather us into your arms as
            a shepherd gathers her lambs. Help us to demonstrate
            your gentleness with one another. May we gather
            together the diverse peoples among us and prepare to
            make way for your coming. We ask this through your
            tender care and mercy for us, God without end. Amen.

DAYTIME PRAYER

Ant 1 Comfort, comfort my people, says our God.

Ant 2 Every valley shall be lifted up, and every mountain shall be
          made low, and the glory of God shall be revealed.

Ant 3 The grass withers, the flower fades; but the word of our
          God will live forever.

(Prayer as in Morning Prayer)

EVENING PRAYER

READING

Several years before his death in '72, a remarkable rabbi, Abraham
Joshua Heschel, suffered a near-fatal heart attack from which he never
fully recovered. A dear friend visiting him then found him woefully
weak. Just about able to whisper, Heschel said to him: "Sam, when I
regained consciousness, my first feeling was not of despair or anger. I
felt only gratitude to God for my life, for every moment I had lived. I was
ready to depart. 'Take me, O Lord,' I thought, 'I have seen so many
miracles in my lifetime.'" Exhausted by the effort, Heschel paused then
added: "That is what I meant when I wrote [in the preface to his book of
Yiddish poems]: 'I did not ask for success; I asked for wonder. And you
gave it to me.'"

Walter J. Burghardt, SJ, *Still Proclaiming Your Wonders*, p 168, (1)

RESPONSORY

Come to deliver us, gentle and loving God; — **Come...**

Turn your face to us and save us; —**gentle**...
Glory to you, Source of all Being, Eternal Word and Holy Spirit.
  — **Come**...

CANTICLE OF MARY

Ant It is the will of your God that not one of those little ones
  should perish.

INTERCESSIONS

During this season of Advent you remind us that all things are
passing; in trust we pray;
                 Give comfort to us, O God!

You are a sign of eternal life;
  —touch our hearts to recognize and work for lasting values.
In compassion you proclaim your message to us;
  —assist parents to listen to their children and to act out of love.
Help us to be of service to one another;
  —may the love we share be more important than the acquisition
  of material goods.
You search tenderly after the one lost sheep;
  —give us the gift of hospitality that we may open our hearts to
  all who seek you.

PRAYER: O God of Tenderness, you gather us into your arms as
  a shepherd gathers her lambs. Help us to demonstrate
  your gentleness with one another. May we gather
  together the diverse peoples among us and prepare to
  make way for your coming. We ask this through your
  tender care and mercy for us, God without end. Amen.

SECOND WEDNESDAY OF ADVENT
(Psalms and antiphons from Week II, p. 69)
MORNING PRAYER

READING

I [François de Sales] have just come from prayer, where I was
considering the reason we are in this world. I have learned that we are
here only to receive and carry the gentle Jesus: on our tongue by
proclaiming him; in our arms by doing good works; on our shoulders by

supporting the yoke of dryness and sterility in both the interior and exterior senses. Happy are those who carry him gently and with constancy....

Wendy M.Wright, Bond of Perfection, p. 98, (1)

RESPONSORY

Sing to God a new song, give praise from the ends of the earth.
   —Sing to...
Mountains and deserts rejoice; **—give**...
Glory to you, Source of all Being, Eternal Word and Holy Spirit.
   —Sing to...

CANTICLE OF ZECHARIAH

Ant You, O God, are everlasting, the creator of all the earth.

INTERCESSIONS

In your promise, Jesus, you invite us to come to you and find rest for our heavy burdens. In confidence we say:
Come, Lord Jesus!

You invite us to come to you for rest;
   —may we take the time today to sit, reflect and rest in your love
   for us.
You show us the benefits of gentleness;
   —help us to see beyond our personal and national defenses to
   the gentleness in all people and created things.
You remind us that your yoke is easy and your burden is light;
   —enable us to ease the yoke and burdens of one another,
   especially those coping with addictions.
You reflect the love of a caring God;
   —may our lives witness that the time of salvation is now.
You give strength to the weary;
   —be with the women and men who have the courage to
   challenge our unjust structures.

PRAYER: All loving God, you invite us in Jesus to cast aside our heavy burdens and to be gentle of heart. Help us to be open to the tender ways in which your Word of Love touches our being. We ask you to hear our prayer in the name of Jesus who lives with you and the Holy Spirit forever. Amen.

DAYTIME PRAYER

Ant 1 Comfort, comfort my people, says our God.

Ant 2 Every valley shall be lifted up, and every mountain shall be made low, and the glory of God shall be revealed.

Ant 3 The grass withers, the flower fades; but the word of our God will live forever.

(Prayer as in Morning Prayer)

EVENING PRAYER

READING

Mary MacKillop attributed the habit of depending on divine providence to her mother. She reminded her mother that it was she who taught her by example, to trust in Divine Providence. She wrote thus: "It was in hardships, poverty, and even want that you had to rear your children, but in the bitterest trial and greatest need your confidence in Divine Providence never failed." (27 November 1866)

Bl. Mary MacKillop, RSJ, (10)

RESPONSORY

Come to deliver us, gentle and loving God; — **Come...**
Turn your face to us and save us; —**gentle**...
Glory to you, Source of all Being, Eternal Word and Holy Spirit.
    — **Come**...

CANTICLE OF MARY

Ant Jesus said: Come to me, all who labor and are heavy laden, and I will give you rest.

INTERCESSIONS

During this season of Advent we celebrate your coming to be one with us, Jesus. In joy we say:
    The time of salvation is now!

God of Sarah, you know us intimately and call us each by name;
    —give us the strength to respond to your call.
God of Abraham, your ways are hidden and mysterious;
    —may we look beyond the obvious to see with the eyes of faith.
God of Israel, you come with might and power to bring us new life;

—enable us to be a presence of your loving care for all people by
   walking in your light.
God of a new dawn, you soar into our lives on eagles' wings;
   —prepare us for life eternal with you, and may all who die this
   day find the dawn of new life in you.

PRAYER: All loving God, you invite us in Jesus to cast aside our
               heavy burdens and to be gentle of heart. Help us to be
               open to the tender ways in which your Word of Love
               touches our being. We ask you to hear our prayer in
               the name of Jesus who lives with you and the Holy
               Spirit forever. Amen.

SECOND THURSDAY OF ADVENT
(Psalms and antiphons from Week II, p. 76)

MORNING PRAYER

READING

Our faith and our love must stand ready to receive joy when it is given
and to accept its absence when it is not. This may be a part of God's
mysterious design, or it may be a part of our humanness. The important
thing is that we are open to its freedom when joy comes. For it is
possible for us to so constrain ourselves by worry and fear that God's
own liberating joy just barely manages to slip through the cracks—we
never really open the door. It is very important in a life of prayer to
foster that little virtue of hope; hope waits expectantly for joy but also
has the fortitude to wrestle with despair. A poet calls hope "my little girl
that wakes up fresh every morning." Whenever worry and fear want to
enter our house, we should bring in a flower, that is, something nice
that we gather from our surroundings, and set it there for our joy. Then
when the joy of God's own life comes to liberate us we shall be ready for
its freedom.

Miriam Elder, OCD, (11)

RESPONSORY

Sing to God a new song, give praise from the ends of the earth.
   —Sing to...
Mountains and deserts rejoice; **—give**...
Glory to you, Source of all Being, Eternal Word and Holy Spirit.
   —Sing to...

CANTICLE OF ZECHARIAH

Ant It is God who holds your hand and says: Fear not, I will help you.

INTERCESSIONS

In confidence we call upon you, O God, to keep your loving promises to us and so we pray:
Remain with us throughout this day.

Fountain of Love, you provide water for the thirsty;
—may we give thanks for your endless gifts.
Comforting God, in your mercy you drive away our fears;
—grant us the grace to reach beyond the fears that keep us in bondage.
Faithful Companion, you walk with us along our journey;
—enable us to accept the diversities among us and to bless all who walk with integrity a road different from our own.
Liberating God, you make the desert bloom and bring hope and beauty to us;
—free us to bring beauty and hope to people in need of refreshment.

PRAYER: Provident God, you take care to nurture and sustain us with the fruits of the earth and the gifts of one another. Help us to show our gratitude for your gifts in the way we use and respect them. We ask this through Jesus, our brother. Amen.

DAYTIME PRAYER

Ant 1 Comfort, comfort my people, says our God.

Ant 2 Every valley shall be lifted up, and every mountain shall be made low, and the glory of God shall be revealed.

Ant 3 The grass withers, the flower fades; but the word of our God will live forever.

(Prayer as in Morning Prayer)

EVENING PRAYER

READING

Self is always with me, and in a double vocation which should lead me
to sanctity, I cling to faults which many people of the world and in the
world would have corrected in themselves.... It seems to me I have
outlived myself. I see the time coming when I shall be good for almost
nothing. As my health has taken on new vigor, that uselessness will be
harder to bear after I have had so much to do...for although I can read
English, as I know the meaning of the printed words, it is quite a
different thing to understand it when it is spoken, or to speak it myself,
because of the extreme difficulty of the pronunciation, which one can
never master at my age.... So I dread becoming a doting old lady in
second childhood before death catches up with me. In the meantime I
shall have to plant and tend our truck garden. They say we shall have
small success this year, for the ground has been covered with snow
three times since the beginning of this month.... I find in this quiet work
one very great advantage—it brings such peace of soul, and this arises,
no doubt, from contact with the beauty of nature, which lifts one up to
the Creator.

Louise Callan, RSCJ, *Philippine Duchesne*, p. 598, (13)

RESPONSORY

Come to deliver us, gentle and loving God; — **Come...**
Turn your face to us and save us; —**gentle**...
Glory to you, Source of all Being, Eternal Word and Holy Spirit.
   — **Come**...

CANTICLE OF MARY

Ant Heed carefully what you hear!

INTERCESSIONS

O God, you joyfully embraced humanity for our sake. With
gratitude we pray:
Come, Christ our Savior!

Christ our Savior, you come into our world to bring peace:
   —may peace in our world be the fruit of peace in our hearts and
      homes.
Christ our Savior, you walk with us in steadfast love;
   —help us to show concern for just causes and to let go of
      smallness of heart.

Christ our Savior, you lead us to the waters of everlasting life;
—refresh our spirits and make us eager to share our fruitful
abundance with one another.
Christ our Savior, your time of fulfillment is present among us;
—enable us to live fully in the present, to remember our past
lovingly, and to embrace our future confidently.

PRAYER: Provident God, you take care to nurture and sustain us
with the fruits of the earth and the gifts of one another.
Help us to show our gratitude for your gifts in the way
we use and respect them. We ask this through Jesus,
our brother. Amen.

SECOND FRIDAY OF ADVENT
(Psalms and antiphons from Week II, p. 84)
MORNING PRAYER

READING

Every Advent each of us is a new person, and every Advent our concept
of the Jesus we wait for has changed too. But whether we have doubted
our way from last December to this Advent or thrilled to the wonder of it
all, we know that the child of Christmas still challenges us to live like
God in the flesh. Advent is the bridge between Ordinary Time and
Christmas. Tread lightly on this holy crossing, and listen. Let the past
below echo its history of heroic waiting in faith.

Elizabeth Meluch, ocd, (11)

RESPONSORY

Sing to God a new song, give praise from the ends of the earth.
—**Sing to...**
Mountains and deserts rejoice; —**give...**
Glory to you, Source of all Being, Eternal Word and Holy Spirit.
—**Sing to...**

CANTICLE OF ZECHARIAH

Ant Thus says your redeemer: I am your God, who leads you in
the way you should go.

INTERCESSIONS

With patience we wait for your coming and in joy we exclaim:
Come, Lord Jesus!

The world awaits your coming in joy;
  —may your grace refresh every heart and mind.
Our voices proclaim your presence among us;
  —may our lives reveal your saving work.
You come to show us your mercy;
  —forgive us for our half-heartedness.
You called us to freedom in God's will;
  —help us to listen to the gentle stirrings of the Spirit.

PRAYER: You, O God, are a loyal friend; help us to be people of
            wisdom. May we discern our actions in the light of our
            relationship with you and with one another. Grant this
            through Jesus who lives with you, Source of all
            Wisdom, in the unity of the Holy Spirit. Amen.

DAYTIME PRAYER

Ant 1 Comfort, comfort my people, says our God.

Ant 2 Every valley shall be lifted up, and every mountain shall be
          made low, and the glory of God shall be revealed.

Ant 3 The grass withers, the flower fades; but the word of our
          God will live forever.

(Prayer as in Morning Prayer)

EVENING PRAYER

READING

[Jesus] is the risen and glorified Lord whom the Church is now awaiting,
raised to God's right hand by his passion and his rising: kyrios Jesus;
the same who will come to judgment at the end of time as Lord in
glory.... His mere presence passes judgment on the evil in us because
that presence is love, because evil is its opposite. Love sets free the
powers of redeemed life, the love of God given to us. What faith and
baptism had grounded in us and sin restricted can grow and develop
once more. "Our salvation is nearer than when we came to believe." The
judgment which this coming of Christ in the Mystery brings can cause
the growth of our redemption until the other judgment gives it
completion. So the Church goes joyfully into Advent, "look up, and lift
up your heads; it means that the time draws near for your deliverance."

Aemiliana Löhr, *The Mass Through the Year*, p. 7, (13)

RESPONSORY

Come to deliver us, gentle and loving God; — **Come...**
Turn your face to us and save us; —**gentle**...
Glory to you, Source of all Being, Eternal Word and Holy Spirit.
— **Come...**

CANTICLE OF MARY

Ant Jesus said to the crowds: You condemned John and rejected
me, but in time, wisdom and truth will be revealed.

INTERCESSIONS

God of Unconditional Love, we ask you to enlighten our minds
and expand our hearts; and so we pray:
Be with your people, O God.

To hear your word and follow it will bring us to life;
—may we listen to you as you speak to us in the ordinary and
not so ordinary happenings of our daily life.
You promise never to forsake us;
—help all lonely, isolated people to experience hope.
You teach us the path of holiness;
—assist all teachers to share the fruits of their insights.
You share with us of your bounty;
—enable those who are prosperous to see beyond their own
interests that they may help those in need.

PRAYER: You, O God, are a loyal friend; help us to be people of
wisdom. May we discern our actions in the light of our
relationship with you and with one another. Grant this
through Jesus who lives with you, Source of all
Wisdom, in the unity of the Holy Spirit. Amen.

SECOND SATURDAY OF ADVENT
(Psalms and antiphons from Week II, p. 91)
MORNING PRAYER

READING

Mary is therefore the model of prayer for all Christians. Prayer is getting
in touch with reality, letting it speak to us, and incarnating the word
which comes to us. We let it happen in our lives. Saying yes to God in

prayer...means changing our lives in accordance with what we have heard. It means engaging that word with our whole being, and letting it alter our existence. For prayer is a dialogue between life and life, between divine life and human life, between the life of the Spirit and the life of the flesh. Unless we enflesh the word of God and let it become incarnate in us, it cannot become real in the world.

Joseph Martos and Richard Rohr, OFM, "Mary in Luke's Gospel," (4)

RESPONSORY

Sing to God a new song, give praise from the ends of the earth.
  —Sing to...
Mountains and deserts rejoice; **—give**...
Glory to you, Source of all Being, Eternal Word and Holy Spirit.
  —Sing to...

CANTICLE OF ZECHARIAH

Ant The reign of God is at hand: heal the sick, raise the dead,
      cleanse the lepers, cast out demons.

INTERCESSIONS

In trust, O God of Hosts, we await your coming and we pray:
          Come and save us, Holy One of God!

Word of God, you inflame our hearts with desire for you;
  —may we share your love with one another.
Word of God, you invite us each day to a change of heart;
  —help us to be responsive to your stirrings within us.
Word of God, you call us by name and give us new life;
  —assist all church leaders to respect the freedom and
    differences among their people.
Word of God, you call us to peace and wholeness;
  —may those people who have died for justice inspire us with
    their courage.

PRAYER: Be with us, O God of Life, and help us to be faithful to
        our respective calls. In your love you invite us each by
        name to participate in the fullness of your life. We ask
        you to bless us in your goodness and in the name of
        Jesus. Amen.

DAYTIME PRAYER

Ant 1 Comfort, comfort my people, says our God.

Ant 2 Every valley shall be lifted up, and every mountain shall be made low, and the glory of God shall be revealed.

Ant 3 The grass withers, the flower fades; but the word of our God will live forever.

(Prayer as in Morning Prayer)

THIRD SUNDAY OF ADVENT

EVENING PRAYER I
(Psalms from Sunday, Week III, p. 96)

Ant 1 God indeed is my savior; with joy all will draw water at the fountain of salvation, alleluia.

Ant 2 The savior who is to come will baptize you in the Holy Spirit and in fire.

Ant 3 O Emmanuel, Lamb of God, come and save us; free us from our sin.

READING

In [Phil] 4:4–7, [Paul] gives a model for Christian life.... The first mark of the life Paul advocates is rejoicing (4:7). Joy is not a by-product of life in Jesus, but its first characteristic. The word "rejoice" in Greek bears an interesting linguistic relation to the word for "grace" or "mercy," that is, a special manifestation of divine presence or blessing. Leon Bloy has written that the "most infallible presence of God in a person is joy." Here in Germany, if the royal family is in residence in the castle, the family standard or flag is flown from the tower. Joy is the flag we fly from our tower when God is in residence in our hearts.
Bonnie Bowman Thurston, PhD, "Paul's Fundamentals of Faith," (4)

RESPONSORY

O God, guide us into the way of peace and love. —**O God**...
And give light to our darkness; —**into**...
Glory to you, Source of all Being, Eternal Word and Holy Spirit.
    —**O God**...

CANTICLE OF MARY

Ant God will shine on you; all the earth will see your splendor.

INTERCESSIONS

In anticipation of your promise, O God, we pray:
Drop down dew, you heavens from above;
let the clouds rain down the Just One.

Gentle God, you satisfy our thirsty hearts;
   —may we respond to the needs of those thirsting for justice.
Loving God, you give us bread for our table and bread for our
spirit;
   —may we share our bread generously; may it never be used as
   a weapon in the hands of the powerful.
Peaceful God, you desire harmony for us;
   —may we be free from our selfish and defensive ways.
Comforting God, you give sight to the blind;
   —may we see with new eyes your life in our midst.
Liberating God, you set the captives free;
   —may we support those people who are imprisoned for the sake
   of justice.

PRAYER: In joy and gladness we give praise to you, O God, for
you come to share life with us. Come and assist us to
see your loving care in the midst of our daily struggles.
May you continue to grant us peace and joy that
surpasses all understanding. We ask these gifts in the
mystery of our God, Source of all life. Amen.

MORNING PRAYER

Ant 1 You who know God, rejoice, for the Just One is coming.

Ant 2 A star from Judah will arise to redeem the people.

Ant 3 The desert and the land will exult; they shall bloom with
an abundance of flowers, for God, Emmanuel, is coming.

READING

Rejoice in [God] always; again I will say, Rejoice. Let your gentleness
be known to everyone. The [Most High] is near. Do not worry about
anything, but in everything by prayer and supplication with

thanksgiving, let your requests be made known to God. And the peace of God, which surpasses all understanding, will guard your hearts and your minds in Christ Jesus.

Phil 4:4–7

RESPONSORY

Loving God, in you abides the womb of all life; show us your love and
    mercy. —**Loving**...
Be with us in our waiting; —**show us**...
Glory to you, Source of all Being, Eternal Word and Holy Spirit.
    —**Loving**...

CANTICLE OF ZECHARIAH

Ant The Holy Spirit will come upon you, and the child to be born
    will be called holy, the child of God.

INTERCESSIONS

In hope we have waited for your coming, O Jesus; in confidence we pray:
    Most Holy One, bring us your salvation!

Strengthen our hearts and hands;
    —help us to appreciate the wonder of birth and bless the
    wombs of all expectant mothers.
Open our eyes to your ways;
    —assist us to see beyond the borders of our vision and to cut
    through the prejudices that keep us in isolation.
Release us from bondage;
    —may we be ready to free ourselves and others from the
    oppression that keeps us in slavery.
Loosen our tongues to sing your praise;
    —may we proclaim your message in the way we speak to and
    treat one another.
Free our ears to hear your word;
    —grant us a readiness to listen attentively to your voice, and
    assist all pastoral ministers to bear witness to your word
    among the poor.

PRAYER: In joy and gladness we give praise to you, O God, for you come to share life with us. Come and assist us to see your loving care in the midst of our daily struggles. May you continue to grant us peace and joy that surpasses all understanding. We ask these gifts in the mystery of our God, Source of all life. Amen.

DAYTIME PRAYER

Ant 1 Comfort, comfort my people, says our God.

Ant 2 Every valley shall be lifted up, and every mountain shall be made low, and the glory of God shall be revealed.

Ant 3 The grass withers, the flower fades; but the word of our God will live forever.

(Prayer as in Morning Prayer)

EVENING PRAYER II

Ant 1 Jesus Christ will come to save all people, alleluia.

Ant 2 Let the mountains rejoice and the seas rise up in joy for our Light comes to bring us peace.

Ant 3 Let us prepare for Christ's coming with lives rooted in hope.

READING

I will greatly rejoice in [you, O God], my whole being shall exult in [you]; for [you have] clothed me with the garments of salvation, [you have] covered me with the robe of righteousness, as a bridegroom decks himself with a garland, and as a bride adorns herself with her jewels. For as the earth brings forth its shoots, and as a garden causes what is sown in it to spring up, so [will you, O God], cause righteousness and praise to spring forth before all the nations.

Is 61:10–11

RESPONSORY

Sing to God a new song, give praise from the ends of the earth.
  —**Sing to**...
Mountains and deserts rejoice; —**give**...
Glory to you, Source of all Being, Eternal Word and Holy Spirit.
  —**Sing to**...

CANTICLE OF MARY

Ant The Holy Spirit will come upon you and the power of the Most High will overshadow you, alleluia.

INTERCESSIONS

Jesus, you are the one born of Mary, and in joy we pray with eager hearts:

Maranatha! Come, Lord Jesus!

You, Jesus, are our savior;
—may we proclaim your message willingly and participate in bringing about your reign in our world.
You are the fountain of living water;
—be with all peoples who are preparing to receive baptism.
You are the Holy One of Israel;
—grant shelter to the homeless, especially children, who need food, care, and companionship.
You are hope in our weariness;
—free us from our selfishness and give courage to all children and adults who are handicapped.

PRAYER: In joy and gladness we give praise to you, O God, for you come to share life with us. Come and assist us to see your loving care in the midst of our daily struggles. May you continue to grant us peace and joy that surpasses all understanding. We ask this for the glory and praise of your name. Amen.

THIRD MONDAY OF ADVENT
(If today is December 17 or 18, for weekdays begin using p. 251 or p. 254 instead)
(Psalms and antiphons from Week III, p. 104)

MORNING PRAYER

READING

We can produce works that will call forth admiration and praise, but if the work we have done has not made us more holy—more like our Lord [Jesus]—it is of small value. If in doing it, there has been little effort to overcome our own will and judgment, our overeagerness;... if we show irritation under interruptions or when things do not please us, sensitiveness if our work doesn't satisfy; these and similar reactions show the presence of [self], and unless this is combated, we shall do little for God however perfect our works may appear.

Mother Aloysius Rogers, OCD, *Fragrance from Alabaster*, p. 31, (6)

RESPONSORY

Sing to God a new song, give praise from the ends of the earth.
  —Sing to...
Mountains and deserts rejoice; **—give**...
Glory to you, Source of all Being, Eternal Word and Holy Spirit.
  —Sing to...

CANTICLE OF ZECHARIAH

Ant From heaven you come, O Most High; to you we give honor
    and glory.

INTERCESSIONS

O God, you share your life with us in the mystery of the Word
Incarnate. In joy, let us pray:
        Come, hope of all peoples!

In your light, Christ Jesus, we can walk in freedom;
  —may we follow your way of truth without counting the cost.
Our hearts are open to receive you;
  —enable us to be compassionate in working with one another.
You come as a fragile child;
  —empower religious leaders to respond effectively from the
    experience of their personal vulnerability.
Teach us your law of love and mercy;
  —assist all missionaries in their efforts to give birth to your
    love.

PRAYER: In you, Jesus, lies the gift of wisdom and the power of
          authority. You share these gifts with us in a caring,
          gentle way as given to you by God, our Mother and
          Father. Assist us in recognizing humbly the source of
          our gifts and enable us to use them in praise of you,
          one with the Source of all life. Amen.

DAYTIME PRAYER

Ant 1 Comfort, comfort my people, says our God.

Ant 2 Every valley shall be lifted up, and every mountain shall be
      made low, and the glory of God shall be revealed.

Ant 3 The grass withers, the flower fades; but the word of our God will live forever.

(Prayer as in Morning Prayer)

EVENING PRAYER

READING

For the world and time are the dance of the Lord in emptiness. The silence of the spheres is the music of a wedding feast. The more we persist in misunderstanding the phenomena of life, the more we analyze them out into strange finalities and complex purposes of our own, the more we involve ourselves in sadness, absurdity, and despair. But it does not matter much, because no despair of ours can alter the reality of things, or stain the joy of the cosmic dance which is always there. Indeed, we are in the midst of it, and it is in the midst of us, for it beats in our very blood, whether we want it to or not. Yet the fact remains that we are invited to forget ourselves on purpose, cast our awful solemnity to the winds and join in the general dance.

Thomas Merton, *New Seeds of Contemplation*, p. 297, (16)

RESPONSORY

Come to deliver us, gentle and loving God; — **Come...**
Turn your face to us and save us; —**gentle**...
Glory to you, Source of all Being, Eternal Word and Holy Spirit.
    — **Come**...

CANTICLE OF MARY

Ant Every age will honor me; God, Most High, has favored me.

INTERCESSIONS

In you, O God, we rejoice, for you invite us to new heights and to climb your holy mountain. In joy we proclaim:
    Let us walk in your light, O God!

You are our refuge in time of need;
    —protect the homeless and give refuge to those who leave their
    homelands to find peace.
You are our shade in the heat of the day;
    —give hope to the elderly so that they may experience fullness
    in their years of apparent diminishment.

You are a light to guide us on our journey;
—may your people find meaning in their youthful years, and a
desire to create a peaceful future.
You are our shelter from storm and rain;
—grant us the insight to see your provident care in all our
struggles.
You are the source of our peace;
—may all who die today experience peace in your light.

PRAYER: In you, Jesus, lies the gift of wisdom and the power of
authority. You share these gifts with us in a caring,
gentle way as given to you by God, our Mother and
Father. Assist us in recognizing humbly the source of
our gifts and enable us to use them in praise of you,
one with the Source of all life. Amen.

THIRD TUESDAY OF ADVENT
(If today is December 17 or 18, for weekdays begin using p. 251 or p. 254 instead)
(Psalms and antiphons from Week III, p. 111)
MORNING PRAYER

READING

Christian prayer is an expression of vigilance for God's coming into our
human history. [Jesus] teaches us at the same time prayer and
vigilance. "Be on the alert and pray at all times for strength" (Lk 21:36).
Especially in all decisive moments we must pray; but we cannot pray if
we are not willing to be alert and ready for the coming of the Lord
[Jesus] in the hour of decision. But neither can we be truly ready to
receive him in the decisive moments without a spirit of prayer.

Bernard Häring, *Prayer: The Integration of Faith and Life*, p. 101, (8)

RESPONSORY

Sing to God a new song, give praise from the ends of the earth.
—Sing to...
Mountains and deserts rejoice; **—give**...
Glory to you, Source of all Being, Eternal Word and Holy Spirit.
—Sing to...

CANTICLE OF ZECHARIAH

Ant Let the earth open, that salvation may come forth and justice
may spring up from the earth.

INTERCESSIONS

O Giver of all gifts, you continue to reveal your goodness to us
and in faith we pray:
May your spirit rest gently upon us!

O Spirit of Wisdom, you give us insight;
—grant all people the wisdom to choose effective ways to
develop their human potential through their respective
governments.
O Spirit of Understanding, you show us mercy;
—help us to reach out in compassion to one another.
O Spirit of Counsel and of Strength, you give us courage;
—may we be open to your loving challenges and strengthened in
our desire to be of service.
O Spirit of Knowledge, you instruct us in your ways;
—assist us to know ourselves and to be open to your
continuous revelation in our midst.

PRAYER: O God of Forgiveness, you are close to the brokenhearted and to all who call upon you. As we approach
the celebration of Christmas, help us to be patient with
our own shortcomings, and to extend forgiveness and
peace to our neighbors. Grant us this grace in the
name of Jesus, our brother. Amen.

DAYTIME PRAYER

Ant 1 Comfort, comfort my people, says our God.

Ant 2 Every valley shall be lifted up, and every mountain shall be
made low, and the glory of God shall be revealed.

Ant 3 The grass withers, the flower fades; but the word of our
God will live forever.

(Prayer as in Morning Prayer)

EVENING PRAYER

READING

I live my Advent in the womb of Mary.
And on one night when a great star swings free
from its high mooring and walks down the sky

to be the dot above the *Christus i,*
I shall be born of her by blessed grace.
I wait in Mary-darkness, faith's walled place,
with hope's expectance of nativity.

I knew for long she carried me and fed me,
guarded and loved me, though I could not see.
But only now, with inward jubilee,
I come upon earth's most amazing knowledge:
someone is hidden in this dark with me.

"Advent," in *Selected Poetry of Jessica Powers,* p. 81, (5)

RESPONSORY

Come to deliver us, gentle and loving God; — **Come...**
Turn your face to us and save us; —**gentle**...
Glory to you, Source of all Being, Eternal Word and Holy Spirit.
   — **Come...**

CANTICLE OF MARY

Ant Jesus said: Truly, sinners enter the fullness of God before
   the self-righteous.

INTERCESSIONS

O God of Love, hear the cry of the poor; listen to us as we pray:
   Come and save your people!

O God, you invite us to work in the vineyard;
   —may all peoples know the true dignity of work.
You call us to serve one another in love;
   —may we be open to hear the needs of those around us.
You give us the image of peace, the wolf as a guest of the lamb;
   —grant us the courage to work for peace and to support all
   peacemakers.
You love justice and are close to the afflicted;
   —assist all women and men in their search for just institutional
   structures.

PRAYER: O God of Forgiveness, you are close to the broken-
            hearted and to all who call upon you. As we approach
            the celebration of Christmas, help us to be patient with
            our own shortcomings, and to extend forgiveness and
            peace to our neighbors. Grant us this grace in the
            name of Jesus, our brother. Amen.

THIRD WEDNESDAY OF ADVENT
(If today is December 17 or 18, for weekdays begin using p. 251 or p. 254 instead)
(Psalms and antiphons from Week III, p. 117)

MORNING PRAYER

READING

Advent is God entering into history...into us. It is light piercing our
world and us. And there is something asked of us...the Baptist tells us,
we must be ready...we must be cleansed...we must change to make
ready for him who has been promised. Thomas Merton says: "What is
uncertain is not the coming of Christ but our own reception of him, our
own response to him, our own readiness and capacity to 'go forth and to
meet him.'" This is why John preaches the way he does...and why we
need to meet him...to be startled by him...on our way to the cradle.

Paul H. Harkness, "Our Journey to the Cradle," (4)

RESPONSORY

Sing to God a new song, give praise from the ends of the earth.
   —Sing to...
Mountains and deserts rejoice; **—give**...
Glory to you, Source of all Being, Eternal Word and Holy Spirit.
   —Sing to...

CANTICLE OF ZECHARIAH

Ant Thus says God who formed earth and heaven: I am your
    God, there is no other.

INTERCESSIONS

God of our salvation, you come bringing us nourishment and joy
and we exclaim:

Jesus, you are the joy of our salvation!

Jesus, you are the light in our darkness;
   —may we see meaning in our struggles.
You bring bread to feed us;
   —assist us to move beyond our selfish desires to be a leaven for
   others.
In healing and forgiveness you wipe away our tears;
   —help us to be a sign of healing within the brokenness around
   us.

You made this earth your home;
  —enlighten us to discover creative ways for preserving and
  renewing our environment.
You taught us to have a deep respect for life;
  —be with all expectant parents and enable them to bring forth
  life.

PRAYER: O God, may the celebration of this holy birth fill us
with the life-giving waters from your holy womb. You
call us to life once again and we ask you to renew our
desire to serve you in one another. Grant this in the
name of the Incarnate Word who lives with you and the
Holy Spirit for all ages to come. Amen.

DAYTIME PRAYER

Ant 1 Comfort, comfort my people, says our God.

Ant 2 Every valley shall be lifted up, and every mountain shall be
made low, and the glory of God shall be revealed.

Ant 3 The grass withers, the flower fades; but the word of our
God will live forever.

(Prayer as in Morning Prayer)

EVENING PRAYER

READING

If Christmas is going to mean something to us this year, we must try
through its celebration to become more like Jesus. It is true that we
need friends who are agreeable and helpful to us; even Jesus had
special friends. And in this sense charity begins at home, but it only
begins there. Our love and concern must spread beyond a small circle of
companions. We cannot treat everyone in the same way, but we must
not deliberately exclude anyone from our love and respect, whether it be
because of [his or her color, religion, nationality], or just plain old
orneriness. In fact, if we want to be more like Jesus, the "undesirables"
of this world have a special claim on us.

Charles E. Miller, CM, and John A. Grindel, CM, *Until He Comes*, p. 48, (17)

RESPONSORY

Come to deliver us, gentle and loving God; — **Come...**
Turn your face to us and save us; —**gentle...**

Glory to you, Source of all Being, Eternal Word and Holy Spirit.
— **Come...**

CANTICLE OF MARY

Ant Go tell John what you see and hear: the blind see, the lame walk, the lepers are cleansed.

INTERCESSIONS

You, O God, are a loving father and mother as you share your life, your table, and your inheritance with us. In gratitude we pray:
Show us the way, O God!

You promise us a banquet of choice food;
  —may all people find the food they need this day.
You give us guidance in your compassionate understanding;
  —assist us to discern faithfully your word for us.
You invite us to choose freely the way we use our gifts and the fruits of the earth;
  —help us to allow our sisters and brothers the opportunity to live in your freedom and love.
You are a God of hospitality and you welcome us to share in your inheritance;
  —enable us to be faithful to your invitation to growth, freedom, and love.

PRAYER: O God, may the celebration of this holy birth fill us with the life-giving waters from your holy womb. You call us to life once again and we ask you to renew our desire to serve you in one another. Grant this in the name of the Incarnate Word who lives with you and the Holy Spirit for all ages to come. Amen.

THIRD THURSDAY OF ADVENT
(If today is December 17 or 18, for weekdays begin using p. 251 or p. 254 instead)
(Psalms and antiphons from Week III, p. 124)

MORNING PRAYER

READING

And now this is what our Creator...decided...."I myself shall continue to dwell above the sky, and that is where those on the earth will end their thanksgiving. They will simply continue to have gratitude for everything they see that I created on the earth, and for everything they see that is growing.... The people moving about on the earth will have love; they will simply be thankful. They will begin on the earth, giving thanks for all they see. They will carry it upward, ending where I dwell. I shall always be listening carefully to what they are saying, the people who move about. And indeed I shall always be watching carefully what they do, the people on the earth." (A Seneca Thanksgiving Address)

Native North American Spirituality of the Eastern Woodlands, p. 67, (1)

RESPONSORY

Sing to God a new song, give praise from the ends of the earth.
  —Sing to...
Mountains and deserts rejoice; **—give**...
Glory to you, Source of all Being, Eternal Word and Holy Spirit.
  —Sing to...

CANTICLE OF ZECHARIAH

Ant My steadfast love shall not depart from you, and my
        covenant of peace shall not be removed, says our God.

INTERCESSIONS

O God of Goodness, you invite us to a covenant of peace and love.
In faith we pray:
         Show us your kindness forever!

O God, you call us to be one in you;
  —give us the grace to live in your love.
You walk among us in the poor and lonely;
  —help us to serve you in our sisters and brothers.
You bless the Church with the gift of your Spirit;
  —may we place our gifts at the service of all.
You are our messenger of light;
  —assist us with the courage to share our faith life with one
     another.

PRAYER: Compassionate God, you look upon our brokenness
         with mercy and kindness. Help us to extend your
         goodness to one another. Hear our prayer, for you are
         our God; Creator, Redeemer, and Sanctifier. Amen.

DAYTIME PRAYER

Ant 1 Comfort, comfort my people, says our God.

Ant 2 Every valley shall be lifted up, and every mountain shall be made low, and the glory of God shall be revealed.

Ant 3 The grass withers, the flower fades; but the word of our God will live forever.

(Prayer as in Morning Prayer)

EVENING PRAYER

READING

This is what the Sky Dwellers did: They told us that we should always have love, we who move about on the earth. And this will always be first when people come to gather, the people who move on the earth. It is the way it begins when two people meet. They first have the obligation to be grateful that they are happy.... This is what our Creator...decided, "The people moving about on the earth will simply come to express their gratitude...." "I shall establish the earth, on which the people will move about...and there will be a relationship when they want to refer to the earth: They will say 'Our mother, who supports our feet.'" (A Seneca Thanksgiving Address)

Native North American Spirituality of the Eastern Woodlands, p. 58 (1)

RESPONSORY

Come to deliver us, gentle and loving God; — **Come...**
Turn your face to us and save us; —**gentle**...
Glory to you, Source of all Being, Eternal Word and Holy Spirit.
    — **Come...**

CANTICLE OF MARY

Ant I send my messenger before you, who shall prepare the way.

INTERCESSIONS

Christ, you are the Light that the darkness cannot overcome; in confidence we pray:
Come, Light of Life!

You were present at the creation of the world;
    —by your coming as one of us renew the earth.

You who dwell in the heart of God;
  —come and teach us the love of God.
John the Baptist was imprisoned for the cause of truth;
  —free those imprisoned for the sake of your name.
You are always attentive to us in our every need;
  —help us to comfort the poor by our loving efforts.

PRAYER: Compassionate God, you look upon our brokenness
with mercy and kindness. Help us to extend your
goodness to one another. Hear our prayer, for you are
our God; Creator, Redeemer, and Sanctifier. Amen.

THIRD FRIDAY OF ADVENT

(If today is December 17 or 18, for weekdays begin using p. 251 or p. 254 instead)
(Psalms and antiphons from Week III, p. 131)

MORNING PRAYER

READING

To do justice, to love kindness, to walk humbly with God—these may
embody all that we need to know in order to be faithful and to be
human. They are not three "virtues." They are not "things to do." Rather,
they speak of three dimensions of a life of faithfulness, each of which
depends on and is reinforced by the other two. To *love kindness (hesed)*
means to enter into relationships of abiding solidarity. It means to make
commitments and to keep commitments. And so the questions come:
With whom? And in what way? The New Testament struggles with the
question of the limits of solidarity. In Luke 10:29, the neighbor question
is the overriding question for the community, as it still is.... We learn
how to practice solidarity by discerning the ways in which God practices
solidarity.... The solidarity of God's *hesed* is not a powerful, overriding
solidarity, but it is a patient, attentive, waiting, hoping solidarity.

Walter Brueggemann, Sharon Parks, Thomas H. Groome,
To Act Justly, Love Tenderly, Walk Humbly, pp. 14–15, (1)

RESPONSORY

Sing to God a new song, give praise from the ends of the earth.
  —Sing to...
Mountains and deserts rejoice; **—give**...
Glory to you, Source of all Being, Eternal Word and Holy Spirit.
  —Sing to...

CANTICLE OF ZECHARIAH

Ant My house shall be called a house of prayer for all peoples.

INTERCESSIONS

Gracious Spirit, you share with us your life and light; in trust we say:

Have mercy on us!

Christ, you gave us the commandment to love one another;
—help us to live in this covenant of love.
You send your Spirit of hope into our hearts;
—may our lives be signs of hope for others.
Give world leaders the wisdom to work for justice;
—that peace may become a reality for all people.
We await the celebration of Christ's birth;
—may every family experience joy and harmony.

PRAYER: O holy Womb of God, guide us with your love as we await the birthing of Jesus in our hearts. Keep us faithful that we may be nurtured through life and brought to salvation. We ask this in the name of this same Jesus, God-with-us. Amen.

DAYTIME PRAYER

Ant 1 Comfort, comfort my people, says our God.

Ant 2 Every valley shall be lifted up, and every mountain shall be made low, and the glory of God shall be revealed.

Ant 3 The grass withers, the flower fades; but the word of our God will live forever.

(Prayer as in Morning Prayer)

EVENING PRAYER

READING

...God's solidarity (*hesed*) is not just an act of humble solidarity. It is also an active intervention that changes things. So one is enjoined to *do justice*, as God does justice. And when God does justice, it is not modest or polite or understated. It is an act of powerful intervention. It is like Moses in the court of Pharaoh insisting on freedom. It is like Nathan sent to David (2 Sam 12) who will not tolerate such rapacious action. It is like Elijah thundering against Ahab and Jezebel when Naboth has been done in, for the sake of land (1 Kgs 21). God is a lover of justice,

which means God intervenes for the poor and weak against the powerful
who have too much.

Walter Brueggemann, Sharon Parks, Thomas H. Groome,
To Act Justly, Love Tenderly, Walk Humbly, p. 15, (1)

RESPONSORY

Come to deliver us, gentle and loving God; — **Come...**
Turn your face to us and save us; —**gentle**...
Glory to you, Source of all Being, Eternal Word and Holy Spirit.
    — **Come...**

CANTICLE OF MARY

Ant My words bear witness that God has sent me.

INTERCESSIONS

We rejoice in you, God of our salvation; you call our blindness to
sight and our deafness to hearing. In joy we proclaim:

Hear our prayer, O God!

God of Love, you invite us to trust in your saving mercy;
   —help us to be confident of your continuous love for us,
     especially in times of doubt and distress.
God of Light, increase our vision;
   —help us to see the beauty around us and to celebrate it each
     day.
God of Wonders, you come to us in simplicity;
   —enable us to be content with our basic needs.
God of Joy, increase our openness to celebrating life;
   —may all children experience acceptance, love, and care.

PRAYER: O holy Womb of God, guide us with your love as we
await the birthing of Jesus in our hearts. Keep us
faithful that we may be nurtured through life and
brought to salvation. We ask this in the name of this
same Jesus, God-with-us. Amen.

FOURTH SUNDAY OF ADVENT

EVENING PRAYER I

(Psalms from Sunday, Week IV, p. 143)

Ant 1 Say to the daughters of Zion: your salvation comes; rejoice, for the time is near, alleluia.

Ant 2 A virgin shall be with child, and will bear a son, and shall name him Emmanuel.

Ant 3 O Come, Emmanuel, promise of God; Jesus, the Word, come!

READING

...the Holy Spirit inspires all the commandments and all the new testimonies, giving before the Incarnation of the Lord the law of his glorious mysteries, and then showing the same glory in the Incarnation itself. And the Spirit's inspiration is a golden splendor and a high and excellent illumination, and by this outpouring It makes known, as was said, the mystical secrets of God's Only-Begotten to the ancient heralds who showed the Son of God through types and marveled at his coming from [God] and his miraculously arising in the dawn of the perpetual Virgin. And thus the Spirit in Its power fused the Old Testament and the Gospels into one spiritual seed, from which grew all justice.

Hildegard of Bingen, Scivias, III:4.14, (1)

RESPONSORY

O God, guide us into the way of peace and love. **—O God...**
And give light to our darkness; **—into...**
Glory to you, Source of all Being, Eternal Word and Holy Spirit.
  —O God...

CANTICLE OF MARY

(See the special antiphons for December 17–23)

INTERCESSIONS

God of a New Dawn, you are born of Mary. In confidence let us pray:
  Come, Lord Jesus, and be one with us.

You became human and were born in a troubled land;
  —come and liberate all peoples suffering oppression.
Like us, you faced the reality of death;

—be our comfort at the hour of death, and give courage to the
terminally ill.
You came to judge the poor with justice;
—save us from our blindness and place a new spirit within us.
Your came as a child to call us to gentleness and simplicity;
—free us from false pretenses and from the burden of self-
aggrandizement.
Your death brought us the hope of resurrection;
—grant new life to all who have died this day.

PRAYER: In eagerness we await your coming, Desired One
among all peoples. May we come to realize with Mary
that we are your highly favored ones and that you
desire to be with us. Increase our faith and put a new
spirit in our hearts so that we may bear your word to
the world. We ask this in your name. Amen.

MORNING PRAYER
(Psalms from Sunday, Week IV, p. 145)

Ant 1 God shall reign forever, O Zion, throughout all generations.

Ant 2 Joseph, son of David, do not fear to take Mary as your
wife.

Ant 3 Behold, a virgin will conceive and bear a son and name
him Emmanuel.

READING

But you, O Bethlehem of Ephrathah, who are one of the little clans of
Judah, from you shall come forth for me one who is to rule in Israel,
whose origin is from of old, from ancient days. Therefore, [the Most
High] shall give them up until the time when she who is in labor has
brought forth; then the rest...shall return to the people of Israel. And
[the Anointed] shall stand and feed [the] flock in the strength of the
[Most High], in the majesty of the name of the [Most High God.] And
they shall live secure, for now [their ruler] shall be great to the ends of
the earth....

Mi 5:2–4

RESPONSORY

Come to deliver us, gentle and loving God. **—Come**...
Turn your face to us and save us; **—gentle**...

Glory to you, Source of all Being, Eternal Word and Holy Spirit.
—**Come**...

CANTICLE OF ZECHARIAH

Ant The Savior of the world shall appear like the sun and descend into the Virgin's womb as rain on the grass.

INTERCESSIONS

We await your coming and with joyful hearts we pray:
Come, Lord Jesus!

You come to bring us hope and courage;
—may we support people who feel rejected and hopeless in their present struggles.
You come as a radiant reflection of God's love;
—assist us to be prayerful and reflective women and men before we take steps of action for the sake of justice.
You come to speak the human word of God's care and tenderness;
—help us to show our care for one another, our environment and all our endangered species
You come to show us how to be more fully human in our giving to a needy world;
—may we share our gifts freely and willingly in a manner that gives dignity to the poor among us.

PRAYER: In eagerness we await your coming, Desired One among all peoples. May we come to realize with Mary that we are your highly favored ones and that you desire to be with us. Increase our faith and put a new spirit in our hearts so that we may bear your word to the world. We ask this in your name. Amen.

DAYTIME PRAYER

Ant 1 Comfort, comfort my people, says our God.

Ant 2 Every valley shall be lifted up, and every mountain shall be made low, and the glory of God shall be revealed.

Ant 3 The grass withers, the flower fades; but the word of our God will live forever.

(Prayer as in Morning Prayer)

EVENING PRAYER II

Ant 1 Jesus will appear in glory, and will come without delay.

Ant 2 Prepare the way for our God; make ready our hearts for the Holy One.

Ant 3 The reign of God will cover the earth; the compassion of our God will embrace all creation.

READING

The [Most High God] spoke to Ahaz saying, Ask a sign of [your God]; let it be deep as Sheol or high as heaven. But Ahaz said, I will not ask, and I will not put [my God] to the test. Then Isaiah said, "Hear then, O house of David! Is it too little for you to weary mortals, that you weary my God also? Therefore [the Most High God] will give you a sign. Look, the young woman is with child and shall bear a son, and shall name him Immanuel."

Is 7:10–14

RESPONSORY

The time has come; the day is at hand, and salvation shall be ours. —**The time**...
The one who frees us will be our ruler; —**and salvation**...
Glory to you, Source of all Being, Eternal Word and Holy Spirit.
    —**The time**...

CANTICLE OF MARY

Ant O Emmanuel, giver of a new law to all nations, come and save us, for you are our God.

INTERCESSIONS

O God of Wisdom, you come to walk with us and give us the opportunity to choose the good and the holy each day, and so we pray:

We rejoice in your coming, Jesus!

O Jesus, our brother, grant us the gift of understanding;
    —may we welcome the stranger in our midst.
O Word of God, you have come to be one with us in our humanity;
    —assist us to be open to our individual and communal differences.

O Light of God's radiance, you come to enlighten our darkness;
—enable us to hear the prophets of our time and to discern
their message.
Proclaimer of God's love, you come to invite us to share your
covenantal love;
—grant us the grace to be faithful in our commitments and
covenants with one another.

PRAYER: In eagerness we await your coming, Desired One
among all peoples. May we come to realize with Mary
that we are your highly favored ones and that you
desire to be with us. Increase our faith and put a new
spirit in our hearts so that we may bear your word to
the world. We ask this in your name. Amen.

DECEMBER 17
(Psalms and antiphons from the current week)
MORNING PRAYER

READING

As in the Gospel of John, Christ is the Word, the divine utterance from
the mouth of the Most High (Jn 1:1–14). According to Paul, he is the
divine Wisdom that presides at the new creation (Heb 1:3). What John
expresses in terms of a "new birth" (Jn 3:3–7), Paul puts in terms of a
"new creation," of which Christ is the source, the new Adam, and also
the creator and redeemer. According to Paul, the mission of divine
Wisdom supposes and entails a cosmic dimension of salvation that is
tied to the function of Christ as redeemer: all have been created in
Christ and for Christ; all have been made heirs of Christ and saved by
him and for him (Col 1:15–20). As for the abundance of divine gifts
brought together in Wisdom and the promise that [God's] spirit would be
upon the Messiah (Is 11:1–2), in Christ it is an abundance that is
poured out: "Of his fullness we have all had a share—love following
upon love" (Jn 1:16).

Days of the Lord, Vol. 1, pp. 185–86, (9)

RESPONSORY

Lift up your eyes, Jerusalem; the glory of God is dawning on you.
—**Lift up**...
Darkness has covered the earth and thick clouds the people;
—**the glory**...

Glory to you, Source of all Being, Eternal Word and Holy Spirit.
—**Lift up**...

CANTICLE OF ZECHARIAH

Ant Your God is coming, O Zion, to rejoice over you with
gladness and renew you in tender love.

INTERCESSIONS

Jesus Christ comes as our Savior; we rejoice in you and say:
Renew in us the light of hope.

You call all nations to universal peace;
  —deliver us from all forms of violence.
You come to show us the face of love;
  —give us a readiness to forgive those who have hurt us.
May the elderly find hope and meaning;
  —and comfort from those who care.
You accepted with trust and love the reality of being human;
  —help all who are nearing their passage through death.

PRAYER: O God of Wisdom, you who fill our hearts but
transcend our thoughts, give us all things in the
gift of your Incarnate Word. Make us discerning
persons with formed consciences and the freedom
to recognize your invitations to grow. We ask this
through Jesus, Emmanuel, God with us forever. Amen.

DAYTIME PRAYER

Ant 1 Our Savior will come like rain on the grass, like showers
that water the earth.

Ant 2 Christ will have dominion from sea to sea, and from the
river to the ends of the earth.

Ant 3 In your day justice will flourish and peace abound until
the moon be no more.

(Prayer as in Morning Prayer)

EVENING PRAYER

READING

There is in all visible things an invisible fecundity, a dimmed light, a
meek namelessness, a hidden wholeness. This mysterious Unity and

Integrity is Wisdom, the Mother of all, *Natura naturans.* There is in all things an inexhaustible sweetness and purity, a silence that is a fount of action and joy. It rises up in wordless gentleness and flows out to me from the unseen roots of all created being, welcoming me tenderly, saluting me with indescribable humility. This is at once my own being, my own nature, and the Gift of my Creator's Thought and Art within me, speaking as Hagia Sophia, speaking as my sister, Wisdom. I am awakened, I am born again at the voice of this my Sister, sent to me from the depths of the divine fecundity.

"Hagia Sophia" in *The Collected Poems of Thomas Merton,* p. 363, (16)

RESPONSORY

Show us, O God, your steadfast love, and grant us your salvation.
   —Show us...
Restore us again that we may rejoice, **—and grant...**
Glory to you, Source of all Being, Eternal Word and Holy Spirit.
   —Show us...

CANTICLE OF MARY

Ant   O Wisdom, Holy Word of God, you reach from one end of the earth to the other with providential and tender care. Come and teach us to live in your ways.

INTERCESSIONS

You have revealed the Christ, O God, as the goal of human history. We pray to you:
       Enlighten our minds and hearts.

Your children, O God, are burdened with uneasiness;
   —strengthen our spirits as we try to better our world.
It is your will that all people come to the knowledge of truth;
   —raise up models of integrity to point the way.
You are the desired One of all the nations;
   —we cannot rest until we rest in you.
You have written your law in our hearts;
   —help us to love what is good and avoid what is evil.

PRAYER: O God of Wisdom, you who fill our hearts but transcend our thoughts, give us all things in the gift of your Incarnate Word. Make us discerning persons with formed consciences and the freedom to recognize your invitations to grow. We ask this through Jesus, Emmanuel, God with us forever. Amen.

DECEMBER 18

(Psalms and antiphons from the current week)

MORNING PRAYER

READING

Christmas is appealing to us because it makes God so close to us. Jesus is indeed "Immanuel," God with us in a simple, human way. But we should never allow the simplicity and humanness of Christmas to dull our sense of wonder and awe. We would do well to imitate Joseph in his humility because we are really much less worthy than he, a great saint, to take part in so holy a reality. Humility does not mean backing off in fear from the mystery of Christmas; rather it should move us to praise God for God's goodness in calling us to be so close...in the person of [Jesus] made flesh. As we prepare to celebrate the birth of Jesus Christ our hearts should be filled with wonder and praise.

Charles E. Miller, CM and John A. Grindel, CM, *Until He Comes*, p. 62, (17)

RESPONSORY

Lift up your eyes, Jerusalem; the glory of God is dawning on you.
  —**Lift up**...
Darkness has covered the earth and thick clouds the people;
  —**the glory**...
Glory to you, Source of all Being, Eternal Word and Holy Spirit.
  —**Lift up**...

CANTICLE OF ZECHARIAH

Ant Look up and raise your heads because your redemption is drawing near.

INTERCESSIONS

Jesus, you came to witness to the truth. With trust in you we pray:
  May the truth make us free.

Look with compassion on the sick and suffering;
  —may their faith in you make them whole.
At your coming all things rejoice;
  —give us respect for all living things.
You call us to deeper fidelity to the gospel;
  —free us from all forms of blindness.
You come to show us our dignity as God's children;
  —show us the way to a social order that can incarnate it.

PRAYER: O God of the Universe, your vastness is beyond our power to imagine, but you have come among us and revealed yourself in Christ. As we celebrate this coming, may we recognize again our dignity and serve one another with respect for the diversity of your gifts to us. We ask this for all creation in union with Christ who radiates in all and through all to your honor and glory forever. Amen.

DAYTIME PRAYER

Ant 1 You will deliver the needy when they call, the poor and those who have no helper.

Ant 2 All peoples will be blessed in you, all nations call you blessed.

Ant 3 You will draw water in joy from the Savior's fountain.

(Prayer as in Morning Prayer)

EVENING PRAYER

READING

Mystery is necessarily lonely because of its profundity, not its incomprehensibility. Nothing is more meaningful than mystery in its essence, but because of our finite minds and constricted hearts, mystery throws us into the land of loneliness. Standing on the ocean shore, even surrounded by friends, draws us deep into the darkness of not knowing infinity; gazing at the horizon from a mountain peak plunges our imaginations into the experience of immensity; contemplating the fingers of a newborn child or pondering the death of a life-time friend—the mysteries of life and death—drives us into an inarticulateness. Mystery means not to know and that space is lonely. No one can enter into the uniqueness of our experience even though blessed with compassion. All of us stutter and stumble in the presence of a sunset, a friendship, a star. Such is life.

Robert F. Morneau, *Mantras from a Poet: Jessica Powers*, pp. 58–59, (5)

RESPONSORY

Show us, O God, your steadfast love, and grant us your salvation.
    —**Show us**...
Restore us again that we may rejoice, —**and grant**...

Glory to you, Source of all Being, Eternal Word and Holy Spirit.
—**Show us...**

CANTICLE OF MARY

Ant   O Adonai and Leader of the house of Israel, who appeared to Moses in flames of a burning bush and gave him your Law on Sinai, come and free us with your outstretched arm.

INTERCESSIONS

O God, Source of all Good, we pray to you:
Renew your gifts in our hearts.

You have given us Jesus to lead us to the fullness of life;
—we welcome in him the news of salvation.
Help us to recognize the signs of the times;
—and to judge all things in the light of your truth.
We are aware that we are one family in you;
—tear down the barriers that divide us.
Through Christ the riddles of sorrow and death grow meaningful;
—comfort the grieving; console the dying.

PRAYER: O God of the Universe, your vastness is beyond our power to imagine, but you have come among us and revealed yourself in Christ. As we celebrate this coming, may we recognize again our dignity and serve one another with respect for the diversity of your gifts to us. We ask this for all creation in union with Christ who radiates in all and through all to your honor and glory forever. Amen.

DECEMBER 19
(Psalms and antiphons from the current week)

MORNING PRAYER

READING

"Make your home in me as I make mine in you" (Jn 15:40).... Our first home was in the womb of our earthly mother, but the womb of God is our "forever" home.... Living in God's womb is living in the heart of the Trinity. Nicodemus asked Jesus if a grown person could enter again the mother's womb. In the womb of God, our Eternal Mother, we can indeed enter and find again the source of our being, the font of life-giving waters, the life of our life. God is pregnant with us—holding us, nourishing us, delighting in us, bringing us into birth at each new moment—yet enveloping and embracing us forever in the fold of this Holy Womb. It is our refuge, our place of repose, our home.

Teresa M. Boersig, OCD, "Christmas Reverie," (4)

RESPONSORY

Lift up your eyes, Jerusalem; the glory of God is dawning
　　on you. —**Lift up**...
Darkness has covered the earth and thick clouds the people;
　　—**the glory**...
Glory to you, Source of all Being, Eternal Word and Holy Spirit.
　　—**Lift up**...

CANTICLE OF ZECHARIAH

Ant　Let us wait for God's word as we wait for rain; may it
　　descend upon us as dew on the grass.

INTERCESSIONS

O Christ, you are our light, the image of God and the firstborn of all creation. We pray to you:
　　Come and illumine the mystery of life.

In you we have been reconciled to God and among ourselves;
　　—help us to work as one family for the liberation of all.
You are the center of all life;
　　—renew us and free us from dullness of mind and heart.
Yours is the earth and its fullness;
　　—help us to respect and care for our planet.
You died for all humankind;
　　—may all come to live in the light of the paschal mystery.

PRAYER:　O God, your holy Word became enfleshed in the Virgin
　　Mary. With her this Advent we have reflected on the
　　angel's promises. We know you are always coming into
　　our lives and that we bring you forth in works of mercy
　　and love. Help us today to live by this faith. We ask
　　this through the intercession of all who revealed your
　　compassionate love and now live with you in eternal
　　joy. Amen.

DAYTIME PRAYER

Ant 1 Behold, a virgin shall conceive and bear a son and shall call his name Emmanuel.

Ant 2 Sing aloud, O daughter of Zion. Rejoice and exult with all your heart.

Ant 3 Do not fear, O Zion, your God is in your midst.

(Prayer as in Morning Prayer)

EVENING PRAYER

READING

Divine Wisdom surely revealed a new part of its plan during David's dynasty. Israel will have a country, a capital, even a temple that will symbolize the divine presence in the midst of the people of the promise. In the person of the king, it also receives a leader, a guarantor of the covenant and servant of the divine will.... David's line will remain a standard, a sign raised to rally the nations as well as the exiles of Israel and Judah.... Nathan's prophecy...has no other purpose than to keep alive the faith of his readers in the promise of God, at a time when hardly anything remained that had been accomplished.

Days of the Lord, Vol. 1, pp. 186–87, (9)

RESPONSORY

Show us, O God, your steadfast love, and grant us your
    salvation. **—Show us...**
Restore us again that we may rejoice, **—and grant...**
Glory to you, Source of all Being, Eternal Word and Holy Spirit.
    —Show us...

CANTICLE OF MARY

Ant O Root of Jesse, you stand as a sign for all people. Before you rulers keep silence; from you all nations seek help. O come to free us and do not make us wait.

INTERCESSIONS

O God, you call us in Christ to holiness, grace, and peace. We pray to you and say:

Help us to live with grateful hearts.

Your word is in harmony with our deepest desires;
—restore hope to the doubtful and despairing.
Give us a living and vibrant faith;
—animating us to works of justice for the poor and the
oppressed.
Your Spirit directs the unfolding of time;
—renew the face of the earth.
You have created us all in love;
—give us light to recognize that you are our true destiny.

PRAYER: O God, your holy Word became enfleshed in the Virgin
Mary. With her this Advent we have reflected on the
angel's promises. We know you are always coming into
our lives and that we bring you forth in works of mercy
and love. Help us today to live by this faith. We ask
this through the intercession of all who revealed your
compassionate love and now live with you in eternal
joy. Amen.

DECEMBER 20

(Psalms and antiphons from the current week)

MORNING PRAYER

READING

The people of Advent are "us." The Baptist prods us on to newness, and
the Zachary in us resists until our Elizabeth insists. Our Joseph lets it
happen, and the young Mary in us seizes the gift and runs with it. It
must be so if the Christ in us is to be born.

Elizabeth Meluch, OCD, (11)

RESPONSORY

Lift up your eyes, Jerusalem; the glory of God is dawning
on you. **—Lift up...**
Darkness has covered the earth and thick clouds the people;
—the glory...
Glory to you, Source of all Being, Eternal Word and Holy Spirit.
—Lift up...

CANTICLE OF ZECHARIAH

Ant The angel Gabriel was sent to Mary, a virgin engaged to a man named Joseph.

INTERCESSIONS

Jesus, you come that we might walk in newness of life. To you we pray:

Come, Lord Jesus, come.

Be a deliverer to those countries ravaged by war;
   —help us to see the way to peace.
You are the center of all life;
   —teach us our responsibility for human development.
You come from God to save us from sin;
   —free us from the evil we find in our hearts.
We remember all who have died;
   —welcome them home to everlasting joy.

PRAYER: O God, Source of all peace, we have heard again your promises of old and your vision for all humankind. In the coming of Christ, we recognize the one who can free us from all that prevents their fulfillment. Help us to respond wholeheartedly to this liberating presence. This we ask through Jesus, the Eternal Word, who lives with you and the Holy Spirit forever. Amen.

DAYTIME PRAYER

Ant 1 Our God will come from the holy place to free us from oppression.

Ant 2 Nation shall not lift up sword against nation; nor shall they learn war anymore.

Ant 3 Teach us your ways that we may walk in paths of peace.

(Prayer as in Morning Prayer)

EVENING PRAYER

READING

For believers, God's plan in governing and saving...humankind, is a gift to be gratefully received and admired and an obligatory goal to strive for.

The fact that even fervent believers and communities can approach it only gradually and discover only step by step all the implications does not at all mean that it is just a matter of a virtue going beyond what is commanded or required. It is a central goal-commandment for everyone in one's interpersonal relationships and community life, and finally also for one's mission to be salt for the earth and light to the world (Mt 5: 13–6). The whole world should benefit by the gospel of peace through the example and commitment of Christians to overcome the curse of violence.

Bernard Häring, The Healing Power of Peace and Nonviolence, p. 60, (1)

RESPONSORY

Show us, O God, your steadfast love, and grant us your
  salvation. **—Show us**...
Restore us again that we may rejoice, **—and grant**...
Glory to you, Source of all Being, Eternal Word and Holy Spirit.
  —Show us...

CANTICLE OF MARY

Ant O Key of David and Scepter of the house of Israel. You open
  and no one shuts. You close and no one opens. Come and
  deliver us from the prisons that hold us, for we are seated in
  darkness, oppressed by the shadows of death.

INTERCESSIONS

O God, your delight is to be with the children of earth. One with you in Christ, we pray:

  Glory and praise to our God!

When we lack human resources and power;
  —deepen our trust in the power of your Spirit.
We are often in darkness and aware of our weakness;
  —kindle within us the light of the gospel.
You have put us at the service of your creation;
  —help us to use our gifts for the good of all creatures.
Sustain us in love and devotion to you;
  —that we may live fully according to the truth.

PRAYER: O God, Source of all peace, we have heard again your
  promises of old and your vision for all humankind. In
  the coming of Christ, we recognize the one who can free
  us from all that prevents their fulfillment. Help us to

respond wholeheartedly to this liberating presence.
This we ask through Jesus, the Eternal Word, who lives
with you and the Holy Spirit forever. Amen.

DECEMBER 21
(Psalms and antiphons from the current week)
MORNING PRAYER

READING

The Day of the Lord is announced as a day of joy and deliverance for all
those who hope for salvation: "The people that walked in darkness have
seen a great light" (Is 9:1). How could joy not accompany the dazzling
clarity of the endless Day that vanquishes all errors and lies?... God's
chosen ones will bask in the "sun of justice with its healing rays." When
Zechariah salutes the dawn of the messianic day, along with his
celebration of John the Baptist's birth, he appeals in his canticle
(*Benedictus*) to the "Sun of justice"....

Days of the Lord, Vol. 1, p. 188, (9)

RESPONSORY

Lift up your eyes, Jerusalem; the glory of God is dawning on you.
   —Lift up...
Darkness has covered the earth and thick clouds the people;
   —the glory...
Glory to you, Source of all Being, Eternal Word and Holy Spirit.
   —Lift up...

CANTICLE OF ZECHARIAH

Ant There is no cause for fear. In five days our God will be
        coming to us.

INTERCESSIONS

O God, in the gift of Jesus, we see the face of Love:
   Help us to reveal this love to others.

Enlighten all church leaders and those of nations;
   —may your Spirit fill the earth.
Look with compassion on the tired, disillusioned and discouraged;
   —may faith enkindle new vision in the darkness.
You have blessed us with freedom for we are made in your image;
   —keep our consciences true and our choices wise.

You call us to commune with you and to share your happiness;
—may this gift of friendship be realized in our lives.

PRAYER: O God, Source of all good, you constantly broke
through our history calling us to love, peace, and
justice. Your Word made flesh in Jesus is a new call
and a new beginning. This Advent we ask to renew this
vision and our fidelity to Jesus who is the way. We ask
this in Jesus' name. Amen.

DAYTIME PRAYER

Ant 1 Come let us walk in the light of our God.

Ant 2 The night is far gone; the day is at hand.

Ant 3 Let us cast off the works of darkness and put on the armor
of light.

(Prayer as in Morning Prayer)

EVENING PRAYER

READING

The most powerful metaphor [for God] for me is Creator.... If I could
create a symbol to express the helping, nourishing, feeding role of God-
with-us, it would be a massive, gentle earth mother who enfolds her
offspring with warmth and love, protecting them from outside harm; a
nursing mother who never pushes her child away, a goddess of great
wisdom and beauty, a simple kind of beauty, eyes that smile Love into
anyone receiving their gaze. Life-giver is feminine; it's flesh and blood
delivery and deliverance from the darkness of our lives, it's Spirit
breathed into me at the moment of my coming into the world.

Paula Farrell Sullivan, *The Mystery of My Story.* p. 80, p. 81, (1)

RESPONSORY

Show us, O God, your steadfast love, and grant us your salvation.
  —Show us...
Restore us again that we may rejoice, **—and grant...**
Glory to you, Source of all Being, Eternal Word and Holy Spirit.
  —Show us...

CANTICLE OF MARY

Ant O Rising Sun, splendor of Eternal Light and brilliant Sun of
Justice, come and light up the darkness concealing from us
the path to life.

INTERCESSIONS

You have revealed the Christ, O God, as the goal of human
history. We pray to you:
Enlighten our minds and hearts.

You draw to yourself the marginal and the alienated;
—heal all families, communities, and nations that have lost
your Spirit as the bond of union.
You alone search the heart;
—deliver us from all harmful judgments of ourselves and
others.
May new possibilities in science and technology;
—lead to wise and moral choices.
We recognize our freedom but also new kinds of social slavery;
—come and save us from all forms of death.

PRAYER: O God, Source of all good, you constantly broke
through our history calling us to love, peace, and
justice. Your Word made flesh in Jesus is a new call
and a new beginning. This Advent we ask you to renew
in us this vision and our fidelity to Jesus who is the
way. We ask this in Jesus' name. Amen.

DECEMBER 22
(Psalms and antiphons from the current week)

MORNING PRAYER

READING

Advent is the season of the secret, the secret of the growth of Christ, of
Divine Love growing in silence. It is the season of humility, silence, and
growth. For nine months Christ grew in His Mother's body. By His own
will she formed Him from herself, from the simplicity of her daily life.
She had nothing to give Him but herself.... He asked for nothing else.
She gave Him herself. Working, eating, sleeping, she was forming His
body from hers. His flesh and blood. From her humanity she gave Him
His humanity.

Caryll Houselander, *The Reed of God*, pp. 38–39, (5)

RESPONSORY

Lift up your eyes, Jerusalem; the glory of God is dawning
  on you. **—Lift up**...
Darkness has covered the earth and thick clouds the people;
  —the glory...
Glory to you, Source of all Being, Eternal Word and Holy Spirit.
  —Lift up...

CANTICLE OF ZECHARIAH

Ant When the voice of your greeting came to my ears, the babe in
  my womb leaped for joy.

INTERCESSIONS

O Christ, we long for your coming as we say:
  Come, Lord Jesus, come!

As Sarah longed for Isaac;
  —our barren and sorrow-laden world longs for your fullness.
As Hannah longed for Samuel;
  —our deafened ears long to hear your voice.
As Elizabeth rejoiced in the babe in her womb;
  —let all expectant mothers rejoice in their fruitfulness.
As Zachary sang a song of blessing for his son;
  —let all expectant fathers rejoice in the gift of new life.
As Mary waited in mystery and longing;
  —may all who await your second coming be born into eternal
  life.

PRAYER: O God of tender mercy, your love for us has drawn you
  to be one with us in Christ. You are breaking down the
  barriers between nations by the force of that love in our
  hearts. Help us always to be persons of peace in union
  with those who actively build it in society. Grant this
  through your Christ whose gift is the blessing of peace
  in the midst of chaos. Amen.

DAYTIME PRAYER

Ant 1 No one has seen a God like you who rewards those who
  await you.

Ant 2 You bless the ones who joyfully work for justice, who
         remember you and your ways.

Ant 3 The days are coming when I will fulfill the promise I made
         to the house of Judah and the house of Israel.

(Prayer as in Morning Prayer)

EVENING PRAYER

READING

Mary greets her cousin and Elizabeth becomes ecstatic. Joy is
everywhere in the house because it comes from the one who is coming
into the world to give birth to joy. Mary sings, inspired by the Spirit
animating her child. Elizabeth exults with the joy of the forerunner who
has not yet been born. John the Baptist expresses his joy already—even
before he has been born. Joy is born of the promise. It is given to us
when we come to life like the child born of hope.... [Those] who will live
in the grace of faith will dance every evening. [They] will feel the Spirit
and life itself trembling within [them], even when everything seems
barren.

Marcel Bastin, Ghislain Pinckers, Michel Teheux, *God Day by Day, Vol. 4*, p. 61, (1)

RESPONSORY

Show us, O God, your steadfast love, and grant us your
    salvation. **—Show us...**
Restore us again that we may rejoice, **—and grant...**
Glory to you, Source of all Being, Eternal Word and Holy Spirit.
    —Show us...

CANTICLE OF MARY

Ant O Ruler of all nations and true desire of our hearts! You are
        the cornerstone binding us all into a home for God. Come
        and free us whom you formed from earth.

INTERCESSIONS

O God, you made the world in the image of your Word; with
grateful hearts we pray:

Come, Lord Jesus, come!

In the image of the Word all things were made;
    —teach us to reverence all of creation.

Your hands fashioned the moon and the stars;
—may our adventures into space further the cause of peace.
You created the waters and all that dwell in them;
—may we keep them free of all pollution.
The birds and animals reflect the joy of your bounty;
—may we respect their rights to survive for their own sake
rather than ours.
You created us as your own children;
—may your image shine forth in us.

PRAYER: O God of tender mercy, your love for us has drawn you
to be one with us in Christ. You are breaking down the
barriers between nations by the force of that love in our
hearts. Help us always to be persons of peace in union
with those who actively build it in society. Grant this
through your Christ whose gift is the blessing of peace
in the midst of chaos. Amen.

DECEMBER 23
(Psalms and antiphons from the current week)
MORNING PRAYER
READING

The great antiphons reach their highest point with the invocation of
Emmanuel.... The presentiment that God is not only the Most High, but
also the Omnipresent (Pss 119; 148), the creator God present to
[creation] (Wis 11:25), the savior God present to [the] people (Exod 19:4),
climaxes in the person of Emmanuel, i.e., God-with-us, already
obscurely announced in the prophecy of Almah (Is 7:14). So the great
yearning of faith that longed for Wisdom to dwell among us finally found
its fulfillment in the conception of the Son of God, in Mary, by the power
of the Holy Spirit.... Concrete presence—in the flesh—of God as [one of
us], the actual Word of God, come to pitch [a] tent among us (Jn 1:14)!
The final, ultimate presence of God, who will remain with the Church
forever (Mt 28:20), until the full acceptance by all nations of the One
who fills the universe by the power of his resurrection!

Days of the Lord, Vol. 1, p. 189, (9)

RESPONSORY

Lift up your eyes, Jerusalem; the glory of God is dawning
on you. **—Lift up**...

Darkness has covered the earth and thick clouds the people;
  —the glory...
Glory to you, Source of all Being, Eternal Word and Holy Spirit.
  —Lift up...

CANTICLE OF ZECHARIAH

Ant Behold, all things spoken to Mary by an angel have now
  been completed.

INTERCESSIONS

To the One who is and who is to come, we pray:
  O Come, O Come, Emmanuel!

Because we are poor and needy;
  —we long for your fullness.
Because your people are oppressed and in chains;
  —teach us how to break the bonds that enslave them.
Because your word falls on barren ground;
  —send us the saving waters that we may make barren land
  fruitful.
Because our hearts are stone and our eyes are blind;
  —create in us hearts of flesh to see your suffering world.
Because we await your coming at the dawning of each day;
  —may those who await your final coming see the dawn of
  eternal life.

PRAYER: O God of Life, Mary became the mother of Jesus by
  embracing your will with a full heart. Help us to enter
  into the mystery of salvation by an active and
  responsible obedience. Free us from the attitudes that
  limit our responses to your inspirations. We ask this in
  union with all who journey with Jesus to fullness of
  life. Amen.

DAYTIME PRAYER

Ant 1 In those days I will cause a branch to spring forth for
  David. Justice will be seen in the land.

Ant 2 Proclaim to all peoples the glad tidings. God, our Savior, is
  coming to us.

Ant 3 Behold, a virgin shall conceive and bear a son and shall call his name Emmanuel.

(Prayer as in Morning Prayer)

EVENING PRAYER

READING

Before every prayer,...the Church expresses the wish "The Lord be with you". May Christmas help us to understand this, for ever since the feast of the Incarnation, which is also the beginning of the divinization of men and women, the tremendous desire for a salvation is open to all, along with the great desire for God that is offered to all....

> O God, you are life,
> you are salvation,
> you are health,
> you are immortality,
> you are beatitude,
> you are illumination...
> for you take delight
> in nothing other
> than the salvation of [humankind].   (Gregory Narek)

Days of the Lord, Vol. 1, pp. 189–90, (9)

RESPONSORY

Show us, O God, your steadfast love, and grant us your
   salvation. **—Show us...**
Restore us again that we may rejoice, **—and grant...**
Glory to you, Source of all Being, Eternal Word and Holy Spirit.
   —Show us...

CANTICLE OF MARY

Ant O Emmanuel, Giver of a new law to all nations, come and
   save us, for you are our God.

INTERCESSIONS

To Christ who longed to live among us, we pray:
   Glory to you, Lord Jesus Christ!

Leaping from the eternal womb of God, you come into our world;
   —may we reverence this world that you love.
Encircled in the loving womb of Mary, you graced her life;
   —may we reverence all children born into this world.

Experiencing our weakness and littleness, you taught us true greatness;
   —teach us to reverence the sick, the elderly, and the lonely.
Enjoying the blessings of family life, you knew the gift of sharing;
   —give comfort to the homeless, the abandoned, and the
     forgotten.
Returning to the One you loved and served, you sent us your Spirit;
   —may all who die know your welcoming and loving embrace.

PRAYER: O God of Life, Mary became the mother of Jesus by embracing your will with a full heart. Help us to enter into the mystery of salvation by an active and responsible obedience. Free us from the attitudes that limit our responses to your inspirations. We ask this in union with all who journey with Jesus to fullness of life. Amen.

DECEMBER 24

(Psalms and antiphons from the current week)

MORNING PRAYER

READING

What shall I wish you for Christmas? I think the best Christmas wish is that some holy and lovely thought may come to your heart with your Christmas Communion, and make its home with you and stay to strengthen you and help you to "walk forty days and forty nights" like the heavenly bread of Elias. God only knows the bread to give [God's] creatures, and when [God] says one word it makes the impossible possible, and the unlovely lovely, and the unmeaning become a revelation. (Janet Erskine Stuart, RSCJ)

Maud Monahan, *Life and Letters of Janet Erskine Stuart*, p. 258, (15)

RESPONSORY

Tomorrow our sinfulness will be taken away and salvation shall
   be ours. **—Tomorrow...**
The one who frees us will be our ruler;
   —and salvation...
Glory to you, Source of all Being, Eternal Word and Holy Spirit.
   —Tomorrow...

CANTICLE OF ZECHARIAH

Ant The Savior of the world shall appear like the sun and descend into the Virgin's womb as rain on the grass.

INTERCESSIONS

The time has come; the day is at hand. With joyful hearts we pray:
Today is the day of salvation!

We eagerly await your coming;
—come to all your people, especially those who are most destitute.
We eagerly await your coming;
—to the homeless, the addicted, and all held in bondage.
We eagerly await your coming;
—to free the waters, the animals, and the plants from human destruction and negligence.
We eagerly await your coming;
—to those longing to be taken to their eternal home.
We eagerly await your coming;
—to praise the One who sent you, the Source of all Life and fruitfulness.

PRAYER: Most loving God, in the stillness of this Advent season we have contemplated the mystery of your coming in Christ. We thank you for your great mercy and for the hope that gives meaning to all our striving. Renew that hope in our hearts at the dawning of each day that we may not tire in the work we must do. Grant this through Jesus, the Incarnate Word who lives with you and the Spirit for all eternity. Amen.

DAYTIME PRAYER

Ant 1 The child to be born will be called holy, the holy one of God.

Ant 2 Blessed is she who has believed in the word spoken to her from God.

Ant 3 O that you would rend the heavens and come down, that the mountains would quake at your presence.

(Prayer as in Morning Prayer)

CHRISTMAS

EVENING PRAYER I

Ant 1 Christ, our peace, comes in glory; the universe welcomes its redeemer. (Ps 113, p. 96)

Ant 2 This day God sends forth the Eternal Word to the earth. (Ps 47, p. 24)

Ant 3 O Eternal Word, for our salvation you emptied yourself and became one of us. (Phil 2:6–11, p. 2)

READING

Jesus is the summit toward which past sacred history converges, as does our history, which begins with his birth. From beginning to end, this history is lived out by men and women from generation to generation. In some way, Joseph and Mary show the road to follow by outlining the general path, which will become specific in the lives of all people according to the way they respond to their vocation.... In a way certainly different from Joseph's, but no less real, we have an irreplaceable role to fulfill. God waits for us to do what [we are told], not by the voice of an angel, but by that of Scripture and the Church at first, and later through unexpected situations and people who come into our lives. Jesus receives the name that Joseph gives to him. We have to acknowledge it and pass it on. Then, "the glory of [God] will be revealed, and all [humankind] will see the saving power of God."... Let us rise up, let us go forward with songs of joy. The celebration of Christmas is about to begin.

Days of the Lord, Vol. 1, pp. 198–99, (9)

RESPONSORY

Today you will see the coming of the Promised One. **—Today**...
At dawn you will see God's glory, **—the coming**...
Glory to you, Source of all Being, Eternal Word and Holy Spirit.
    —Today...

CANTICLE OF MARY

Ant At sunrise you will see the coming of the Most High. Like the morning star, God will shine in our darkness.

INTERCESSIONS

A child is born in Bethlehem, alleluia.
                Come, let us rejoice, alleluia, alleluia.

This is the day we have long awaited, the reality foretold by all the prophets;

—We thank you, we praise you, we rejoice in you.

You are our God who shares divinity with us;

—We thank you, we praise you, we rejoice in you.

You are our God, Emmanuel, ever in our hearts and lives each day;

—We thank you, we praise you, we rejoice in you.

PRAYER: O God, the long-awaited day has come when your Eternal Word becomes one of us in Jesus. May every child born into this world also incarnate your Word, that the good news of your life with us and in us may be relived in every time and every age, today and forever. Amen.

MORNING PRAYER
(Psalms from Sunday, Week I, p. 3)

Ant 1 Shepherds, tell us what you have seen and heard. We saw the newborn savior, and hosts of angels singing God's praises, alleluia.

Ant 2 The angels said to them: "I bring you good news of great joy; to you is born this day Christ the savior, alleluia."

Ant 3 To us a child is born; today the Mighty God shares our humanity, alleluia.

READING

Flocks feed by darkness with a noise of whispers,
In the dry grass of pastures,
And lull the solemn night with their weak bells.

The little towns upon the rocky hills
Look down as meek as children:
Because they have seen come this holy time.

God's glory, now, is kindled gentler than low candlelight
Under the rafters of a barn:
Eternal Peace is sleeping in the hay,
And Wisdom's born in secret in a straw-roofed stable.

And O! Make holy music in the stars, you happy angels.
You shepherds, gather on the hill.
Look up, you timid flocks, where the three kings
Are coming through the wintry trees;

While we unnumbered children of the wicked centuries
Come after with our penances and prayers,
And lay them down in the sweet-smelling hay
Beside the wise men's golden jars.

"Carol" in *The Collected Poems of Thomas Merton*, p. 89, (16)

RESPONSORY

Christ has made known our salvation, alleluia, alleluia.
   —Christ...
Salvation by our God, **—alleluia...**
Glory to you, Source of all Being, Eternal Word and Holy Spirit.
   —Christ...

CANTICLE OF ZECHARIAH

Ant Glory to God in the highest; peace to all people on earth,
   alleluia.

INTERCESSIONS

In the beginning was the Word, and the Word was God, who
became flesh and dwells among us this day.
                    Christ shall be called Wonderful!
                    Christ shall be called Peace!

On this day new joy entered our world;
   —may we try by our lives to share joy with others each day.
On this day fresh hope entered our world;
   —may we bring hope to those who are heavily burdened.
On this day love was visible in a child;
   —may we show our love for others in concrete ways of
   friendship and service.
On this day the promise of peace on earth was proclaimed;
   —may we be lovers of peace and demonstrate this love by
   reflective responses to life's challenges and trials.

PRAYER: Morning has broken with new glory this Christmas
            day; we rejoice in our brother, Jesus. May we deepen
            our relationships with God and with one another in

ever-growing love and reverence. This we ask through Jesus, born this day and through all ages. Amen.

DAYTIME PRAYER

Ant 1 The parents of Jesus were filled with awe at all that was said of him, alleluia. (Ps 19:7–14, p. 12)

Ant 2 Mary kept all these things, pondering them in her heart, alleluia. (Ps 47, p. 24)

Ant 3 My eyes have seen your salvation, which you have prepared in the presence of all peoples, alleluia. (Ps 48, p. 30)

PRAYER: At this noontime hour we thank you for the time you offer us to praise you anew and to grow in knowing, loving, and serving you in one another. May all know your gift of peace in the midst of chaos. Grant this through Jesus who promised us peace the world cannot give. Amen.

EVENING PRAYER II

Ant 1 You are honored by the Most High; before the dawning of time, before the creation of the sun, you were begotten, alleluia. (Ps 110:1–5, 7, p. 53)

Ant 2 The love of God is eternal; the power of the Most High will not fail. (Ps 130, p. 143)

Ant 3 In the beginning was the Word, who is God; today the Word comes to save the world. (Col 1:12–20, p. 122)

READING

We have a tendency to read the infancy stories differently from the way they were intended. We read them with especial attention to the infancy, the virginity of Mary, and the historicity of the occurrences. But the stories are not particularly meant to provide information about any of these details. The point of the infancy narratives is not the infancy but the Christology involved in identifying and accepting the mature Jesus. The virginity of Mary is a theological statement about Jesus

rather than a gynecological statement about Mary. It tells us that the
Spirit responsible for the ministry and resurrection of Jesus was active
in the origins of Jesus and that Jesus must be explained not in terms of
human agency alone but in terms that are extraordinary and
exceptional. The historicity of the various items in the infancy stories is
marginal. These are stories that deal, instead, with symbol and
meaning, with theological reflection and cultural continuity.

Anthony T. Padavano, Christmas to Calvary, p. 12, (1)

RESPONSORY

The Word was made flesh, alleluia, alleluia. **—The Word**...
And dwelt among us, **—alleluia**...
Glory to you, Source of all Being, Eternal Word and Holy Spirit.
   —The Word...

CANTICLE OF MARY

Ant Your Christ is born today and has appeared among us. All
      creation joins in song with angel choirs to sing your praise.
      Today your people delight in your glory, alleluia.

INTERCESSIONS

With bright hope we confide our weary, war-torn, suffering world
to you, son of Mary, Word of God.
   May your birth bring new peace to all.

O God, we confide all young people to you;
   —increase their faith in your love so that they find more joy
   in life and more courage in the challenge of following your
   ways.
We confide all the suffering of our world to you;
   —may they know your presence and healing grace at this
   difficult time.
We confide the unemployed, the homeless, the suicidal to your
tender concern;
   —be light in the darkness of their pain and grant them
   hope.
We confide all the elderly to you;
   —may they be strengthened and comforted by faith in the
   eternal life that lies ahead of them.

We confide all the children of the world to you;
—may they experience love and compassion, food and
shelter, and the joy of carefree play.

PRAYER: O Holy Womb of God, birth each of us into your image
and likeness that Christ may again reveal your love
and concern to our world. We pray especially for all
who are most vulnerable that they may experience your
care. Grant this in the name of Jesus and through the
intercession of all the children who play with you in
your eternal home. Amen.

HOLY FAMILY SUNDAY
Sunday in the Octave of Christmas
EVENING PRAYER I

Ant 1 Jacob was the father of Joseph, the husband of Mary, of
whom Jesus was born, who is called the Christ.
(Ps 113, p. 96)

Ant 2 Joseph, son of David, do not fear to take Mary as your
wife, for the one who is conceived in her is of the Holy
Spirit. (Ps 147:12–20, p. 85)

Ant 3 The shepherds went with haste and found Mary and
Joseph, and the babe lying in a manger.
(Eph 1:3–10, p. 14)

READING

With the beloved mother looking for her beloved Son, do not cease
searching until you have found him. O, how you would weep if with
devotion you could look upon so venerable a lady, so charming a girl, in
a foreign country with so tender and handsome a little boy; or if you
could hear the sweet complaint of the loving mother of God: *Son, why
have you done this to us?*

Bonaventure, *The Tree of Life*, p. 132, (1)

RESPONSORY

The Word was made flesh, alleluia, alleluia. **—The Word...**
And dwelt among us; **—alleluia,...**
Glory to you, Source of all Being, Eternal Word and Holy Spirit.
—The Word...

CANTICLE OF MARY

Ant The boy Jesus stayed behind in Jerusalem. His parents did
not know it, but supposing him to be among their friends
and relatives, they went a day's journey.

INTERCESSIONS

O God, you image life in relationship through the gift of our
families, and so we pray:
> **Blessed are you, Most Holy Trinity.**

O God, beloved Father, giver of all gifts;
— we thank you for your provident care.
O God, beloved Mother, birthing us into new life;
— we thank you for life-giving waters.
O God, Word made flesh in Jesus;
— we thank you for drawing us into the mystery of
incarnating Christ in our lives.
O Holy Trinity,
— grant that we may be generative and fruitful bearers of
your life-giving Spirit.

PRAYER: O God, you call us to life in relationship. Help us to
know ourselves that we may be compassionate to
others. Forgive the many times we have failed to be
forgiving to those nearest us, and grant us the humility
to ask pardon. This we ask through the intercession of
Jesus, Mary, and Joseph. Amen.

MORNING PRAYER
(Psalms from Sunday, Week I, p. 3)

Ant 1 The parents of Jesus went to Jerusalem every year at the
feast of the Passover.

Ant 2 The child grew and became strong and filled with wisdom;
the favor of God was with him.

Ant 3 His father and mother marveled at what was said about
their child.

READING

And this is He whom Heaven hymns,
All trembling in His white young limbs,
Whom choirs adore and seraphs bless—
Unspeakable His helplessness.
A Baby's cheek the wind would kindle.
Ah, holy weaver and blessed spindle,
That spun the little swaddling clothes
To sheathe so sweet, so fair a rose!
Dull stable-lamp, my love you are—
Shine bright and be His morning star.
Full many a moon would give her light
To hang upon your beam tonight,
And flood the wondrous sanctuary
And shine on Him and His Mother Mary.

Leonard Feeney, SJ, In Towns and Little Towns, p. 97, (23)

RESPONSORY

Christ, come forth from the living God, have mercy on us.
   —Christ...
Obedient to Mary and Joseph, **—have mercy**...
Glory to you, Source of all Being, Eternal Word and Holy Spirit.
   —Christ...

CANTICLE OF ZECHARIAH

Ant Son, why have you treated us so? Your father and I have
   been anxiously looking for you.

INTERCESSIONS

Christ, you came to us from the depths of Mystery. Your vision
always drew you forward and so we pray:
   May we seek our God in sincerity of heart.

Christ, our brother and companion, teach us how to communicate
with gentle understanding and love;
   —be with us each day in our families and communities as
   we try to grow in loving relationships.
You were obedient to Mary and Joseph;
   —may we learn to follow you by listening to each other with
   discerning hearts.

You showed your love for your parents;
— let us be creative and generous in responding to those
   who fostered and nurtured us.
Be with those families wounded by alienation and pain;
— enable them to understand differences and support one
   another in suffering.
Comfort loved ones who grieve for missing, kidnapped, or run-
away children;
— give them strength to keep the light of hope burning in
   their homes and in their hearts.

PRAYER: Most Holy Trinity, look with compassion on all families
where love and understanding have long been absent.
In your merciful kindness, bring peace, comfort, and
joy to all members today. Let all families take
inspiration and courage from Jesus, Mary, and Joseph.
So may we praise you now and forever. Amen.

DAYTIME PRAYER
(Psalms from Sunday, Week I, p. 6)

Ant 1 Mary and Joseph marveled at what was spoken of Jesus.

Ant 2 The mother of Jesus kept these words in her heart.

Ant 3 My eyes have seen your salvation which you have prepared
in the presence of all peoples.

PRAYER: Creator, Redeemer, and Sanctifier, bless all family
units this day and give them strength in forgiving one
another in patient love, so that they will daily find
comfort and encouragement in their homes. This we
ask through the intercession of all our family members
who live with you in the communion of saints. Amen.

EVENING PRAYER II

Ant 1 After three days, Mary and Joseph found Jesus in the
temple, sitting among the teachers, listening to them and
asking them questions. (Ps 122, p. 143)

Ant 2 Jesus went with his parents to Nazareth and was obedient
to them. (Ps 127, p. 122)

Ant 3 Jesus increased in wisdom and stature, in the favor of God and of the people. (Eph 1:3–10, p. 109)

READING

I look upon my vows as a means of expressing and living out my total commitment to God in faith and love. When I made my vows some forty-five years ago, it was with the uneasy intuition that I did not appreciate their meaning or grasp the full import of what I was doing.... My concept of consecration to God and union with Christ was pretty individualistic. I see my dedication now as a process of death and resurrection, and a journey toward freedom made with others and for them.... Christ's surrender to God in obedience and love is both the inspiration of my own obedience and the ground from which I perceive its value. This keeps me striving to adapt myself to others in community. I feel that I experience the reality of obedience when I listen and respond to the voice of the community or individual, and I consider this a form of service, not just to an individual or to the community, but to the church and society. For I believe that in serving my own community, I do, in part, serve all humankind. This is a deep conviction with me.

Miriam Elder, OCD, p. 23, (11)

RESPONSORY

Let us adore the Christ who was pleased to be born of a virgin.
   —Let us...
Flesh of our flesh; **—who was...**
Glory to you, Source of all Being, Eternal Word and Holy Spirit.
   —Let us...

CANTICLE OF MARY

Ant All who heard him were amazed at his understanding and his answers.

INTERCESSIONS

O God, you image life in relationship through the gift of our families, and so we pray:
   Blessed are you, Most Holy Trinity.

O God, beloved Father, giver of all gifts;
   —we thank you for your provident care.
O God, beloved Mother, birthing us into new life;
   —we thank you for life-giving waters.

O God, Word made flesh in Jesus;
  —we thank you for drawing us into the mystery of
    incarnating Christ in our lives.
O Holy Trinity,
  —grant that we may be generative and fruitful bearers of
    your life-giving Spirit.

PRAYER: Most Holy Trinity, look with compassion on all
              families where love and understanding have long been
              absent. In your merciful kindness, bring peace,
              comfort, and joy to all members today. Let all families
              take inspiration and courage from Jesus, Mary, and
              Joseph. So may we praise you now and forever.
              Amen.

DECEMBER 26
FEAST OF ST. STEPHEN

MORNING PRAYER
(Psalms from Sunday, Week I, p. 3)

Ant 1 I have been faithful to you, my God, even in the face of
          death.

Ant 2 Filled with the Holy Spirit, Stephen gazed into heaven
          and saw the glory of God.

Ant 3 Stephen saw Jesus standing at the side of the Most High.

READING

Closest to the newborn Savior we see St. Stephen. What secured the
first martyr of the Crucified this place of honor? In youthful
enthusiasm he accomplished what the Lord said upon his entrance
into the world, "A body you have prepared for me. Behold, I come to
fulfill your will."... He followed the Lord in what may be by nature the
most difficult for the human heart, and even seems impossible: He
fulfilled the command to love one's enemies as did the Savior himself.
The Child in the manger...sees before him in spirit all who will follow
[God's] will, follow him on this way. His heartbeat goes out to the
youth whom he will one day await with a palm as the first to reach
[God's] throne. His little hand points him out to us as an example, as if
to say, "See the *gold* that I expect from you."

Edith Stein: The Hidden Life, p.113, (3)

RESPONSORY

The heavens opened, and Stephen beheld your glory.
  —The heavens...
Forgiving those who stoned him; **—Stephen...**
Glory to you, Source of all Being, Eternal Word and Holy Spirit.
  —The heavens...

CANTICLE OF ZECHARIAH

Ant Stephen prayed, "Lord, receive my spirit." He entered
    heaven and was crowned the first of martyrs.

INTERCESSIONS

In Christ, O God, we have received every spiritual blessing; we
lift our hearts and pray:
    May your perfect love cast out all fear.

We praise you and ask for the courage to accept life's sufferings;
  —hide us in the shelter of your wings.
We give you thanks for Stephen and all the early martyrs;
  —may we learn to be nonviolent when we are challenged
    and confronted.
We give you thanks for the martyrs of today;
  —give them strength and courage in their time of trial.
You taught us in Jesus to forgive those who hurt us;
  —turn our hearts of stone to hearts of flesh.

PRAYER: O God, as we celebrate your coming into our world,
    we also celebrate the feast of your martyr, Stephen,
    born into eternal life. Give us the grace to understand
    both the joy and the cost of discipleship. We pray
    especially for all of our sisters and brothers who are
    serving you in life-threatening situations. Be their
    strength and comfort. This we ask through the
    intercession of Stephen and all who gave their lives for
    you. Amen.

DAYTIME PRAYER
(Psalms from the current weekday of Week I)

Ant 1 Mary and Joseph marveled at what was spoken of Jesus.

Ant 2 The mother of Jesus kept these words in her heart.

Ant 3 My eyes have seen your salvation which you have prepared in the presence of all peoples.

PRAYER: Christ Jesus, give us the courage to forgive and love those who harm us and our sisters and brothers anywhere in the world. Then, like your martyr, Stephen, may we one day rejoice in your presence, beholding the glory of God Most Holy. Amen.

EVENING PRAYER

Ant 1 You are honored by the Most High; before the dawning of time, before the creation of the sun, you were begotten, alleluia. (Ps 110:1–5, 7, p. 53)

Ant 2 The love of God is eternal; the power of the Most High will not fail. (Ps 130, p. 143)

Ant 3 In the beginning was the Word, who is God; today the Word comes to save the world. (Col 1:12–20, p. 122)

READING

At the Last Supper Jesus prayed that we all may be one. In fact we are one, and the challenge for us is to realize our unity and our connectedness, to realize that everything we do affects the entire world. My move to understand, to forgive, and to be compassionate toward another who annoys me can mobilize to mercy a soldier who is thousands of miles away. It can inspire mediation among world leaders. At any moment I can pour into the world either love or hate energy. I can build or I can destroy. We are born of God's love, and we bear the power of that love.

Carmelites of Indianapolis, Hidden Friends, p. 95, (5)

RESPONSORY

The Word was made flesh, alleluia, alleluia. **—The Word**...
And dwelt among us, **—alleluia,**...
Glory to you, Source of all Being, Eternal Word and Holy Spirit.
    —The Word...

CANTICLE OF MARY

Ant In the silent darkness of night, the Word of God came down from heaven.

INTERCESSIONS

O God, you have come to earth that we might live with you for all eternity. Let us sing out in joy:
Glory to God in the highest!

God of compassion, you did not condemn Paul at the time of Stephen's death;
— teach us to withhold judgment and give us patient hearts.

You chose Stephen to serve the needs of your people;
— may all called to ministry be enabled to serve your people according to their gifts.

You graced Stephen with the gifts of wisdom and goodness;
— help us to appreciate and affirm the gifts of our friends and companions.

You enabled Stephen to forgive those who persecuted him;
— give us the gift of compassion toward those who misunderstand or oppress us.

PRAYER: O God, as we celebrate your coming into our world, we also celebrate the feast of your martyr, Stephen, born into eternal life. Give us the grace to understand both the joy and the cost of discipleship. We pray especially for all of our sisters and brothers who are serving you in life-threatening situations. Be their strength and comfort. This we ask through the intercession of Stephen and all who gave their lives for you. Amen.

DECEMBER 27
ST. JOHN, APOSTLE AND EVANGELIST

MORNING PRAYER
(Psalms from Sunday, Week I, p. 3)

Ant 1 John, evangelist and apostle, was beloved of Christ.

Ant 2 Christ on the cross put the care of his mother, Mary, into the hands of John.

Ant 3 The disciple whom Jesus loved said: It is the Lord!

READING

I have been speaking mainly of the wine (of suffering). Now I want to speak of the oil of joy. It was of this oil that Saint John said, "But you have an anointing from the Holy One, and all of you know the truth. I do not write to you because you do not know the truth, but you know it and because no lie comes from the truth," etc. (1 Jn 1: 20–21). And then a little later he says, the anointing you have received from God remains with you, and you have no need of someone to teach you. What the anointing teaches you is truth and not falsehood. So hold fast to what you have been taught.

Leonhard Schiemer, *Early Anabaptist Spirituality*, pp. 93–94, (1)

RESPONSORY

The Word was made flesh, alleluia, alleluia. **—The Word**...
And dwelt among us, **—alleluia,**...
Glory to you, Source of all Being, Eternal Word and Holy Spirit.
    —The Word...

CANTICLE OF ZECHARIAH

Ant   The Word became flesh and dwelt among us, and we have witnessed the glory of God bestowed on Jesus.

INTERCESSIONS

Christ Jesus, you chose women and men to preach the good news, and so we pray:
         Give us the grace of discipleship.

You called John to preach the gospel of love;
  —break down the barriers that separate us from others.
Your disciples, Mary and John, stood beneath the cross;
  —give us the courage to be faithful in times of trial.
You entrusted to John the care of your mother;
  —help us to grow in trust toward one another.
John was called a "Son of Thunder";
  —teach us to accept ourselves as we are and to appreciate the gifts we have been given.

PRAYER: O God, may the celebration of the birth of Jesus enkindle our desires to be his disciples. Teach us to be loving and responsive to those in need, and help us to grow in intimacy with you. This we ask in the name of Jesus, God-with-us, now and forever. Amen.

DAYTIME PRAYER

(Psalms from the current weekday of Week I)

Ant 1 Mary and Joseph marveled at what was spoken of Jesus.

Ant 2 The mother of Jesus kept these words in her heart.

Ant 3 My eyes have seen your salvation which you have prepared in the presence of all peoples.

(Prayer as in Morning Prayer)

EVENING PRAYER

Ant 1 You are honored by the Most High; before the dawning of time, before the creation of the sun, you were begotten, alleluia. (Ps 110:1–5, 7, p. 53)

Ant 2 The love of God is eternal; the power of the Most High will not fail. (Ps 130, p. 143)

Ant 3 In the beginning was the Word, who is God; today the Word comes to save the world. (Col 1:12–20, p. 122)

READING

Through John we know how we are to participate as our destiny in the life of Christ—as a branch of the divine vine—and in the life of the triune God. While he was alive, he was permitted to see the Incarnate God as the judge of the world in order to paint for us the mighty, enigmatic images of the mysterious revelation of the final days. He showed us this in that book which, like none other, can teach us to understand the chaos of this time as a part of the great battle between Christ and the Antichrist, a book of relentless solemnity and consoling promise.

Edith Stein: The Hidden Life, p.114, (3)

RESPONSORY

The Word was made flesh, alleluia, alleluia. **—The Word**...
And dwelt among us, **—alleluia,**...
Glory to you, Source of all Being, Eternal Word and Holy Spirit.
   —The Word...

CANTICLE OF MARY

Ant The prophet's words, O Mary, have been fulfilled through you; Christ was born of a virgin.

INTERCESSIONS

Your Word, O God, came down from heaven to set us free, and so we pray:

Glory to God in the highest!

Through the mouths of children, you perfected praise;
  —teach us to be meek and humble of heart.
John preached the message: Love one another;
  —help us to persevere in our efforts to grow in relationship.
John accepted the cup you asked him to drink;
  —give us the courage to accept the circumstances of our
    daily lives.
You chose women and men to witness to your coming;
  —may we give witness to our world that you still live
    among us.

PRAYER: O God, as evening comes, we thank you for the gift of Christ, the Light of the World. We thank you for the early followers of Jesus who passed the light on to us. May we be light for our world that all may know you live and dwell among us. Grant this through Jesus and all who preached in his name. Amen.

DECEMBER 28
HOLY INNOCENTS, MARTYRS

MORNING PRAYER
(Psalms from Sunday, Week I, p. 3)

Ant 1 These holy ones, who shed their blood for Christ, will dwell in heaven forever.

Ant 2 By their death and not by words, do these infants proclaim their witness to the gospel.

Ant 3 Out of the mouths of children you have found perfect praise, O God.

READING

The poverty of the birth is described in royal terms because, later, the poverty of the cross will be delineated in the light of Easter. The history of this child, from impoverished crib to imperial cross, will be as seamless as the garment taken from him as he was executed.

Christmas is suffused with the joy of the child in the manger and the
heartache of the children in the massacre. Grace and violence,
blessing and bloodshed intermingle. The passion narratives are
already begun on the first day of the child's life.

Anthony T. Padavano, Christmas to Calvary, p. 14, (1)

RESPONSORY

In the heavens, O God, your friends praise you forever. —**In the**...
You have prepared a place for them; —**your friends**...
Glory to you, Source of all Being, Eternal Word and Holy Spirit.
   —**In the**...

CANTICLE OF ZECHARIAH

Ant We praise you, O God; the glorious company of martyrs
      acclaim you.

INTERCESSIONS

O God, at the birth of Jesus the angels sang songs of glory and
peace:
   Grant us peace the world cannot give.

As Rachel mourned her children;
   —comfort all parents who mourn the death of their
      children.
As Jacob wept for Joseph;
   —bring solace and hope to those whose children are
      missing or have run away.
The Israelites in Egypt grieved over the slaughter of their
children;
   —protect children from all forms of violence.
Mary and Joseph fled with the child into Egypt;
   —may all exiled and refugee children find loving care and
      support.
Through the intercession of Joachim and Anne;
   —give patience and wisdom to young mothers and fathers.

PRAYER: Most loving God, the Holy Innocents were martyrs for
      Christ. May we, in our lives, bear witness to our love
      for you, showing by our deeds what we profess with
      our lips. Grant courage to women and men who strive
      by nonviolent action to influence others for the good
      of those suffering and deprived. This we ask through

the intercession of those who were victims of violence and now share eternal life with you. Amen.

DAYTIME PRAYER
(Psalms from the current weekday of Week I)

Ant 1 Mary and Joseph marveled at what was spoken of Jesus.

Ant 2 The mother of Jesus kept these words in her heart.

Ant 3 My eyes have seen your salvation which you have prepared in the presence of all peoples.

(Prayer as in Morning Prayer)

EVENING PRAYER

Ant 1 You are honored by the Most High; before the dawning of time, before the creation of the sun, you were begotten, alleluia. (Ps 110:1–5, 7, p. 53)

Ant 2 The love of God is eternal; the power of the Most High will not fail. (Ps 130, p. 143)

Ant 3 In the beginning was the Word, who is God; today the Word comes to save the world. (Col 1:12–20, p. 122)

READING

We carry the infant Christ and we carry the suffering Christ as well. At times, Christ is silent in me, moving the Spirit to leap in others, and sometimes the Christ leaps in me as I encounter the Spirit in another. As a community or as a family, the whole Christ becomes incarnate. In some, Christ comes to birth; in others, Christ advances in age, and grace, and wisdom. Still others are Christ suffering, or lying in a tomb. To embrace it all is to embrace the whole Christ. Christmas enables me to believe that when Christ is in the tomb of my heart, it is an advent time. The living waters will come and the tomb becomes a womb, waiting to burst forth into a living Christ.

Carmelites of Indianapolis, *Hidden Friends*, p. 17, (5)

RESPONSORY

The Word was made flesh, alleluia, alleluia. **—The Word...**
And dwelt among us, **—alleluia,...**
Glory to you, Source of all Being, Eternal Word and Holy Spirit.
    —The Word...

CANTICLE OF MARY

Ant God took flesh of the holy Virgin and became her only child. Let us worship God who is our salvation.

INTERCESSIONS

Today innocent people suffer because of jealousy and fear, and so we pray:

Create in us a new heart, O God.

Christ Jesus, you answered insult with silence;
—teach us how to be nonviolent in our responses.
You forbade Peter to use the sword;
—enable us to resolve conflicts between nations and persons through dialogue rather than violence.
You invited the children to come to you;
—may all children come to know their worth and their dignity.
You came to forgive our sins;
—forgive all who have perpetrated violence in any way, and give them the help they need to live peacefully.
You call us to justice;
—give us discerning hearts that we may follow your example.

PRAYER: Merciful God, we ask your blessing on young people who are tempted to end their lives because of the experience of abuse or the loss of meaning to their lives. Send them a friend who can encourage or enlighten them and share their burdens with them. We ask this through Jesus who is our way, our truth, and our life. Amen.

DECEMBER 29

MORNING PRAYER
(Psalms from Sunday, Week I, p. 3)

Ant 1 Shepherds, tell us what you have seen and heard. We saw the newborn savior, and hosts of angels singing God's praises, alleluia.

Ant 2 The angel said to them: I bring you good news of great joy; to you is born this day Christ the savior, alleluia.

Ant 3 To us a child is born; today the Mighty God shares our humanity, alleluia.

READING

Now, then, my soul, embrace that divine manger; press your lips upon and kiss the boy's feet. Then in your mind keep the shepherds' watch, marvel at the assembling host of angels, join in the heavenly melody, singing with your voice and heart: *Glory to God in the highest and on earth peace to [all] of good will.*

Bonaventure, The Tree of Life, p. 129, (1)

RESPONSORY

Christ has made known our salvation, alleluia, alleluia.
  —Christ...
Salvation by our God, **—alleluia,...**
Glory to you, Source of all Being, Eternal Word and Holy Spirit.
  —Christ...

CANTICLE OF ZECHARIAH

Ant The shepherds said to one another, "Let us go over to Bethlehem and see this thing that has happened which God has made known to us."

INTERCESSIONS

The Word of God lives among us. Let us cry out in joy:
  Praise be to you, Christ Jesus.

In you we find true peace;
  —give patient endurance to all who work for justice and
  peace between peoples and nations.
You spoke words of truth in the midst of hostility;
  —may all those who disseminate information speak with
  integrity and honesty.
You treated all people with respect and reverence;
  —teach us to appreciate diversity in persons and cultures.
You fully entered into family and social gatherings;
  —lift our burdens of stress and help us to enjoy family and
  friends.

You commended yourself into the hands of God;
  —may all who die this day find themselves in God's
  embrace.

PRAYER: Most Loving God, in Jesus you gave us the best of
gifts. He is our companion on the way, leading us
toward fullness of life in you. May we respond each day
to the way you lure us in the many choices that we
make, and so incarnate your life in us. We ask this
through Jesus, our bread of life. Amen.

DAYTIME PRAYER
(Psalms from the current weekday of Week I)

Ant 1 Mary and Joseph marveled at what was spoken of Jesus.

Ant 2 The mother of Jesus kept these words in her heart.

Ant 3 My eyes have seen your salvation which you have prepared
in the presence of all peoples.

(Prayer as in Morning Prayer)

EVENING PRAYER

Ant 1 You are honored by the Most High; before the dawning of
time, before the creation of the sun, you were begotten,
alleluia. (Ps 110:1–5, 7, p. 53)

Ant 2 The love of God is eternal; the power of the Most High will
not fail. (Ps 130, p. 143)

Ant 3 In the beginning was the Word, who is God; today the
Word comes to save the world. (Col 1:12–20, p. 122)

READING

I had some very bitter trouble over Christmas—...I felt almost as near
despairing as I could do. I do not mean despairing of God's mercy, but of
my work ever doing anything but go awry and give pain.... But when I
saw you getting the lights for your little crib, and being, in a real, lovely
sense "the father" in your little family, it somehow gathered every spark
of what capacity for joy I had left into a point—a point of light, the little
light by your crib. And then I had a deep peace in spite of everything,
and saw visibly how nothing matters so long as Christ is born again in
the souls of [people].... So...a Christmas which might have been among

the saddest has been one which I shall remember always as particularly
lovely....

The Letters of Caryll Houselander, p. 49, (5)

RESPONSORY

The Word was made flesh, alleluia, alleluia. **—The Word**...
And dwelt among us, **—alleluia,**...
Glory to you, Source of all Being, Eternal Word and Holy Spirit.
   —The Word...

CANTICLE OF MARY

Ant O Christ, you humbled yourself by taking on our humanity
       that you might restore humanity to the inheritance of
       heaven.

INTERCESSIONS

As evening comes, we sing a new song to our God, for a light has
shone in our darkness. In confidence we pray:
           In your light we find life.

Christ our Light, we rejoice in your redeeming love;
   —may we share our resources, our time, and our gifts with
     one another, and especially with those in need of love.
Christ our Light, we give thanks for your compassion;
   —enlighten our hearts that we may understand and
     lovingly support the many people who are burdened with
     emotional trauma during this season.
Christ our Light, we are touched by your humility;
   —assist us in our efforts to act with integrity and justice
     and to speak truthfully.
Christ our Light, we are honored with your humanity;
   —teach us to respect and care for our bodies, and by
     reverencing ourselves to embrace all life.
Christ our Light, we are humbled by your simplicity;
   —show us creative ways to live simply and to conserve our
     natural resources for future generations.

PRAYER: Most Loving God, you shared your Word with us as a
            light in our darkness. May we be open to the awe and
            mystery of life that surrounds us in so many ways.
            Help us to recognize the light of Christ in our own inner

poverty and to reach out courageously to share our
light with others. We pray this in the wonder of your
love. Amen.

DECEMBER 30

MORNING PRAYER
(Psalms from Sunday, Week I, p. 3)

Ant 1 Shepherds, tell us what you have seen and heard. We saw
the newborn savior, and hosts of angels singing God's
praises, alleluia.

Ant 2 The angel said to them: I bring you good news of great joy;
to you is born this day Christ the savior, alleluia.

Ant 3 To us a child is born; today the Mighty God shares our
humanity, alleluia.

READING

Only love can bring individual beings to their perfect completion, as
individuals, by uniting them one with another, because only love takes
possession of them and unites them by what lies deepest within them.
This is simply a fact of our everyday experience. For indeed at what
moment do lovers come into the most complete possession of
themselves if not when they say they are lost in one another?... And
why should not what is thus daily achieved on a small scale be repeated
one day on world-wide dimensions? Humanity, the spirit of the earth,
the synthesis of individuals and peoples, the paradoxical conciliation of
the element with the whole, of the one with the many...if we would see
them made flesh in the world what more need we do than imagine our
power to love growing and broadening till it can embrace the totality of
[all peoples] and of the earth?

Teilhard de Chardin, Hymn of the Universe, p. 145, (14)

RESPONSORY

Christ has made known our salvation, alleluia, alleluia.
    —**Christ**...
Salvation by our God, —**alleluia,**...
Glory to you, Source of all Being, Eternal Word and Holy Spirit.
    —**Christ**...

CANTICLE OF ZECHARIAH

Ant   Angels sang to greet the birth of Christ: Glory to God and to the Anointed One, alleluia.

INTERCESSIONS

In the birth of Christ we are reminded of our own fragile humanity and God's enduring love, and so we pray:
Word of God, stay with us.

Word of God, the prophet Anna spoke of our redemption;
—open our hearts to listen to the prophets of today.
Word of God, the parents of young children need your comfort;
—grant all parents the patience and wisdom to nurture their children.
Word of God, you call us to live in this world but to challenge its values;
—help us to carry out our business affairs with integrity.
Word of God, you remind us that we belong to you;
—touch our hearts that we may have confidence in your love and live in your freedom.
Word of God, you call us to eternal life;
—give comfort to the dying and be with all who mourn the death of their loved ones this season.

PRAYER: O Holy Word of God, you call us to walk with you each day in the mystery of your love. We are often anxious and worried about our own well-being. Help us to put aside false anxiety and to trust in your care for us. Grant us the grace to discern wisely, to act confidently, and to let go courageously. We ask this in your name, Word Incarnate among us. Amen.

DAYTIME PRAYER
(Psalms from the current weekday of Week I)

Ant 1   Mary and Joseph marveled at what was spoken of Jesus.

Ant 2   The mother of Jesus kept these words in her heart.

Ant 3   My eyes have seen your salvation which you have prepared in the presence of all peoples.

(Prayer as in Morning Prayer)

EVENING PRAYER

Ant 1 You are honored by the Most High; before the dawning of time, before the creation of the sun, you were begotten, alleluia. (Ps 110:1–5, 7, p. 53)

Ant 2 The love of God is eternal; the power of the Most High will not fail. (Ps 130, p. 143)

Ant 3 In the beginning was the Word, who is God; today the Word comes to save the world. (Col 1:12–20, p. 122)

READING

I now choose with tears, in reparation for those faults and for the root of them all,...that for the love of our [God] you relieve me of the care of others, take away my preaching and my study, leaving me only my Breviary, and bid me come to Rome, begging my way, and there put me to work in the kitchen, or serving table, or in the garden, or at anything else. And when I am no longer good for any of this, put me in the lowest class of grammar and that until death, without any more care for me (in external things), as I have said, than you have for an old broom.

Letters of St. Ignatius of Loyola, p. 273, (19)

RESPONSORY

The Word was made flesh, alleluia, alleluia. —**The Word**...
And dwelt among us, —**alleluia,**...
Glory to you, Source of all Being, Eternal Word and Holy Spirit.
   —**The Word**...

CANTICLE OF MARY

Ant Holy Mary, mother of our Redeemer, we praise you; watch over all those saved by your son.

INTERCESSIONS

In joy and thanksgiving we call to you, Christ Jesus:
   May we find hope in your birth.

Christ, be our strength in our struggle for justice;
   —may oppressed and abused children find hope in your birth.
Be our wisdom in our efforts to further world progress;
   —may we use our gifts wisely and treat one another justly.

Be our vision of wholeness in our search for integration;
  —may we bind up our own wounds and in our healing
    find hope in your birth.
Be our sign of grace in times of despair;
  —in times of rejection may young people find hope in us
    and choose life.
You are the Light of the World. Be a light to us;
  —that we may experience joy in one another's gifts and
    find hope in your birth.

PRAYER: O Giver of Hope, you delight us with the birth of
Christ in whom we find strength, wisdom, and grace.
Renew our vision during this season that we may
reach out to the needs of others in our families, our
neighborhoods, and places of work. In confidence we
pray that we may always find hope in your birth.
Amen.

DECEMBER 31

MORNING PRAYER

(Psalms from Sunday, Week I, p. 3)

Ant 1 Shepherds, tell us what you have seen and heard. We
saw the newborn savior, and hosts of angels singing
God's praises, alleluia.

Ant 2 The angel said to them: I bring you good news of great
joy; to you is born this day Christ the savior, alleluia.

Ant 3 To us a child is born; today the Mighty God shares our
humanity, alleluia.

READING

...A year has passed. Tonight people will wish each other a "happy new
year" without knowing whether it will be or not. Shall we, children of
God, be able to face the future with no other luggage than our faith? It
is, after all, our faith in Christ that distinguishes us from all [those]
who want to lead us astray on ways that are not those of the Word that
is new every day. Only Christ is the Alpha and the Omega, the
beginning and the end.

    Marcel Bastin, Ghislain Pinckers, Michel Teheux, *God Day by Day,* Vol 4, p. 92, (1)

RESPONSORY

Christ has made known our salvation, alleluia, alleluia.
—**Christ**...
Salvation by our God, —**alleluia,**...
Glory to you, Source of all Being, Eternal Word and Holy Spirit.
—**Christ**...

CANTICLE OF ZECHARIAH

Ant And suddenly there was with the angel a multitude of the heavenly host praising God and saying: Glory to God in the highest—peace, good will to all.

INTERCESSIONS

In the fullness of time you came to share life with us. With the evangelist we proclaim in awe:
The Word became flesh and dwells among us.

In the beginning was the Word; you, O God, are timeless and your patience is without end;
—grant inner peace to all who are in prison for their beliefs.
The Word was in God's presence; you, O God, are with us always;
—may we live and work mindful of your presence, and may our actions reflect your love.
The Word was God; you, O God, are wonder in the flesh;
—assist us to respect all forms of life and to support efforts to improve the quality of life among the poor.
Through you, O God, all things come into being;
—may we make time today to reflect upon your generosity to us, and to show compassion to those with heavy burdens.
You are the true light, O God, that enlightens each of us;
—shed light this day upon those places within us that cry out for healing, that we may find wholeness in you.

PRAYER: O Christ, you are the Word become flesh, you are our God. You know both the love and the struggle experienced in human families. Teach us to extend ourselves beyond our immediate families to embrace a broader vision of your gospel challenge. May this day

be a time of reflection on our past gifts and a time of
conversion to hear your continuous call. Amen.

DAYTIME PRAYER
(Psalms from the current weekday of Week I)

Ant 1 Mary and Joseph marveled at what was spoken of Jesus.

Ant 2 The mother of Jesus kept these words in her heart.

Ant 3 My eyes have seen your salvation which you have
prepared in the presence of all peoples.

(Prayer as in Morning Prayer)

JANUARY 1
MARY, MOTHER OF GOD

EVENING PRAYER I

Ant 1 Great is your love, O God. You were born of the virgin
Mary to share in our humanity, so that we may become
one with you in your divinity. (Ps 113, p. 96)

Ant 2 The Scriptures have been fulfilled, O Christ, in your birth
to a virgin; you have come like dew upon the earth to
refresh your people. (Ps 147:12–20, p. 85)

Ant 3 The burning bush on Sinai symbolizes your faithful
virginity, O Mary. Pray for us who look to you for help.
(Eph 1:3–10, p. 61)

READING

A new year at the hand of the Lord [Jesus]—we do not know whether
we shall experience the end of this year. But if we drink from the fount
of the Savior each day, then each day will lead us deeper into eternal
life and prepare us to throw off the burdens of this life easily and
cheerfully at some time when the call of the Lord sounds. The Divine
Child offers us his hand to renew our [commitment]. Let us hurry to
clasp this hand. [God] is my light and my salvation—of whom shall I be
afraid?

Edith Stein, The Hidden Life, p. 115, (3)

RESPONSORY

The Word was made flesh, alleluia, alleluia. **—The Word...**

And dwelt among us, —**alleluia**...
Glory to you, Source of all Being, Eternal Word and Holy Spirit.
   —**The Word**...

CANTICLE OF MARY

Ant In the depth of your love for us, O God, you sent your
      Word, born of Mary, to take on mortal flesh and live under
      the law of Moses.

INTERCESSIONS

Most Loving God, you sent forth Jesus to share your life with us,
and so we pray:
      Christ Jesus, born of Mary, hear our prayer.

Breath of Life, you continue to sustain your people;
   —may we reverence the gift of life within ourselves, our
      companions, and all of creation.
God, our Father, you show your compassion for us in the gift of
Jesus;
   —may we be grateful for your mercy and extend your
      tenderness to those living in our midst who are
      oppressed.
God, our Mother, you share with us the strength and beauty of
giving birth;
   —may we draw upon your strength in times of birthing new
      energy, insight, and integrity into our institutional
      structures.
God of Wonder, you surprise us with the mystery of your love
and joy;
   —may we delight in the good humor that surrounds us and
      calls us to shed light where there is darkness.
Womb of God, you surround us with sustenance and life-giving
water;
   —may we use fruitfully the gifts of nourishment; may those
      burdened by addictions find hope and help this day.

PRAYER: You, O God, are the Holy One who gathers us
            together in the womb of our earth. May we reverence
            the life you give us in Jesus through Mary, our
            mother. We give thanks, for you bring us life and

salvation through Jesus, our way, our truth, and our life. We ask you to bless us as we celebrate your life with us in the name of Jesus. Amen.

MORNING PRAYER
(Psalms from Sunday, Week I, p. 3)

Ant 1 God became the child of Mary; we have been made the children of God.

Ant 2 John saw Jesus and said: "Behold the Lamb of God, who takes away the sin of the world."

Ant 3 Mary, virgin and mother, treasured in her heart what was spoken of her son, Jesus.

READING

Your voice speaks:
> Little child out of Eternity, now will I sing to thy mother!
> The song shall be fair as dawn-tinted snow.
Rejoice Mary Virgin, daughter of my earth, sister of my soul,
> rejoice, O joy of my joy!
I am as one who wanders through the night, but you are a
> house under stars.
I am a thirsty cup, but you are God's open sea.
Rejoice Mary Virgin, blessed are those who call you blessed,
> never more shall child of [ours] lose hope.
I am one love for all, I shall never cease from saying: one of you
> has been exalted by [our God].
Rejoice Mary Virgin, wings of my earth, crown of my soul,
> rejoice joy of my joy!
Blessed are those who call you blessed.

Gertrude von LeFort, "Christmas," Hymns to the Church, p. 40, (5)

RESPONSORY

Christ has made known our salvation, alleluia, alleluia.
  —Christ...
Salvation by our God, **—alleluia**...
Glory to you, Source of all Being, Eternal Word and Holy Spirit.
  —Christ...

CANTICLE OF ZECHARIAH

Ant God has renewed us by becoming one of us in Jesus. We rejoice at this wondrous work of love.

INTERCESSIONS

A new dawn gives us joy as we celebrate Mary, Mother of God, who brings peace in Christ to all people, and so we pray:
Christ, be a sign of peace to all.

Christ, way of peace, enlighten our hearts to embrace the ways of non-violence;
—may we resist violence within our hearts and within our homes.

Christ, giver of peace, share your gifts this day with all leaders;
—may they find ways to pursue peaceful solutions to issues of justice.

Christ, proclaimer of peace, enable us to speak honestly and truthfully for the sake of peace and justice;
—may all peoples working in justice systems be open to the ways of non-violence.

Christ, sign of peace, be with us in our efforts to be women and men with peaceful hearts;
—may the prayers of contemplative people bring peace to those in need of healing.

Christ, teacher of peace, spur us on today to take renewed steps as people of peace;
—may all parents and teachers strive to show and share attitudes of peace with our youth.

PRAYER: You, O God, are the Holy One who gathers us together in the womb of our earth. May we reverence the life you give us in Jesus through Mary, our mother. We give thanks, for you bring us life and salvation through Jesus, our way, our truth, and our life. We ask you to bless us as we celebrate your life with us in the name of Jesus. Amen.

DAYTIME PRAYER

Ant 1 Mary and Joseph marveled at what was spoken of Jesus. (Ps 147:12–20, p. 85)

Ant 2 Mary kept all these things, pondering them in her heart. (Ps 127, p. 122)

Ant 3 My eyes have seen your salvation, which you have prepared in the presence of all peoples. (Ps 131, p. 116)

(Prayer as in Morning Prayer)

EVENING PRAYER II

Ant 1 Great is your love, O God. You were born of the virgin Mary to share in our humanity, so that we may become one with you in your divinity. (Ps 122, p. 143)

Ant 2 The Scriptures have been fulfilled, O Christ, in your birth to a virgin; you have come like dew upon the earth to refresh your people. (Ps 127, p. 122)

Ant 3 The burning bush on Sinai symbolizes your faithful virginity, O Mary. Pray for us who look to you for help. (Eph 1:3–10, p. 109)

READING

Hence, *the pillar you see beyond the tower of anticipation of God's will* designates the ineffable mystery of the Word of God; for in that true Word, the Son of God, all the justice of the New and Old Testaments is fulfilled. This justice was opened to believers for their salvation by divine inspiration, when the Son of the Supreme [God] deigned to become incarnate of the sweet Virgin; and the virtues showed themselves to be powerful in the anticipation of God's will, which was the beginning of the circumcision. Then the mystery of the Word of God was also declared in strict justice by the voice of the...prophets, who foretold that He would be manifest in justice and godly deeds and great severity, doing the justice of God and leaving no injustice free to evade the commands of the Law.

Hildegard of Bingen, Scivias, III:4, 1, (1)

RESPONSORY

The Word was made flesh, alleluia, alleluia. **—The Word...**
And dwelt among us, **—alleluia...**
Glory to you, Source of all Being, Eternal Word and Holy Spirit.
   —**The Word...**

CANTICLE OF MARY

Ant Blessed is your mother, O Christ, for she heard the word of God and kept it, alleluia.

INTERCESSIONS

You are blessed among all people, for you are the mother of God, and so we pray:
Christ, born of Mary, hear us.

Sun of Justice, show us new ways to be people of justice;
—may we protect the rights of peoples, animals and all
   creation.
You are called Wonderful, Counselor, O God; you share the
wonder of life with women and men in the parenting of children;
—may we support parents of the young in word and deed.
Christ, you gladden our hearts with the announcement of
salvation;
—may all who proclaim your gospel of peace receive the
   unction of your joy.
In Mary you found warmth, love, and nourishment for your
journey among us;
—may all mothers be blessed with creative insight and
   wisdom and find delight in their children.
You are our comforter in time of affliction;
—be with those who are dying today and bring them to
   your dwelling place.

PRAYER: You, O God, are the Holy One who gathers us
together in the womb of our earth. May we reverence
the life you give us in Jesus through Mary, our
mother. We give thanks, for you bring us life and
salvation through Jesus, our way, our truth, and our
life. We ask you to bless us as we celebrate your life
with us in the name of Jesus. Amen.

FROM JANUARY 2 TO EPIPHANY

MONDAY
(Psalms and antiphons from the current weekday)
MORNING PRAYER

READING

Recollection is just looking at Jesus more and more. It is our sweet
occupation throughout the day. It has its consummation at our hours
of prayer. The way to the possession of Jesus is in each hourly duty

assigned to us. It is the thousand details and actions of daily life. We have only to bring to each of them a spirit of faith, and each moment will hold for us grace, and will hold for us God.

Mother Aloysius Rogers, OCD, *Fragrance from Alabaster*, p. 28, (6)

RESPONSORY

Jesus revealed in glory, alleluia, alleluia. —**Jesus**...
The salvation by our God, —**alleluia,**...
Glory to you, Source of all Being, Eternal Word and Holy Spirit.
    —**Jesus**...

CANTICLE OF ZECHARIAH

Ant A child is given to us, the Eternal Word of God.

INTERCESSIONS

At the name of Jesus, every knee must bend in heaven and on earth, and so we pray:
                Come, let us adore.

Jesus, in your name our sins are forgiven and we are healed;
    —let your name in our minds and hearts protect us from
        harm.
In your name those deprived of sight, hearing, and speech are healed;
    —give us the grace to use our faculties with reverence, as
        instruments of praise to you.
In your name the hungry are fed and anxious hearts are comforted;
    —teach us to share our bread, your word, and ourselves,
        that all may have what they need.
For the sake of your name, the disciples faced suffering and death;
    —help us to endure whatever is necessary for the sake of
        truth and justice.

PRAYER: O God, you have called us to follow Jesus as a model
        of dedication to you. Have mercy on our weakness
        and give us the insight and strength we need to grow
        in grace and wisdom before you. This we ask in the
        name of Jesus. Amen.

DAYTIME PRAYER

Ant 1 Joseph and Mary, the parents of Jesus, wondered at what was said of him.

Ant 2 Mary, the mother of Jesus, kept all these things, pondering them in her heart.

Ant 3 My eyes have seen your salvation, which you have prepared in the presence of all people.

(Prayer as in Morning Prayer)

EVENING PRAYER

READING

When, for the fifteenth year, Tiberius Caesar
Cursed, with his reign, the Roman world,
Sharing the Near-East with a tribe of tetrarchs,
The Word of God was made in far-off province:
Deliverance from the herd of armored cattle,
When, from the desert, John came down to Jordan.

But his prophetic messages
Were worded in a code the scribes were not prepared
    to understand.
Where, in their lexicons, was written: "Brood of vipers,"
Applied, that is, to them?...

"St. John the Baptist" in *The Collected Poems of Thomas Merton*, pp. 122-23, (16)

RESPONSORY

The Word became flesh, alleluia, alleluia. **—The Word...**
And dwelt among us, **—alleluia,...**
Glory to you, Source of all Being, Eternal Word and Holy Spirit.
    —The Word...

CANTICLE OF MARY

Ant O glorious child, you brought light and healing to us at your birth, coming to us like the sun rising in the east.

INTERCESSIONS

Child of God, child of the poor, named by God: they named him Jesus. In faith we proclaim:
        Child of Bethlehem, you are the Christ of God.

Mary and Joseph were faithful to the law; Jesus was
circumcised on the eighth day;
>   —O God, guide us to formulate laws that serve the needs of
>   the people.

Jesus, you submitted to the rites asked of every child;
>   —deliver us from the corruption of pride and vainglory.

Mary, your mother, was full of grace; Joseph was called "just";
>   —bless all children with good parents and guides.

Jesus, in your name your mother will suffer much; you will one
day be her widow's mite;
>   —draw us to give all that we have to be one with you.

PRAYER: O God, you have called us to follow Jesus as a model
of dedication to you. Have mercy on our weakness
and give us the insight and strength we need to grow
in grace and wisdom before you. This we ask in the
name of Jesus. Amen.

TUESDAY
(Psalms and antiphons from the current weekday)
MORNING PRAYER

READING

..."Who is this Lamb, Whose love
Shall fall upon His people like an army:
Who is this Savior, Whose sandal-latchet
This furious Precursor is afraid to loose?"

His words of mercy and of patience shall be flails
Appointed for the separation of the wheat and chaff.
But who shall fear the violence
And crisis of His threshing floor
Except the envious and selfish heart?
Choose to be chaff, and fear the Winnower,
For then you never will abide His Baptism of Fire and Spirit....
>   "St. John the Baptist" in *The Collected Poems of Thomas Merton*, p. 123, (16)

RESPONSORY

Jesus revealed in glory, alleluia, alleluia. **—Jesus**...
The salvation by our God, **—alleluia,**...
Glory to you, Source of all Being, Eternal Word and Holy Spirit.
>   **—Jesus**...

CANTICLE OF ZECHARIAH

Ant The Word became flesh and dwelt among us, from whose fullness we have all received.

INTERCESSIONS

Prophets and rulers, exiles and slaves, all people had awaited the coming of the savior. You come as a child, O Christ, and your name is Jesus, and so we pray:
Blessed be the name of Jesus.

To those who seek you with a sincere heart;
—grant the light of faith and the courage to embrace it.
To those who wait for deliverance in our prisons;
—bring peace of heart, and send caring personnel who will enable their rehabilitation.
To all who serve you in the single life;
—grant the support of human companionship and the awareness of your presence.
To our hidden poor;
—give the opportunity to find adequate employment and all that is needed for their livelihood and development.

PRAYER: O God, you delight to be with the children of the earth. We know your love and we praise you for your goodness to us. Keep us open to your Spirit. Let our joy be in doing your will that we may praise you now and forever. Amen.

DAYTIME PRAYER

Ant 1 Joseph and Mary, the parents of Jesus, wondered at what was said of him.

Ant 2 Mary, the mother of Jesus, kept all these things, pondering them in her heart.

Ant 3 My eyes have seen your salvation, which you have prepared in the presence of all people.

(Prayer as in Morning Prayer)

EVENING PRAYER

READING

The shepherds of the galaxies, the Hubble Telescope astronomers,
have released photos of the universe from fourteen billion years ago.
As I attempt to fathom the very notion of billions of years, my gaze
settles on a large maple tree outdoors. Nestled in the fork of the trunk
and a snow-covered limb, a squirrel wrapped in its tail is sleeping. Its
ability to slumber while so precariously balanced is as mind boggling
as the distance of light years—equally deserving of the "I-don't-know-
what" of God. Awareness is a gift. Meditation on God's mystery,
whether it be the creation of the universe or the ingenuity of providing
squirrels with tails for winter sleeping, is gift. The presence of God in
one's life is a gift.

Carmelites of Indianapolis, *Hidden Friends*, p. 67, (5)

RESPONSORY

The Word became flesh, alleluia, alleluia. **—The Word...**
And dwelt among us, **—alleluia,...**
Glory to you, Source of all Being, Eternal Word and Holy Spirit.
   —The Word...

CANTICLE OF MARY

Ant The presence of Jesus among us fills us with song. Our
      salvation has come, alleluia.

INTERCESSIONS

Jesus, the new high priest, calls us all to share in his
priesthood. We pray:
         O God, we come to do your will.

For your church;
      —may those who are guided by your Spirit be enabled to
      serve as leaders.
For the people of all nations, large or small;
      —teach us to live as sisters and brothers born of your love.
For all minorities;
      —may their voices be heard and their persons be respected
      as children of God.
To those who plan and wait for a better future;
      —send your Spirit that they may renew the face of the
      earth.

PRAYER: O God, you delight to be with the children of the earth. We know your love and we praise you for your goodness to us. Keep us open to your Spirit. Let our joy be in doing your will that we may praise you now and forever. Amen.

WEDNESDAY
(Psalms and antiphons from the current weekday)
MORNING PRAYER
READING

The only thing separating us from the love of God is our own recognition of it! If one knew it, that God is the highest of all which is good, it would be impossible not to love God alone above all else. In fact, to know God truly is to love God so dearly that it would be impossible to hold something else dear beside God, even if threatened with eternal punishment! Yes, if I knew God truly, I would experience in my soul and spirit such a pure joy that this joy would surge through my body and make even my body wholly without pain or suffering, immortal and glorified.

Leonhard Schiemer, *Early Anabaptist Spirituality*, p. 92, (1)

RESPONSORY

Jesus revealed in glory, alleluia, alleluia. —**Jesus**...
The salvation by our God, —**alleluia,**...
Glory to you, Source of all Being, Eternal Word and Holy Spirit.
   —**Jesus**...

CANTICLE OF ZECHARIAH

Ant For love of us, O Christ our God, you emptied yourself and took on our nature, restoring our humanity, alleluia.

INTERCESSIONS

O God, you have created us and all your ways are holy. With gratitude we pray:
Make us a holy people.

You call us to unity but we are a church divided;
   —break the barriers among us and bring us to truth.
The earth is yours and all it contains;
   —teach us to use its resources with reverence and discipline.

You delight in all your creatures: animals and plants, fish and fowl;
  —help us to share the earth with them in responsible ways.
Your rain sings the song of the heavens;
    —forgive our pollution of the seas and rivers, and make us generous and persevering in restoring and preserving them.

PRAYER: O God, you called us to be your people, inviting us to fullness of life and joy in your presence. Let us never forget your mercy to us throughout the ages. Make us ever attentive to your Spirit. This we ask in the name of Jesus who lives with you and the Spirit, now and forever. Amen.

DAYTIME PRAYER

Ant 1 Joseph and Mary, the parents of Jesus, wondered at what was said of him.

Ant 2 Mary, the mother of Jesus, kept all these things, pondering them in her heart.

Ant 3 My eyes have seen your salvation, which you have prepared in the presence of all people.

(Prayer as in Morning Prayer)

EVENING PRAYER

READING

We have not grasped the ultimate seriousness and sacredness of a single human act because we have not understood how absolutely unique every human being really is. To be unique is not a matter of peculiar differences but of outstanding fidelity. When all is said and done that is what the spiritual life is all about, *fidelity*: to myself and the God who calls me to become more and more gracefully myself, my very best self; not in isolation but in communion with the whole human race. My passion must go on mounting until I am so faithful that God will look on me with pleasure and say: "This is my beloved [child]" (Mt. 3:17).

William McNamara, OCD, *Mystical Passion*, p. 124, (1)

RESPONSORY

The Word became flesh, alleluia, alleluia. **—The Word**...
And dwelt among us, **—alleluia,**...
Glory to you, Source of all Being, Eternal Word and Holy Spirit.
   —The Word...

CANTICLE OF MARY

Ant I have come into the world to do not my will but the will of
   the One who sent me.

INTERCESSIONS

Jesus, son of God, son of David, son of Mary, you are flesh of
our flesh. We pray:
   O Christ, you are the glory of our race.

O Christ, you fulfilled the desires of your people;
   —deepen in us the desire for union with you.
Enslaved, your people dreamed of your coming in power;
   —let the power of your love transform the hearts of all
   oppressors.
Your people renewed their hope through prayer and song;
   —help us to keep alive the hope of your gospel.
The hope of your birth, O Christ, brought joy and courage;
   —let our lives incarnate your message to the world.

PRAYER: O God, you called us to be your people, inviting us to
   fullness of life and joy in your presence. Let us never
   forget your mercy to us throughout the ages. Make us
   ever attentive to your Spirit. This we ask in the name
   of Jesus who lives with you and the Spirit, now and
   forever. Amen.

THURSDAY
(Psalms and antiphons from the current weekday)
MORNING PRAYER

READING

...Our true life is to be found only through conversion, and there is no
other way to enter upon it (1 Tm 6:19). As the same Lord says, "Unless

you are converted and become like little children, you will not enter the [kindom] of heaven" (Mt 18:3). Truly, only little children will enter, for it is a little child who leads them (Is 9:6), he who was born and given to us for this very end.

Bernard of Clairvaux, *On Conversion*, p. 66, (1)

RESPONSORY

Jesus revealed in glory, alleluia, alleluia. —**Jesus**...
The salvation by our God, —**alleluia,**...
Glory to you, Source of all Being, Eternal Word and Holy Spirit.
—**Jesus**...

CANTICLE OF ZECHARIAH

Ant You have come to your people, O God, to release them from
sorrow and sin.

INTERCESSIONS

God, you hide yourself from the worldly wise and show yourself to the lowly, and so we pray to you:
Make us meek and humble of heart.

Your Spirit abides in all who believe in you;
  —teach us to listen to one another with openness and
    respect.
To all who labor to open to us the lessons of history;
  —send your Spirit with gifts of understanding and wisdom.
To all who share wealth, time, and talents to serve
underdeveloped countries;
  —give insight and creativity in all their endeavors.
To all who are mentally ill or handicapped;
  —grant your peace, and help us to facilitate a wholesome
    life for them.

PRAYER: O God, our Creator, you have given us the freedom
to choose between good and evil. Have mercy on our
blindness and let the coming of Jesus enlighten us.
Fill our minds with his truth and our memories with
his goodness. Let our hearts be totally dedicated to
you. This we ask in the name of Jesus who is our
way. Amen.

DAYTIME PRAYER

Ant 1 Joseph and Mary, the parents of Jesus, wondered at what was said of him.

Ant 2 Mary, the mother of Jesus, kept all these things, pondering them in her heart.

Ant 3 My eyes have seen your salvation, which you have prepared in the presence of all people.

(Prayer as in Morning Prayer)

EVENING PRAYER

READING

When Jesus was born, I don't think Mary or Joseph thought about anything but the joy of having and holding the child. At that blessed midnight moment, the future did not exist: the rejection, betrayal, misunderstanding, the violence of scourging and crucifixion. There was only joy and gratitude. What was to come could not impinge on what was present. We all need times like that—midnight moments—when the wonder of the present fills our being and the past and the future cease to exist.

Carmelites of Indianapolis, *Hidden Friends*, p. 15, (5)

RESPONSORY

The Word became flesh, alleluia, alleluia. **—The Word**...
And dwelt among us, **—alleluia,**...
Glory to you, Source of all Being, Eternal Word and Holy Spirit.
—The Word...

CANTICLE OF MARY

Ant Mary and Joseph named the child, Jesus, for he would save his people from their sins.

INTERCESSIONS

Jesus, at your birth, angels sang of peace, and shepherds rejoiced at your coming; and now, we, your people, pray to you:
O Christ, grant us the peace that the world cannot give.

To those who proclaim war as a way to peace;
—grant the heart and mind of Jesus.

To those who oppose the destruction of human life in any way;
  —grant the courage of their convictions and let their efforts
     bear fruit.
To all who bear the wounds of war;
  —grant your peace and consolation.
For all who have died in war;
  —bless their generosity and courage with eternal life.

PRAYER: O God, our Creator, you have given us the freedom
           to choose between good and evil. Have mercy on our
           blindness and let the coming of Jesus enlighten us.
           Fill our minds with his truth and our memories with
           his goodness. Let our hearts be totally dedicated to
           you. This we ask in the name of Jesus who is our
           way. Amen.

FRIDAY
(Psalms and antiphons from the current weekday)

MORNING PRAYER

READING

...through the Church's liturgy, we have the opportunity to
contemplate year after year the marvelous testimony of the Spirit, the
water and the blood. The *Spirit* fulfills the memory of the Scriptures
and answers our most desperate prayers. The *Water* of Baptism
introduces us into the eternal life shared with Jesus, God's incarnate
Word. *Blood* symbolizes the fullness of life and the consummate love of
Jesus crucified. There on the cross after his death, "one of the soldiers
thrust a lance into his side, and immediately blood and water flowed
out" (Jn 19:34).

Carroll Stuhlmueller, CP, Biblical Meditations for Advent and the Christmas Season, p. 119, (1)

RESPONSORY

Jesus revealed in glory, alleluia, alleluia. **—Jesus**...
The salvation by our God, **—alleluia,**...
Glory to you, Source of all Being, Eternal Word and Holy Spirit.
  —Jesus...

CANTICLE OF ZECHARIAH

Ant Jesus Christ came by water, blood, and Spirit.

INTERCESSIONS

In Christ, you have called us each by name, and so we pray:
Open our minds to your way, your truth, and your life.

By your birth, human life is raised to a new dignity;
—make us diligent in preserving and enabling quality of
life for all.
You were sent by God, not to judge, but to bring us to new life;
—give us the grace to hear and to live your gospel.
By your birth you filled the lives of Mary and Joseph with joy;
—bless with the gift of new life all who desire to have
children.
You were called the son of Joseph;
—give joy and fulfillment to adopted and foster children and
bless their families.
By your birth, you revealed the fidelity of God;
—make us worthy of your promises.
By your birth, human life is changed forever;
—open our minds and hearts to transformation. Make us
witnesses of your love.

PRAYER: O God, giver of all gifts, you clothe us with love and
lead us to truth. Let us realize the wonder of your call
to life. Let us respond by giving all to you and by
sharing life creatively with one another. Grant this
through Jesus, who lives and reigns with you, Source
of all Being, and with your Holy Spirit, forever and
ever. Amen.

DAYTIME PRAYER

Ant 1 Joseph and Mary, the parents of Jesus, wondered at
what was said of him.

Ant 2 Mary, the mother of Jesus, kept all these things,
pondering them in her heart.

Ant 3 My eyes have seen your salvation, which you have
prepared in the presence of all people.

(Prayer as in Morning Prayer)

EVENING PRAYER

READING

Luke for his part stresses the presence of the Holy Spirit and the almost stunned reaction of the ecstatic prayer. He alone in recounting Jesus' baptism states with emphasis, "Jesus was at *prayer* after likewise being baptized." With Luke we have moved away from study about Jesus to contemplative union with him as a voice from heaven is heard to say, "*You* are my beloved Son. *On you* my favor rests." Christianity is not to be identified with correct doctrine about Jesus; teaching is intended to lead us into a mystery of life that reaches into our deepest hopes in the person of Jesus.

Carroll Stuhlmueller, CP, *Biblical Meditations for Advent and the Christmas Season*, p. 224, (1)

RESPONSORY

The Word became flesh, alleluia, alleluia. **—The Word...**
And dwelt among us, **—alleluia,...**
Glory to you, Source of all Being, Eternal Word and Holy Spirit.
   —The Word...

CANTICLE OF MARY

Ant   The Spirit descended upon Jesus, and a voice from heaven proclaimed: You are my beloved; with you I am well pleased.

INTERCESSIONS

Jesus, named by an angel, you will be obedient unto death. We pray:
      Your law, O God, is a light to our path.

Jesus, born a helpless child, cared for by Mary and Joseph;
   —have compassion on children who are abused. Heal them
     and those who abuse them.
Jesus, mighty in God's love for you;
   —enlighten all who look upon themselves with disdain. Let
     them know your love and care.
Jesus, marked by circumcision a child of Israel;
   —claim us as your own. Make us true disciples.
Jesus, open to life and death, given totally to God's will;
   —make us fearless in following you.

PRAYER: O God, giver of all gifts, you clothe us with love and lead us to truth. Let us realize the wonder of your call to life. Let us respond by giving all to you and by sharing life creatively with one another. Grant this through Jesus, who lives and reigns with you, Source of all Being, and with your Holy Spirit, forever and ever. Amen.

SATURDAY

(Psalms and antiphons from the current weekday)

MORNING PRAYER

READING

Every cycle has its prophets—as guiding stars; and they are the burning candles of the Lord to light the spiritual temple on earth, for the time being. When they have done their work, they will pass away; but the candlesticks will remain, and other lights will be placed in them.

Antoinette Doolittle, *The Shakers*, p. 351, (1)

RESPONSORY

Jesus revealed in glory, alleluia, alleluia. —**Jesus**...
The salvation by our God, —**alleluia,**...
Glory to you, Source of all Being, Eternal Word and Holy Spirit.
    —**Jesus**...

CANTICLE OF ZECHARIAH

Ant You are the One of whom the prophets wrote: In Israel the Anointed One is born; eternal will be your reign.

INTERCESSIONS

You, O Christ, are just and all your ways are holy; we pray to you:
    You have the words of eternal life.

By your coming, you break through the clouds of our darkness;
    —help us to know and to live the truth that is our peace.
By your coming, you brought a marvelous love into the world;
    —heal the wounds of the past, and let us run toward the
    lure of God's call.

By your coming, you conquer sin and death;
> —give us the courage to stop the flow of anger and revenge
> by returning good for evil.

By your coming, you revealed the equality of all women and men;
> —guide us to the unity that you share with God.

PRAYER: O God, you sent Jesus to save us and to teach us to love one another. Heal our prejudices; expand our hearts. Give us a hunger to see the beauty and goodness that you see in us. Let the birth of Jesus be a new birth for us, that we may be children in whom you are well pleased. This we ask in Jesus' name. Amen.

DAYTIME PRAYER

Ant 1   Joseph and Mary, the parents of Jesus, wondered at what was said of him.

Ant 2   Mary, the mother of Jesus, kept all these things, pondering them in her heart.

Ant 3   My eyes have seen your salvation, which you have prepared in the presence of all people.

(Prayer as in Morning Prayer)

EPIPHANY

EVENING PRAYER I

Ant 1   Begotten before the daystar and before the ages, Jesus our savior has appeared this day to our world.
(Ps 135 I, p. 136)

Ant 2   Your light has come, Jerusalem; the glory of our God has risen upon you; the nations shall walk by your light, alleluia. (Ps 76, p. 148)

Ant 3   That star, like a flame of fire, pointed the way to God, Ruler of rulers; the Magi saw the star and brought their gifts in homage.

Canticle 1 Timothy 3:16

Praise our Savior, all you
nations.
Christ manifested in the flesh,
Christ justified by the Spirit.

Praise our Savior, all you
nations.
Christ seen by the angels,
Christ proclaimed to
unbelievers.

Praise our Savior, all you
nations.
Christ believed in by the world,
Christ taken up in glory.

Praise our Savior, all you
nations.
Glory to you...

READING

Do not now turn away from the brilliance of that star in the east which
guides you. Become a companion of the holy kings; accept the
testimony of the Jewish Scriptures about Christ and avert the evil of
the treacherous king. With gold, frankincense and myrrh, venerate
Christ the King as true God and [true human]. Together with the first
fruits of the Gentiles to be called to faith, adore, confess, and praise
this humble God lying in a manger.

Bonaventure, *The Tree of Life*, p. 130, (1)

RESPONSORY

All humankind will be blessed in Jesus, people of every race.
   —**All humankind...**
Every nation will glorify Christ, —**people of...**
Glory to you, Source of all Being, Eternal Word and Holy Spirit.
   —**All humankind...**

CANTICLE OF MARY

Ant   The Magi, seeing the star, said to one another, "This is the
sign of the great king! Let us go and seek him, bringing him
our gifts of gold, frankincense and myrrh," alleluia.

INTERCESSIONS

Led by the light of a star, magi came to worship the child. In our
longing for truth, let us pray:
   Guide all who seek you, O God.

Creator of the world, complete the work which you have begun;
   —help us to hear and live the message of Jesus.

God of the nations, you see us all as your children;
  —draw us to unity that mirrors your own.
Source of all truth, you dwell within us, the light of our minds;
  —let us never silence your voice.
Word of God made flesh, the magi adored you in a Child;
  —help us to recognize you in one another.
Eternal God, you know our needs and you care for us;
  —help us to see the things that you see.

PRAYER: Lord Jesus, you are the star inviting all nations to
fullness of life. Give us the wisdom to follow you and
to lead others to walk in your light. This we ask in
your name. Amen.

MORNING PRAYER
(Psalms from Sunday, Week I, p. 3)

Ant 1 The magi worshipped the child and offered him their
treasures of gold, frankincense and myrrh, alleluia.

Ant 2 Bless God, seas and rivers; springs and fountains exalt
God forever, alleluia.

Ant 3 Arise, shine, O Jerusalem, for your light has come, the
glory of God dawns upon you; nations shall come to your
light, alleluia.

READING

When strangers come into our lives, as they did to Herod and
Jerusalem or to Jesus, they can be our brothers and sisters, our sons
and daughters, because of Jesus.... *At least* we ought to pay attention
to those important signals by which people try to break down the
barriers between us—signals of forgiveness, signals of hope and
kindliness, signals of need and desires. These are like the star and the
dream which led the Magi to Jesus. If Jerusalem had known well the
prophecy of Isaiah, then it would have been prepared by this signal
that God wanted gentiles to be co-heirs with them—that all men and
women must eventually belong to one family, our very own!
Carroll Stuhlmueller, CP, *Biblical Meditations for Advent and the Christmas Season*, p. 220, p. 221, (1)

RESPONSORY

All the rulers of the earth will come to adore.—**All the...**
Men and women of every nation, **—will come...**

Glory to you, Source of all Being, Eternal Word and Holy Spirit.
—**All the...**

CANTICLE OF ZECHARIAH

Ant This day earth unites with heaven, for Christ has become one with us and has revealed God's glory to the people.

INTERCESSIONS

Jesus, son of God, son of Mary, you are the glory of our race. To you we pray:

Come and set us free.

You are the revelation of God to us;
—help us to be your revelation to one another.
Splendor of God's glory, you came as a child;
—teach us to see you in the great and the small.
Your light drew the magi to a foreign land;
—open our minds to new insights, new vision.
Your parents received the magi with the courtesy of the poor;
—be with us as we encourage those who seek you.

PRAYER: Lord Jesus, you are the star inviting all nations to fullness of life. Give us the wisdom to follow you and to lead others to walk in your light. This we ask in your name. Amen.

DAYTIME PRAYER
(Psalms from Sunday, Week I, p. 6)

Ant 1 Rise in splendor, Jerusalem! Your light is come, the glory of God has dawned upon you.

Ant 2 Raise your eyes! See, they all gather and come to you; your sons come from afar, and your daughters rise up at your side.

Ant 3 All shall come bearing gold, frankincense and myrrh, and proclaiming the praises of God.

(Prayer as in Morning Prayer)

EVENING PRAYER II

Ant 1 Jesus, our peace, you come in glory; you are ruler of all the earth, alleluia. (Ps 110:1–5, 7, p. 53)

Ant 2 Daylight has dawned upon God's people; you, O Christ, bring us grace, mercy, and justice, alleluia. (Ps 112, p. 149)

Ant 3 All nations shall come and worship you, for your justice has been revealed, alleluia. (Rev 15:3–4, p. 89)

READING

How different from Herod's is the power of the infant child in Bethlehem. The child will lay down all claims to superiority *over* others, demonstrating rather a power that is *for* others—a new form of power, one not manifested in the manner of the principalities and powers. It is the divine power to heal others (Lk 5:17), the power of reconciling love that is capable of meeting the darkness of the world and overcoming it. And that is why the world, represented by the wise men, can find hope in this child.

Proclamation 4: Epiphany, p. 11, (24)

RESPONSORY

All humankind will be blessed in Jesus, people of every race.
   —All humankind...
Every nation will glorify Christ, **—people of**...
Glory to you, Source of all Being, Eternal Word and Holy Spirit.
   —All humankind...

CANTICLE OF MARY

Ant Seeing the star the magi were filled with joy, and entering the house, they offered the child gold, frankincense and myrrh, alleluia.

INTERCESSIONS

Led by the light of a star, magi came to worship the child. In our longing for truth let us pray:
   Guide all who seek you, O God.

Creator of the world, complete the work which you have begun;
   —help us to hear and live the message of Jesus.

God of the nations, you see us all as your children;
  —draw us to unity that mirrors your own.
Source of all truth, you dwell within us, the light of our minds;
  —let us never silence your voice.
Word of God made flesh, the magi adored you in a child;
  —help us to recognize you in one another.
Eternal God, you know our needs and you care for us;
  —help us to see the things that you see.

PRAYER: Lord Jesus, you are the star inviting all nations to fullness of life. Give us the wisdom to follow you and to lead others to walk in your light. This we ask in your name. Amen.

MONDAY

(Psalms and antiphons from the current weekday)

MORNING PRAYER

READING

It is God's desire to become manifest to us, but...God wills to take created forms for this manifestation—forms of persons, events, circumstances, which call for faith if we are to recognize the Divine presence, a faith that can discern through and in the human. For each one of us, the star is shining in the heaven of our souls pointing out to us the place where we shall find Jesus. It is the star of grace contained in the Will of God of every moment, that Will which leads us to God.

Mother Aloysius Rogers, OCD, *Fragrance from Alabaster*, p. 28, (6)

RESPONSORY

All the rulers of the earth will come to adore. **—All the...**
Women and men of every nation, **—will come...**
Glory to you, Source of all Being, Eternal Word and Holy Spirit.
  —All the...

CANTICLE OF ZECHARIAH

Ant From the East the magi came to worship the Savior, offering gold to Christ our Ruler, frankincense to Christ our God, and myrrh to Christ our Redeemer, alleluia.

INTERCESSIONS

The Word became flesh bringing light out of darkness. Come let us adore:

Glory to you, O God.

Your light, O Christ, means life to us;
—make us bearers of life to others.
Your light, O Christ, reveals the mysteries of God to us;
—help us to recognize the "gifts of God."
Your light, O Christ, brings healing to our hearts;
—teach us to be compassionate with one another.
Your light, O Christ, brings peace to our world;
—have mercy on us lest we cloud it with conflict.

PRAYER: Jesus, you light our way through the centuries, you guide us day by day. Give us the courage to remain steadfast in our commitment to you when our weakness darkens the way. We ask this in your holy name. Amen.

DAYTIME PRAYER

Ant 1 Rise in splendor, Jerusalem! Your light is come, the glory of our God has dawned upon you.

Ant 2 Raise your eyes! See, they all gather and come to you; your sons come from afar, and your daughters rise up at your side.

Ant 3 All shall come bearing gold, frankincense, and myrrh, and proclaiming the praises of God.

(Prayer as in Morning Prayer)

EVENING PRAYER

READING

[Isaac] Hecker's esteem for human beings derived from his faith in creation, but it was mainly enhanced by his faith in the Incarnation, which was central in his religious experience. Even before he finished his zigzagging itinerary in the church of Rome, Hecker had spoken of the incarnation as a mystery inclusive of everything that is positively human. Later he would speak of the church as an extension of the incarnation (the expression seems to have come from Bossuet), as a channel of grace in the world and for the world, and he would present Christianity as the source of the highest humanity. This would lead him to struggle for a spirituality in the world.

John Manuel Lozano, *Grace and Brokenness in God's Country*, pp. 44–45, (1)

RESPONSORY

All humankind will be blessed in Jesus, people of every race.
—**All humankind...**
Every nation will glorify Christ, —**people of...**
Glory to you, Source of all Being, Eternal Word and Holy Spirit.
—**All humankind...**

CANTICLE OF MARY

Ant When the magi saw the star, they rejoiced; going into the house, they offered the child gifts: gold, frankincense, and myrrh, alleluia.

INTERCESSIONS

Jesus, the Sun of Justice, is born for our salvation. We pray to him:

Draw us, O Christ, we will follow you.

In your light our sins are forgiven and we are healed;
—help us to forgive one another.
In your light all who seek will find you;
—deliver us from all that blinds us to you.
In your light our hope is renewed and nourished;
—teach us how to encourage one another.
In your light the poor discover the way to fullness of life;
—teach us to discern and cherish true human values.
Your light is eternal;
—keep us faithful to your teaching.

PRAYER: Jesus, you light our way through the centuries, you guide us day by day. Give us the courage to remain steadfast in our commitment to you when our weakness darkens the way. We ask this in your holy name. Amen.

TUESDAY

(Psalms and antiphons from the current weekday)

MORNING PRAYER

READING

This is my prayer—
That, though I may not see,
I be aware
Of the Silent God
Who stands by me.
That, though I may not feel,
I be aware
Of the Mighty Love
Which doggedly follows me.
That, though I may not respond,
I be aware
That God—my Silent, Mighty God,
Waits each day.
Quietly, hopefully, persistently,
Waits each day and through each night
For me,
For me—alone.

Edwina Gateley, "Silent God," in Psalms of a Laywoman, p. 22, (51)

RESPONSORY

All the rulers of the earth will come to adore. **—All the...**
Women and men of every nation, **—will come...**
Glory to you, Source of all Being, Eternal Word and Holy Spirit.
   —All the...

CANTICLE OF ZECHARIAH

Ant The magi offered the child their treasures, alleluia.

INTERCESSIONS

Jesus, Word made flesh, you came bringing peace, yet rulers would seek to destroy you. Hear us as we pray:
   Have mercy on us.

Your peace, O Christ, is a challenge to our lethargy;
   —call us again to be your disciples.
In your peace we can hear the voice of your Spirit;
   —make us faithful to your call.

In your peace we die and rise daily;
—give us the courage to live this mystery.
Your peace, O Christ, is peace the world cannot give;
—let our lives be open to your gifts.

PRAYER: Jesus, our Savior, you knew the homage of the wise and the wrath of rulers. Bless all who must flee from their homeland. Guide and protect those who are displaced by war or poverty. Show us the way to justice for all. This we ask in your name and through the intercession of those who have given their lives for the sake of others. Amen.

DAYTIME PRAYER

Ant 1 Rise in splendor, Jerusalem! Your light is come, the glory of our God has dawned upon you.

Ant 2 Raise your eyes! See, they all gather and come to you; your sons come from afar, and your daughters rise up at your side.

Ant 3 All shall come bearing gold, frankincense, and myrrh, and proclaiming the praises of God.

(Prayer as in Morning Prayer)

EVENING PRAYER

READING

Love, then, consists in this: not that we have loved God, but that he has loved us (1 Jn 4:10)....God's love implants life within us, so that we can imitate Jesus and respond in ways beyond our normal strength and endurance.

Carroll Stuhlmueller, *Biblical Meditations for Advent and the Christmas Season,* p. 128, p. 129, (1)

RESPONSORY

All humankind will be blessed in Jesus, people of every race.
   —All humankind...
Every nation will glorify Christ, **—people of...**
Glory to you, Source of all Being, Eternal Word and Holy Spirit.
   —All humankind...

CANTICLE OF MARY

Ant Christ, our Light, when you dawned upon the nations, the magi offered you their gifts, alleluia.

INTERCESSIONS

Jesus, Word made flesh, is revealed to the shepherds and the sages; let us praise God as we say:

O God, we long to see your face.

Christ Jesus, you reveal yourself to the singlehearted;
  —help us to seek and to do your will all the days of our lives.
You promise your fullness to the poor in spirit;
  —help us to hear the cry of the poor.
You chose to live among the poor and the lowly;
  —make us humble of heart.
You answer all who call upon you;
  —let us walk in the way of your mercy.

PRAYER: Jesus, our Savior, you knew the homage of the wise and the wrath of rulers. Bless all who must flee from their homeland. Guide and protect those who are displaced by war or poverty. Show us the way to justice for all. This we ask in your name and through the intercession of those who have given their lives for the sake of others. Amen.

WEDNESDAY

(Psalms and antiphons from the current weekday)

MORNING PRAYER

READING

The principle of unity which saves our guilty world, wherein all is in process of returning to dust, is Christ. Through the force of his magnetism, the light of his ethical teaching, the unitive power of his very being, Jesus establishes again at the heart of the world the harmony of all endeavors and the convergence of all beings.

Teilhard de Chardin, *Hymn of the Universe*, p. 147, (14)

RESPONSORY

All the rulers of the earth will come to adore. **—All the...**

Women and men of every nation, **—will come**...
Glory to you, Source of all Being, Eternal Word and Holy Spirit.
—All the...

CANTICLE OF ZECHARIAH

Ant We have seen the star in the East, and have come to
worship the Savior.

INTERCESSIONS

A child is born for us; God has visited the people of the earth.
Let us pray:
Come let us adore.

Word of God, you came to save us, born in a stable;
—teach us to see you in the poor and lowly.
You came to make all things new;
—liberate us from the prison of the familiar.
You revealed yourself to magi from a foreign land;
—save us from our hidden prejudices.
Visitors from the East brought you royal gifts;
—help us to give you the best of our lives.

PRAYER: Jesus, our Savior, you came as a child to bring new
life to the world. Open our minds and hearts to the
message of your life. Transform our lives and make us
instruments of your peace. Grant this through the
power of your name. Amen.

DAYTIME PRAYER

Ant 1 Rise in splendor, Jerusalem! Your light is come, the glory
of our God has dawned upon you.

Ant 2 Raise your eyes! See, they all gather and come to you;
your sons come from afar, and your daughters rise up at
your side.

Ant 3 All shall come bearing gold, frankincense, and myrrh,
and proclaiming the praises of God.

(Prayer as in Morning Prayer)

EVENING PRAYER

READING

In regard to evil, he [Clement of Alexandria] further suggests that fear of [God] is good even"...if bitter. Sick, we truly stand in the need of the Savior; having wandered, of one to guide us; blind, of one to lead us to light; thirsty, of the fountain of life of which whosoever partakes shall no longer thirst; dead, we need life; sheep, we need a shepherd; we who are children need a tutor while universal humanity stands in need of Jesus. (Clement of Alexandria, *Paedagogus* I, 9)

Mary E. Penrose, *Roots Deep and Strong*, p. 37, (1)

RESPONSORY

All humankind will be blessed in Jesus, people of every race.
   —All humankind...
Every nation will glorify Christ, **—people of...**
Glory to you, Source of all Being, Eternal Word and Holy Spirit.
   —All humankind...

CANTICLE OF MARY

Ant The magi said to Herod: We saw the star of the Savior rise
     in the East; its brightness fills the heavens and the earth.

INTERCESSIONS

The Word of God has come to satisfy the longing of all people from ages past. With one voice let us pray:
   Be praised forever, O Christ.

Through your coming, Christ Jesus, we know the way to fullness of life;
   —teach us to be poor in spirit.
Through your coming we see the face of God;
   —teach us to see you in one another.
Through your coming we share the Bread of Life;
   —give us the courage to share your cross.
Through your coming our sins are forgiven, and our lives renewed;
   —we thank and praise you for your mercy and love.

PRAYER: Jesus, our Savior, you came as a child to bring new
      life to the world. Open our minds and hearts to the

message of your life. Transform our lives and make us instruments of your peace. Grant this through the power of your name. Amen.

THURSDAY
(Psalms and antiphons from the current weekday)
MORNING PRAYER

READING

...the sweetness of the Holy Spirit is boundless and swift to encompass all creatures in grace, and no corruption can take away the fullness of its just integrity. Its path is a torrent, and streams of sanctity flow from it in its bright power, with never a stain of dirt in them; for the Holy Spirit Itself is a burning and shining serenity, which cannot be nullified, and which enkindles ardent virtue so as to put all darkness to flight.

Hildegard of Bingen, *Scivias,* II:4, 2, (1)

RESPONSORY

All the rulers of the earth will come to adore. **—All the...**
Women and men of every nation, **—will come**...
Glory to you, Source of all Being, Eternal Word and Holy Spirit.
  —All the...

CANTICLE OF ZECHARIAH

Ant All nations will come from afar bearing their gifts, alleluia.

INTERCESSIONS

Jesus is born in Bethlehem. Angels sing and shepherds adore; let us join them as we say:
  Glory to God in the highest!

We praise you, O God, in the gift of Jesus, our way;
  —keep us ever true to his teaching.
We praise you in the angels and saints;
  —following their example, may we also lead others to you.
We praise you for the daily bread of life that you give us;
  —give us the wisdom to nourish and support one another.
We praise you for your constant mercy;
  —fill our minds with understanding and our hearts with compassion.

PRAYER: O God, we marvel at your goodness to us. We are the work of your hands and you invite us to labor with you in building the city of God. Keep us faithful to you, and may our service be worthy of our calling. Grant this in the name of Jesus who lives with you and the Holy Spirit. Amen.

DAYTIME PRAYER

Ant 1 Rise in splendor, Jerusalem! Your light is come, the glory of our God has dawned upon you.

Ant 2 Raise your eyes! See, they all gather and come to you; your sons come from afar, and your daughters rise up at your side.

Ant 3 All shall come bearing gold, frankincense, and myrrh, and proclaiming the praises of God.

(Prayer as in Morning Prayer)

EVENING PRAYER

READING

This One who is from David and before David
This Word of God, looking beyond lyre and harp,
        mindless instruments,
   By his Holy Spirit tunes the Cosmos,
Especially this little cosmos, the human person,
        mind and body;
And he sings to God with this many-voiced instrument—
   He accompanies his song with the instrument
        of the human person.
What then does this instrument, the Word of God, the Lord, the New Song desire? To open the eyes of the blind and unstop the ears of the deaf; to lead the lame or the erring to righteousness; to exhibit God to the foolish; to put a stop to corruption; to conquer death; to reconcile disobedient children to [God] their [Mother/Father]. (Clement of Alexandria—*Exhortation to the Heathen*)

Mary E. Penrose, *Roots Deep and Strong*, p. 40, (1)

RESPONSORY

All humankind will be blessed in Jesus, people of every race.
  —All humankind...
Every nation will glorify Christ, **—people of...**
Glory to you, Source of all Being, Eternal Word and Holy Spirit.
  —All humankind...

CANTICLE OF MARY

Ant All are coming from every land! They bear gold and
     frankincense, alleluia.

INTERCESSIONS

God guides the humble to truth; God protects the stranger. In
gratitude we pray:
  Loving Guardian of us all, may you be praised forever.

Jesus, our brother, you loved the poor and lived among them;
  —help us to serve those who cannot support themselves.
Jesus, faithful friend, grazing animals first befriended you and
your parents;
  —teach us to respect the animals of our world and give
    them the care and space they need.
A rocky cave housed you and straw gave you warmth;
  —help us to give our planet, its plants, rocks, and all of its
    substances the reverence that we owe to all that you
    have created.
You were the son of a carpenter and you labored with your
hands;
  —bless all people with labor and wages sufficient for a
    wholesome life.

PRAYER: O God, we marvel at your goodness to us. We are the
       work of your hands and you invite us to labor with
       you in building the city of God. Keep us faithful to
       you, and may our service be worthy of our calling.
       Grant this in the name of Jesus who lives with you
       and the Holy Spirit. Amen.

FRIDAY

(Psalms and antiphons from the current weekday)

MORNING PRAYER

READING

There are two things you should know: first, what you are; second, that you are not what you are by your own power. Then you will boast, but not in vain.... So we should greatly fear that ignorance which makes us think less of ourselves than we should. But no less, indeed rather more, should we fear the ignorance which makes us think ourselves better than we are. This is what happens when we are deceived into thinking that some good in us originates from ourselves.

Bernard of Clairvaux, On Loving God, pp. 176–77, (1)

RESPONSORY

All the rulers of the earth will come to adore. **—All the**...
Women and men of every nation, **—will come**...
Glory to you, Source of all Being, Eternal Word and Holy Spirit.
  —All the...

CANTICLE OF ZECHARIAH

Ant Those who were once in darkness will come to adore you.

INTERCESSIONS

Jesus, your law is love and your gospel is peace. Savior of the world we implore you:
Come and set us free.

By the power of your life you raised the human race to new dignity;
  —help us to free all women and men who are denied their
    human rights.
By the power of your love you taught us that love is stronger than death;
  —give us the courage to risk our lives, if necessary, to be
    faithful to you.
Your power is just and merciful;
  —give us leaders who are capable, honest, and
    compassionate.
By the power of your death and resurrection, you have overcome the world;
  —enable us to hope and to give hope to others.

PRAYER: O God of peace and love, you raise up the lowly and call sinners to repentance. Heal our weakness and show us how to use our gifts for the good of others. Transform our lives that we, too, may live by the power of love. Grant this that your reign may be manifested today and for all eternity. Amen.

DAYTIME PRAYER

Ant 1 Rise in splendor, Jerusalem! Your light is come, the glory of our God has dawned upon you.

Ant 2 Raise your eyes! See, they all gather and come to you; your sons come from afar, and your daughters rise up at your side.

Ant 3 All shall come bearing gold, frankincense, and myrrh, and proclaiming the praises of God.

(Prayer as in Morning Prayer)

EVENING PRAYER

READING

Prayer alone is that which vanquishes God. Christ has willed that it be operative for no evil.... It knows nothing save how to recall the souls of the departed from the very path of death, to transform the weak, to restore the sick, to purge the possessed, to open prison bars, to loose the bonds of the innocent. Likewise it washes away faults, repels temptations, extinguishes persecutions, consoles the fainthearted, cheers the high-spirited, escorts travelers, appeases waves, makes robbers stand aghast, nourishes the poor, governs the rich, upraises the fallen, arrests the falling, confirms the standing. (Tertullian, *On Prayer*)

Mary E. Penrose, *Roots Deep and Strong*, p. 51, (1)

RESPONSORY

All humankind will be blessed in Jesus, people of every race.
    —All humankind...
Every nation will glorify Christ, **—people of...**
Glory to you, Source of all Being, Eternal Word and Holy Spirit.
    —All humankind...

CANTICLE OF MARY

Ant Warned in a dream, the magi departed to their own country by another way.

INTERCESSIONS

Bountiful God, all that you do is done with love. In joy we sing of your care:

God has done marvelous deeds for us.

You are our God, and you call us to union with you;
—lead us out of our selfishness; we cannot do it alone.
You are our Creator, and you share this world with us;
—help us to heal the inequities that scar our society.
You sent your Word, not to judge, but to call us to fullness of life;
—teach us how to take your message to the ends of the earth.
You are love, O God, and those who seek you live in you;
—fill our hearts with longing, that living in you, we may reveal your love in our lives.

PRAYER: O God of peace and love, you raise up the lowly and call sinners to repentance. Heal our weakness and show us how to use our gifts for the good of others. Transform our lives that we, too, may live by the power of love. Grant this that your reign may be manifested today and for all eternity. Amen.

SATURDAY

(Psalms and antiphons from the current weekday)

MORNING PRAYER

READING

I often think that our Lord must have been terribly bored with the disciples very often, humanly speaking. Certainly, he wasn't picking out brilliant, accomplished, pleasing personalities with whom to live. Isn't it in [one of the gospels] where the mother of James and John wanted the best place for her two sons? So even the relatives were hanging on to see what they could get out of the situation. He certainly had to get away from them every now and then and do a lot of praying. They say a mystic is someone who is in love with God, again using that comparison as the kind of love we should feel. This is one of the most absorbing problems of all the world, this relationship we have to all those around us, the tie that holds us all around the [world] together.

Dorothy Day, *Meditations*, pp. 97–98, (1)

RESPONSORY

All the rulers of the earth will come to adore. —**All the...**
Women and men of every nation, —**will come...**
Glory to you, Source of all Being, Eternal Word and Holy Spirit.
   —**All the...**

CANTICLE OF ZECHARIAH

Ant Jesus worked the first of his signs at Cana in Galilee, and manifested his glory; his disciples believed in him.

INTERCESSIONS

Jesus Christ, born of a woman, has revealed the love of God to us. Let us pray:
   Savior of the world, come and set us free.

O God, you called a humble virgin to be the mother of the savior;
   —help us to respond to your call as Mary did.
Magi, persecution, and exile wove a cloak of mystery around the child;
   —give us the faith to live the questions in our lives.
You sent a savior for all the nations, yet many do not know you;
   —inspire teachers and preachers to take the gospel to the whole world.
You sent a savior to give us life;
   —have mercy on the dying and those who are in pain.

PRAYER: Mother and God, God and Father, you revealed yourself to us in Jesus, our brother. You call us to recognize all humanity as your children, our sisters and brothers. Help us to reverence each other. May the diversity that exists among us not be a cause of division but of enrichment. Grant this in Jesus' name. Amen.

DAYTIME PRAYER

Ant 1 Rise in splendor, Jerusalem! Your light is come, the glory of our God has dawned upon you.

Ant 2 Raise your eyes! See, they all gather and come to you; your sons come from afar, and your daughters rise up at your side.

Ant 3 All shall come bearing gold, frankincense, and myrrh, and proclaiming the praises of God.

(Prayer as in Morning Prayer)

BAPTISM OF THE LORD JESUS
FIRST SUNDAY OF ORDINARY TIME

EVENING PRAYER I

Ant 1 Today is the mystery, hidden from all ages, revealed to us. (Ps 135 I, p. 136)

Ant 2 Arise, Jerusalem, your light is come and the glory of our God is risen upon you, alleluia. (Ps 100, p. 132)

Ant 3 Today, when Jesus was baptized in the Jordan, a voice from the clouds thundered: This is my Beloved, in whom I am well pleased.

Canticle 1 Timothy 3:16

Praise our Savior, all you
  nations.
Christ manifested in the flesh,
Christ justified by the Spirit.

Praise our Savior, all you
  nations.
Christ seen by the angels,
Christ proclaimed to
  unbelievers.

Praise our Savior, all you
  nations.
Christ believed in by the world,
Christ taken up in glory.

Praise our Savior, all you
  nations.
Glory to you...

READING

You also, accompany him faithfully; and once regenerated in [Jesus], explore his secrets so that "on the banks of the Jordan you may discern the [Most High] in the voice, the [Christ] in the flesh and the Holy Spirit in the dove, and when the heaven of the Trinity is opened to you," you will be taken up into God.

Bonaventure, *The Tree of Life*, p. 133, (1)

RESPONSORY

O Christ, anointed of God, hear the plea of your people.
—**O Christ**...
Let your living water flow for us, —**hear**...
Glory to you, Source of all Being, Eternal Word and Holy Spirit.
—**O Christ**...

CANTICLE OF MARY

Ant Our Savior came to John to be baptized in the Jordan.
Through these cleansing waters we are restored to new life,
our sinful nature is healed, and we are clothed in holiness.

INTERCESSIONS

Jesus was baptized in the river Jordan by John, and the heavens opened. We cry out in expectation:
Come, Holy Spirit.

Jesus, beloved of God, you were led by the Spirit throughout your mission;
—teach us to follow that same Spirit on our way through life.
Jesus, Word of God, you embraced our humanity totally;
—help us to live your gospel and so transform our lives.
Jesus, son of Mary, you left your family and home to proclaim God's love;
—draw us to follow you in the service of others.
Jesus, sent by God to teach us, you went to John as a disciple to a master;
—teach us to respect all people, whatever their age or state in life.
Jesus, our Savior, you allowed John to cover you with the waters of baptism;
—give us a spirit of reverence that we may heal and encourage one another.

PRAYER: Jesus, sent by God to save us, you so loved the world that your every deed was inspired by the Holy Spirit.

Your mission was God's mission, and you gave your life
to fulfill it. Teach us to listen to the Spirit in our hearts.
Help us to love as you have loved us that we may
continue your mission. We ask this in your name.
Amen.

MORNING PRAYER
(Psalms from Sunday, Week I, p. 3)

Ant 1 In those days, Jesus came from Nazareth of Galilee and
was baptized in the Jordan, alleluia.

Ant 2 When Jesus came out of the water, the heavens opened
and the Spirit descended upon him, alleluia.

Ant 3 Rivers of water were made holy as Christ Jesus revealed
the glory of our God to the world, alleluia.

READING

Today's feast of the Baptism of Jesus reminds all of us that we are—in
the words of Pope Pius XII—"spiritually Semites." Just as the baptism of
Jesus did not cancel out his earlier life as a Jew but brought it to
perfection, likewise our own baptism did not eradicate who we were
from our natural birth. The sacrament, instead, consecrated our lives
with all its potential and goodness. Baptism perfects what otherwise
would remain underdeveloped, isolated, and frustrated.

Carroll Stuhlmueller, CP, *Biblical Meditations for Advent and the Christmas Season*, p. 223, (1)

RESPONSORY

Lord Jesus Christ, have mercy on us.—**Lord Jesus**...
Make known your ways to us, —**have**...
Glory to you, Source of all Being, Eternal Word and Holy Spirit.
    —**Lord Jesus**...

CANTICLE OF ZECHARIAH

Ant You springs and fountains, rivers and seas, clap your hands,
    for your Creator has manifested a sign of salvation in you.

INTERCESSIONS

The Holy Spirit hovered over Jesus and a voice declared him the
beloved One of God. We pray to him:
        Blessed be God who comes to save us.

Jesus, servant of God, you listened to the Spirit and were led to the Jordan to be baptized;

—open our minds and hearts to your call to conversion.

Jesus, Word made flesh, you listened to the Spirit and were led to the desert to prepare for your mission;

—teach us to pray that our ministry may proclaim the good news of the fullness of life.

Jesus, savior of us all, you listened to the Spirit and encouraged John in his time of doubt;

—help us to live the truth of our own baptism so deeply that we may be guides to one another.

Jesus, our peace, you listened to the spirit and were covered with the waters of the Jordan;

—bless all who are dying and enfold them in your mercy.

PRAYER: Jesus, sent by God to save us, you so loved the world that your every deed was inspired by the Holy Spirit. Your mission was God's mission, and you gave your life to fulfill it. Teach us to listen to the Spirit in our hearts. Help us to love as you have loved us, that we may continue your mission. We ask this in your name. Amen.

DAYTIME PRAYER
(Psalms from Sunday, Week I, p. 6)

Ant 1 When Jesus had been baptized and was praying, the heavens were opened.

Ant 2 You purged our guilt by fire and the Holy Spirit. We praise you, our God and Savior.

Ant 3 John bore witness: I saw the Spirit descend as a dove from heaven and it remained on him.

(Prayer as in Morning Prayer)

EVENING PRAYER II

Ant 1 A wondrous mystery has been made manifest this day. We praise you, our God. Alleluia! (Ps 110:1-5, 7, p. 53)

Ant 2 We have seen and have borne witness, this is the anointed of God, alleluia. (Ps 112, p. 149)

Ant 3 Seas and rivers, mountains and hills, all you living
creatures sing with us the praises of our God, alleluia.
(Rev 15:3–4, p. 89)

READING

After his baptism,...Matthew tells us that Jesus was led by the Spirit
into the desert in order to be tempted. When I experience my own
desert times—times of alienation, barrenness, or aloneness, I tend to
forget that I may have been led there by the Spirit to face my own
demons, to let them emerge and rise before me, and to learn my own
powerlessness and weakness, to enable me to see my oneness with
others who feel alienated, rejected, barren, alone. I need to recognize
and acknowledge those whom I have kept at a distance as those who
can broaden my vision, who can stretch my boundaries and free me
from the trap of judging who or what is "acceptable." My demons can
minister to me if I acknowledge them, and those others whom I hold at a
distance may well be the angels who will bring me to wholeness.

Carmelites of Indianapolis, *Hidden Friends*, p. 22–23, (5)

RESPONSORY

Jesus comes in water, blood and Spirit. —**Jesus**...
The Christ who saves us, —**in water**...
Glory to you, Source of all Being, Eternal Word and Holy Spirit.
   —**Jesus**...

CANTICLE OF MARY

Ant The one on whom the Spirit descends and remains, this is
the one who baptizes with the Holy Spirit.

INTERCESSIONS

Jesus was baptized in the river Jordan by John, and the heavens
opened, and so we pray:
Come, Holy Spirit.

Jesus, beloved of God, you were led by the Spirit throughout your
mission;
   —teach us to follow that same Spirit on our way through life.
Jesus, Word of God, you embraced our humanity totally;
   —help us to live your gospel and so transform our lives.
Jesus, son of Mary, you left your family and home;
   —draw us to follow you in the service of others.

Jesus, sent by God to teach us, you went to John as a disciple to a master;

—teach us to respect all people, whatever their age or state in life.

Jesus, our savior, you allowed John to cover you with the waters of baptism;

—give us a spirit of reverence that we may heal and encourage one another.

PRAYER: Jesus, sent by God to save us, you so loved the world that your every deed was inspired by the Holy Spirit. Your mission was God's mission, and you gave your life to fulfill it. Teach us to listen to the Spirit in our hearts. Help us to love as you have loved us, that we may continue your mission. We ask this in your name. Amen.

SECOND SUNDAY IN ORDINARY TIME

EVENING PRAYER I
(Psalms and Antiphons from Sunday, Week II, p. 47)

READING

We point to Christ in different ways, and we point to Christ in one same way. We point to Christ in different ways, because he calls us to *do* different things. Stephen, first to be martyred, pointed to Christ with his blood; Augustine and Aquinas, gifted minds, pointed to Christ with their theology. Teresa of Avila pointed to Christ as a mystic in action...people in professions point to Christ by penetrating technology with the gospel; civil servants, by planning passionately for peace.... Amid all this diversity, we point to Christ in one same way, because Christ calls all of us to *be* one person. Whatever you are called to *do*, you point to Christ ultimately by who you *are*; and in the concrete this means you point to Christ in the measure that you are Christlike.

Walter J. Burghardt, sj, *Lovely in Eyes Not His*, p. 70, (1)

RESPONSORY

In love and thanksgiving, we praise you, Holy God. —**In love...**
Your name is written in our hearts; —**we praise...**
Glory to you, Source of all Being, Eternal Word and Holy Spirit.
    —**In love...**

CANTICLE OF MARY

Ant. Forever I will sing your praise.

INTERCESSIONS and PRAYER: (from Sunday, Week II, p. 49)

MORNING PRAYER
(Psalms from Sunday, Week II, p. 49)

Ant 1 John looked at Jesus who was walking by, and said, "Behold the Lamb of God."

Ant 2 I will give you as a light to the nations that my salvation may reach to the ends of the earth.

Ant 3 To each is given the manifestation of the Spirit for the common good.

READING

John testified, "I saw the Spirit descending from heaven like a dove, and it remained on him. I myself did not know him, but the one who sent me to baptize with water said to me, 'He on whom you see the Spirit descend and remain is the one who baptizes with the Holy Spirit.' And I myself have seen and have testified that this is the Son of God."

Jn 1:32–34

RESPONSORY

There are varieties of gifts, but the same Spirit.—**There are**...
There are varieties of service, —**but the**...
Glory to you, Source of all Being, Eternal Word and Holy Spirit.
   —**There are**...

CANTICLE OF ZECHARIAH

Ant Here I am, O God, I come to do your will.

INTERCESSIONS (from Sunday, Week II, p. 51)

PRAYER: O God, you draw us to yourself through signs and wonders, through the ordinary events and encounters of the day, and through the silent word spoken in the depths of our hearts. Keep us ever open to your call; let us approach one another and all of your creatures with reverence and humility. Help us to seed our days with silent moments of presence to you. Make us worthy messengers of your Word Incarnate, Jesus Christ, one with you and the Holy Spirit, now and forever. Amen.

DAYTIME PRAYER

Ant 1 I will make you a light to the nations, that my salvation may reach to the ends of the earth.

Ant 2 Jesus asked his disciples, "What are you looking for?"

Ant 3 As bride and groom rejoice, so shall your God rejoice in you.

(Prayer as in Morning Prayer)

EVENING PRAYER II
(Psalms from Sunday, Week II, p. 53)

Ant 1 This is the one of whom I said, "After me comes one who ranks before me, one that was before me."

Ant 2 You are not your own; you were bought at a great price.

Ant 3 His mother said to the servants, "Do whatever He tells you."

READING

To each is given the manifestation of the Spirit for the common good. To one is given through the Spirit the utterance of wisdom, and to another the utterance of knowledge according to the same Spirit, to another faith by the same Spirit, to another gifts of healing by the one Spirit, to another the working of miracles, to another prophecy, to another the discernment of spirits, to another various kinds of tongues, to another the interpretation of tongues. All these are activated by one and the same Spirit, who allots to each one individually just as the Spirit chooses.

I Cor 12:7–11

RESPONSORY

I waited for you, O God, and you heard my cry. —**I waited**...
You put a new song into my mouth, —**you heard**...
Glory to you, Source of all Being, Eternal Word and Holy Spirit.
   —**I waited**...

CANTICLE OF MARY

Ant You have been consecrated in Christ Jesus and called to be a holy people.

INTERCESSIONS (from Sunday, Week II, p. 55)

PRAYER: O God, you draw us to yourself through signs and wonders, through the ordinary events and encounters of the day, and through the silent word spoken in the depths of our hearts. Keep us ever open to your call; let us approach one another and all of your creatures with reverence and humility. Help us to seed our days with silent moments of presence to you. Make us worthy messengers of your Word Incarnate, Jesus Christ, one with you and the Holy Spirit, now and forever. Amen.

THIRD SUNDAY IN ORDINARY TIME
EVENING PRAYER I
(Psalms and Antiphons from Sunday, Week III, p. 96)

READING

To those who practice discursive reflection, I say they should not pass
the whole time thinking. For, although discursive reflection is very
meritorious, they don't seem to realize that since their prayer is
delightful there should ever be a Sunday or a time in which one is not
working; but they think such a time is lost. I consider this loss a great
gain. But, as I have said, they should put themselves in the presence of
Christ and, without tiring the intellect, speak with and delight in Him
and not wear themselves out in composing syllogisms; rather, they
should show Him their needs and the reason why He doesn't have to
allow us to be in His presence.

Teresa of Avila, Life, 13.11, (3)

RESPONSORY

Shelter us, O God, in the safety of your dwelling place. —**Shelter...**
Your name is forever blessed; —**in the...**
Glory to you, Source of all Being, Eternal Word and Holy Spirit.
   —**Shelter...**

CANTICLE OF MARY

Ant. I long for you God of my life.

INTERCESSIONS and PRAYER: (from Sunday, Week III, p. 97)

MORNING PRAYER
(Psalms from Sunday, Week III, p. 98)

Ant 1 The people who walked in darkness have seen a great
    light.

Ant 2 From that time Jesus began to preach, saying, "Repent, for
    the reign of God is at hand."

Ant 3 Now you are the body of Christ and individually members
    of it.

READING

Brothers and sisters, the appointed time has grown short; from now on,
let even those who have spouses be as though they had none, and those
who mourn as though they were not mourning, and those who rejoice

as though they were not rejoicing, and those who buy as though they had no possessions, and those who deal with the world as though they had no dealings with it. For the present form of this world is passing away.

1 Cor 7:29–31

RESPONSORY

In the morning, O God, you hear my voice. **—In the...**
While I am watching and waiting, **—you hear...**
Glory to you, Source of all Being, Eternal Word and Holy Spirit.
   —In the...

CANTICLE OF ZECHARIAH

Ant To each is given the manifestation of the Spirit for the common good.

INTERCESSIONS (from Sunday, Week III, p. 100)

PRAYER: Spirit of God, you manifested yourself in the life of Jesus, directing his steps to the very end. Help us to realize your presence in our lives, and let us know the love, joy, peace and patience that are the fruits of your work in us. Enable us to inspire one another with the image of God that you continue to recreate in us. Let our lives tell of our baptism into the body of Christ, reflecting the unity that you share with God, our Creator, and that same Jesus Christ, now and forever. Amen.

DAYTIME PRAYER

Ant 1 Just as the body is one and has many members, and all the members of the body, though many, are one body, so it is with Christ.

Ant 2 Those who dwelt in the land of deep darkness, on them has light shined.

Ant 3 This day is holy to our God; do not be grieved, for the joy of God is your strength.

(Prayer as in Morning Prayer)

EVENING PRAYER II
(Psalms from Sunday, Week III, p. 102)

Ant 1 You have brought abundant joy, O God, and great rejoicing.

Ant 2 Jesus said to them, "Follow me and I will make you fishers of people."

Ant 3 The Spirit of God is upon me, because the Most High has anointed me to preach good news to the poor.

READING

Just as the body is one and has many members, and all the members of the body, though many, are one body, so it is with Christ. For in the one Spirit we were all baptized into one body—Jews or Greeks, slaves or free—and we were all made to drink of one Spirit. Indeed, the body does not consist of one member but of many. Now you are the body of Christ and individually members of it.

1 Cor 12:12–14, 27

RESPONSORY

You take delight in your people, O God; you adorn the humble with victory. **—You take...**
Let the faithful exult in their glory; **—you adorn...**
Glory to you, Source of all Being, Eternal Word and Holy Spirit.
—You take...

CANTICLE OF MARY

Ant God has sent me to proclaim release to the captives and to set at liberty those who are oppressed.

INTERCESSIONS (from Sunday, Week III, p. 104)

PRAYER: Spirit of God, you manifested yourself in the life of Jesus, directing his steps to the very end. Help us to realize your presence in our lives, and let us know the love, joy, peace and patience that are the fruits of your work in us. Enable us to inspire one another with the image of God that you continue to recreate in us. Let our lives tell of our baptism into the body of Christ, reflecting the unity that you share with God, our Creator, and that same Jesus Christ, now and forever. Amen.

FOURTH SUNDAY IN ORDINARY TIME

EVENING PRAYER I

(Psalms and Antiphons from Sunday, Week IV, p. 143)

READING

There remain, therefore, faith, hope and love—these three. But the greatest of these is love. So says Paul. But we could also translate this: Faith, hope, and love constitute that which is definitive and final. Perhaps it has been shown that hope is not simply the attitude of one who is weak and at the same time hungering for a fulfillment that has yet to be achieved, but rather the courage to commit oneself in thought and deed to the incomprehensible and the uncontrollable which permeates our existence, and, as the future to which it is open, sustains it. Perhaps it has also been shown that such courage has the power to dare more than what can be arrived at merely by planning and calculations. Perhaps it has been shown that in the final and definitive consummation hope still prevails and endures, because this definitive consummation is God.

Karl Rahner, *The Practice of Faith*, p. 260, (2)

RESPONSORY

We call to you in our need, O God, for you hear the cry of the poor.
   —**We call...**
You will not leave us orphans; —**for you...**
Glory to you, Source of all Being, Eternal Word and Holy Spirit.
   —**We call...**

CANTICLE OF MARY

Ant. Be mindful of your mercy to us, O loving God.

INTERCESSIONS and PRAYER: (from Sunday, Week IV, p. 144)

MORNING PRAYER

(Psalms from Sunday, Week IV, p. 145)

Ant 1 God is the source of your life in Christ Jesus, who is our wisdom, our righteousness, our sanctification and our redemption.

Ant 2 The people were astonished at his teaching for he taught them as one having authority.

Ant 3 Love bears all things, believes all things, hopes all things, endures all things.

READING

Consider your own call, brothers and sisters; not many of you were wise by human standards, not many were powerful, not many were of noble birth. But God chose what is foolish in the world to shame the wise; God chose what is weak in the world to shame the strong; God chose what is low and despised in the world, things that are not, to reduce to nothing things that are, so that no one might boast in the presence of God.

1 Cor 1:26–29

RESPONSORY

You bless your people, O God; you fill our mouths with gladness.
   —You bless...
Holy is your name; **—you fill...**
Glory to you, Source of all Being, Eternal Word and Holy Spirit.
   —You bless...

CANTICLE OF ZECHARIAH

Ant Let the one who boasts, boast in the Lord Jesus Christ.

INTERCESSIONS (from Sunday, Week IV, p. 147)

PRAYER: Jesus, you were a blessing to the poor, the meek, the wounded, and to all who received you. Help us to be open to you and to know the meaning of your words. Turn our minds and our very world of thought around, that we may creatively bring dignity and healing to our people and our planet. Give us faith in the more that lies within and beyond what we can see and hear. Teach us to care for one another as you have cared for us, that like you, we may be a blessing for our world and praise to God our Creator now and forever. Amen.

DAYTIME PRAYER

Ant 1 Seek God, all you humble of the land, who do God's command.

Ant 2 I will raise up for them a prophet like you from among their brothers and sisters, in whose mouth I put my words.

Ant 3 Before I formed you in the womb I knew you, and before you were born I consecrated you.

(Prayer as in Morning Prayer)

EVENING PRAYER II

(Psalms from Sunday, Week IV, p. 149)

Ant 1 Today, this Scripture has been fulfilled in your hearing.

Ant 2 I say this for your own benefit, to promote good order and to secure your undivided devotion to God.

Ant 3 Blessed are the merciful, for they shall obtain mercy.

READING

Love never ends. But as for prophecies, they will come to an end; as for tongues, they will cease; as for knowledge, it will come to an end. For we know only in part, and we prophesy only in part; but when the complete comes, the partial will come to an end. When I was a child, I thought like a child, I reasoned like a child; when I became an adult, I put an end to childish ways. For now we see in a mirror, dimly, but then we will see face to face. Now I know only in part; then I will know fully, even as I have been fully known. And now faith, hope, and love abide, these three; and the greatest of these is love.

1 Cor 12:8–13

RESPONSORY

My soul clings to you, O God, your hand upholds me.—**My soul...**
In the shadow of your wings I sing for joy, —**your hand...**
Glory to you, Source of all Being, Eternal Word and Holy Spirit.
  —**My soul...**

CANTICLE OF MARY

Ant Love bears all things, believes all things, hopes all things, endures all things.

INTERCESSIONS (from Sunday, Week IV, p. 150)

PRAYER: Jesus, you were a blessing to the poor, the meek, the wounded, and to all who received you. Help us to be open to you and to know the meaning of your words. Turn our minds and our very world of thought around, that we may creatively bring dignity and healing to our people and our planet. Give us faith in the more that lies within and beyond what we can see and hear. Teach us to care for one another as you have cared for us, that like you, we may be a blessing for our world and praise to God our Creator now and forever. Amen

FIFTH SUNDAY IN ORDINARY TIME

EVENING PRAYER I

(Psalms and Antiphons from Sunday, Week I, p. 1)

READING

The philosoper Eliade states that the cycle of life, death, and rebirth, or
resurrection is the deepest myth of reality. Creation lives this reality
from cosmic evolution to the autumn leaves decomposing into life-giving
soil. We might well meditate on the backyard compost heap as weeds
and vegetable scraps break down for the enrichment of next year's crop.
This paradox of nature lives itself out in the Christian tradition.

Vilma Seelaus, OCD, "Kenosis in the Carmelite Tradition," (4)

RESPONSORY

We sing to you, O God, and bless your name. —**We sing...**
Tell of your salvation day after day; —**and bless...**
Glory to you, Source of all Being, Eternal Word and Holy Spirit.
    —**We sing...**

CANTICLE OF MARY

Ant. You have helped your servant, Israel, remembering your
    mercy.

INTERCESSIONS and PRAYER: (from Sunday, Week I, p. 3)

MORNING PRAYER

(Psalms from Sunday, Week I, p. 3)

Ant 1 I decided to know nothing among you except Jesus Christ
    and him crucified.

Ant 2 When Simon Peter saw it, he fell down at Jesus' knees,
    saying, "Depart from me, for I am a sinful man, O Lord."

Ant 3 Jesus said to Simon, "Do not be afraid, henceforth you will
    be catching people."

READING

Is not this the fast that I choose: to loose the bonds of injustice, to undo
the thongs of the yoke, to let the oppressed go free, and to break every
yoke? Is it not to share your bread with the hungry, and bring the
homeless poor into your house; when you see the naked to cover them,
and not to hide yourself from your own kin? Then your light shall break

forth like the dawn, and your healing shall spring up quickly; your vindicator shall go before you, the glory of God shall be your rear guard.

Is 58:6–8

RESPONSORY

I cried to you for help, O God, and you healed me.—**I cried**...
You have given me back my life, —**and you**...
Glory to you, Source of all Being, Eternal Word and Holy Spirit.
   —**I cried**...

CANTICLE OF ZECHARIAH

Ant If you pour yourself out for the hungry and satisfy the desire of the afflicted, then shall your light rise in the darkness.

INTERCESSIONS (from Sunday, Week I, p. 5)

PRAYER: God our creator and guide, each week you invite us to a day of rest and special presence to you and to one another. Bless those who cannot rest—whose needs demand overwork. Bless those who cannot work. Show us effective ways to distribute the fruits of the earth for the good of all. Remind us that true unity means noticing, caring, and sharing when others have less than they need. Give us the wisdom and courage to be poor in spirit and to serve those who are poor indeed. We ask this in Jesus' name. Amen.

DAYTIME PRAYER

Ant 1 I have made myself a servant to all, that I might win the more.

Ant 2 "Holy, holy, holy are you, O God; the whole earth is full of your glory."

Ant 3 Let your light so shine before others, that they may see your good works and give glory to God who is in heaven.

(Prayer as in Morning Prayer)

EVENING PRAYER II
(Psalms from Sunday, Week I, p. 7)

Ant 1 I have become all things to all people, that I might by all means save some.

Ant 2 The whole city was gathered together about the door. He healed many who were sick with various diseases.

Ant 3 By the grace of God I am what I am, and God's grace toward me was not in vain.

READING

Do not human beings have a hard service on earth, and are not their days like the days of a laborer? Like a slave who longs for the shadow, and like laborers who look for their wages, so I am allotted months of emptiness, and nights of misery are apportioned to me. When I lie down I say, "When shall I rise?" But the night is long, and I am full of tossing until dawn. My days are swifter than a weaver's shuttle, and come to their end without hope. Remember that my life is a breath; my eye will never again see good.

                                                                    Job 7:1–4, 6–7

RESPONSORY

My vows to you I will make, O God; I will give you thanks. —**My vows**...
That I may walk before you in the light of life; —**I will**...
Glory to you, Source of all Being, Eternal Word and Holy Spirit.
    —**My vows**...

CANTICLE OF MARY

Ant Peter said to Jesus, "Teacher, we toiled all night and took nothing! But at your word I will let down the nets."

INTERCESSIONS (from Sunday, Week I, p. 9)

PRAYER: God our creator and guide, each week you invite us to a day of rest and special presence to you and to one another. Bless those who cannot rest—whose needs demand overwork. Bless those who cannot work. Show us effective ways to distribute the fruits of the earth for the good of all. Remind us that true unity means noticing, caring, and sharing when others have less than they need. Give us the wisdom and courage to be poor in spirit and to serve those who are poor indeed. We ask this in Jesus' name. Amen.

SIXTH SUNDAY IN ORDINARY TIME

EVENING PRAYER I

(Psalms and Antiphons from Sunday, Week II, p. 47)

READING

[Poverty] has none of that attachment which, like a band, binds the heart to earth and to earthly things and deprives us of that ease in rising and turning once more to God. It enables us to hear better in all things the voice—that is, the inspiration—of the Holy Spirit by removing the obstructions which hinder it. It gives greater efficacy to our prayers in the sight of God because "[God] hath heard the desire of the poor." It speeds us on our way along the path of virtue, like a traveler who has been relieved of all burdens. It frees us from that slavery common to so many of the world's great ones, in which everything obeys or serves money.

Letters of St. Ignatius of Loyola, pp. 148–49, (19)

RESPONSORY

From daybreak to sunset, we praise your name, O God.
   —From daybreak...
Your glory fills the heavens; **—we praise...**
Glory to you, Source of all Being, Eternal Word and Holy Spirit.
   —From daybreak...

CANTICLE OF MARY

Ant. Blessed are the pure of heart, for they shall see God.

INTERCESSIONS and PRAYER: (from Sunday, Week II, p. 49)

MORNING PRAYER

(Psalms from Sunday, Week II, p. 49)

Ant 1 For great is the wisdom of God, who is mighty in power and sees everything.

Ant 2 Whether you eat or drink, or whatever you do, do all to the glory of God.

Ant 3 No eye has seen nor ear heard, nor human heart conceived, what has been prepared for those who love God.

READING

If you choose, you can keep the commandments, and to act faithfully is a matter of your own choice. God has placed before you fire and water; stretch out your hand for whichever you choose. Before each person are life and death, and whichever one chooses will be given. For great is the wisdom of God; who is mighty in power and sees everything; whose eyes are on those who fear the Most High, and who knows every human action. God has not commanded anyone to be wicked, and has not given anyone permission to sin.

Sir 15:15–20

RESPONSORY

Restore me to health, make me live! —**Restore**...
You are the hope of all the earth; —**make me**...
Glory to you, Source of all Being, Eternal Word and Holy Spirit.
   —**Restore**...

CANTICLE OF ZECHARIAH

Ant I say to you, everyone who is angry with a sister or brother shall be liable to judgment.

INTERCESSIONS (from Sunday, Week II, p. 51)

PRAYER: O God, you have given us the gift of freedom that we prize as much as life itself. Give us the grace to honor the gift by employing it with justice and mercy. Bless all who are enslaved in any way. Give comfort and strength to those who are ill, imprisoned, confused, or caught in some form of selfishness. Give us all freedom of heart. Enable us to live creatively. Let the mystery of the cross lead us to the hope of resurrection through Jesus Christ, who lives with you and the Holy Spirit forever. Amen.

DAYTIME PRAYER

Ant 1 Blessed are they who trust in God, whose hope is the Most High.

Ant 2 A leper came to Jesus beseeching him, and kneeling said to him, "If you will, you can make me clean."

Ant 3 Blessed are you poor, for yours is the reign of God.

(Prayer as in Morning Prayer)

EVENING PRAYER II

(Psalms from Sunday, Week II, p. 53)

Ant 1 Think not that I have come to abolish the law and the prophets; I have come not to abolish them but to fulfill them.

Ant 2 Christ has been raised from the dead, the first fruits of those who have fallen asleep.

Ant 3 Jesus was moved with pity and stretching out his hand he touched the man and said, "I will, be clean."

READING

So whether you eat or drink, or whatever you do, do everything for the glory of God. Give no offense to Jews or to Greeks or to the church of God, just as I try to please everyone in everything I do, not seeking my own advantage, but that of many, so that they may be saved. Be imitators of me, as I am of Christ.

1 Cor 10:31–11:1

RESPONSORY

May all who seek you, O God, rejoice and be glad.—**May all**...
May all who love your salvation —**rejoice**...
Glory to you, Source of all Being, Eternal Word and Holy Spirit.
  —**May all**...

CANTICLE OF MARY

Ant Blessed are you that hunger now, for you shall be satisfied.

INTERCESSIONS (from Sunday, Week II, p. 55)

PRAYER: O God, you have given us the gift of freedom that we prize as much as life itself. Give us the grace to honor the gift by employing it with justice and mercy. Bless all who are enslaved in any way. Give comfort and strength to those who are ill, imprisoned, confused, or caught in some form of selfishness. Give us all freedom of heart. Enable us to live creatively. Let the mystery of the cross lead us to the hope of resurrection through Jesus Christ, who lives with you and the Holy Spirit forever. Amen.

SEVENTH SUNDAY IN ORDINARY TIME

EVENING PRAYER I

(Psalms and Antiphons from Sunday, Week III, p. 96)

READING

There are many ways to become open to our Divine Source so that we may be healed. There is life itself. Clearly the Divine Mystery can touch us in people, in nature, in music, in art.... Whatever spiritual disciplines we undertake, they are no band aid. The heavy and stubborn patterns which overlay our souls don't magically go away. Spiritual practice is essential, not for its own sake, but to link us up to God and to God's health which lives at the center of each of us. There is no way we can get out of God's love or away from the deep-seated health. We have resources available to us that are mightier than all the powers of the world, even that in us which is resistant to the light and the best interests of our own souls. What is needful is not perfect spiritual practice but our *willingness* to let God's gift of deep health come out of its hiding place and become the operative principle of our lives.

John P. Gorsuch, An Invitation to the Spiritual Journey, pp. 64–65, (1)

RESPONSORY

Shelter us, O God, in the safety of your dwelling place. **—Shelter...**
Your name is forever blessed; **—in the safety...**
Glory to you, Source of all Being, Eternal Word and Holy Spirit.
   —Shelter...

CANTICLE OF MARY

Ant. You are faithful to your word, forever.

INTERCESSIONS and PRAYER: (from Sunday, Week III, p. 97)

MORNING PRAYER

(Psalms from Sunday, Week III, p. 98)

Ant 1 You shall be holy, for I your God am holy.

Ant 2 Love your enemies that you may be children of God.

Ant 3 Judge not, and you will not be judged; condemn not, and you will not be condemned.

READING

Do you not know that you are God's temple and that God's Spirit dwells in you? If anyone destroys God's temple, God will destroy that person.

For God's temple is holy, and you are that temple. Do not deceive yourselves. If you think that you are wise in this age, you should become fools so that you may become wise. For the wisdom of this world is foolishness with God. So let no one boast about human leaders. For all things are yours, whether Paul or Apollos or Cephas or the world or life or death or the present or the future—all belong to you, and you belong to Christ, and Christ belongs to God.

1 Cor 3:16–19a, 21–23

RESPONSORY

God's temple is holy, and you are God's temple.**—God's temple**...
God's Spirit dwells in you; **—and you**...
Glory to you, Source of all Being, Eternal Word and Holy Spirit.
   —God's temple...

CANTICLE OF ZECHARIAH

Ant God makes the sun rise on those who do evil and on the good, and sends rain on the just and the unjust.

INTERCESSIONS (from Sunday, Week III, p. 100)

PRAYER: O God, our mother and father, we praise you in the wonder of your all-embracing love. Your compassion extends to all as you forgive us again and again. Give us the humility and love to forgive one another, living the prayer of your Divine Son—to forgive as we are forgiven. Make us sacraments of your healing love, bearers of the promise of Jesus, who lives with you and the Holy Spirit now and forever. Amen.

DAYTIME PRAYER

Ant 1 You shall love your neighbor as yourself: I am your God.

Ant 2 I am the One who blots out your transgressions for my own sake, and I will not remember your sins.

Ant 3 Just as we have borne the image of the creature of dust, we shall also bear the image of the One come down from heaven.

(Prayer as in Morning Prayer)

EVENING PRAYER II
(Psalms from Sunday, Week III, p. 102)

Ant 1 You, therefore must be perfect as your Creator in heaven is perfect.

Ant 2 God has put a seal upon us and has given us the Spirit in our hearts as a guarantee.

Ant 3 When Jesus saw their faith, he said to the paralytic, "My child, your sins are forgiven."

READING

Do not remember the former things, or consider the things of old. I am about to do a new thing; now it springs forth, do you not perceive it? I will make a way in the wilderness and rivers in the desert. The people whom I formed for myself so that they might declare my praise. Yet you did not call upon me, O Jacob; but you have been weary of me, O Israel! You have not brought me sweet cane with money, or satisfied me with the fat of your sacrifices. But you have burdened me with your iniquities. I, I am the One who blots out your transgressions for my own sake, and I will not remember your sins.

Is 43:18–19, 21–22, 24–25

RESPONSORY

Love your enemies; do good to those who hate you. **—Love your**...
Pray for those who persecute you **—do good**...
Glory to you, Source of all Being, Eternal Word and Holy Spirit.
    —Love your...

CANTICLE OF MARY

Ant The wisdom of this world is folly with God.

INTERCESSIONS (from Sunday, Week III, p. 104)

PRAYER: O God, our mother and father, we praise you in the wonder of your all-embracing love. Your compassion extends to all as you forgive us again and again. Give us the humility and love to forgive one another, living the prayer of your Divine Son—to forgive as we are forgiven. Make us sacraments of your healing love, bearers of the promise of Jesus, who lives with you and the Holy Spirit now and forever. Amen.

EIGHTH SUNDAY IN ORDINARY TIME

EVENING PRAYER I

(Psalms and Antiphons from Sunday, Week IV, p. 143)

READING

Let us consider, beloved, how [God] continually proves to us that there shall be a future resurrection, of which [God] has rendered the Lord Jesus Christ the first-fruits by raising him from the dead. Let us contemplate, beloved, the resurrection which is at all times taking place. Day and night declare to us a resurrection. The night sinks to sleep, and the day arises; the day again departs, and the night comes on. (St. Clement of Rome)

Mary E. Penrose, *Roots Deep and Strong*, p. 9, (1)

RESPONSORY

Living source of light and wisdom, be with us always. —**Living...**
In you we find new life; —**be with...**
Glory to you, Source of all Being, Eternal Word and Holy Spirit.
   —**Living...**

CANTICLE OF MARY

Ant. You are faithful to your promise, God of all the ages.

INTERCESSIONS and PRAYER: (from Sunday, Week IV, p. 144)

MORNING PRAYER

(Psalms from Sunday, Week IV, p. 145)

Ant 1 Seek first God's realm and way of holiness, and all else will be given you besides.

Ant 2 No one can serve two masters.

Ant 3 Christ will bring to light what is hidden in darkness and manifest the intentions of hearts.

READING

But Zion said, "The Most High has forsaken me, my God has forgotten me." Can a woman forget her nursling child, or show no compassion for the child of her womb? Even these may forget, yet I will not forget you.

Is 49:14–15

RESPONSORY

God is my stronghold, I shall not be disturbed; —**God is...**

My refuge and my salvation; —**I shall**...
Glory to you, Source of all Being, Eternal Word and Holy Spirit.
    —**God is**...

CANTICLE OF ZECHARIAH

Ant Our sole credit is from God, who has made us qualified
ministers of a new covenant.

INTERCESSIONS (from Sunday, Week IV, p. 147)

PRAYER: Bountiful God, we are filled with wonder and gratitude
as we strive to realize our calling to tell the message of
the gospel with our lives. Let the promises of Christ give
us the freedom to leave behind all that hinders the
coming of your realm on earth. Give us the courage and
peace of heart that comes from confidence in your care.
Dispel the darkness of our lives with healing truth;
make us ready for the new wine of the future. We ask
this of you, God of time and eternity. Amen.

DAYTIME PRAYER

Ant 1 Can a woman forget her suckling child? Even these may
forget, yet I will not forget you.

Ant 2 Our competence is from God who has made us competent
to be ministers of a new covenant.

Ant 3 Out of the abundance of the heart the mouth speaks.

(Prayer as in Morning Prayer)

EVENING PRAYER II
(Psalms from Sunday, Week IV, p. 149)

Ant 1 I will betroth you to me in faithfulness; and you shall know
your God.

Ant 2 Look at the birds of the air; they neither sow nor reap nor
gather into barns, and yet your Father/Mother in heaven
feeds them.

Ant 3 The fruit discloses the cultivation of a tree; so the
expression of a thought discloses the cultivation of a
person's mind.

READING

Therefore, I will now allure her, and bring her into the wilderness, and speak tenderly to her. There she shall respond as in the days of her youth, as at the time when she came out of the land of Egypt. And I will take you for my wife forever; I will take you for my wife in righteousness and in justice, in steadfast love, and in mercy. I will take you for my wife in faithfulness; and you shall know the Most High.

Hos 2:14–15, 19–20

RESPONSORY

Why look at the speck in another's eye, when you miss the
　　plank in your own? —**Why look**...
How can you say to another, "Let me remove the speck from
your eye?" —**When you**...
Glory to you, Source of all Being, Eternal Word and Holy Spirit.
　　—**Why look**...

CANTICLE OF MARY

Ant Each tree is known by its yield.

INTERCESSIONS (from Sunday, Week IV, p. 150)

PRAYER: Bountiful God, we are filled with wonder and gratitude as we strive to realize our calling to tell the message of the gospel with our lives. Let the promises of Christ give us the freedom to leave behind all that hinders the coming of your realm on earth. Give us the courage and peace of heart that comes from confidence in your care. Dispel the darkness of our lives with healing truth; make us ready for the new wine of the future. We ask this of you, God of time and eternity. Amen.

NINTH SUNDAY IN ORDINARY TIME

EVENING PRAYER I

(Psalms and Antiphons from Sunday, Week I, p. 1)

READING

The lives of the other ascetics he (Anthony the Great) knew became the training ground for his own practices:
　　He observed the graciousness of one, the earnestness at prayer in another; studied the even temper of one and the kindheartedness of

another; fixed his attention on the vigils kept by one and on the studies pursued by another; admired one for his patient endurance, another for his fasting and sleeping on the ground; watched closely this person's meekness and the forbearance shown by another; and in one and all alike he marked especially devotion to Christ and the love they had for one another. (*Life of Anthony*)

Mary E. Penrose, *Roots Deep and Strong*, p. 68, (1)

RESPONSORY

You create us in your image, O God, we are co-creators with you.
  —You create...
We are nothing without you; **—we are...**
Glory to you, Source of all Being, Eternal Word and Holy Spirit.
  —You create...

CANTICLE OF MARY

Ant. I rejoice in your greatness, O God.

INTERCESSIONS and PRAYER: (from Sunday, Week I, p. 3)

MORNING PRAYER
(Psalms from Sunday, Week I, p. 3)

Ant 1 The centurion said to Jesus, "Lord, I am not worthy to have you come under my roof, but only say the word, and my servant will be healed."

Ant 2 While we live we are always being given up to death for Jesus' sake, so that the life of Jesus may be manifested in our mortal flesh.

Ant 3 You are my rock and my fortress; for your name's sake lead me and guide me.

READING

See, I am setting before you today a blessing and a curse: the blessing, if you obey the commandments of the Most High God that I am commanding you today; and the curse if you do not obey the commandments of the Most High God, but turn from the way that I am commanding you today to follow other gods that you have not known.

Deut 11:26–28

RESPONSORY

We praise your name, O God; all your servants give praise.
—**We praise**...
Those who stand in your holy house; —**all your**...
Glory to you, Source of all Being, Eternal Word and Holy Spirit.
—**We praise**...

CANTICLE OF ZECHARIAH

Ant We have this treasure in earthen vessels, to show that the transcendent power belongs to God and not to us.

INTERCESSIONS (from Sunday, Week I, p. 5)

PRAYER: Eternal Wisdom, you have written your law of love in our hearts. Remove from our lives all that blinds us to your life-giving truth. Help us to transcend the fear and selfishness that would direct us away from you. Make us willing to pay the price of love that will bless the world with the mercy and healing it knew in the life of Jesus. May all that we do give praise to you now and forever. Amen.

DAYTIME PRAYER

Ant 1 For we hold that a person is justified by faith apart from works of law.

Ant 2 Observe the Sabbath day, to keep it holy, as your God, the Most High commanded you.

Ant 3 When Jesus heard this he marveled at him, saying "Not even in Israel have I found such faith."

(Prayer as in Morning Prayer)

EVENING PRAYER II
(Psalms from Sunday, Week I, p. 7)

Ant 1 Jesus said, "Not everyone who says to me, 'Lord, Lord,' shall enter the realm of heaven, but the one who does the will of God who is in heaven."

Ant 2 Am I now seeking the favor of people, or of God? If I were still pleasing people, I should not be a servant of Christ.

Ant 3 Jesus said, "Is it lawful on the sabbath to do good or to do harm, to save life or to kill?"

READING

It is the God who said, "Let light shine out of darkness," who has shone in our hearts to give the light of the knowledge of the glory of God in the face of Jesus Christ. But we have this treasure in clay jars, so that it may be made clear that this extraordinary power belongs to God and does not come from us. We are afflicted in every way, but not crushed; perplexed, but not driven to despair; persecuted, but not forsaken; struck down, but not destroyed; always carrying in the body the death of Jesus, so that the life of Jesus may also be made visible in our bodies. For while we live, we are always being given up to death for Jesus' sake, so that the life of Jesus may be made visible in our mortal flesh.

2 Cor 4:6–11

RESPONSORY

O God, your name endures forever; you will work justice for your people.
   —O God...
You have compassion on your servants, **—you will...**
Glory to you, Source of all Being, Eternal Word and Holy Spirit.
   —O God...

CANTICLE OF MARY

Ant The sabbath was made for the people, not the people for the sabbath; and so the Christ is head even of the sabbath.

INTERCESSIONS (from Sunday, Week I, p. 9)

PRAYER: Eternal Wisdom, you have written your law of love in our hearts. Remove from our lives all that blinds us to your life-giving truth. Help us to transcend the fear and selfishness that would direct us away from you. Make us willing to pay the price of love that will bless the world with the mercy and healing it knew in the life of Jesus. May all that we do give praise to you now and forever. Amen.

ASH WEDNESDAY
(Psalms from Friday, Week III, p. 131)
MORNING PRAYER

Ant 1 Rend your hearts and not your garments.

Ant 2 You, O God, are slow to anger and rich in compassion.

Ant 3 A contrite and humble heart, O God, you will not spurn.

READING

You are a people holy to [God Most High]; [God] has chosen you out of all the peoples on earth to be [God's] people, [God's] treasured possession. It was because [God] loved you and kept the oath that [was sworn] to your ancestors, that [God] has brought you out with a mighty hand, and redeemed you from the house of slavery, from the hand of Pharaoh king of Egypt. Know therefore that the [Most High God] is God, the faithful God who maintains covenant loyalty with those who love [God] and keep [the] commandments to a thousand generations.

Dt. 7:6, 8–9

RESPONSORY

Spare us, O God, and have pity on your people. —**Spare us**...
We have sinned against you, —**have pity**...
Glory to you, Source of all Being, Eternal Word and Holy Spirit.
   —**Spare us**...

CANTICLE OF ZECHARIAH

Ant When you fast, do not look gloomy like the hypocrites.

INTERCESSIONS

We pray that we will be filled with the Holy Spirit, that our hearts will be renewed, and our vision clarified in love, and so we ask:
   O loving Creator, fill us with your Spirit.
O God, grant that we may be sensitive to your presence in our lives;
   —by taking time to pause for reflection and remembrance.
May we use the freedom you have given us;
   —to liberate those with burdens too heavy to bear.
Give us world leaders who govern with integrity and honesty;
   —so that all people may live their lives in peaceful
      environments.

Strengthen our inner resources with your power;
  —that we may grow in gentleness when our lives are confronted
    with difficulties.
Be with those who are terminally ill;
  —and grant them peace of mind as they await your coming.

PRAYER: As we begin Lent, O holy God, strengthen us in our
endeavors against evil. Bless our efforts to live in union
with you and all the people of the world. Help us to
discover whatever interferes with loving each other. We
ask this in union with all people who begin this season
in your name. Amen.

DAYTIME PRAYER

Ant 1 The season of deliverance has come; the time of salvation
is at hand.

Ant 2 Turn to me with all your heart, says our God.

Ant 3 Believing in God's strength and mercy, let us be fortified
with patience.

(Prayer as in Morning Prayer)

EVENING PRAYER

Ant 1 Wash me from my guilt and cleanse me of my sin.

Ant 2 I acknowledge my offense; my sins are before me always.

Ant 3 I turn to you, O God, and seek your salvation.

READING

Work out your own salvation with fear and trembling; for it is God who
is at work in you, enabling you both to will and to work for [God's] good
pleasure. Do all things without murmuring and arguing, so that you
may be blameless and innocent, children of God without blemish.

Phil 2:12b–15a

RESPONSORY

Have mercy on me, O God in your goodness. **—Have**...
In the greatness of your compassion, wipe out my offense, **—O God,**...
Glory to you, Source of all Being, Eternal Word and Holy Spirit.
  —Have...

CANTICLE OF MARY

Ant A clean heart create for me, O God, and a steadfast spirit renew within me.

INTERCESSIONS

O God, giver of life, we ask during this lenten time to be united with the suffering, death, and resurrection of Jesus. We raise our hearts to you in prayer:
Draw us ever closer to you.

O God, you desire peace and harmony for all;
—comfort those who are experiencing the devastation of war.
Your Christ healed the sick and forgave sins;
—bless all in this world who relieve psychological and physical pain.
Through the ministry of Jesus, the poor were fed and the blind given sight;
—refresh all those who continue to work with the helpless and the needy.
Strengthen all those dedicated to your service;
—that their lives may give witness to your love and compassion.
You look with gracious mercy on all who seek you;
—ease the burdens of the elderly and all who are in need of your help.

PRAYER: Make us reconciled to you, O God, that we may put on the holiness of Christ and give you glory. Help us to live this season as true disciples on our way to transformation and fullness of life. Grant this as we journey to you with Jesus, our brother. Amen.

THURSDAY AFTER ASH WEDNESDAY
(Antiphons and Psalms from Thursday, Week IV, p. 172)

MORNING PRAYER

READING

And sometimes the heart is dry and feels nothing, or else, by the temptation of our enemy, reason and grace drive the soul to implore our Lord with words, recounting his blessed Passion and his great goodness. And so the power of our Lord's word enters the soul and enlivens the heart and it begins by his grace faithful exercise, and makes the soul to pray most blessedly, and truly to rejoice in our Lord. This is a most loving thanksgiving in his sight.

Julian of Norwich, Showings, p. 60, (1)

RESPONSORY

Spare us, O God, and have pity on your people. **—Spare**...
We have sinned against you, **—have pity**...
Glory to you, Source of all Being, Eternal Word and Holy Spirit.
   —Spare...

CANTICLE OF ZECHARIAH

Ant Happy are they who walk in your ways.

INTERCESSIONS

O God, we pray that we may grow in your Spirit during these days of Lent, and so we say:
   Renew our hearts and fill us with your love.

May leaders of nations choose life for their people;
   —that all may have employment, food, and shelter for their
      families.
May church leaders choose life for the faithful;
   —that consciences be not burdened but formed to make
      reflective decisions.
May parents choose life for their children;
   —that they may grow in wisdom and reverence for others.
May all peoples of this earth choose life for our planet;
   —that our natural resources may be preserved and all species
      continue to exist.
May all of us choose life now and for all time;
   —that we may live in your presence for all eternity.

PRAYER: O God, grant us the strength to bear our sufferings and
         our weaknesses. Help us to carry our burdens with a
         renewed faith and continued belief in your love for us.
         Give us lightness of heart and compassion for those we
         live and work with. This we ask in Jesus' name. Amen.

DAYTIME PRAYER

Ant 1 The season of deliverance has come; the time of salvation is at hand.

Ant 2 Turn to me with all your heart, says our God.

Ant 3 Believing in God's strength and mercy, let us be fortified with patience.

(Prayer as in Morning Prayer)

EVENING PRAYER

READING

Through your passion and death, make me die unto myself and live unto you alone. Through your glorious resurrection and wonderful ascension make me advance daily from strength to strength.

The Exercises of Saint Gertrude, p. 39, (13)

RESPONSORY

Have mercy on me, O God in your goodness. —**Have**...
In the greatness of your compassion, wipe out my offense, —**O God,**...
Glory to you, Source of all Being, Eternal Word and Holy Spirit.
   —**Have**...

CANTICLE OF MARY

Ant Happy are they who delight in God's law and meditate on it night and day.

INTERCESSIONS

In your mercy look on us with kindness. Hear our prayer as we say:
   Increase our faith and fill us with your Spirit.

God of compassion, look with tender mercy on all who grieve the loss of a loved one;
   —comfort them in their affliction.
God of wisdom, inspire scientists and those engaged in research;
   —to find cures for fatal illnesses and to promote quality of human life in ethical ways.
God of the universe, give us a lively curiosity;
   —that we may explore the planets and the atoms in ways that benefit all of creation.

God of providence, order our minds and hearts;
  —that our daily choices will further the coming of your reign on
    earth.
God of the living, receive those who die this day;
  —that they may see you face to face.

PRAYER: O God, grant us the strength to bear our sufferings and
our weaknesses. Help us to carry our burdens with a
renewed faith and continued belief in your love for us.
Give us lightness of heart and compassion for those
with whom we live and work. This we ask in Jesus'
name. Amen.

FRIDAY AFTER ASH WEDNESDAY
(Antiphons and Psalms from Friday, Week IV, p. 179)
MORNING PRAYER

READING

We must not let ourselves be surpassed in love by anybody. It is the
first, the greatest, the divine virtue. Our example is Jesus, bleeding on
the Cross with a thousand wounds. Whoever wants to win over the
world to higher ideals, must have the courage to come into conflict with
it. (The world) in the end runs after [the one] who has the courage to do
that which it lacked the courage to do. But this conflict with the world is
hard. It caused Christ to die on the Cross.
The Beatification of Father Titus Brandsma, Carmelite, p. 126, (12)

RESPONSORY

Spare us, O God, and have pity on your people. **—Spare**...
We have sinned against you, **—have pity**...
Glory to you, Source of all Being, Eternal Word and Holy Spirit.
  —Spare...

CANTICLE OF ZECHARIAH

Ant A broken, humble heart, O God, you will not scorn.

INTERCESSIONS

During this lenten season, O God, you enlighten us to walk in
truth and love. Lead us to share the blessings we receive with
others. We pray:
        Guide us into the path of goodness.

Uplift those who suffer the anguish of mental illness;
  —and fill those who care for them with strength and
   compassion.
Inspire lawyers and judges to be just in all circumstances;
  —so that the welfare of all may become their main concern.
Liberate all men and women who are suffering persecution;
  —help them to be faithful and fill them with the love that
   conquers hatred.
Dissipate our inertia of mind and body;
  —strengthen our efforts toward wholeness.

PRAYER: O God, in your gentle way, free us from the sin that
keeps us bound to the familiar and the comfortable.
May the light of Easter joy encourage us in the way of
discipleship. We ask this in the name of Jesus who
died for us and was raised to new life. Amen.

DAYTIME PRAYER

Ant 1   The season of deliverance has come; the time of salvation
is at hand.

Ant 2   Turn to me with all your heart, says our God.

Ant 3   Believing in God's strength and mercy, let us be fortified
with patience.

(Prayer as in Morning Prayer)

EVENING PRAYER

READING

I wonder if pain does not keep us close to God? In the ordinary sense
pain can unfit us for prayer. We simply cannot pray. But in another
sense, suffering *becomes* prayer. Suffering accepted becomes a mighty
cry in the ears of God. It was in pain that Christ redeemed us; our pain
continues the redemption. We are not asked to do more than we can.

Miriam Elder, OCD, (11)

RESPONSORY

Have mercy on me, O God in your goodness. **—Have...**
In the greatness of your compassion, wipe out my offense, **—O God,...**
Glory to you, Source of all Being, Eternal Word and Holy Spirit.
  —Have...

CANTICLE OF MARY

Ant Save your servant who trusts in you.

INTERCESSIONS

O God, accept our lenten efforts. May they bear fruit in the ways we relate to others and to our planet. Fill us with your compassion and tenderness as we say:

Cleanse us and heal our brokenness.

Grant to artists, musicians, and writers;
—the ability to lift our hearts to the Source of all harmony and beauty.
Give parents patience, tolerance, and happiness;
—as they meet the daily challenge of their problems and possibilities.
Instill in each of us the desire to be responsible;
—for the preservation of all living things within our environment.
Enkindle within our hearts;
—a cheerfulness of spirit as we approach each day.

PRAYER: O God, in your gentle way, free us from the sin that keeps us bound to the familiar and the comfortable. May the light of Easter joy encourage us in the way of discipleship. We ask this in the name of Jesus who died for us and was raised to new life. Amen.

SATURDAY AFTER ASH WEDNESDAY
(Antiphons and Psalms from Saturday, Week IV, p. 186)

MORNING PRAYER

READING

From the crib to the cross suffering, poverty, misunderstanding were his portion. His whole life was directed to teaching people how differently God sees suffering, poverty, and misunderstanding on the part of people from the false wisdom of [the world]. Suffering is the way to heaven. Oh, that we would realize this very day, the value God has included for us in the sufferings [God] sends upon us, [God] who nevertheless is the All-bountiful.

The Beatification of Father Titus Brandsma, Carmelite, p. 125, (12)

RESPONSORY

Spare us, O God, and have pity on your people. —**Spare**...
We have sinned against you, —**have pity**...
Glory to you, Source of all Being, Eternal Word and Holy Spirit.
  —**Spare**...

CANTICLE OF ZECHARIAH

Ant God will renew your strength.

INTERCESSIONS

God of abundant life, you call us to become a loving people. We
pray with confidence:
  Give us your Holy Spirit.

You are life for our searching minds;
  —give wisdom and insight to educators.
You are love for our hungry hearts;
  —help us to be patient with our brokenness.
You are the truth that sets us free;
  —help those seeking truth to bring integrity and accuracy to the
    media.
You are the dawn when the night is over;
  —welcome into your joy all those who have died.

PRAYER: God, our Creator, as we fast and pray and share our
      resources with those in need, may we dedicate
      ourselves anew to walk in the way of truth as Jesus
      has taught us. We ask this in his name. Amen.

DAYTIME PRAYER

Ant 1 The season of deliverance has come; the time of salvation
    is at hand.

Ant 2 Turn to me with all your heart, says our God.

Ant 3 Believing in God's strength and mercy, let us be fortified
    with patience.

(Prayer as in Morning Prayer)

FIRST SUNDAY OF LENT

EVENING PRAYER I

(Antiphons and Psalms from Sunday, Week I, p. 1)

READING

The image of Jesus on the cross is the image of human sin in its most desecrated form.... The cross thus becomes an image of defilement, a gross manifestation of collective human sin. Jesus, then does not conquer sin through death on the cross. Rather, Jesus conquers the sin of temptation in the wilderness by resistance—by resisting the temptation to value the material over the spiritual ([you] shall not live by bread alone) by resisting death...(if you are the son of God throw yourself down); by resisting the greedy urge of monopolistic ownership.... Jesus therefore conquered sin in life, not in death. In the wilderness he refused to allow evil forces to defile the balanced relation between the material and the spiritual, between life and death, between power and the exertion of it.

Delores S. Williams, *Sisters in the Wilderness*, p. 166, (22)

RESPONSORY

My soul waits for God; in your word I hope. **—My soul...**
For with you there is steadfast love, **—in your...**
Glory to you, Source of all Being, Eternal Word and Holy Spirit.
   —My soul...

CANTICLE OF MARY

Ant Jesus was in the wilderness forty days, and was tempted by
   Satan.

INTERCESSIONS

Let us praise Jesus Christ, bread of life and living water. In homage we pray:

You alone are holy.

By your prayer and fasting;
   —teach us to rid our lives of all that blinds us to your Holy
   Spirit.
By your faithfulness to the word of God;
   —help us to keep your gospel alive and meaningful in our
   culture.
You revealed yourself to the woman at the well and she became your disciple announcing your truth to others;

—let the voices of women be heard in your church, that your message to them may be given to the world.

You are the temple destroyed by human hands;
 —help us to remember that we are temples of the Holy Spirit.

PRAYER: Jesus, our Savior, you bore hunger, thirst, and temptation as you prepared to preach the good news to your people. You offer the bread of heaven and living water to those who hear you with faith. During this holy season of Lent, let us hunger and thirst anew for your word. Grant us all that we need to be totally dedicated to you, that we may live with you forever. Amen.

MORNING PRAYER
(Psalms from Sunday, Week I, p. 3)

Ant 1 Jesus was in the wilderness for forty days and was tempted by Satan.

Ant 2 You shall worship the Most High God, and God only shall you serve.

Ant 3 Christ also died for sins once for all, the righteous for the unrighteous, that he might bring us to God.

READING

This day is holy to the [Most High], your God; do not mourn or weep. For all the people wept when they heard the words of the law. For this day is holy to our [God]; and do not be grieved, for the joy of [the Most High] is your strength.

Neh 8:9, 10b

RESPONSORY

My soul waits for God; in your word I hope. —**My soul**...
For with you there is steadfast love, —**in your**...
Glory to you, Source of all Being, Eternal Word and Holy Spirit.
 —**My soul**...

CANTICLE OF ZECHARIAH

Ant You shall worship God alone; you shall serve only your God.

INTERCESSIONS

Let us praise Jesus Christ, model of faithfulness, hope of our salvation. With sincere hearts we pray:
O Christ, guide us to truth.

You knew the burden of temptation;
— make us strong in resisting evil.
You drove away those who desecrated the temple of God;
— help us to make our worship pleasing to you and a blessing for all.
Moses was called to lead his people to water in the desert;
— lead those who thirst for truth to the words of the gospel.
You taught your disciples patience and long-suffering;
— teach us to set aside our own convenience and comfort to enable the growth of others.

PRAYER: Jesus, our Savior, you bore hunger, thirst, and temptation as you prepared to preach the good news to your people. You offer the bread of heaven and living water to those who hear you with faith. During this holy season of Lent, let us hunger and thirst anew for your word. Grant us all that we need to be totally dedicated to you, that we may live with you forever. Amen.

DAYTIME PRAYER

Ant 1 The season of deliverance has come; the time of salvation is at hand.

Ant 2 Turn to me with all your heart, says our God.

Ant 3 Believing in God's strength and mercy, let us be fortified with patience.

(Prayer as in Morning Prayer)

EVENING PRAYER II

Ant 1 You cannot live by bread alone, but by every word that proceeds from the mouth of God.

Ant 2 The time is fulfilled, the realm of God is at hand; repent and believe in the Good News.

Ant 3 You shall not tempt God Most High.

READING

Brothers and sisters, we ask and urge you in the Lord Jesus that, as you learned from us how you ought to live and to please God, (as you are doing), you should do so more and more. For God did not call us to impurity but in holiness.

1 Thess 4:1, 7

RESPONSORY

Christ, Chosen One of the living God, have mercy on us. —**Christ**...
Delivered up to death on a cross, —**have mercy**...
Glory to you, Source of all Being, Eternal Word and Holy Spirit.
   —**Christ**...

CANTICLE OF MARY

Ant The time is fulfilled, the reign of God is at hand; repent and believe the good news.

INTERCESSIONS

Let us praise Jesus Christ, model of faithfulness, hope of our salvation. With sincere hearts we pray:
        O Christ, guide us to truth.

Jesus, you turned away from the honor of this world;
   —help us to seek only the glory that is your presence in our
      lives.
Lent is the season to renew our lives;
   —may your Spirit help and guide us.
You were tempted to change stones into bread;
   —may your Holy Spirit inspire us with ways of distributing the
      world's goods equitably.
Through fear and distrust we lean upon weapons of war;
   —lead the world into the path of true peace.

PRAYER: Jesus, our Savior, you bore hunger, thirst, and
          temptation as you prepared to preach the good news to
          your people. You offer the bread of heaven and living
          water to those who hear you with faith. During this

holy season of Lent, let us hunger and thirst anew for
your word. Grant us all that we need to be totally
dedicated to you, that we may live with you forever.
Amen.

FIRST MONDAY OF LENT
(Antiphons and Psalms from Week I, p. 10)
MORNING PRAYER

READING

Our life is authentically Christian to the extent that we know Christ and
listen to his word with a readiness to respond with our whole being.
Christian life needs prayer: the integration of faith and life. In its full
meaning, prayer is joyous acceptance of life's greatest gift, the Lord's
friendship, and the return of the gift of one's self to God in the service of
[all].

Bernard Häring, *Prayer: The Integration of Faith and Life*, p. 1, (8)

RESPONSORY

Spare us, O God, and have pity on your people.—**Spare us**...
We have sinned against you, **—have pity**...
Glory to you, Source of all Being, Eternal Word and Holy Spirit.
   —Spare us...

CANTICLE OF ZECHARIAH

Ant. You shall be holy, as I, your God, am holy.

INTERCESSIONS

We praise you, O Christ, for your fidelity unto death. We cry out
in hope:
Fill us with the fullness of life.

You count as done to you all that we do for others;
   —help us to love others as you love them.
You did not spare yourself in the service of those in need;
   —show us the way to spend ourselves for others, for their
   welfare and your glory.
You bore insult and abuse from the people of your own town;
   —teach us to respect people and things that are familiar to us,
   ever open to hidden truths.

You came to set us free from our small ideas and from our limited notions of God;
  —let your forgiving love and healing word enlighten our minds and change our hearts.

PRAYER: O God, we thank you for your mercy and love. Your law of love guides our way, and your mercy heals and restores our courage. Help us to persevere in our lenten efforts to serve you more faithfully. This we ask through Jesus who showed us the way. Amen.

DAYTIME PRAYER

Ant 1 The season of deliverance has come; the time of salvation is at hand.

Ant 2 Turn to me with all your heart, says our God.

Ant 3 Believing in God's strength and mercy, let us be fortified with patience.

(Prayer as in Morning Prayer)

EVENING PRAYER

READING

O great, incomprehensible God, who fills all, be my heaven in which my new birth in Christ Jesus might live. Let my spirit be the stringed instrument, music, and joy of the Holy Spirit. Play on me in Your reborn image and lead my harmony into Your divine [kindom] of joy, into the great praise of God, into the wonders of your glory and majesty, into the community of the holy angelic harmony, and establish in me the holy city of Zion in which we, as the children of Christ, shall all live in one city that is Christ in us. I sink myself fully and completely into You. Do in me what you will. Amen.

Jacob Boehme: The Way to Christ, p. 53, (1)

RESPONSORY

Have mercy on me, O God, in your goodness. — **Have...**
In the greatness of your compassion wipe out my offense,
  —**O God...**
Glory to you, Source of all Being, Eternal Word and Holy Spirit.
  — **Have...**

CANTICLE OF MARY

Ant. Come and receive your inheritance, for I was hungry and you gave me food; I was thirsty and you gave me drink.

INTERCESSIONS

When the Word made flesh comes again in glory, we will stand before your holiness. We cry out to you:
Have mercy on us in that day.

Jesus, you come each day in glory, your Spirit abides in our hearts;
—help us to minister to those in need.
You bless those who clothe the naked and shelter the homeless.
—bless, too, our fashion-conscious culture, and enlighten our use of our resources.
Our spirits, hungry and thirsty for your inspiration, are weakened by our own selfishness;
—break through the resistance of our fears and apathy; renew our will and strength to serve you.
You care for the least of us as well as the greatest;
—heal our pride, dissolve our prejudices; let us love as we are loved.

PRAYER: O God, we thank you for your mercy and love. Your law of love guides our way, and your mercy heals and restores our courage. Help us to persevere in our lenten efforts to serve you more faithfully. This we ask through Jesus who showed us the way. Amen.

FIRST TUESDAY OF LENT
(Antiphons and Psalms from Week I, p. 16)

MORNING PRAYER

READING

Every good impulse, every noble deed we perform is of God. Christ in us. At the very same time there is an evil, complacent nagging going on, trying to discourage us, trying to impugn our motives, trying to spoil everything of good we do. This complacency, self-satisfaction, is to be scorned and silenced. It shows pride even to be surprised and grieved at the baseness, like sediment, at the bottom of every good deed. As long as we live there will be a war, a conflict between nature and grace, nature again and again getting the upper hand for the moment, only to be put down rigidly. If we have faith and hope it is impossible to be discouraged.

The Dorothy Day Book, p. 95, (21)

RESPONSORY

Spare us, O God, and have pity on your people.—**Spare us**...
We have sinned against you, —**have pity**...
Glory to you, Source of all Being, Eternal Word and Holy Spirit.
   —**Spare us**...

CANTICLE OF ZECHARIAH

Ant. The word that goes forth from my mouth shall not return to me empty.

INTERCESSIONS

Let us praise God who forgives us our sins and gives us the power to forgive one another. In gratitude we pray:
       May you be blessed forever, O God.

Jesus, you reveal God to us as father and mother;
   —help us to respond with confidence and love.
You teach us to ask for our daily bread;
   —give us the generosity to share what we have with those in need.
You were put to the test; you were delivered into the hands of evil;
   —give us the wisdom to shun evil, and to choose what is good for ourselves and others.
You prayed for the fidelity of your disciples;
   —pray for us that we will stand firm in time of trial.

PRAYER: God, our Creator, you care for us with the love of a father and a mother. You know our weakness, and you raise us up. You know our strength, and you challenge us to grow. Teach us to love and forgive one another with patience and good will. Make us worthy to be called your children. We ask this in the name of Jesus, our brother. Amen.

DAYTIME PRAYER

Ant 1 The season of deliverance has come; the time of salvation is at hand.

Ant 2 Turn to me with all your heart, says our God.

Ant 3 Believing in God's strength and mercy, let us be fortified
with patience.

(Prayer as in Morning Prayer)

EVENING PRAYER

READING

Keep in mind that each of you has your own vineyard. But every one is
joined to your neighbors' vineyards without any dividing lines. They are
so joined together, in fact, that you cannot do good or evil for yourself
without doing the same for your neighbors.

Catherine of Siena, The Dialogue, p. 62, (1)

RESPONSORY

Have mercy on me, O God, in your goodness. — **Have...**
In the greatness of your compassion wipe out my offense, —O God...
Glory to you, Source of all Being, Eternal Word and Holy Spirit.
— Have...

CANTICLE OF MARY

Ant. If you forgive the sins of others, God will forgive you.

INTERCESSIONS

O God, a contrite and humble heart is pleasing to you, more than
holocausts of rams on your altars. We pray to you:
We praise you for your mercy.

Jesus, those who trust in you are never disappointed;
—teach us to realize our limitations and to live in peace with the
limitations of others.
You teach us to forgive our sisters and brothers seventy times
seven times;
—help us to bring peace by being nonjudgmental toward one
another.
You call us to abide in you as branches on the vine;
—guide us in our efforts to live the truths of your gospel.
We did not choose you; you have chosen us to follow you;
—make us generous and creative in sharing the gift of your
word.

PRAYER: God, our Creator, you care for us with the love of a father and a mother. You know our weakness, and you raise us up. You know our strength, and you challenge us to grow. Teach us to love and forgive one another with patience and good will. Make us worthy to be called your children. We ask this in the name of Jesus, our brother. Amen.

FIRST WEDNESDAY OF LENT
(Antiphons and Psalms from Week I, p. 23)

MORNING PRAYER

READING

I am no longer my own, but yours. Put me to what you will, rank me with whom you will; put me to doing, put me to suffering; let me be employed for you or laid aside for you, exalted for you or brought low for you; let me be full, let me be empty; let me have all things, let me have nothing; I freely and heartily yield all things to your pleasure and disposal.

John Wesley, John and Charles Wesley, p. 387, (1)

RESPONSORY

Spare us, O God, and have pity on your people.—**Spare us**...
We have sinned against you, —**have pity**...
Glory to you, Source of all Being, Eternal Word and Holy Spirit.
    —**Spare us**...

CANTICLE OF ZECHARIAH

Ant. Create in me a clean heart, O God, and put a new spirit within me.

INTERCESSIONS

Jesus, you are the sign of Jonah; death will not destroy you, and so we proclaim:
        Glory and praise to you.

You came with truth and healing, but the crowds asked for a sign;
    —open our eyes to the life-giving message of the gospel.
You ministered to all who came to you;
    —help us to see through our prejudices and free ourselves to serve all people.

You suffered from the dullness of your followers and the unbelief
of the crowds;
> —strengthen us when our labor seems fruitless and we doubt
> your call.

Remember all who have brought your word to us: our parents,
teachers, clergy, religious, and friends;
> —let them know the gift of God they have been to us.

PRAYER: O God, our hearts are longing for your peace, and the
whole world cries out for justice and mercy. During this
season of Lent, give us the grace to deepen our efforts
to make peace among ourselves. Let us fan the flames
of justice so that the starving will be fed, the naked
clothed, and all in need will know your saving power.
We ask this in the name of Jesus who lived and walked
among us. Amen.

DAYTIME PRAYER

Ant 1   The season of deliverance has come; the time of salvation
is at hand.

Ant 2   Turn to me with all your heart, says our God.

Ant 3   Believing in God's strength and mercy, let us be fortified
with patience.

(Prayer as in Morning Prayer)

EVENING PRAYER

READING

The problems and differences we see as insurmountable are not so in
God's eyes. It is difficult to accept that people we don't like and who may
want to harm us are invited in the [Kindom]. But the Gospel urges us to
recognize in the stranger and the enemy the children of God. That very
insight would give us a fresh start. And we could work from there.

Bishop Thomas Gumbleton, "Worth Pondering...," (4)

RESPONSORY

Have mercy on me, O God, in your goodness. **— Have...**
In the greatness of your compassion wipe out my offense, **—O God...**
Glory to you, Source of all Being, Eternal Word and Holy Spirit.
> **— Have**...

CANTICLE OF MARY

Ant. As Jonah became a sign for the people of Nineveh, so will the Christ be a sign to this generation.

INTERCESSIONS

Jesus is the fulfillment of the law; his love is everlasting. Let us pray with confidence:
>**Christ Jesus, lead us on the path of salvation.**

Jesus, you are never alone; God is always with you;
>—help us to realize the presence of God in our lives.

You came to cast fire upon the earth;
>—enkindle in our hearts a love that bears fruit in service and praise.

You came that we might have life, now and forever;
>—awaken us to our responsibility to build a world based on justice and compassion.

You are the way, the truth, and the life;
>—come to the aid of those who search for meaning in life.

PRAYER: O God, our hearts are longing for your peace, and the whole world cries out for justice and mercy. During this season of Lent, give us the grace to deepen our efforts to make peace among ourselves. Let us fan the flames of justice so that the starving will be fed, the naked clothed, and all in need will know your saving power. We ask this in the name of Jesus who lived and walked among us. Amen.

FIRST THURSDAY OF LENT
(Antiphons and Psalms from Week I, p. 29)

MORNING PRAYER

READING

Fidelity is the hallmark of true progress in the spiritual life. It must mark those times we experience God's presence and activity within and around us; and, it must mark those times we experience nothing of God in our life. Regardless of the specific form our discipline of personal prayer takes, fidelity to that discipline is the expression of our willingness to maintain a loving attentiveness to [God].

Joel Giallanza, CSC, "Loving Attention to the Lord," (4)

RESPONSORY

Spare us, O God, and have pity on your people.—**Spare us**...
We have sinned against you, —**have pity**...
Glory to you, Source of all Being, Eternal Word and Holy Spirit.
   —**Spare us**...

CANTICLE OF ZECHARIAH

Ant. Ask and it will be given you, seek and you will find, knock
    and it will be opened to you.

INTERCESSIONS

You, O Christ, have come to call sinners and not the just. With
contrite hearts, we pray:
       Be merciful for we have sinned.

You call us to turn from sin through persons, events, and inner
urgings;
   —strengthen us in the way of your truth.
You were led by the Spirit into the wilderness;
   —give us courage to face the emptiness of our lives.
You call us to works of justice and mercy;
   —let us see your face in the poor and homeless.
By your passion and death you have opened the gates of heaven;
   —draw to yourself all those who have died.

PRAYER: God of mercy, as we begin this season of Lent, opening
      ourselves to your grace, we ask that you will guide us
      into a true change of heart and reorientation of our
      lives. We ask this in the name of Jesus. Amen.

DAYTIME PRAYER

Ant 1 The season of deliverance has come; the time of salvation
    is at hand.

Ant 2 Turn to me with all your heart, says our God.

Ant 3 Believing in God's strength and mercy, let us be fortified
    with patience.

(Prayer as in Morning Prayer)

EVENING PRAYER

READING

No effort should be spared to shun all unnecessary sufferings both physiological and psychological, but when this has been faithfully done, and there still remains a residuum...it is wise and prudent to make a strong effort to pass into the realm of sweet resignation at once, and there remain in patience and prayer until we have become perfectly passive under the stroke of our affliction....

Oliver C. Hampton, *The Shakers*, p. 350, (1)

RESPONSORY

Have mercy on me, O God, in your goodness. — **Have...**
In the greatness of your compassion wipe out my offense, —**O God**...
Glory to you, Source of all Being, Eternal Word and Holy Spirit.
— **Have...**

CANTICLE OF MARY

Ant. How much more will God who loves you give good things to those who ask.

INTERCESSIONS

The God of peace is preparing a new dwelling place and a new earth where justice will abide. Let us pray with confidence:
In you, O God, we place all our hope.

Jesus has given us a pledge of hope and strength in the Eucharist;
—may we always walk in the strength of this food.
O God, you have sent your Christ to preach the good news to the poor;
—free us from our prisons and our blindness.
We remember those who are lost, frightened, and despairing;
—send forth your Spirit to comfort their hearts.
We will one day overcome death and be raised in Christ;
—what was sown in weakness will be raised in power.

PRAYER: God of mercy, as we begin this season of Lent, opening ourselves to your grace, we ask that you will guide us into a true change of heart and reorientation of our lives. We ask this in the name of Jesus. Amen.

FIRST FRIDAY OF LENT
(Antiphons and Psalms from Week I, p. 36)
MORNING PRAYER

READING

Only my soul hangs on thy promises
With face and hands clinging unto thy breast,
Clinging and crying, crying without cease
    Thou art my rock, thou art my rest.

George Herbert, *Perseverance*, p. 332, (1)

RESPONSORY

Spare us, O God, and have pity on your people.—**Spare us**...
We have sinned against you, —**have pity**...
Glory to you, Source of all Being, Eternal Word and Holy Spirit.
    —**Spare us**...

CANTICLE OF ZECHARIAH

Ant. Unless your holiness exceeds that of the scribes and
        Pharisees, you will never enjoy the fullness of life.

INTERCESSIONS

Led by the Spirit into the desert of Lent, we are called to purify
and renew ourselves. Let us earnestly pray:
    May the light of Christ shine brightly on our world.

May we hear and interpret the many voices of our age;
    —and judge them in the light of your word.
You raised Jesus from the dead;
    —Christ is the center of our life, the joy of every heart, and the
    answer to our yearnings.
We remember the elderly who feel useless or forgotten;
    —have mercy on your people, and let them know your love.
Teach us to be simple and disciplined in our needs;
    —and to share our abundance with those in want.

PRAYER: Jesus, you are God's own compassion. You are one
        with the victimized, the wounded, the weak, and the
        forgotten. May we abandon our struggles for power and
        learn to minister in a spirit of service and self-

emptying. We ask this in your holy name, for you are one with our Source and with the Spirit, for all ages. Amen.

DAYTIME PRAYER

Ant 1 The season of deliverance has come; the time of salvation is at hand.

Ant 2 Turn to me with all your heart, says our God.

Ant 3 Believing in God's strength and mercy, let us be fortified with patience.

(Prayer as in Morning Prayer)

EVENING PRAYER

READING

I pray you, then, to follow eagerly after this humble stirring of love in your heart. It will be your guide in this life, and will bring you to grace in the next. It is the substance of all good living, and without it no good work can be begun or ended. It is nothing else but a good will that is directed to God, and a kind of satisfaction and gladness that you experience in your will concerning all that [God] does.

The Cloud of Unknowing, pp. 214–15, (1)

RESPONSORY

Have mercy on me, O God, in your goodness. — **Have...**
In the greatness of your compassion wipe out my offense, —**O God**...
Glory to you, Source of all Being, Eternal Word and Holy Spirit.
   — **Have...**

CANTICLE OF MARY

Ant. First be reconciled to your sister or brother, and then come and offer your gift.

INTERCESSIONS

Christ Jesus, you call us to share in your mission and to deepen our belief in the mystery of creation and redemption. We wish to be sensitive to your Spirit, and so we pray:
   Renew your gifts in our hearts.

We believe the life of each person in our world is sacred;
  —may we incarnate your love in a global way.
We confess to you our sins and addictions;
  —forgive us and lead us on the path to life.
You have given us the gift of life;
  —help us live with grateful hearts.
Look upon all countries divided by fear and hatred;
  —may their people know the gift of peace.

PRAYER: Jesus, you are God's own compassion. You are one
with the victimized, the wounded, the weak, and the
forgotten. May we abandon our struggles for power and
learn to minister in a spirit of service and self-
emptying. We ask this in your holy name, for you are
one with our Source and with the Spirit, for all ages.
Amen.

FIRST SATURDAY OF LENT
(Antiphons and Psalms from Week I, p. 43)

MORNING PRAYER

READING

The essence of real Christian prayer always consists in "going out of
oneself in order to meet the Other." In contrast with an attitude that
might appear as egoism or as an evasion of reality and responsibilities,
true prayer is a supreme act of abnegation and forgetfulness of self in
order to meet Christ and his demands in others. In this sense prayer is
related to the classic themes of death, and the cross—"death to self in
order to live for God"—which implies the crucifixion of egoism. That is
why Christian mysticism goes through loneliness and aridity which
causes egoism to die and leads us out of ourselves in order to find the
Other.

Segundo Galilea, *Following Jesus*, p. 61, (22)

RESPONSORY

Spare us, O God, and have pity on your people.—**Spare us**...
We have sinned against you, **—have pity**...
Glory to you, Source of all Being, Eternal Word and Holy Spirit.
  —Spare us...

CANTICLE OF ZECHARIAH

Ant. Love your enemies, and pray for those who persecute you so that you may be children of the One who makes the sun rise on the evil and on the good.

INTERCESSIONS

As disciples we are called to a change of heart expressed in praise of God and in deeds of justice and service. We pray:
Help us and heal us, O God.

Enable us to grow in a spirit of self-giving;
—showing care and concern for all people.
Break through the evil in our hearts and our social structures;
—we are burdened with a sense of guilt.
Teach us to pray and to know the beauty of silence;
—fill us with your faithful love.
Enlighten the leaders of nations;
—to make the choices that lead to peace.

PRAYER: Merciful God, in this season of Lent we wish to discipline ourselves so that we can learn to say a fuller yes to all you call us to become. We ask for this grace in the name of Jesus, your Incarnate Word, who lives with you in the Holy Spirit, now and forever. Amen.

DAYTIME PRAYER

Ant 1 The season of deliverance has come; the time of salvation is at hand.

Ant 2 Turn to me with all your heart, says our God.

Ant 3 Believing in God's strength and mercy, let us be fortified with patience.

(Prayer as in Morning Prayer)

SECOND SUNDAY OF LENT

EVENING PRAYER I

(Antiphons and Psalms from Sunday, Week II, p. 47)

READING

Do not be ashamed, then, of the testimony about our Lord or of me his prisoner, but join with me in suffering for the gospel, relying on the power of God, who saved us and called us with a holy calling, not according to our works, but according to [God's] own purpose and grace. This grace was given to us in Christ Jesus before the ages began, but it has now been revealed through the appearing of our Savior Christ Jesus, who abolished death and brought life and immortality to light through the gospel.

2 Tim 1:8–10

RESPONSORY

My soul waits for God; in your word I hope. —**My soul**...
For with you there is steadfast love, —**in your**...
Glory to you, Source of all Being, Eternal Word and Holy Spirit.
     —**My soul**...

CANTICLE OF MARY

Ant I will indeed bless you, and I will multiply your descendants as the stars of heaven and as the sands on the shore.

INTERCESSIONS

Let us praise God who at various times and places is revealed to us. Let us rejoice in the revelation of Jesus. In God's presence let us acclaim:
     It is good for us to be here.

You called Abraham to serve you with obedience and love and did not allow the death of his son;
     —teach us to discern what is pleasing to you, always
     keeping the welfare and rights of others in mind.
You chose David, a youthful shepherd, to lead your people;
     —help us to look beyond outward appearances as we choose
     our leaders.
You made Jesus a vessel of your healing love;
     —show us how to reach out to the sick in healing ways, with
     respect and reverence.

You sent manna for your people to eat in the desert;
  —let your word nourish our minds and enkindle our hearts
    toward the transformation of our lives.

PRAYER: O God, we praise you for your call to renew our lives
during this season of Lent. Make us ready and eager
to accept your invitation to grow. We confess our
weakness and ask for new strength to serve you more
faithfully. Let our efforts be pleasing to you. This we
ask through Jesus, who is our way, our truth, and our
life. Amen.

MORNING PRAYER
(Psalms from Sunday, Week II, p. 49)

Ant 1 Jesus took Peter, James, and John and led them up a
high mountain apart by themselves, and he was
transfigured before them.

Ant 2 Master, it is good that we are here.

Ant 3 A bright cloud overshadowed them, and a voice from the
cloud said, "This is my Beloved Son, with whom I am well
pleased; Listen to him."

READING

As they were coming down the mountain, [Jesus] ordered them to tell
no one what they had seen, until the [Chosen One of God] had risen
from the dead. So they kept the matter to themselves, questioning what
this rising from the dead could mean.

Mk 9:9–10

RESPONSORY

Spare us, O God, and have pity on your people.**—Spare**...
We have sinned against you, **—have**...
Glory to you, Source of all Being, Eternal Word and Holy Spirit.
  —Spare...

CANTICLE OF ZECHARIAH

Ant If God is for us, who can be against us?

INTERCESSIONS

As Moses lifted up the serpent in the desert, so Jesus was lifted up on the cross for our salvation. In homage we pray:
We adore you, O Christ!

Whoever believes in you will not be condemned;
—we do believe, help our unbelief.
You have come to reconcile us to God and to one another;
—make us effective ambassadors of your mission of peace.
You seek out those who are lost, forgiving us again and again;
—let our lives so mirror your compassion that those who are wounded by sin will be drawn to you.
Your mercy reached out to all in need;
—bless the sick and the dying; let them know your presence.

PRAYER: O God, we praise you for your call to renew our lives during this season of Lent. Make us ready and eager to accept your invitation to grow. We confess our weakness and ask for new strength to serve you more faithfully. Let our efforts be pleasing to you. This we ask through Jesus, who is our way, our truth, and our life. Amen.

DAYTIME PRAYER

Ant 1 The season of deliverance has come; the time of salvation is at hand.

Ant 2 Turn to me with all your heart, says our God.

Ant 3 Believing in God's strength and mercy, let us be fortified with patience.

(Prayer as in Morning Prayer)

EVENING PRAYER II

Ant 1 On the mountain, there appeared to the disciples Elijah with Moses, and they were talking to Jesus.

Ant 2 Peter said to Jesus, "Let us make here three booths, one for you and one for Moses and one for Elijah."

Ant 3 As they were coming down the mountain, Jesus commanded them, "Tell no one the vision until the Anointed One of God is raised from the dead."

READING

Give heed to me, [O God], and listen to what my adversaries say! Is evil a recompense for good? Yet they have dug a pit for my life. Remember how I stood before you to speak good for them, to turn away your wrath from them.

Jer 18:19–20

RESPONSORY

Have mercy on me, O God, in your goodness. **—Have**...
In the greatness of your compassion wipe out my offense,
   —O God...
Glory to you, Source of all Being, Eternal Word and Holy Spirit.
   —Have...

CANTICLE OF MARY

Ant When they lifted up their eyes, they saw no one but Jesus.

INTERCESSIONS

O God, you are rich in mercy, sending leaders and prophets and your Eternal Word to lead us to life. With hope and trust we pray:
   We will serve you all the days of our lives.

Abraham and Sarah believed and you made them the founders of your people;
   —give us faith in you that will bear fruit a hundredfold in
    your service.
God of Wonders, we marvel at the miracles of life;
   —enable us to enter joyously and fully into our personal
    and communal commitments.
Jesus, you taught your disciples patience and long-suffering;
   —teach us to set aside our own convenience and comfort to
    encourage the growth of others.
You knew that your death would mean suffering for your friends;
   —give us the courage to follow God's will through the
    mystery of pain throughout the world.

PRAYER: O God, we praise you for your call to renew our lives
during this season of Lent. Make us ready and eager
to accept your invitation to grow. We confess our
weakness and ask for new strength to serve you more
faithfully. Let our efforts be pleasing to you. This we
ask through Jesus, who is our way, our truth, and our
life. Amen.

SECOND MONDAY WEEK OF LENT
(Antiphons and Psalms from Week II, p. 55)
MORNING PRAYER
READING

The capacity to forgive is one of the infallible signs of Christian
maturity, or holiness, the proof that we are growing in virtue and
wisdom. What is wisdom ultimately but perspective, and what is virtue
but a life conformed to wisdom or perspective, a person given over to
grace.... When we forgive others, we step out of this time-bound
condition, with all its imperfection, selfishness, pettiness, and
ignorance, becoming more deeply established in God's love.

Wayne Teasdale, "The Mystery of Forgiveness," (4)

RESPONSORY

Spare us, O God, and have pity on your people.—**Spare us**...
We have sinned against you, —**have pity**...
Glory to you, Source of all Being, Eternal Word and Holy Spirit.
   —**Spare us**...

CANTICLE OF ZECHARIAH

Ant. To you, O God, belong mercy and forgiveness.

INTERCESSIONS

Jesus Christ, you have shown us the narrow gate and promised
that it is the entrance to life. With trust we pray:
   Lead us and we will follow.

You showed us the way of mercy and compassion;
   —give us understanding and patience with the weaknesses
   of others.

You had pity on public sinners and shared their ignominy;
—enlighten governments that claim an eye for an eye and a
life for a life.
You call us to conversion to life, not to death;
—enlighten our lenten efforts that they may enrich our lives
and give praise to you.
For a father's faith, you healed a child, increase our faith;
—let our belief be a sharing in your life and healing ministry.

PRAYER: O God, you keep your merciful covenant of love with
us even when we sin and fail you generation after
generation. During this lenten season, as we renew our
efforts to serve you and to love one another, give us the
grace we need to persevere in our resolutions. Free us
from all that separates us from you; help us to follow
the way of Jesus, your incarnate Word, who lives with
you in the unity of the Holy Spirit. Amen.

DAYTIME PRAYER

Ant 1 The season of deliverance has come; the time of salvation
is at hand.

Ant 2 Turn to me with all your heart, says our God.

Ant 3 Believing in God's strength and mercy, let us be fortified
with patience.

(Prayer as in Morning Prayer)

EVENING PRAYER

READING

The cross...is the symbol of the rejection and violation of the sacred
rights of God and the human being. It is the product of hatred. There
are those who, committing themselves to the struggle to abolish the
cross of the world, themselves have to suffer and bear the cross. The
cross is imposed upon them, inflicted on them, by the creators of
crosses. But this cross is accepted. Not because a value is seen in it,
but because there are those who burst asunder the logic of its violence
by their love. To accept the cross is to be greater than the cross. To live
thus is to be stronger than death.

Leonardo Boff, *Passion of Christ, Passion of the World*, p. 131, (22)

RESPONSORY

Have mercy on me, O God, in your goodness. —**Have...**
In the greatness of your compassion wipe out my offense,
  —**O God...**
Glory to you, Source of all Being, Eternal Word and Holy Spirit.
  —**Have...**

CANTICLE OF MARY

Ant. Give and it shall be given to you; for the measure you give
  will be the measure you receive.

INTERCESSIONS

Jesus has come, creating a new heaven and a new earth; let us
praise him saying:
  O Christ, all your works are wonderful.

By your life among us you have taught us how to live;
  —during this season of Lent, let us put aside all that keeps us
  from being your disciples.
You sought out what was lost; you blessed the poor in spirit;
  —hear us as we plead for zeal and direction for without you we
  can do nothing.
Only you are just and all your ways are holy;
  —forgive us for our self-righteous ways; let us see ourselves in
  truth.
You guard the weak and care for the lowly;
  —have pity on all children who have no one to care for them;
  help us to come to their aid.

PRAYER: O God, you keep your merciful covenant of love with
  us even when we sin and fail you generation after
  generation. During this lenten season, as we renew our
  efforts to serve you and to love one another, give us the
  grace we need to persevere in our resolutions. Free us
  from all that separates us from you; help us to follow
  the way of Jesus, your incarnate Word, who lives with
  you in the unity of the Holy Spirit. Amen.

SECOND TUESDAY OF LENT
(Antiphons and Psalms from Week II, p. 62)

MORNING PRAYER

READING

To be "spiritual" means to know, and to live according to the knowledge, that there is more to life than meets the eye. To be "spiritual" means, beyond that, to know, and to live according to the knowledge, that God is present to us in grace as the principle of personal, interpersonal, social, and even cosmic transformation. To be "open to the Spirit" is to accept explicitly who we are and who we are called always to become, and to direct our lives accordingly.

Richard P. McBrien, *Catholicism: Study Edition*, p. 1057, (14)

RESPONSORY

Spare us, O God, and have pity on your people.—**Spare us**...
We have sinned against you, —**have pity**...
Glory to you, Source of all Being, Eternal Word and Holy Spirit.
   —**Spare us**...

CANTICLE OF ZECHARIAH

Ant. Cease to do evil, learn to do good; seek justice, correct oppression; defend the orphan, plead for the helpless.

INTERCESSIONS

God promises forgiveness: though your sins are like scarlet, they shall be as white as snow. Let us pray with confidence:
Save us, O God.

Jesus, your yoke is easy and your burden is light;
   —show us the way to live your gospel in sincerity and truth.
You did not seek a name or place of honor;
   —help us to simplify our lives and the trends of our culture.
You were persecuted for healing on the sabbath;
   —console and enlighten those who are called to choose between law and mercy.
You, O God, hear our secret prayer, you are present to us always;
   —help us to remember your love and to live in hope in times of doubt and pain.

PRAYER: O God, no sin is so great that it cannot be forgiven when we come to you in faith. In times of doubt, help us to see that the whole world is a message of your sustaining love. You do not leave us orphans. You are present to our every thought and desire. Help us to let you fill our lives with grace and to draw us to the fullness of joy, that we may live with you forever and ever. Amen.

DAYTIME PRAYER

Ant 1 The season of deliverance has come; the time of salvation is at hand.

Ant 2 Turn to me with all your heart, says our God.

Ant 3 Believing in God's strength and mercy, let us be fortified with patience.

(Prayer as in Morning Prayer)

EVENING PRAYER

READING

Only in trustful and persevering prayer do we come gradually to the full knowledge of the name of Jesus, and thus, to the experience of that love of which St. Paul says, "There is no limit to its trust" (1 Cor 13:3). And if we unite with others in calling upon the name of Jesus, the Savior of all, then we hope for each other, encourage each other, give credit to each other, respect and love each other.

Bernard Häring, *Prayer: The Integration of Faith and Life*, p. 5, (8)

RESPONSORY

Have mercy on me, O God, in your goodness. —**Have...**
In the greatness of your compassion wipe out my offense,
   —O God...
Glory to you, Source of all Being, Eternal Word and Holy Spirit.
   —Have...

CANTICLE OF MARY

Ant. Those who exalt themselves will be humbled; those who humble themselves will be exalted.

INTERCESSIONS

Eternal life is knowing God, and Jesus Christ whom God has sent, and so we pray:
Christ Jesus, you have the words of eternal life.

You taught your disciples to pray in your name;
—in your name, we ask for the grace to persevere in your love.
You spoke the truth in love; your words were words of life;
—help us to guard our tongue by using the gift of speech with responsibility and reverence.
You were held in derision and contempt;
—teach us how to serve the outcasts of society, and how to respect and accept their gifts.
You hid from those who would destroy you and falsify your message;
—come to the aid of those who are abused by the misuse of law and who have no one to defend them.

PRAYER: O God, no sin is so great that it cannot be forgiven when we come to you in faith. In times of doubt, help us to see that the whole world is a message of your sustaining love. You do not leave us orphans. You are present to our every thought and desire. Help us to let you fill our lives with grace and to draw us to the fullness of joy, that we may live with you forever and ever. Amen.

SECOND WEDNESDAY OF LENT
(Antiphons and Psalms from Week II, p. 69)
MORNING PRAYER

READING

I am reading (Simone Weil's) essays as part of my Lenten reading....
She says that we "...must experience every day, both in the spirit and the flesh, the pains and humiliations of poverty...and further we must do something which is harder than enduring in poverty, we must renounce all compensations: in our contacts with the people around us we must sincerely practice the humility of a naturalized citizen in the country which has received us."

I keep reminding the young people who come to work with us that they
are not naturalized citizens.... They are not really poor. We are always
foreigners to the poor. So we have to make up for it by "renouncing all
compensations...."

The Dorothy Day Book, p. 11, (21)

RESPONSORY

Spare us, O God, and have pity on your people.—**Spare us**...
We have sinned against you, —**have pity**...
Glory to you, Source of all Being, Eternal Word and Holy Spirit.
   —**Spare us**...

CANTICLE OF ZECHARIAH

Ant. One who wishes to be great must serve the needs of all.

INTERCESSIONS

Jesus came not to be served but to serve and to give his life as a
ransom for many. We cry out to you:
    O Christ, you are the savior of the world.

Your call is a call to service;
   —inspire people of all ages to work in your vineyard.
Bless those who are difficult to serve, those who harm
themselves, and the people who minister to them;
   —may they have the courage to trust and the willingness
      to endure.
Bless our families; give them the material sustenance they need;
   —enable them to hear your word and keep it with a joyful
      spirit.
Bless the aging and the dying;
   —help us to make their last years a time of contentment
      and peace.

PRAYER: Jesus, you came among us as a servant, lording it
over no one, wielding only the power of love. Help us to
care as much for the concerns of others as we do for
our own. Let us hear your voice in every cry for help;
to think your thoughts, and love what pleases you.
This we ask through the power of your holy name.
Amen.

DAYTIME PRAYER

Ant 1 The season of deliverance has come; the time of salvation is at hand.

Ant 2 Turn to me with all your heart, says our God.

Ant 3 Believing in God's strength and mercy, let us be fortified with patience.

(Prayer as in Morning Prayer)

EVENING PRAYER

READING

I would have you know that every [good], whether perfect or imperfect, is acquired and made manifest in me. And it is acquired and made manifest by means of your neighbor.... If you have received my love sincerely without self-interest, you will drink your neighbor's love sincerely. It is just like a vessel that you fill at the fountain. If you take it out of the fountain to drink, the vessel is soon empty. But if you hold your vessel in the fountain while you drink, it will not get empty. Indeed, it will always be full. So the love of your neighbor, whether spiritual or temporal, is meant to be drunk in me, without any self-interest.

Catherine of Siena, *The Dialogue*, p. 120, (1)

RESPONSORY

Have mercy on me, O God, in your goodness. —**Have...**
In the greatness of your compassion wipe out my offense,
     —**O God...**
Glory to you, Source of all Being, Eternal Word and Holy Spirit.
     —**Have...**

CANTICLE OF MARY

Ant. Jesus said: "You do not know what you ask. Are you able to drink the cup I am to drink?"

INTERCESSIONS

The goodness and kindness of God follows us all the days of our lives. With trust in your word we pray:
     O God, all our hope is in your promise.

Jesus, your days were long with work and prayer;
  —free those who must labor beyond their strength.
You are the living bread come down from heaven;
  —help us to discern those things that nourish us and those
    that destroy our bodies and minds.
You reign from the cross but your realm is not of this world;
  —give men and women the courage and creativity to lead our
    nations in ways of peace and justice.
Your word is a light for our way; you know our weakness;
  —send your Spirit to those who interpret your gospel, lest they
    burden the consciences of those seeking truth.

PRAYER: Jesus, you came among us as a servant, lording it
over no one, wielding only the power of love. Help us to
care as much for the concerns of others as we do for
our own. Let us hear your voice in every cry for help;
to think your thoughts, and love what pleases you.
This we ask through your holy name. Amen.

SECOND THURSDAY OF LENT
(Antiphons and Psalms from Week II, p. 76)
MORNING PRAYER

READING

Do not serve God with sighs. Gladly and of good heart show the truth of
the words: My yoke is sweet and my burden is light. Be of good cheer
and see grief in a higher light, in which it becomes a free choice and a
motive for gladness. Joy is not a virtue, but an effect of love.

Essays on Titus Brandsma, p. 126, (12)

RESPONSORY

Spare us, O God, and have pity on your people.—**Spare us**...
We have sinned against you, —**have pity**...
Glory to you, Source of all Being, Eternal Word and Holy Spirit.
  —**Spare us**...

CANTICLE OF ZECHARIAH

Ant. Amend your ways and your doings and do not trust in
deceptive words, says our God.

INTERCESSIONS

Christ is at work in our hearts through the energy of the Spirit, renewing the face of the earth, and so we pray:
Let us walk each day in love.

We remember those whose search for justice has led to the cross;
 —strengthen them in the light of the resurrection.
You taught us wisdom by using examples from daily life;
 —bless all teachers dedicated to educating youth.
Free us from the love of self;
 —to bring our gifts into the service of humanity.
May leaders of nations work in harmony for the good of the earth;
 —be for all the way, the truth, and the life.

PRAYER: We are aware, O God, of our sin which inhibits a free response to your grace and word. We confess our failures but look to the promise given to us in the death and resurrection of Jesus. As we share his cross, may we share his glory. We ask this in his name. Amen.

DAYTIME PRAYER

Ant 1 The season of deliverance has come; the time of salvation is at hand.

Ant 2 Turn to me with all your heart, says our God.

Ant 3 Believing in God's strength and mercy, let us be fortified with patience.

(Prayer as in Morning Prayer)

EVENING PRAYER

READING

When I am in pain, I think of prisoners who have no voice concerning their food, medicines, or the temperature of their cells. My discomfort becomes the occasion to pray for those who know no comfort.

A Carmelite

RESPONSORY

Have mercy on me, O God, in your goodness. —**Have...**
In the greatness of your compassion wipe out my offense,
   —O God...
Glory to you, Source of all Being, Eternal Word and Holy Spirit.
   —Have...

CANTICLE OF MARY

Ant.   If you do not hear Moses and the prophets you will not be
   convinced if some one should rise from the dead.

INTERCESSIONS

Christ, you have entrusted to your church the mystery of God
and the meaning of our existence, and so we pray to you:
   Teach us to worship in spirit and in truth.

You are the fully human one;
   —in following you may we come to the fullness of our
    humanity.
May world endeavors be penetrated by the spirit of the gospel;
   —open our eyes to see what is false.
You healed the sick by the touch of your hands;
   —bless all those who serve us in hospitals and nursing homes.
Help us to overcome all forms of violence between nations, races,
and ideologies;
   —strengthen those human associations which are just and
    impartial.

PRAYER: We are aware, O God, of our sin which inhibits a free
       response to your grace and word. We confess our
       failures but look to the promise given to us in the
       death and resurrection of Jesus. As we share his
       cross, may we share his glory. We ask this in his
       name. Amen.

SECOND FRIDAY OF LENT
(Antiphons and Psalms from Week II, p. 84)

MORNING PRAYER

READING

In our life of prayer silence is unquestionably part of the environment. The din and roar of the incessant noises of our daily world is enough to drown out both the impulse to prayer and its interiority. In the midst of so much noise the impetus to pray is eventually lost. We are swept away on the sounds and we move further away from that center where we know the presence of God.

Jay C. Rochelle, "The Environment of Prayer," (4)

RESPONSORY

Spare us, O God, and have pity on your people.—**Spare us**...
We have sinned against you, —**have pity**...
Glory to you, Source of all Being, Eternal Word and Holy Spirit.
   —**Spare us**...

CANTICLE OF ZECHARIAH

Ant. When Joseph came to his brothers, they stripped him of his robe, and they took him and cast him into a pit.

INTERCESSIONS

In God we live and move and have our being. Immersed in the mystery of this presence we humbly pray:
Let us cling to you in love.

May we see your will in every event, see Christ in every person;
   —and judge all things in the light of faith.
Your love is poured forth in our hearts by the Holy Spirit;
   —help us to live the spirit of the beatitudes in our lives.
We remember those imprisoned because of their convictions;
   —let them know your saving help.
Into your hands we commend the dead and the dying;
   —may they see your face in glory.

PRAYER: God of peace, purify our hearts through fasting, prayer, words, and works of kindness, that we may be new people who celebrate the paschal mystery. We ask

this in the name of Jesus, the Eternal Word, who lives
with you and the Holy Spirit, now and forever. Amen.

DAYTIME PRAYER

Ant 1 The season of deliverance has come; the time of salvation
is at hand.

Ant 2 Turn to me with all your heart, says our God.

Ant 3 Believing in God's strength and mercy, let us be fortified
with patience.

(Prayer as in Morning Prayer)

EVENING PRAYER

READING

Just as no one comes to wisdom except through grace, justice and
knowledge, so no one comes to contemplation except by penetrating
meditation, a holy life and devout prayer. Since grace is the foundation
of the rectitude of the will and of the penetrating light of reason, we
must first pray, then live holy lives and thirdly concentrate our
attention upon the reflections of truth. By concentrating there, we must
ascend step by step until we reach the height of the mountain *where
the God of gods is seen in Sion* (Ps. 83:8).

Bonaventure, The Soul's Journey into God, p. 63, (1)

RESPONSORY

Have mercy on me, O God, in your goodness. **—Have...**
In the greatness of your compassion wipe out my offense,
    —O God...
Glory to you, Source of all Being, Eternal Word and Holy Spirit.
    —Have...

CANTICLE OF MARY

Ant. Jesus said to them: "Have you never read in the scriptures:
'The very stone which the builders rejected has become the
cornerstone'?"

INTERCESSIONS

We are called to a new hope and to a new vision that we must live without fear and without oversimplification. Aware of our weakness, we pray:
Jesus, make us free.

We are aware of the challenge of this moment in history;
—form your church as a model of justice.
Renew in us the grace of baptism;
—draw us to deeper friendship with you.
May we renounce our selfishness and bear our daily cross;
—open our hearts to live with your compassion.
We remember those who have died and those who grieve;
—may the light of Christ shine in their hearts.

PRAYER: God of peace, purify our hearts through fasting, prayer, words, and works of kindness, that we may be new people who celebrate the paschal mystery. We ask this in the name of Jesus, the Eternal Word, who lives with you and the Holy Spirit, now and forever. Amen.

SECOND SATURDAY OF LENT
(Antiphons and Psalms from Week II, p. 91)

MORNING PRAYER

READING

There is no form of Christian life that has as much potential to bring the spirit of the gospel into the world, into neighborhoods and communities, than Christian family life. And the most basic way a family (or religious community) can do this is to allow the gospel to constantly transform, in practical ways, its lifestyle/spirituality.
Mitch and Kathy Finley, "The Home Front," (4)

RESPONSORY

Spare us, O God, and have pity on your people.—**Spare us**...
We have sinned against you, —**have pity**...
Glory to you, Source of all Being, Eternal Word and Holy Spirit.
    —**Spare us**...

CANTICLE OF ZECHARIAH

Ant. While he was yet at a distance, his father saw him and had compassion. He ran and embraced him and kissed him.

INTERCESSIONS

We believe in the redemptive love of God. As those who have experienced God's forgiving mercy in Christ we pray:
You have redeemed us and set us free.

May your mother, Mary, draw us to reflect on your gifts to us;
—and to join with her in a song of praise.
You learned obedience by the things you suffered;
—give us patience and a spirit of wisdom.
Comfort the elderly and those who feel useless;
—renew in them an undying hope.
May the remembrance of what God has done in you through the Spirit;
—be a wellspring of creativity for the future.

PRAYER: Jesus, in a fullness of knowledge and trust you embraced the reality and truth of being human. Help us by our lenten renewal to be free of our illusions and evasions. We ask this of our God in your name. Amen.

DAYTIME PRAYER

Ant 1 The season of deliverance has come; the time of salvation is at hand.

Ant 2 Turn to me with all your heart, says our God.

Ant 3 Believing in God's strength and mercy, let us be fortified with patience.

(Prayer as in Morning Prayer)

THIRD SUNDAY OF LENT

EVENING PRAYER I

(Antiphons and Psalms from Week III, p. 96)

READING

Hope does not disappoint us, because God's love has been poured into
our hearts through the Holy Spirit that has been given to us. For while
we were still weak, at the right time Christ died for the ungodly. Indeed,
rarely will anyone die for a righteous person— though perhaps for a
good person someone might actually dare to die. But God proves
[God's] love for us in that while we still were sinners Christ died for us.

Rom 5:5-8

RESPONSORY

My soul waits for God; in your word I hope. **—My soul...**
For with you there is steadfast love, **—in your...**
Glory to you, Source of all Being, Eternal Word and Holy Spirit.
    —My soul...

CANTICLE OF MARY

Ant God said to Moses: Strike the rock, and water shall come
       out of it, that the people may drink!

INTERCESSIONS

Let us praise Jesus Christ, bread of life and living water. In
homage we pray:
        You alone are holy.

By your prayer and fasting;
    —teach us to rid our lives of all that blinds us to your
    Holy Spirit.
By your faithfulness to the word of God;
    —help us to keep your gospel alive and meaningful in our
    culture.
You revealed yourself to the woman at the well and she became
your disciple announcing your truth to others;
    —let the voices of women be heard in your church, that your
    message to them may be given to the world.
You are the temple destroyed by human hands;
    —help us to remember that we are temples of the Holy Spirit.

PRAYER: O God, you shepherd us with tender care and you draw us to yourself in a covenant of love. Help us to heed the words of Jesus to follow the call of your Spirit. Let this season of Lent be a turning point in our lives toward greater fidelity to you. We ask this in Jesus' name. Amen.

MORNING PRAYER
(Psalms from Sunday, Week III, p. 98)

Ant 1 The water that I shall give will become in you a spring of water welling to eternal life.

Ant 2 You shall not make the house of God a house of trade.

Ant 3 My food is to do the will of the One who sent me and to accomplish the work I was sent to do.

READING

We proclaim Christ crucified, a stumbling block to Jews and foolishness to Gentiles, but to those who are the called, both Jews and Greeks, Christ the power of God and the wisdom of God. For God's foolishness is wiser than human wisdom, and God's weakness is stronger than human strength.

1 Cor 1:23–25

RESPONSORY

Create in me a clean heart, O God; put a steadfast spirit within me.—**Create...**
Cast me not from your presence, —**put a...**
Glory to you, Source of all Being, Eternal Word and Holy Spirit. —**Create...**

CANTICLE OF ZECHARIAH

Ant To those who are called, Christ is the power of God.

INTERCESSIONS

Let us praise Jesus Christ, model of faithfulness, hope of our salvation. With sincere hearts we pray:

O Christ, guide us to truth.

You knew the burden of temptation;
—make us strong in resisting evil.

You drove away those who desecrated the temple of God;
  —help us to make our worship pleasing to you and a blessing
    for all.
Moses was called to lead his people to water in the desert;
  —lead those who thirst for truth to the words of the gospel.
You taught your disciples patience and long-suffering;
  —teach us to set aside our own convenience and comfort to
    enable the growth of others.

PRAYER: O God, you shepherd us with tender care and draw us
to yourself in a covenant of love. Help us to heed the
words of Jesus to follow the call of your Spirit. Let this
season of Lent be a turning point in our lives toward
greater fidelity to you. We ask this in Jesus' name.
Amen.

DAYTIME PRAYER

Ant 1 The season of deliverance has come; the time of salvation
is at hand.

Ant 2 Turn to me with all your heart, says our God.

Ant 3 Believing in God's strength and mercy, let us be fortified
with patience.

(Prayer as in Morning Prayer)

EVENING PRAYER II

Ant 1 Jesus said, "Destroy this temple, and in three days I will
raise it up."

Ant 2 If you knew the gift of God, and who it is that is saying to
you, "Give me a drink," you would have asked him, and
he would have given you living water.

Ant 3 The woman said to him, "I know that the Messiah is
coming, who will show us all things." Jesus said to her, "I
who speak to you am he."

READING

[God] said, "I have observed the misery of my people who are in Egypt; I have heard their cry on account of their taskmasters. Indeed, I know their sufferings, and I have come down to deliver them from the Egyptians, and to bring them up out of that land to a good and broad land, a land flowing with milk and honey."

Ex 3: 7–8

RESPONSORY

Deliver me from death, O God of my salvation. **—Deliver**...
And my tongue will sing out your saving help; **—O God**...
Glory to you, Source of all Being, Eternal Word and Holy Spirit.
   —Deliver...

CANTICLE OF MARY

Ant Jesus knew human nature and needed no one to explain it
   to him; he knew what was in the human heart.

INTERCESSIONS

God of abundant life, you call us to become a loving people. We pray with confidence:
Send us your Holy Spirit.

You led the Israelites through the desert to the promised land;
   —may the discipline of prayer and fasting bring us joy of
      heart.
You seek to satisfy the deepest longings of the human heart;
   —help us to discern what is of real value in our lives.
Strengthen all who are committed to living the gospel of Jesus
   —let their lives bear witness to your love and compassion.
You look with mercy on all who strive to do your will;
   —refresh those who labor to ease the burdens of others.

PRAYER: O God, you shepherd us with tender care and draw us
      to yourself in a covenant of love. Help us to heed the
      words of Jesus to follow the call of your Spirit. Let this
      season of Lent be a turning point in our lives toward
      greater fidelity to you. We ask this in Jesus' name.
      Amen.

THIRD MONDAY OF LENT
(Antiphons and Psalms Week III, p. 104)

MORNING PRAYER

READING

Consider life as a Way of the Cross, but take the cross on your
shoulders with joy and courage, for Jesus with his example and grace
made it light.... Let us follow Jesus on the royal way of the cross, not
with repugnance like Simon of Cyrene, but with joy and gladness for we
are royal children.

Essays on Titus Brandsma, p. 126, (12)

RESPONSORY

Spare us, O God, and have pity on your people.—**Spare us**...
We have sinned against you, —**have pity**...
Glory to you, Source of all Being, Eternal Word and Holy Spirit.
    —**Spare us**...

CANTICLE OF ZECHARIAH

Ant. Now I know that there is no God but you in all the earth.

INTERCESSIONS

We praise you, O Christ, for your fidelity unto death. We cry out
in hope:
        Fill us with the fullness of life.

You count as done to you all that we do for others;
    —help us to love others as you love them.
You did not spare yourself in the service of those in need;
    —show us the way to spend ourselves for others, for their
        welfare and your glory.
You bore insult and abuse from the people of your own town;
    —teach us to respect people and things that are familiar to
        us, ever open to hidden truths.
You came to set us free from our small ideas and from our limited
notions of God;
    —let your forgiving love and healing word enlighten our
        minds and change our hearts.

PRAYER: O God, each morning we awaken anew to your gift of
            life. In this season of Lent grant us also the gift of
            renewed fervor in following your way of truth and love.

Give us the mind and heart of Jesus and never let us
be separated from you. We ask this in his name.
Amen.

DAYTIME PRAYER

Ant 1 The season of deliverance has come; the time of salvation
is at hand.

Ant 2 Turn to me with all your heart, says our God.

Ant 3 Believing in God's strength and mercy, let us be fortified
with patience.

(Prayer as in Morning Prayer)

EVENING PRAYER

READING

In everything Christ does, he is guided by the Spirit. The Spirit leads
him into the desert where he lives "on every word that comes from the
mouth of God." The Spirit comes visibly upon him in his baptism in the
Jordan where he shows his readiness to bear the burden of all...and to
be the brother of all people. It is by the power of the Holy Spirit that
Jesus drives out evil spirits and cures the sick. Through the power of
the Spirit he is the Poor One, the Blessed who brings the [kindom] of
God.

Bernard Häring, *Prayer: The Integration of Faith and Life*, p. 7, (8)

RESPONSORY

Have mercy on me, O God, in your goodness. —**Have...**
In the greatness of your compassion wipe out my offense,
  —**O God...**
Glory to you, Source of all Being, Eternal Word and Holy Spirit.
  —**Have...**

CANTICLE OF MARY

Ant. Jesus came to Nazareth and spoke to the people in the
synagogue.

INTERCESSIONS

When the Word made flesh comes again in glory, we will stand before your holiness. We cry out to you:
Have mercy on us in that day.

Jesus, you come each day in glory, your Spirit abides in our hearts;
—help us to minister to those in need.
You bless those who clothe the naked and shelter the homeless.
—bless, too, our fashion-conscious culture, and enlighten our use of our resources.
Our spirits, hungry and thirsty for your inspiration, are weakened by our own selfishness;
—break through the resistance of our fears and apathy; renew our will and strength to serve you.
You care for the least of us as well as the greatest;
—heal our pride, dissolve our prejudices; let us love as we are loved.

PRAYER: O God, this evening we give you thanks for the life given us this day. In this season of Lent grant us the gift of gratitude for all the gifts received each and every day, and we ask for a renewed fervor in following your way of truth and love. Give us the mind and heart of Jesus and never let us be separated from you. We ask this in his name. Amen.

THIRD TUESDAY OF LENT

(Antiphons and Psalms from Week III, p. 111)

MORNING PRAYER

READING

It is the purpose of the environment of prayer to provide us with the necessary time and space for reflection so that we are attuned to the Holy Trinity—and for that, community is and will remain central to the life of prayer, a community in which—even in the worst and most confusing of times—the presence of the Transcendent One is celebrated and upheld.

Jay C. Rochelle, "The Environment of Prayer," (4)

RESPONSORY

Spare us, O God, and have pity on your people.—**Spare us**...
We have sinned against you, —**have pity**...
Glory to you, Source of all Being, Eternal Word and Holy Spirit.
   —**Spare us**...

CANTICLE OF ZECHARIAH

Ant. Deliver us by your marvelous works, O God, and give glory
      to your name.

INTERCESSIONS

Let us praise God who forgives us our sins and gives us the
power to forgive one another. In gratitude we pray:
              May you be blessed forever, O God.

Jesus, you reveal God to us as father and mother;
   —help us to respond with confidence and love.
You teach us to ask for our daily bread;
   —give us the generosity to share what we have with those
   in need.
You were put to the test; you were delivered into the hands of
evil;
   —give us the wisdom to shun evil, and to choose what is
   good for ourselves and others.
You prayed for the fidelity of your disciples;
   —pray for us that we will stand firm in time of trial.

PRAYER: O God, you have created us all, and all that we have
         belongs to you. Help us to share what we now have, to
         heal old wounds, and to free one another from the
         bondage of debt. Raise up leaders for the nations and
         for the church who will bring us to unity and peace.
         This we ask in the name of Jesus, who promised peace
         the world cannot give. Amen.

DAYTIME PRAYER

Ant 1 The season of deliverance has come; the time of salvation
       is at hand.

Ant 2 Turn to me with all your heart, says our God.

Ant 3 Believing in God's strength and mercy, let us be fortified
with patience.

(Prayer as in Morning Prayer)

EVENING PRAYER

READING

Forgiveness is transformative, much like the process of composting
garbage. Just as garbage, under the right conditions of heat, moisture,
and fermentation will break down into a rich soil, so too will our own
negativity be transformed, under the spiritually vital conditions of
conversion, humility, surrender, and forgiveness. This rich soil will
then be love itself.

Wayne Teasdale, "The Mystery of Forgiveness," (4)

RESPONSORY

Have mercy on me, O God, in your goodness. **—Have...**
In the greatness of your compassion wipe out my offense, **—O God...**
Glory to you, Source of all Being, Eternal Word and Holy Spirit.
    —Have...

CANTICLE OF MARY

Ant. You must forgive from your heart those who wrong you as
God forgives you.

INTERCESSIONS

O God, a contrite and humble heart is pleasing to you, more than
holocausts of rams on your altars. We pray to you:
    We praise you for your mercy.

Jesus, those who trust in you are never disappointed;
    —teach us to realize our limitations and to live in peace
    with the limitations of others.
You teach us to forgive our sisters and brothers seventy times
seven times;
    —help us to bring peace by being nonjudgmental toward
    one another.
You call us to abide in you as branches on the vine;
    —guide us in our efforts to live the truths of your gospel.

We did not choose you; you have chosen us to follow you;
— make us generous and creative in sharing the gift of
   your word.

PRAYER: O God, you have created us all, and all that we have
            belongs to you. Help us to share what we now have, to
            heal old wounds, and to free one another from the
            bondage of debt. Raise up leaders for the nations and
            for the church who will bring us to unity and peace.
            This we ask in the name of Jesus, who promised peace
            the world cannot give. Amen.

THIRD WEDNESDAY OF LENT
(Antiphons and Psalms from Week III, p. 117)

MORNING PRAYER

READING

...that means trying to see things, persons, and choices from the angle
of eternity; and dealing with them as part of the material in which the
Spirit works. This will be decisive for the way we behave as to our
personal, social, and national obligations. It will decide the papers we
read, the movements we support, the kind of administrators we vote
for, our attitude to social and international justice. For though we may
renounce the world for ourselves...we have to accept it as the sphere in
which we are to cooperate with the Spirit and try to do [God's] will.

Evelyn Underhill, The Spiritual Life, pp. 80–81, (62)

RESPONSORY

Spare us, O God, and have pity on your people.**—Spare us**...
We have sinned against you, **—have pity**...
Glory to you, Source of all Being, Eternal Word and Holy Spirit.
   —Spare us...

CANTICLE OF ZECHARIAH

Ant.   Moses said to the people: Give heed to the statutes and
       ordinances I teach you and do them, that you may live.

INTERCESSIONS

Jesus, you are the sign of Jonah; death will not destroy you, and
so we proclaim:
                Glory and praise to you.

You came with truth and healing, but the crowds asked for a sign;
—open our eyes to the life-giving message of the gospel.

You ministered to all who came to you;
—help us to see through our prejudices and free ourselves to serve all people.

You suffered from the dullness of your followers and the unbelief of the crowds;
—strengthen us when our labor seems fruitless and we doubt your call.

Remember all who have brought your word to us: our parents, teachers, clergy, religious, and friends;
—let them know the gift of God they have been to us.

PRAYER: O God, you created all things, the great and the small. Your care extends to all. During this season of Lent, help us to see your sustaining presence everywhere. Teach us to live responsibly, sharing the gifts of creation with discipline and reverence as well as with satisfaction and joy. Grant this through Jesus, your Word of life, who teaches us the way. Amen.

DAYTIME PRAYER

Ant 1 The season of deliverance has come; the time of salvation is at hand.

Ant 2 Turn to me with all your heart, says our God.

Ant 3 Believing in God's strength and mercy, let us be fortified with patience.

(Prayer as in Morning Prayer)

EVENING PRAYER

READING

So many rather dream of a mysticism full of sweetness and blissful rest, without reflecting that God who seeks our union followed the way of suffering, contempt, and death. True mysticism leads to Calvary, only to rest dying in the embrace of the Cross upon the bloodless heart of Jesus.

Essays on Titus Brandsma, p. 125, (12)

RESPONSORY

Have mercy on me, O God, in your goodness. —**Have...**
In the greatness of your compassion wipe out my offense,
   —O God...
Glory to you, Source of all Being, Eternal Word and Holy Spirit.
   —Have...

CANTICLE OF MARY

Ant. Till heaven and earth pass away, nothing will pass from the
   law until all is accomplished.

INTERCESSIONS

Jesus is the fulfillment of the law; his love is everlasting. Let us
pray with confidence:
      Christ Jesus, lead us on the path of salvation.

Jesus, you are never alone; God is always with you;
   —help us to realize the presence of God in our lives.
You came to cast fire upon the earth;
   —enkindle in our hearts a love that bears fruit in service
   and praise.
You came that we might have life, now and forever;
   —awaken us to our responsibility to build a world based on
   justice and compassion.
You are the way, the truth, and the life;
   —come to the aid of those who search for meaning in life.

PRAYER: O God, you created all things, the great and the small.
Your care extends to all. During this season of Lent,
help us to see your sustaining presence everywhere.
Teach us to live responsibly, sharing the gifts of
creation with discipline and reverence as well as with
satisfaction and joy. Grant this through Jesus, your
Word of life, who teaches us the way. Amen.

THIRD THURSDAY OF LENT
(Antiphons and Psalms from Week III, p. 124)
MORNING PRAYER

READING

If we can, we should occupy ourselves in looking upon [Jesus] who is
looking at us; keep him company; talk with him; pray to him; humble
ourselves before him; have our delight in him.... Anyone who can do
this, though...but a beginner in prayer, will derive great benefit from it,
for this kind of prayer brings many benefits: at least, so my soul has
found.

Teresa of Avila, Life, Ch. XIII, p. 83, (5)

RESPONSORY

Spare us, O God, and have pity on your people.—**Spare us**...
We have sinned against you, —**have pity**...
Glory to you, Source of all Being, Eternal Word and Holy Spirit.
   —**Spare us**...

CANTICLE OF ZECHARIAH

Ant. Obey my voice; I will be your God and you shall be my
       people.

INTERCESSIONS

Jesus, you have come to call sinners and not the just. With
contrite hearts, we pray:
       Be merciful for we have sinned.

Through people, events, and inner urgings, you call us to turn
from sin;
   —strengthen us in the way of your truth.
You were led by the Spirit into the wilderness;
   —give us courage to face the emptiness of our lives.
You call us to works of justice and mercy;
   —let us see your face in the poor and homeless.
By your passion and death you have opened the gates of heaven;
   —draw to yourself all those who have died.

PRAYER: O Christ, you have taught us to let go and to love to
       the end, persevering to the other side of death which
       is resurrection. During this lenten season, call us to

prayer that will make our hearts ready for this depth of love. We ask this grace in your name. Amen.

DAYTIME PRAYER

Ant 1 The season of deliverance has come; the time of salvation is at hand.

Ant 2 Turn to me with all your heart, says our God.

Ant 3 Believing in God's strength and mercy, let us be fortified with patience.

(Prayer as in Morning Prayer)

EVENING PRAYER

READING

The firm and faithful hope for love's final conquest constitutes the very substance of Christianity. It is not worthwhile to dedicate one's life for any cause inferior to that of love or to work hard for anything that is not inspired by redeeming love and does not serve its cause. But the cause of love for which Christ came is, indeed, worth all dedication and even all suffering. This is the one precious pearl that is worth more than all else. The reward for those who have given everything away for love's sake is...the abode of love for all eternity.

Bernard Häring, C.SS.R., *Heart of Jesus*, pp. 130–31, (55)

RESPONSORY

Have mercy on me, O God, in your goodness. —**Have...**
In the greatness of your compassion wipe out my offense,
   —**O God...**
Glory to you, Source of all Being, Eternal Word and Holy Spirit.
   —**Have...**

CANTICLE OF MARY

Ant. They who are not with me are against me, and they who do not gather with me scatter.

INTERCESSIONS

The God of peace is preparing a new dwelling place and a new earth where justice will abide. Let us pray with confidence:

      In you, O God, we place all our hope.

Jesus has given us a pledge of hope and strength in the Eucharist;
   —may we always walk in the strength of this food.
O God, you have sent your Christ to preach the good news to the poor;
   —free us from our prisons and our blindness.
We remember those who are lost, frightened, and despairing;
   —send forth your Spirit to comfort their hearts.
We will one day overcome death and be raised in Christ;
   —what was sown in weakness will be raised in power.

PRAYER: O Christ, you have taught us to let go and to love to the end, persevering to the other side of death which is resurrection. During this lenten season, call us to prayer that will make our hearts ready for this depth of love. We ask this grace in your name. Amen.

THIRD FRIDAY OF LENT
(Antiphons and Psalms from Week III, p. 131)
MORNING PRAYER

READING

Where there is charity and wisdom, there is neither fear nor ignorance. Where there is patience and humility, there is neither anger nor disturbance. Where this is poverty with joy, there is neither covetousness nor avarice. Where there is inner peace and meditation, there is neither anxiousness nor dissipation.... Where there is mercy and discernment, there is neither excess nor hardness of heart.

Francis of Assisi, *Francis and Clare*, p. 35, (1)

RESPONSORY

Spare us, O God, and have pity on your people.—**Spare us**...
We have sinned against you, —**have pity**...
Glory to you, Source of all Being, Eternal Word and Holy Spirit.
   —**Spare us**...

CANTICLE OF ZECHARIAH

Ant. I will heal their faithfulness; I will love them freely, for my anger has turned from them.

INTERCESSIONS

Led by the Spirit into the desert of Lent, we are called to purify and renew ourselves. Let us earnestly pray:
May the light of Christ shine brightly on our world.

May we hear and interpret the many voices of our age;
—and judge them in the light of your word.
You raised Jesus from the dead;
—Christ is the center of our life, the joy of every heart, and the answer to our yearnings.
We remember the elderly who feel useless or forgotten;
—have mercy on your people, and let them know your love.
Teach us to be simple and disciplined in our needs;
—and to share our abundance with those in want.

PRAYER: Christ Jesus, may we join you in your passion by letting go of our selfish ways and plans. Help us to learn true sacrifice and thus prepare for our union with you in the victory of resurrection. We ask this in your name. Amen.

DAYTIME PRAYER

Ant 1 The season of deliverance has come; the time of salvation is at hand.

Ant 2 Turn to me with all your heart, says our God.

Ant 3 Believing in God's strength and mercy, let us be fortified with patience.

(Prayer as in Morning Prayer)

EVENING PRAYER

READING

Each human being is like a mirror of every other and of the whole universe; personality is the crossroad of the entire world. And the Logos who is in God, who is God, who is the mirror in whom God...is reflected in the oneness of their Spirit, is also the mirror of every human being.

Jean Leclercq, "Solitude and Solidarity," p. 81, (7)

RESPONSORY

Have mercy on me, O God, in your goodness. —**Have...**
In the greatness of your compassion wipe out my offense,
   —**O God...**
Glory to you, Source of all Being, Eternal Word and Holy Spirit.
   —**Have...**

CANTICLE OF MARY

Ant. You shall love your God with all your heart, with all your
      soul, with all your mind, and with all your strength.

INTERCESSIONS

Christ Jesus, you call us to share in your mission and to deepen
our belief in the mystery of creation and redemption. We wish to
be sensitive to your Spirit, and so we pray:
      Renew your gifts in our hearts.

We believe the life of each person in our world is sacred;
   —may we incarnate your love in a global way.
We confess to you our sins and addictions;
   —forgive us and lead us on the path to life.
You have given us the gift of life;
   —help us live with grateful hearts.
Look upon all countries divided by fear and hatred;
   —may their people know the gift of peace.

PRAYER: Christ Jesus, may we join you in your passion by
         letting go of our selfish ways and plans. Help us to
         learn true sacrifice and thus prepare for our union
         with you in the victory of resurrection. We ask this in
         your name. Amen.

THIRD SATURDAY OF LENT
(Antiphons and Psalms from Week III, p. 138)

MORNING PRAYER

READING

Christ is the Lord, the source of joy for all people. By the power of the
Spirit he took the burden of our sins upon himself: "Yet it was our
infirmities that he bore, our sufferings that he endured, while we

thought of him as stricken, as one smitten by God and afflicted. But he was pierced for our offenses, crushed for our sins. Upon him was the chastisement that makes us whole. By his stripes we were healed." (Is 53:4-6).

Bernard Häring, *Prayer: The Integration of Faith and Life*, p. 9, (8)

RESPONSORY

Spare us, O God, and have pity on your people.—**Spare us**...
We have sinned against you, —**have pity**...
Glory to you, Source of all Being, Eternal Word and Holy Spirit.
   —**Spare us**...

CANTICLE OF ZECHARIAH

Ant. Those who exalt themselves will be humbled and those who humble themselves will be exalted.

INTERCESSIONS

Our vocation as disciples calls us to a change of heart, a conversion expressed in praise of God and in deeds of justice and service. We turn to God and pray:

Help us and heal us, O God.

Enable us to grow in a spirit of self-giving;
   —showing care and concern for all people.
Break through the evil in our hearts and our social structures;
   —we are burdened with a sense of guilt.
Teach us to pray and to know the beauty of silence;
   —fill us with your faithful love.
Enlighten the leaders of nations;
   —to make the choices that lead to peace.

PRAYER: God of mercy and love, may the discipline of Lent strengthen us to say yes to the hard choices that lead to life. We ask this in union with Jesus who has shown us the way. Amen.

DAYTIME PRAYER

Ant 1 The season of deliverance has come; the time of salvation is at hand.

Ant 2 Turn to me with all your heart, says our God.

Ant 3 Believing in God's strength and mercy, let us be fortified with patience.

(Prayer as in Morning Prayer)

FOURTH SUNDAY OF LENT
(Antiphons and Psalms from Week IV, p. 143)
EVENING PRAYER I

READING

The Christian option is not for poverty, because poverty as such does not exist. The option is for the poor, above all for the permanently poor in my path and part of my society, the one who has the right to expect something from me. The fact of the poor as a collective neighbor gives to [familial] charity its great social and political demand. For the Gospel the socio-political commitment of the Christian is because of the poor person. Politics means the liberation of the needy.

Segundo Galilea, *Following Jesus*, p. 27, (22)

RESPONSORY

My soul waits for God; in your word I hope. —**My soul**...
For with you there is steadfast love, —**in your**...
Glory to you, Source of all Being, Eternal Word and Holy Spirit.
  —**My soul**...

CANTICLE OF MARY

Ant The Most High is my shepherd; I shall dwell in the house of God all the days of my life.

INTERCESSIONS

Let us praise God who at various times and places is revealed to us. Let us rejoice in the revelation of Jesus. In God's presence let us acclaim:
  It is good for us to be here.

You called Abraham to serve you with obedience and love and did not allow the death of his son;
  —teach us to discern what is pleasing to you, always keeping the welfare and rights of others in mind.
You chose David, a youthful shepherd, to lead your people;
  —help us to look beyond outward appearances as we choose our leaders.

You made Jesus a vessel of your healing love;
  —show us how to reach out to the sick in healing ways, with
    respect and reverence.
You sent manna for your people to eat in the desert;
  —let your word nourish our minds and enkindle our hearts
    toward the transformation of our lives.

PRAYER: O God, you are our light and without you, all our ways
        are darkness. Heal our blindness and lead us to the
        light of your truth. Help us to overcome all that keeps
        us from following your commandments. During this
        season of Lent, may we grow in love for you and for
        one another. This we ask through Christ Jesus, the
        light of the world. Amen.

MORNING PRAYER
(Psalms from Sunday, Week IV, p. 145)

Ant 1 As long as I am in the world, I am the light of the world.

Ant 2 As Moses lifted up the serpent in the wilderness, so must I
      myself be lifted up, that whoever believes in me may have
      eternal life.

Ant 3 It was fitting to make merry and be glad, for this your
      brother was dead, and is alive; he was lost and is found.

READING

God, who is rich in mercy, out of the great love with which [we are
loved] even when we were dead through our trespasses, made us alive
together with Christ—by grace you have been saved—and raised us up
with him and seated us with him in the heavenly places in Christ
Jesus, so that in the ages to come [God] might show the immeasurable
riches of [God's own] grace in kindness toward us in Christ Jesus.

Eph 2:4–7

RESPONSORY

Who will deliver us, O God, from our weakness and sin? **—Who**...
Jesus Christ has saved us **—from**...
Glory to you, Source of all Being, Eternal Word and Holy Spirit.
  —Who...

CANTICLE OF ZECHARIAH

Ant Once you were in darkness, but now you are light in Christ
Jesus.

INTERCESSIONS

As Moses lifted up the serpent in the desert, so Jesus was lifted
up on the cross for our salvation. In homage we pray:
We adore you, O Christ!

Whoever believes in you will not be condemned;
—we do believe, help our unbelief.
You have come to reconcile us to God and to one another;
—make us effective ambassadors of your mission of peace.
You seek out those who are lost, forgiving us again and again;
—let our lives so mirror your compassion that those who are
wounded by sin will be drawn to you.
Your mercy reached out to all in need;
—bless the sick and the dying; let them know your presence.

PRAYER: O God, you are our light, and without you all our ways
are darkness. Heal our blindness and lead us to the
light of your truth. Help us to overcome all that keeps
us from following your commandments. During this
season of Lent, may we grow in love for you and for
one another. This we ask through Christ Jesus, the
light of the world. Amen.

DAYTIME PRAYER

Ant 1 The season of deliverance has come; the time of salvation
is at hand.

Ant 2 Turn to me with all your heart, says our God.

Ant 3 Believing in God's strength and mercy, let us be fortified
with patience.

(Prayer as in Morning Prayer)

EVENING PRAYER II

Ant 1 Jesus said, "For judgment I came into this world, that those who do not see may see, and that those who see may become blind."

Ant 2 For God sent the Anointed One into the world, not to condemn the world, but that the world might be saved through the One God sent.

Ant 3 While she was yet at a distance, her mother saw her and had compassion, and ran and embraced her and kissed her.

READING

If anyone is in Christ, there is a new creation: everything old has passed away; see, everything has become new! All this is from God, who reconciled us to [God's own self] through Christ, and has given us the ministry of reconciliation; that is, in Christ God was reconciling the world to [God's self], not counting their trespasses against them, and entrusting the message of reconciliation to us.

2 Cor 5:17–19

RESPONSORY

Lord Jesus Christ, your yoke is easy and your burden is
  light. **—Lord**...
In you we will find rest, **—for your**...
Glory to you, Source of all Being, Eternal Word and Holy Spirit.
  —Lord...

CANTICLE OF MARY

Ant Jesus said: "I have come into the world, that those who do not see may be given light."

INTERCESSIONS

As Moses lifted up the serpent in the desert, so Jesus was lifted up on the cross for our salvation. In homage we pray:
We adore you, O Christ.

Whoever believes in you will not be condemned;
  —we do believe, help our unbelief.
You have come to reconcile us to God and to one another;
  —make us effective ambassadors of your mission of peace.

You seek out those who are lost, forgiving us again and again;
—let our lives so mirror your compassion that those who are
  wounded by sin will be drawn to you.
Your mercy reached out to all in need;
—bless the sick and the dying; let them know your presence.

PRAYER: O God, you are our light and without you, all our ways
are darkness. Heal our blindness and lead us to the
light of your truth. Help us to overcome all that keeps
us from following your commandments. During this
season of Lent, may we grow in love for you and for
one another. This we ask through Christ Jesus, the
light of the world. Amen.

FOURTH MONDAY OF LENT
(Antiphons and Psalms from Week IV, p. 151)
MORNING PRAYER

READING

Just as ordinary bread and water are the materials of the Christian
sacraments, Underhill states that the ordinary events, the joys and
sorrows, choices and renunciations, all the humdrum jobs of the
"ground floor" life can be dignified by our "upstairs" life if the fire of
charity burns there. That our daily work can be, indeed should be, true
prayer gains significance when we try to incarnate in our workaday
world the spiritual truths by which we attempt to live.

Mary Brian Durkin, OP, *Teresian Wisdom in Selected Writings of Evelyn Underhill*, p. 28, (20)

RESPONSORY

Spare us, O God, and have pity on your people.—**Spare us...**
We have sinned against you, —**have pity...**
Glory to you, Source of all Being, Eternal Word and Holy Spirit.
  —**Spare us...**

CANTICLE OF ZECHARIAH

Ant. For behold, I create a new heaven and a new earth.

INTERCESSIONS

Jesus Christ, you have shown us the narrow gate and promised
that it is the entrance to life. With trust we pray:
  Lead us and we will follow.

You showed us the way of mercy and compassion;
  —give us understanding and patience with the weaknesses
  of others.
You had pity on public sinners and shared their ignominy;
  —enlighten governments that claim an eye for an eye and a
  life for a life.
You call us to conversion to life, not to death;
  —enlighten our lenten efforts that they may enrich our lives
  and give praise to you.
For a father's faith, you healed a child, increase our faith;
  —let our belief be a sharing in your life and healing ministry.

PRAYER: O God, be with us during this season of Lent as we
seek to serve you more faithfully. Bless our country
and our world. Enlighten our leaders; make them
instruments of your peace. Bless all in research;
reward their efforts with healing for our people and
regeneration for our environment. Let this be a time of
salvation for us and of glory and praise to you. We ask
this in Jesus' name. Amen.

DAYTIME PRAYER

Ant 1 The season of deliverance has come; the time of salvation
is at hand.

Ant 2 Turn to me with all your heart, says our God.

Ant 3 Believing in God's strength and mercy, let us be fortified
with patience.

(Prayer as in Morning Prayer)

EVENING PRAYER

READING

Almighty, eternal, just and merciful God, grant us in our misery [the
grace] to do for You alone what we know You want us to do, and always
to desire what pleases You. Thus, inwardly cleansed, interiorly
enlightened, and inflamed by the fire of the Holy Spirit, may we be able
to follow in the footprints of your beloved Son, our Lord Jesus Christ.
And by your grace alone, may we make our way to You, Most High, Who

live and rule in perfect Trinity and simple Unity, and are glorified God all-powerful forever and ever. Amen.

Francis of Assisi, *Francis and Clare*, p. 61, (1)

RESPONSORY

Have mercy on me, O God, in your goodness. —**Have...**
In the greatness of your compassion wipe out my offense,
   —**O God...**
Glory to you, Source of all Being, Eternal Word and Holy Spirit.
   —**Have...**

CANTICLE OF MARY

Ant. The royal official believed the word that Jesus spoke to him
   and went his way.

INTERCESSIONS

Jesus has come, creating a new heaven and a new earth; let us praise him saying:
   O Christ, all your works are wonderful.

By your life among us you have taught us how to live;
   —during this season of Lent, let us put aside all that keeps
   us from being your disciples.
You sought out what was lost; you blessed the poor in spirit;
   —hear us as we plead for zeal and direction for without you
   we can do nothing.
Only you are just and all your ways are holy;
   —forgive us for our self-righteous ways; let us see ourselves
   in truth.
You guard the weak and care for the lowly;
   —have pity on all children who have no one to care for them;
   help us to come to their aid.

PRAYER: O God, be with us during this season of Lent as we
   seek to serve you more faithfully. Bless our country
   and our world. Enlighten our leaders; make them
   instruments of your peace. Bless all in research;
   reward their efforts with healing for our people and
   regeneration for our environment. Let this be a time of
   salvation for us and of glory and praise to you. We ask
   this in Jesus' name. Amen.

FOURTH TUESDAY OF LENT
(Antiphons and Psalms from Week IV, p. 158)

MORNING PRAYER

READING

...For us, too, Christ is still a promise, because we are still on our way
and the world is still longing for the final liberation. But Christ is with
us on our way. He comes constantly into our life as the promise
"already" realized and the firm but "not-yet" totally fulfilled hope. As we
discover his presence in our life more and more vitally, we long more
and more to stay near him, to be with him.

Bernard Häring, Prayer: The Integration of Faith and Life, p. 28, (8)

RESPONSORY

Spare us, O God, and have pity on your people.—**Spare us**...
We have sinned against you, —**have pity**...
Glory to you, Source of all Being, Eternal Word and Holy Spirit.
   —**Spare us**...

CANTICLE OF ZECHARIAH

Ant. I saw the water issuing from the temple, flowing from the
   temple to renew the world.

INTERCESSIONS

God promises forgiveness: though your sins are like scarlet, they
shall be as white as snow. Let us pray with confidence:
Save us, O God.

Jesus, your yoke is easy and your burden is light;
   —show us the way to live your gospel in sincerity and truth.
You did not seek a name or place of honor;
   —help us to simplify our lives and the trends of our culture.
You were persecuted for healing on the sabbath;
   —console and enlighten those who are called to choose
   between law and mercy.
You, O God, hear our secret prayer, you are present to us always;
   —help us to remember your love and to live in hope in times
   of doubt and pain.

PRAYER: O God, in this season of Lent, we recall the suffering of
         Jesus. Our pain and struggle is very present to us.
         Help us to remember the power of Jesus' resurrection,

that eye has not seen nor ear heard what you have
prepared for those who love you. Help us to persevere
in our service to you and to one another. We ask this
in Jesus' name, who is our companion on the way.
Amen.

DAYTIME PRAYER

Ant 1 The season of deliverance has come; the time of salvation
is at hand.

Ant 2 Turn to me with all your heart, says our God.

Ant 3 Believing in God's strength and mercy, let us be fortified
with patience.

(Prayer as in Morning Prayer)

EVENING PRAYER

READING

Christ has many services to be done; some are easy, others more
difficult; some bring honor, others bring reproach; some are suitable to
our natural inclinations and temporal interests, others are contrary to
both. In some we may please Christ and please ourselves; but there are
others in which we cannot please Christ except by denying ourselves.
Yet the power to do this is assuredly given us in Christ. We can do all
things in him who strengthens us.

John Wesley, *John and Charles Wesley*, p. 386, (1)

RESPONSORY

Have mercy on me, O God, in your goodness. —**Have...**
In the greatness of your compassion wipe out my offense,
  —**O God...**
Glory to you, Source of all Being, Eternal Word and Holy Spirit.
  —**Have...**

CANTICLE OF MARY

Ant. Jesus said: "Do you want to be healed? Rise, take up your
mat and walk."

INTERCESSIONS

Eternal life is knowing God, and Jesus Christ whom God has sent, and so we pray:
> **Christ Jesus, you have the words of eternal life.**

You taught your disciples to pray in your name;
> —in your name, we ask for the grace to persevere in your love.

You spoke the truth in love; your words were words of life;
> —help us to guard our tongue by using the gift of speech with responsibility and reverence.

You were held in derision and contempt;
> —teach us how to serve the outcasts of society, and how to respect and accept their gifts.

You hid from those who would destroy you and falsify your message;
> —come to the aid of those who are abused by the misuse of law and who have no one to defend them.

PRAYER: O God, in this season of Lent, we recall the suffering of Jesus. Our pain and struggle is very present to us. Help us to remember the power of Jesus' resurrection, that eye has not seen nor ear heard what you have prepared for those who love you. Help us to persevere in our service to you and to one another. We ask this in Jesus' name, who is our companion on the way. Amen.

FOURTH WEDNESDAY OF LENT
(Antiphons and Psalms from Week IV, p. 165)

MORNING PRAYER

READING

Forgiveness is love in pain. A trusting self-abandon is the total de-centration of ourselves and our total recentering on Someone who infinitely transcends us. Forgiveness and self-surrender mean risking Mystery, throwing in our lot with that ultimate vessel of Meaning in which we participate more than we dream. This is the opportunity offered to human freedom. Men and women can take advantage of the offer, and rest secure. Or they can let it slip by, and founder in despair.

Forgiveness and trust are our tools for not letting hopelessness have the last word. They constitute the supreme deed of human grandeur.

Leonardo Boff, *Passion of Christ, Passion of the World*, pp. 131-32, (22)

RESPONSORY

Spare us, O God, and have pity on your people.—**Spare us**...
We have sinned against you, —**have pity**...
Glory to you, Source of all Being, Eternal Word and Holy Spirit.
—**Spare us**...

CANTICLE OF ZECHARIAH

Ant. Sing for joy, O heavens, and exult, O earth; break forth, O
mountains, into song.

INTERCESSIONS

Jesus came not to be served but to serve and to give his life as a
ransom for many. We cry out to you:
O Christ, you are the savior of the world.

Your call is a call to service;
—inspire people of all ages to work in your vineyard.
Bless those who are difficult to serve, those who harm
themselves, and the people who minister to them;
—may they have the courage to trust and the willingness to
endure.
Bless our families; give them the material sustenance they need;
—enable them to hear your word and keep it with a joyful
spirit.
Bless the aging and the dying;
—help us to make their last years a time of contentment
and peace.

PRAYER: Christ Jesus, to follow you is to follow the way of the
cross to new life. In this season of Lent, give us the
grace to take up the challenge of each day and to live
as your faithful disciples. Strengthen us when we
waver and help us to persevere in our efforts to grow.
Through our lives let the world hear your words and
see your good works. May all one day live with you
forever in the unity of the Holy Trinity. Amen.

DAYTIME PRAYER

Ant 1 The season of deliverance has come; the time of salvation is at hand.

Ant 2 Turn to me with all your heart, says our God.

Ant 3 Believing in God's strength and mercy, let us be fortified with patience.

(Prayer as in Morning Prayer)

EVENING PRAYER

READING

The virtues of faith and love are within the reach of all of us. They are the two wings by which we can fly to God on countless occasions, and these occasions are provided by [God] just to have us do so. In using these happenings, we shall find countless opportunities for overcoming our natural self, so given to irritation when things contradict our will, and so ready to think that annoying circumstances justify our showing annoyance.... It is only the light of faith that can enable us to see *through* the various circumstances we meet.... To one under the influence of [the Spirit] instead of her own, these little trials show her...what she must work at, what she must overcome....

Mother Aloysius Rogers, OCD *Fragrance from Alabaster*, p. 10, (6)

RESPONSORY

Have mercy on me, O God, in your goodness. **—Have...**
In the greatness of your compassion wipe out my offense,
   —O God...
Glory to you, Source of all Being, Eternal Word and Holy Spirit.
   —Have...

CANTICLE OF MARY

Ant. Even if a mother forgets her child and be without tenderness, I will never forget you, says our God.

INTERCESSIONS

The goodness and kindness of God follows us all the days of our lives. With trust in your word we pray:
      O God, all our hope is in your promise.

Jesus, your days were long with work and prayer;
  —free those who must labor beyond their strength.

You are the living bread come down from heaven;
  —help us to discern those things that nourish us and those
  that destroy our bodies and minds.
You reign from the cross but your realm is not of this world;
  —give men and women the courage and creativity to lead
  our nations in ways of peace and justice.
Your word is a light for our way; you know our weakness;
  —send your Spirit to those who interpret your gospel, lest
  they burden the consciences of those seeking truth.

PRAYER: Christ Jesus, to follow you is to follow the way of the
cross to new life. In this season of Lent, give us the
grace to take up the challenge of each day and to live
as your faithful disciples. Strengthen us when we
waver and help us to persevere in our efforts to grow.
Through our lives let the world hear your words and
see your good works. May all one day live with you
forever in the unity of the Holy Trinity. Amen.

FOURTH THURSDAY OF LENT
(Antiphons and Psalms from Week IV, p. 172)

MORNING PRAYER

READING

This is one way the symbol of a suffering God can help: by signaling
that the mystery of God is here in solidarity with those who suffer. In
the midst of the isolation of suffering the presence of divine compassion
as companion to the pain transforms suffering, not mitigating its evil
but bringing an inexplicable consolation and comfort.

Elizabeth Johnson, *She Who Is*, p. 267, (2)

RESPONSORY

Spare us, O God, and have pity on your people.—**Spare us**...
We have sinned against you, —**have pity**...
Glory to you, Source of all Being, Eternal Word and Holy Spirit.
  —**Spare us**...

CANTICLE OF ZECHARIAH

Ant. My judgment is just because I seek not my own will but the
will of the One who sent me.

INTERCESSIONS

Christ is at work in our hearts through the energy of the Spirit,
renewing the face of the earth, and so we pray:
Let us walk each day in love.

We remember those whose search for justice has led to the cross;
— strengthen them in the light of the resurrection.
You taught us wisdom by using examples from daily life;
— bless all teachers dedicated to educating youth.
Free us from the love of self;
— to bring our gifts into the service of humanity.
May leaders of nations work in harmony for the good of the earth;
— be for all the way, the truth, and the life.

PRAYER: O God, you have given us this life to know you, to love
you, and to be at home with you. Help us to experience
you in our hearts as we find you anew in the words
and deeds of Jesus. This we ask through Jesus who is
our way to you. Amen.

DAYTIME PRAYER

Ant 1 The season of deliverance has come; the time of salvation
is at hand.

Ant 2 Turn to me with all your heart, says our God.

Ant 3 Believing in God's strength and mercy, let us be fortified
with patience.

(Prayer as in Morning Prayer)

EVENING PRAYER

READING

So...journey on the road of life in harmony with your conscience. Do so
always. Do not say "I will begin on such and such a day," but start right
now. Remember that everything can be retrieved except time with
which we see our life passing. Time rushes on, carrying your life with it,
yet you let it go.

Francisco de Osuna, *The Third Spiritual Alphabet*, p. 59, (1)

RESPONSORY

Have mercy on me, O God, in your goodness. —**Have...**
In the greatness of your compassion wipe out my offense,
   —**O God...**
Glory to you, Source of all Being, Eternal Word and Holy Spirit.
   —**Have...**

CANTICLE OF MARY

Ant. How can you believe: you, who receive glory from one
   another, and do not seek the glory that comes from the one
   true God?

INTERCESSIONS

Christ, you have entrusted to your church the mystery of God
and the meaning of our existence, and so we pray to you:
   Teach us to worship in spirit and in truth.

You are the fully human one;
   —in following you may we come to the fullness of our
   humanity.
May world endeavors be penetrated by the spirit of the gospel;
   —open our eyes to see what is false.
You healed the sick by the touch of your hands;
   —bless all those who serve us in hospitals and nursing homes.
Help us to overcome all forms of violence between nations, races,
and ideologies;
   —strengthen those human associations which are just and
   impartial.

PRAYER: O God, you have given us this life to know you, to love
   you, and to be at home with you. Help us to experience
   you in our hearts as we find you anew in the words
   and deeds of Jesus. This we ask through Jesus who is
   our way to you. Amen.

FOURTH FRIDAY OF LENT
(Antiphons and Psalms from Week IV, p. 179)

MORNING PRAYER

READING

I am far from capable of holding the office you impose on me. I bow my head in submission, but I realize my incapacity. ... here all thought is but confusion when I want to do good—poor blockhead that I am—old, without talents, without lovable qualities, without virtue.... I desire to live only in order to sacrifice my life to the hardest labor. I realize that repose is not for this life. One must put one's body on the rack and one's heart in the wine press. If I can be useful in the least little work for the glory of the Sacred Heart, I am willing to spend a long old age here, without success, without friends, as my only means of imitating the Sacred Heart.

Louise Callan, RSCJ, *Philippine Duchesne*, pp. 426–27, (13)

RESPONSORY

Spare us, O God, and have pity on your people.—**Spare us**...
We have sinned against you, —**have pity**...
Glory to you, Source of all Being, Eternal Word and Holy Spirit.
   —**Spare us**...

CANTICLE OF ZECHARIAH

Ant. "Let us condemn him to a shameful death." Their sin blinded them; they did not know the secret purposes of God.

INTERCESSIONS

In God we live and move and have our being. Immersed in the mystery of this presence we humbly pray:
        Let us cling to you in love.

May we see your will in every event, see Christ in every person;
   —and judge all things in the light of faith.
Your love is poured forth in our hearts by the Holy Spirit;
   —help us to live the spirit of the beatitudes in our lives.
We remember those imprisoned because of their convictions;
   —let them know your saving help.
Into your hands we commend the dead and the dying;
   —may they see your face in glory.

PRAYER: Merciful God, may we imitate Jesus in the deep
love revealed in his passion and accept the kind of
suffering that leads to true freedom and resurrection.
We ask this in the name of Jesus, the Eternal Word,
who lives with you and with the Holy Spirit. Amen.

DAYTIME PRAYER

Ant 1 The season of deliverance has come; the time of salvation
is at hand.

Ant 2 Turn to me with all your heart, says our God.

Ant 3 Believing in God's strength and mercy, let us be fortified
with patience.

(Prayer as in Morning Prayer)

EVENING PRAYER

READING

It came to me like a blinding flash of light that Christ did not resist evil,
that he allowed *Himself* to be violently done to death, that when He
gave *Himself* to be crucified, He knew that the exquisite delicacy and
loveliness of the merest detail of Christian life would survive the
Passion, that indeed, far from being destroyed by it, it depended on it.
And so it is now: that which is holy, tender, and beautiful will not be
swept away or destroyed by war; on the contrary, we can still say,
"Ought not Christ to suffer these things and so enter into His glory?"

The Letters of Caryll Houselander, p. 24, (5)

RESPONSORY

Have mercy on me, O God, in your goodness. —**Have...**
In the greatness of your compassion wipe out my offense,
    —**O God...**
Glory to you, Source of all Being, Eternal Word and Holy Spirit.
    —**Have...**

CANTICLE OF MARY

Ant. I have not come of my own accord. The One who sent me is
true and unknown by you.

INTERCESSIONS

We are called to a new hope and to a new vision that we must live without fear and without oversimplification. Aware of our weakness, we pray:

Jesus, make us free.

We are aware of the challenge of this moment in history;
—form your church as a model of justice.
Renew in us the grace of baptism;
—draw us to deeper friendship with you.
May we renounce our selfishness and bear our daily cross;
—open our hearts to live with your compassion.
We remember those who have died and those who grieve;
—may the light of Christ shine in their hearts.

PRAYER: Merciful God, may we imitate Jesus in the deep love revealed in his passion and accept the kind of suffering that leads to true freedom and resurrection. We ask this in the name of Jesus, the Eternal Word, who lives with you and with the Holy Spirit. Amen.

FOURTH SATURDAY OF LENT
(Antiphons and Psalms from Week IV, p. 186)

MORNING PRAYER

READING

We must have compassion for others and show the sympathy we feel for the weakness or difficulty of another, even if it seems slight to us. A small thing can cause one person as much pain as a great trial would cause someone else. There are people who by their natures are distressed at slight things. In these matters let us not judge by comparison with ourselves at a time when perhaps without any effort on our part, God gave us greater strength. Rather let us think of ourselves as we were at our weakest.

Mother Aloysius Rogers, OCD, *Fragrance from Alabaster*, p. 29, (6)

RESPONSORY

Spare us, O God, and have pity on your people.—**Spare us...**
We have sinned against you, —**have pity...**
Glory to you, Source of all Being, Eternal Word and Holy Spirit.
   —**Spare us...**

CANTICLE OF ZECHARIAH

Ant. When they heard these words, some of the people said, "This is really the prophet." Others said, "This is the Christ."

INTERCESSIONS

We believe in the redemptive love of God. As those who have experienced God's forgiving mercy in Christ we pray:
You have redeemed us and set us free.

May your mother, Mary, draw us to reflect on your gifts to us;
—and to join with her in a song of praise.
You learned obedience by the things you suffered;
—give us patience and a spirit of wisdom.
Comfort the elderly and those who feel useless;
—renew in them an undying hope.
May the remembrance of what God has done in you through the Spirit;
—be a wellspring of creativity for the future.

PRAYER: God, our Creator, may our lenten journey teach us not to fill the void of our incompleteness with material things, but to find hope in the brightness of your promises. We ask this through Jesus Christ who lives and reigns with you, the Source of all Being, and with your Holy Spirit, forever and ever. Amen.

DAYTIME PRAYER

Ant 1 The season of deliverance has come; the time of salvation is at hand.

Ant 2 Turn to me with all your heart, says our God.

Ant 3 Believing in God's strength and mercy, let us be fortified with patience.

(Prayer as in Morning Prayer)

FIFTH SUNDAY OF LENT
(Antiphons and Psalms from Week I, p. 1)

EVENING PRAYER I

READING

Suffering is what happens when we realize that we and the rest of the world are not yet whole. It makes us conscious of the fact that we will not become whole without one another and without God. Transformation happens when we decide that we want to be whole so much, want to be finished so much, that we follow Jesus to the death where "It is finished," and where resurrection and new life begin in a way we cannot imagine.

Elizabeth Meluch, OCD, (11)

RESPONSORY

My soul waits for God; in your word I hope. **—My soul...**
For with you there is steadfast love, **—in your...**
Glory to you, Source of all Being, Eternal Word and Holy Spirit.
　—My soul...

CANTICLE OF MARY

Ant Unless a grain of wheat falls into the earth and dies, it remains alone; but if it dies, it bears much fruit.

INTERCESSIONS

Christ Crucified is the power of God and the wisdom of God. With trust we pray to him:
Save us by your Holy Cross.

You are one with God in glory;
　—help us to serve and follow you.
You wanted to gather your people as a hen gathers her young;
　—free us from the forces that divide us.
Through you a new law is written in our hearts;
　—may our thoughts and actions spring from love.
You cured Lazarus and brought him to life;
　—heal the sick and comfort the dying.

PRAYER: Compassionate One, free us from the sins and attachments that keep us from the fullness of life you have given us in Christ. May our fidelity be strengthened in him who was obedient unto death on a cross. Amen.

MORNING PRAYER
(Psalms from Sunday, Week I, p. 3)

Ant 1 I am the Resurrection and the life, those who believe in me, though they die, yet shall they live, and whoever lives and believes in me shall never die.

Ant 2 I say to you, unless a grain of wheat falls into the ground and dies, it remains alone, but if it dies, it bears much fruit.

Ant 3 Let those who are without sin among you be the first to throw a stone at her.

READING

In the days of his flesh, Jesus offered up prayers and supplications, with loud cries and tears, to the one who was able to save him from death, and he was heard because of his reverent submission. Although he was a Son, he learned obedience through what he suffered, and having been made perfect, he became the source of eternal salvation for all who obey him.

Heb 5:7–9

RESPONSORY

When the cares of my heart are many, your consolations cheer my soul. —**When**...
You have become my stronghold; —**your**...
Glory to you, Source of all Being, Eternal Word and Holy Spirit. —**When**...

CANTICLE OF ZECHARIAH

Ant Jesus said to his disciples, "Our friend, Lazarus, has fallen asleep. Let us go to awaken him."

INTERCESSIONS

We are not our own; we were bought with a price, and so we proclaim:
> **We are yours, O Christ, and you are God's!**

O God, we are burdened with our own concerns and forget the needs of others;
—make us caring people.
We are confused by a multitude of voices;
—give us discerning hearts.
We are drawn in opposite ways from our deepest yearnings;
—strengthen us in truth.
We feel the loss of many whom we love;
—bring them to eternal life in you.

PRAYER: Compassionate God, free us from the sins and attachments that keep us from the fullness of life you have given us in Christ. Bless all who are preparing for baptism. May our fidelity be strengthened in Jesus, who was obedient unto death on a cross. We ask this in his name. Amen.

DAYTIME PRAYER

Ant 1 The season of deliverance has come; the time of salvation is at hand.

Ant 2 Turn to me with all your heart, says our God.

Ant 3 Believing in God's strength and mercy, let us be fortified with patience.

EVENING PRAYER

Ant 1 Jesus cried out with a loud voice, "Lazarus, come forth." He then said to them, "Unbind him, and let him go."

Ant 2 When I am lifted up from the earth, I will draw all people to myself.

Ant 3 Jesus said, "Neither do I condemn you; go and do not sin again."

READING

"My [brothers and sisters], you descendants of Abraham's family, and others who fear God, to us the message of this salvation has been sent. Because the residents of Jerusalem and their leaders did not recognize him or understand the words of the prophets that are read every sabbath, they fulfilled those words by condemning him. Even though they found no cause for a sentence of death, they asked Pilate to have him killed. When they had carried out everything that was written about him, they took him down from the tree and laid him in a tomb. But God raised him from the dead.

Acts 13:26–30

RESPONSORY

I will give heed to the way that is blameless. When will you
    come to me? —**I will**...
I will walk with integrity of heart within my house.
    —**When**...
Glory to you, Source of all Being, Eternal Word and Holy Spirit.
    —**I will**...

CANTICLE OF MARY

Ant When I am lifted up from the earth, I will draw all people to
    myself.

INTERCESSIONS

O God of Salvation, you have raised Christ Jesus. We, too, shall
be raised by your power, and so we pray:
    Help us to live in union with you.

Lent is the season to renew our lives;
    —may your Spirit help and guide us.
You have given us a world rich in resources;
    —encourage those who see solutions to the problem of
    equitable distribution.
Through fear and distrust we collect weapons of war;
    —lead us into the path of peace.
You led the Israelites through the desert to the promised land;
    —may the discipline of prayer and fasting bring us joy of heart.

PRAYER: Compassionate God, free us from the sins and
    attachments that keep us from the fullness of life you
    have given us in Christ. Bless all who are preparing for
    baptism. May our fidelity be strengthened in Jesus,
    who was obedient unto death on a cross. We ask this
    in his name. Amen.

FIFTH MONDAY OF LENT
(Antiphons and Psalms from Week I, p. 10)

MORNING PRAYER

READING

Death is vanquished when it ceases to be the terrifying specter that
prevents us from living and proclaiming the truth. Now death is
accepted. It is simply inserted into the project of the just person and
true prophet. It can be expected. It must be expected. Jesus' greatness
consists in having refused to yield to the spirit of comfort and
convenience. Even on the cross, overwhelmed by a conviction of
abandonment by the God he has so earnestly and steadfastly served,
Jesus refuses to give over to resignation. He forgives, and he keeps
believing and hoping.... Here is a hope that transcends the bounds of
death. Here is the perfect deed of liberation. Here Jesus has delivered
himself entirely from himself, in order to be completely God's.

Leonardo Boff, *Passion of Christ, Passion of the World*, p. 65, (22)

RESPONSORY

Christ, Chosen One of the living God, have mercy on us.
—**Christ,**...
Delivered up to death on a cross, —**have mercy**...
Glory to you, Source of all Being, Eternal Word and Holy Spirit.
—**Christ**...

CANTICLE OF ZECHARIAH

Ant. The one who follows me will not walk in darkness, but will
have the light of life.

INTERCESSIONS

We pray to you, O Christ, whose death has brought life to the
world.
Remove our sins from us.

You know the recesses of the human heart;
—help us to seek God's will in all things.
We are aware of dark forces in our world;
—remind us that in you victory is already ours.
You stood for truth against the pain of opposition;
—we pray for integrity in those who lead us.

Because you trusted God, you accepted the cross;
—may the promise of resurrection help us through the
narrow gate.

PRAYER: Christ Jesus, you emptied yourself and appeared in
human likeness. Lead us always in the way of truth
and a loving acceptance of the burdens of life. We ask
this in the power of your name. Amen.

DAYTIME PRAYER

Ant 1 The season of deliverance has come; the time of salvation
is at hand.

Ant 2 Turn to me with all your heart, says our God.

Ant 3 Believing in God's strength and mercy, let us be fortified
with patience.

(Prayer as in Morning Prayer)

EVENING PRAYER

READING

Dear Mother: please will [you] allow me to offer myself to the heart of
Jesus as a sacrifice of propitiation for true peace, that the dominion of
the Antichrist may collapse, if possible, without a new world war, and
that a new order may be established? I would like it [my request]
granted this very day because it is the twelfth hour. I know that I am a
nothing, but Jesus desires it, and surely he will call many others to do
likewise in these days.

Edith Stein: Self-Portrait in Letters, p. 305, (3)

RESPONSORY

My soul waits for God; in your word I hope. —**My soul...**
For with you there is steadfast love, —**in your...**
Glory to you, Source of all Being, Eternal Word and Holy Spirit.
—**My soul...**

CANTICLE OF MARY

Ant. I bear witness to myself, and the One who sent me bears
witness to me.

INTERCESSIONS

Most loving God, you have given us, in Jesus, the bread of life
and the cup of salvation. We turn to him and say:
We proclaim your death until you come!

Jesus was led like a sheep to the slaughter;
—comfort those who face a cruel death.
May our fasting from food and self-indulgence;
—free us to love you and one another.
Jesus died that we all may be one;
—free us from the prejudices that divide women and men,
races and nations.
You call us to intimate union with you;
—encourage those who seek you in silence and solitude.

PRAYER: Christ Jesus, you emptied yourself and appeared in
human likeness. Lead us always in the way of truth
and a loving acceptance of the burdens of life. We ask
this in the power of your name. Amen.

FIFTH TUESDAY OF LENT
(Antiphons and Psalms from Week I, p. 16)
MORNING PRAYER

READING

Lent is, above all, a process of conversion. It involves both giving up and
giving more, and it hopefully creates some sort of indelible mark on our
spiritual selves so that we are never quite the same again. We become,
in the hands of God, like a piece of cloth which the dyer dyes using the
method known as batik—in some places the color is denied, in others it
is deep and glorious, but never is that piece of cloth ever just a white
sheet again.

Kay Winchester, "The Home Front," (4)

RESPONSORY

Christ, Chosen One of the living God, have mercy on us.
—**Christ,**...
Delivered up to death on a cross, —**have mercy**...
Glory to you, Source of all Being, Eternal Word and Holy Spirit.
—**Christ**...

CANTICLE OF ZECHARIAH

Ant. You are from below, I am from above; you are of this world, I am not of this world.

INTERCESSIONS

Lord Jesus, you were baptized by the Spirit and missioned to call us to union with God. We pray as one people:
May your Spirit help and guide us.

For those in difficult periods of transition;
  —we pray for trust.
For victims of mass starvation;
  —we pray for relief and a change in the inequitable possession of our world's resources.
For those addicted to drugs and alcohol;
  —we pray for healing and freedom.
For our beloved dead;
  —we pray for life eternal.

PRAYER: Jesus, our Brother, you are the cornerstone rejected by builders but exalted by God. Help us to believe that the power of Love at work in our world is in all things and above all things to the glory of God's name. Amen.

DAYTIME PRAYER

Ant 1 The season of deliverance has come; the time of salvation is at hand.

Ant 2 Turn to me with all your heart, says our God.

Ant 3 Believing in God's strength and mercy, let us be fortified with patience.

(Prayer as in Morning Prayer)

EVENING PRAYER

READING

The little world of each of us with its persons and places, its sunshine and shadows, its joys and its pain, is the one and only Holy of Holies, in which is tabernacled the Divine Will, the chosen temple in which alone [God] accepts our worship. "I shall dwell in their midst" was [the] promise, and [God] is present in every happening.

Mother Aloysius Rogers, OCD, *Fragrance from Alabaster*, p. 16, (6)

RESPONSORY

My soul waits for God; in your word I hope. —**My soul...**
For with you there is steadfast love, —**in your...**
Glory to you, Source of all Being, Eternal Word and Holy Spirit.
    —**My soul...**

CANTICLE OF MARY

Ant. The One who sent me is with me, never leaving me alone, because I always do God's will.

INTERCESSIONS

You are the truthful One who sends us the gift of our salvation in the living word of Jesus, therefore we proclaim:
    Blessed are you, Lord Jesus Christ!

Strengthen leaders of church and state;
    —help them to see new and creative possibilities in problem areas.
There are many who are sick in mind as well as in body;
    —be light in their darkness and help us to lessen the stress and enervating tensions in which we live.
Help us to transform our sinful ways;
    —so that we may be of service to one another.
Give hope to all people who are oppressed;
    —enable them to find freedom and support within their communities and families.

PRAYER: Jesus, our Brother, you are the cornerstone rejected by builders but exalted by God. Help us to believe that the power of Love at work in our world is in all things and above all things to the glory of God's name. Amen.

FIFTH WEDNESDAY OF LENT
(Antiphons and Psalms from Week I, p. 23)

MORNING PRAYER

READING

Never has my own heart so proved to me that the direct "contemplation" of Christ in [people], in the world—done not only through our minds, but through our bodies also—is the way to Him, the way to heaven on earth: and now I see how, without more than a necessary amount of egoism, we can contemplate Him in our own life and come closer to Him through it. This last means a more intense living and perhaps a more intense dying. I am confident now that the poetry, the beauty of life, which is nothing else but our divine Lord living in human souls, will go on, and that our lives though they seem to leave no visible trace, will not have been in vain.

The Letters of Caryll Houselander, pp. 24–25, (5)

RESPONSORY

Christ, Chosen One of the living God, have mercy on us.
  —**Christ,...**
Delivered up to death on a cross, —**have mercy**...
Glory to you, Source of all Being, Eternal Word and Holy Spirit.
  —**Christ**...

CANTICLE OF ZECHARIAH

Ant. If you live by my word, you are truly my disciples; and you
    will know the truth, and the truth will make you free.

INTERCESSIONS

You, O liberating God, call us from slavery to freedom and from death to life. In joy we cry out:
    We come to do your will.

You invite us to be slaves no longer;
  —free us from the selfishness that keeps us in bondage.
You call us to a life of freedom;
  —help us to bear the tension necessary to develop and grow
    in wholesome ways.
You draw us from death to life;
  —enable us to confront our addictions and to support one
    another in our process of recovery.
God of our freedom, we are open to your will;
  —help us to discern your ways for us.

PRAYER: God of love, you have called us to the life of
    resurrection by raising us, in Christ, from the dead.
    Strengthen us and those preparing for baptism to be
    wholly given to the Easter mystery. We ask this is
    Jesus' name. Amen.

DAYTIME PRAYER

Ant 1 The season of deliverance has come; the time of salvation is at hand.

Ant 2 Turn to me with all your heart, says our God.

Ant 3 Believing in God's strength and mercy, let us be fortified with patience.

(Prayer as in Morning Prayer)

EVENING PRAYER

READING

We persevere in the hope that we shall be well established some day. But just now the clouds are too thick to let us even glimpse that day. We know by experience that happiness can be combined with much suffering. We are satisfied with our lot; we have no regrets; and we are even disposed to abide in peace in the midst of failure. Poverty costs us little when it means merely privation for ourselves. It is the debts that stab the heart. But we embrace our poverty—abject, dependent, repugnant though it be—because it is like the poverty of our Lord and comes to us from the Heart of Jesus.

Louise Callan, RSCJ, *Philippine Duschesne*, p. 319, (13)

RESPONSORY

My soul waits for God; in your word I hope. —**My soul...**
For with you there is steadfast love, —**in your...**
Glory to you, Source of all Being, Eternal Word and Holy Spirit.
   —**My soul**...

CANTICLE OF MARY

Ant. Now you seek to kill me, a man who has told the truth which I heard from God.

INTERCESSIONS

O God of our ancestors, in Christ we are sisters and brothers to one another, and so we pray:
May we be one in you!

O God, you are a father to us;
   —help us to break down the barriers that keep us from respecting our differences.

You are a mother to us;
   —aid us in our efforts to care for our earth and to protect
   our environment for future generations.
You, most faithful companion, journey with us;
   —enable us to serve one another in humility.
You, Spirit of Life, breathe your life within us;
   —may all preparing for baptism find support in their
   faith communities.

PRAYER: God of love, you have called us to the life of
resurrection by raising us, in Christ, from the dead.
Strengthen us and those preparing for baptism to be
wholly given to the Easter mystery. We ask this is
Jesus' name. Amen.

FIFTH THURSDAY OF LENT
(Antiphons and Psalms from Week I, p. 29)

MORNING PRAYER

READING

True humility...is an outgrowth of a very different soil—a healthy mulch
of self-knowledge, of woundedness in the darkness of sin, coupled with
an intense awareness of the healing light of God's abiding presence and
love. The flower that grows out of this soil has a beauty and fragrance
that pierce the heavens, thus accomplishing the miracle that is finally
needed. The heavens must be pierced to that through the opening, no
matter how infinitesimal, a ray of divine light and love can escape... To
be a conduit for the all-penetrating, all-conquering rays of divine
love—this was God's original idea for all of us.

Mary Roman, OCD, "Christian: Wimp or Saint?," (4)

RESPONSORY

Christ, Chosen One of the living God, have mercy on us.
   —**Christ,**...
Delivered up to death on a cross, —**have mercy**...
Glory to you, Source of all Being, Eternal Word and Holy Spirit.
   —**Christ**...

CANTICLE OF ZECHARIAH

Ant. Jesus said to them: They who are of God hear the words of
God; the reason why you do not hear them is that you are
not of God.

INTERCESSIONS

Most loving God, you invite us to a covenantal relationship with you and with one another. In confidence we proclaim:
Your faithfulness will last forever!

You promise to keep your covenant with us throughout the ages;
  —give hope to children who do not experience love and care.
You give us the land as part of our inheritance;
  —may we design a future where peace will reign.
You gift us through our ancestors, our cultural heritage, and our relationships with one another;
  —bring us to a growing awareness of interdependence in
  our global family.
You mystify us in being the I AM, our God;
  —increase our faith in you, Holy Mystery, triune God.

PRAYER: God of mercy, you light up what is hidden in darkness and reveal the purposes of the heart. Give us the mind and heart of Christ that our thoughts and inclinations may lead to work worthy of you. Grant this in the power of Jesus' name. Amen.

DAYTIME PRAYER

Ant 1 The season of deliverance has come; the time of salvation is at hand.

Ant 2 Turn to me with all your heart, says our God.

Ant 3 Believing in God's strength and mercy, let us be fortified with patience.

(Prayer as in Morning Prayer)

EVENING PRAYER

READING

Teach us, O Lord, to pray truthfully in your name. Free us from our foolish trust in ourselves and in the works of our hands and minds. Help us to pray in absolute trust that whatever you send us is for our good; and help us to accept the surprising things for which we have not prayed. Give us the trust that all events, even suffering and death, are for us occasions to glorify you and, with you, the [One who sent you].

Bernard Häring, *Prayer: Integration of Faith and Life*, p. 30, (8)

RESPONSORY

My soul waits for God; in your word I hope. —**My soul...**
For with you there is steadfast love, —**in your**...
Glory to you, Source of all Being, Eternal Word and Holy Spirit.
   —**My soul**...

CANTICLE OF MARY

Ant. You are not yet fifty years old, and have you seen Abraham?
   Truly, I say to you, before Abraham was, I am.

INTERCESSIONS

Jesus, you are the way, the truth, and the life. In confidence we
say:
   May we walk in the light of your life.

Jesus, seeker of truth, you spoke your truth and yet they
attempted to stone you;
   —may we have the courage to speak honestly in the face of
   violence and oppression.
Jesus, sign of peace, your suffering gives us your gift of peace;
   —help us to transform our suffering and to recognize its
   redemptive qualities.
Jesus, seeker of justice, your life challenges all oppressors to face
their destructive ways;
   —may we be open to look at the subtle ways that we oppress
   one another.
Jesus, source of light, you are a beacon in our darkness;
   —enable all leaders within church communities to offer
   credible, just, and collegial leadership.

PRAYER: God of mercy, you light up what is hidden in darkness
   and reveal the purposes of the heart. Give us the mind
   and heart of Christ that our thoughts and inclinations
   may lead to work worthy of you. Grant this in the
   power of Jesus' name. Amen.

FIFTH FRIDAY OF LENT
(Antiphons and Psalms from Week I, p. 36)

MORNING PRAYER

READING

I do not find anything in the world, good or bad, for which we cannot bless God if we just examine it carefully. Doing this we will join the angels in glorifying and blessing God in all things as their source and ascribing them to either [God's] mercy or justice, for in both cases we find [God] worthy of praise.

Francisco de Osuna, The Third Spiritual Alphabet, p. 96, (1)

RESPONSORY

Christ, Chosen One of the living God, have mercy on us.
   —Christ,...
Delivered up to death on a cross, **—have mercy...**
Glory to you, Source of all Being, Eternal Word and Holy Spirit.
   —Christ...

CANTICLE OF ZECHARIAH

Ant. I have shown you many good works from the One who sent me. For which of these do you seek to kill me?

INTERCESSIONS

Your works, Christ Jesus, reflect the goodness of the Holy One who sent you. In faith let us pray:

Show us your mercy!

God of holiness, you give us the healing gifts of Jesus;
   —may all who experience the incurable illnesses of our day
     find comfort in your healing touch.
Most provident God, in Jesus we know the effects of fruitful ministry;
   —help us to work diligently and prayerfully to be signs of
     your living presence.
God of wonders, we marvel at the everyday miracles of life;
   —enable us to enter joyously and fully into our personal and
     communal commitments.
Spirit of God, you broke the bonds of death;
   —may all who die this day experience the fullness of life.

PRAYER: Everlasting God, you have brought us into union with Christ Jesus, who is our way to you. By him we have become your people and are set free. May we always rejoice in your love until we behold you in glory. Amen.

DAYTIME PRAYER

Ant 1 The season of deliverance has come; the time of salvation is at hand.

Ant 2 Turn to me with all your heart, says our God.

Ant 3 Believing in God's strength and mercy, let us be fortified with patience.

(Prayer as in Morning Prayer)

EVENING PRAYER

READING

I am more and more convinced that life is meant to be burdensome and toilsome and extraordinarily like traveling with an ox wagon in South Africa at the rate of about two miles a day.... So I am more doubtful about things that go smoothly than when they are troublesome from morning till night. Never mind, the arrival will be worth it all, and it is not so far now—to see [God's] overflowing gladness of welcome as each poor battered heart-sick child comes home for the everlasting homecoming, and to see all that [God] thought of the struggles and troubles, and accidents of the way. (Janet Erskine Stuart, RSCJ)

Maud Monahan, *Life and Letters of Janet Erskine Stuart*, p. 482, (15)

RESPONSORY

My soul waits for God; in your word I hope. —**My soul...**
For with you there is steadfast love, —**in your...**
Glory to you, Source of all Being, Eternal Word and Holy Spirit.
   —**My soul...**

CANTICLE OF MARY

Ant. If I do the works of God, even though you do not believe me, believe my works.

INTERCESSIONS

In the mystery of faith we are invited to be one with you, gracious God. In awe we pray:

You, O God, are our strength!

Jesus, you show us how much God, your father, loves us;
  —in times of doubt increase our faith.
You show us the love of God as mother;
  —enable health care ministers to show gentleness and love
  to all in their service, especially the dying.
You present God to us as a steadfast friend;
  —may we respond to the fullness of life to which we are
  called.
You reflect the image of the compassionate God;
  —help all teachers and leaders of youth to guide those
  under their care with justice and mercy.

PRAYER: Everlasting God, you have brought us into union with Christ Jesus, who is our way to you. By him we have become your people and are set free. May we always rejoice in your love until we behold you in glory. Amen.

FIFTH SATURDAY OF LENT
(Antiphons and Psalms from Week I, p. 43)

MORNING PRAYER

READING

I am impatient to send you a few hurried lines, rejoicing that our sorrowful meditations are at an end, and humbly imploring God to impart to us all some portion of those precious gifts and graces which our Dear Redeemer has purchased by His bitter sufferings, that we may endeavor to prove our love and gratitude by bearing some resemblance to Him, copying some of the lessons he has given us during His mortal life, particularly those of His passion.

The Correspondence of Catherine McAuley 1827–1841, No. 203, p. 220, (63)

RESPONSORY

Christ, Chosen One of the living God, have mercy on us.
  —Christ,...
Delivered up to death on a cross, **—have mercy...**

Glory to you, Source of all Being, Eternal Word and Holy Spirit.
—**Christ...**

CANTICLE OF ZECHARIAH

Ant. Jesus dies to bring together into one body all the scattered
children of God.

INTERCESSIONS

O God, you make your dwelling place with us and give us the
promise of your fidelity; in trust we proclaim:
You have redeemed us and set us free.

You promise to make a covenant of peace with us;
—enable all women and men to put aside their defenses
and weapons to make peace a reality.
Your dwelling place is with us in the midst of our struggles;
—give us the insight to recognize that you dwell with all your
people and that each person has the right to be treated
with respect and dignity.
You, indeed, are our God; there is no other God but you;
—help us to place our trust in you, to put aside the idols of
consumerism, and all that inhibits us from allowing you
to be our God.
You call us to a covenantal relationship as your people;
—may all who experience brokenness in relationships find
healing and forgiveness in their faith communities.

PRAYER: O God, Source of all blessings, we have not received
the spirit of the world but the Spirit which is from you.
May our lenten path of penance open us to a renewal of
life in the Spirit. We ask this in Jesus' name. Amen.

DAYTIME PRAYER

Ant 1 The season of deliverance has come; the time of salvation
is at hand.

Ant 2 Turn to me with all your heart, says our God.

Ant 3 Believing in God's strength and mercy, let us be fortified
with patience.

(Prayer as in Morning Prayer)

PASSION SUNDAY (PALM SUNDAY)
(Antiphons and Psalms from Week II, p. 47)

EVENING PRAYER I

READING

In its highest and most general sense, the doctrine of the Cross is that
to which all...adhere who believe that the vast movement and agitation
of human life opens on to a road which leads somewhere, and that road
climbs upward.... The final stages of the ascent to which it calls us
compel us to cross a threshold, a critical point, where we lost touch with
the zone of the realities of the senses.... Towards the peaks, shrouded in
mist from our human eyes, whither the Cross beckons us, we rise by a
path which is the way of universal progress. The royal road of the Cross
is no more nor less than the road of human endeavor supernaturally
righted and prolonged.

Teilhard de Chardin, *The Divine Milieu*, p. 102, p. 103, p. 103–104, (14)

RESPONSORY

We adore you, O Christ, and we bless you. **—We adore**...
By your death you redeemed the world, **—we bless**...
Glory to you, Source of all Being, Eternal Word and Holy Spirit.
　　—We adore...

CANTICLE OF MARY

Ant O Just One, the world has not known you, but I have known
　　you because you have sent me.

INTERCESSIONS

Jesus wept for his people in their blindness; he mourned their
future destruction. When his time had come he entered the city of
Jerusalem. Let us greet him saying:
　　Praise to you, O Christ, our Savior.

Jesus, many whom you had healed and consoled would betray
you;
　　—make us grateful for the gift of your life and death, and
　　keep us faithful to you.
Your disciples would leave you when glory changed to scorn;
　　—help us to sustain the cost of discipleship.
You received the praise of children and would not let them be
silenced;
　　—make us pure of heart, ever open to your truth.

You freely exchanged a political throne for the reign of love on the cross;
—give us the wisdom to know and the courage to live by the values of the gospel.

PRAYER: Jesus, our Savior, you came with a message of love and forgiveness; you offered us joy and fullness of life. Generation after generation we have scorned your love and destroyed your life among us. Have mercy on us. Let your Holy Spirit overcome our weakness that we may rise courageously to the challenge of following you. This we ask in your name, Eternal Word, one with the Source of all Being and with the Holy Spirit for all ages. Amen.

MORNING PRAYER
(Psalms from Sunday, Week II, p. 49)

Ant 1 Blessed is the One who comes in the name of our God! Peace in heaven and glory in the highest!

Ant 2 Now as they were eating, Jesus took bread and blessed, and broke it, and gave it to his friends and said, "Take, eat; this is my body."

Ant 3 Abba, all things are possible to you; remove this cup from me; yet not what I will, but what you will.

READING

The next day the great crowd that had come to the festival heard that Jesus was coming to Jerusalem. So they took branches of palm trees and went out to meet him, shouting, "Hosanna! Blessed is the one who comes in the name of [our God], the King of Israel!" Jesus found a young donkey and sat on it; as it is written: "Do not be afraid, daughter of Zion. Look, your king is coming, sitting on a donkey's colt!"

Jn 12:12–15

RESPONSORY

Hosanna on high, Christ our Savior.—**Hosanna**...
You gave your life for us; —**Christ**...
Glory to you, Source of all Being, Eternal Word and Holy Spirit.
—**Hosanna**...

CANTICLE OF ZECHARIAH

Ant The multitude, gathered for the feast, cried out: "Blessed be the one who comes in the name of our God! Hosanna in the highest!"

INTERCESSIONS

Jesus enters Jerusalem riding on a donkey; the people would make him king. Let us join the children and sing:
Hosanna to the Son of David!

Jesus, your kindom is not of this world;
　—help us to build here a world of justice and love.
You knew the hearts of those who hailed you as king;
　—show us our true selves and keep us faithful to you.
You came as giver of mercy and love and disdained a political crown;
　—bless our leaders with integrity and wisdom.
You declared your beliefs openly even in the face of death;
　—give us the courage to seek and live the truth no matter what the cost.

PRAYER: Jesus, our Savior, you came with a message of love and forgiveness; you offered us joy and fullness of life. Generation after generation we have scorned your love and destroyed your life among us. Have mercy on us. Let your Holy Spirit overcome our weakness that we may rise courageously to the challenge of following you. This we ask in your name, Eternal Word, one with the Source of all Being and with the Holy Spirit for all ages. Amen.

DAYTIME PRAYER

Ant 1 The Hebrew children bearing olive branches went out to meet Jesus, crying: "Hosanna in the highest!"

Ant 2 The people spread their garments on the road shouting: "Hosanna to the son of David! Blessed be the one who comes in the name of our God!"

Ant 3 To you, God, defender of my life, I have entrusted my cause.

(Prayer as in Morning Prayer)

EVENING PRAYER II

Ant 1 Let the greatest among you become as the least, and the leader as one who serves.

Ant 2 Christ Jesus, who, though he was in the form of God, did not count equality with God something to be grasped, but emptied himself, taking the form of a servant, being born in human likeness.

Ant 3 At the name of Jesus every knee should bow, in heaven, on earth and under the earth, and every tongue confess that Jesus Christ is Lord, to the glory of God.

READING

We are at the beginning of Holy Week. If we want truly to be Christian, this week ought to be a time when we share in a special way in the passion of Christ. We do this not so much by indulging in pious feelings, but by bearing the burdens of our life with simple fortitude and without ostentation. For we share by faith in the passion of our Lord precisely by realizing that our life is a participation in his destiny. We find this difficult, because so often we fail to understand that the bitterness and burden of our own life do—or should—give us a mysterious share in the destiny of all human beings.... If we were aware of this...we would understand that his passion is the unique acceptance of the passion of humankind, in which it is accepted, suffered, redeemed, and freed into the mystery of God.

Karl Rahner, *The Great Church Year*, pp. 140–41, (2)

RESPONSORY

We adore you, O Christ, and we bless you. —**We adore**...
By your death you redeemed the world; —**we bless**...
Glory to you, Source of all Being, Eternal Word and Holy Spirit.
—**We adore**...

CANTICLE OF MARY

Ant It is written: I will strike the shepherd, and the sheep of the flock will be dispersed. But after I have risen, I will go before you into Galilee. There you will see me.

INTERCESSIONS

Jesus wept for his people in their blindness; he mourned their future destruction. When his time had come he entered the city of Jerusalem. Let us greet him saying:

Praise to you, O Christ, our Savior.

Jesus, many whom you had healed and consoled would betray you;
　—make us grateful for the gift of your life and death and
　keep us faithful to you.
Your disciples would leave you when the glory changed to scorn;
　—help us to sustain the cost of discipleship.
You received the praise of children and would not let them be silenced;
　—make us pure of heart, ever open to your truth.
You freely exchanged a political throne for the reign of love on the cross;
　—give us the wisdom to know and the courage to live by the
　values of the gospel.

PRAYER: Jesus, our Savior, you came with a message of love and forgiveness; you offered us joy and fullness of life. Generation after generation we have scorned your love and destroyed your life among us. Have mercy on us. Let your Holy Spirit overcome our weakness that we may rise courageously to the challenge of following you. This we ask in your name, Eternal Word, one with the Source of all Being and with the Holy Spirit for all ages. Amen.

MONDAY OF HOLY WEEK
(Antiphons and Psalms from Week II, p. 55)

MORNING PRAYER

READING

...one understands so well now our dear Lord's prayer in Gethsemane, his fear, and his courage. But whatever happens in the future, it seems to me that in this which we are *now* experiencing, he is saying, "Fear not, it is I." I can't explain, but several times today, when I felt I could really cave in, suddenly, right in the midst of *myself,* his voice seemed to say that, "Fear not, it is I," and I felt vaguely that somehow or other our *becoming* Christ—the consummation of our love for him—has to take this form of knowing something of his Passion, so that even the feeling of fear, and the awful moments when one just wants to cry and cry like a child, need not shame us, because they are all part of Christ's own experience in us.

The Letters of Caryll Houselander, p. 23, (5)

RESPONSORY

Hosanna on high, Christ our Savior.—**Hosanna**...
You gave your life for us, —**Christ**...
Glory to you, Source of all Being, Eternal Word and Holy Spirit.
 —**Hosanna**...

CANTICLE OF ZECHARIAH

Ant. O God, glorify me in your presence with the glory I had with
   you before the world was made.

INTERCESSIONS

Jesus, you came a gentle savior, not breaking the bruised reed, not quenching the smoldering wick. We pray to you:
   Show us your mercy, O Christ.

Jesus, before your passion you welcomed the company of friends;
   —help us to recognize those in need of consolation and to
   know how to support them.
You let Mary anoint your feet with perfume in preparation for your
burial;
   —give us the grace to serve the sick selflessly.
You knew your time had come;
   —have mercy on those on death row who count the
   remaining days of their lives.

You hid from your enemies and could not walk freely in your own land;

   —give strength, patience, and courage to all who are in prison.

PRAYER: Jesus, on the eve of your passion and death, you found comfort in the company of your friends. In the truest sign of friendship, you gave your life for them and for us. Help us to live the call of the gospel more deeply. Let our relationship with one another be a sign of your presence. Help us to live and die in your love, that we may live with you forever. Amen.

DAYTIME PRAYER

Ant 1 With you at my side, of whom shall I be afraid?

Ant 2 O God, you have pleaded the cause of my soul; you the defender of my life.

Ant 3 My people, what have I done to you, or in what have I grieved you? Answer me.

(Prayer as in Morning Prayer)

EVENING PRAYER

READING

A true and faithful friend of God...will have [a heart] strengthened...to be able to carry the cross of Christ. All that such a person suffers is Christ's suffering and not our own. For we are one body in Christ in many members, united and bound together by the bond of love. Christ accepts such a person as part of his own body. He witnessed to this when he said..."whatever you do to the least of these my own, you do to me." The affliction of Christ must be fulfilled in every member until the suffering Christ is brought to completion. Just as Christ is the lamb who was slain since the beginning of the world, so he will also be crucified until the end of the world. In this way the body is perfected in length, width, depth, and height in the love of Christ. This passes all understanding, for in this Christ will be filled with all the fullness of God.

Hans Hut, *Early Anabaptist Spirituality*, p. 75, (1)

RESPONSORY

We adore you, O Christ, and we bless you. —**We adore**...
By your death you redeemed the world, —**we bless**...
Glory to you, Source of all Being, Eternal Word and Holy Spirit.
    —**We adore**...

CANTICLE OF MARY

Ant. You would have no power over me unless it were given you
    from above.

INTERCESSIONS

Six days before the Passover, Jesus came to Bethany, where
Lazarus was, whom Jesus had raised from the dead. Let us pray:
    We remember your mercies, O Christ.

Jesus, faithful to the end, you blessed the house of Lazarus;
    —give us the grace to live lovingly in union with one another.
You defended Mary and received her costly gift;
    —give us the wisdom to judge values in the light of your
    truth.
You would remain the faithful servant of God to the end;
    —give us all the gift of perseverance in following you.
You knew that your death would mean suffering for your friends;
    —give us the courage to follow God's will through all of the
    mystery of suffering for ourselves and others.

PRAYER: Jesus, on the eve of your passion and death, you found
    comfort in the company of your friends. In the truest
    sign of friendship, you gave your life for them and for
    us. Help us to live the call of the gospel more deeply.
    Let our relationship with one another be a sign of your
    presence. Help us to live and die in your love, that we
    may live with you forever. Amen.

TUESDAY OF HOLY WEEK
(Antiphons and Psalms from Week II, p. 62)
MORNING PRAYER

READING

The Christ who went to the poor like steel to a magnet was poor himself.
He was poor in his origins and in his birth, but even more so when he

left behind the uncertain but more or less stable life of a village
tradesman and took to wandering about the country without job, home,
or income. Yet finally even that was not enough, for cultural and
economic poverty only symbolize the deeper poverty of human beings.
The deepest poverty is the lack of God, and only a poor God could be
vulnerable enough to share that, a God who had 'emptied himself' and
become 'obedient even to death', as the poor have to be, who die young
at the will of others. The poor Christ is not just the wandering preacher
who had nowhere to sleep unless somebody took him in, he is above all
the one who died.

Rosemary Haughton, The Passionate God, p. 328, (1)

RESPONSORY

Hosanna on high, Christ our Savior.—**Hosanna**...
You gave your life for us, —**Christ**...
Glory to you, Source of all Being, Eternal Word and Holy Spirit.
　—**Hosanna**...

CANTICLE OF ZECHARIAH

Ant.　Before the festival day of the Passover, Jesus knew that his
hour had come to depart from this world. Having loved his
own who were in the world, he loved them to the end.

INTERCESSIONS

Jesus said to his disciples: Where I am going, you cannot follow
me now. Later on you shall come after me. Let us pray to him:
Draw us, we shall come after you.

Jesus, you knew that Peter would deny you three times, yet you
forgave him;
　—help us to be forgiving of one another.
All would betray you; your only refuge was in God;
　—be with us when we have no one to help us.
Your disciples were without understanding even to the end;
　—we praise you for your patience with us as we strive to
　　follow you.
You remained steadfast in your mission when all seemed doomed
to failure;
　—let us choose faithfulness to you above worldly success.

PRAYER: O God, we praise you in the gift of Jesus, given to us for
our salvation. We ask you to forgive us for our sins and

failings that prevent the coming of your reign and continue to nail his followers to a cross. Give us the grace to change our lives and to let the life of Jesus bear fruit in us. We ask this in his name. Amen.

DAYTIME PRAYER

Ant 1 With you at my side, of whom shall I be afraid?

Ant 2 O God, you have pleaded the cause of my soul; you the defender of my life.

Ant 3 My people, what have I done to you, or in what have I grieved you? Answer me.

(Prayer as in Morning Prayer)

EVENING PRAYER

READING

The cross is to be understood as God's solidarity with men and women in the condition of human suffering—not to eternalize it, but to suppress it. And the manner in which God seeks to suppress it is not by domination, but by love. Christ preached and lived this new dimension. He was rejected by a "world" oriented toward the preservation of power. He succumbed to these forces. But he never abandoned his project of love. The cross is the symbol of human power—and the symbol of Jesus' love and fidelity. Love is stronger than death, and power collapses before it. The loyalty of the cross, then, the love on the cross, has triumphed. The name for this is resurrection: a life stronger than the life of power, biological life, the life of the ego.

Leonardo Boff, *Passion of Christ, Passion of the World*, p. 110, (22)

RESPONSORY

We adore you, O Christ, and we bless you. —**We adore...**
By your death you redeemed the world, —**we bless...**
Glory to you, Source of all Being, Eternal Word and Holy Spirit.
  —**We adore...**

CANTICLE OF MARY

Ant. I have the power to lay my life down and I have power to take it up again.

INTERCESSIONS

Jesus, Truth itself, confronts the Prince of Lies. Let us pray:
O Christ, be our light.

O Christ, generation upon generation awaited your coming, and now you die unknown;
—keep us in your truth that we may never deny you.
You spent yourself in healing and preaching to the people;
—give us the generosity to serve you and others without seeking a reward.
You spent many nights in prayer during the time of your ministry;
—teach us to make prayer the foundation of our service to you.
You knew that your passion and death would pierce your mother's heart;
—bless all parents who suffer with their children.

PRAYER: O God, we praise you in the gift of Jesus, given to us for our salvation. We ask you to forgive us for our sins and failings that prevent the coming of your reign and continue to nail his followers to a cross. Give us the grace to change our lives and to let the life of Jesus bear fruit in us. We ask this in his name. Amen.

WEDNESDAY OF HOLY WEEK
(Antiphons and Psalms from Week II, p. 69)

MORNING PRAYER

READING

My title, the happy one given to me at my Profession, implies a life of crosses and afflictions.... (7 June 1870) The Cross is my portion, it is also my sweet rest and support. I could not be happy without it, I could not lay it down for all the world would give. With the Cross I am happy, but without it I would be lost. The only way I have of trying to show my gratitude to God for all that [God] has done for those I love, and for all in general, is in the cross. But I often fail in bearing it as I ought, and will do so still unless I am wonderfully aided by the prayers of others. (26 February 1872)

Bl. Mary MacKillop, RSJ, (10)

RESPONSORY

Hosanna on high, Christ our Savior.—**Hosanna**...
You gave your life for us, —**Christ**...
Glory to you, Source of all Being, Eternal Word and Holy Spirit.
—**Hosanna**...

CANTICLE OF ZECHARIAH

Ant. Simon, are you asleep? Could you not watch one hour with
me?

INTERCESSIONS

At the name of Jesus, every knee should bow, in heaven, on
earth, and under the earth. In adoration we proclaim:
Jesus Christ is Lord.

Jesus, you shared your bread with one who would betray you;
—teach us the ways of non-violence.
The betrayer broke your heart, but you did not condemn him;
—help us to give one another time to rise from weaknesses.
You were sold for thirty pieces of silver;
—give us the courage always to prefer you above all worldly
things.
You celebrated the paschal meal with your friends on the eve of
your death;
—as we share bread and wine with one another, renew our
desire for reconciliation with and reverence for all our
sisters and brothers.

PRAYER: Jesus, you spent the years of your ministry sharing
the word of God and your healing power with all who
would receive them. You approached your passion with
a heart broken by sorrow but overflowing with love for
God and for us. Have mercy on us. Keep us faithful to
your gospel that we may end our days faithful to you.
We ask this for the glory of your name. Amen.

DAYTIME PRAYER

Ant 1 With you at my side, of whom shall I be afraid?

Ant 2 O God, you have pleaded the cause of my soul; you the
defender of my life.

Ant 3 My people, what have I done to you, or in what have I grieved you? Answer me.

(Prayer as in Morning Prayer)

EVENING PRAYER

READING

For this we can say to the whole world, we have wronged no [one's] person or possessions, we have used no force nor violence against any [person], we have been found in no plots, nor guilty of sedition. When we have been wronged, we have not sought to revenge ourselves, we have not made resistance against authority, but wherein we could not obey for conscience' sake, we have suffered even the most of any people in the nation. We have been accounted as sheep for the slaughter, persecuted, and despised, beaten, stoned, wounded, stocked, whipped, imprisoned, haled out of synagogues, cast into dungeons and noisome vaults where many have died in bonds, shut up from our friends, denied needful sustenance for many days together, with other like cruelties.

George Fox, *Quaker Spirituality*, p. 106, (1)

RESPONSORY

We adore you, O Christ, and we bless you. —**We adore**...
By your death you redeemed the world, —**we bless**...
Glory to you, Source of all Being, Eternal Word and Holy Spirit.
   —**We adore**...

CANTICLE OF MARY

Ant. The woman said to Peter: Surely you are one of them for even your speech betrays you.

INTERCESSIONS

Your heart was broken with insults, O Christ. You looked for comfort and there was none. With contrite hearts. we pray:
        Come, let us adore.

Jesus, your love is stronger than death;
   —help us to overcome our selfishness; give us hearts of flesh.
Light of the world, you were forced to hide from your enemies;
   —bless all who are exiled for their works of justice.

You suffered the ignominy of a captured criminal;
—give us the creativity and generosity to improve the lives of all prisoners and to reverence their right to life.
You became obedient for us, even to death;
—give us the grace to seek and do the will of God all the days of our lives.

PRAYER: Jesus, you spent the years of your ministry sharing the word of God and your healing power with all who would receive them. You approached your passion with a heart broken by sorrow but overflowing with love for God and for us. Have mercy on us. Keep us faithful to your gospel that we may end our days faithful to you. We ask this for the glory of your name. Amen.

HOLY THURSDAY
(Antiphons and Psalms from Week II, p. 76)
MORNING PRAYER

READING

Enter into the mystery of being master and servant. Look at your neighbors and pick up the towel. With authority grounded in humility, kneel before them and wash off the dirt of daily living. If you are the neighbor in need of washing, lay aside your pride and, like Peter, accept the service of the one kneeling before you. Then go, and do likewise. Be blessed as you wash the feet of others and reveal the face of the Master through the towel in your hands.

Alma L. Maish, "Master and Servant," (4)

RESPONSORY

Hosanna on high, Christ our Savior.—**Hosanna**...
You gave your life for us, —**Christ**...
Glory to you, Source of all Being, Eternal Word and Holy Spirit.
—**Hosanna**...

CANTICLE OF ZECHARIAH

Ant. Now his betrayer had given them a sign, saying: "Whomsoever I kiss, that is he. Hold him!"

INTERCESSIONS

Jesus rose from supper and began to wash the feet of his
disciples, and so we pray:
                Free us from our sins.

You came to serve and not to be served;
   —help us to realize the nobility of serving you and one
      another.
In your final hours you were lonely, even among friends;
   —be present to all who face death alone and afraid.
You are the Good Shepherd, who dies for the sheep;
   —raise up leaders who will facilitate the processes that
      enable people to live wholesome lives.
The disciple whom you loved rested his head on your breast; he
would stand beneath the cross;
   —give us the grace to live and die faithful to your calling.

PRAYER: Christ Jesus, our Savior, you have given us a memorial
            of your life and death. As we are nourished by your
            body and blood, open our minds and hearts to your
            Spirit that we too may give ourselves totally to the
            salvation of your people. Let the bread of life make us
            one with you and with one another. Amen.

DAYTIME PRAYER

Ant 1 With you at my side, of whom shall I be afraid?

Ant 2 O God, you have pleaded the cause of my soul; you the
          defender of my life.

Ant 3 My people, what have I done to you, or in what have I
          grieved you? Answer me.
(Prayer as in Morning Prayer)

EVENING PRAYER
(Evening prayer is said only by those who do not participate
in the evening Eucharist)

READING

God did not intend the surrogacy roles [black women] have been forced
to perform. God did not intend the defilement of their bodies during the
slavocracy.... Rape is defilement, and defilement means wanton
desecration. Worse, deeper and more wounding than alienation, the sin

of defilement is the one of which today's technological world is most guilty. Nature...[is] every day defiled by humans.... The oceans are defiled by oil spills, and industrial waste destroys marine life. The rain forest is being defiled. The cross is a reminder of how humans have tried throughout history to destroy visions of righting relationships.... As Christians, black women cannot forget the cross, but neither can they glorify it. To do so is to glorify suffering and to render their exploitation sacred.

Delores S. Williams, Sisters in the Wilderness, pp. 166–67, (22)

In place of the responsory, the following is said:

Ant Christ Jesus humbled himself and became obedient unto death, even death on a cross.

CANTICLE OF MARY

Ant. Jesus said to them: "How I have longed to eat this Passover with you before I suffer, for I tell you I shall not eat it again until all is finished."

INTERCESSIONS

Jesus sat at table with his companions and said: I have earnestly desired to eat this Passover with you before I suffer. Let us pray:
> **How can we repay you for your goodness to us?**

You gave us your body and blood in the sacrament of thanksgiving;
—let this sign of your love transform us into true followers of your gospel.
You would shield your people as a mother hen hides her nestlings, but there was no one to comfort you in your suffering;
—forgive us and awaken us to the many who suffer from our mindless neglect.
You sweat blood in fear and sorrow for our sins;
—strengthen all who live in fear of any kind.
You asked that the cup of suffering might be removed from you, yet you acquiesced to God's will for you;
—let us always begin and complete all we do in accord with God's will for the salvation of our world.
You prayed that we all may be one as you are one with the One who sent you;
—make us instruments of your peace, signs of your love on earth.

PRAYER: Christ Jesus, our Savior, you have given us a memorial of your life and death. As we are nourished by your body and blood, open our minds and hearts to your Spirit that we too may give ourselves totally to the salvation of your people. Let the bread of life make us one with you and with one another. Amen.

GOOD FRIDAY

MORNING PRAYER

Ant 1 They divided my garments among them and for my vesture they cast lots. (Ps 51, p. 36)

Ant 2 Daughters of Jerusalem, weep not for me but for your children.

Canticle: Habakkuk 3:2–4, 13a, 15–19

O God, I have heard reports of
    you and your work, O God, I
    fear.
In the course of the years renew
    it;
In the course of the years make it
    known.
In your wrath remember mercy!

God came from Teman;
the Holy One from Mount Paran.
Your glory covered the heavens,
and the earth was full of your
    praise.

Your brightness was like the
    light,
rays flashed from your hand;
there you veiled your power.
You went forth for the salvation of
    your people,
to save the anointed.

You trampled the sea with your
    horses,
amid the surging of mighty
    waters.—

I hear, and my body trembles,
my lips quivered at the sound.

Decay enters into my bones,
my steps totter beneath me.
I will wait for the day of reckoning
to come upon the earth.

Though the fig tree does not
    blossom
nor fruit be on the vines,
the produce of the olive fail
and the fields yield no food,

the flock be cut off from the fold
and there be no herd in the stalls,
yet will I rejoice in you, Most
    High,
and rejoice in the God of my
    salvation.

For you, O God, are my strength;
you make my feet like hinds' feet,
and make me tread upon high
    places. **Glory...**

Ant 3 Truly, I say to you, today you will be with me in paradise.
(Ps 147:12–20, p. 85)

READING

The cry of Jesus on the cross at the very end was, therefore the cry of
awareness that all was indeed accomplished, brought to its
consummation. He knew that he could, at last, give back to the One he
loved the unshackled fullness of love, and in so doing *carry with him* on
the surge of that passion the love which is the essential being of all
creation. This is, in a sense, the moment of resurrection, or rather it is
the moment at which that process begins, for the resurrection is not a
single event but the ever-extending 'outflow' of the energy previously
dammed up by the power of sin and death.

Rosemary Haughton, The Passionate God, p. 153, (1)

In place of the responsory, the following is said:

Ant Christ Jesus humbled himself and became obedient unto
death, even death on a cross.

CANTICLE OF ZECHARIAH

Ant. Let every spirit praise you, Most Holy Trinity, who has given
us victory through the cross.

INTERCESSIONS

We adore you, O Christ, for by the wood of the cross, you brought
joy to the world:
> **Glory and praise to you, Lord Jesus Christ.**

Jesus, you were taken prisoner in the darkness of night; all your
friends abandoned you;
> —be with all who are abducted and strengthen all who
> mourn those who are missing.

You were crowned with thorns and beaten by soldiers;
> —help us to end torture throughout the world; have pity
> on those so afflicted.

Your face was covered with spittle and you wore a robe of shame;
> —heal the wounds that make us act less than human;
> remind us that we are made in the image of God.

You accepted the help of Simon and Veronica;
> —awaken us to the ways that we can help those who are
> suffering, and be grateful to those who minister to us.

Carrying your cross, you continued to show concern for others,
for those who would come after you;
   —let our burdens make us compassionate toward the
   burdens of others.

PRAYER: Merciful God, you so loved the world that you sent
Jesus to save us. He showed his love for us by his life
and his death on the cross. Give us the grace to
respond with all our minds and hearts with a love that
transforms us into a people worthy of you. Teach us to
live in you and for one another as Jesus taught us.
Amen.

DAYTIME PRAYER

Ant 1 And when they crucified him, they divided his garments
among them by casting lots; they sat down and kept watch
over him. (Ps 40:2–14, 17–18, p. 58)

Ant 2 Now at the sixth hour there was darkness over all the land.
(Ps 54:1–6, 8–9, p. 66)

Ant 3 Standing by the cross were the mother of Jesus and his
mother's sister, Mary, the wife of Clopas, and Mary
Magdalen. (Ps 88, p. 161)

(Prayer as in Morning Prayer)

EVENING PRAYER

Ant 1 Into your hands, O God, I commend my spirit.
(Ps 116:10–19, p. 96)

Ant 2 Behold the Lamb of God. (Ps 143:1–11, p. 172)

Ant 3 They took the body of Jesus, bound it in linen cloth and
spices and laid it in a tomb. (Phil 2:6–11, p. 96)

READING

...Jesus, on the Cross is both the symbol and the reality of the immense
labor of the centuries which has little by little, raised up the created
spirit and brought it back to the depths of the divine *milieu*. He
represents (and in a true sense, he is) creation, as, upheld by God, it
reascends the slopes of being, sometimes clinging to things for support,

sometimes tearing itself from them in order to pass beyond them, and always compensating, by physical suffering, for the setbacks caused by its moral downfalls.

Teilhard de Chardin, *The Divine Milieu*, p. 104, (14)

In place of the responsory, the following is said:

Ant Christ, for our sake, became obedient to death, even to death on a cross.

CANTICLE OF MARY

Ant. When Jesus had taken the wine he said: It is consummated! And bowing his head, he gave up his spirit.

INTERCESSIONS

Mary, the mother of Jesus, stood before the cross of her dying son, and so we pray:

Blessed is she who has believed.

Jesus, you entrusted the care of your mother to the disciple whom you loved;

—instill in us a deep respect and love for the aging and the abandoned.

You forgave Peter with a look of love and you promised the believing thief the fullness of life;

—give us undying faith in your mercy; let us never turn from you in our sins.

At your death, the veil of the temple was rent in two;

—protect your church from all blindness; keep us ever open to the truth that leads us forward.

You hung naked on the cross, at the mercy of those who reviled you;

—heal victims of rape and those who molest them. Give our society a respect for life.

In derision you were hailed as a king, king of fools;

—Ruler of the nations, bless all nations with just and wise leaders, that the people of the earth may become your glory.

PRAYER: Merciful God, you so loved the world that you sent Jesus to save us. He showed his love for us by his life and his death on the cross. Give us the grace to respond with all our minds and hearts with a love that

transforms us into a people worthy of you. Teach us to
live in you and for one another as Jesus taught us.
Amen.

HOLY SATURDAY

MORNING PRAYER

Ant 1   Truly he has borne our iniquities and carried our sorrows.
(Ps 64, p. 94)

Ant 2   Our Shepherd who led us to living waters is gone; at his
passing the sun was darkened.
(Is 38:10–14, 17–20, p. 63)

Ant 3   In peace I shall sleep and take my rest, for my body rests
in hope. (Ps 150, p. 50)

READING

We know from our own experience of pain, that it can free us for
creative transformation, or it can embitter us to the point of rebellion by
its lack of meaning. It can be destructive or creative. Whether suffering
becomes a source of creativity depends in part on how the individual
treats it and reacts to it. One of the outstanding marks of a mature
person is seeking value in the face of suffering. Never to seek the
suffering, but *its meaning* when suffering seeks us! For suffering *is* a
meaning. The instance of this that will forever be our hope is Christ's
despairing cry and prayer from the cross, "My God, why have you
forsaken me?" and that utterly tender surrender, "Into your hands I
commit my spirit." This is the one who on the very night that *he was
betrayed* gave himself for us. Betrayal can break a person, but Jesus
accepted being broken and told us plainly: "This body which is broken is
given for you."

Miriam Elder, OCD, (11)

In place of the responsory, the following is said:

Ant   Christ Jesus humbled himself and became obedient unto
death, even death on a cross. Therefore God also exalted him
and gave him a name above all other names.

CANTICLE OF ZECHARIAH

Ant.   The women sitting at the sepulcher were weeping and
lamenting.

INTERCESSIONS

The body of Jesus was taken from the cross and wrapped in a linen shroud and laid in a rock-hewn tomb, where no one had ever yet been laid. We cry to you:
Spare us, O God.

Jesus, your betrayer despaired of your love;
—let us never lose hope of forgiveness, however grave our
 guilt.
Your mother held your broken body; her heart was pierced with sorrow;
—have pity on all mothers who must bury their children or
 lose them by abduction.
Jesus, covered with wounds, you died for a wounded world;
—heal us, bring light out of our darkness, let us know the
 things that are to our peace.
One with the Creator of the earth, by your burial you became one with the earth;
—teach us to reverence our earth and all its resources.
The women who had followed you prepared spices for your anointing;
—bless all women who minister to your people at the risk
 of their reputations and their lives.

PRAYER: O God, by his life and his death on the cross, Jesus
              has revealed the depth of your love for us. One in
              our flesh, he became one in our dying and burial.
              Have mercy on us, forgive us our sins, and once again
              call us to life that we may be one with him in his
              resurrection. This we ask through Jesus, who lives and
              reigns with you and the Holy Spirit, one God, forever.
              Amen.

DAYTIME PRAYER

Ant 1 They shall mourn for him as for an only child; for the
          savior who is innocent has been slain! (Ps 27, p. 26)

Ant 2 O death, I will be your death! Hell, I will be your
          destruction! (Ps 30, p. 33)

Ant 3 I know that my Redeemer lives and in my flesh I shall see God. (Ps 76, p. 52)

(Prayer as in Morning Prayer)

EVENING PRAYER

Ant 1 Now in the place where Jesus was crucified there was a garden, and in the garden a new tomb where no one had ever lain. (Ps 116:10–19, p. 96)

Ant 2 The women who had come from Galilee followed, and saw the tomb and how the body was laid. Then they returned and prepared spices and ointments. (Ps 143:1–11, p. 172)

Ant 3 Joseph of Arimathea laid the body in his own new tomb, rolled a great stone to the door of the tomb and departed. (Phil 2:6–11, p. 96)

READING

When we call upon Christ the Redeemer, we join our efforts with his intention to free [humankind] from the slavery of sin and the sin of slavery. We pray in his name for the great gift of the liberty of the sons and daughters of God. Christ is the redeemer not only of souls and of separate individuals; he is the redeemer of the whole person and of the whole world. He wants to restore [our] wholeness and liberty.... We can pray and act in the name of Christ the Redeemer when we are truly freeing ourselves and are working not only for an individualized freedom but for freedom for all, especially those most oppressed, most discriminated against and outcast.

Bernard Häring, Prayer: The Integration of Faith and Life, p. 38, (8)

In place of the responsory, the following is said:

Ant Christ Jesus humbled himself and became obedient unto death, even death on a cross. Therefore God also exalted him and gave him a name above all other names.

CANTICLE OF MARY

Ant. After three days I will rise again.

INTERCESSIONS

Jesus, son of God, come to set us free, lies bound in the earth. All who hoped in him await a new day, and so we pray:
O Christ, deliver us.

Jesus, you died to set us free;
—give true freedom to those bound because of race, sex, creed, or way of life.
You died that we might have life to the full;
—inspire and encourage women in their quest for equality.
You died revealing God's love for us;
—enlighten those who have no love for themselves; befriend and heal them.
You died leaving your mother in the care of another;
—bless those who leave all to serve you in their respective ways of life; encourage and comfort their families.
Death released you from the agony of the cross;
—be present to all who are ill; have pity on the elderly and the dying.

PRAYER: O God, by his life and his death on the cross, Jesus has revealed the depth of your love for us. One in our flesh, he became one in our dying and burial. Have mercy on us, forgive us our sins, and once again call us to life that we may be one with him in his resurrection. This we ask through Jesus, who lives and reigns with you and the Holy Spirit, one God, forever. Amen.

CALENDAR OF FEASTS

December 1
CHARLES de FOUCAULD

MORNING/EVENING PRAYER
(Psalms from Sunday, Week I, p. 3)

Ant 1 Prepare the way. Make straight in the desert a highway for our God.

Ant 2 Take no gold, nor silver, nor copper in your belts, no bag for your journey, nor two tunics, nor sandals, nor a staff.

Ant 3 When you pray, go into your room and shut the door and pray to your God in secret.

READING

I have known the balm of solitude at all times—ever since I was twenty years old and could enjoy it. Even in the days when I was not a believing Christian, I relished the solitude of nature and now I do so all the more. I appreciate that, deprived of human company, one is never alone. The soul is not made for noise, but for quiet meditation, and life must be a preparation for heaven, not only by worthwhile actions but by contemplation of God. (Charles de Foucauld)

Ronald Victor Courtenay Bodley, *The Warrior Saint*, p. 250, (37)

RESPONSORY

In your presence, O God, I will find all my joy. —**In your**...
When I see you face to face, —**I will**...
Glory to you, Source of all Being, Eternal Word and Holy Spirit.
   —**In your**...

CANTICLE

Ant Christ I proclaim, not by my voice, but by my way of living!

INTERCESSIONS

Charles was orphaned at the age of six;
   —instill a sense of belonging in all children left orphaned
      either physically or psychologically.
A Trappist in three different monasteries, a Franciscan tertiary, a hermit who could not stay in one hermitage, a founder of a religious order which no one of his day would join, a priest without a parish;
   —bless the seeker in each of us and companion those called
      to walk beyond familiar structures for the sake of the Gospel.

Charles became the Christ to nomadic and marginal peoples in
the Sahara;
   —give us generous hearts to embrace all who are outcast or
      marginalized by society.
An explorer and a writer, Charles also served with great
dedication and discipline as a soldier in the military;
   —protect all who serve their countries in military duty.
Charles was murdered at the hands of tribal raiders;
   —give us a spirit of forgiveness toward people who victimize
      those who serve them. Free us from the temptation to seek
      vengeance.

PRAYER: O God, you inspire us through the lives of those who
         embrace the gospel of Jesus and reflect his life and his
         love. Bless all who seek to serve you in unconventional
         paths and give them the courage to follow their vision.
         Strengthen them and give them peace of heart in the
         face of misunderstanding. We ask this in the name of
         Jesus who has shown us the way. Amen.

December 2
MAURA CLARKE, MM, ITA FORD, MM,
DOROTHY KAZEL, OSU, AND JEAN DONOVAN

MORNING/EVENING PRAYER

Ant 1 Our lips will praise you, for sweeter than life is your
       merciful love. (Jer 14:17–21, p. 132)

Ant 2 They girded themselves with your strength. The light they
       have kindled will never go out. (Ps 72, p. 81)

Ant 3 Give them the reward of their deeds, for they served you in
       the poor. (Ps 72, II, p. 81)

READING

On the evening of December 2, 1980, two Maryknoll Sisters, Maura
Clarke and Ita Ford, were returning to El Salvador from a retreat in
Nicaragua. They were picked up at the airport by an Ursuline Sister,
Dorothy Kazel, and a young lay woman, Jean Donovan, who worked in
the refugee camps. On the road from the airport, they were stopped at a
military roadblock. They were taken to a remote spot along a side road,
brutally abused, and then executed. They have become part of the
martyrology of the Christian communities throughout Latin America. In

her eulogy, Sr. Melinda Roper of Maryknoll said: "...God, in His/Her loving kindness, has raised up witnesses in our midst. God is calling each of us to a more radical discipleship—one which will not be understood by the powerful of our day. We must be wise as serpents in naming and denouncing the evil which pervades our world. We must be filled with compassion for those for whom suffering from lack of basic necessities has become a way of life. We must be moved to action which will clearly identify us with the poor. Above all, let us not be filled with fear. Let us be filled with courage and hope, for "in the tender compassion of our God, the dawn shall break upon us, to shine on those who dwell in darkness and the shadow of death, to guide our feet into the way of peace."

RESPONSORY

Our God is a stronghold for the oppressed, a stronghold in times
   of trouble. — **Our**...
Those who know your name put their trust in you; —**a stronghold**...
Glory to you, Source of all Being, Eternal Word and Holy Spirit.
   — **Our God**...

CANTICLE

Ant You shall love your God with all your heart, and with all your
   soul and with all your mind, and your neighbor as yourself.
   Do this and you will live.

INTERCESSIONS

O God, you have inspired many women to follow Jesus, your
Incarnate Word, who gave his life that we may have life. We lift
our voices and say:
   **Blessed are they who suffer persecution for
   the sake of the gospel.**

Through the witness of Maura Clarke, Ita Ford, Dorothy Kazel,
and Jean Donovan;
   —may more people be inspired to serve the homeless and the
      oppressed.
May all who have died in Latin America for the sake of justice;
   —be seeds of liberty for all the oppressed.
God of freedom, protect the poor and the helpless;
   —from the greed of large corporations and those seeking
      personal profit.

Jesus, you lived in a land held captive by imperial Rome;
—grant all peoples the right of self-determination that they
may forge their own destinies.
God of the Americas, Christ of the Andes, Our Lady of Guadalupe;
—look with love and compassion on the peoples of Central
and South America, and grant them freedom from all
oppression.

PRAYER: O God, Lover of the poor and oppressed, in our
remembrance of these four courageous women, may we
honor all the nameless women, men, and children
whose lives were forfeited by violence and hatred. May
they now know your peace and the joy of seeing you
face to face. We ask this through the intercession of all
these victims who now stand before the Lamb, singing
your praises. Amen.

December 3
ST. FRANCIS XAVIER

MORNING/EVENING PRAYER
(Psalms from Sunday, Week I, p. 3)

Ant 1 How beautiful upon the mountains are the feet of those
who bring glad tidings.

Ant 2 I will change the speech of the peoples to a pure speech,
that all of them may call on the name of God.

Ant 3 O God, your love overwhelmed me, and I was conquered.
In my heart was kindled a burning fire.

READING

At some convenient time each day I shall occupy myself for an hour or
more with the following points. First, I am to cultivate great humility in
my preaching, attributing all the good of it to God very perfectly.
Secondly, I shall keep before my eyes the good people who listen to me,
remembering that it is God who gives them the devotion to hear me out,
and to me the devotion to preach. Thirdly, I must strive to acquire a
great love for my people, remembering the obligation I bear towards
them.... Fourthly, I shall consider how the grace of being able to preach
comes to me through the prayers and merits of my brethren in the
Society who with humble, charitable love beg God's blessing on the
efforts of such as myself, for the greater glory of God and the salvation of
souls.... I shall beg God earnestly to make me realize the obstacles

which I put in the way of those who might make better use of me but have to refrain because I am what I am.... Before God who sees into the hearts of [all] I shall humble myself mightily, and take the very greatest care never to be a cause of scandal to the people in my preaching or my conversation or my work....

James Brodrick, SJ, St. Francis Xavier, pp. 478–79, (16)

RESPONSORY

All nations shall come to adore you and glorify your name: you who
    alone are God. **—All nations**...
For you are great and do marvelous deeds; **—you who**...
Glory to you, Source of all Being, Eternal Word and Holy Spirit.
    —All nations...

CANTICLE

Ant As long as I was with them, I guarded them with your name
    which you gave me.

INTERCESSIONS

O God, you sent Francis to preach the good news to the nations of
the Indies;
    —may we also preach the gospel with our lives.
Francis touched others by his cheerfulness and happy
disposition;
    —may our hope in you enable us to bring new life and comfort
      to others.
Francis worked tirelessly for the instruction of children and for
the care of the sick;
    —give us the wisdom to heal the wound of child abuse and
      lack of health care that mars our society.
With only one Brother for his company in the midst of persecuting
enemies, Francis labored day and night for the good of others;
    —in times of loneliness and distress, help us to remember
      your presence in our lives, and uphold us in your service.

PRAYER: God our Creator, you sent Francis Xavier to make
known your unbounded love to the peoples of the East.
As we honor him today, grant us some part of his zeal
for your glory, his love for the poor, and his constant
fidelity to your call. Let our lives bear fruit in the
spread of your gospel and the salvation of others. We
ask this in Jesus' name. Amen.

December 8
IMMACULATE CONCEPTION
EVENING PRAYER I

Ant 1 God has done marvelous deeds, let us sing a new song to
the Most High. (Ps. 113, p. 96)

Ant 2 You have called me, O God, to serve you in holiness.
(Ps. 147:12–20, p. 85)

Ant 3 Mother of mercy and holy hope, be near to those who pray
to you. (Eph. 1:3–10, p. 61)

READING

Mary is...an outsider brought in to the center of the story by the power
of God, the unexpected "non-person" who brought the messiah to life. In
this context, the virginal conception of Jesus as presented in Matthew
is, at the most profound theological level, an insight into the strange
patterns of history: God working to bring about salvation through people
and circumstances that secure and self-satisfied human beings tend to
ignore or disparage. Narrative remembrance of *this* Mary rearranges
one's vision of what is possible despite hardened historical "givens" and
turns "outsiders" toward action on behalf of their own dignity.

Elizabeth A. Johnson, "Reconstructing a Theology of Mary," p. 82, (1)

RESPONSORY

O Mary, Mother of the Christ, intercede for us. **—O Mary**...
God preserved you from sin; **—intercede**...
Glory to you, Source of all Being, Eternal Word and Holy Spirit.
  —O Mary...

CANTICLE OF MARY

Ant You who are mighty have made me great; holy be your name.

INTERCESSIONS

Let us praise God who has given us Mary as a model of holiness.
We pray to her:
  Mother of Christ, teach us to hear the word of God.

O Christ, be praised in Mary, comforter of the afflicted;
  —teach us to be a healing presence in the lives of others.
Be praised in Mary, queen of martyrs;
  —let all who bear the cross for your name's sake know her
  help and protection.

Be praised in Mary, queen of confessors;
—let all who confess your name in word or deed find justice
and encouragement in the church.
Be praised in Mary, queen of peace;
—give us forgiving hearts and bless our world with the peace
that only you can give.

PRAYER: O God, you have given us Mary, the mother of Jesus,
to encourage and guide us on our way to union with
you. Let her life of loving obedience and humble prayer
be a beacon of light and courage for us as we seek to
follow your Christ. This we ask in the name of that
same Jesus Christ, the Eternal Word, who lives with
you and with the Holy Spirit, forever. Amen.

MORNING PRAYER
(Psalms from Sunday, Week I, p. 3)

Ant 1 Mother of the Word Incarnate, through you we received the
Bread of Life.

Ant 2 Mother of the Word Incarnate, your holy womb was the
chalice of our salvation.

Ant 3 Mother of the Word Incarnate, you gave us the body and
blood of Jesus, the Christ, the Holy One of God.

READING

Mary exemplifies how the Christian man and woman must shape their
life during the quest for meaning and fulfillment.... She is the kind of
person who listens to the word of God, ponders it in her heart, and
keeps it despite difficulties. She recognizes the call of God—that
movement of the Spirit which all humans can recognize, be they
Christian or non-Christian, in the things of creation, the things that
happen in life, which are the call of being (Heidegger) or the voice of
God.... She perseveres through the cross to the resurrection, through
difficulties to meaning—and not only to delayed gratification. She sows
and reaps, but goes deeper into her human soil than superficial
gratifications.

Walter Brennan, OSM, *The Sacred Memory of Mary*, pp. 91–92, (1)

RESPONSORY

You have made me a vessel of salvation; a font of living water.
—You have...

Within my womb springs forth **—a font**...
Glory to you, Source of all Being, Eternal Word and Holy Spirit.
   —You have...

CANTICLE OF ZECHARIAH

Ant   O Mary, you are the Dawn; through you all creation will see
      the Light of the World.

INTERCESSIONS

Let us praise the Holy Spirit who throughout the centuries has
inspired the faithful to call upon God through the intercession of
Mary:
      Lead us in the way of truth.

O God, be praised through Mary, help of Christians;
   —help us all to proclaim the gospel with our lives.
Be praised through Mary, refuge of sinners;
   —teach us to support one another in our efforts to follow
      your will.
Be praised in Mary, ark of the covenant;
   —let our lives bear witness to your abiding presence in us.
Be praised in Mary, mother of good counsel;
   —form us to be discerning people.

PRAYER: O God, you have given us Mary, the mother of Jesus,
      to encourage and guide us on our way to union with
      you. Let her life of loving obedience and humble prayer
      be a beacon of light and courage for us as we seek to
      follow your Christ. This we ask in the name of that
      same Jesus Christ, the Eternal Word, who lives with
      you and with the Holy Spirit, forever. Amen.

DAYTIME PRAYER

Ant 1   Blessed are you, O Mary, for in you God's promise was
      fulfilled. (Ps. 120, p. 155)

Ant 2   Rejoice, O highly favored daughter; the Holy Spirit has
      overshadowed you. (Ps. 121, p. 89)

Ant 3   Blessed are you above all God's people; in you the Word
      became flesh. (Ps. 131, p. 116)

(Prayer as in Morning Prayer)

EVENING PRAYER II

Ant 1 God has raised up the lowly and filled the hungry with good things. (Ps. 122, p. 143)

Ant 2 Blessed are you among women, and blessed is the fruit of your womb. (Ps. 127, p. 122)

Ant 3 You are the new Eve, the beginning of a new creation. (Eph. 1:3–10, p. 109)

READING

...to think of Mary today as a model of faith in the pilgrim church is to think of her as a model for all Christians, women and men, in the journey of faith. This understanding of Mary as a model of the Christian on the path from unbelief to belief, a model of the slow and often painful growth of faith as it discerns responsible action in the tangled web of human life in time, can truly represent the pilgrim church today. A new, fully human understanding of Mary as the one who receives and communicates the grace of Christ in the Spirit corresponds with the description of the church as pilgrim, and all of us as persons in the community that is on the way.

We can appreciate the images of the past tradition about Mary, reading in them the history of Christ's church and of human perceptions of the life of the Spirit in the church. And we can add to that tradition the understanding of Mary today as fully human, growing in faith, receptive to the Spirit of Christ, a saint in the communion of saints.

Anne Carr, "Mary: Model of Faith," p. 20, (1)

RESPONSORY

You are the mother of holy hope, the glory of Jerusalem **—You**...
The fairest daughter of Israel; **—the glory**...
Glory to you, Source of all Being, Eternal Word and Holy Spirit.
    —You...

CANTICLE OF MARY

Ant In you all women have been blessed; in you all creation has found hope.

INTERCESSIONS

Let us praise God who has given us Mary as a model of holiness. We pray to her:
      Mother of Christ, teach us to hear the word of God.

O Christ, be praised in Mary, comforter of the afflicted;
  —teach us to be a healing presence in the lives of others.
Be praised in Mary, queen of martyrs;
  —let all who bear the cross for your name's sake know her
    help and protection.
Be praised in Mary, queen of confessors;
  —let all who confess your name in word or deed find justice
    and encouragement in the church.
Be praised in Mary, queen of peace;
  —give us forgiving hearts and bless our world with the peace
    that only you can give.

PRAYER: O God, you have given us Mary, the mother of Jesus,
         to encourage and guide us on our way to union with
         you. Let her life of loving obedience and humble prayer
         be a beacon of light and courage for us as we seek to
         follow your Christ. This we ask in the name of that
         same Jesus Christ, the Eternal Word, who lives with
         you and with the Holy Spirit, forever. Amen.

December 10
THOMAS MERTON

MORNING/EVENING PRAYER
(Psalms from Sunday, Week I, p. 3)

Ant 1 Blessed are the peacemakers for they shall be called
children of God.

Ant 2 You made us for yourself, O God; our hearts are restless
until they rest in you.

Ant 3 I lift up my eyes to your holy mountain.

READING

It would perhaps be too much to say that the world needs another
movement such as that which drew these [hermits] into the deserts of
Egypt and Palestine.... We cannot do exactly what they did. But we must
be as thorough and as ruthless in our determination to break all
spiritual chains, and cast off the domination of alien compulsions, to
find our true selves, to discover and develop our inalienable spiritual
liberty and use it to build, on earth, the [Kindom] of God. This is not the
place in which to speculate what our great and mysterious vocation
might involve. That is still unknown. Let it suffice for me to say that we

need to learn from these [people of the desert] of the fourth century how to ignore prejudice, defy compulsion and strike out fearlessly into the unknown.

Thomas Merton, The Wisdom of the Desert, p. 23, p. 24, (16)

RESPONSORY

I have trusted in your steadfast love. **—I have**...
My heart shall rejoice in your salvation, **—in your**...
Glory to you, Source of all Being, Eternal Word and Holy Spirit.
　—I have...

CANTICLE

Ant Wisdom is radiant and unfading, easily discerned by those
　　who love her, and found by those who seek her.

INTERCESSIONS

Strengthen those whose unique service to humanity is a life of
contemplation;
　　—that others may be encouraged to seek intimacy with God
　　in the way they are called.
Encourage us to go beyond clear and comfortable ideas of God;
　　—to a deeper trust, purer love, and more complete surrender
　　to One beyond our understanding.
Lead us through contemplation to spiritual understanding,
freedom, and a new capacity to love;
　　—that our action in and for the world may spring from you.
Help us to value prayer and solitude;
　　—that we may live in your presence and always walk in
　　truth.

PRAYER:　O God, enable us to live in the love that invites us to
　　　　union with you and all creation. May we be enriched by
　　　　the depths that contemplative love unfolds for us in our
　　　　world and have the courage to surrender in total
　　　　freedom to the God of our life. Amen.

December 12
OUR LADY OF GUADALUPE

MORNING/EVENING PRAYER

Ant 1 I am the ever-virgin Mary, Mother of the God who gives life
　　and maintains it. (Ps 113, p. 96)

Ant 2 I will show my compassion to your people and to all
        people. (Ps 147:12–20, p. 85)

Ant 3 What is troubling you, my little one? Are you not under my
        protection? (Eph 1:3–10, p. 61)

READING

Of the forty-five popes who have reigned since the creation of the
miraculous portrait (of Our Lady of Guadalupe), twenty-five have issued
decrees concerning it. The earliest recorded decree is that of Pope
Gregory XIII, dated 1575, that extended the indulgences granted by his
predecessors. This implies that indulgences were granted shortly after
the apparitions of 1531. Our Lady of Guadalupe was appointed National
Patroness by Pope Benedict XIV in 1754. December 12 was set aside as
a Day of Obligation, with an octave which could be celebrated with a
special Mass and Office. The same pontiff wrote: "In the image
everything is miraculous, an image emanating from flowers gathered on
completely barren soil on which only prickly shrubs can grow...an image
in no manner deteriorated, neither in her supreme loveliness nor in its
sparkling color...God has not done likewise to any other nation."

Joan Carroll Cruz, Miraculous Images of Our Lady, p. 296, (53)

RESPONSORY

Hail Mary, full of grace, the Lord is with you. **—Hail Mary**...
Blessed are you among women; **—the Lord**...
Glory to you, Source of all Being, Eternal Word and Holy Spirit.
    —Hail Mary...

CANTICLE

Ant From this day all generations will call me blessed.

INTERCESSIONS

O God, through Mary, our Mother, you revealed your compassion
to the Hispanic people;
    —bless all peoples with the awareness of your tender mercy.
O God, you choose the anawim of the world to confound the
mighty;
    —give us true humility of spirit.
The image of the Mother and your Son was imprinted on the
garment of Juan Diego with features of his race;
    —imprint within us a fearless acceptance of all races and
        peoples.

In Jesus, the Incarnate Word, you have showed us that you are
ever close to us;
    —have mercy on the downtrodden, the abused and
      neglected of the world.
Through Juan Diego, you showed your love for the simple and the
humble;
    —forgive us for the injustices imposed on native peoples of
      the earth and redress the wrongs they have suffered.

PRAYER: O God, of infinite compassion, you have revealed your
most tender mercy in the consoling words spoken to
your servant, Juan Diego, by our Lady of Guadalupe.
Bless all the native peoples of the Americas and of
every land and may we all come to realize that our true
and lasting integrity is in Jesus, our loving Savior.
Amen.

December 14
ST. JOHN OF THE CROSS

MORNING/EVENING PRAYER
(Psalms from Sunday, Week I, p. 3)

Ant 1 O living flame of love.... How gently and lovingly You wake
in my heart, where in secret You dwell alone.

Ant 2 Pouring out a thousand graces, he passed these groves in
haste; and having looked at them, with his image alone,
clothed them in beauty.

Ant 3 O guiding night! O night more lovely than the dawn! O
night that has united the Lover with His beloved,
transforming the beloved in her Lover.

READING

Mine are the heavens and mine is the earth. Mine are the nations, the
just are mine, and mine the sinners. The angels are mine, and the
Mother of God, and all things are mine; and God...is mine and for me,
because Christ is mine and all for me. What do you ask, then, and seek,
my soul? Yours is all of this, and all is for you. Do not engage yourself in
something less, nor pay heed to the crumbs which fall from [the] table.
Go forth and exult in your Glory! Hide yourself in It and rejoice, and you
will obtain the supplications of your heart.
      "Prayer of a Soul Taken with Love" in *The Collected Works of St. John of the Cross*, pp. 87–88, (3)

RESPONSORY

As the lover in the beloved, each lived in the other. **—As the**...
And the Love that unites them is one with them, **—each**...
Glory to you, Source of all Being, Eternal Word and Holy Spirit.
    —As the...

CANTICLE

Ant   O spring like crystal! If only, on your silvered-over face, You
would suddenly form the eyes I have desired, which I bear
sketched deep within my heart. (*The Spiritual Canticle* #12)

INTERCESSIONS

The son of a poor widow, John served the sick poor with tender
compassion;
    —may our own suffering inspire us to understand and
      support others in their pain.
He sought Truth in the Inspired Word through study and in the
depth of his heart through prayer;
    —help us to realize the life of Your Spirit within us.
You blessed John with the gift of contemplative prayer and the
ability to instruct others in the ways of prayer;
    —give us the grace to persevere in prayer and to desire its
      fruits.
John's disciplined life yielded a spirit of deep joy for himself and
for those he served;
    —lead us in the way of true and lasting happiness.
Imprisoned and abused, he forgave his tormentors;
    —may we also be numbered among those who thus imitate
      the crucified.

PRAYER: O God, you blessed John of the Cross with a love for
you that burst forth into a flame that burns brightly in
our lives. We thank you for the inspiration of his life
and for his writings. Grant us a share in his spirit, that
our lives, too, may enrich and heal a needy world. We
ask this in the name of Jesus for the glory of your
name. Amen.

January 4
ST. ELIZABETH ANN BAYLEY SETON

MORNING/EVENING PRAYER
(Psalms from Sunday, Week I, p. 3)

Ant 1 God has done great things for me; may God be forever praised, alleluia.

Ant 2 The valiant woman is a pearl of great price—all generations will call her blessed, alleluia.

Ant 3 What you have done for the least of my sisters and brothers, you have done for me, alleluia.

READING

Elizabeth Seton, widow, mother, and convert to Roman Catholicism, is the first native born American saint. She founded the American Sisters of Charity, established the first free Catholic day school, and opened the first Catholic orphanage. She was known for her works of mercy and charity. She wrote: "...You know I am as a mother encompassed by many children of different dispositions, not all equally amiable or congenial; but bound to love, instruct and provide for the happiness of all, to give the example of cheerfulness, peace, resignation, and consider individuals more as proceeding from the same origin and tending to the same end than in the different shades of merit or demerit."* Elizabeth Seton died January 4, 1821.

*Joseph Dirvin, *Mrs. Seton*, p. 287, (30)

RESPONSORY

Those who sow in tears shall reap with shouts of joy. —**Those**...
She who goes forth weeping; —**shall**...
Glory to you, Source of all Being, Eternal Word and Holy Spirit.
   —**Those**...

CANTICLE

Ant Many waters cannot quench love, neither can floods drown it.

INTERCESSIONS

O God, you raised up Elizabeth Seton to be an inspiration for many. In thanksgiving for the gift of her life, we pray:
Blessed be God forever!

Elizabeth Seton was widowed at an early age;
   —may all who sorrow and are lonely be comforted.
She was the mother of five children;
   —grant those entrusted with the rearing of children the wisdom
     to guide them.
Through the intercession of Elizabeth Seton, a convert to
Catholicism;
   —may we come to more understanding of and appreciation for
     our differences in our efforts to live the gospel.
You inspired her to found the Sisters of Charity;
   —help us to be faithful to our religious commitment, that we
     may be transformed into Christ.
You filled her with zeal for the education of youth;
   —guide all teachers and educators to enable students to grow
     in knowledge and to become good citizens of the earth and
     heirs of heaven.

PRAYER: O God, we give you thanks for the life of Elizabeth
              Seton. May the values she cherished be realized in our
              world that all may enjoy a better quality of life. May the
              holiness of her life inspire us to serve you and work
              only for your glory. Bless all the Sisters of Charity that
              they may faithfully continue the work she began. We
              ask this in the name of Jesus. Amen.

January 5
ST. JOHN NEUMANN

MORNING/EVENING PRAYER
(Psalms from Sunday, Week I, p. 3)

Ant 1 I will give you shepherds after my own heart; they will
           nourish you with knowledge and sound teaching.

Ant 2 I shall feed my flock; I shall search for the lost and lead
           back those who have strayed.

Ant 3 My life is at the service of the Gospel; God has given me
           this grace.

READING

St. John Nepomucene Neumann was born in Bohemia in 1811. He came
to the United States as a missionary cleric and was ordained in New

York in 1836. He entered the Congregation of the Most Holy Redeemer, and in 1852 he was consecrated bishop of Philadelphia where he promoted the establishment of public schools and founded many parishes for the numerous immigrants. Devoted as he was to these endeavors, he was noted even more for his care of the poor. "One class of people were his special concern—the poor. His generosity to them became so proverbial that those working in the rectory complained that the poor imposed upon him, oftentimes overdoing appeals for aid. He had a skillful way of slipping money into the hands of the poor; when his pocket was empty, he would look around for something at hand and give clothes, linens or shoes." * St. John Neumann died in 1860 and was canonized in 1977.

*Rev. Michael J. Curley, C.SS.R., *Bishop John Neumann*, C.SS.R., p. 366, (18)

RESPONSORY

May God answer you in the day of trouble. **—May God**...
May God grant you your heart's desire; **—in the**...
Glory to you, Source of all Being, Eternal Word and Holy Spirit.
    —May God...

CANTICLE

Ant Our Gospel came to you not only in word, but also in power and in the Holy Spirit and with full conviction.

INTERCESSIONS

O God, you selected some to be leaders of your people: to teach, strengthen, and support them. We lift our hearts and pray:
    Send down your Spirit on those you have chosen.

O God, your Church has given us John Neumann as an example of priestly holiness;
    —may he be an inspiration for all in positions of authority.
Through the intercession of Blessed John Neumann;
    —may the work of Christian educators be fruitful.
As bishop of Philadelphia, he served the many immigrants in his diocese:
    —help all bishops in their efforts to serve the alienated and the poor.
Christ, you washed the feet of your followers;
    —may our bishops be strengthened by your example as they carry out their mission of service to the people of God.
The blessed live with you in glory;
    —may all who die share eternal happiness with you.

PRAYER: O God, you lived among us as one who served. Teach us how to empty ourselves of pride, selfishness, and vainglory that we may be filled with your fullness. May all in authority be clothed in Christ's Spirit so that once again the lame will walk, the blind will see, and the poor will have the gospel preached to them. We ask this through Jesus who is our way, our truth, and our life. Amen.

January 6
BL. BROTHER ANDRÉ BESSETTE

MORNING/EVENING PRAYER
(Psalms from Sunday, Week I, p. 3)

Ant 1 Come to me all who are weary and I will give you rest.

Ant 2 These signs will accompany those who believe; in my name they will cure the sick.

Ant 3 Those who exalt themselves shall be humbled; and those who humble themselves shall be exalted.

READING

Alfred Bessette was born August 9, 1845. Though uneducated and frail, he had a great love of prayer and an ardent devotion to St. Joseph. In 1870, he was admitted into the Congregation of the Holy Cross where he was given the name Brother André. He was dedicated to serving the sick and poor and many cures were attributed to him. He was responsible for building a shrine to St. Joseph on Mount Royal. It became a place of healing and pilgrimage. At the blessing of the Oratory, Archbishop Bruchesi said: "What shall I say of the miracles which take place here? If I deny them, these crutches and braces, witnesses of all the donors, will speak in my place. I had no need of the inquiry. It is certain that extraordinary things have taken place here, and even greater prodigies than physical cures...the greater things are the spiritual healings...."* Brother Andre died on January 6, 1937, and was beatified in May, 1982.
*Quote reprinted by permission of the Oratory, (34)

RESPONSORY

Ask and you shall receive; God gives all that we need. —**Ask**...
Seek and you will find; —**God**...
Glory to you, Source of all Being, Eternal Word and Holy Spirit.
    —**Ask**...

CANTICLE

Ant What you have hidden from the wise and the learned, you
have revealed to the merest children.

INTERCESSIONS

Most gentle God, you continue to reveal your love for us through
your faithful friends. In confidence we implore you:
> **Heal us and anoint us in your love.**

Through the intercession of Brother André, increase our faith in
you;
   —that we may be vessels of your healing and reconciling love.
You inspired Brother André to cure the sick in the name of St.
Joseph.
   —enable us to serve the sick and the oppressed in humility and
   with grateful hearts.
You call some to minister among us as religious brothers;
   —may they experience your presence in their ministries and be
   signs of faith in our world.
You remind us that in you all things are possible.
   —assist all who work in apparent difficulty to find equitable
   and just solutions through discerning faith in you.

PRAYER: Most gracious God, as Brother André revealed your
love and compassion in the ordinary routines of daily
life, help us to witness to you as we go about our
everyday tasks. Fill us with the zeal and understanding
that we serve you as we serve the sick and the
oppressed. We ask this grace in the name of Jesus.
Amen.

January 12
ST. MARGUERITE BOURGEOYS*

MORNING/EVENING PRAYER
(Psalms from Sunday, Week I, p. 3)

Ant 1 All that I have ever desired is that the great precept of the
love of God and neighbor be written in every heart.

Ant 2 Charcoal that is fired all the way to the center is not
extinguished, but is consumed.

Ant 3 It is only the love of the lover that penetrates the heart of
    God.

READING

St. Marguerite Bourgeoys left her native France in 1653 for the newly
founded colony of Ville Marie, the present-day city of Montreal in
Canada, where she played a vital role in the lives of young couples and
their families. In 1658 she opened the first school, a renovated stone
stable, for the children of the native people and the French colonists,
and soon became lovingly known as the "Mother of the Colony." That
same year she founded the Congregation of Notre Dame, the first
uncloistered community of women in the New World. She wrote to her
Sisters: "...so it was that the Blessed Virgin who was, after the death of
her Son, the only superior of this first community, as she is ours today,
formed these happy Christians. In the same way, we ought to be
perfectly united in the Congregation. Without this union, we cannot
flatter ourselves that we are living under the auspices of this good
Mother.... God is not satisfied if we preserve the love we owe our
neighbor; we must preserve our neighbor in the love she ought to have
for us." Canonized in 1982, she stands as an inspiration and a challenge
to women disciples in our contemporary Church and world.

RESPONSORY

All that I have ever desired is that the great precept of the love of God
    above all things be written in every heart. —**All that**...
And of the love of neighbor as oneself; —**be written**...
Glory to you, Source of all Being, Eternal Word and Holy Spirit.
    —**All that**...

CANTICLE

Ant The woman said, "Go, I will not abandon you," and I knew it
    was the Blessed Virgin.

INTERCESSIONS

Spirit of the living God, confirm the awareness of your presence
alive and active in us and among us as we celebrate this feast of
Marguerite Bourgeoys. Let us pray:
    We praise you for the gift of her life.

You gifted Marguerite with a love for your Church and a desire
that it be a faithful witness of Christ among your people;
    —may you enable us to respond with love and compassion to
    the special needs of the Church in our time.

You inspired her to found the Sisters of the Congregation of Notre Dame to live and proclaim the gospel as educators;
  —guide all teachers and educators as they enable others to grow in knowledge, wisdom, and gospel values.
You gifted her with a special love for those who are needy and poor;
  —enable us to reflect her spirit in our presence and service among those who are needy and poor in our time.
You filled her with a desire to imitate the life that Mary led throughout her time on earth;
  —may we be graced, like Mary, to live in openness to the Spirit and to respond with courage to your call in our daily lives.

PRAYER: O God, you called Marguerite Bourgeoys to leave her country to extend your realm by educating your people in the Christian way of life. Grant that, inspired by her example and assisted by her prayer, we may proclaim by our word and action the presence of Jesus to all who seek paths that lead to you. Bless especially the Sisters of the Congregation of Notre Dame, that they may be given the grace to live faithfully in the spirit and vision of Marguerite Bourgeoys and to be transformed by it. We ask you this in the name of Jesus. Amen.

* Composed by the Sisters of the Congregation of Notre Dame, Ottawa.

January 19
MOTHER JOSEPH OF THE SACRED HEART*

MORNING/EVENING PRAYER
(Psalms from Sunday, Week I, p. 3)

Ant 1 How admirable are the ways in which Providence directs our lives.**

Ant 2 Whatever concerns the poor is always our affair.**

Ant 3 The ways of Divine Providence are sweet and gentle and move slowly.**

READING

Mother Joseph of the Sacred Heart (Esther Pariseau) was born on April 16, 1823, near Montreal, Quebec. In 1843, she entered the Sisters of Providence, founded by Bishop Ignace Bourget and a young widow, Mother Emilie Gamelin. At the request of Bishop Augustine Magloire Blanchet, Mother Joseph led four sisters to the West in 1856, to help the Bishop with his new diocese of Nisqually in the Washington Territory. From her base at Fort Vancouver, on the Columbia River, Mother Joseph, architect and builder, laid the foundations for her schools, orphanages, hospitals, places of refuge, and asylums for the mentally ill. Traveling across mountains, along rivers of the Northwest, collecting funds for the poor, the sick, and the homeless, she emphasized that the poor were the responsibility of all. In a male-dominated age, when gold, exploration, and adventure were the motivating drives, Mother Joseph safeguarded the resources of the poor. This early pioneer woman had no financial reserves. Her only reserve was her deep understanding of the Church's mission and her mandate to educate, to care for the Native American, and to reach out to the sick and those with special needs. On January 19, 1902, Mother Joseph of the Sacred Heart died, leaving a legacy which continues to be a challenge. In addition to being recognized as the first architect of the Pacific Northwest, and the first Northwestern artist to work in the medium of wood, she was chosen, in 1980, as one of the two representatives of Washington State. Her statue stands in the nation's capital with that of Marcus Whitman.

RESPONSORY

There is a river whose streams bring joy to the city of God.
    —There...
The holy place where the Most High dwells;**—bringing joy**...
Glory to you, Source of all Being, Eternal Word and Holy Spirit.
    —There...

CANTICLE

Ant Unless you, O God, build the house, in vain do its builders labor.

INTERCESSIONS

O God, you hear the cry of the poor;
    —imprint on our minds and hearts the importance of serving as advocates of the poor, especially for those minorities who are deprived of their rights.

Jesus, you sent your apostles to preach the Good News to the whole world;
>—give us the grace to look beyond the geographical borders of our ministries and maintain a Christian sensitivity to the needs of people everywhere.

You made yourself available to everyone in need;
>—show us the way to mirror your care for the sick, the elderly, and for the young who look to us for education.

Your Spirit prays in us, asking for what we hardly know we need;
>—in times of uncertainty, give us the faith to rely on Divine Providence.

Following your call, courageous women and men pioneered their way through dangerous regions and across unbroken paths;
>—let their lives be an ongoing inspiration to all religious today, keeping them aware of their mission and of directions yet to be taken.

PRAYER: O God, we believe that your Providence is always with us through the difficult directions our lives may take. Keep us searching for, and responding to those who have deep needs, to those whom our society often moves to the sidelines, to those who face a lifetime of anxieties and concerns. Keep alive in religious women and men, as well as in their associates, the flame of your love. We ask this in Jesus' name. Amen.

* composed by Mary Gleason, SP, Seattle, WA., (40)
**From the unpublished writings of Mother Joseph of the Sacred Heart

January 23
MARY WARD

MORNING/EVENING PRAYER
(Psalms from Sunday, Week I, p. 3)

Ant 1 Blessed are you when people revile you and say all manner of evil against you; your reward shall be great.

Ant 2 My God, cast us not away from your face, and take not your Spirit from us.

Ant 3 You have broken my bonds; so I will offer to you a sacrifice of praise.

READING

Mary Ward was born in England in 1585; she died there in 1645. The
years between took her on a journey of faith to found and shape a new
kind of religious life for women. In order to be better adapted to the
needs of the times, it would be free of enclosure and governed by
women. Gropingly, tentatively, painfully, she began the loneliness of the
long journey that led to the fulfillment of her own prophecy that women
would share actively in the church's ministry. Her companions today are
known as members of the Institute of the Blessed Virgin Mary. She
wrote to one of her sisters: "I think, dear child, the trouble and the long
loneliness you hear me speak of is not far from me, which whensoever it
is, happy success will follow...."* And to Pope Urban: "...if a greater
punishment bejudged necessary than publicly to be declared a heretic,
a schismatic, an obstinate rebel against Holy Church; to be taken and
imprisoned as such; to have been at the gates of death...if all this is too
little, I offer my poor and short life...."* Mary Ward died January 30,
1645.

*Mary Oliver, IBVM, *Mary Ward,* p. 106, p. 159, (5)

RESPONSORY

Suffering without sin is no burden; into your hands I commend my spirit
   —**Suffering**...
Show me your mercy and grant me your salvation; —**into your**...
Glory to you, Source of all Being, Eternal Word and Holy Spirit.
   —**Suffering**...

CANTICLE

Ant God will assist and help you, it is no matter the who but the
        what; and when God shall enable me to return, I will serve
        you.

INTERCESSIONS

Christ Jesus, you were rejected by your own but your love never
failed. In hope we pray:
   Shelter us in the shadow of your wings.

O God, your daughter Mary was labeled as "heretic, schismatic,
rebel to Holy Church," and her congregation was suppressed;
   —grant courage to those misunderstood or misjudged by
      ecclesiastical or civil authorities.
O God, in spite of failure and exile, Mary accepted all with
patience and a sense of humor;

—grant us hearts that are humble and help us to not take ourselves too seriously.

Imprisoned, Mary was refused the sacraments even when she was thought to be dying;

—comfort all who are unjustly imprisoned and give them hope.

O God, you gifted Mary with vision and courage;

—support all those whose vision and gifts further the work of bringing this world to fullness of life especially in their times of trial.

PRAYER: O God, purify our hearts and give us courage to work for the coming of your reign in our hearts. Knowing that the work we do is yours to accomplish, let us not be discouraged by lack of results. We thank you for all those who have faithfully persevered in spite of adversity and ask them to intercede for us. Grant this through Jesus who is our Way, our Truth, and our Life. Amen.

January 24
ST. FRANCIS de SALES

MORNING/EVENING PRAYER
(Psalms from Sunday, Week I, p. 3)

Ant 1 To desire to love God is to love to desire God, and hence to love, for love is the root of all desire.

Ant 2 You must love God with your whole heart and your neighbor as yourself.

Ant 3 God must increase and I must decrease.

READING

Francis de Sales was born in 1567. He was chosen bishop of Geneva, and was known for his pastoral care of his priests and people. He directed many by his writings which enabled the ordinary Christian to find the path to holiness. He wrote: "...So [this good person] says that there is no need to employ the imagination in order to envision the sacred humanity of the Savior. Not, perhaps, for those who are already far advanced along the mountain of perfection. But for those of us who are still in the valleys, although desirous of mounting, I think it expedient to employ all our faculties, including the imagination. Nonetheless, I have already stressed in another letter that this imagining must be very simple and, like a humble seamstress, thread affections and resolutions onto our spirits."* Francis collaborated with Jane Frances de Chantal in the founding of the Visitation Order. He died at Lyons in 1622.

*Wendy Wright, *Bond of Perfection*, p. 79, (1)

RESPONSORY

The just shall stand like a cedar of Lebanon. **—The just...**
With hands raised in glory; **—like a...**
Glory to you, Source of all Being, Eternal Word and Holy Spirit.
   —The just...

CANTICLE

Ant A heart indifferent to all things is like a ball of wax in the hands of God; it does not place its love in the things which God wills, but in the will of God who decrees them.

INTERCESSIONS

Francis drank deeply from the springs of mystical tradition;
   —we give thanks for the lives and writings of those who have shown us the way to holiness.
Through the writings of Francis many have entered more deeply into following the Christian way of life;
   —grant journalists and writers of our day the integrity and courage to express themselves without bias or prejudice from societal or political pressures.
Francis was enriched by his spiritual friendship with Jane Frances de Chantal;
   —may our friendships be the leaven for all to experience the love of God.
He made himself all things to all people that he might lead them to Christ;
   —detach us from our own selfishness that we may become more fully present to all our sisters and brothers.
Francis was deeply concerned with the spiritual direction of others;
   —enable those who companion others on the spiritual journey to lead with gentleness and care.

PRAYER: O God, you inspired Francis de Sales with a burning love for yourself and your people. Let love press us on as we journey through life. Give us a heart to embrace all people and a passion to live fully for you. Give us humble and compassionate hearts that all may come to know your gentle care and concern. We ask this in the name of Jesus who was meek and humble of heart. Amen.

January 27
ST. ANGELA MERICI

MORNING/EVENING PRAYER
(Psalms from Sunday, Week I, p. 3)

Ant 1 Have hope and firm faith that God will help you in all things.

Ant 2 Blessed are those who sincerely take up the work of serving God's people.

Ant 3 Let your first refuge always be at the feet of Jesus Christ.

READING

Angela Merici, born in Italy in the latter part of the fifteenth century, dedicated herself to catechetical and religious works as a young woman. Going to Brescia in her forties, she sought to support young girls in leading a Christian life in a decadent society. In her early sixties, she founded the Ursulines, a group of women who originally lived in their own homes, served the needy, and met monthly for mutual support. Angela sought to transform society through the renewal of family life and Christian education. In [Angela's] reckoning, a mother is loving, but also demanding; tough as well as flexible; able to embody both divine mercy and divine judgment.... She was able to look into the mirror and see herself and her daughters as powerful even as they committed themselves to lives of service. She managed for most of her life to be what many of us hope eventually to become, self-accepting, aware of life's bleak realities without being defined by them, and so quietly self-confident that it seems not to have occurred to her that she would not be able to do what needed to be done.... She died in 1540.

Mary Jo Weaver, (54)

RESPONSORY

Angela joyfully served others for the glory of God alone. —**Angela**...
She lived in wisdom and holiness; —**for the**...
Glory to you, Source of all Being, Eternal Word and Holy Spirit.
    —**Angela**...

CANTICLE

Ant Cling together with the bonds of love, esteeming, helping and supporting one another in Christ Jesus.

INTERCESSIONS

O God, through your daughter Angela, you promised to provide for all our needs. In confidence we turn to you and say:
Hear our prayer and help us.

Angela told us that the more united we are, the more God is among us;
   —teach us to overcome the obstacles of prejudice, selfishness, and fear, and to enable all people to know that you are present to them.
Angela worked to live and teach your gospel;
   —help all missionaries and teachers to spread your reign by word and action.
You blessed Angela with the gift of understanding the scriptures;
   —grant us the grace to know and live your word.
Many and varied are the ways you are served by those who claim Angela as their founder;
   —give the Church unity in its diversity and trust in the presence of your Spirit.

PRAYER: Loving God, in St. Angela you give us an example of prayerful and dedicated service to your people. May her prayers for us help us to live your gospel as witnesses to your presence in the world. We ask this through her intercession and the intercession of all her faithful followers who now live with you. Amen.

February 1
ST. BRIGID OF KILDARE

MORNING/EVENING PRAYER
(Psalms from Sunday, Week I, p. 3)

Ant 1 Since I first fixed my mind on God, I have never taken it off.

Ant 2 As the outcome of your faith you obtain the salvation of your souls.

Ant 3 Come to that living stone, rejected by humankind, but in God's sight chosen and precious.

READING

St. Brigid of Kildare was born about the year 450 in a place called Faughart on the east coast of Ireland. A Christian by birth through her mother, a slave, she was also knowledgeable of the Druid ways of her father. With several other young women, she began Ireland's first convent of nuns and eventually became an abbess governing both women and men. Brigid's gifts to the Christian world include helping lay the foundations of education for the laity through monastery schools, which developed into the universities of the Middle Ages. Moreover, she gave the women of her country the opportunity to use their energies and intellect in a way previously not open to them. For many generations after her, Kildare would continue to be ruled by a double line of abbesses and abbot-bishops. Only in medieval times were convents placed entirely under the jurisdiction of men. She is a patron saint of Ireland.

Based on Joanne Turpin, *Women in Church History*, pp. 45–52, (50)

RESPONSORY

Wisdom reaches mightily from one end of the earth to the other.
　—**Wisdom**...
She orders all things well, —**from one**...
Glory to you, Source of all Being, Eternal Word and Holy Spirit.
　—**Wisdom**...

CANTICLE

Ant You are a chosen race, a royal priesthood, a holy nation, God's own people.

INTERCESSIONS

O God, you favored Ireland with the brilliant leadership of St. Brigid;
　—grant all nations a leader after your own heart.
Brigid's love for learning and respect for freedom gave new quality of life to women and to all people;
　—give us the grace to remain open to growth all the days of our lives.
Her holiness was magnified by her deep joy;
　—may our love and dedication to you be so manifest.

Brigid's sweet disposition and delicate ways made her loved by
all;
  —help us to meet difficult personalities with patience and
    understanding.
She was lavish in her love for the poor;
  —let love be the measure of our giving in the fullness of your
    being.

PRAYER: O God, we praise and thank you for the life of St.
          Brigid. She gave to the Christian world the foundations
          of education for the laity and the opportunity for
          women of Ireland to use their energies and intellect in a
          way previously not open to them. An "ascetic with a
          smile," she helped lay the foundations of a golden age
          of learning and missionary endeavor. May she continue
          to be a beacon of light and courage to all women who
          labor to lead others to the freedom of the gospel. We
          ask this in Jesus' name. Amen.

February 2
PRESENTATION OF THE LORD JESUS

EVENING PRAYER I

Ant 1 The parents of Jesus brought him to Jerusalem to present
      him to God according to the Law of Moses.
      (Ps 113, p. 96)

Ant 2 Open your hearts, people of God, to receive your redeemer.
      (Ps 147:12-20, p. 85)

Ant 3 Simeon and Anna, prophets of God, gave witness to Christ,
      the fulfillment of God's promises. (Phil 2:6-11, p. 96)

READING

Lumen
Ad revelationem gentium.

Look kindly, Jesus, where we come,
New Simeons, to kindle,
Each at Your infant sacrifice [one's] own life's candle.

And when Your flame turns into many tongues,
See how the One is multiplied, among us, hundreds!
And goes among the humble, and consoles our sinful kindred.

It is for this we come,
And, kneeling, each receive one flame:
Ad revelationem gentium....

"The Candlemas Procession" in *The Collected Poems of Thomas Merton*, p. 92, (16)

RESPONSORY

You reveal, O God, your salvation for us. **—You reveal**...
In the sight of all you have prepared, **—your**...
Glory to you, Source of all Being, Eternal Word and Holy Spirit.
   —You reveal...

CANTICLE OF MARY

Ant You, Most High, have prepared your salvation in the
      presence of all the people.

INTERCESSIONS

Mary and Joseph brought Jesus to the temple to be presented to
God. Let us pray:

Christ, be our light.

Jesus, light of the world, you revealed the love of God to us;
   —let our lives lead others to the truth of God's mercy.
Jesus, longed for savior, you are presented with the gifts of the
poor;
   —help us to dedicate our lives to those in need.
Jesus, child of mystery, your mother's heart was pierced by
prophecy;
   —strengthen all women whose dedication to you brings pain
      and sorrow.
Jesus, child of promise, Simeon had waited and prayed for your
coming;
   —give us patience and hope as we pray for the fulfillment of
      your gospel.
Jesus, joy of all who seek God, Anna had given you lifelong
service;
   —bless the elderly and teach us how to give them joy and
      encouragement.

PRAYER: Bountiful God, you are father and mother to us. You
         receive the dedication of the infant Son, Jesus, with
         two turtle doves. You inspire aged Simeon and Anna to
         bless and announce his mission. O gentle, strong God,

we rejoice in your care for us. Help us to draw those
who turn away from you in fear. Let the saving light of
Jesus bring truth and peace to our world. This we ask
in his name. Amen.

MORNING PRAYER
(Psalms from Sunday, Week I, p. 3)

Ant 1 Simeon, just and devout, looked for the consolation of
Israel.

Ant 2 Anna gave thanks to God for the child and spoke of him to
all who were looking for the redemption of Jerusalem.

Ant 3 Inspired by the Holy Spirit, they received the child in their
arms and gave thanks to God.

READING

Rejoice, then, with that blessed old man and the aged Anna; walk forth
to meet the mother and Child. Let love overcome your bashfulness; let
affection dispel your fear. Receive the Infant in your arms and say with
the bride: *I took hold of him and would not let him go.* Dance with the
holy old man and sing with him: *Now dismiss your servant,...according to
your word in peace.*

Bonaventure, The Tree of Life, p. 131, (1)

RESPONSORY

We adore you, O God, and bow down before you.—**We**...
We sing your praise, —**and bow**...
Glory to you, Source of all Being, Eternal Word and Holy Spirit.—**We**...

CANTICLE OF ZECHARIAH

Ant You grant peace to your servant, O God, according to your
word.

INTERCESSIONS

Jesus was presented in the temple; Anna and Simeon gave praise
to God. Let us proclaim:
            God has come to save us.

Jesus, you were dedicated to God in the temple, and Simeon
blessed you;

—have mercy on children who have no one to guide them in the path of holiness.

Jesus, hope of the ages, women and men of good will prayed for and longed for you for generations;

—show your compassion to all who are exiled or cut off from their roots.

Jesus, light of the world, your people longed for freedom;

—enlighten and change the hearts of governments that enslave others.

Jesus, infant son, you embraced our human helplessness;

—bless all who are in need, and fill us all with compassion for them.

PRAYER: Bountiful God, you are father and mother to us. You receive the dedication of the infant Son, Jesus, with two turtle doves. You inspire aged Simeon and Anna to bless and announce his mission. O gentle, strong God, we rejoice in your care for us. Help us to draw those who turn away from you in fear. Let the saving light of Jesus bring truth and peace to our world. This we ask in his name. Amen.

DAYTIME PRAYER

Ant 1 You have prepared in the presence of all, a light of revelation to the nations. (Ps 123, p. 109)

Ant 2 Blessed are you, O God, who have fulfilled your word to your people. (Ps 124, p. 109)

Ant 3 The child Jesus grew and became strong, and the favor of God was upon him. (Ps 125, p. 115)

(Prayer as in Morning Prayer)

EVENING PRAYER II

Ant 1 It had been revealed to Simeon by the Holy Spirit that he should not see death before he saw the Christ of God. (Ps 110:1–5, 7, p. 149)

Ant 2 Simeon prayed: Your salvation is a light of revelation to the nations and the glory of your people. (Ps 130, p. 143)

Ant 3 Joseph and Mary marveled at what was said about the
child. (Col 1:12–20, p. 122)

READING

Through what obscure, half-comprehending night
Thou shinest, Christ, for light!
Candle and flame Thou art,
Set in the candelabrum of my heart.

Sr. M. Madeleva, csc, "Candlemas Day," p. 64, (1)

RESPONSORY

You reveal, O God, your salvation for us. **—You reveal**...
In the sight of all, you have prepared, **—your**...
Glory to you, Source of all Being, Eternal Word and Holy Spirit.
   —You reveal...

CANTICLE OF MARY

Ant This day, Mary brought the child Jesus into the temple.

INTERCESSIONS

Mary and Joseph brought Jesus to the temple to be presented to
God. Let us pray to him:
Christ, be our light.
Jesus, light of the world, you revealed the love of God to us;
   —let our lives lead others to the truth of God's mercy.
Jesus, longed for savior, you are presented with the gifts of the
poor;
   —help us to dedicate our lives to those in need.
Jesus, child of mystery, your mother's heart was pierced by
prophecy;
   —strengthen all women whose dedication to you brings pain
     and sorrow.
Jesus, child of promise, Simeon had waited and prayed for your
coming;
   —give us patience and hope as we pray for the fulfillment of
     your gospel.
Jesus, joy of all who seek God, Anna had given you lifelong
service;
   —bless the elderly and teach us how to give them joy and
     encouragement.

PRAYER: Bountiful God, you are father and mother to us. You receive the dedication of the infant Son, Jesus, with two turtle doves. You inspire aged Simeon and Anna to bless and announce his mission. O gentle, strong God, we rejoice in your care for us. Help us to draw those who turn away from you in fear. Let the saving light of Jesus bring truth and peace to our world. This we ask in his name. Amen.

February 10
ST. SCHOLASTICA

MORNING/EVENING PRAYER
(Psalms from Sunday, Week I, p. 3)

Ant 1 She opens her mouth with wisdom, and the teaching of kindness is on her tongue.

Ant 2 Let us love one another, because love is of God.

Ant 3 Make my joy complete by your unanimity, praising the one love, united in Spirit and ideals.

READING

St. Scholastica was born at Nursia in Italy in about 480. She and her brother, St. Benedict, originated the two branches of the Benedictine Order, which is still flourishing after fourteen centuries. St. Scholastica's whole life was devoted to "seeking God" and is summed up in the twofold maxim of loving justice and hating iniquity. She died in 547.

RESPONSORY

I rejoice heartily in my God in whom is the joy of my soul. —**I rejoice**...
For God has clothed me with the robe of salvation; —**in whom**...
Glory to you, Source of all Being, Eternal Word and Holy Spirit.
   —**I rejoice**...

CANTICLE

Ant We have come to know and believe in the love God has for us.

INTERCESSIONS

To those who are pure of heart you manifest yourself, O God. In joyful expectation, we pray:
  Prepare our minds and our lips to praise your holy name.

Through the intercession of Scholastica, teach us to pray and to trust in your care for us;
  —teach us to live by the law of love.
Your servant Scholastica pondered your word and knew the value of work;
  —give us the grace always to be people of prayer and to do our work with reverence and creativity.
Scholastica had a deep love for her brother, Benedict;
  —grant that all families may grow closer in love and trust.
Bless all who derive their rule of life from Benedict and Scholastica;
  —keep them faithful to their calling and let them also bear fruit in abundant life for the church.

PRAYER: Loving God, in your daughter, Scholastica, love was stronger than adherence to rule, and you heard her prayer because of her great trust in you. Bless all those who have been gifted with the charism of Scholastica: a gift to the Church of prayer and universal charity. In your mercy, raise up in our day those who are so dedicated to you, that they, too, will guide and nourish all who seek you in spirit and in truth. This we ask in Jesus, who is your Incarnate Word. Amen.

March 3
BL. KATHARINE DREXEL, SBS

MORNING/EVENING PRAYER
(Psalms from Sunday, Week I, p. 3)

Ant 1 I want to enter into and be permeated with Jesus' desire to save all—all the world throughout the centuries.

Ant 2 It is easy to see [Jesus] when our net is full of fish, but hard to recognize him when we have caught nothing.

Ant 3 Out of our common todays and yesterdays, we are building for eternity.

READING

Katharine Drexel was born in Philadelphia on November 26, 1858. Through her father, a well-known banker and philanthropist, Katharine learned early on that wealth was to be shared with those in need. When she experienced the destitution of Native Americans, she began her lifelong vocation of serving them. In 1891, she founded the Sisters of the Blessed Sacrament whose mission was to share the gospel with Native and African Americans. She wrote in her retreat notes: "Resolve: Generously with no half-hearted, timorous dread of the opinions of Church and [men or women] to *manifest my mission.* To speak only and when it pleases God; but to lose no opportunity of speaking before priests and bearded men. Manifest yourself. You have no time to occupy your thoughts with that complacency or consideration of what others will think. Your business is simply, 'What will [God] in Heaven think.'"*
She died on March 3, 1955, and was beatified November 20, 1988.

*Consuela Marie Duffy, sbs, *Katharine Drexel*, p. 246, (39)

RESPONSORY

Sell what you have and give to the poor. —**Sell what**...
Come follow me; —**and give**...
Glory to you, Source of all Being, Eternal Word and Holy Spirit.
   —**Sell what**...

CANTICLE

Ant The offspring of this intensity of love for our Eucharistic Lord should be a consuming zeal for the gathering of souls into the fold of Christ.

INTERCESSIONS

All day long I abide with [Christ] and must watch him whom I am to imitate;
   —Jesus, help us to keep you in mind and to live in the present moment.
It is only by entering into oneself in prayer and meditation that the soul can be restored to its true poise...and the value of unimportant things be seen in its true light;
   —Spirit of God, teach us to pray.
It is a lesson we all need—to let alone the things that do not concern us;
   —O God, teach us the things that are to our peace.

Kind words, by their power of producing happiness, have also a power of producing holiness;

—let our words, O God, bear your love and creativity.

Beware of sadness, for it is contrary to love in diminishing and destroying its power of affection;

—let us find courage in your cross, Lord Jesus, and joy in your resurrection.

PRAYER: Ever loving God, you called Blessed Katharine Drexel to share the message of the Gospel and the life of the Eucharist with the poor and oppressed among Native and African American peoples. Through her intercession, may we grow in the faith and love that will enable us to be united as sisters and brothers in you. Inspired by her zeal may we strive for greater unity, justice, and peace. We pray this in Jesus' name. Amen.

March 15
ST. LOUISE DE MARILLAC*

MORNING/EVENING PRAYER
(Psalms from Sunday, Week I, p. 3)

Ant 1 After having seen the beauty of virtue, we must proceed to resolve to practice it; otherwise prayer is not well made.

Ant 2 The virtue of cordiality should not stand alone for it is in need of another virtue, which is respect.

Ant 3 Prayer and mortification are two sisters who are so closely united together that one will never be found without the other.

READING

Louise was born in Paris, France, on August 12, 1591. Her mother died soon after her birth. When she was seventeen years old she had a desire to become a Poor Clare nun, but her confessor discouraged her due to her frail health and the austere rule of the Capuchin order. In 1613, at the age of twenty-two, she married Antoine Le Gras. After a year of marriage they had a son. Both she and her husband had a love for the poor. When her husband became very ill, she lovingly cared for him and was at his bedside when he died on Christmas Eve, 1625. After the death of her husband, she met Vincent de Paul who became her spiritual director. On November 29, 1633, after years of collaboration, they cofounded the Daughters of Charity. The following year, her desire to commit herself to God by vow was realized.

RESPONSORY

You have given us an example of love and service; help us to be faithful.
— **You have**...
Walk in humility and confidence; — **help us**...
Glory to you, Source of all Being, Eternal Word and Holy Spirit.
— **You have**...

CANTICLE

Ant It is into hearts who seek God alone that God is pleased to pour forth the most excellent lights and great graces.

INTERCESSIONS

O God, through Louise, you taught us a deeper love and respect for the poor and so we entreat you:
Help us to serve them, respecting their dignity.

Christ Jesus, you inspired the daughters of Louise to be women of compassion and empathy in their service to humankind;
—help us to grow in mercy and understanding.
Loving Creator, we thank you for the example of untiring collaboration of Louise with Vincent in the formation of works of charity;
—may we follow her example in our service of the church.
Louise transformed adversity into positive energy for the service of the unfortunate;
—help us to see with the eyes of faith and the mind of Christ.
O God, send laborers into your harvest to mirror the gospel values of justice and love of Christ;
—may our lives give you glory and praise.

PRAYER: O God, you inspired Louise de Marillac with the spirit of charity for the poor. In response to her call, she envisioned a new way of living the vows. Her daughters' cloister would be the streets of the city or the wards of hospitals, their cell a hired room, and their grill, obedience. Grant us the grace to serve those whose lives we touch with the same spirit of love, and may the family of Louise continue to grow and multiply throughout the world. Amen.

*Based on "Paper from the Symposium Louise de Marillac," (41)

March 17
ST. PATRICK

MORNING/EVENING PRAYER
(Psalms from Sunday, Week I, p. 3)

Ant 1 My soul clings fast to you; your hand holds me.

Ant 2 Sing praises to God on the lyre and the harp.

Ant 3 You shall be my witness to the ends of the earth.

READING

I, Patrick, a sinner, a most simple countryman, the least of all the faithful and most contemptible to many, had for father the deacon Calpurnius, son of the late Potitus, a priest, of the settlement [vicus] of Bannavem Taburniae; he had a small villa nearby where I was taken captive. I was at that time about sixteen years of age. I did not, indeed, know the true God; and I was taken into captivity in Ireland with many thousands of people, according to our deserts, for quite drawn away from God, we did not keep [God's] precepts, nor were we obedient to our priests who used to remind us of our salvation. And [God]...scattered us among many nations, even to the ends of the earth, where I, in my smallness, am now to be found among foreigners.... Therefore, indeed, I cannot keep silent—nor would it be proper, so many favors and graces has the [Most High] deigned to bestow on me in the land of my captivity. For after chastisement from God, and recognizing [God, our way to repay is to exalt and confess God's] wonders before every nation under heaven. (St. Patrick)

Brian De Breffny, *In the Steps of St. Patrick*, p. 153, (43)

RESPONSORY

Go to all the nations; sharing the good news of Christ Jesus. **—Go to...**
Announce liberty to the captives; **—sharing...**
Glory to you, Source of all Being, Eternal Word and Holy Spirit.
 —Go to...

CANTICLE

Ant We give thanks to God for you always, remembering before our God your work of faith and labor of love.

INTERCESSIONS

O God, you call us to arise each day in the light of your sun and in the radiance of your moon. In faith we pray:
Christ be with us!

Christ within us;
—breathe into our hearts a renewed faith that seeks peace and justice for all peoples.
Christ beside us;
—give us the confidence that you are with us in all we do.
Christ in danger;
—sustain us and let the light of your passion bring meaning to our difficulties.
Christ in quiet;
—enkindle our hearts as we seek you in prayer.
Christ to comfort and restore us;
—be with us at the hour of death.

PRAYER: O God, we celebrate in Patrick your gifts of holiness, service, and leadership. May he continue to call us to a deeper faith and to a renewed zeal for living and sharing the gospel. Bless the country of Ireland which he loved with the mind and heart of Christ. We ask this through the same Jesus Christ who lives with you and the Holy Spirit, Trinity in Unity, now and forever. Amen.

March 19
ST. JOSEPH

EVENING PRAYER I

Ant 1 Joseph, the husband of Mary, was a just man (alleluia). (Ps 113, p. 96)

Ant 2 Do not fear to take Mary as your wife, for that which is conceived in her is of the Holy Spirit (alleluia). (Ps 146, p. 166)

Ant 3 Joseph did as God told him and took Mary as his wife, (alleluia). (Eph 1:3–10, p. 157)

READING

In our pursuit of perfection we have St. Joseph's humble and hidden life as our model. He was highly honored as the spouse of the Immaculate Mother of God and representative of the Eternal [Father /Mother] to [the] divine Son on earth, yet he was ever humble, simple, and retiring.... In the exercise of his duties as a poor artisan he knew what real poverty was. Never was there one so poor in spirit or desire as St. Joseph, never one in whom the virtue of poverty shone with more splendor in the sight of heaven. (19 March 1893)

Bl. Mary MacKillop, RSJ, (10)

RESPONSORY

You spoke your word to Joseph, O God, and he fulfilled your will.
　　—You spoke...
You blessed him with holiness, **—and he...**
Glory to you, Source of all Being, Eternal Word and Holy Spirit.
　　—You spoke...

CANTICLE OF MARY

Ant　Praise to you, O God, who chose Joseph to be the faithful protector and provider of Jesus, the Word made flesh, (alleluia).

INTERCESSIONS

Let us give praise for Joseph the just man, who was called the father of Jesus, the Christ:
　　Blessed are those whom you choose, O God.

O God, you chose Joseph to be the guide and teacher of the child, Jesus;
　　—direct our minds and hearts as we strive to instruct children in your ways.
Through the intercession of Joseph, spouse of Mary;
　　—give husbands and wives the grace to relate to each other with reverence and mutual respect.
Joseph supported his family with the work of his hands;
　　—grant meaningful employment and an adequate wage to all.
Joseph knew the joys and sorrows of parenthood;
　　—bless all parents with the courage and patience to care for their children with love and compassion.

PRAYER: O God, you gave Joseph the ineffable joy of joining Mary in caring for the child, Jesus. Through his intercession, grant us the grace to nurture the life of Christ in our lives. Help us to guide and support one another in truth and in love, and so build up the body of your church. We ask this in the name of Jesus who lives with you, Source of all Being, and with the Holy Spirit. Amen.

MORNING PRAYER
(Psalms from Sunday, Week I, p. 3)

Ant 1 In a dream Joseph was told to take the child and his mother into Egypt (alleluia).

Ant 2 Joseph rose and took Mary and Jesus at night into Egypt (alleluia).

Ant 3 An angel appeared to Joseph in a dream telling him to return to Israel (alleluia).

READING

I took for my advocate and lord the glorious St. Joseph and earnestly recommended myself to him. I saw clearly...this father and lord of mine came to my rescue in better ways than I knew how to ask for. I don't recall up to this day ever having petitioned him for anything that he failed to grant. It is an amazing thing the great many favors God has granted me through the mediation of this blessed saint, the dangers I was freed from both of body and soul. For with other saints it seems [God] has given them grace to be of help in one need, whereas with this glorious saint I have experience that he helps in all our needs and that the Lord wants us to understand that just as he was subject to St. Joseph on earth—for since bearing the title father, being the Lord's tutor, Joseph could give the Child commands—so in heaven God does whatever he commands.

Teresa of Avila, *Life*, 6.6, (3)

RESPONSORY

O God, you spoke your word to Joseph, and he fulfilled your will.
　— **O God,...**
You blessed him with holiness, —**and he**...
Glory to you, Source of all Being, Eternal Word and Holy Spirit.
　— **O God**...

CANTICLE OF ZECHARIAH

Ant They said of Jesus: isn't this the son of Joseph, the carpenter?

INTERCESSIONS

O God, you direct the life of the church through the guidance of the Holy Spirit. We have named Joseph, its guardian and protector, and so we pray:
Help us to walk the ways of your holy ones.

In praise of Joseph we recall his humility and goodness;
—deliver us from harmful ambition and self-seeking.
Joseph entered into the mysteries of the life of Jesus;
—grant us the faith to recognize and follow the call of your Spirit in our lives.
Joseph cared for his family in an occupied land;
—be merciful to those who are in bondage and grant them freedom and peace.
Joseph died knowing the love of Jesus and Mary;
—give us the grace to die at peace with our families and with confidence in your mercy.

PRAYER: O God, you gave Joseph the ineffable joy of joining Mary in caring for the child, Jesus. Through his intercession, grant us the grace to nurture the life of Christ in our lives. Help us to guide and support one another in truth and in love, and so build up the body of your church. We ask this in the name of Jesus who lives with you, Source of all Being, and with the Holy Spirit. Amen.

DAYTIME PRAYER

Ant 1 Through Joseph and his spouse, Mary, God fulfilled the covenant promised to Abraham and Sarah, (alleluia). (Ps 120, p. 155)

Ant 2 In the hills of Nazareth, you fulfilled your plan for us in silent and hidden ways, (alleluia). (Ps 121, p. 89)

Ant 3 Joseph grew strong in faith, giving glory to God (alleluia). (Ps 122, p. 143)

(Prayer as in Morning Prayer)

EVENING PRAYER II

Ant 1 Jesus and his parents went to Jerusalem every year at the feast of Passover, (alleluia). (Ps 15, p. 14)

Ant 2 As they returned to Jerusalem, Jesus remained behind, and they searched three days for him, (alleluia). (Ps 112, p. 149)

Ant 3 The parents of Jesus found him among the teachers, listening to them and asking them questions, (alleluia). (Rev 15:3–4, p. 41)

READING

Contemporary Christians might find their way back to what is best in them if the individuality of this man [Joseph], their patron, were again producing more stature in them.... A nation needs men and women of lifelong performance of duty, of clearheaded loyalty, of discipline of heart and body. A nation needs men and women who know that true greatness is achieved only in selfless service to the greater and holy duty that is imposed upon each life.... A nation needs men and women who do not lose confidence in God's grace, even when they have to seek it as lost, as Joseph once sought the divine child. Such individuals are urgently needed in every situation and in every class.... Joseph lives...for the communion of saints is near and the seeming distance is only appearance.... We, however, will experience the blessing of his protection if we, with God's grace, open our heart and our life to his spirit and the quiet power of his intercession.

Karl Rahner, *The Great Church Year*, pp. 326–27, (2)

RESPONSORY

O God, you spoke your word to Joseph, and he fulfilled your will.
   — O God...
You blessed him with holiness, **—and he...**
Glory to you, Source of all Being, Eternal Word and Holy Spirit.
   — O God...

CANTICLE OF MARY

Ant Jesus returned to Nazareth with his parents and was obedient to them, (alleluia).

INTERCESSIONS

Let us give praise for Joseph the just man, who was called the
father of Jesus, the Christ:
> **Blessed are those whom you choose, O God.**

O God, you chose Joseph to be the guide and teacher of the child,
Jesus;
>   —direct our minds and hearts as we strive to instruct children
>   in your ways.

Through the intercession of Joseph, spouse of Mary;
>   —give husbands and wives the grace to relate to each other
>   with reverence and mutual respect.

Joseph supported his family with the work of his hands;
>   —grant meaningful employment and an adequate wage to all.

Joseph knew the joys and sorrows of parenthood;
>   —bless all parents with the courage and patience to care for
>   their children with love and compassion.

PRAYER: O God, you gave Joseph the ineffable joy of joining
Mary in caring for the child, Jesus. Through his
intercession, grant us the grace to nurture the life of
Christ in our lives. Help us to guide and support one
another in truth and in love, and so build up the body
of your church. We ask this in the name of Jesus who
lives with you, Source of all Being, and with the Holy
Spirit. Amen.

March 24
OSCAR ROMERO

MORNING/EVENING PRAYER

Ant 1 Unless a grain of wheat falls into the ground and dies, it
remains just a single grain; but if it dies, it will bear much
fruit. (Jer 14:17–21, p. 132)

Ant 2 His faith was founded on solid rock; he feared no wicked
threats. (Ps 72 I, p. 81)

Ant 3 Whatever you have done for the least of my people you
have done for me. (Ps 72 II, p. 81)

READING

I have frequently been threatened with death. I should tell you that as a Christian, I do not believe in death without resurrection. If they kill me I will come to life again in the Salvadoran people. If they kill me, from this moment I offer my blood to God for the redemption and resurrection of El Salvador. My death will be for the liberation of my people and as a testimony of hope for the future.

                                    Oscar Romero (assassinated Mar. 24, 1980)

RESPONSORY

You have lifted me up from the gates of death, that I may give you praise.
   —You...
Be gracious to me, O God, **—that I...**
Glory to you, Source of all Being, Eternal Word and Holy Spirit. **—You...**

CANTICLE

Ant When the days drew near for Jesus to be taken up to
         heaven, he set his face to go to Jerusalem.

INTERCESSIONS

O Christ, you gave us the example that one can have no greater love than to lay down one's life for one's friend, and so we pray:
   Teach us to love one another as you have loved us.

Christ Jesus, you inspired your servant, Oscar Romero, to speak fearlessly your gospel of love;
   —give us the grace to stand up for our convictions in the face of
      adversity.
You enabled Archbishop Romero to become attentive to the cries of the poor;
   —keep our hearts open that we may hear your voice and follow
      it.
You promised your followers a peace that the world cannot give;
   —may nations learn that peace cannot be achieved through
      war or acts of violence.
You have told us that the meek will inherit the earth;
   —may there be true land reform in countries where ownership
      is controlled by the rich and powerful.
Grant all those who have been killed by acts of violence;
   —eternal peace and joy in your presence.

PRAYER: O God, you have given us women and men, who like Jesus, have preached the gospel with their lives. May their example spur us on to be more committed to the cause of justice and peace. Help us so live your gospel in our lives that its effects will influence the political and economic decisions that affect the quality of life for all peoples on this earth. We ask this through the intercession of those who have died for the sake of justice and now live with you for all eternity. Amen.

March 25
ANNUNCIATION

EVENING PRAYER I

Ant 1 A virgin shall conceive and bear a child and the child shall be called Emmanuel (alleluia). (Ps 113, p. 96)

Ant 2 Sacrifice and offerings you have not desired, but a body you have prepared for me (alleluia). (Ps 147:12–20, p. 85)

Ant 3 As the rain falls from heaven and does not return until it has given growth to the seed, so shall my word accomplish my purpose (alleluia). (Phil 2:6–11, p. 96)

READING

It seems that the moment of breakthrough for Mary was also the beginning of the breakthrough of salvation for all creation....a moment came at which a unique demand was made on her.... Her response was a self-giving so total that she was, as it were, subsumed in that giving. It *was* herself. But the event we are talking about is the conception of a baby, which is above all a bodily event.... Mary, mother of the Word, had much to learn, later. She made mistakes, she did not understand, she suffered. But from that time her being, her very body, was the Being of the One to whom she had assented.

Rosemary Haughton, The Passionate God, pp. 133–34, (1)

RESPONSORY

You are the honor of our race, you are the joy of our people. **—You are..**
The promise has been fulfilled, **—you are the joy**...
Glory to you, Source of all Being, Eternal Word and Holy Spirit.
    —You are...

CANTICLE OF MARY

Ant The angel of God declared unto Mary, and she conceived by the Holy Spirit (alleluia).

INTERCESSIONS

Mary, full of grace, is called to be the mother of Jesus. We rejoice in you, O God, as we say:

You are the honor of your people, O blessed virgin, Mary.

Mary is blessed among women with the joy all ages have awaited;
—through her intercession free all women who are in bondage and who lead lives less than human.
Mary chose freely to become the mother of the savior;
—grant to all people the freedom to choose their way of life.
Mary rejoiced at the mystery of her motherhood;
—grant your grace and guidance to mothers who do not want their children.
Mary went in haste to support and to share the mystery of new life with her cousin, Elizabeth;
—teach us how to share with others, the fruit of your Spirit in our lives.

PRAYER: O God, in the fullness of time, you called the virgin, Mary, to be the mother of Jesus. As we celebrate this mystery of the annunciation, of Mary's entrance into the mystery of redemption, grant us the grace of opening our lives to all that you would call us to be. Give us the mind and heart of Mary that we too may bear Christ to the world. We ask this through Jesus Christ, the Incarnate Word, one with you, Source of all life, and with the Holy Spirit. Amen.

MORNING PRAYER
(Psalms from Sunday, Week I, p. 3)

Ant 1 The angel Gabriel said to Mary: Hail full of grace, the Most High is with you (alleluia).

Ant 2 Favored daughter of Israel, you have found favor with God (alleluia).

Ant 3 You will give birth to Jesus who will save his people from their sins (alleluia).

READING

Oh, if you could feel in some way the quality and intensity of that fire sent from heaven, the refreshing coolness that accompanied it, the consolation it imparted; if you could realize the great exaltation of the Virgin Mother, the ennobling of the human race, the condescension of the divine majesty; if you could hear the Virgin singing with joy.... If you could see the sweet embrace of the Virgin and the woman who had been sterile and hear the greeting in which the tiny servant recognized his Lord,...then I am sure you would sing in sweet tones with the Blessed Virgin that sacred hymn: *My soul [proclaims your greatness, O my God,]* and with the tiny prophet you would exalt, rejoice and adore the marvelous virginal conception.

Bonaventure, The Tree of Life, p. 127, (1)

RESPONSORY

Mother of our savior, mother pierced with a lance, pray for us who trust in you. —**Mother**...
You are the cause of our joy, —**pray for**...
Glory to you, Source of all Being, Eternal Word and Holy Spirit.
   —**Mother**...

CANTICLE OF ZECHARIAH

Ant I am God's handmaid, be it done to me according to your word (alleluia).

INTERCESSIONS

The mercies of God endure from age to age, working marvels for the people. With grateful hearts we pray:
   O God, holy is your name.

You blessed the holiness of Mary with the joy of your call;
   —give us the grace to persevere in faith and in prayer when our efforts seem fruitless.
Mary's fiat brings salvation to the world;
   —let all of our choices promote life and give you praise and glory.
Mary heard the word of God and entered the mystery of redemption;
   —give us the grace to follow the lure of your call to growth.
Mary's "yes" to God brought motherhood and martyrdom of heart;

—bless all parents who bear deep suffering in their children; be their refuge and strength.

PRAYER: O God, in the fullness of time, you called the virgin, Mary, to be the mother of Jesus. As we celebrate this mystery of the annunciation, of Mary's entrance into the mystery of redemption, grant us the grace of opening our lives to all that you would call us to be. Give us the mind and heart of Mary that we too may bear Christ to the world. We ask this through Jesus Christ, the Incarnate Word, one with you, Source of all life, and with the Holy Spirit. Amen.

DAYTIME PRAYER

Ant 1 I delight to do your will, O God; your law is within my heart (alleluia). (Ps 120, p. 155)

Ant 2 All generations shall call me blessed; most holy is your name (alleluia). (Ps 121, p. 89)

Ant 3 You have favored the lowliness of your handmaid and have lifted up the powerless (alleluia). (Ps 122, p. 143)

(Prayer as in Morning Prayer)

EVENING PRAYER II

Ant 1 Blessed is she who believed that God's word in her would be fulfilled (alleluia). (Ps 110:1–5, 7, p. 53)

Ant 2 The power of the Most High overshadowed Mary, and the Spirit came upon her (alleluia). (Ps 130, p. 143)

Ant 3 The Holy One born of you shall be called the Son of God (alleluia). (Col 1:12–20, p. 171)

READING

...The girl prays by the bare wall
Between the lamp and the chair.
(Framed with an angel in our galleries
She has a richer painted room, sometimes a crown.
Yet seven pillars of obscurity
Build her to Wisdom's house, and Ark, and Tower.
She is the Secret of another Testament
She owns their manna in her jar.)

Fifteen years old—
The flowers printed on her dress
Cease moving in the middle of her prayer
When God, Who sends the messenger,
Meets [this] messenger in her Heart.
Her answer, between breath and breath,
Wrings from her innocence our Sacrament!
In her white body God becomes our Bread....

"The Annunciation" in *The Collected Poems of Thomas Merton*, p. 284, (16)

RESPONSORY

Blessed are you among women and blessed is the fruit of your womb.
   —Blessed...
Hail, ark of the covenant, **—blessed is...**
Glory to you, Source of all Being, Eternal Word and Holy Spirit.
   —Blessed...

CANTICLE OF MARY

Ant My spirit rejoices in God, my savior (alleluia).

INTERCESSIONS

Mary, full of grace, is called to be the mother of Jesus. We rejoice
in you, O God, as we say:
   You are the honor of your people, O blessed virgin, Mary.

Mary is blessed among women with the joy all ages have awaited;
   —through her intercession free all women who are in bondage
      and who lead lives less than human.
Mary chose freely to become the mother of the savior;
   —grant to all people the freedom to choose their way of life.
Mary rejoiced at the mystery of her motherhood;
   —grant your grace and guidance to mothers who do not want
      their children.
Mary went in haste to support and to share the mystery of new
life with her cousin, Elizabeth;
   —teach us how to share with others, the fruit of your Spirit in
      our lives.

PRAYER: O God, in the fullness of time, you called the virgin,
            Mary, to be the mother of Jesus. As we celebrate this
            mystery of the annunciation, of Mary's entrance into
            the mystery of redemption, grant us the grace of
            opening our lives to all that you would call us to be.

Give us the mind and heart of Mary that we too may bear Christ to the world. We ask this through Jesus Christ, the Incarnate Word, one with you, Source of all life, and with the Holy Spirit. Amen.

April 7
ST. JULIE BILLIART

MORNING/EVENING PRAYER
(Psalms from Sunday, Week I, p. 3)

Ant 1 If you would follow me, take up your cross.

Ant 2 All will go right or not; if it does not go right, the good God will open a way for us.

Ant 3 May our good Jesus and his holy cross live in us!

READING

Julie Billiart, born in France in 1751, founded the congregation of Sisters of Notre Dame de Namur. Though afflicted by many physical sufferings and the political unrest of the French Revolution, Julie Billiart was a woman of courage with outstanding faith. She wrote: "The good God asks these very simple and easy tasks: that our soul be united to [God] by charity; that we do our duty as perfectly as possible...that we do the most common things in an uncommon manner."* Julie Billiart died April 7, 1816.

Themes of Julie Billiart, p. 8, (44)

RESPONSORY

Do not be frightened, God will never fail you. —**Do not...**
In joy or adversity, — **God...**
Glory to you, Source of all Being, Eternal Word and Holy Spirit.
   —**Do not...**

CANTICLE

Ant As gold in the furnace, God proved her.

INTERCESSIONS

You use the weak ones of the earth to accomplish your works, O God, and so we pray:
   Blessed are they who suffer persecution for your sake.

O God, through the intercession of Julie Billiart;
  —may all threatened by revolutions and political unrest know
     the peace the world cannot give.
For nearly twenty years of her adult life, Julie was a cripple;
  —give courage to those who are injured and physically
     disabled.
She was a "soul of prayer" and a woman of sound common sense;
  —help us all to use our gifts of nature and grace for your glory.
Julie persevered in her dedication to your call in spite of civil,
ecclesiastic, and domestic persecution;
  —comfort all who suffer misunderstanding as they follow the
     guidance of the Spirit.

PRAYER: Most loving God, you blessed your daughter, Julie,
           with humility and wisdom in the midst of struggle and
           misunderstanding. Through her, many came to know
           your love and concern. Bless her followers, the Sisters
           of Notre Dame de Namur, that they may continue the
           work you began in her. We ask this in the names of
           Jesus and his mother, Mary. Amen.

April 10
TEILHARD DE CHARDIN

MORNING/EVENING PRAYER

Ant 1 We rejoice in the works of your hands. (Ps 8, p. 92)

Ant 2 The universe reflects your glory, O God. You reveal its
        secrets to the wise and simple. (Ps 148, p. 99)

Ant 3 All creation sings your glory; even the stones shout for joy.
        (Ps 65, p. 63)

READING

Since today, Lord, I your priest have neither bread nor wine nor altar, I
shall spread my hands over the whole universe and take its immensity
as the matter of my sacrifice. Is not the infinite circle of things the one
final Host that it is your will to transmute? The seething cauldron in
which the activities of all living and cosmic substance are brewed
together—is not that the bitter cup that you seek to sanctify?... Let
creation repeat to itself again today, and tomorrow, and until the end of

time, so long as the transformation has not run its full course, the divine saying: "This is my body."

Teilhard deChardin, *The Prayer of the Universe*, p. 157, p. 158, (60)

RESPONSORY

I will give thanks to God with my whole heart. —**I will**...
I will tell of all your wonders; —**with my**...
Glory to you, Source of all Being, Eternal Word and Holy Spirit.
    —**I will**...

CANTICLE

Ant Christ is the goad that urges creatures along the road of effort, of elevation, of development.

INTERCESSIONS

O Cosmic Christ, you are present in the heart of the world;
    —may we reverence you in all your works.
Unifying Center of the world, you draw all things to yourself;
    —bring all creation to the fullness of being.
Redeemer of the world;
    —help us to protect our environment for future generations.
God of the heavens;
    —may our ventures into space be for the good of all humankind and in accord with gospel values.
Christ, the Alpha and the Omega;
    —may all who have died enjoy the glory of resurrection and aid us on our way.

PRAYER: We give you thanks, Creator God, for your servant, Teilhard, and for all those who help us to see you in your universe. May creation be continually transformed that all may share in the life, death, and resurrection of God become human, our Lord Jesus Christ. Amen.

April 17
ANNA DENGEL, SCMM

MORNING/EVENING PRAYER
(Psalms from Sunday, Week I, p. 3)

Ant 1 The impossible of today is the work of tomorrow.

Ant 2 I was fire and flame.... I was determined to become a mission doctor.

Ant 3 A religious community has a task to do...to be an arm of the Church, to reach out in the name of Christ to the hundred and one human needs.

READING

Anna Marie Dengel was born on March 16, 1892, in Steeg, Austria. In her late teens, she heard that women and children were dying needlessly in another land because their customs would not allow them to be treated by men. She responded by becoming a doctor and eventually founding the Medical Mission Sisters, a community for whom she obtained permission to "practice medicine in its full scope." When Mother Dengel died in April, 1980, the Medical Mission Sisters were serving the sick and needy on five continents, and through them the vision of their founder continues to expand throughout the world today.

RESPONSORY

Every person has an inherent right to live a fully human life.
  —Every person...
Justice is essential to the healing that enables all people;
  —to live...
Glory to you, Source of all Being, Eternal Word and Holy Spirit.
  —Every person...

CANTICLE

Ant All the ends of the earth have seen the saving power of God.

INTERCESSIONS

Throughout her life, Anna Dengel had a passion for possibilities;
  —O God, increase our faith.
Mother Dengel taught her sisters to be a healing presence among people in need;
    —help us to remove anything in our lives that blocks your life-giving Spirit.
She dreamed of a world where no boundaries existed, where women and men, Christian and Muslim...all people had access to what would make them fully human;
    —Spirit of God, open our hearts and minds to the reality of your Presence in every person.

Her deep compassion inspired others to serve the sick in cultures
where women had formerly been left untreated;

—Jesus our Savior, awaken us to the hidden needs of others.

To the advantage of those she taught and served, Mother Dengel
combined religious life in the Church with medical
professionalism;

—Creator God, give us the generosity and perseverance to do all
things well.

PRAYER: O God, Anna Dengel transformed the challenges of her
life and the needs of others into a means of healing and
salvation for people throughout the world. Her
compassion and deep faith enabled her to break
through ecclesiastic and cultural barriers to allow
religious women to serve the needy as medical doctors.
Through her intercession, we ask for the wisdom and
courage we need to grant all women and men their true
dignity in the human family. We ask this for the praise
and glory of your name. Amen.

COMMEMORATION OF A HOLY WOMAN

MORNING/EVENING PRAYER

(Psalms from Sunday, Week I, p. 3)

Ant 1 God has done great things for her, and holy is God's name.

Ant 2 The water that I shall give them will become a spring of
living water welling up to eternal life.

Ant 3 Where shall I go from your Spirit? Or where shall I flee
from your presence?

READING

[Jesus] brings salvation through his life and Spirit, restoring women to
full personal dignity in the reign of God, and inspiring their liberation
from structures of domination and subordination. This is a challenging
christology, as is every form of liberation theology. It signals a genuine
Copernican revolution, this time not dethroning the earth in favor of the
sun, but patriarchy in favor of a community of genuine mutuality. If it is
good news to those oppressed, it can be a fearful thing to the oppressor.
The call once again is for conversion of hearts, minds, and structures, so
that the reign of God may take firmer hold in this world.

Elizabeth A. Johnson, *Consider Jesus,* p. 112, (2)

RESPONSORY

She opens her mouth with wisdom, and the teaching of kindness
    is on her tongue. **—She opens**...
She holds her hands out to the poor, **—and the**...
Glory to you, Source of all Being, Eternal Word and Holy Spirit.
    —She opens...

CANTICLE

Ant You are a chosen race, a royal priesthood, a holy nation,
    God's own people.

INTERCESSIONS

O God, you have blessed us with valiant women in every age;
    —show us the way to encourage women today in their efforts
    to build the kindom.
The majority of the homeless are women and children;
    —teach us practical ways to end their suffering.
Lord Jesus, you were nurtured and taught by Mary;
    —bless mothers and teachers who guide our children today.
You had compassion on the sick
    —be with women in all of the helping professions; may their
    insights be heeded and their ministry appreciated.
You sent a woman to proclaim your resurrection to the other
disciples;
    —let the women you send today be heard by the church.

PRAYER: O God, you created woman in your image and called
            Mary to enflesh the body and blood of your Divine Son.
            Awaken your Spirit in your people today. Give us all
            the freedom to worship you in spirit and in truth, that
            the life of Jesus may be good news for the world as
            never before. We ask this in his name. Amen.

COMMEMORATION OF A HOLY MAN
MORNING/EVENING PRAYER
(Psalms from Sunday, Week I, p. 3)

Ant 1 Behold my servant whom I have chosen. He will not break a bruised reed or quench a smoldering wick.

Ant 2 I have chosen you to bear much fruit and to glorify the one who sent me.

Ant 3 Whatever you have done for the least of my people, you have done to me.

READING

The early disciples, after the resurrection and the outpouring of the Holy Spirit, preached and witnessed to Jesus Christ, giving him names out of their cultural contexts, so too today, disciples are still inspired by the power of the Holy Spirit and, guided by the tradition generated through the experiences of the early communities, should be engaged in active following, in writing the fifth gospel so to speak.

Elizabeth A. Johnson, *Consider Jesus*, p. 61, (2)

RESPONSORY

Lord Jesus, you have given us an example of love and service; help us to be faithful. —**Lord Jesus,**...
Teach us to pray; —**help us**...
Glory to you, Source of all Being, Eternal Word and Holy Spirit. —**Lord Jesus,**...

CANTICLE

Ant Eye has not seen nor ear heard nor has it entered into the heart of anyone what you have prepared for those who love you.

INTERCESSIONS

O God, from time immemorial you have showered your graces upon your people;
May you be praised forever!

Jesus, you died to set us free;
—strengthen those who risk their lives to free those who are enslaved by poverty and prejudice.

You spent yourself to preach the good news;
  —grant wisdom and words to ministers of your word today.
Your compassion for the sick knew no bounds;
  —bless all who work to heal and ease the pain of others.
Spirit of God, you dwell in our hearts;
  —awaken in each of us an outpouring of your gifts.

PRAYER: O God, you sent your son, Jesus, for the salvation of
all your people. We praise you for the gift of those who
have followed him faithfully toward the building of your
kindom. Help us to be faithful as they were faithful.
Show us the way to proclaim the gospel with our lives.
We ask this in Jesus' name. Amen.

INDEX OF PSALMS

	Ps Wk	1997	1998	1999	2000	2001	2002
Sun Cycle		B	C	A	B	C	A
Wkdy Cycle		1	2	1	2	1	2
1-Adv	1	1 Dec 96	30 Nov 97	29 Nov 98	28 Nov 99	3 Dec 00	2 Dec 01
2-Adv	2	8 Dec	7 Dec	6 Dec	5 Dec	10 Dec	9 Dec
3 Adv	3	15 Dec	14 Dec	13 Dec	12 Dec	17 Dec	16 Dec
4 Adv	4	22 Dec	21 Dec	20 Dec	19 Dec	24 Dec	23 Dec
Christmas	Proper	25 Dec	25 Dec	25 Dec	25 Dec	25 Dec	25 Dec
Holy Family	1	29 Dec	28 Dec	27 Dec	26 Dec	31 Dec	30 Dec
Moth.of God	Proper	1 Jan	1 Jan	1 Jan	1 Jan	1 Jan	1 Jan
Epiphany	2	5 Jan	4 Jan	3 Jan	2 Jan	7 Jan	6 Jan
Baptism	1	12 Jan	11 Jan	10 Jan	9 Jan	8 Jan	13 Jan
2-Ord	2	19 Jan	18 Jan	17 Jan	16 Jan	14 Jan	20 Jan
3-Ord	3	26 Jan	25 Jan	24 Jan	23 Jan	21 Jan	27 Jan
4-Ord	4	2 Feb	1 Feb	31 Jan	30 Jan	28 Jan	3 Feb
5-Ord	1	9 Feb	8 Feb	7 Feb	6 Feb	4 Feb	10 Feb
6-Ord	2	–	15 Feb	14 Feb	13 Feb	11 Feb	–
7-Ord	3	–	22 Feb	–	20 Feb	18 Feb	–
8-Ord	4	–	–	–	27 Feb	25 Feb	–
9-Ord	1	–	–	–	5 Mar	–	–
Ash Wed	4	12 Feb	25 Feb	17 Feb	8 Mar	28 Feb	13 Feb
1 Lent	1	16 Feb	1 Mar	21 Feb	12 Mar	4 Mar	17 Feb
2 Lent	2	23 Feb	8 Mar	28 Feb	19 Mar	11 Mar	24 Feb
3 Lent	3	2Mar	15 Mar	7 Mar	26 Mar	18 Mar	3 Mar
4 Lent	4	9 Mar	22 Mar	14 Mar	2 Apr	25 Mar	10 Mar
5 Lent	1	16 Mar	29 Mar	21 Mar	9 Apr	1 Apr	17 Mar
Passion Sun	2	23 Mar	5 Apr	28 Mar	16 Apr	8 Apr	24 Mar
Easter	Proper	30 Mar	12 Apr	4 Apr	23 Apr	15 Apr	31 Mar
2 Easter	2	6 Apr	19 Apr	11 Apr	30 Apr	22 Apr	7 Apr
3 Easter	3	13 Apr	26 Apr	18 Apr	7 May	29 Apr	14 Apr
4 Easter	4	20 Apr	3 May	25 Apr	14 May	6 May	21 Apr
5 Easter	1	27 Apr	10 May	2 May	21 May	13 May	28 Apr
6 Easter	2	4 May	17 May	9 May	28 May	20 May	5 May
Ascension	Proper	8 May	21 May	13 May	1 Jun	24 May	9 May
7 Easter	3	11 May	24 May	16 May	4 Jun	27 May	12 May
Pentecost	Prop	18 May	31 May	23 May	11 Jun	3 Jun	19 May
Trinity Sun	Prop	25 May	7 Jun	30 May	18 Jun	10 Jun	26 May
Corpus Christi	Prop	1 Jun	14 Jun	6 Jun	25 Jun	17 Jun	2 Jun
10-Ord	2	8 Jun	–	–	–	–	9 Jun
11-Ord	3	15 Jun	–	13 Jun	–	–	16 Jun
12-Ord	4	22 Jun	21 Jun	20 Jun	–	24 Jun	23 Jun
13-Ord	1	29 Jun	28 Jun	27 Jun	2 Jul	1 Jul	30 Jun
14-Ord	2	6 Jul	5Jul	4 Jul	9 Jul	8 Jul	7 Jul
15-Ord	3	13 Jul	12 Jul	11 Jul	16 Jul	15 Jul	14 Jul
16-Ord	4	20 Jul	19 Jul	18 Jul	23 Jul	22 Jul	21 Jul
17-Ord	1	27 Jul	26 Jul	25 Jul	30 Jul	29 Jul	28 Jul
18-Ord	2	3 Aug	2 Aug	1 Aug	6 Aug	5 Aug	4 Aug
19-Ord	3	10 Aug	9 Aug	8 Aug	13 Aug	12 Aug	11 Aug
20-Ord	4	17 Agu	16 Aug	15 Aug	20 Aug	19 Aug	18 Aug
21-Ord	1	24 Aug	23 Aug	22 Aug	27 Aug	26 Aug	25 Aug
22-Ord	2	31 Aug	30 Aug	29 Aug	3 Sep	2 Sep	1 Sep
23-Ord	3	7 Sep	6 Sep	5 Sep	10 Sep	9 Sep	8 Sep
24-Ord	4	14 Sep	13 Sep	12 Sep	17 Sep	16 Sep	15 Sep
25-Ord	1	21 Sep	20 Sep	19 Sep	24 Sep	23 Sep	22 Sep
26-Ord	2	28 Sep	27 Sep	26 Sep	1 Oc	30 Sep	29 Sep
27-Ord	3	5 Oct	4Oct	3 Oct	8 Oct	7 Oct	6 Oct
28-Ord	4	12 Oct	11 Oct	10 Oct	15 Oct	14 Oct	13 Oct
29-Ord	1	19 Oct	18 Oct	17 Oct	22 Oct	21 Oct	20 Oct
30-Ord	2	26 Oct	25 Oct	24 Oct	29 Oct	28 Oct	27 Oct
31-Ord	3	2 Nov	–	31 Oct	5 Nov	4 Nov	3 Nov
32-Ord	4	9 Nov	8 Nov	7 Nov	12 Nov	11 Nov	10 Nov
33-Ord	1	16 Nov	15 Nov	14 Nov	19 Nov	18 Nov	17 Nov
34-Ord	2	23 Nov	22 Nov	21 Nov	26 Nov	25 Nov	24 Nov

	Ps Wk	2003	2004	2005	2006	2007	2008
Sun Cycle		B	C	A	B	C	A
Wkdy Cycle		1	2	1	2	1	2
1-Adv	1	1 Dec 02	30 Nov 03	28 Nov 04	27 Nov 05	3 Dec 06	2 Dec 07
2-Adv	2	8 Dec	7 Dec	5 Dec	4 Dec	10 Dec	9 Dec
3 Adv	3	15 Dec	14 Dec	12 Dec	11 Dec	17 Dec	16 Dec
4 Adv	4	22 Dec	21 Dec	19 Dec	18 Dec	24 Dec	23 Dec
Christmas	Proper	25 Dec	25 Dec	25 Dec	25 Dec	25 Dec	25 Dec
Holy Family	1	29 Dec	28 Dec	26 Dec	30 Dec	31 Dec	30 Dec
Moth.of God	Proper	1 Jan	1 Jan	1 Jan	1 Jan	1 Jan	1 Jan
Epiphany	2	5 Jan	4 Jan	2 Jan	8 Jan	7 Jan	6 Jan
Baptism	1	12 Jan	11 Jan	9 Jan	9 Jan	8 Jan	13 Jan
2-Ord	2	19 Jan	18 Jan	16 Jan	15 Jan	14 Jan	20 Jan
3-Ord	3	26 Jan	25 Jan	23 Jan	22 Jan	21 Jan	27 Jan
4-Ord	4	2 Feb	1 Feb	30 Jan	29 Jan	28 Jan	3 Feb
5-Ord	1	9 Feb	8 Feb	6 Feb	5 Feb	4 Feb	–
6-Ord	2	16 Feb	15 Feb	–	12 Feb	11 Feb	–
7-Ord	3	23 Feb	22 Feb	–	19 Feb	18 Feb	–
8-Ord	4	2 Mar	–	–	26 Feb	–	–
9-Ord	1	–	–	–	–	–	1 Jun
Ash Wed	4	5 Mar	25 Feb	9 Feb	1 Mar	21 Feb	6 Feb
1 Lent	1	9 Mar	29 Feb	13 Feb	5 Mar	25 Feb	10 Feb
2 Lent	2	16 Mar	7 Mar	20 Feb	12 Mar	4 Mar	17 Feb
3 Lent	3	23 Mar	14 Mar	27 Feb	19 Mar	11 Mar	24 Feb
4 Lent	4	30 Mar	21 Mar	6 Mar	26 Mar	18 Mar	2 Mar
5 Lent	1	6 Apr	28 Mar	13 Mar	2 Apr	25 Mar	9 Mar
Passion Sun	2	13 Apr	4 Apr	20 Mar	9 Apr	1 Apr	16 Mar
Easter	Proper	20 Apr	11 Apr	27 Mar	16 Apr	8 Apr	23 Mar
2 Easter	2	27 Apr	18 Apr	3 Apr	23 Apr	15 Apr	30 Mar
3 Easter	3	4 May	25 Apr	10 Apr	30 Apr	22 Apr	6 Apr
4 Easter	4	11 May	2 May	17 Apr	7 May	29 Apr	13 Apr
5 Easter	1	18 May	9 May	24 Apr	14 May	6 May	20 Apr
6 Easter	2	25 May	16 May	1 May	21 May	13 May	27 Apr
Ascension	Proper	29 May	20 May	5 May	25 May	17 May	1 May
7 Easter	3	1 Jun	23 May	8 May	28 May	20 May	4 May
Pentecost	Prop	8 Jun	30 May	15 May	4 Jun	27 May	11 May
Trinity Sun	Prop	15 Jun	6 Jun	22 May	11 Jun	3 Jun	18 May
Corpus Christi	Prop	22 Jun	13 Jun	29 May	18 Jun	10 Jun	25 May
10-Ord	2	–	–	5 Jun	–	–	8 Jun
11-Ord	3	–	–	12 Jun	–	17 Jun	15 Jun
12-Ord	4		20 Jun	19 Jun	25 Jun	24 Jun	22 Jun
13-Ord	1	29 Jun	27 Jun	26 Jun	2 Jul	1 Jul	29 Jun
14-Ord	2	6 Jul	4 Jul	3 Jul	9 Jul	8 Jul	6 Jul
15-Ord	3	13 Jul	11 Jul	10 Jul	16 Jul	15 Jul	13 Jul
16-Ord	4	20 Jul	18 Jul	17 Jul	23 Jul	22 Jul	20 Jul
17-Ord	1	27 Jul	25 Jul	24 Jul	30 Jul	29 Jul	27 Jul
18-Ord	2	3 Aug	1 Aug	31 Jul	6 Aug	5 Aug	3 Aug
19-Ord	3	10 Aug	8 Aug	7 Aug	13 Aug	12 Aug	10 Aug
20-Ord	4	17 Aug	Assum	14 Aug	20 Aug	19 Aug	17 Aug
21-Ord	1	24 Aug	22 Aug	21 Aug	27 Aug	26 Aug	24 Aug
22-Ord	2	31 Aug	29 Aug	28 Aug	3 Sep	2 Sep	31 Aug
23-Ord	3	7 Sep	5 Sep	4 Sep	10 Sep	9 Sep	7 Sep
24-Ord	4	14 Sep	12 Sep	11 Sep	17 Sep	16 Sep	14 Sep
25-Ord	1	21 Sep	19 Sep	18 Sep	24 Sep	23 Sep	21 Sep
26-Ord	2	28 Sep	26 Sep	25 Sep	1 Oct	30 Sep	28 Sep
27-Ord	3	5 Oct	3 Oct	2 Oct	8 Oct	7 Oct	5 Oct
28-Ord	4	12 Oct	10 Oct	9 Oct	15 Oct	14 Oct	12 Oct
29-Ord	1	19 Oct	17 Oct	16 Oct	22 Oct	21 Oct	19 Oct
30-Ord	2	26 Oct	24 Oct	23 Oct	29 Oct	28 Oct	26 Oct
31-Ord	3	2 Nov	31 Oct	30 Oct	5 Nov	4 Nov	2 Nov
32-Ord	4	9 Nov	7 Nov	6 Nov	12 Nov	11 Nov	9 Nov
33-Ord	1	16 Nov	14 Nov	13 Nov	19 Nov	18 Nov	16 Nov
34-Ord	2	23 Nov	21 Nov	20 Nov	26 Nov	25 Nov	23 Nov

	Ps Wk	2009	2010	2011	2012	2013	2014
Sun Cycle		IB	C	A	B	C	A
Wkdy Cycle		1	2	1	2	1	2
1-Adv	1	30 Nov 08	29 Nov 09	28 Nov 10	27 Nov 11	2 Dec 12	1 Dec 13
2-Adv	2	7 Dec	6 Dec	5 Dec	4 Dec	9 Dec	8 Dec
3 Adv	3	14 Dec	13 Dec	12 Dec	11 Dec	16 Dec	15 Dec
4 Adv	4	21 Dec	20 Dec	19 Dec	18 Dec	23 Dec	22 Dec
Christmas	Proper	25 Dec	25 Dec	25 Dec	25 Dec	25 Dec	25 Dec
Holy Family	1	28 Dec	27 Dec	26 Dec	30 Dec	30 Dec	29 Dec
Moth.of God	Proper	1 Jan	1 Jan	1 Jan	1 Jan	1 Jan	1 Jan
Epiphany	2	4 Jan	3 Jan	2 Jan	8 Jan	6 Jan	5 Jan
Baptism	1	11 Jan	10 Jan	9 Jan	9 Jan	13 Jan	12 Jan
2-Ord	2	18 Jan	17 Jan	16 Jan	15 Jan	20 Jan	19 Jan
3-Ord	3	25 Jan	24 Jan	23 Jan	22 Jan	27 Jan	26 Jan
4-Ord	4	1 Feb	31 Jan	30 Jan	29, Jan	3 Feb	2 Feb
5-Ord	1	8 Feb	7 Feb	6 Feb	5 Feb	10 Feb	9 Feb
6-Ord	2	15 Feb	14 Feb	13 Feb	12 Feb	–	16 Feb
7-Ord	3	22 Feb	–	20 Feb	19 Feb	–	23 Feb
8-Ord	4	–	–	27 Feb	–	–	2 Mar
9-Ord	1	–	–	–	–	–	–
Ash Wed	4	25 Feb	17 Feb	9 Mar	22 Feb	13 Feb	5 Mar
1 Lent	1	1 Mar	21 Feb	13 Mar	26 Feb	17 Feb	9 Mar
2 Lent	2	8 Mar	28 Feb	20 Mar	4 Mar	24 Feb	16 Mar
3 Lent	3	15 Mar	7 Mar	27 Mar	11 Mar	3 Mar	23 Mar
4 Lent	4	22 Mar	14 Mar	3 Apr	18 Mar	10 Mar	30 Mar
5 Lent	1	29 Mar	21 Mar	10 Apr	25 Mar	17 Mar	6 Apr
Passion Sun	2	5 Apr	28 Mar	17 Apr	1 Apr	24 Mar	13 Apr
Easter	Proper	12 Apr	4 Apr	24 Apr	8 Apr	31 Mar	20 Apr
2 Easter	2	19 Apr	11 Apr	1 May	15 Apr	7 Apr	27 Apr
3 Easter	3	26 Apr	18 Apr	8 May	22 Apr	14 Apr	4 May
4 Easter	4	3 May	25 Apr	15 May	29 Apr	21 Apr	11 May
5 Easter	1	10 May	2 May	22 May	6 May	28 Apr	18 May
6 Easter	2	17 May	9 May	29 May	13 May	5 May	25 May
Ascension	Proper	21 May	13 May	2 Jun	17 May	9 May	29 May
7 Easter	3	24 May	16 May	5 Jun	20 May	12 May	1 Jun
Pentecost	Prop	31 May	23 May	12 Jun	27 May	19 May	8 Jun
Trinity Sun	Prop	7 Jun	30 May	19 Jun	3 Jun	26 May	15 Jun
Corpus Christi	Prop	14 Jun	6 Jun	26 Jun	10 Jun	2 Jun	22 Jun
10-Ord	2	–	–	–	–	9 Jun	–
11-Ord	3	–	13 Jun	–	17 Jun	16 Jun	–
12-Ord	4	21 Jun	20 Jun	–	24 Jun	23 Jun	–
13-Ord	1	28 Jun	27 Jun	–	1 Jul	30 Jun	29 Jun
14-Ord	2	5 Jul	4 Jul	3 Jul	8 Jul	7 Jul	6 Jul
15-Ord	3	12 Jul	11 Jul	10 Jul	15 Jul	14 Jul	13 Jul
16-Ord	4	19 Jul	18 Jul	17 Jul	22 Jul	21 Jul	20 Jul
17-Ord	1	26 Jul	25 Jul	24 Jul	29 Jul	28 Jul	27 Jul
18-Ord	2	2 Aug	1 Aug	31 Jul	5 Aug	4 Aug	3 Aug
19-Ord	3	9 Aug	8 Aug	7 Aug	12 Aug	11 Aug	10 Aug
20-Ord	4	16 Aug	15 Aug	14 Aug	19 Aug	18 Aug	17 Aug
21-Ord	1	23 Aug	22 Aug	21 Aug	26 Aug	25 Aug	24 Aug
22-Ord	2	30 Aug	29 Aug	28 Aug	2 Sep	1 Sep	31 Aug
23-Ord	3	6 Sep	5 Sep	4 Sep	9 Sep	8 Sep	7 Sep
24-Ord	4	13 Sep	12 Sep	11 Sep	16 Sep	15 Sep	14 Sep
25-Ord	1	20 Sep	19 Sep	18 Sep	23 Sep	22 Sep	21 Sep
26-Ord	2	27 Sep	26 Sep	25 Sep	30 Sep	29 Sep	28 Sep
27-Ord	3	4 Oct	3 Oct	2 Oct	7 Oct	6 Oct	5 Oct
28-Ord	4	11 Oct	10 Oct	9 Oct	14 Oct	13 Oct	12 Oct
29-Ord	1	18 Oct	17 Oct	16 Oct	21 Oct	20 Oct	19 Oct
30-Ord	2	25 Oct	24 Oct	23 Oct	28 Oct	27 Oct	26 Oct
31-Ord	3	All Saints	31 Oct	30 Oct	4 Nov	3 Nov	2Nov
32-Ord	4	8 Nov	7 Nov	6 Nov	11 Nov	10 Nov	9 Nov
33-Ord	1	15 Nov	14 Nov	13 Nov	18 Nov	17 Nov	16 Nov
34-Ord	2	22 Nov	21 Nov	20 Nov	25 Nov	24 Nov	23 Nov

	Ps Wk	2015	2016	2017	2018	2019	2020
Sun Cycle		B	C	A	B	C	A
Wkdy Cycle		1	2	1	2	1	2
1-Adv	1	30 Nov 14	29 Nov 15	27 Nov 16	3 Dec 17	2 Dec 18	1 Dec 19
2-Adv	2	7 Dec	6 Dec	4 Dec	10 Dec	9 Dec	8 Dec
3 Adv	3	14 Dec	13 Dec	11 Dec	17 Dec	16 Dec	15 Dec
4 Adv	4	21 Dec	20 Dec	18 Dec	24 Dec	23 Dec	22 Dec
Christmas	Proper	25 Dec	25 Dec	25 Dec	25 Dec	25 Dec	25 Dec
Holy Family	1	28 Dec	27 Dec	2 Jan	31 Dec	30 Dec	29 Dec
Moth. of God	Proper	1 Jan	1 Jan	1 Jan	1 Jan	1 Jan	1 Jan
Epiphany	2	4 Jan	3 Jan	8 Jan	7 Jan	6 Jan	5 Jan
Baptism	1	11 Jan	10 Jan	9 Jan	14 Jan	13 Jan	12 Jan
2-Ord	2	18 Jan	17 Jan	15 Jan	21 Jan	20 Jan	19 Jan
3-Ord	3	25 Jan	24 Jan	22 Jan	28 Jan	27 Jan	26 Jan
4-Ord	4	1 Feb	31 Jan	29 Jan	4 Feb	3 Feb	2 Feb
5-Ord	1	8 Feb	7 Feb	–	–	10 Feb	9 Feb
6-Ord	2	15 Feb	–	–	–	17 Feb	16 Feb
7-Ord	3	–	–	5 Feb	–	24 Feb	23 Feb
8-Ord	4	–	–	12 Feb	–	3 Mar	–
9-Ord	1	–	–	19 Feb	–	–	–
Ash Wed	4	18 Feb	10 Feb	26 Feb	14 Feb	6 Mar	22 Feb
1 Lent	1	22 Feb	14 Feb	5 Mar	18 Feb	10 Mar	1 Mar
2 Lent	2	1 Mar	21 Feb	12 Mar	25 Feb	17 Mar	8 Mar
3 Lent	3	8 Mar	28 Feb	19 Mar	4 Mar	24 Mar	15 Mar
4 Lent	4	15 Mar	6 Mar	26 Mar	11 Mar	31 Mar	22 Mar
5 Lent	1	22 Mar	13 Mar	2 Apr	18 Mar	7 Apr	29 Mar
Passion Sun	2	29 Mar	20 Mar	9 Apr	25 Mar	14 Apr	5 Apr
Easter	Proper	5 Apr	27 Mar	16 Apr	1 Apr	21 Apr	12 Apr
2 Easter	2	12 Apr	3 Apr	23 Apr	8 Apr	28 Apr	19 Apr
3 Easter	3	19 Apr	10 Apr	30 Apr	15 Apr	5 May	26 Apr
4 Easter	4	26 Apr	17 Apr	7 May	22 Apr	12 May	3 May
5 Easter	1	3 May	24 Apr	14 May	29 Apr	19 May	10 May
6 Easter	2	10 May	1 May	21 May	6 May	26 May	17 May
Ascension	Proper	17 May	8 May	28 May	13 May	2 June	24 May
7 Easter	3	24 May	15 May	4 Jun	20 May	9 Jun	31 May
Pentecost	Prop	31 May	22 May	11 Jun	27 May	16 Jun	7 Jun
Trinity Sun	Prop	7 Jun	29 May	18 Jun	3 Jun	23 Jun	14 Jun
Corpus Christi	Prop	14 Jun	5 Jun	25 Jun	10 Jun	30 Jun	21 Jun
10-Ord	2	–	–	–	–	–	–
11-Ord	3	–	12 Jun	–	17 Jun	–	–
12-Ord	4	21 Jun	19 Jun	–	24 Jun	–	–
13-Ord	1	28 Jun	26 Jun	2 Jul	1 Jul	–	28 Jun
14-Ord	2	5 Jul	3 Jul	9 Jul	8 Jul	7 Jul	5 Jul
15-Ord	3	12 Jul	10 Jul	16 Jul	15 Jul	14 Jul	12 Jul
16-Ord	4	19 Jul	17 Jul	23 Jul	22 Jul	21 Jul	19 Jul
17-Ord	1	26 Jul	24 Jul	30 Jul	29 Jul	28 Jul	26 Jul
18-Ord	2	2 Aug	31 Jul	6 Aug	5 Aug	4 Aug	2 Aug
19-Ord	3	9 Aug	7 Aug	13 Aug	12 Aug	11 Aug	9 Aug
20-Ord	4	16 Aug	14 Aug	20 Aug	19 Aug	18 Aug	16 Aug
21-Ord	1	23 Aug	21 Aug	27 Aug	26 Aug	25 Aug	23 Aug
22-Ord	2	30 Aug	28 Aug	3 Sep	2 Sep	1 Sep	30 Aug
23-Ord	3	6 Sep	4 Sep	10 Sep	9 Sep	8 Sep	6 Sep
24-Ord	4	13 Sep	11 Sep	17 Sep	16 Sep	15 Sep	13 Sep
25-Ord	1	20 Sep	18 Sep	24 Sep	23 Sep	22 Sep	20 Sep
26-Ord	2	27 Sep	25 Sep	1 Oct	30 Sep	29 Sep	27 Sep
27-Ord	3	4 Oct	2 Oct	8 Oct	7 Oct	6 Oct	4 Oct
28-Ord	4	11 Oct	9 Oct	15 Oct	14 Oct	13 Oct	11 Oct
29-Ord	1	18 Oct	16 Oct	22 Oct	21 Oct	20 Oct	18 Oct
30-Ord	2	25 Oct	23 Oct	29 Oct	28 Oct	27 Oct	25 Oct
31-Ord	3	1 Nov	30 Oct	5 Nov	4 Nov	3 Nov	1 Nov
32-Ord	4	8 Nov	6 Nov	12 Nov	11 Nov	10 Nov	8 Nov
33-Ord	1	15 Nov	13 Nov	19 Nov	18 Nov	17 Nov	15 Nov
34-Ord	2	22 Nov	20 Nov	26 Nov	25 Nov	24 Nov	22 Nov

CANTICLE OF ZECHARIAH

Blessed are you, God of Israel
for you have visited and redeemed your people,
and have raised up a horn of salvation for us
in the house of your servant.

As you spoke through the mouths
of your holy prophets from of old,
that we should be saved from our enemies,
and from the hand of all who oppress us;

to perform the mercy promised to our ancestors,
and to remember your holy covenant,

the oath you swore to Abraham and Sarah,
to grant us deliverance from evil,
that we might serve you without fear,
in holiness and righteousness
all the days of our lives.

And you, child,
will be called the prophet of the Most High,
for you will go before the Holy One
to prepare God's ways,

to give knowledge of salvation to God's people
in the forgiveness of their sins,

through the tender mercy of our God
when the day shall dawn upon us from on high

to give light to those who sit in darkness
and in the shadow of death,
to guide our feet
into the way of peace.   Glory...